Sri Lanka

Verity Campbell
Christine Niven

LONELY PLANET PUBLICATIONS
Melbourne • Oakland • London • Paris

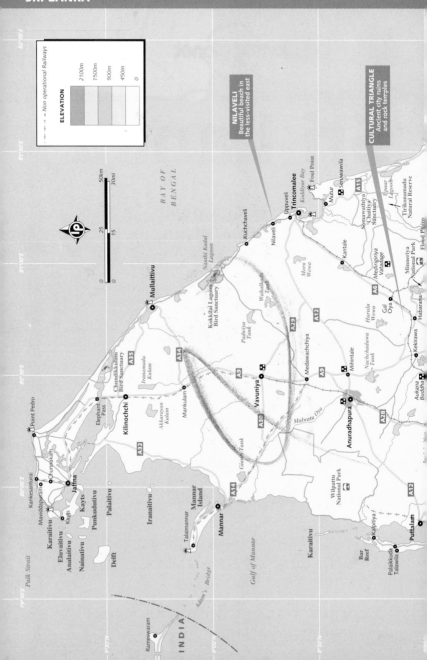

ELEVATION

2100m
1500m
900m
450m
0

- + - = Non operational Railways

NILAVELI
Beautiful beach in
the less-visited east

CULTURAL TRIANGLE
Ancient city ruins
and rock temples

BAY OF
BENGAL

50km
30mi

Point Pedro

Kankesanturai
Mavidappuram
Chunnakam
Jaffna
Kayts
Karaitivu
Eluvaitivu
Analaitivu
Nainativu
Delft

Palk Strait

Rameswaram

INDIA

Adam's Bridge

Talaimannar

Mannar Island

Mannar

Gulf of Mannar

Karaitivu

Iranaitivu

Punkudutivu

Palaitivu

Mullaittivu

Chundikkulam
Bird Sanctuary

Elephant
Pass

Kilinochchi

Iranamadu
Kulam

Akkarayan
Kulam

Mankulam

Giant's Tank

Nanthi Kadal
Lagoon

Kokkilai Lagoon
Bird Sanctuary

Kuchchaveli

Nilaveli
Uppuveli
Trincomalee
Koddiyar Bay
Foul Point

Mutur

Seruwawila

Padaviya
Tank

Wahalkada
Tank

Mora
Wewa

Kantale

Somawathiya
'Chaitiya'
Sanctuary

Upaar
Lagoon

Tirikonamadu
Natural Reserve

A9

Vavuniya

Malwatu Oya

Medawachchiya

Horuwa
Wewa

Gal
Oya

Medirigiriya
Vatadage

Minneriya
National Park

Flood Plains

Habarana

Mihintale

Nachchaduwa
Tank

Anuradhapura

Aukana
Buddha

Kekirawa

Wilpattu
National Park

Bar
Reef

Palaikkuda
Talawila

Kalpitiya

Puttalam

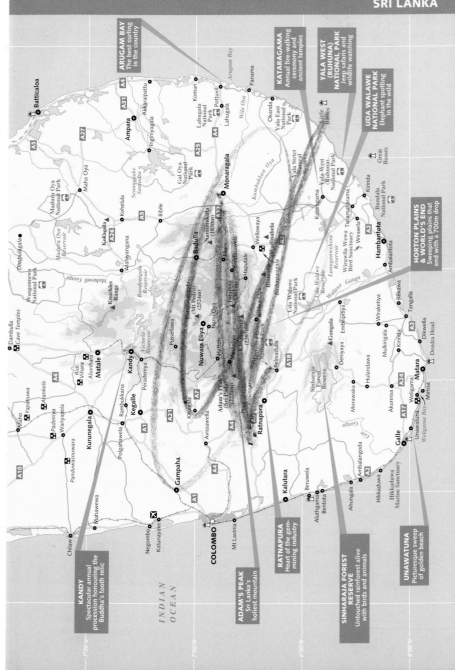

SRI LANKA

Sri Lanka
8th edition – August 2001
First published – February 1980

Six-monthly upgrades of this title available free on
www.lonelyplanet.com/upgrades

Published by
Lonely Planet Publications Pty Ltd ABN 36 005 607 983
90 Maribyrnong St, Footscray, Victoria 3011, Australia

Lonely Planet Offices
Australia Locked Bag 1, Footscray, Victoria 3011
USA 150 Linden St, Oakland, CA 94607
UK 10a Spring Place, London NW5 3BH
France 1 rue du Dahomey, 75011 Paris

Photographs
Many of the images in this guide are available for licensing from
Lonely Planet Images.
email: lpi@lonelyplanet.com.au
Web site: www.lonelyplanetimages.com

Front cover photograph
Cyclist and palm trees silhouetted against a red sky at sunset, Midigama
(Mark Daffey)

Wildlife Guide title page photograph
The sociable mingling of an elephant herd (Michael Aw)

ISBN 1 74059 039 2

text & maps © Lonely Planet Publications Pty Ltd 2001
photos © photographers as indicated 2001

Printed by Craft Print International Ltd, Singapore

Contents – Text

Contents – Maps

MAPS

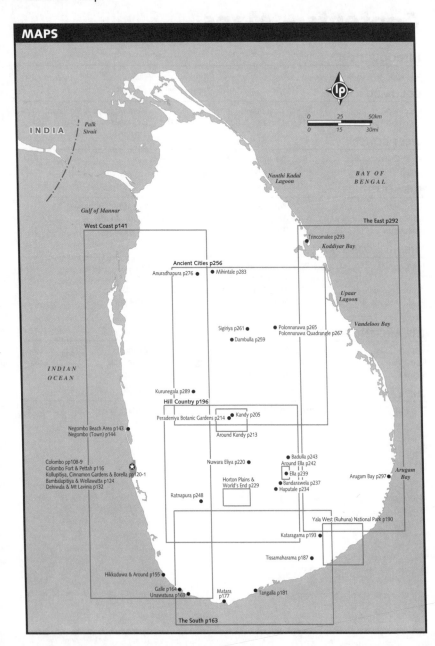

INDIA

Palk Strait

Gulf of Mannar

0 25 50km
0 15 30mi

Nanthi Kadal Lagoon

BAY OF BENGAL

West Coast p141

The East p292

Trincomalee p293
Koddiyar Bay

Ancient Cities p256

Anuradhapura p276 ● ● Mihintale p283

Upaar Lagoon

Vandeloos Bay

Sigiriya p261 ● ● Polonnaruwa p265
Polonnaruwa Quadrangle p267

● Dambulla p259

INDIAN OCEAN

Kurunegala p289 ●

Hill Country p196

Peradeniya Botanic Gardens p214 ● ● Kandy p205

Around Kandy p213

Negombo Beach Area p143 ●
Negombo (Town) p144

Colombo pp108-9
Colombo Fort & Pettah p116
Kollupitiya, Cinnamon Gardens & Borella pp120-1
Bambalapitiya & Wellawatta p124
Dehiwala & Mt Lavinia p132

Nuwara Eliya p220 ●

● Badulla p243
Around Ella p242

● Ella p239

● Bandarawela p237
Haputale p234 ●

Arugam Bay p297 ● *Arugam Bay*

Horton Plains & World's End p229

Ratnapura p248 ●

Yala West (Ruhuna) National Park p190

Kataragama p193 ●

Tissamaharama p187 ●

Hikkaduwa & Around p155 ●

Galle p164 ●
Unawatuna p169 ●

Matara p177 ●

● Tangalla p181

The South p163

The Authors

Verity Campbell
Verity has been travelling ever since her mother yelled, 'we're outta here'. (Melbourne, Australia, that was.) Struggling to fight the travel bug, she went to uni and studied landscape architecture. A year later she quit her graduate job and wrestled Tony Wheeler to the ground to land a job at Lonely Planet's Melbourne office. After four years of office life Verity has ventured into the authoring world. Despite her mother's protests, her home is in Melbourne, where she lives in a small flat that she shares with her ageing pooch Max and too many balls of dog hair.

Christine Niven
Christine grew up in New Zealand but a bad case of wanderlust has meant she has spent most of her time abroad. Her first long trip was overlanding from Europe to India. This was followed by forays into Japan, China, the Middle East – and India, again. She has authored LP's *India*, *South India*, *Sri Lanka*, *New Zealand* and *Auckland* guides.

5

FROM THE AUTHOR

Verity Campbell

Without the help and hospitality of many Sri Lankans this update would not have been possible. In no particular order, thanks to: Charmarie Maelge at the Ceylon Tourist Board, Robyn, Padmini, Vesak and the two welcoming families at Long Beach and Hill Top. Three-wheelers often saved the day – special thanks to MD Jayantha, S Srikanihan and P Ranawaka. Thanks also to the travellers I met (and letters you sent) – your contributions were invaluable.

Back home, Brigitte Ellemor provided an inexhaustible amount of encouragement and help; Panduka from the High Commission was always at hand; and Jenny Mullaly, Heath Comrie, Evan Jones, Hilary Rogers, Amanda Sierp, Hilary Ericksen, Adriana Mammarella and Geoff Stringer at LP worked hard yards to get the tome to the printers. Thanks also to Michael for morning cups of tea and much more. Finally, I'm almost embarrassed to say I'm indebted to my mother, but I am – she 'kept the wheels on the bus'.

This Book

Tony Wheeler wrote and researched the first three editions of this book. John Noble tackled the fourth edition in 1986, and, together with Susan Forsyth, updated the fifth edition. Christine Niven updated the sixth and seventh editions. This eighth edition of *Sri Lanka* was updated by Verity Campbell.

FROM THE PUBLISHER

This edition of *Sri Lanka* was edited in Lonely Planet's Melbourne office by Jenny Mullaly, with assistance from Evan Jones and Hilary Rogers. Amanda Sierp coordinated the mapping, with assistance from Heath Comrie. Amanda also coordinated the design and layout. Shahara Ahmed prepared the climate charts and did additional research for the health section. Jenny Jones designed the front cover. Matt King assisted with the illustrations, while Annie Horner from Lonely Planet Images assisted with the photographs. Lindsay Brown wrote the Wildlife Guide and Quentin Frayne compiled the Language chapter.

Thanks to Maxime Bodin and Oenone Chadburn for taking time out of their busy lives as volunteers to answer questions about life in Jaffna, and to Verity for answering all our extra questions with diligence and charm. Many thanks to Hilary Ericksen, senior editor, and Adriana Mammarella, senior designer, for overseeing the project so ably at the same time as juggling four other Indian subcontinent-related titles.

THANKS

Many thanks to the travellers who used the last edition and wrote to us with helpful hints, advice and interesting anecdotes. Your names appear in the back of this book.

Foreword

ABOUT LONELY PLANET GUIDEBOOKS

The story begins with a classic travel adventure: Tony and Maureen Wheeler's 1972 journey across Europe and Asia to Australia. Useful information about the overland trail did not exist at that time, so Tony and Maureen published the first Lonely Planet guidebook to meet a growing need.

From a kitchen table, then from a tiny office in Melbourne (Australia), Lonely Planet has become the largest independent travel publisher in the world, an international company with offices in Melbourne, Oakland (USA), London (UK) and Paris (France).

Today Lonely Planet guidebooks cover the globe. There is an ever-growing list of books and there's information in a variety of forms and media. Some things haven't changed. The main aim is still to help make it possible for adventurous travellers to get out there – to explore and better understand the world.

At Lonely Planet we believe travellers can make a positive contribution to the countries they visit – if they respect their host communities and spend their money wisely. Since 1986 a percentage of the income from each book has been donated to aid projects and human rights campaigns.

Updates Lonely Planet thoroughly updates each guidebook as often as possible. This usually means there are around two years between editions, although for more unusual or more stable destinations the gap can be longer. Check the imprint page (following the colour map at the beginning of the book) for publication dates.

Between editions up-to-date information is available in two free newsletters – the paper *Planet Talk* and email *Comet* (to subscribe, contact any Lonely Planet office) – and on our Web site at www.lonelyplanet.com. The *Upgrades* section of the Web site covers a number of important and volatile destinations and is regularly updated by Lonely Planet authors. *Scoop* covers news and current affairs relevant to travellers. And, lastly, the *Thorn Tree* bulletin board and *Postcards* section of the site carry unverified, but fascinating, reports from travellers.

Correspondence The process of creating new editions begins with the letters, postcards and emails received from travellers. This correspondence often includes suggestions, criticisms and comments about the current editions. Interesting excerpts are immediately passed on via newsletters and the Web site, and everything goes to our authors to be verified when they're researching on the road. We're keen to get more feedback from organisations or individuals who represent communities visited by travellers.

Lonely Planet gathers information for everyone who's curious about the planet – and especially for those who explore it first-hand. Through guidebooks, phrasebooks, activity guides, maps, literature, newsletters, image library, TV series and Web site we act as an information exchange for a worldwide community of travellers.

Research Authors aim to gather sufficient practical information to enable travellers to make informed choices and to make the mechanics of a journey run smoothly. They also research historical and cultural background to help enrich the travel experience and allow travellers to understand and respond appropriately to cultural and environmental issues.

Authors don't stay in every hotel because that would mean spending a couple of months in each medium-sized city and, no, they don't eat at every restaurant because that would mean stretching belts beyond capacity. They do visit hotels and restaurants to check standards and prices, but feedback based on readers' direct experiences can be very helpful.

Many of our authors work undercover, others aren't so secretive. None of them accept freebies in exchange for positive write-ups. And none of our guidebooks contains any advertising.

Production Authors submit their raw manuscripts and maps to offices in Australia, USA, UK or France. Editors and cartographers – all experienced travellers themselves – then begin the process of assembling the pieces. When the book finally hits the shops, some things are already out of date, we start getting feedback from readers and the process begins again...

WARNING & REQUEST

Things change – prices go up, schedules change, good places go bad and bad places go bankrupt – nothing stays the same. So, if you find things better or worse, recently opened or long since closed, please tell us and help make the next edition even more accurate and useful. We genuinely value all the feedback we receive. A well-travelled team reads and acknowledges every letter, postcard and email and ensures that every morsel of information finds its way to the appropriate authors, editors and cartographers for verification.

Everyone who writes to us will find their name in the next edition of the appropriate guidebook. They will also receive the latest issue of *Planet Talk*, our quarterly printed newsletter, or *Comet*, our monthly email newsletter. Subscriptions to both newsletters are free. The very best contributions will be rewarded with a free guidebook.

Excerpts from your correspondence may appear in new editions of Lonely Planet guidebooks, the Lonely Planet Web site, *Planet Talk* or *Comet*, so please let us know if you *don't* want your letter published or your name acknowledged.

Send all correspondence to the Lonely Planet office closest to you:

Australia: Locked Bag 1, Footscray, Victoria 3011
USA: 150 Linden St, Oakland, CA 94607
UK: 10a Spring Place, London NW5 3BH
France: 1 rue du Dahomey, 75011 Paris

Or email us at: talk2us@lonelyplanet.com.au

For news, views and updates see our Web site: www.lonelyplanet.com

HOW TO USE A LONELY PLANET GUIDEBOOK

The best way to use a Lonely Planet guidebook is any way you choose. At Lonely Planet we believe the most memorable travel experiences are often those that are unexpected, and the finest discoveries are those you make yourself. Guidebooks are not intended to be used as if they provide a detailed set of infallible instructions!

Contents All Lonely Planet guidebooks follow roughly the same format. The Facts about the Destination chapters or sections give background information ranging from history to weather. Facts for the Visitor gives practical information on issues like visas and health. Getting There & Away gives a brief starting point for researching travel to and from the destination. Getting Around gives an overview of the transport options when you arrive.

The peculiar demands of each destination determine how subsequent chapters are broken up, but some things remain constant. We always start with background, then proceed to sights, places to stay, places to eat, entertainment, getting there and away, and getting around information – in that order.

Heading Hierarchy Lonely Planet headings are used in a strict hierarchical structure that can be visualised as a set of Russian dolls. Each heading (and its following text) is encompassed by any preceding heading that is higher on the hierarchical ladder.

Entry Points We do not assume guidebooks will be read from beginning to end, but that people will dip into them. The traditional entry points are the list of contents and the index. In addition, however, some books have a complete list of maps and an index map illustrating map coverage.

There may also be a colour map that shows highlights. These highlights are dealt with in greater detail in the Facts for the Visitor chapter, along with planning questions and suggested itineraries. Each chapter covering a geographical region usually begins with a locator map and another list of highlights. Once you find something of interest in a list of highlights, turn to the index.

Maps Maps play a crucial role in Lonely Planet guidebooks and include a huge amount of information. A legend is printed on the back page. We seek to have complete consistency between maps and text, and to have every important place in the text captured on a map. Map key numbers usually start in the top left corner.

Although inclusion in a guidebook usually implies a recommendation we cannot list every good place. Exclusion does not necessarily imply criticism. In fact there are a number of reasons why we might exclude a place – sometimes it is simply inappropriate to encourage an influx of travellers.

Introduction

It's easy to think of Sri Lanka as a tropical island offshoot of India – with the difference being that the majority of people are Buddhist, not Hindu, and that there aren't so many of them, but their quarrels are bloodier. In fact Sri Lanka is totally different from India and has its own qualities.

Marco Polo thought that Sri Lanka was the finest island of its size in all the world, and you won't have trouble agreeing with him once you've explored any of Sri Lanka's delights. What takes your fancy? Beaches? The coastal stretch south of Colombo has palm-lined beach after palm-lined beach. Culture? Try the Kandyan dances, a procession of elephants or the masked devil dances. Ruins? There's more than enough to see at the ruined ancient cities of Anuradhapura and Polonnaruwa.

Scenery? Head for the hill country where the heat of the plains and the coast fades away to reveal gorgeous rolling hills often carpeted with tea plantations. Surfing? Many rave about the waves at Arugam Bay. Wildlife? The island is teeming with bird life, monkeys are often at hand to steal your lunch, and the plethora of nature reserves is home to elephants, leopards and deer, to name just a few. To top it off, these goodies come with the added bonus of welcoming, friendly people, good food, pleasant places to stay and reasonably low costs – all wrapped up in an easy-to-navigate, compact package.

CEYLON OR SRI LANKA?

Changing the country's name from Ceylon to Sri Lanka in the 1970s caused considerable

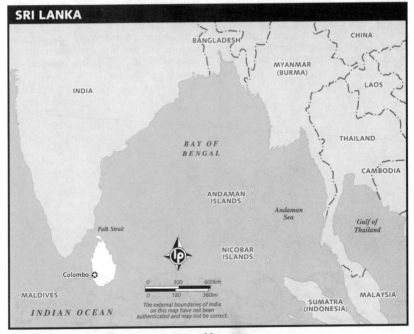

Is it Safe?

Many potential visitors have been scared away from Sri Lanka by the violent ethnic conflict that has periodically rendered the north and east of the island off limits since 1983. These areas are still troubled, and it's not safe to travel to Jaffna and other parts of the north. In May 2000, the Liberation Tigers of Tamil Eelam (LTTE) captured the strategic position of Elephant Pass, the gateway to the Jaffna peninsula, and gained further ground in an ongoing attempt to take Jaffna and create a separate homeland in the north and the east of the island.

The long-term situation for travellers remains up in the air until the conflict comes to a decisive end. Safety cannot be guaranteed in Colombo, where there are a number of suicide bombings every year. When travelling on the west and south coasts (which include Hikkaduwa, Unawatuna and Tangalla), in the hill country (Kandy, Adam's Peak and Sinharaja) and in the Cultural Triangle (Anuradhapura, Dambulla and Polonnaruwa), however, you'd barely know there was a war on. Although fighting continues in the north and east of the island, a handful of travellers continue to visit Trincomalee in the north-east, while many more head east to the surf at Arugam Bay.

Over 400,000 tourists visit Sri Lanka each year, but as things can change quickly, you should check the latest situation with your embassy before you leave.

confusion, but in fact it has always been known to the Sinhalese (the majority people of Sri Lanka) as Lanka, and to the Tamils as Ilankai. Indeed the 2000-year-old Hindu epic, the Ramayana, tells of Rama's beautiful wife being carried away by the evil king of Lanka. Later, the Romans knew it as Taprobane and Muslim traders talked of the island of Serendib, from which was derived the word 'serendipity' – the faculty of making happy and unexpected discoveries by accident. The Portuguese called it Ceilão, a corruption of Sinhala-dvipa, the native name. In turn, the Dutch altered this name to Ceylan and the British to Ceylon. In 1972 the original Lanka was restored with the addition of Sri, which means 'auspicious' or 'resplendent' in the Sinhalese language.

Facts about Sri Lanka

HISTORY

Sri Lanka is one of those places where history seems to fade into the mists of legend. Is not Adam's Peak said to be the very place where Adam set foot on earth, having been cast out of heaven? Isn't that his footprint squarely on top of the mountain to prove it? Or is it the Buddha's footprint on Sri Pada, visiting an island halfway to paradise? And isn't Adam's Bridge (the chain of islands linking Sri Lanka to India) the very series of stepping stones that Rama skipped across to rescue Sita from the clutches of the evil demon Rawana, King of Lanka, in the epic Ramayana?

It is probable that the story of the Ramayana actually does have some frail basis in reality, for Sri Lanka's history recounts many invasions from southern India. Perhaps some early, punitive invasion provided the background for the story of Rama and his beautiful wife, a story that is recounted over and over again all around Asia.

Whatever the legends, the reality points towards the first Sinhalese people (who probably originated in North India) arriving in Sri Lanka around the 5th or 6th century BC, gradually replacing the prior inhabitants, the Wanniyala-aetto or Veddahs.

The Rise & Fall of Anuradhapura

The Sinhalese kingdom of Anuradhapura developed in the dry, northern plain region of the island in the 4th century BC. Later, other Sinhalese kingdoms were built in the south and west, but Anuradhapura remained the strongest. It was in the 3rd century BC that Mahinda, the son of the great Buddhist emperor Ashoka (who reigned in India), came to the island to spread the Buddha's teachings. He soon converted the Anuradhapuran king and his followers to Buddhism, and his sister, Sangamitta, planted a sapling of the sacred Bodhi Tree *(Ficus religiosa)* under which the Buddha attained enlightenment in Bodhgaya in northern India. It can still be seen flourishing in Anuradhapura today.

Buddhism went through a rejuvenation in Sri Lanka and it was here that the Theravada school of Buddhism developed, later spreading to other Buddhist countries. Even today, Buddhists of the Theravada school in Myanmar (Burma), Thailand and other countries look to Sri Lanka for spiritual leadership.

Buddhism gave the Sinhalese people a sense of national purpose and identity, and also inspired the development of their culture and literature, which were to become important in the tumultuous centuries that followed. Anuradhapura was the centre of Sinhalese kingdoms for almost 1500 years, from around the 4th century BC to the 10th century AD. But it suffered as a result of its proximity to South India, where Hinduism continued to flourish. There were repeated invasions and takeovers of Anuradhapura by south Indian kingdoms, and self-defeating entanglements in south Indian affairs by Anuradhapura's rulers.

A number of Sinhalese heroes arose to repel the invaders, two of the most famous being Dutugemunu (2nd century BC) and Vijayabahu I (11th century AD). It was Vijayabahu I who finally decided to abandon Anuradhapura and make Polonnaruwa, farther south-east, his capital.

Today, the majestic ruins of these two cities are not the only reminders of this period of Sri Lankan history. Scattered over the country are enormous 'tanks', artificial lakes developed for irrigation purposes in the dry regions of Sri Lanka. Even today they would be considered amazing engineering feats.

The Rise & Fall of Polonnaruwa

Polonnaruwa survived as a Sinhalese capital for over two centuries and provided two other great kings after Vijayabahu I. His nephew Parakramabahu I (r. AD 1153–86), not content with Vijayabahu's expulsion of south Indian Chola rulers from Sri Lanka, carried the fight to South India and even made a raid on Myanmar. Internally he indulged in an orgy of building at his capital, and constructed many new tanks around the country. But his warring and architectural extravagances wore the country out, and probably shortened Polonnaruwa's lifespan.

His successor, Nissanka Malla (r. 1187–96), was the last great king of Polonnaruwa. He was followed by a series of weak rulers, until a south Indian kingdom arose once again in the north of the island. Tanks were neglected or destroyed, malaria started to spread due to the decay of the irrigation system and finally, like Anuradhapura before it, Polonnaruwa was abandoned.

The Portuguese Period

The centre of Sinhalese power shifted to the south-west of the island, and between AD 1253 and 1400 there were five Sinhalese capitals. During this period Sri Lanka also suffered attacks by Chinese and Malayans, as well as periodic incursions from South India. Finally, the Portuguese arrived in 1505.

At this time Sri Lanka had three main kingdoms: the Tamil kingdom of Jaffna in the north (which originated in South India), and the Sinhalese kingdoms of Kandy in the central highlands and Kotte, which was the most powerful, in the south-west. When the Portuguese Lorenço de Almeida arrived in Colombo, he established friendly relations with the king of Kotte and gained a monopoly on the spice and cinnamon trade for Portugal, which soon became enormously important in Europe. Attempts by Kotte to capitalise on the strength and protection of the Portuguese resulted in Portugal taking over and ruling not only their regions but also the rest of the island, apart from the central highlands around Kandy. Because the highlands were remote and inaccessible, the kings of Kandy were always able to defeat attempts by the Portuguese to annex them, and on a number of occasions drove the Portuguese right back down to the coast. The Tamil kingdom of Jaffna was the last Portuguese stronghold on the island.

The Dutch Period

Portuguese rule was at its worst characterised by greed, cruelty and intolerance, but attempts by Kandy to enlist Dutch help in expelling the Portuguese only resulted in the substitution of one European power for another. By 1658, 153 years after the first Portuguese contact, the Dutch had taken control over the coastal areas of the island. During their 140 years' rule the Dutch, like the Portuguese, were involved in repeated unsuccessful attempts to bring Kandy under their control. The Dutch were much more interested in trade and profits than the Portuguese, who were more focused on spreading their religion and extending their physical control.

The British Period

The French revolution resulted in a major shake-up among the European powers, and in 1796 the Dutch were easily supplanted by the British, who in 1815 also managed to win control of the kingdom of Kandy, thus becoming the first European power to rule the whole island. Until 1802 the British administered Sri Lanka from Chennai (Madras) in India, but in that year Sri Lanka became a crown colony and in 1818 a unified administration for the island was set up.

In 1832 sweeping changes in property laws opened the doors to British settlers – at the expense of the Sinhalese, who in the eyes of the British did not have clear title to their land. Soon the country was dotted with coffee, cinnamon and coconut plantations and a network of roads and railways was built to handle this new economic activity. English became the official language, and is still widely spoken today.

Coffee was the main cash crop and the backbone of the colonial economy, but when a leaf blight virtually wiped it out in the 1870s, the plantations were quickly switched over to tea or rubber.

The British, unable to persuade the Sinhalese to work cheaply and willingly on the plantations, imported large numbers of Tamil labourers from South India. Sinhalese peasants in the hill country lost land to the estates, and today friction between the hill-country Tamils and their Sinhalese neighbours still leads to occasional outbreaks of violence.

Independence

Following WWII, in the wake of independence for India, it was evident that Sri Lanka would be granted independence very soon. In February 1948 Sri Lanka, or Ceylon as it was still known, became an independent member of the British Commonwealth. The first independent government was formed by DS Senanayake and his United National Party (UNP). His main opponents were Tamil parties from the north of the country and from the tea plantations, and communists.

At first everything went smoothly. The economy remained strong; tea prices, running at a high level from WWII, were further bolstered by the Korean conflict. The government concentrated on strengthening social services and weakening the opposition. Having disenfranchised the hill-country Tamils by depriving them of citizenship, it certainly did achieve the latter. (Eventually deals in the 1960s and 1980s between Sri Lanka and India allowed some of the hill-country Tamils to be 'repatriated' to India while others were granted Sri Lankan citizenship.)

In 1952, DS Senanayake was killed in an accident and was succeeded by his son Dudley Senanayake. This, the first of his four periods as prime minister,was very short lived. One of the first policies instituted after independence had been free rations of rice to every Sri Lankan as well as subsidies for imports of this staple. But the price of rice had started to escalate worldwide and the balance of payments started to run the wrong way. An attempt in 1953 to increase the rice price resulted in mass riots, many deaths and the declaration of a state of emergency. Dudley Senanayake resigned.

Sir John Kotelawala, his uncle, replaced him, and the UNP earned the nickname 'Uncle Nephew Party'. Kotelawala was easily defeated in the 1956 general election by the Mahajana Eksath Peramuna (MEP) coalition led by SWRD Bandaranaike.

SWRD Bandaranaike

Bandaranaike defeated the UNP primarily on nationalistic issues that harked back to the Dharmapala movement of the late 19th and early 20th centuries (see Religion later in this chapter).

Nearly 10 years after independence was granted, English remained the national language and the country continued to be ruled by an English-speaking, mainly Christian, elite. Many Sinhalese thought the elevation of their language to 'official' status, to be used in government and official work, would increase their power and job prospects.

Caught in the middle of this disagreement (English versus Sinhala, and Christian versus Buddhist) were the Tamils, whose mother tongue was Tamil. When Banaranaike enacted the 'Sinhala Only' law, making Sinhalese the official language of the country, Tamil protests were followed by violence and deaths. The Tamils began pressing for a federal system of government with greater local autonomy in the main Tamil-populated areas, the north and east.

Sri Lanka's serious Sinhalese-Tamil difficulties really date from this time, although they had started simmering during the jockeying for position when the end of colonial rule came in sight. From the mid-1950s, when the economy slowed, competition for wealth and work – intensified by the high expectations created by Sri Lanka's fine education system – exaggerated Sinhalese-Tamil jealousies. The main political parties, particularly when in opposition, played on Sinhalese paranoia that their religion, language and culture could all be swamped by the Hindu and non-Sinhala-speaking peoples of India, who were thought to be the natural allies of the Tamils in Sri Lanka. The Tamils began to see themselves as a threatened minority.

Bandaranaike also launched a program of nationalisation and creation of state monopolies. The most visible of these was the Ceylon Transport Board (CTB), which took over every private bus line in the country and managed to make bus travel an uncomfortable and thoroughly chaotic experience.

Bandaranaike was assassinated by a Buddhist monk in 1959, and to this day is looked upon as a national hero who brought the government of Sri Lanka back to the common people.

Sirimavo Bandaranaike

In the 1960 general election, the Sri Lanka Freedom Party (SLFP), led by SWRD Bandaranaike's widow, Sirimavo, swept to power. She was the first female prime minister in the world.

Sirimavo Bandaranaike pressed on with her husband's nationalisation policies and soured relations with the USA by taking over the Sri Lankan oil companies. But the economy was going from bad to worse and an attempt to abolish the rice policy met with massive opposition.

In the 1965 election Dudley Senanayake scraped back into power, but his reluctance to turn back the clock on the SLFP's nationalisation program soon lost him much support. The UNP was massively defeated by the SLFP in the 1970 elections.

JVP Uprising Sirimavo Bandaranaike again failed to come to grips with the economic crisis. Then in 1971 a Sinhalese Marxist insurrection broke out, led by a dropout from Moscow's Lumumba University, Rohana Wijeweera, under the banner of the Janatha Vimukthi Peramuna (JVP, People's Liberation Army). The poorly organised rebels, mostly students and young people, were quickly and ruthlessly eradicated by the army, at a cost of many thousand lives. North Korea was accused of aiding the revolt.

The revolt handed the government a mandate for sweeping changes, including strengthened armed forces, a new constitution, and a new Sinhalese name, Sri Lanka, for the country. However, the economy continued to deteriorate. Attempts to continue the supply of free rice at all costs led to drastic shortages of almost everything else. Long queues became commonplace in shops all over the country and in the 1977 elections the SLFP (under its new guise as the United Left Front) went down in a stunning defeat at the hands of the UNP.

Tamil Unrest Meanwhile the Tamils were growing more alienated, with two pieces of legislation causing particular grievance. The first, passed in 1970, was designed to cut their numbers in universities – previously,

Tamils had tended to gain a disproportionate number of university places. The second was the new 1972 constitution's declaration that Buddhism had the 'foremost place' and that it was the state's duty to 'protect and foster' Buddhism.

When unrest grew among northern Tamils, a state of emergency was imposed on their areas for several years from 1971. Since the police and army that enforced the state of emergency now included few Tamils (partly because of the 'Sinhala Only' law) and were often undisciplined and heavy-handed, they came to be seen more and more as an enemy force by Tamils.

In the mid-1970s, some mostly left-wing young Tamils started to take to violence, fighting for an independent Tamil state, Eelam. The Tamil United Liberation Front (TULF), founded in 1976, also campaigned for Eelam.

JR Jayewardene

Economic Change The new UNP prime minister elected in 1977, Junius Richard (JR) Jayewardene, back-pedalled on the Bandaranaike nationalisation programs and made an all-out effort to lure back some of the foreign investment chased away by Sirimavo Bandaranaike. He cut subsidies, devalued the rupee to help exports, opened the country up on a large scale to tourism and foreign imports and investment (especially by setting up a free-trade zone north of Colombo near the airport at Katunayake). He also speeded up the Mahaweli project, in which a series of dams were constructed on Sri Lanka's longest river to provide hydroelectricity and irrigation. Steps were taken to improve agricultural output, and some state companies were sold off to the private sector.

These measures yielded some successes: Unemployment was halved by 1983, Sri Lanka became self-sufficient in rice production in 1985, and tourism and the large numbers of Sri Lankans working in the Middle East began bringing in foreign currency. On the other hand, inflation rose until it peaked at 40% in 1979–80 (though it was down below 10% by 1986); prices of major exports such as tea and rubber were unstable; and while some people made fast money from tourism and trade, many people's incomes stood still or were eaten into by inflation.

Political Developments Jayewardene took a number of steps said to be aimed at achieving the political stability needed to counter left-wing subversion, but which were also criticised as undemocratic. In 1978 he introduced a new constitution (Sri Lanka's third), which conferred greatest power on the new post of president, to which he himself was elected by parliament.

In 1980 parliament found Sirimavo Bandaranaike guilty of 'abuse of power' while in office, and her civic rights were removed for seven years. This meant she could no longer be a member of parliament. (Jayewardene restored her rights in 1986.)

In 1982 Jayewardene was re-elected president in national polls (after amending his own constitution to bring the voting forward two years) and then in the same year won a referendum to bypass the 1983 general election and leave the existing parliament in office until 1989. As usual there were allegations of electoral skulduggery.

Tamil Rebellion Jayewardene promoted Tamil to the status of a 'national language' to be used in official work in Tamil-majority areas, and also introduced greater local control in government. But these measures didn't stop the clashes between Tamil 'boys' and the security forces from growing into a pattern of killings, reprisals, reprisals for reprisals, etc. All too often the victims were civilians.

The 1983 Riots The powder keg finally exploded in 1983. The spark was the ambush and massacre of an army patrol by Tamil 'Tiger' secessionists in the northern Jaffna region, the heartland of the island's Tamil population. For several days afterwards, Sinhalese mobs and gangs indulged in an orgy of killing, burning and looting against Tamils and their property in towns all over the island. Somewhere between 400

and 2000 Tamils were killed and some areas with large Tamil populations – such as Colombo's Pettah district and the business districts of some hill-country towns – were virtually levelled.

The government, the police and the army were unable, and in some cases, unwilling, to stop the violence. There had been similar, smaller-scale, anti-Tamil outbursts in 1958, 1977 and 1981, but this was the worst and for many it marked the point of no return. Tens of thousands of Tamils fled to safer, Tamil-majority areas while many others left the country altogether; Sinhalese started to move out of Jaffna and other areas dominated by Tamils.

Escalation of Violence Both sides grew more violent and there were several large-scale massacres – probably the worst being the May 1985 Anuradhapura massacre in which about 150 people (mainly Sinhalese) were gunned down by terrorists. The government was condemned by Amnesty International and others over torture and disappearances, but it pointed to the intimidation and violence against civilians (including Tamils) by the Tamil fighters, and the help and training India allowed them to receive in its Tamil areas. The Indian government was reluctant to clamp down on this for fear of losing the votes of Indian Tamils.

The area claimed by the Tamil militants for the independent state of Eelam was Sri Lanka's Northern and Eastern Provinces – roughly speaking, the region to the north of Vavuniya as well as a strip all the way down the east coast. This amounted to about one-third of Sri Lanka's land area, which the government couldn't even contemplate conceding given the strength of Sinhalese feeling. While Tamils were the overwhelming majority in the Northern Province, in the east Muslims, Sinhalese and Tamils were present in nearly equal numbers (although Tamils argued that the Sinhalese numbers had only been bumped up to this level due to newcomers settled on lands opened by the Mahaweli irrigation schemes).

The limited self-government the Tamils were offered in the mid-1980s was too little, too late. Tamil feeling had hardened and the militants' grip over the Tamil population had tightened. At the same time, the sometimes undisciplined government forces alienated many moderate Tamils.

By the end of 1985 fighting had spread not only throughout the north but also down most of the east coast, where the strongest and most hardline Tamil armed group, the Tigers (officially the Liberation Tigers of Tamil Eelam or LTTE), attacked Sinhalese villages, leading of course to reprisals on Tamil inhabitants. Clashes also began between Tamils and Muslims in the east. Around 50,000 people (Tamils, Sinhalese and Muslims) were in refugee camps in Sri Lanka, according to the government, and about 100,000 Tamils were in camps in India. Thousands more Tamils had left for other countries.

The violence cost Sri Lanka's economy dearly. Many businesses were destroyed and tourism slumped badly after 1983. The government had to put crippling amounts of money into defence; aid-giving countries threatened to cut assistance because of the ill-treatment of Tamils. Just to add to the woes, tea prices dived.

Indo–Sri Lankan Accord

In 1987 government forces pushed the LTTE back into Jaffna city, only to provoke increasingly serious threats of Indian intervention on the Tamil side. Jayewardene turned round and struck a deal with India by which the Sri Lankan army would return to barracks while an Indian Peace Keeping Force (IPKF) would disarm Sri Lanka's Tamil rebels and keep the peace in the north and east. A single provincial council would be elected to govern the east and north with substantial autonomy for a trial period.

Opposition to the deal came not just from the secessionist LTTE – which complied initially, but only because India gave it no choice – but also from the ranks of Muslims and Sinhalese, including the SLFP, the reviving JVP and a number of important Buddhist monks, who feared Indian influence and considered the deal a sell-out of non-Tamils in the east. Colombo was hit by Sinhalese riots

and the LTTE carried out some savage attacks on Sinhalese villages in the east. The IPKF laid into the LTTE and took Jaffna city with hundreds dead on both sides.

JVP Rebellion

Just as the lid was put on the Tamil insurgency, a Sinhalese rebellion broke out in the south and centre of the country. In 1987–88 the Marxist JVP, which had threatened Sirimavo Bandaranaike's government in 1971, re-emerged to launch a series of political murders and strikes enforced on pain of death. By late 1988 the centre and south of the country were terrorised and the economy was crippled. At one critical point tourists were flown out of the country in their thousands, killing the tourism industry stone dead. The military had to force employees of essential services to go to work at gunpoint.

At the end of 1988 Jayewardene retired. His successor as UNP leader, Ranasinghe Premadasa, defeated Sirimavo Bandaranaike in the new presidential election, and the UNP went on to win a general election in February 1989. Premadasa's ruthless answer to the JVP, after both Jayewardene and he had failed to persuade it to join mainstream politics, was death squads that went round killing JVP suspects. By late 1989 most of the JVP leadership were killed, including Wijeweera, or captured. JVP activity tailed off in 1990 but the method of eliminating it resulted in pressure from aid-giving Western countries for improved human rights in Sri Lanka. It is estimated that up to 17,000 were killed in the three-year insurrection.

Indian Withdrawal

One of Premadasa's main electoral promises, which had won him the support of Sinhalese nationalists, was the removal of the Indian peacekeepers from Sri Lanka, despite the fact that they had seemingly almost eliminated the LTTE. Premadasa soon set about securing his goal. The LTTE, desperate to see the back of the peacekeepers, agreed to a cease-fire with the government to help speed up the Indian withdrawal, but at the same time began to gear up for another war. The peacekeepers completed their withdrawal in March 1990. At its peak, the peacekeeping force had numbered 80,000 men and in three years it lost over 1000 lives. In June the LTTE attacked several police stations in the east, and, it's thought, massacred hundreds of police. The war between the LTTE and the Sri Lankan government began all over again. By the end of 1990, while the LTTE held much of the north, the east was largely back under government control, though still subject to LTTE attacks on Sinhalese and Muslim villagers, which were aimed at diverting government forces from the north.

New War in the North

The new war reached a peak in mid-1991 – soon after the assassination of India's prime minister, Rajiv Gandhi, by a suspected Tamil Tiger in Tamil Nadu – with a series of battles around Jaffna, but then tailed off as the LTTE suffered some reverses. The LTTE's support among Tamils was declining. By early 1992 it seemed ready to consider some kind of federal arrangement, which would involve giving self-control to a united north and east within a unitary Sri Lankan state. The mood among Tamil and Sinhalese people seemed to favour peace. But Sinhalese nationalists, who thought the Tigers were simply buying time, blocked any chance of the government coming to talks.

In mid-1992 the army, after doubling in size in nine years to 75,000 and being better armed and trained than ever before, launched a big new assault in the north. It was also reportedly conducting a 'hearts and minds' effort in areas it captured by giving protection to the Tamil inhabitants – an important change, if genuine, because it still had a reputation for senseless killings of Tamil civilians. The LTTE, relying increasingly on women fighters after heavy losses of its 'boys', declared that even if it lost a conventional war it would fight on as an urban guerrilla army. By the end of 1992, tens of thousands of people had died since the 1983 Tamil insurrection and 700,000 people had been displaced. Over 200,000 Sri Lankans were living in the Indian state of Tamil Nadu, about half of them in refugee camps.

Assassinations & Elections

President Premadasa was assassinated at a May Day rally in 1993. The LTTE was suspected, but never claimed responsibility. Prime Minister Dingiri Banda Wijetunge took his place, but in the meantime there was jockeying for position within both the UNP and the SLFP parties in anticipation of elections. Gamini Dissanayake, who had quit the UNP along with several other disaffected members in late 1991 to form the Democratic United Nations Front (DUNF), returned to the fold, eventually becoming the party's presidential candidate.

At the same time Chandrika Bandaranaike Kumaratunga, daughter of SLFP leader Sirimavo Bandaranaike, made a successful challenge for the leadership of the SLFP. As leader, Kumaratunga became head of the People's Alliance (PA), a coalition that included the SLFP and smaller parties. The PA narrowly won the parliamentary elections in August 1994. But just weeks before the November presidential elections an LTTE suicide bomber killed Dissanayake and a number of senior party members. Kumaratunga won the elections, becoming Sri Lanka's first female president, appointing her mother prime minister.

Peace Talks Break Down

The PA had promised to end the civil war, and things indeed looked promising when peace talks began in January 1995 and there was a halt to hostilities. But it all came to an end in April in a hail of accusations and counter-accusations.

In late 1995 tens of thousands of government troops swarmed into the Jaffna peninsula in Operation Riviresa (Operation Sunshine). Jaffna city was taken in December, but not before a major exodus of its inhabitants. A major thrust to establish a land route from Vavuniya to Jaffna was begun in May 1997 (Operation Sure Victory). In September 1998 the army captured Mankulam, 40km from Vavuniya. The LTTE made a tactical withdrawal from Mankulam and went on to capture Kilinochchi and part of Paranthan.

The first local elections since 1983 were held in Jaffna in January 1998; the majority of the 17 local councils were won by a former militant group, the Eelam People's Democratic Party (EPDP). In May 1998 the mayor of Jaffna (a member of the pro-government Tamil United Liberation Front) was assassinated, with many claiming it was the work of the Tigers. In August 1998 the government imposed a nationwide state of emergency; the following month the Tigers offered to restart peace talks on the condition that there should be third-party mediation. This was rejected by the government. In 1999 provincial elections went ahead in six provinces. Neither major party, the PA or the UNP, gained a majority of votes. The PA coalition depended on minor parties, including the JVP, which had joined mainstream politics, to govern in these provinces.

Kumaratunga was the target of a suicide bomber just days before the December 1999 presidential election. She survived the attack, but lost the sight of one eye, and won the election for a second term in office.

Resumed Peace Talks

In May 2000, the LTTE captured the strategic Elephant Pass, the gateway to the Jaffna peninsula. The Sri Lankan army, fighting low morale, feared the LTTE would move to take the peninsula including Jaffna city, which was taken from them in 1995. The situation looked bleak. With parliamentary elections looming in October, President Kumaratunga reacted by pushing a reformed constitution aimed at giving more power to the provincial councils. Although she failed to get this devolution package through parliament, she was hopeful the election would be a kind of referendum on the issue; if the PA won enough of the 225 seats she would have the majority to change the constitution. But there's no doubt Kumaratunga would have been disappointed with the election results: a narrow victory, with the UNP winning 89 seats and the minor parties, including the JVP, gaining ground.

Sirimavo Bandaranaike, the president's mother and three-time prime minister of Sri Lanka, died shortly after casting her vote at the October election.

In late 2000, a Norwegian peace envoy, led by Erik Solheim, was invited to bring the LTTE and the government to the negotiating table. Progress has been extremely slow with both sides battling extremist views and long-held prejudices. The fighting continues, despite cease-fires, though the Jaffna peninsula still remains in the hands of the Sri Lankan army.

Sri Lanka spends more than US$720 million a year on the war effort. So far more than 60,000 people have died and more than a million have been displaced.

GEOGRAPHY

Sri Lanka is shaped like a teardrop falling from the southern end of India. It stretches over 433km from north to south (latitudes 5°55' north and 9°51' north); it's only 244km at its widest point (longitudes 79°41' east to 81°53' east). Its area of 66,000 sq km is about the same as that of Ireland, or of Tasmania in Australia.

The central hill country rises a little south of the centre of the island and is surrounded by a coastal plain. The flat north-central and northern plain extends from the hill country all the way to the northern tip of the island – this region is much drier than the rest of the island. The best beaches are on the southwest, south and east coasts.

The highest mountain in the beautiful hill-country region is Pidurutalagala (2524m), which rises above Nuwara Eliya. Adam's Peak, at 2224m, is far better known and much more spectacular. The Mahaweli Ganga, Sri Lanka's longest river, has its source close to Adam's Peak and runs into the sea near Trincomalee. In the north-west of the country Mannar Island, joined to the mainland by a bridge, is almost connected to Rameswaram in southern India by a long chain of sandbanks and islets called Adam's Bridge.

CLIMATE

Sri Lanka is a typically tropical country in that there are distinct dry and wet seasons, but the picture is somewhat complicated by the fact that it is subject to two monsoons. From May to August the south-west monsoon brings rain to the south- and west-coast regions and the central highlands. This season is called *Yala*. The dry season in these regions is from December to March. The north-east monsoon blows from October to January – the *Maha* season – bringing rain to the north and east of the island. The dry season in the north-east is from May to September. There is also an inter-monsoonal period in October and November when rain and thunderstorms can occur in many parts of the island.

This peculiar monsoon pattern means that it is always the 'right' season somewhere on the island – though this advantage has been undermined by the troubles in the east. Don't count on the weather following the rules though – it often seems to be raining where it should be sunny and sunny where it should be raining, and like many other parts of the world, Sri Lanka has suffered some unusual weather conditions in recent years, with a serious drought in 1992 and another in 1996.

The south, south-west and central highlands are much wetter than the north and north-central regions. In the latter area annual rainfall averages only 100cm and the many tanks, some built over a thousand years ago to provide irrigation water, indicate that this is by no means a new problem. In the wetter part of the country annual rainfall reaches 400cm or more.

Colombo and the low-lying coastal regions have an average temperature of 27°C. The temperatures rapidly fall with altitude, so if you don't feel like cooling off in the sea you simply have to go up into the hill country. At Kandy (altitude 500m) the average temperature is 20°C and at Nuwara Eliya (at 1889m) you're down to 16°C. Up in the hills it can get warm during the day but you should come prepared for chilly evenings.

The highest temperatures in the south, south-west and central highlands are usually from February to May, but the mercury rarely climbs above 33°C. However, the

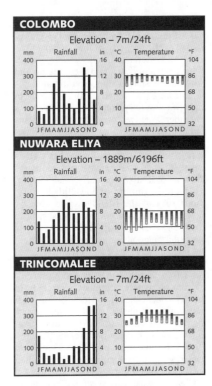

humidity in these months routinely reaches 75%, which will make you feel a few degrees hotter than the recorded temperature. November to January is usually the coolest time of the year. The sea can be counted upon to remain at around 27°C year-round, although it is much less suitable for swimming in during the monsoon period (May to August) when it can be choppy and murky.

ECOLOGY & ENVIRONMENT

More than 2000 years ago royalty ensured certain areas were protected from any human activity by declaring them sanctuaries. Almost every province in the kingdom of Kandy had such *udawattakelle* (sanctuaries), and they were overseen by specially designated officials. All animals, plants and birds in sanctuaries were to be left undisturbed, the taking of life being anathema to

Buddhist beliefs. But the worst violation was killing an elephant; elephants were regarded as the property of the Crown and as such, were sacred.

Large-scale destruction of fauna and flora really started during colonial times when forest was felled in the wet zone to make way for tea plantations, and elephants and other large creatures were shot for sport and to protect these plantations. Since independence, a growing population and an ever-increasing demand for food as well as a rush to industrialise have put enormous strain on Sri Lanka's resources and wildlife.

At the beginning of the 20th century, about 70% of the island was covered by natural forest. By 1998 this had shrunk to about 24%. *Chena* (shifting cultivation) is blamed for a good part of this deforestation, but huge areas in the east were also cleared under the Mahaweli irrigation scheme in the late 1970s, and clearance for paddy and cultivation elsewhere continues, especially in the dry zone. Since independence, clearing in the dry zone has proceeded at an escalating rate. The amount of land under cultivation was 1.35 million hectares in 1956; by 1995 this had increased to 2.02 million hectares. Selective logging and illicit felling have also taken their toll.

Clearing, especially slash-and-burn farming, and the increasing use of marginal land on steep slopes for vegetable crops such as tomatoes and potatoes (grown with heavy applications of chemical fertilisers), have created serious erosion problems.

Gem mining, sand mining and the destruction of coral reefs to feed lime kilns have also degraded the environment. On the west coast, between Chilaw and Puttalam, prawn farming has done major damage to the coastal ecology.

Some 82% of the land is controlled by the state in some form or other; the majority of natural forests are under state jurisdiction. The relevant government departments, the Department of Wildlife & Conservation and the Forestry Department, play an important role in conservation. Coastal resource management is under the jurisdiction of the Coast Conservation Department.

There is a raft of legislation to combat destructive activity and to protect sensitive areas. Sri Lanka is a signatory to the Ramsar Convention on Wetlands and Bundala NP has been recognised internationally under this convention. Sinharaja Forest Reserve is a World Heritage site – saved after being logged during the early 1970s. Sri Lanka has two marine sanctuaries: the Bar Reef (west of Kalpitiya peninsula) and the Hikkaduwa Marine Sanctuary. The Coast Conservation Department's 1996 Special Area Management Plans were targeted at Hikkaduwa and Rekawa, seeking to involve local stakeholders in managing the coastal resources. The Crown Lands Ordinance has banned the removal of coral since 1929, and the Forest Ordinance allows authorities to act against people who illicitly cut mangroves. There are laws against marine pollution, trade in endangered species, and the illegal felling of trees.

Despite all these measures, degradation continues due to a growing population that demands more land to be cleared for settlement and cultivation. However, things may be looking up for Sri Lanka's environment. In 2001, the government budgeted Rs 3.5 billion for a conservation and reafforestation project aimed at Sri Lankans living in rural areas.

Some of the most encouraging stories to emerge on the conservation front come from small communities in isolated areas. The Sri Lanka Environmental Journalists Forum (e slefj@sri.lanka.net) has published a book, *Environment is Their Mission*, which details numerous such projects around the country. Its office is at 174/4 Stanley Tillakaratne Mawatha, Nugegoda and its Web site is at www.oneworld.org/slejf.

In early 2001, Sri Lanka hosted an ecotourism conference as part of the government's push to market the potential of Sri Lanka in this increasingly popular and fashionable field. Niche markets being explored include adventure travel, health resorts and Ayurvedic resorts, but little is being said about what positive effects this will have on the environment. Indeed, at this stage the program seems somewhat tokenistic, driven by an urge to expand the tourist industry rather than protect the environment.

Energy

Sri Lanka lacks reserves of fossil fuels and as a result 95% of its electricity is hydro-generated. However, biomass (fuel wood gathered from forests and plantations, as well as paddy husks and coconut husks and shells) provides about 55% of the energy used. Only about 44% of households in Sri Lanka have access to electricity, and it's mostly used for lighting.

By far the biggest hydro project ever launched in Sri Lanka is the Mahaweli scheme, which was designed to provide irrigation for 365,000 hectares of land and yield a 470MW generating capacity. The first phase of the 30-year project was completed in 1978 (a 40MW hydro power plant at Ukauwela). The Accelerated Mahaweli Program, a revision of the master plan, started in 1977 and the headworks are finished, but the scheme has been riddled with criticism. To encourage settlement in the newly irrigated areas, settlers were promised 2½ acres of land. Few have received the land, and those who have complain that it isn't irrigated sufficiently, or at all. Many people have been displaced, for example the Wanniyala-aetto or Veddahs near Maduru Oya National Park, while compensation is still to be paid in many cases. There are also allegations of waterfall destruction. Adding salt to the wound, inefficiencies in the up-and-running irrigation systems have one report stating that one-third of the water is lost due to leakages.

The Sri Lanka Mahaweli Restructuring and Rehabilitation Project has been launched at a cost of US$74.2 million, supported by a World Bank loan of US$57 million, but this is seen by many as a band-aid approach to a fundamentally flawed vision.

Meanwhile, alternatives to hydropower are back on the drawing board. A privately owned power station, which would be the country's largest, has been proposed for the Colombo region. The project would be wholly funded by foreign interests.

FLORA & FAUNA

Sri Lanka not only has an exciting and varied range of animal and plant life – with elephants and leopards to the fore – but also an extensive national parks and reserves system.

Flora

The south-western wet zone is tropical rainforest with characteristic dense undergrowth and a tall canopy of hardwood trees, including ebony, teak and silkwood. Here also are some of the most spectacular orchids and many of the plants used in traditional Ayurvedic medicine. The central hill zone, which includes Horton Plains, is typical of cool, damp highland areas, with hardy grasslands, rhododendron and elfin (stunted) forests, and trees often draped in Spanish moss. The remainder of the island forms the arid dry zone, with a sparser cover of trees and shrubs, and grasslands that may erupt into bloom with the first rains.

Spice Gardens Spices are integral to Sri Lanka's cuisine and Ayurvedic traditions. A visit to a spice garden is an excellent way to discover the alternative uses of spices you've probably been using for years. You'll see cinnamon, cloves, nutmeg, vanilla beans, cardamom and black pepper, to name just a few. You can buy the pure products, oils or Ayurvedic potions. The sales teams are efficacious, and even if you walk in feeling fine, you'll come out laden with slimming drops, cough syrups and herbal sex stimulants. Watch the prices, and check in local markets beforehand to get an idea of costs.

Fruit Trees You'll see fruit trees such as mangoes, papayas and bananas growing in many private gardens in Sri Lanka, but two trees will certainly catch your eye, the jackfruit and the *del* or breadfruit. The jackfruit *(Artocarpus integrifolia)* is a tall evergreen tree with the world's largest fruit. These green, knobbly-skinned fruit, which sometimes weigh up to 30kg, hang close to the trunk of the tree. The tree also provides wood, frequently used for furniture. The breadfruit *(Artocarpus incisa)* is its smaller relative, is also large and ungainly.

Ayurveda – the Herbs for Good Health

Ayurveda (pronounced *eye-yer-veda*) – or the science of life – is an ancient system of medicine that uses herbs and oils to heal and rejuvenate. Heavily influenced by the system of the same name in India, Ayurveda is widely used in Sri Lanka for a range of ailments. Essentially, it postulates that the five elements (earth, air, ether, water and light) are linked to the five senses and these in turn shape the nature of an individual's constitution – their *dosha* or life force. These doshas are referred to in Sanskrit as *vata*, *pitta* and *kapha*. Each has a cluster of qualities that distinguish it from the others. Disease and illness occurs when they are out of balance. The purpose of Ayurvedic treatment is to restore the balance and thus good health.

Therapeutic treatments generally take some time; the patient must be prepared to make a commitment of weeks or months and be willing to concoct the often time-consuming preparations. It would be rare that a visitor underwent such a course of treatment. More commonly tourists avail themselves of one of the growing number of Ayurvedic massage centres attached to major hotels. The full treatment involves a head massage with oil, an oil body massage and a steam bath followed by a herbal bath (leaves and all). But this sort of regime is really only for relaxation.

Ayurvedic herbs, many of which are collected from the wild, are available for purchase at pharmacies all over the island. Siddhalepa Hospital in Mt Lavinia (Colombo) produces a range of Ayurvedic potions; its pleasantly pungent balm is a favourite with pilgrims tackling Adam's Peak and indeed there is a Siddhalepa stall halfway up that sells it. Other popular treatments include *paspanguwa*, the collection of plant seeds, leaves and twigs boiled in water and reduced to an acrid-tasting brew to treat colds. Packets of a more pleasant instant *peyava* (cold treatment) are available at *kades* (corner shops).

Ayurvedic physicians generally practise from their homes, which can usually be picked out from all the other similar looking places around them by the swastika signs outside (the swastika is an ancient protective symbol). For places to try Ayurvedic massage, see the Colombo and Hill Country chapters for details.

Common Trees The sacred bodhi tree *(Ficus religiosa)* was brought from India at the time Mahinda introduced the teachings of the Buddha to Sri Lanka. Saplings are planted in most Buddhist temples in Sri Lanka. The shape of a turned over leaf is said to have inspired the shape of the dagoba (Buddhist temple).

Also often found around Buddhist temples is the *sal*, also known as the cannonball tree *(Couroupita guianensis)*. You'll understand how the tree got its name when you see the huge woody fruits clinging to the trunk. The frangipani *(Plumeria spp)* is common throughout the island; its sweet-scented white, pink or yellow flowers are used as Buddhist temple offerings. You'll also see plenty of scarlet and magenta bougainvilleas in gardens. In the hill country there are many eucalyptus trees, which have often been planted to provide shade at tea estates.

Fauna

Mammals Sri Lanka has 86 mammal species including the famous elephant, leopards and monkeys including the long-tailed grey langur and the toque macaque. Other interesting mammals include sloth bears, loris, porcupines, jackals, dugongs and flying foxes. For more details see the 'Wildlife Guide' colour section.

Fish & Reptiles Some 54 species of fish are found in the waterways and marshlands, including prized aquarium varieties such as the red scissor-tail barb and the ornate paradise fish. The British introduced several kinds of fish, including trout, which are still common around Horton Plains. Then there are the myriad colourful tropical marine fish.

Also present are 40 species of frogs and toads, and the large variety of reptiles includes two species of crocodile (so watch where you swim!) and five of turtles. Most reptiles, however, are land dwellers, including the beautiful star tortoise and the infamous cobra. Of the 83 species of snakes recorded, only five are poisonous – the cobra, Russell's viper, the Indian and Sri Lankan krait and the saw-scaled viper – but these five are relatively common, especially in the dry-zone region around Anuradhapura and Polonnaruwa. Be careful if you are wandering around ruins off the main paths or cycling. (See Health in the Facts for the Visitor chapter for information on treating snake bites.)

Endangered Species

The World Conservation Union (formerly the IUCN) *Red Databook* lists 43 animal species as threatened in Sri Lanka. They include Sri Lanka's own subspecies of Asian elephant *(Elephas maximus)*, the sloth bear *(Melursus ursinus)* and the leopard *(Panthera pardus)*. All five of Sri Lanka's turtle species are threatened, as is the estuarine crocodile (killed for its meat) and the mild-mannered dugong (a protected animal that is nevertheless killed for its meat, which is supposed to taste like pork). Several species of birds, fish and insects are also under threat.

Elephants Elephants occupy a special place in Sri Lankan culture. In ancient times elephants were Crown property and killing one was a terrible offence. Legend has it that elephants stamped down the foundations of the great dagobas (Buddhist monuments) at Anuradhapura, and elephant iconography is common in Sri Lankan religious and secular art. Even today elephants are held in great affection and the Maligawa tusker, which carries the tooth relic on the final night of the Kandy Esala Perahera, is perhaps the most venerated of all.

But elephants are endangered, and although they are protected by law, they continue to be at risk. Habitat destruction and ongoing human-elephant conflict mean this huge creature faces a bleak future. There are some 2500 wild elephants in Sri Lanka (compared with 12,000 at the beginning of the 20th century), plus about 300 domesti-cated elephants (of which most were born in the wild).

Most at risk are the so-called pocketed herds, which, cut off from their normal feeding areas by development around them, find themselves trapped and vulnerable. The best-known pocketed herd is at Handapangala Tank, 9km out of Wellawaya. This herd has been trapped around a tank, unable to browse in its normal feeding areas. Attempts to relocate the herd have largely failed, and the elephants continue to pose a danger to the local villagers. Unless a solution is found, this herd will probably die out.

Some claim that Sri Lanka's total elephant population is falling at a rate of about 6% annually. It takes about 5 sq km of land to support an elephant in the wild. As the existing protected areas cover only 12.5% of the land area, there is only enough room for 1600 elephants within them.

For farmers in elephant country, this means an ever-present threat from animals that may trample their crops, destroy their buildings and even take their lives. To scare off the unwelcome raiders during the cultivation season, farmers conduct round-the-clock vigils for up to three months. It's understandable that for farmers on the breadline, elephants are a luxury they can't afford. Swift and adequate compensation for elephant-inflicted damage is one solution to the problem. The arming of farmers is occasionally mooted, but this would surely hasten the demise of elephants in Sri Lanka. Another option is creating elephant corridors. Problem elephants are sometimes relocated, but seem to have a knack for finding their way back.

Marine Turtles Sri Lanka has five species of marine turtle, all endangered: the leathery, the olive Ridley, the loggerhead, the hawksbill and the green. Though protected, they face significant threats from poachers, and environmental hazards from pollution and coastal exploitation. The hawksbill turtle is slaughtered for its beautifully patterned shell, which is made into combs, cigarette cases and other trinkets. Turtle eggs are dug up and sold in markets.

National Parks & Reserves

Bundala National Park (6216ha)
Location: On the south coast between Hambantota and Tissamaharama
Bundala is the end of the line for migrant birds. It is one of the best places to watch birds, with flamingos a star attraction. It can also be good for viewing elephants. See The South chapter.

Chundikkulam Bird Sanctuary (11,150ha)
Location: North-east coast
On Sri Lanka's eastern bird-migration route, this sanctuary attracts spectacular numbers of birds during spring and autumn. At other times there are still large numbers of birds and other wildlife. At the time of research the sanctuary was closed.

Flood Plains National Park (17,350ha)
Location: North-east of Polonnaruwa
This park was established in 1984 under the Mahaweli irrigation scheme. The Mahaweli Ganga flows through the park, and the marshy depressions along it are home to the endangered estuarine crocodile. Also found are elephants, fishing cats, jungle cats, jackals, wild boar, spotted deer, water buffaloes and migrant and resident waterfowl. At the time of research this park was closed.

Gal Oya National Park (62,936ha)
Location: North-west of Arugam Bay
This isolated park surrounds a large tank, the Senanayake Samudra, and provides an important sanctuary for elephants and a variety of other wildlife including sloth bears, leopards, deer and water buffaloes. See The East chapter for details.

Horton Plains National Park (3160ha)
Location: In the south-central hill country
The forests at this altitude (over 2000m) have unusual plant and animal life adapted to a cooler climate. The spectacular World's End precipice is just one feature of this unusual landscape. See the Hill Country chapter for details.

Kokkilai Lagoon Bird Sanctuary (2995ha)
Location: On the north-east coast
This sanctuary has a similar landscape and bird life to the Chundikkulam Bird Sanctuary. At the time of research it was closed.

Lahugala National Park (1554ha)
Location: Near Pottuvil, on the east coast
This small park protects tanks that attract good numbers of elephants. It's also very good for bird life. The park is officially closed, but see The East chapter for details.

Maduru Oya National Park (58,850ha)
Location: West of Batticaloa, east Sri Lanka
Created in 1983 under the Mahaweli irrigation scheme, this park contains an 8km range of rocky mountains in the south-west. It's considered one of Sri Lanka's most valuable conservation areas for elephants and endemic birds. Other wildlife includes sloth bears, water buffaloes, leopards, slender loris, toque macaques, fishing cats and wild boar. At the time of research the park was closed.

Minneriya National Park (8890ha)
Location: North-west of Polonnaruwa
The park is dominated by the Minneriya Tank. Toque macaques, sambar deer and elephants (in numbers up to 200) are regularly seen. There is plenty of bird life too. See the Ancient Cities chapter.

National Parks & Reserves

Sinharaja Forest Reserve (18,899ha)
Location: In the south-west, just south of Pelmadulla near Ratnapura
This is Sri Lanka's last remaining patch of virgin rainforest and the richest in endemic flora and fauna. It has spectacular rainforest scenery and the highest concentration of animals unique to Sri Lanka. Sinharaja has been declared a World Heritage site by Unesco. See the Hill Country chapter.

Somawathiya Chaitiya National Park (37,762ha)
Location: South-west of Trincomalee on the east coast
This park, adjacent to the Flood Plains National Park, is an important habitat for elephants. About 75 species of migrant birds winter here. At the time of research this park was closed.

Uda Walawe National Park (30,821ha)
Location: 200km south-east of Colombo, close to the southern end of the highlands; can be reached from Ratnapura or Embilipitiya
This park contains the Uda Walawe Reservoir. Elephants are the highlight; there are also spotted deer, water buffaloes and wild boar. See the Hill Country chapter for details.

Udawattakelle Sanctuary (105ha)
Location: Beside Kandy
This ancient reserve offers pleasant walking as well as opportunities to see birds and other wildlife. You may not have to go far to see the toque macaques here, as they usually come to you. See the Hill Country chapter for more information.

Wasgomuwa National Park (37,063ha)
Location: South-east of Polonnaruwa
Previously a sanctuary, Wasgomuwa was declared a national park under the Mahaweli scheme. It has a population of elephants as well as estuarine crocodiles, primates, sloth bears, deer and wild boar. At the time of research this park was closed.

Wilpattu National Park (131,693ha)
Location: 176km north of Colombo
This is Sri Lanka's largest park, most famous for its leopards, bears and bird life. At the time of research it was closed.

Wirawila Wewa Bird Sanctuary (4150ha)
Location: Near Tissamaharama
An extensive network of bird-covered lagoons forms this sanctuary, which is centred on Wirawila Wewa. See The South chapter for details.

Yala East National Park (18,149ha)
Location: Divided from Yala West National Park by a strict natural reserve into which visitors aren't allowed
Containing the Kumana mangrove swamp, this park has a variety of waterbirds in spectacular numbers. It is officially closed but see The East chapter for details.

Yala West (Ruhuna) National Park (14,101ha)
Location: 305km south-east of Colombo; conveniently approached from the south coast or the hill country
The open, undulating country of this park is studded with rocky formations and lagoons. Famous for elephants, the park is also home to sloth bears, leopards and water buffaloes. See the West Coast chapter for details.

101 Uses for a Coconut

The scrape-scraping sound of an *ekel* broom on bare earth is one that becomes very familiar very quickly in Sri Lanka. Ekel brooms, made from the tough mid-rib of the coconut frond, are plied on gardens and driveways all over the country every day. It's just one application of the extraordinarily versatile coconut palm tree, every part of which seems to have one use or other.

Sri Lankan cuisine wouldn't be what it is without the rich, white flesh of the coconut kernel. Grated coconut is made into *pol sambol* (*pol* means coconut in Sinhala), a fiery condiment laced with chilli. But minus the chilli it can be sprinkled over a curry to reduce it to something less explosive. Dried, the scrapings are known as *copra*, which is exported and used to make confectionery. Coconut oil is extracted from copra locally, and *poonac* (the desiccated residue) is used as fodder for animals.

The flesh of a newly opened coconut can be squeezed to produce a creamy white milk that adds a silky richness to curries; *pol hodda*, for example, is a spicy gravy made from coconut milk. *Kiri bath* (rice cooked in coconut milk) is not only delicious but ritually significant. It's traditionally the first solid food fed to a baby and is essential at weddings and other social events.

The bud on top of the stem, called the *bada*, can be pickled and eaten.

Piles of *thambli* (golden coconuts) are a familiar sight along roadsides. The liquid they contain is sweet and refreshing, and is cheaper and healthier than soft drink. *Kurumba* (green coconuts), actually younger versions of those used for cooking, are also good for drinking, but are slightly less sweet.

The sap of the coconut palm is extracted by agile toddy tappers who move from tree to tree like tightrope artists. (Toddy is the drink made from the sap.) Toddy trees are not permitted to bear fruit; the opened flowers are bound and bent over, and their sap is drawn off after about three weeks. Every morning and evening the toddy tappers go from flower to flower, changing the pots. One palm yields an average of 270 litres of toddy annually and a good tapper can get about a month's sap from one flower. Toddy can be boiled down to form a type of brown sugar called *jaggery*. Fermented and distilled, toddy becomes *arrack*, a popular honey-coloured alcoholic drink that's especially nice mixed with ginger ale. Vinegar is a by-product of distillation.

As for the rest of the tree, it seems to have 101 uses. In rural areas you can still see *cadjan* (coconut frond), fencing made from dried coconut branches, and roof supports of coconut wood. Bowls made from polished coconut shells are widely available. The fibrous husk that clings to the nut is stripped off, soaked in pits and then beaten to separate the fibres. These are woven into surprisingly strong coir ropes, or are used to make matting and upholstery, brushes and brooms. The shells are sculpted into tacky souvenirs such as monkeys and elephants. The versatile coconut shell also fulfils a spiritual role – it's often smashed at temples to bring good fortune.

MICK WELDON

Sand mining has scoured some beaches to the point where they are too steep for turtles to land. Bright lights and noise from tourist developments on the coast also discourage egg-laden females from landing.

As a visitor to Sri Lanka you should never buy turtle-shell products or turtle eggs, and if you see a swimming turtle, leave it alone. If you want to find out more about Sri Lanka's marine turtles and their conservation, see the boxed text 'Saving the Turtles' in The South chapter.

Flora The Trincomaleewood *(Berrya cordifolia),* satinwood *(Chloroxylon swietenia)* and ebony *(Diospyros ebenum)* are on the endangered list, a direct result of clearing forest for agriculture. The variegated ebony *(Diospyros quaesita)* is considered to be threatened with extinction. Many plant species used in Ayurvedic medicine are now also scarce, due to habitat destruction and over-collection.

Parks & Reserves

The early edicts of the country's Buddhist leaders and the Sinhalese culture itself kept much of the island's natural richness undisturbed for centuries. Sri Lanka can boast the world's first wildlife sanctuary, created by King Devanampiya Tissa in the 3rd century BC. One proclamation carved in Polonnaruwa for King Nissanka Malla (r. AD 1187–96) called for a ban on killing all animals within seven *gaw* (39km) of the city. These rulers were also aware of the importance of undisturbed forests and set aside large *thahanankalle* (forbidden forests) as wilderness areas and watersheds. Some of these ancient reserves still exist today, including the spectacular Sinharaja Forest Reserve and the Udawattakelle Sanctuary.

Today's system of parks and reserves is mostly a synthesis of traditionally protected areas and those established by the British. Nearly 100 protected areas are acknowledged by the government. There are three types of protected areas, though the distinctions can be blurred: national parks, strict natural reserves where no visitors are allowed and nature reserves, in which human habitation is permitted.

Sadly, owing mainly to the ethnic violence, many of Sri Lanka's national parks and reserves are closed to visitors. Some information on these parks is included in this book in the hope that they will reopen in the not-too-distant future. See the boxed text 'National Parks & Reserves', for more details.

GOVERNMENT & POLITICS

The Democratic Socialist Republic of Sri Lanka, which gained independence from Britain in February 1948, adopted its first republican constitution in 1972 and its current constitution in August 1978. Sri Lanka's executive president is elected for a period of six years and has the power to appoint or dismiss members of the cabinet, including the prime minister, and to dissolve parliament. Members of the 225 seat unicameral parliament are elected by popular vote via a modified proportional representation system for a six-year term.

The country is divided into eight provinces: Central, North-Central, North-Eastern, North-Western, Sabaragamuwa, Southern, Uva and Western.

The legal system is a complex mix of English common law and Roman-Dutch, Muslim, Sinhalese and customary law. For details on the major political parties and their evolution, see the History section earlier in this chapter.

ECONOMY

Before independence Sri Lanka's economy centred on plantation crops (tea, rubber and coconut products) – a legacy of the colonial regime. While plantation crops remain important, the economy today is considerably more diverse. The top earner now is the garment sector, which accounts for more than 30% of manufacturing employment and more than 32% of exports.

Sri Lanka's main export crops are tea and coconut products (agriculture accounts for 18.4% of GDP). The main markets for Sri Lankan tea are Russia and the Middle East; in 2000 tea accounted for 14% of exports (compared with 2% for coconut products). Sri Lanka exports 300 metric tons of fish and fish products (mainly prawns) annually. Fish consumption is some 15kg per capita a year. The fishing industry employs about 145,000 people, but the sector is yet to fully develop.

A major source of income is repatriated money earned by Sri Lankans in the Middle East and elsewhere. Some claim that it is, after garments, the country's second-highest source of income.

Tourism contributes about US$275 million per year to Sri Lanka's economy. Most tourists are from Western Europe (63%); only about 3% are from Australia.

At the time of research, inflation was about 11.7%. The economy has grown an average of 5.3% over the past five years and unemployment is at 8.9%. There is a heavy expenditure on defence – around US$720 million annually.

Sri Lanka has a small population earning big money, but the majority earns little. A tea picker earns around Rs 125 per day, while a batik artist gets Rs 100 per day, as does a worker in the garment manufacturing trade. A three-wheeler costs Rs 169,000, and a three-wheeler driver earns around Rs 100 per day – on this wage it's easy to understand why few own their own vehicles. A journalist can expect to start on around Rs 300 per day, while a bank manager should be pretty happy bringing home Rs 1400 per day. When you weigh these wages up against the average cost of basic food items such as rice (Rs 23 per kilogram), beef (Rs 123) or potatoes (Rs 45), you can appreciate how many people are struggling to make ends meet.

POPULATION & PEOPLE

Sri Lanka has a population of over 19 million; the resulting population density of some 280 people per sq km is one of the highest in Asia. In 1948 the population was only seven million, but between 1963 and 1972 it increased at an average of 2.3% annually, this rate falling to 1.5% in the 1990s. In 2000 the increase was 1.4%. About a third of the population is under the age of 15.

The welfare policies of most of the post-independence governments have given Sri Lanka a creditable literacy and health record. Adult literacy (ie, people 10 years of age and over who can read and write) is a little over 86% (90.5% for men, 82.4% for women). The life expectancy for men is 70 years and for women 75.4 years.

Ethnic Groups

You can hardly fail to notice that Sri Lanka's ethnic jigsaw is currently its biggest problem. But despite claims that the Sinhalese and Tamils have been fighting each other for 2000 years and are 'natural enemies', there was little trouble between them during the colonial years and in the first few years after independence.

Although the first Sinhalese settlers in Sri Lanka almost certainly came from North India, and the ancestors of most Tamils came from South India, their ranks have been mixed over the centuries with each other and with Sri Lanka's other ethnic groups. The late Sinhalese politician, Sirimavo Bandaranaike, for instance, listed a Tamil and a European in her family tree.

From appearances you certainly can't do more than guess whether a person is Sinhalese or Tamil, although Sri Lankans say they can make the distinction. Language and religion are two important aspects in which the two groups do differ.

Sinhalese The Sinhalese constitute about 74% of the population. They speak Sinhala, are predominantly Buddhist and have a reputation for being easy-going. Their forebears probably came from somewhere around the northern Bay of Bengal. Their chronicles state that the first Sinhalese king, Vijaya, arrived in Sri Lanka with a small band of followers in the 6th century BC.

The Sinhalese have a caste system, although it is not as important as in India. Sinhalese see themselves as either 'low country', or 'Kandyan', and the Kandyan Sinhalese have a pride – some would say snobbishness – that stems from the time when the hill country was the last bastion of Sinhalese rulers against European colonists.

Tamils The Tamils are the second-largest group, constituting about 18% of the population. There are sometimes claims that the percentage is higher and that there is a Sinhalese plot to underestimate their numbers. Tamils are predominantly Hindu and speak Tamil. About 50 million more Tamils – far more than the entire population of Sri Lanka – live across the Palk Strait in India.

There are two distinct groups of Tamils in Sri Lanka. The origins of the so-called 'Sri Lanka' or 'Ceylon' Tamils go back to the southern Indians who started coming to Sri Lanka during the centuries of conflict between Sinhalese and south Indian kingdoms a thousand or more years ago. These Tamils are concentrated in the north, where they now form nearly all the Tamil population, and down the east coast, where they are present in roughly equal numbers with Sinhalese and Muslims.

The other group is the 'hill country' or 'plantation' Tamils whose ancestors were brought from India by the British to work on the tea plantations in the 19th century. The hill-country Tamils and the Sri Lankan Tamils are separated by geography, history and caste (the hill-country Tamils come mainly from lower Indian castes and have largely kept out of the bloody conflict with the Sinhalese over the past 18 years). Caste distinctions among the Tamils are more important than among the Sinhalese, although still nowhere near as important as in India.

Muslims About 7% of the population is Muslim. Most of these Muslims are so-called 'Sri Lanka Moors', whose presence goes back to Portuguese times and who are probably the descendants of Arab or Indian Muslim traders. They are scattered all over the island, perhaps more thinly in the south and north, and are still particularly active in trade and business. Tamil is the mother tongue for most of them.

Muslims have largely steered clear of the Sinhalese-Tamil troubles, though there has been some conflict between Tamils and Muslims in the east. The Malays are a smaller group of Muslims; many of their ancestors came with the Dutch from Java. They still speak Malay and there's a concentration of them in Hambantota. The 'Indian Moors' form a second small group; they are more recent Muslim arrivals from India and Pakistan.

Wanniyala-aetto The Wanniyala-aetto (People of the Forest) are usually referred to in Sri Lanka as Veddahs. They are the original inhabitants of the country, and their story is one of great tragedy. Some claim that Wanniyala-aetto no longer exist, that they are so intermarried and absorbed into the mainstream culture that they can no longer claim to exist as a distinct and unique group. Others hotly deny this. Whatever the truth of these claims, the whole debate surrounding these people remains extremely sensitive.

The Sinhalese word Veddah implies 'uncivilised' or 'backward'. According to the *Mahavamsa* or Great Chronicle (written by monks in about 500 BC), when the Indian prince Vijaya and his followers arrived in Sri Lanka, they found the land inhabited by *yakkhas,* a Sinhalese name for demons or evil spirits. Vijaya took a yakkha princess for his wife and exploited this alliance to become master of the entire island. Having achieved this, he sent his yakkha wife and children back to their people and married an Indian princess. His first wife, regarded by the yakkhas as a traitor, was killed. Her son and daughter fled into the forest, eventually marrying each other and producing children of their own – the ancestors of the present-day Wanniyala-aetto.

The Wanniyala-aetto are by no means a homogenous group, sharing a common religion, language and culture. And this is one of the reasons some people claim they actually don't exist. Central to the whole issue are the traditional hunting grounds of the Wanniyala-aetto in what is now the national park of Maduru Oya. The park was created in 1983 to serve as a refuge for wildlife displaced by the giant Mahaweli irrigation scheme. The law specifically prohibits hunting and gathering in national parks. Five Wanniyala-aetto villages were included in the area set aside for the park.

Sri Lanka's Dances & Masks

Dances

Sri Lanka has a rich dance heritage comprising three main schools: Kandyan, *kolam* (masked drama) and devil dancing. Although traditional dance has declined as many look to the West and India for inspiration, it is being kept alive by a small group of dedicated teachers and students. If you go to Kandy you'll certainly have the opportunity to witness Kandyan dance performances – a riot of movement, colour and sparkles fed by the arrhythmic pounding of drums. Kolam is a series of dance-theatre pieces exploring the themes of everyday life, while devil dancing is performed to exorcise evil spirits. You're most likely to see kolam and devil dancing at Ambalangoda (see the West Coast chapter for details).

Kandyan Dance This dance form flourished under the Kandyan kings and is today considered the national dance of Sri Lanka. There are four types: *pantheru, naiyaki, udekki* and *ves*. In addition there are 18 *vannamas* (representations in dance of animals and birds). These include the *gajaga vannama* (elephant) and the *mayura vannama* (peacock). The Ramayana has provided plenty of material for the dances, especially Rama's dash to Lanka to save Sita, aided by the loyal Hanuman. But over the centuries other stories have been absorbed including those about kings and heroes. Under the Kandyan kings, the dance became so beautiful and refined that Buddhist monks admitted it to their temple courtyards and it became an integral part of the great Kandy Esala Perahera (see Public Holidays & Special Events in the Facts for the Visitor chapter for information about this procession).

The best-known costume of the typical male Kandyan dancer is a wide skirt-like garment. The dancer's bare chest is covered with necklaces of silver and ivory, and bangles of beaten silver are worn on the arms and ankles. These performances are extremely athletic, with great leaps and back flips. The dancers are accompanied by drummers who beat out complex rhythms on the *geta bera,* a double-sided drum that tapers towards the ends – one end is covered with monkey hide and the other with cow hide in order to yield different tones.

Masked Drama There are four folk-drama forms: *kolam, sokari, nadagam* and *pasu*. Best known is the *kolam* (kolam is a Tamil word meaning costume or guise). Kolam has many characters – one estimate puts them at 53 – many of which are grotesque, with exaggerated deformities. These are the demons, who may have a cobra emerging from one nostril, bulging eyes or tusks.

Performances were traditionally held at the New Year, over a period of three to five nights. Included in the cast of performers are singers, two drummers and a master of ceremonies. The whole thing kicks off with songs in praise of the Buddha. The master of ceremonies then explains how the kolam began (an Indian king's wife had cravings while pregnant to see a masked dance-drama). The cast of characters is then introduced.

Of the many kolam plays, the two best-known are the *Sandakinduru Katava* and the *Gothayimbala Katava*. In the first, two creatures, half-bird half-human, live in the forest. A king out hunting kills the man-bird, who is later restored to life by the Buddha. In the second, a demon who falls in love with a beautiful woman is beheaded by the revenging husband. But the demon is able to regenerate itself over and over again, until the husband is rescued from his dilemma by the forest deity.

Devil Dance Devil dancing is performed to free a person from demons, evil spirits or just plain bad luck caused by malignant spirits. The devil dancers themselves belong to a low-caste community and specialise in this art form.

Counting the beat: a *geta bera* drummer

Just keep those plates spinning...

Moving to the rhythm of a different drum

Kandyan dancers in full regalia

A mask carver painstakingly adds colour to a mask.

A fearsome visage: a *naga raksha* (cobra) mask

Fine detail on a *kolam* (masked drama) mask

One of *kolam's* less elegant characters

Sri Lanka's Dances & Masks

There are many types of devil dance. One, the *sanni yakku,* is performed to exorcise the disease demon. The demon is represented by a range of characters including a pregnant woman and a mother. Other dances include the *kohomba kankariya,* which is performed to ensure prosperity, and the *bali,* which is performed for the benefit of heavenly beings.

Three beings must be propitiated in these ceremonies: demons, deities and semidemons. Before the dance begins, palm-leaf shrines dedicated to each of the beings are built outside the victim's house. The beings must be tempted out of these and into the arena. The dancers (all men) go through an extraordinarily athletic routine. Strips of palm leaves hang down from a red cloth tied around their heads; the white cloth wound tightly round their hips stays firm despite their gyrations. All the while bare-chested drummers beat out a frantic rhythm on the *yak bera* (a double-sided, cylindrical drum). From time to time there is a break in the dancing while others perform mimes and magic. At the climax of their routine, the dancers put on masks representing the demons and explain who they are and why they've come. The demon that is considered to be causing the victim's distress or disease enters that person and the chief exorcist questions, exhorts and threatens the demon. He may even try to bribe it to make it leave.

Masks

There are three basic types of mask: *kolam, sanni* and *raksha.*

The kolam mask – literally a mask or form of disguise – is used in kolam masked drama in which all the characters wear masks. Kolam masks generally illustrate a set cast of characters, and although these masks are still made for dance performances, and some new characters are being introduced, they are not produced for tourist consumption.

The second type, sanni, is the devil-dancing mask that dancers wear in order to impersonate disease-causing demons and to thus exorcise them. The '18 disease' sanni mask depicts a demon figure, clutching one or more victims (often with another clenched in his teeth), flanked by 18 faces – each used to exorcise a different disease ranging from rheumatism, earache or boils to blindness or the 'morbid state of wind, bile and phlegm'. The whole grotesque ensemble is bordered by two cobras, with others sprouting from the demon's head.

Raksha masks are used in processions and festivals. There are about 25 varieties, including the more common *naga raksha* (cobra) masks, in which a demonic face complete with protruding eyeballs, lolling tongue and pointed teeth is topped with a 'coiffure' of writhing cobras.

Legend has it that Sri Lanka was once ruled by a race called the Rakshasas, whose king was Rawana of the Ramayana story. The Rakshasas could assume the form of cobras to terrify and subjugate their enemies. Their victims, however, would sometimes plead for help from the *gurulu,* a bird that preys on snakes, and today the *gurulu raksha* is another frequently seen type of mask.

Buying Masks Most masks are made from a light balsa-type wood *(Strychnos nux-vomica)* called *kaduru,* which is smoke-dried before the mask is carved out of it. Yellow is applied as the base colour, with other colours being added as desired. The final stage of the process is the application of a mixture of resin powder and oil.

Ambalangoda is the best place to see kolam masks being made, and there's a museum here that explains how it all works. The town also has a handful of quality mask shops, though you'll find masks in the government-run Laksala stores all over the country. See the Ambalangoda section in the West Coast chapter for details.

All but one community eventually moved outside the park borders. Those who had made the move became unhappy with the situation. They could no longer hunt and gather on their ancestral lands, and wanted to go back. In 1990 an area inside the park was set aside for them, and they began to return, only to discover that the allocated area did not encompass all five villages, nor did it provide sufficient area to sustain them. In August 1998 the government agreed to set aside more of the park for the Wanniyala-aetto and hunting-and-gathering permits were allowed. Too few permits were given and in early 1999 a Wanniyala-aetto was shot by a ranger for allegedly hunting in the park. The Wanniyala-aetto continue to appeal for improved rights to the Maduru Oya National Park.

Others The Burghers are Eurasians, primarily descendants of the Portuguese and Dutch – more frequently the former than the latter. For a time, even after independence, the Burghers had a disproportionate influence over the political and business life of Sri Lanka, but growing Sinhalese and Tamil nationalism has reduced their advantage and many Burghers have moved abroad. Nevertheless, names such Fernando, de Silva and Perera are still very common.

There are also small Chinese and European communities and a small, downtrodden group of low-caste south Indians brought in to perform the most menial tasks.

EDUCATION

From about the 3rd century BC, formal learning primarily took place in monasteries. The present-day system, however, has been shaped by European, particularly British, influences. Free education from kindergarten to university was introduced shortly after WWII, and state education remains free to this day. There are also many private institutions from preschool and up. These private schools are often referred to as 'English-medium' schools.

A good education is greatly valued, and this is reflected in the high level of literacy in Sri Lanka. Schoolchildren heading to and from school, immaculately turned out in their pressed white uniforms (despite the fact many children possess one uniform only), are a common sight all over the island. Around 4.5 million children are enrolled at school, almost equally divided between male and female.

The first university was established in 1942 at Peradeniya near Kandy. Today there are 12 universities, plus an open university, and more than 28 technical colleges. Preschool education is an area of federal government responsibility, unlike the rest of the education system. There are 10,191 schools of which 235 are run by the Ministry of Education & Higher Education. The rest are administered by provincial councils. There are 63 private schools and 509 *pirivenas* (centres of learning attached to monasteries).

ARTS
Dance & Theatre
Sri Lanka's famous Kandyan dance and *kolam* (masked dance-drama) have their origins in South India, but have developed a uniquely local character. The devil dancing of the low country almost certainly predates Buddhism. See the boxed text 'Sri Lanka's Dances & Masks' for more information.

Modern Theatre It wasn't until the 19th century that theatre started to move into the cities. The first inroads were made by a Parsi theatrical company from Bombay (present-day Mumbai) that introduced *nurti* (literally 'new theatre') to Colombo audiences. Nurti was a blend of European and Indian theatrical conventions: stage scenery, painted backdrops and wings; an enclosed theatre; costumes, music and song. And it spawned a new profession – play writing. Until the arrival of nurti, writers had focused on prose and poetry, but now they drew on Sanskrit classical drama and other sources including Shakespeare for inspiration.

The arrival of cinema all but killed off theatre until after independence, with the biggest breakthrough coming in 1956 following the premiere of *Maname* (King's Name), a play written by university professor Ediriweera Sarachchandra. This used a *jataka* (a tale from the Buddha's life) as its theme, although the tale was altered somewhat, and was staged in the traditional *nadagam* style. The combination of familiar folk tale and popular staging made the play an instant hit and marked the beginning of a new era of experimentation and creativity.

Literature

Although inscriptions that predate Christ have been found, the earliest texts date from the 10th century AD. These are primarily aids for the study of the Pali (Sanskrit) texts on Buddhism. One striking aspect of Sinhalese literature is its early focus on the recording of history. The *Mahavamsa* (Great Chronicle) and the *Culavamsa* (Minor Chronicle), which detail the exploits of successive kings and nobles from the time of the arrival of Prince Vijaya from India (about 200 years before Buddhism spread throughout Sri Lanka), were compiled by monks. Together with such documents as the *Thupavamsaya* (Chronicle of the Great Stupa) they record the history of all great Buddhist monuments in Sri Lanka.

Poetry was certainly an early literary form; the graffiti on the Sigiriya mirror wall attest to that. Tales from the Buddha's past lives were also expressed poetically in Jataka Tales. A genre that proved very popular in Sri Lanka was *samdesha* literature. This originated in Hindu India and centred on the theme of an exiled lover sending a message to his beloved on the monsoon clouds. Eulogies (to the Buddha and secular figures) and poems about war also existed.

Until the mid-19th century, literary endeavours were mostly religious in nature, but at this time there was a flurry of activity, aided by access to printing presses, including translations of works such as *Pilgrims Progress*, *Gulliver's Travels* and *The Arabian Nights* and the advent of newspapers and periodicals in the vernacular. The Bible was translated into Sinhalese and Tamil at this time.

The first Sinhalese novel, *Meena*, appeared in 1905. Written by a Christian priest, Issac D Silva, its theme of young love didn't go down well in a conservative society. Other works appearing shortly thereafter, notably those by Buddhist writer and political activist Piyadasa Sirisena, as well as Martin Wickramasinghe (arguably the best among his contemporaries) and WA Silva, were more favourably received, and fiction as a literary form became established. Much of Sri Lanka's modern literature centres on the ramifications of the civil war that has ravaged the country. For more information about books, including fiction and nonfiction, see the Books section in the Facts for the Visitor chapter.

Architecture

Sri Lanka's most famous contemporary architect is Geoffrey Bawa. His work is particularly accessible to visitors as it includes several well-known hotels, including the Lighthouse in Galle, the Kandalama Hotel in Dambulla, the YWCA at Rotunda Gardens and the Bentota Beach Hotel.

At the other end of the scale, the *cadjan* (coconut frond) dwellings that one sees today were probably similar to the type of structures favoured in ancient times by ordinary people. Cadjan dwellings have a timber frame over which are placed woven coconut frond mats. This is a type of building particularly suited to Sri Lanka's climate. It's also inexpensive, although the cadjan needs replacing every three years or so.

Buddhist One of the most striking features of Sri Lanka's architectural landscape is the dagoba (stupa). The smooth, lime-washed mounds protrude above the tree line along the coast, and dot the dry zone at Anuradhapura. In the intense tropical sun they give off an eerie glow.

Dagobas, sometimes located inside caves, are classified into six basic shapes resembling a heap of paddy, a bell, a bubble and so on. Above the mound is a square box-like structure called a *hataraes kotuwa*, which in the early days of dagoba building contained relics. Rising from this is the furled ceremonial parasol called the *chatta*. Because the staff left little room for relics in the hataraes kotuwa, they were eventually lodged inside an area of hollowed out brickwork, just below the staff. A piece of granite (the mystic stone) with nine squares scooped out of its surface held the relics and offerings. These stones can be seen at museums in Anuradhapura, Mihintale and elsewhere. Dagobas are made of solid brick, then plastered and lime-washed. There is very often a *vahalakadas* (platform) surrounding the dagoba, used by devotees to make a clockwise circuit; stairways to the pathway pass through gates situated at the cardinal points.

Early dagobas were probably very simple structures, but became increasingly sophisticated during the time of the ancient kingdoms of the dry zone. Dagobas built in the 2nd century AD by King Dutugemunu – Ruvanvelisaya and Mirisavatiya in Anuradhapura – had their foundations established well below ground (stamped down by elephants, legend has it). The Jetavanarama dagoba in Anuradhapura, dating from the 3rd century AD and the focus of a gigantic reconstruction project in recent times, is nearly as high as Egypt's Cheops pyramid. The 19th-century travel writer Emerson Tennant estimated that it contained enough material to form a wall at least 'one foot in thickness and 10 feet in height, reaching from London to Edinburgh'. Dagobas have been subject to constant renovation over the centuries, which is problematic for scholars who wish to unlock their hidden secrets.

A uniquely Sinhalese architectural concept is the *vatadage* or circular relic house. Today you can see vatadages in Anuradhapura and Polonnaruwa – perhaps the finest example is at Medirigiriya. They consist of a small central dagoba flanked by Buddha images and encircled by columns. Long ago these columns held up a wooden roof, but all traces of wooden architecture have long disappeared from the remains of the ancient cities, and you must get your imagination into top gear to picture how things really were. The museum at Polonnaruwa, however, has a reconstructed model of the vatadage. Only important buildings were constructed of stone – everything else was made of wood.

Another peculiarly Sinhalese style is the *gedige* – a hollow temple with extremely thick walls topped by a 'corbelled' (trussed) roof. Often the walls are so thick that stairways can be built right into them. There are a number of such gediges in Anuradhapura and Polonnaruwa, and a restored one at Nalanda – with the exception of the latter almost all of their roofs collapsed long ago.

A distinction to bear in mind is that between the *vihara* and the *devale*. The former is generally a Buddhist complex that includes a shrine containing a statue of the Buddha, a congregational hall and a monks' house. A devale is a complex designed for worshipping either a Hindu deity or a local Sri Lankan one. At Polonnaruwa, devales are quite separate from Buddhist shrines, but in later centuries many Buddhist temples also had devales.

Hindu Hindu temples are called *kovils* in Sri Lanka and are mostly dedicated to Shaivite (Shiva) worship. Essentially they consist of a prayer hall and shrine room. There is a covered space that allows worshippers to take a ritual walk clockwise around the hall and shrine room. Towering above all is the *sikhara*, a central edifice, usually dome- or pyramid-shaped, that rises above the shrine room. Some temples also have *gopurams*, or ornate towering gateways. Both tend to be elaborately sculpted and brightly coloured.

European The Europeans all made an impact on Sri Lanka's architectural styles. The Portuguese influence can be seen in certain conventions such as high pitched roofs and covered verandas. Interestingly, Portuguese style continued well after the Dutch defeated them because the Portuguese, barred from administrative duties, turned to the building trade to earn a living. Dutch influence is, however, far more apparent. The historic Fort in Galle has many wonderful examples of Dutch style. When the Dutch took over they changed the Portuguese forts, and the English continued the tradition, bringing their own ecclesiastic and secular architectural fashions with them as well. The buildings in hill stations such as Nuwara Eliya positively cry out 'England'.

Sculpture & Painting

Images of the Buddha dominate the work of Sri Lankan sculptors. Limestone, which is plentiful, was used for early works (which means they haven't weathered well), but a variety of other materials has been used over the centuries, including jade, rock crystal, marble, emerald, pink quartz, ivory, coral and sometimes wood or metal. The Buddha is represented in three poses – sitting, standing or lying – with his hands arranged in various *mudras,* or positions: *dhyana mudra* is a meditative pose where the hands are cupped and resting lightly in the lap (the right hand overlaps the left); in *abhaya mudra,* the right hand is raised (conveying protection); in the *vitarka mudra* the index finger touches the thumb (a gesture symbolising teaching). Other notable examples of sculpture include the four solid panels of sculture or *vahalkadas* at the Kantaka Chetiya at Mihintale (see the Ancient Cities chapter for details).

Staircases at Sri Lanka's ancient temples and palaces reveal a wealth of finely sculpted detail, the semicircular, elaborately carved moonstones (only one rectangular moonstone has been discovered – at the Alahana Pirivena in Polonnaruwa) being a notable feature. A moonstone comprises a series of rings, enclosed within flames of purifying fire, which contain various symbolic motifs including the elephant (representing birth), the horse (old age), the lion (illness), the bull (death and decay), geese (purity) and serpents (lust and desire). In the centre sits the sacred lotus flower.

On either side of the foot of these staircases are guardstones (which have their origin in Indian art and depict the Naga king and his dwarf attendants) and, as you ascend, dwarfs that appear to hold up each stair. A mythical beast (a cross between a lion, a pig and an elephant) called a *makara* often decorates the balustrade.

Painting, like dance and music, was not approved of by orthodox Buddhists who saw no good in art for art's sake. Yet artists (influenced by Indian conventions) did paint, the best-known example of their efforts appearing in the form of shapely nymphs on the walls of the Sigiriya fortress, although it's not known exactly who painted these. On the whole, painting centred on Buddhist themes, with the best examples to be seen in Dambulla and Polonnaruwa. By the 13th century, painting as an art form appears to have declined.

Cinema

Cinemas started to appear in Sri Lanka at the beginning of the 20th century, but as there was no local film industry at that stage, offerings were imported from India and the UK. Silent-screen actors from this era who proved enormously popular in Sri Lanka included Rudolf Valentino and Douglas Fairbanks Sr. With the arrival of sound in the 1920s, Indian films, with their songs and dances and familiar language, drew the biggest audiences. The first Sri Lankan–made film, *Kadavunu Poronduwa* (Broken Promise) was shown in Colombo in 1947, when audiences heard Sinhala spoken on screen for the first time. After its release, movies continued to be mostly produced in Indian studios, until the director Sirisena Wimalaweera opened a studio in Sri Lanka in 1951. Lester James Peries' first feature film, *Rekawa* (Line of Destiny) is known as the first truly Sinhalese film. It attempted to realistically portray Sri Lankan life and used its filming technique to express this – it was the first film in Sri Lanka shot outside a studio. Other notable and prolific local directors include Dharmasena Pathiraja, Vasantha Obeysekera and Peries' wife, Sumithra Peries.

Contemporary Sri Lankan directors tend to explore themes directly relating to the war. *Death on a Full Moon Day*, made in 2000 by Prasanna Vithanage, is a recent production about a father who refuses to accept the death of his soldier son. The film is currently banned in Sri Lanka by the government (the reason cited is that it may have a negative affect on soldiers' morale).

Sri Lanka has also provided a setting for a number of visiting film directors. The first

Finding a Perfect Match is All in the Stars

'Respectable Buddhist Govi parents in Colombo seek educated professional partner for their pretty University Graduate daughter, 25, 5'5''. Well mannered and cultured. Dowry in cash or land, jewellery and household items. Reply with copy of horoscope.'

Marriage is probably the strongest expectation placed on young Sri Lankans of all castes and classes, religions and ethnic groups. Children, especially daughters, are conditioned and brought up to be 'looked after' by their future husbands. Single middle-aged people face the question of who will care for them in their old age, an obligation traditionally fulfilled by children, and unmarried people may also be regarded as odd because of their nonconformity. Although 'affairs' that lead to 'love marriages' increasingly occur, arranged marriages are still common. If a man or woman is not married by the age of 30, parents make every effort to facilitate a match. If they're still single at 35, parents may fear it may be too late to find an appropriate marriage partner.

Parents consult marriage proposal advertisements in newspapers or on the Internet, as well as traditional village matchmakers, relatives and friends in the business of searching for a suitable husband or wife. Eligible children are 'signed up' to commercial matchmakers who use computerised horoscope readings and family background to propose alliances. Research by the Voice of Women, a Colombo-based NGO, of almost 8000 marriage advertisements in the *Sunday Observer* showed arranged marriages in Sri Lanka were still influenced by caste, ethnicity and religion, and that a horoscope match and dowry formed part of most negotiations. Dowries provided by the bride typically consist of land, a house, cash or jewellery and contributions from the male partner are also considered favourably. A husband with a house is a better option than a husband without assets!

When a promising partner is found, a formal meeting with parents and the couple in question is arranged, usually at the woman's family home. If both parties express interest and the parents are agreeable, another meeting is planned. The couple may be left alone in the room after a couple of

▲ ▲ ▲ ▲ ▲ ▲ ▲ ▲ ▲ ▲ ▲ ▲ ▲ ▲ ▲ ▲ ▲

film made by a foreigner to achieve acclaim abroad was *Song of Ceylon*, made in 1934 by Englishman Basil Wright. This film was actually commissioned by the Empire Marketing Board as a propaganda piece on tea. The end result was a production that included compelling footage of Sri Lanka and its people, sounds that European audiences had never heard before (Kandyan drumming and music, jungle noises) and a narration (in English, but with Sinhala included) by Colombo artist Lionel Wendt. The film won first prize for best documentary at the 1935 International Film Festival in Brussels. Other films shot on location in Sri Lanka include *Elephant Walk*, which starred Elizabeth Taylor and Peter Finch, and David Lean's *Bridge on the River Kwai*. More recently Sri Lanka has been used as a setting in *Mountbatten: The Last Viceroy*, *Light over the Water*, *Tarzan the Apeman* and *The Iron Triangle*.

SOCIETY & CONDUCT

Sri Lanka is a multicultural society and visitors should try to be sensitive to this. If you are unsure about how to conduct yourself in a situation, ask. Sri Lankans are invariably happy to explain. Overall, visitors are accorded great tolerance and your unwitting mistakes will usually be politely overlooked.

Traditional Society

Rites of Passage Sri Lanka is a tremendously family-oriented society. The birth of a child is a great event, greeted by relatives near and far with joy. Everyone comes to visit the new baby, bearing gifts. The next important event is when the child takes its first solid food. *Kiri bath* (milk rice) is the traditional food given at this time, but it can be anything that's mild and chilli free. Another important milestone in the life of a child is when they first learn the alphabet.

Finding a Perfect Match is All in the Stars

meetings, but once they venture out in public together, the association is considered serious and on the path towards a wedding. Pulling out of the 'arrangement' at this stage may affect the woman's future marriageability.

The courtship poses other difficulties, especially for people having an 'affair'. Privacy is hard to find in a society where physical affection is rarely expressed in public. Public parks and the beach stretching from Colombo to Mt Lavinia and beyond are crowded with 'umbrella lovers' – couples seeking privacy and intimacy under umbrellas, beyond disapproving gazes and gossiping neighbours. The intimacy can only go so far though, and brides are generally expected to be virgins. Sometimes, in the south of the country, the mother-in-law may check bedclothes after the wedding night to determine whether the bride has passed the 'virginity test'.

Critics of arranged marriages say it disempowers women and enforces traditional stereotypes and gender roles. Factors such as caste and class are strong determinants of possible partners and the process does not allow couples to get to know each other beyond the confines of the family home before they must make a serious decision about their future together. Pragmatists say the system provides the opportunity to meet possible partners and point out that most Western couples are similarly matched according to class, interests and material status. And how many times have single people in the West complained about how difficult it is to meet others? The Sri Lankan system does, however, tend to affect women more than men, because men enjoy a greater level of autonomy before and after the marriage and are less likely to be judged on their moral behaviour.

'A pretty bride is sought by Buddhist Karawe parents for their very handsome and professional son aged 30, accountant in a well-known firm. Educated at a leading school in Colombo. Owns assets. Horoscope essential.'

Brigitte Ellemor

Birthdays were not traditionally celebrated but are now celebrated as a result of European influence.

In days gone by, traditional families would keep their daughter in the house for the duration of her first period, but this custom isn't really adhered to today. Coming-of-age parties are held to mark the occasion though, and the girl may receive gifts including jewellery from parents and other relatives.

Marriages in Sri Lanka are traditionally arranged, and astrology certainly does play a part – see the boxed text 'Finding a Perfect Match is All in the Stars'.

There are three main events in a Sri Lankan marriage: the engagement, the wedding reception (where gifts are given) and the homecoming. At the wedding everyone is dressed in their best; in the past a wedding was the occasion for the purchase of new clothes. The celebrations can go on all night and generally involve a band of musicians. Wedding cakes are tremendously popular, and enormous care goes into their presentation.

Traditional Buddhist weddings take place on a *poruwa* (square platform) in the wedding room. The bride and groom stand on the platform, which is decorated with pots full of coconut flowers and a canopy made of flowers. Buddhist priests do not officiate at weddings, so a special layperson chants religious stanzas in Sinhala and Pali. The master of ceremonies gives the groom betel leaves and the groom and bride pass some of these to their parents. After this rings and gifts are exchanged. Then comes the kiri bath (the ritual milk rice); the bride and groom ceremonially feed each other a small quantity. The bride's little finger on her right hand is tied with a gold thread to the little finger of the groom's left hand and the master of ceremonies pours water over their fingers. Young girls dressed in white sing a series of stanzas in Pali – these describe qualities of the Buddha that may bless the couple. As the couple leaves the poruwa, a coconut is sometimes broken behind it. The bride and groom then sign a register and sit at the wedding feast table. Toasts are made and the couple is congratulated.

In old age, security comes from the family. The aged are accorded more respect than is often the case in the West, and remain an integral part of the extended family. Generally, an ageing parent will live with a son or daughter.

Buddhists and Hindus cremate their dead rather than bury them, while Christians may do either. Among Buddhists, Hindus and Muslims, the body may lie in the house of an immediate family member until the funeral. In Buddhist cremations, the elder son will touch off the pyre. Mourners invariably wear white, and white funeral flags are a fairly common sight at Hindu and Buddhist funerals in Sri Lanka; they are strung along fences and poles, providing a guided pathway to the place where the body is to be buried.

The Caste System Although Buddhism discourages distinctions based on caste, a caste system does exist among Sri Lankan Buddhists, although it is not as marked as it once was. Unlike the orthodox Hindu system, there is no Brahmin or Kshatriya caste. Instead, the highest rung is occupied by the Govigama caste, who are descendants of landowners and cultivators. The Bandaras and Radalas were subgroups within this caste. Lower down came the Karava (fishing folk), the Hakurus (jaggery makers), the Berawaya (drummers), the Paduvua (palanquin bearers), the Radhu (washer folk) and at the bottom, the Rodiya (itinerant entertainers). However, these distinctions are virtually irrelevant today. More commonly you'll hear people making a distinction between low country Sinhalese and Kandyans.

Among Jaffna Tamils the Brahmin is the highest caste. Next come the Vellalas, who are cultivators and landlords. Beneath these two castes are various others with occupations involving varying degrees of ritual pollution (eg, barbers, washer folk). The hill-country Tamils mainly come from these lower castes. The activities of 19th-century Christian missionaries provoked a reaction among Hindus who wished to maintain traditional ways, and until legislation tried to reduce its influence in the 1950s, the caste system perpetuated the power of the Vellalas.

Dos & Don'ts

Temple Etiquette When visiting a Buddhist temple you should remove your shoes and hat and, if carrying an umbrella, furl it. Your legs and shoulders should be covered; never enter a temple in beach wear (ie, shorts or singlets). You should walk around the stupa in a clockwise direction. Some places don't like you taking photos; if in doubt, ask. You should never take a photo of a monk without asking permission.

Hindu temples also require you to remove your shoes and headwear. There is no circumambulation requirement, but you should be respectful. And as in Buddhist temples, you should cover your legs and shoulders.

In most temples you will be asked for a donation. The traditional practice is that you make a donation only if you wish to. If you decide to give money, the best place to put it is in the donation box.

Visiting Homes If you're invited to someone's home, it's customary to bring a small gift. Don't bring flowers as they're not considered special and certainly don't offer frangipani flowers, which are associated with death. A packet of tea or quality sweetmeats will do. Don't be offended if the gift vanishes without comment; it's considered rude to inspect a gift in front of its giver. You'll be expected to dress decently; freshly laundered, pressed clothes are the minimum requirement, and you should cover your legs and shoulders. Remove your shoes before entering; some hosts waive this rule for foreigners, but it's polite to do it nevertheless.

The Right Hand Rule Always give, receive and eat with your right hand. The left hand is used for and associated with unclean functions and it is extremely bad mannered to use it for eating.

Bathing Nudity is absolutely not allowed anywhere. This includes on the beach. You'll notice people bathing in streams and tanks all over the country, but you'll also notice they do so covered with thin cloths and they manage to soap and rinse themselves without removing the cloth.

Treatment of Animals

Buddhism abhors the taking of life and traditionally animals have enjoyed respect and protection because of this. Killing for sport was introduced with the European colonials and it was at this time that elephants, leopards and other creatures were shot, not just by trophy hunters, but by planters seeking to protect their plantations. These days many creatures are protected by law and the notion that taking life can be considered a sporting activity is, thankfully, no more. Generally, animals are respected and left to go their own way. Despite the crowded roads, drivers are careful to let any living thing that crosses their paths pass safely. This courtesy is extended to all things, from poisonous snakes to stray dogs. See the Flora & Fauna section earlier in this chapter for more information about Sri Lanka's fauna.

RELIGION

Buddhism is the dominant creed of the largest ethnic group, the Sinhalese, and is followed by 70% of the population. It plays an extremely important role in the country both spiritually and culturally. Sri Lanka's literature, art and architecture are to a large extent a product of its Buddhist basis. About 15% of the population, mainly Tamils, is Hindu. Muslims and Christians account for about 7.5% each. The Christians include both Sinhalese and Tamil converts.

However, there is much more mixing and melding among religious groups than these census figures would suggest. A Catholic, for example, may well feel the need to pay his respects to the Hindu god Ganesh in order to ensure he has no obstacles or problems in his path in the course of a particular venture. Buddhist, Hindu, Muslim and Christian Sri Lankans all venture to some of the same pilgrimage sites, Adam's Peak and Kataragama in particular.

Buddhism

Strictly speaking, Buddhism is not a religion since it is not centred on a god but is rather a system of philosophy and a code of morality. It covers a wide range of interpretations of the basic beliefs that started with the enlightenment of the Buddha in north India around 2500 years ago. Siddhartha Gautama, born a prince, is said to be the fourth Buddha 'Enlightened one', and is not expected to be the last. Since Buddhists believe achieving enlightenment is the goal of every being, eventually we will all reach Buddhahood.

The Buddha didn't write down his dharma (teachings), and a schism later developed so that today there are two major schools of Buddhism, Theravada and Mahayana. The Theravada 'doctrine of the elders' or 'small vehicle' school holds that to achieve nirvana, the eventual aim of every Buddhist, you must 'work out your own salvation with diligence'. In contrast, the Mahayana, or 'large vehicle', school holds that its belief is enough eventually to encompass all humankind and bear it to salvation. The 'large' and 'small' vehicle terms were coined by the Mahayana school.

The Mahayana school has not rejected the Theravada teachings but claims that it has extended them; the Theravada school sees the Mahayana as a corruption of the Buddha's teachings. It is true that the Mahayana offers the 'soft option' – have faith and all will be well – while the Theravada is more austere and ascetic and is harder to practise.

Ashoka, the great Indian emperor who was a devout Buddhist, sent missions to all the known world, and his son Mahinda brought Buddhism to Sri Lanka. It took a strong hold almost immediately and Sri Lanka has since been looked upon as a centre for Buddhist culture and teaching. It was in Sri Lanka that the Theravada school of Buddhism first developed, and was later passed on to Thailand, Myanmar (Burma), Vietnam, Laos and Cambodia; Mahayana Buddhism is followed in Japan and Vietnam and among Chinese Buddhists. There are also other, sometimes more esoteric, divisions of Buddhism such as the Hindu-Tantric Buddhism of Tibet, also practised in Nepal, or the Zen schools of Buddhism of Japan.

The Buddha taught that life is suffering, and that although there may be happiness in life this is mainly an illusion. To be born is to suffer, to live and toil is to suffer, to die is to suffer. The cycle of life is one of suffering, but humanity's suffering is caused by its ignorance, which makes it crave things to alleviate its pain. This is a mistake, for only by reaching a state of desiring nothing can one attain true happiness. To do this one must turn inward, master one's own mind and find the peace within. This is an evolutionary process through many states of spiritual development until the ultimate goal is reached – death, no further rebirths, and thus entry to nirvana.

The Buddha also taught that supreme enlightenment is the only reality in a world of unreality. All else is illusion and there is no unchanging soul that is reborn after life, but a consciousness that develops and evolves spiritually until it reaches the goal of nirvana or oneness with the all. Central to the doctrine of rebirth is karma, the law of causation; each rebirth results from the actions one has committed in the previous life. Thus in Buddhism each person alone is responsible for his or her life. The Buddha did not claim that his way was the only way, since in the end all beings will find a path because the goal is the same for all.

Modern Sri Lankan Buddhism Since the late 19th century a strand of 'militant' Buddhism has developed in Sri Lanka, centred on the belief that the Buddha – who visited Sri Lanka three times according to tradition – charged the Sinhalese people with the task of making the island a citadel of Buddhism in its purest form. This more campaigning, less tolerant style

of Buddism, perhaps taking its cue from the type of Christianity practised by the British colonial power, emerged under the inspiration of Anagarika Dharmapala. It sees threats to Sinhalese Buddhist culture in both European Christianity and Tamil Hinduism.

Sri Lankan Buddhism has become increasingly intertwined with politics, to the point where the clergy can exert great pressure on politicians by accusing them of failing to look after Buddhism. Some Buddhist monks are among the country's least tolerant people when it comes to compromise with the Tamils. Nor are all monks anything like as pure, virtuous and unworldly as you might imagine! On the other hand, many monks are genuinely dedicated to the personal and spiritual side of Buddhism and many of the people still practise the religion in a simple, gentle way.

Books on Buddhism A good book to start with is Christmas Humphrey's *Buddhism* (Pelican). There are many books on Buddhism available in Sri Lanka; a good place to look is the Buddhist Publication Society in Kandy. There is a library of Buddhism at the Gangaramaya temple's Bhikku Training Centre, 61 Sri Jinarathana Rd, Slave Island (Col 2). The Buddhist Cultural Centre at 125 Anderson Rd, Nedimala, Dehiwala, Colombo also stocks a range of books in English. For more information on places to practise and study meditation and Buddhism, see Kandy in the Hill Country chapter.

Hinduism

Tamil kings and their followers from South India brought Hinduism initially to northern Sri Lanka. Today, there are significant Hindu communities in Colombo, Kandy and the tea plantation areas in the hill country, as well as in the north and east of the island.

Hinduism defies attempts to define it in any specific sense. Some argue that it's more an association of religions. It has no founder, central authority or hierarchy. It's not a proselytising religion. The orthodox view is that you can't be converted; to be a Hindu you must be born one. The strictly orthodox maintain that only a person born in India of Hindu parents can truly claim to be Hindu. Both views are hotly debated.

To outsiders, Hinduism often appears as a complex mix of contradictory beliefs and multiple gods. In theory it happily incorporates all forms of belief and worship. But for Hindus religious truth is ineffable; at its heart, Hinduism does not depend on the belief in the existence or otherwise of any individual or multiple gods. Essentially, all Hindus believe in Brahman, the One without a second, without attributes. Brahman is eternal, uncreated and infinite; everything that exists emanates from Brahman and will ultimately return to it. The multitude of gods and goddesses are merely manifestations – knowable aspects of this formless phenomenon – and one may freely pick and choose among them.

Although beliefs and practices vary widely from region to region, there are several unifying factors. These include common beliefs in reincarnation, karma (conduct or action) and dharma (appropriate behaviour for one's station in life), and in the caste system.

Hindus believe earthly life is cyclical; you are born again and again (a process known as samsara), the quality of these rebirths being dependent upon your karma in previous lives. There is no escaping your behaviour. Living a dharmic life and fulfilling your duty will enhance your chances of being born into a higher caste and better circumstances. Going the other way, rebirth may take animal form, but it's only as a human that you will gain sufficient self-knowledge to escape the cycle of reincarnation and achieve moksha (liberation). Traditionally, women are unable to attain moksha. The best they can do is fulfil their dharma and hope for a male incarnation next time round.

For ordinary Hindus, fulfilling one's ritual and social duties is the main aim of worldly life. The Bhagavad Gita (a Hindu text, part of the Mahabharata) is clear about this; doing your duty is more important than asserting your individuality. That the householder and the renunciate may equally earn religious merit is a notion that was enshrined some 2000 years ago in the Brahmanic *ashrama* system. This kind of merit is only available to the upper three castes.

Gods & Goddesses The Hindu pantheon is prolific; some estimates put the total number of deities at 330 million. Brahman is often described as having three facets, known as the Trimurti: Brahma, Vishnu and Shiva (also known as Mahesh).

Brahma Brahma only plays an active role during the creation of the universe. The rest of the time he is in meditation and is therefore regarded as an aloof figure, unlike the two other members of the Trimurti, Shiva and Vishnu. His consort is Sarasvati, goddess of learning, and his vehicle is a swan. He is sometimes shown sitting on a lotus that rises from Vishnu's navel, symbolising the interdependence of the gods. He is generally depicted with four (crowned and bearded) heads, each turned towards the four points of the compass, and he usually holds the four books of the Vedas in each of his four hands.

Vishnu The preserver or sustainer, Vishnu is associated with 'right action' and behaves as a lawful, devout Hindu. He is usually depicted with four arms, each respectively holding a lotus (whose petals are symbolic of the unfolding of the universe); a conch shell (as it can be blown like a trumpet it symbolises the cosmic vibration from which all existence emanates); a discus; and a mace (a reward for conquering Indra – the god of battle). His consort is Lakshmi, goddess of beauty and fortune. His vehicle is Garuda, a half-bird half-beast creature, and he dwells in a heaven called Vaikuntha. Vishnu has 22 incarnations including Rama, Krishna and Buddha.

Shiva The destroyer, but without whom creation could not occur, Shiva is symbolised by the lingam. With 1008 names Shiva takes many forms including Pashupati, champion of the animals, and Nataraja, lord of the *tandav* (dance), who paces out the creation and destruction of the cosmos.

Shiva is also depicted as lord of yoga; a third eye in his forehead symbolises wisdom. Sometimes he has snakes draped around his neck and is shown holding a trident (representative of the Trimurti) as a weapon while riding Nandi, his bull. Shiva's consort, Parvati, is capable of taking many forms.

Krishna Krishna is an incarnation of Vishnu sent to earth to fight for good and combat evil. He is loyal and generous. His dalliances with the *gopis* (milkmaids) and his love for Radha (a married woman) have inspired countless paintings and songs. Krishna is depicted as being dark blue in colour and usually carries a flute.

Ganesh Chubby and jolly, elephant-headed Ganesh is held in great affection. He is the lord of beginnings, remover of obstacles and patron of scribes (the broken tusk he holds is the very one he used to write down later sections of the Mahabharata). In his other hands he holds an elephant goad, a noose and a bowl of sweetmeats. His animal mount is a rat-like creature, symbolic of Ganesh's light-hearted cunning (the rat is renowned for its slyness).

Hanuman Hero of the Ramayana and loyal ally of Rama, Hanuman embodies the concept of bhakti (devotion). Images of Rama and Sita are said to be emblazoned upon his heart. He is king of the monkeys, but is capable of taking on any form he chooses.

It was Hanuman who discovered where the King of Lanka, Rawana, was hiding Sita. There is a cave at Ella that is claimed to be the site of her captivity.

Skanda (Kataragama) Kataragama, also called Murugan on occasion, has many aspects. He is associated with war (his colour is a brilliant red, and devotees always offer crimson garlands when they visit his shrine) and disease. But he is also viewed as a protective deity by Buddhists, and Sinhalese generally associate him with the struggle in ancient times against South India's Tamils. He is often depicted carrying the *vel* (trident), a symbol identifiable as belonging to Shiva. The ancient and holy shrine of Kataragama in Sri Lanka's south draws a steady stream of pilgrims of all faiths. Each year (usually in July or August), the great festival of Kataragama attracts thousands of devotees, some of whom undergo extraordinary acts of penance.

Kali Known as the 'black one' with the red tongue, Kali is the most fearsome of the Hindu deities. She is often depicted dancing on Shiva's 'corpse' and garlanded with human heads. You will occasionally come upon small Kali shrines in Sri Lanka's hill country.

Islam

Arab traders visiting Sri Lanka from the 8th century on brought Islam to the island. Most Muslims here are Sunnis, although there are communities of Shi'ias who have more recently migrated from the Indian subcontinent.

Islam was founded in Arabia by the Prophet Mohammed in the 7th century. The Arabic term *islam* means to surrender and believers (Muslims) undertake to surrender to the will of Allah (God). The will of Allah is revealed in the scriptures of the Quran (Arabic for reading or recitation) and it was to Mohammed that God revealed his will, spurring him to act as his messenger.

Islam is monotheistic – God is unique and has no equal or partner. There is no concept of a Trinity or Trimurti as encountered in Christianity and Hinduism. Everything is believed to be created by God and is deemed to have its own place and purpose in the universe. Only God is self-sufficient and unlimited. The purpose of all living things is submission to the divine will. Only humans have a choice: whether to obey or disobey. Humankind's weakness is its pride and sense of independence. Although God never speaks to humanity directly, his word is conveyed through messengers (prophets – who are never themselves divine; Mohammed is the most recent prophet) who are charged with calling humanity back to God.

In the years after Mohammed's death a succession dispute split the movement and the legacy today is the Sunnis and the Shi'ahs. The Sunnis, the majority, emphasise the 'well-trodden' path or the orthodox way. They look to tradition and the customs and views of the majority of the community. Shi'iahs believe that only *imams* (exemplary leaders) are able to reveal the hidden and true meaning of the Koran. The orthodox view is that there have been 12 imams, the last being Mohammed. However, since then *mujtahids* (divines) have interpreted law and doctrine under the guidance of the imam, and the imam will return at the end of time to spread truth and justice throughout the world.

All Muslims share a belief in the five pillars of Islam: the shahada or declaration of faith, 'there is no God but Allah; Mohammed is his prophet' (this must be recited aloud at least once in a believer's lifetime, with conviction and true understanding); prayer (five times a day ideally and on one's own if one can't make it to a mosque); the zakat (tax), which today is usually a voluntary donation in the form of charity; fasting (during the month of Ramadan), undertaken by all except the sick, the very young, the elderly and those undertaking arduous journeys; and the hajj (pilgrimage) to Mecca, something every Muslim aspires to do at least once.

Christianity

The Portuguese colonisers introduced Roman Catholicism to Sri Lanka in the 16th century, and the Catholic Church remains strong among the western coastal communities – huge, imposing churches are prominent on the road north to Puttalam or south to Galle. The Dutch brought Protestantism and the Dutch Reformed Church, which has more of a presence in Colombo than elsewhere. Evidence of the British introduction of other denominations can particularly be seen in the hill country, where quaint stone churches dot the landscape.

LANGUAGE

It's easy to get by in Sri Lanka with English. Sinhala and Tamil are both national languages, with English commonly described as a link language. Sri Lanka has its own unique brand of English – 'You are having a problem, isn't it, no?' – which is widely spoken in the main centres. Off the beaten track knowledge of English thins, so it's nice to know a few words of Sinhala or Tamil, and it's pleasant to be able to greet people in their own language anyway. See the Language chapter at the back of the book for useful words and phrases in both Sinhala and Tamil and a gazetteer of place names in Sinhala and Tamil. If you want to know more, get a copy of Lonely Planet's *Sri Lanka phrasebook*.

Facts for the Visitor

HIGHLIGHTS

Sri Lanka has so many highlights that it's unfair to single out a few options. But you probably bought this guidebook to help you sort out the best from the rest, so without further ado check out the following.

Beaches

For many visitors, there's one destination that looms large on any trip to Sri Lanka: the beach. Swaying coconut palms, glistening white sand, shimmering waters – it's the ultimate escape from bleak winters and drab cities. Hikkaduwa and Unawatuna have long, clean beaches lined with restaurants, and Mirissa is so laid-back and the water is so clear, you'll never want to leave. Or, if the security situation is OK, you could head to the spotless sand of Nilaveli beach, a few kilometres north of Trincomalee.

Hill Country

The hill country is a different world: tea plantations, colonial bungalows with fireplaces, crisp mountain air – all within hours of the tropical coast. There is plenty of potential in the hills for keen walkers, and there are tea factories to visit, while the must-do train rides will wind you through exquisite landscapes. An evening stroll by Kandy's lake is a must. For a quieter option choose the tiny Ella nestled in the hills, with stunning views to the plains.

Wildlife

Sri Lanka is blessed with an extraordinary wealth of fauna and flora. Visit Sinharaja Forest Reserve to see a truly magnificently preserved rainforest, or Yala West (Ruhuna) National Park to view elephants, sambar deer and, perhaps if you're lucky, leopards. Lahugala National Park and Uda Walawe National Park attract large numbers of elephants, or you could take the easier (and cheaper) option and see them at the Pinnewala Elephant Orphanage. Twitchers won't need to step far from their hotel room to see birds as the towns, reserves and tanks are home to many feathered friends.

Festivals

Owing to the variety of religious faiths, Sri Lanka has frequent colourful and elaborate festivals. A highlight among these is the Kandy Esala Perahera, which is held in the full-moon month of Esala (July/August). This 10-day event builds up to a crescendo of dancing, drumming and parades of richly caparisoned elephants. At about the same time of year another elaborate festival is held at Kataragama in the south, where days of frenetic activity culminate in devotees walking across beds of glowing cinders.

Ancient Cities

From a small temple hidden by lush vegetation to cities stretching for kilometres, the ancient city region is rich with ruins waiting to be explored. Bicycle along the shady lanes of Polonnaruwa's ancient city – don't miss the reclining Buddha of Gal Vihara – or scramble up the Sigiriya rock fortress, past the saucy frescoes, to a superb view of the countryside. Then there are the less well-known attractions such as Yapahuwa, Dambulla and the Buddha of Aukana.

Activities

Dust off your goggles and fins and save for a scuba diving course – you won't find the best coral in the world but reefs and shipwrecks lie waiting for amateurs and the merely curious. Hikkaduwa and Tangalla are best for scuba diving, while at Unawatuna and Mirissa you can snorkel almost from your doorstep. Surfers will already know about famous Arugam Bay; when the surf bottoms out, head to Hikkaduwa. For hikers, there are plenty of walks in the pretty countryside around Ella. Most enjoy the superb views from World's End at Horton Plains. You shouldn't miss the sweaty slog up Adam's Peak – the dawn views alone make the venture worthwhile.

Shopping

Pad your wallet and get your elbows ready for a trolley-load of options: clothing, fabrics, painted masks, batik, tea, spices and gems, to name a few. You'll find fabrics, trash and flash clothing at Colombo's boutiques; Ratnapura is gem heaven; try Ambalangoda for masks; and save your last rupees for the spices in the Kandy region.

SUGGESTED ITINERARIES

Time and money as well as your particular interests will obviously influence where you go and what you do. Because the country is not that big, it's easy to take in quite a wide variety of places and activities in a relatively short space of time, even if you're using public transport. You don't actually have to be on the move constantly to get the best from Sri Lanka; you can stay put just about anywhere and profitably explore the surrounding area, discovering little temples, villages and other delights that don't appear in any tourist literature or guidebook.

Sri Lanka can be divided into three distinct zones (excluding the north for the time being): the west and south coasts; the hill country down to the east coast; and the ancient cities.

If you have just **one week** and you're travelling by public transport, it would be possible to take in a beach or two before jumping on the train to, say, Kandy in the hills (with maybe a day trip from there to Dambulla and Sigiriya). With a car you could head south and around the coast (taking in a few beaches) to Tissamaharama where you could visit Yala West (Ruhuna) National Park. Or you could head into the hills and the ancient city area.

In **two weeks** using public transport you could easily visit the hill country and the ancient cities or, alternatively, Kandy (with a day trip to the ancient cities), then down through Nuwara Eliya and Ella to, say, Tangalla or Mirissa on the coast, then back up the coast to Colombo. Two weeks with a car and driver will allow you to easily accomplish a circuit of the west and south coasts, the hill country and the ancient cities before heading back to Colombo.

If you have **three weeks** or more, you can afford to spend more time at the places already mentioned as well as taking in more on the way. Or, depending on the political situation, you could head east to Arugam Bay or north-east to Trincomalee and catch sunrays on the quiet beaches.

PLANNING
When to Go

Climatically, the driest and best seasons are from December to March on the west and south coasts and in the hill country, and from May to September for the ancient cities area and the east coast. December to March is the time when most foreign tourists come, the majority of them escaping the European winter. Out-of-season travel has its advantages – not only do the crowds go away but many air fares and accommodation prices drop right down. Nor does it rain *all* the time during the low season. Also, July/August is the time of the Kandy Esala Perahera, the 10-day festival honouring the sacred tooth relic, and the Kataragama Festival in the south.

Maps

One of the best foreign-produced maps is the Nelles Verlag 1:450,000 *Sri Lanka*, which includes city maps of Colombo, Anuradhapura, Kandy and Galle. *Berndston & Berndston Sri Lanka Road Map* is excellent

---

Upgrade This Book

The world can change a lot in a day. Borders may open, hotels close or currencies crash. So before you leave home, check out Upgrades on the LP Web site (www.lonelyplanet.com/upgrades) for significant changes that might have occurred since this book went to press. View or download them, print them and fold them to fit inside the guidebook.

Upgrades are available for over 60 guidebooks, including our most popular titles and those covering countries or regions that are changing rapidly. They are revised every six months until the new, thoroughly updated edition of the book is published.

for detail on routes and sites. It seems more widely available in Europe than in Australia. Globetrotter's 1:600,000 *Sri Lanka* has a decent colour country map and a handful of simplified town maps.

The Sri Lankan government Survey Department's *Road Map of Sri Lanka* at 1:500,000 (1cm = 5km) is an excellent overall map and is clear to read; it also produces a *Road Atlas of Sri Lanka* at the same scale but with 17 town maps at the back. You can buy these maps between 9 am and 4.15 pm on weekdays from the Survey Department Map Sales Centre at 62 Chatham St, Fort (Col 1). The Survey Department has mapped the whole country in British ordnance survey style at three scales, but these excellent maps and many town plans are not for sale for security reasons.

What to Bring

If you are going to spend all your time on the beach, then obviously you can travel very lightly. Clothes (including popular brand names) can be readily bought in Colombo, and if you are in Hikkaduwa, there is plenty of Western-style beach wear on sale (and plenty of tailors who'll run up something for you). Remember, if you visit a temple or other holy sites you should cover your legs and shoulders. Never turn up at a temple in your shorts or beach clothes. A sarong is an acceptable substitute for a long skirt or pair of trousers.

It's not really necessary to bring a sleeping bag or sleeping sheet unless you think you'll be camping or really roughing it. Guesthouses and hotels always provide sheets, pillowslips and blankets where necessary.

Here's a list of essentials:

- underwear and swimming gear
- one pair of cotton trousers
- one pair of shorts (men only)
- one ankle-length cotton skirt (women)
- a few T-shirts or lightweight shirts
- a sweater for cool nights in the hills
- one pair of sneakers or shoes
- a few pairs of socks – useful for visiting temples, when traipsing over areas exposed to the sun
- sandals

- flip-flops (thongs) – to wear when showering
- a set of 'dress up' clothes
- sun hat, sunglasses and sunscreen lotion – Sri Lankans commonly use umbrellas instead of hats, which can be sweaty and uncomfortable; umbrellas can be bought cheaply everywhere

In addition to these things, consider the following list for some handy items to stow away. See the Health section later in this chapter for advice on suggested medical supplies.

- knife (preferably Swiss Army) – it has a whole range of uses, such as peeling fruit
- miniature electric element to boil (and sterilise) water in a cup, a water purification pump system or water purification tablets. Bottled water is readily available but it's usually stale and it invariably tastes a bit like plastic.
- most places provide mosquito nets (sometimes with holes so bring tape) or the electric 'mat' devices. If you need to buy your own, mosquito coils and tablets that you insert into the electric devices are readily available; Keells and Cargills, which are in all the major cities and towns, are good places to buy them. Mosquito repellent is available at pharmacies (Keells and Cargills have good pharmacies).
- torch (flashlight) and/or candles – power cuts are not uncommon
- voltage stabiliser for those travellers bringing sensitive electronic equipment
- spare set of glasses and your spectacle prescription
- if you wear contact lenses, bring enough solution to last your trip
- lip balm may come in handy if you are planning to spend a lot of time on beaches
- length of string; very useful as a makeshift clothes line – double-strand nylon is good to secure your clothes if you have no pegs. You can buy small, inexpensive sachets of washing powder everywhere.
- pair of binoculars if you plan to be wildlife spotting and bird-watching
- high-pitched whistle – some women carry them as a possible deterrent to would-be assailants

RESPONSIBLE TOURISM

You can minimise your impact on the environment by following a few simple rules. Never break coral or brush against it. Coral is basically a colony of living organisms and damaging them can kill them. It's probably best to avoid glass-bottom boats as they tend to scrape over the reefs. If you do use them, encourage the pilot to steer well clear of the coral itself. Never buy coral. See the boxed text 'Responsible Diving & Snorkelling' in the West Coast chapter for information about diving or snorkelling around coral.

Don't buy sea shells or turtle shells (or eggs); all of Sri Lanka's five species of turtle are endangered. If you happen to spot a turtle swimming when you're being taken out in a boat, discourage the driver from circling it; this sort of harassment is very stressful to the turtle. If you wish to learn more about turtles in Sri Lanka and their preservation, refer to the boxed text 'Saving the Turtles' under Tangalla in The South chapter.

Try to minimise your use of plastic. Plastic bags are routinely provided with most purchases but you can decline them. You may go through many plastic bottles of drinking water. Try to dispose of them responsibly – or bring your own water purification equipment so you don't need to use them at all.

Please don't give money, sweets, pens etc to children: it encourages begging. A donation to a recognised project – a health centre or school – is more constructive.

If you are planning to hike in the hills, see the boxed text 'Responsible Hiking' in the Hill Country chapter for a few pointers on minimal-impact hiking.

Unfortunately Sri Lanka attracts paedophiles. Most abusers are local, but a fair few foreigners are involved. It is illegal to have intercourse with anyone under the age of 18 in Sri Lanka, and child abuse is punishable with a maximum 20 years in jail. Two foreigners have been successfully prosecuted in recent times and several more deported. Many countries now have laws in place that allow paedophiles to be prosecuted once they are back in their home country. If you suspect that child offences are being committed by someone you should act immediately: this could prevent further abuse. ECPAT (End Child Prostitution and Trafficking) recommends the following steps:

- Report offences to the local police and Women and Children's Bureau (☎ 01-444444).
- Report offences to the consul at the embassy of the alleged perpetrator, if the perpetrator is a foreigner.
- If the nationality of the perpetrator is unknown, report offences to your own consul/embassy.
- If offences are committed within a hotel or guesthouse, report them to the management.
- Contact the relevant authorities when you return home (if the perpetrator is a foreigner).

You wish to, you can report offences to ECPAT groups in your own country. ECPAT's Web site is www.ecpat.net.

TOURIST OFFICES
Local Tourist Offices

The headquarters and main information office of the Ceylon Tourist Board (☎ 01-437571, fax 440001, ⓔ ctb_dm@sri.lanka.net) is at 80 Galle Rd, Kollupitiya (Col 3), near the Lanka Oberoi Hotel; open from 9 am to 4.45 pm Monday to Friday, until 12.30 pm Saturday. There is also an office in Kandy (☎ 08-222661) as well as a 24-hour information office at the airport in Katunayake (☎ 01-252411). Staff at these offices can help with hotel bookings as well as answer queries and hand out booklets and leaflets. In Colombo, JF Tours' branch office at Fort train station is also helpful.

Among the publications provided by the tourist offices both within and outside Sri Lanka is an *Accommodation Guide*, updated every six months. Establishments have to pay to appear in this, but it's a fairly thorough listing. *Travel Lanka* provides listings of places to stay and various services. *Explore Sri Lanka* has feature articles, information on things to see and places to stay, shop and eat. *The Linc* has information and advertisements specific to Colombo.

Tourist Offices Abroad

Ceylon Tourist Board offices abroad include:

Australia At the time of writing the Ceylon Tourist Bureau office in Australia had closed, but information can still be obtained from the Australia High Commission (☎ 02-6239 7041, fax 6239 6166) 35 Empire Circuit, Forrest, Canberra, ACT 2603

France (☎ 01 42 60 49 99, fax 01 42 86 04 99,
ⓔ ctbparis@compuserve.com) 19 Rue du
Quatre Septembre, 75002 Paris
Germany (☎ 069-287734, fax 288371,
ⓔ CTBFRA@t-online.de) Allerheiligentor
2–4, D-60311 Frankfurt am Main
Japan (☎ 03-328 90771, fax 328 90772) Dowa
Bldg, 7-2-22, Ginza, Chuo-ku, Tokyo
Thailand (☎ 662-332 7761, fax 332 9076,
ⓔ inmark@ksc.th.com) 5/105–6/105 Soi
Rattanaprahm, 2 Sukhumvit Soi 54/2 Bangkok
10250
UK (☎ 020-7930 2627, fax 7930 9070,
ⓔ srilanka@cerbernet.co.uk) 26–27, Clare-
ville House, Oxendon St, London SW1Y 4EL
USA (☎ 212-432 7156, fax 524 9653,
ⓔ ctnUSA@aflusa.com) 1, World Trade
Centre, Suite 4667, New York NY10048

VISAS & DOCUMENTS
Passport
You must have a passport with you all the
time; it is the most basic travel document.
Ensure that it will be valid for the entire
period you intend to remain overseas. If
your passport is lost or stolen, contact your
country's representative (see the Embassies
& Consulates section later in this chapter).

Visas
Most nationalities, including Australians,
New Zealanders, British, French, German
and Americans, receive a tourist visa upon
entry that's valid for 30 days. At the time of
writing it was not possible for travellers to
obtain a visa for longer than 30 days in their
home country. However, you should double
check this before you go, as things can
change.

Visa Extensions Extensions can be made
at the Department of Immigration (☎ 01-
597511), at the seaward end of Station Rd,
near Majestic City shopping centre in Bambalapitiya (Col 4). The office is open from
9 am to 4.30 pm weekdays, but be aware
that the last payments for visa renewals are
received at 3.30 pm. A visa extension gives
you a full three months in the country and
you can apply for your extension almost as
soon as you arrive in the country (your 30-
day visa given upon entry is included in the
three months, or 90 days). A further three-

month extension is apparently possible, but
you must also pay for this and you should
always double check well before your visa
expires, as rules can change. The following
fees apply for the 90-day visa:

nationality	rupees
Australia	Rs 6500
France	Rs 1840
Germany	Rs 1510
The Netherlands	Rs 3440
New Zealand	Rs 2440
Switzerland	Rs 1925
UK	Rs 3795
USA	Rs 3185

The whole process takes about an hour.
First, go to the 1st-floor office and pick up
a visa extension application form from the
counter marked 'Visa Application Receiving Counters'. Fill out the form and return
it. You should have at hand your passport,
foreign exchange receipts and travellers
cheques. You will also be asked to show an
onward ticket. No photos are required. After
this form has been signed by an official go
to a nearby room. At the time of writing the
right place to go was booth No 3 (labelled
Assistant Controller). Get the form signed
and bring it back to the right hand side of
the Visa Application Receiving Counter.
Here you present the signed form and your
passport and receive a payment form, which
you present at the next-door counter. After
paying your fee, you return to the former
counter and hand in the receipt. You will be
given a numbered disc in return. After this
there is about a half-hour wait for your visa
extension to be processed and your passport
to be returned.

Visas for Onward Travel
The cost of a six-month tourist visa to India
is Rs 3190 for Australian, New Zealand,
German, French and UK passport holders;
USA citizens have to pay a whopping Rs
4800. There is a Rs 240 fax fee per application, and you'll need to supply two photographs. It takes at least five working days to
process a tourist visa, but only one day if
you are a foreign resident in Sri Lanka.

The High Commission of India in Colombo (☎ 01-422788) is at 36–38 Galle Rd, Kollupitiya (Col 3). It's open weekdays and tourist visa forms can be submitted between 9.30 am and 1 pm. Expect boring long queues.

The Assistant High Commission of India (☎ 08-222652, Box 47, Kandy), 31 Rajapihilla Mawatha, Kandy, is a good alternative to queuing in Colombo because it's not as busy. Visa applications are accepted between 8.30 and 10.30 am weekdays. Passports can be collected between 4 and 4.45 pm weekdays.

Travel Insurance

A travel insurance policy to cover theft, loss and medical problems is a good idea. The policies with higher medical expense options are chiefly for countries such as the USA, which have extremely high medical costs. There are a wide variety of policies available, so make sure you check the small print.

Some policies specifically exclude 'dangerous activities', which can include scuba diving, motorcycling and even trekking. A locally acquired motorcycle licence is not valid under some policies, so again check the fine print carefully.

You may prefer a policy that pays doctors or hospitals directly rather than you having to pay on the spot and claim later. If you do have to claim later make sure you keep all documentation. Some policies ask you to call (reverse charges) a centre in your home country where an immediate assessment of your problem is made. Check that the policy covers ambulances and an emergency flight home.

Driving Licence & Permits

If you wish to drive yourself, you must obtain a temporary Sri Lankan driving licence, for which you need to show your home-country driving licence and preferably an International Driving Permit too. If you have an International Driving Permit, you simply need to get it endorsed by the Automobile Association of Ceylon (☎ 01-421528/9), 40 Sir Macan Markar Mawatha,

Galle Face, Kollupitiya (Col 3), next to the Holiday Inn. The process takes only a few minutes; the association is open from 8.30 am to 4.30 pm weekdays. If you hire a car the rental company may obtain the endorsement for you for around Rs 50. If you turn up with only your home-country driver's licence, you'll have to pay Rs 600 for a special permit (valid for one month) from the Registrar of Motor Vehicles at Elvitigala Mawatha in Narahenpita, Colombo.

Student & Youth Cards

Bad news folks: an International Student ID Card will not get you much. You can't get a discount on the pricey Cultural Triangle round ticket but you can sometimes get half-price individual site tickets if you sweet talk the ticket seller. See the boxed text 'Cultural Triangle Tickets' in the Ancient Cities chapter for details.

Vaccination Certificate

If you are coming from an area infected with yellow fever you will need to produce a certificate showing you have been vaccinated against yellow fever in order to enter the country. Keeping a record of other vaccinations you've had is a good idea. See the Health section later in this chapter for more information on immunisations.

Copies

All important documents (passport data page and visa page, credit cards, travel-insurance policy, air/bus/train tickets, driving licence etc) should be photocopied before you leave home. Leave one copy with someone at home and keep another with you, separate from the originals.

EMBASSIES & CONSULATES
Sri Lankan Embassies & Consulates

Australia (☎ 02-6239 7041, fax 6239 6166) 35 Empire Circuit, Forrest, Canberra, ACT 2603
Canada (☎ 613-233 8449, fax 238 8448) West Suite 1204, 333 Laurier Ave, Ottawa, Ontario KIP ICI
France (☎ 01 42 66 35 01) 15 Rue d'Astorg, 75008, Paris

Germany (☎ 030-80 90 97 49) Niklasstrasse 19, 14163 Berlin

India
High Commission: (☎ 011-301 0201) 27 Kautilya Marg, Chanakyapuri, New Delhi 110021
Consulate in Chennai: (☎ 044-827 0831) 9D Nawab Habibullah Ave, Anderson Rd
Consulate in Mumbai: (☎ 022-204 8303) Sri Lanka House, 34 Homi Modi St

Italy (☎ 06-855 4560) Via Adige No 2, 00198 Rome

Japan (☎ 03-3440 6911, fax 3440 6914) 21–54 Takanawa, Minato-Ku, Tokyo 108 0074

Maldives (☎ 960-322845) 'Sakeena Manzil', Medhuziyaaraiyh Magu, Male 2005

The Netherlands (☎ 070-365 5910) Jacob de Graefflaan 2, 2517, JM, The Hague

Singapore (☎ 65-250 8662) 13–07/12 Goldhill Plaza, 51 Newton Rd, Singapore 308900

Thailand (☎ 2-254 9200) Ocean Tower II, 13th floor, 75/6–7 Sukhumvit Soi 19, Bangkok 10110

UK (☎ 020-7262 1841, fax 7262 7970) 13 Hyde Park Gardens, London W2 2LU

USA (☎ 202-483 4025, fax 232 7181) 2148 Wyoming Ave NW, Washington DC 20008

Embassies & Consulates in Sri Lanka

It's very important to realise what your own embassy – the embassy of the country of which you are a citizen – can and can't do to help you if you get into trouble. Generally speaking, it won't be much help in emergencies if the trouble you're in is remotely your own fault. Remember that you are bound by the laws of the country you are in. Your embassy will not be sympathetic if you end up in jail after committing a crime locally, even if such actions are legal in your own country.

In genuine emergencies you might get some assistance, but only if other channels have been exhausted. For example, if you need to get home urgently, a free ticket home is exceedingly unlikely – the embassy would expect you to have insurance. If you have all your money and documents stolen, it might assist with getting a new passport, but a loan for onward travel is out of the question.

Some embassies used to keep letters for travellers or have a small reading room with home newspapers, but these days the mail

holding service has usually been stopped, and even newspapers tend to be out of date.

If you are calling from outside Colombo, you will need to add the area code 01 to the following telephone numbers:

Australia (☎ 698767) 3 Cambridge Place, Cinnamon Gardens (Col 7)

Bangladesh (☎ 681310) 47/1 Ernest de Silva Mawatha, Cinnamon Gardens (Col 7)

Belgium (☎ 598678) Police Park Terrace 3/1, Havelock Town (Col 5)

Canada (☎ 695841) 6 Gregory's Rd, Cinnamon Gardens (Col 7)

Delegation of the Commission of European Communities (EEC; ☎ 699745) 81 Barnes Place, Cinnamon Gardens (Col 7)

France (☎ 698815, fax 699039) 89 Rosmead Place, Cinnamon Gardens (Col 7)

Germany (☎ 580431, fax 580440) 40 Alfred House Ave, Kollupitiya (Col 3)
Web site: www.germanembassy.lk

India (☎ 421605) 36–38 Galle Rd, Kollupitiya (Col 3)

Italy (☎ 588388, fax 074-712272) 55 Jawatta Rd, Havelock Town (Col 5)

Japan (☎ 693831, fax 698629) 20 Gregory's Rd, Cinnamon Gardens (Col 7)

Maldives (☎ 580076) 23 Kaviratne Rd, Havelock Town (Col 5)

Nepal (☎ 689656) 153 Kynsey Rd, Borella (Col 8)

The Netherlands (☎ 596914, fax 502855) 25 Torrington Ave, Cinnamon Gardens (Col 7)

Pakistan (☎ 696301) 211 De Saram Place, Maradana (Col 10)

Sweden (☎ 688452, fax 688455) 47/1 Horton Place, Cinnamon Gardens (Col 7)

Switzerland (☎ 695117) 63 Gregory's Rd, Cinnamon Gardens (Col 7)

Thailand (☎ 697406) 43 Dr CWW Kannangara Mawatha (Alexandra Place), Cinnamon Gardens (Col 7)

UK (☎ 437336-43) 190 Galle Rd, Kollupitiya (Col 3)

USA (☎ 448007, fax 437345) 210 Galle Rd, Kollupitiya (Col 3)
Web site: www.usembassy.state.gov/srilanka/

CUSTOMS

You may bring 1.5L of spirits, two bottles of wine, 200 cigarettes or 50 cigars, small quantities of perfume and travel souvenirs into the country as long as all the items don't exceed US$250 in value. You may take out of the country anything you declared upon entering. You can't take out antiques (articles older than 50 years) without seeking a permit from the Director of National Archives and the Archaeological Commissioner. Up to 3kg of tea may be exported duty free.

MONEY
Currency
The Sri Lankan currency is the rupee (Rs), divided into 100 cents. There are coins in denominations of 5, 10, 25 and 50 cents and Rs 1, 2, 5 and 10. Notes come in denominations of Rs 10, 20, 50, 100, 200, 500 and 1000. Break down larger notes (Rs 500 or Rs 1000) when you change money as most vendors never seem to have change. Don't accept very dirty or torn notes as they are often difficult to dispose of, except at a bank.

Exchange Rates
Exchange rates at publication were:

country	unit		rupees
Australia	A$1	=	Rs 46.7
Canada	C$1	=	Rs 56.9
euro	€1	=	Rs 80.7
France	FF1	=	Rs 12.3
Germany	DM1	=	Rs 41.3
India	Rs10	=	Rs 18.6
Italy	1000 lira	=	Rs 41.7
Japan	¥100	=	Rs 73.8
Maldives	Rf1	=	Rs 7.4
The Netherlands	Gl1	=	Rs 36.6
New Zealand	NZ$1	=	Rs 37.9
UK	UK£1	=	Rs 125.8
USA	US$1	=	Rs 86.6

Cash Any bank or exchange bureau will change major currencies including US dollars, deutschmarks and pounds sterling. It's a good idea to change Sri Lankan rupees to foreign currency *before* you leave the country as travellers have reported that many banks outside Sri Lanka will not exchange rupees.

Travellers Cheques You'll have no problem changing travellers cheques at any major bank. Thomas Cook, Visa and American Express (AmEx) are the most widely accepted. Banks charge 10% stamp duty and generally a commission that ranges from around 1% to 8% (the Bank of Ceylon seems to charge the lowest commission). Most banks have a special counter for foreign exchange and you usually won't have to queue.

Both AmEx and Thomas Cook have offices in Colombo (see Money under Information in that chapter for details).

ATMs The HongKong & Shanghai Bank and Standard Chartered Grindlays Bank have ATMs that take Visa and MasterCard for cash advances and Cirrus, Global Access etc facilities for standard withdrawals. There are several ATMs in Colombo and a couple in Kandy (see those chapters for details).

Credit Cards MasterCard and Visa are the most commonly accepted cards. Other major cards such as AmEx and Diners Club are also accepted. Some banks give cash advances (Hatton National Bank and the HongKong & Shanghai Bank accept Visa and MasterCard, and the Bank of Ceylon accepts Visa). AmEx has an office in Colombo.

International Transfers Telegraphic transfer using a major bank or agency with branches worldwide such as Standard Chartered Grindlays or Thomas Cook is, all things being equal, efficient and fast. You can transfer money via Western Union at Seylan Bank in Fort (Col 1).

Moneychangers Moneychangers can be found in Colombo and Hikkaduwa, among other places. They generally don't charge commission and their rates are usually competitive.

Security
Sri Lanka is fairly safe but you still need to take some precautions. The best place for your travellers cheques, spare cash, air ticket and passport is next to your skin, either in a moneybelt or in a pouch worn under your shirt or T-shirt; avoid bulky

'bum' bags as they can attract unwanted attention. It's wise to keep some money (say US$200) stashed away separately from your moneybelt or pouch so that if the worst happens, you at least have enough to tide you over. Keep a separate wallet or purse so you don't have to fish around under your clothing all the time. Remember to always keep a record of your travellers cheque numbers separately from the cheques.

Costs

Sri Lanka is more expensive than India, but is nevertheless reasonably economical. Budget double rooms with bathroom, net and fan cost about Rs 500, although better mid-range accommodation is around Rs 600 to 1000. The cost of accommodation in the touristy beach areas drops considerably out of season. Expect to pay triple the usual accommodation price in Kandy during the perahera and in Nuwara Eliya during the April high season. Public transport is extremely inexpensive: about Rs 1.50 per kilometre by train or bus. Local food is reasonably priced: a rice and curry with chicken costs about Rs 150 to Rs 250, a bottle of cola costs about Rs 15 (or up to Rs 30 at a hotel) and a 1.5L bottle of water costs Rs 50. Entry fees to national parks are US$12 a day; the major ancient city sites such as Anuradhapura, Sigiriya and Polonnaruwa cost US$15 a day.

Two-Level Costs Sri Lanka is no exception to the worldwide phenomenon of locals trying to overcharge tourists for anything from a bus fare to a gemstone necklace, but what really irritates some visitors is that for some things there is an *official* policy of charging foreigners a much higher price than local residents. This applies at places such as the Dehiwala Zoo in Colombo, the ancient cities, Wildlife Department lodges in national parks, and even the Peradeniya Botanic Gardens in Kandy. 'Plain racism!' wrote one disgruntled traveller. The alternative view is that the prices still aren't that high and that tourists, who are well off compared to the average Sri Lankan, might as well do some subsidising.

Tipping & Bargaining

Although a 10% service charge is included in bills for food and accommodation, this usually goes straight to the owner rather than the worker. Tipping is a customary way of showing your appreciation for services rendered. Drivers expect a tip, as do people who 'guide' you through a site. A rule of thumb is to tip 10% of the total amount due. If there's no money involved use your other thumb for this rule: tip around Rs 100 per half hour to an informal guide, Rs 20 for the person who minds your shoes at temples, and Rs 20 to a hotel staff member who helps with your bags.

Unless you are shopping at a fixed price store, you should bargain for goods and services. A precaution before you hit the open markets is to peruse the prices of equivalent items in a fixed price store; this will give you some idea of what to expect to pay. Generally, if someone quotes you a price, halve it. The seller will generally come down about halfway to your price, and the last price will generally be a bit above the halfway point.

Taxes

A 10% service charge is applied to food and accommodation. There is also a GST (Goods and Services Tax) of 12.5%. How this is applied is a bit of a mystery, but generally only top-end places and some upper-mid-range places actually add it to the bill. We have included both the service charge and the GST in all hotel and restaurant prices (where applicable) quoted throughout this book. For example, if you go into a restaurant and order rice and curry from the menu for Rs 250, when you receive your bill you'll end up paying Rs 306 for your meal; the latter price is the one we'll have quoted in this book.

POST & COMMUNICATIONS
Post

It costs Rs 3.50 to post a letter locally and Rs 20 to send a letter up to 10g air mail to the UK, continental Europe or Australia – every additional 10g costs Rs 9. Letters to the USA cost Rs 22, plus Rs 12 for every additional 10g. Postcards to these destinations (including the USA) cost Rs 14 and aerograms are Rs 12. Air-mail matter weighing up to 20g costs Rs 15 (Rs 18 to the USA) and every additional 20g costs Rs 8.50 (Rs 12 to the USA).

Ordinary air mail parcels sent from Sri Lanka can take longer than expected; up to three weeks to Australia. The cost for large parcels to the UK, continental Europe or Australia (Zone C countries) is Rs 60 for up to 100g, Rs 105 for 100g to 250g, Rs 185 for 250g to 500g and Rs 375 for 500g to 1kg. The rate for sending parcels to the USA is around 25% higher.

The Express Mail Service (EMS; ☎ 01-447766) to the UK, continental Europe and Australia costs Rs 30 for handling fees plus Rs 850 for up to 250g, Rs 1100 for 250g to 500g, and Rs 1400 for 500g to 1kg (delivery takes two to five days). If you have something valuable to send home, it may be wiser to use a courier service (see Information in the Colombo chapter for details of courier services).

Apart from the government-run post offices, there are private agencies that also sell stamps. Always ensure your stamps are cancelled, or ask the staff to use the franking machine.

To get up-to-date information on postal rates check out www.lanka.net/slpost

Post offices in larger centres have poste restante, and will generally keep your mail for two months. AmEx also has a mail holding service for its clients (see Money under Information in the Colombo chapter for contact details).

Telephone

To call Sri Lanka from abroad, dial the country code (☎ 94), and omit the 0 at the start of the local area code.

The peak (most expensive) period is from 8 am to 6 pm, the ordinary rate is from 6 am to 8 am and 6 pm to 10 pm while the cheapest rate is from 10 pm to 6 am and all day Sunday. International calls can be made at the main post office in major towns, from communication bureaus or at cardphone booths.

The cheapest calls can be made at post offices but you have to be prepared to wait and use the booking system (expect it to take at least 30 minutes for a connection).

Next in line for price, private communications bureaus are also common and convenient places from which to make calls. Usually you must write the phone number on a piece of paper and let the person at the counter make the call. As an estimate, calls from private bureaus will cost Rs 120 per minute to New Zealand and Australia, Rs 135 per minute to the USA, and Rs 165 to Europe. The rate varies depending on where and when you make the call.

The most expensive option is the cardphone companies such as Lanka Pay (yellow and blue booths) and Metrocard (orange and black booths). Each card is specific to that company's booth so you cannot use a Metrocard in a Lanka Pay phone booth. Cards are sold at newsagents and other small shops; shops usually have a sign indicating which cards they sell.

Cellphones are increasingly popular, and renting a cellphone if you are in Sri Lanka on business is certainly worth considering (see Telephone & Fax under Information in the Colombo chapter for details). Coverage extends to all of Colombo and most major centres, and is gradually increasing.

Area Codes All regions have a two- or three-digit area code. However, new telephone companies operating in Sri Lanka on a wireless loop system also have separate three-digit prefixes, eg, 074. Calls to these phones cost about the same as to a standard telephone. The area code for standard lines is given at the start of each town's entry within this guidebook.

Fax

You can send faxes from some post offices as well as also private bureaus, which are numerous in the major towns and travellers haunts. Prices vary from place to place, but on average you can expect to pay Rs 140 a minute for a fax to New Zealand and Australia, or Rs 165 a minute to the UK, continental Europe and the USA.

Email & Internet Access

You shouldn't have trouble finding Internet facilities in the major tourist towns – even most towns that are off the beaten track have access. The Internet in Colombo is cheap (Rs 3 per minute); elsewhere you can find places that charge Rs 4 per minute, but more often than not you'll have to fork out Rs 7 to Rs 12. Try bargaining, and work offline when you're typing.

INTERNET RESOURCES

The World Wide Web is a rich resource for travellers. You can research your trip, hunt down bargain air fares, book hotels, check on weather conditions or chat with locals and other travellers about the best places to visit (or avoid!).

There's no better place to start your Web explorations than the Lonely Planet Web site (www.lonelyplanet.com). Here you'll find succinct summaries on travelling to most places on earth, postcards from other travellers and the Thorn Tree bulletin board, where you can ask questions before you go or dispense advice when you get back.

Other good Web sites to surf include:

Ceycom Sri Lanka Sri Lanka's major magazines, including *Explore Sri Lanka*, the monthly magazine popular with tourists and expatriates, can be viewed, as well as other newspapers.
www.ccom.lk
The Ceylon Tourist Board The official tourism site is dull, but it's a good starting point.
www.lanka.net/ctb
Daily News The English-language newspaper covers, no surprises here, the daily news, but it also has links to other sites (including sites dedicated to marriage proposals) and has a basic search engine.
www.lanka.net/lakehouse
EalamWeb Get the latest straight from the tiger's mouth (site comes complete with, yes, an online store).
www.tamileelam.com
InfoLanka With links to food, chat lines, news, organisations, nature, entertainment and more.
www.infolanka.com
Official Government Web Site of Sri Lanka This site is dull, but it includes links to the major government departments, and has succinct feature articles.
www.priu.gov.lk

TamilNet Describes itself as 'reporting to the world on Tamil affairs'. It has news, feature articles and a good search engine.
www.tamilnet.com

BOOKS

Imported books are relatively expensive, although they seem to disappear off the shelves quickly. Locally published books are cheaper, but the range is generally limited to nonfiction. Colombo is the only place with good bookshops and a reasonably varied selection of titles; Kandy has a more limited range. Finding books in English outside these cities can be difficult. If you want a cheap novel to read on the beach, try the second-hand bookshops and libraries in places such as Hikkaduwa and other travellers hang-outs.

Most books are published in different editions by different publishers in different countries. As a result, a book might be a hardcover rarity in one country while being readily available in paperback in another. Fortunately, bookshops and libraries search by title or author, so your local bookshop or library can advise you on the availability of the following recommendations.

Lonely Planet

Read This First: Asia & India is essential reading for those tackling Sri Lanka for the first time – even those on a second, third or fourth trip will find it informative for planning itineraries, advice on budgeting and other aspects of travel. *Travel with Children* by Maureen Wheeler contains a chapter on travelling in Sri Lanka as well as plenty of useful tips. Lonely Planet also has a *Sri Lanka phrasebook* as well as a guide to the *Maldives*, which many travellers include on their trip to this region. For those continuing on to India, Lonely Planet puts out guides to *Goa*, *India*, *Indian Himalaya*, *Kerala*, *North India*, *Rajasthan* and *South India*. There are also city guides to *Mumbai* and *Delhi*, as well as *Trekking in the Indian Himalaya*.

Guidebooks

The Ministry of Cultural Affairs has put out a series of books on ancient cities and important sites, including *Anuradhapura*,

Kandy, Nalanda, Polonnaruwa, Ritigala, Sigiriya and *The Temple of the Tooth, Kandy*. At the time of writing, the *The Sri Lanka Travel Manual* by Brigitte Barakat-Siriwardhana was about to be published. It promised to list products and services relevant to the traveller and expat.

For those in search of unusual guides, look out for *A Guide to the Waterfalls of Sri Lanka* by Eberhard Kautzsh (Tisara Prakasakayo, Dehiwala, 1983). For walkers there's the *Trekkers' Guide to Sri Lanka* (Trekking Unlimited of Colombo). Train buffs should get hold of *Sri Lanka by Rail* by Royston Ellis, a practical and interesting guide that will help you arrange your own trip around Sri Lanka.

History & Politics

An Historical Relation of Ceylon by Robert Knox (Tisara Prakasakayo, Colombo) is a fascinating book. Robert Knox was an Englishman captured near Trincomalee in the 17th century and held captive by the king of Kandy for nearly 20 years. His captivity was relatively loosely supervised and he had considerable freedom to wander around the kingdom and observe its operation. When he eventually escaped and returned to England his description of the kingdom of Kandy became a bestseller. It's equally readable today and is far and away the best book on this period of Sri Lankan history.

Dr KM de Silva's monumental *A History of Sri Lanka* brings Sri Lankan history up to modern times. Until its publication there had been something of a gap in books covering the country's post-independence history. *The Story of Ceylon* by EFC Ludowyk (Faber, London, 1962) and *The Modern History of Ceylon* by the same author (Praeger, New York, 1966) provide good introductions to Sri Lankan history.

For prehistory, the most authoritative work is *The Prehistory of Sri Lanka* Parts 1 & 2 by SU Deraniyagala. It's not exactly a light read, though. For an interesting account of the life of one of the most important archaeologists to have worked in Sri Lanka read *HCP Bell; Archaeologist of Ceylon & the Maldives* by Bethia N Bell & Heather M Bell, two of his granddaughters. It is over 300 pages long and has maps. Bell died in Kandy in 1937. His personal collection of antiquities was sold to the National Museum and his library is now housed in the rare books section at the museum.

Only Man is Vile: The Tragedy of Sri Lanka by William McGowan is an excellent account of the modern ethnic troubles, mixing travelogue, history and reportage. It lays the blame for the conflict on the Sinhalese elite and the legacy of British colonialism. *Ethnic & Class Conflicts in Sri Lanka* by Kumari Jayawardena (Centre for Social Analysis, Colombo) is a short readable book that links the current troubles with nearly a century of incidents between the different ethnic groups in Sri Lanka. *Sri Lanka, Island of Terror* by EM Thornton & R Niththyananthan (Eelam Research Organisation, London, 1984) is an account of the 1940s to mid-1980s from a Tamil point of view. *For a Sovereign State: A True Story on Sri Lanka's Separatist War* by Malinga H Gunaratne is another attempt to make sense of the conflict.

Flora & Fauna

A Field Guide to the Trees & Shrubs of Sri Lanka by Mark S Ashton et al is a detailed, well-illustrated hardback on Sri Lanka's flora. *Common Reef Fishes of Sri Lanka* by Dr Charles Anderson is also a well-illustrated guide that will be of interest to divers and snorkellers.

Sinharaja: A Rain Forest in Sri Lanka by Neela de Zoysa & Rhyana Rahem gives details on the flora and fauna you are likely to find if you visit this World Heritage site. *Field Guide to the Mammals of the Indian Subcontinent: Where to Watch Mammals in India, Nepal, Bhutan, Bangladesh, Sri Lanka and Pakistan* by KK Gurung & Raj Singh has a small but useful section on Sri Lanka. For a good introduction to Sri Lanka's elephants, get hold of a copy of *Aliya – Stories of the Elephants of Sri Lanka* by Teresa Cannon & Peter Davis. It's easy to read and is beautifully illustrated. For details of books for bird-watchers, see the 'Birds of Sri Lanka' boxed text in the Facts about Sri Lanka chapter.

Novels, Short Stories & Poems

Running in the Family by Michael Ondaatje is the Canadian writer's humorous account of returning to Sri Lanka in the 1970s after growing up there in the 1940s and '50s. It includes some superb sketches of upper-class life in Ceylon in the first half of this century, and captures precisely many of the little oddities that life in Sri Lanka often seems to be made up of. *Anil's Ghost*, Ondaatje's latest novel, tells the story of a forensic anthropologist exploring the truth behind war murders, but it's also a story about love and identity. Michael Ondaatje's latest collection of poems is featured in *Handwriting*.

Born to Labour by CV Vellupillai tells of the hard lives of the Tamil labourers on the tea estates.

Carl Muller has written a series that centres on the lusty Von Bloss Burgher family: *The Jam Fruit Tree, Yakada Yaka, Once Upon a Tender Time* and *Spit and Polish*. His other books include *A Funny Thing Happened on the Way to the Cemetery, Colombo* and *Children of the Lion*.

Romesh Gunesekera's first book, *Monkfish Moon*, contains nine short stories that centre on the effects of the war on people's lives. His book *Reef*, which also examines lives changed irrevocably by war, was a 1994 Booker Prize nominee. His most recent work is *The Sandglass*.

Shyam Selvadurai's *Funny Boy*, set in the mid-1980s, is an account of a boy's growing awareness of his homosexuality and is skilfully set against a wider background of escalating racism and violence. His most recent work is *Cinnamon Gardens*.

Yasmine Gooneratne's *The Pleasures of Conquest* centres on the so-called Democratic Republic of Amnesia and its attempts to come to terms with its colonial past. It is set in the New Imperial Hotel. She has also written *A Change of Skies*.

When Memory Dies by A Sivanandan won the Commonwealth Writers Prize for the best first-published work. It is an account of the struggles endured by three generations of a family in war-torn Sri Lanka. *Where the Dance Is* is his latest work.

Jean Arasanayagam's *In the Garden Secretly and other Stories* is a recently published collection of short stories. *Reddened Water Flows Clear* is an evocative collection of Arasanayagam's poems. Both examine the ramifications of war.

Ann Ranasinghe is another poet who has examined the implications of Sri Lanka's ethnic strife. *Against Eternity & Darkness* and *Mascot & Symbol* are two of her poetry collections.

First published in 1913, and now available in paperback from Oxford University Press (1981), Leonard Woolf's *The Village in the Jungle* is a readable but depressing story set in Hambantota (southern Sri Lanka) around the early 20th century. Woolf later became a leader of the literary Bloomsbury set between the world wars.

General

Sri Lanka is a photogenic country, and is the subject of many coffee-table books. Among the best are *Sri Lanka* by Tim Page (Lake House); *Sri Lanka: The Resplendent Isle* by Dominic Sansoni & Richard Simon (Times Editions); *Sri Lanka: A Personal Odyssey* by Nihal Fernando; and *Lunuganga* (the story of a garden near Bentota that was 40 years in the making) by Geoffrey Bawa, Christoph Bon & Dominic Sansoni. Exposing the less than attractive face of Sri Lanka's past is *Lanka 1986–1992* by Stephen Champion, with more than 100 black-and-white and colour photos that portray everything from village life to the horrors of war.

The *Architecture of an Island* by R Lewcock, B Sansoni & L Senanayake is a wonderful hardback detailing Sri Lanka's architectural heritage. It's beautifully illustrated with Barbara Sansoni's pen-and-ink drawings. It's available through the Barefoot bookshop in Colombo. Lonely Planet's *Buddhist Stupas in Asia: The Shape of Perfection* is a full colour hardback pictorial that explores the spread of Buddhism and stupa building across India and Asia. *Geoffrey Bawa* by Brian Brace Taylor is a glossy tribute to Sri Lanka's most prominent architect.

For interesting background on more detailed aspects of Sri Lankan history, look out for *A Return to Kandy* and *The Temple of Kelaniya* by Vesak Nanayakkara. Both are available from the Barefoot bookshop in Colombo.

The 43 Group: A Chronicle of Fifty Years in the Arts of Sri Lanka by Neville Weeratne is worthwhile for those interested in the evolution of modern art in Sri Lanka.

The *Palm Leaf Manuscripts of Sri Lanka* by Sirancee Gunawardana is a 327-page exposition on traditional *ola* (palm-leaf) manuscripts. It's well illustrated.

Say it in Sinhala by JB Disanayaka is an excellent reference for English speakers who want to learn a few words and phrases.

NEWSPAPERS & MAGAZINES

English-language newspapers include the popular *Daily News* and *The Island*; there are several weekend papers including the *Sunday Leader*, *Sunday Times* and *Sunday Observer*. The *Lanka Guardian* is a respected publication that appears fortnightly and contains news and commentary on various topical issues.

Magazines with useful information for tourists and expats include *Explore Sri Lanka*, *The Linc* and *Travel Lanka*. *Business Today* and *Lanka Monthly Digest* are both good magazines aimed at the business community. *Infolink – PC World Magazine* has news and background on the local and international computing scene. Regional magazines such as *Frontline*, *The Hindu* and *India Today* regularly have news and editorials. Transnational magazines such as *Time*, *Newsweek*, and *The Far Eastern Economic Review* are available at hotel bookshops and at Lake House and Vijitha Yapa bookshops.

RADIO & TV

Programs in English and Sinhala are broadcast by Sri Lanka's national radio and television network. You can pick up BBC radio broadcasts on 17790khz, 15310khz or 11955khz. Private channels include the boppy English-language Yes FM, as well as TNL and Capitol.

There are seven television channels, including the state-run SLRC (Sri Lanka Rupavahini Corporation), ITN (Independent Television Network) and privately owned ETV-1, ETV-2, MTV, Swarnawahini and TNL. BBC World Service can be picked up on ETV-1 and StarPlus on ETV-2.

VIDEO SYSTEMS

Sri Lanka, like India, the UK, Germany, Italy, Australia and New Zealand, uses the PAL video standard (NTSC is the standard used in the USA and Canada).

PHOTOGRAPHY & VIDEO
Film & Equipment

You can buy transparency and print film in Sri Lanka. Cargills (in Colombo, Kandy, Bandarawela and Nuwara Eliya) generally has a good supply of both. A roll of 100 ASA transparency film (36 exposure) costs about Rs 195. Check the use-by date before you buy. If you want to be certain that film hasn't been affected by the heat, ask for film that's been kept in the fridge. Millers in Fort is a reliable place to have film developed. One traveller has warned that although APS (digital) film is available for purchase in Sri Lanka, it was not processed correctly. His advice was to process this type of film back at home.

Bring any equipment you'll need. There are a few camera sales places in Colombo, but they may not have what you want. For camera repairs, Photoflex (☎ 587824) on the 1st Floor, 451/2 Galle Rd, Kollupitiya (Col 3) has been recommended.

For video, it would be wise to bring with you all your cartridges and anything else you think you may need. Some supplies are available in Colombo, but there's no guarantee you'll find what you're looking for. Few people use video locally, so there isn't much demand.

Technical Tips

Research and planning are the keys to taking good photos. For comprehensive information, *Travel Photography: A Guide to Taking better Pictures* by Richard I' Anson and published by Lonely Planet.

Following is a list of technical tips to help you improve your photography while in Sri Lanka.

- The quality of your photos depends on the quality of light you shoot in. Light is best when the sun is low in the sky – around sunrise and sunset.
- Don't buy cheap equipment, and don't load yourself down with equipment you don't know how to use properly.
- A good single-lens reflex (SLR) camera is advisable, and be aware that the quality of your lenses is the most important thing.
- Zoom lenses are heavier than fixed focal length and the quality isn't as good. An alternative to the zoom is a teleconverter, which fits over your lens and doubles the focal length.
- Always carry a skylight or UV filter. A polarising filter can create dramatic effects and cut glare, but don't fit it over a UV filter.
- Take a tripod and faster film (at least 400 ASA/ISO) rather than a flash, which creates harsh shadows. A cable release is useful for shooting with a tripod.
- Settle on a brand of film and get to know how it works *before* you head off.
- If possible, keep your film in a cool dark place before and after exposure.
- Expose for the main component of a scene and fill the frame with what you are photographing.
- Previsualising is one of the most important elements in photographic vision: You must 'see' your picture clearly before you take it.

Mistakes made by first-time users of camcorders include forgetting there is a microphone attached and having to deal later with all sorts of extraneous, embarrassing sounds that intrude on the footage. Another is being over-enthusiastic with panning and other movement, giving an end result that resembles standing on the deck of a boat in a storm. Think before you shoot and visualise the shot. Don't weigh yourself down with unnecessary equipment; taking the minimum will mean less hassle carrying it around and less stress worrying about it getting stolen or damaged.

The main environmental hazards you'll have to guard your camcorder against are heat, dust, grit and humidity. You can mitigate the effects of the last of these by keeping silicon gel sachets in your camcorder case.

Restrictions
Never take photos of dams, airports, road blocks or indeed anything associated with the military. Don't wave a camera around Colombo Fort, because the area near the port is an especially sensitive zone. The same restrictions apply to both video and photography.

Photographing People & Sacred Sites
Ask permission before taking pictures either of people or the inside of temples and other sacred places. It is forbidden to take photos inside the cave temple complex at Dambulla, for example. Other places may allow photography, but charge a fee. Payment for permission to film with video is usually higher than for still cameras. Never use a flash on murals inside temples and other places; it can damage them. You are not allowed to use a flash on the frescoes at Sigiriya, but even where there is no such ban, please behave responsibly. Never pose beside or in front of a statue of the Buddha (ie, with your back to it): this is considered extremely disrespectful. Tourists are sometimes asked for money for taking photos. Always find out *before* you shoot whether payment is expected.

Airport Security
Airport X-ray machines will not damage film carried in hand luggage. However, if you want to be on the safe side, put it in a lead-lined bag. Some people (usually professional photographers) won't allow their film to go through any X-ray machine, preferring instead to put it in clear plastic containers and carry it through by hand. If you do this be prepared to have each and every canister inspected before you are allowed through security. Never put film in baggage that will go in the hold of aircrafts, as it may be exposed to large doses of X-ray that can damage it.

TIME
Sri Lanka is six hours ahead of GMT, four hours behind Australian EST and 11 hours ahead of American EST.

ELECTRICITY
Voltages & Cycles
The electric current in Sri Lanka is 230V–240V, 50 cycles, alternating current. If you are bringing sensitive electronic equipment into the country (eg, a laptop) take a voltage stabiliser.

Be aware that outside the major cities, power cuts and failures occur reasonably frequently.

Plugs & Sockets
Plugs have three round pins, as in some parts of India. Adaptors are readily available at electrical stores for about Rs 100, but if you want to be better prepared, bring an adaptor with you. If you're bringing a laptop and you want to connect your modem to a phone line, you'll need a TUK, RJ11 phone adaptor.

WEIGHTS & MEASURES
Sri Lanka now uses the metric system, but people commonly refer to the old imperial measures. There are still some roads with markers in miles rather than kilometres. A word you'll hear quite often is *lakh*: one lakh is 100,000 units (of dollars or whatever).

LAUNDRY
All top-end and mid-range places to stay have laundry services, and guesthouses will make arrangements for you if you wish. Expect to pay around Rs 42 for a wash, dry and press for a T-shirt, Rs 75 for a dress. Laundry powder comes in boxes or in small packets for a few rupees and is on sale everywhere. Your guesthouse will happily supply you with a bucket, and you can launder away in the bathroom.

TOILETS
All top-end and mid-range places to stay have sit-down flush toilets, but if you're staying in budget accommodation you'll often find squat toilets (with toilet paper rolls only if you're lucky). Toilet paper can be bought inexpensively in supermarkets and general stores in Sri Lanka. Public toilets are scarce, so you'll have to duck into restaurants and hotels.

HEALTH
Travel health depends on your predeparture preparations, your daily health care while travelling and how you handle any medical problem that does develop. The potential dangers can seem quite frightening, but in reality few travellers experience anything more than an upset stomach. Many risks are avoidable with good preparation and some common-sense measures while you are away.

Predeparture Planning
Immunisations Plan ahead for getting your vaccinations: Some of them require more than one injection, while some vaccinations should not be given together. Note that some vaccinations should not be given to pregnant women or to people with allergies – discuss this with your doctor.

It is recommended you seek medical advice at least six weeks before travel. Be aware that there is often a greater risk of disease with children and during pregnancy.

Discuss your requirements with your doctor, but vaccinations you should consider for this trip include the following (for more details about the diseases themselves, see the individual disease entries later in this section). Carry proof of your vaccinations, as this is sometimes needed to enter some countries.

Diphtheria & Tetanus Vaccinations for these two diseases are usually combined and are recommended for everyone. After an initial course of three injections (usually given in childhood), boosters are necessary every 10 years.

Hepatitis A The vaccine for Hepatitis A (eg, Avaxim, Havrix 1440 or VAQTA) provides long-term immunity (possibly more than 10 years) after an initial injection and a booster at six to 12 months. Alternatively, an injection of gamma globulin can provide short-term protection against hepatitis A – two to six months, depending on the dose given. It is not a vaccine, but a ready-made antibody collected from blood donations. It is reasonably effective and, unlike the vaccine, it is protective immediately, but because it is a blood product, there are current concerns about its long-term safety. Hepatitis A vaccine is also available in a combined form, Twinrix, with hepatitis B vaccine. Three injections over a six-month period are required, the first two providing substantial protection against hepatitis A.

Hepatitis B Travellers who should consider vaccination against hepatitis B include those on a long trip, as well as those visiting countries where there are high levels of hepatitis B infection, where blood transfusions may not be adequately screened or where sexual contact or needle sharing is a possibility. Vaccination involves three injections, with a booster at 12 months. More rapid courses are available if necessary.

Japanese B Encephalitis Consider vaccination against this disease if spending a month or longer in a high-risk area (parts of Asia), making repeated trips to a risk area or visiting during an epidemic. It involves three injections over 30 days.

Polio Everyone should keep up to date with this vaccination, which is normally given in childhood. A booster every 10 years will maintain immunity.

Rabies Vaccination should be considered by those who will spend a month or longer in a country where rabies is common, especially if they are cycling, handling animals, caving or travelling to remote areas, and for children (who may not report a bite). Pretravel rabies vaccination involves having three injections over 21 to 28 days. If someone who has been vaccinated is bitten or scratched by an animal, they will require two booster injections of vaccine; those not vaccinated require more.

Tuberculosis The risk of tuberculosis (TB) to travellers is usually very low, unless you will be living with or closely associated with local people in high-risk areas such as Asia. Vaccination against TB (BCG) is recommended for children and young adults living in these areas for three months or more.

Typhoid Vaccination against typhoid may be required if you are travelling for more than a couple of weeks in most parts of Asia, Africa, central and South America and Central and Eastern Europe. It is now available either as an injection or as capsules to be taken orally. A combined hepatitis A–typhoid vaccine was launched recently but its availability is still limited – check with your doctor to find out its status in your country.

Yellow Fever The only vaccination that is a legal requirement for entry into Sri Lanka is the vaccination against yellow fever. The requirement is usually only enforced in relation to people coming from an infected area such as Central Africa and parts of South America. You may have to go to a special yellow fever vaccination centre.

Malaria Medication Antimalarial drugs do not prevent you from being infected but do kill the malaria parasites during a stage in their development and significantly reduce the risk of becoming very ill or dying. Expert advice on medication should be sought, as there are many factors to consider, including the area to be visited, the risk of exposure to malaria-carrying mosquitoes, the side effects of medication, your medical history and whether you are a child or an adult or pregnant. Travellers to isolated, high-risk areas may like to carry a treatment dose of medication for use if symptoms occur.

Health Insurance Make sure that you have adequate health insurance (see Travel Insurance under Visas & Documents in this chapter for details).

Travel Health Guides Lonely Planet's *Healthy Travel Asia & India* is a handy pocket size and is packed with useful information including pretrip planning, emergency first aid, immunisation and disease information and what to do if you get sick on the road. Lonely Planet's *Travel with Children* also includes advice on travel health for younger children.

There are a number of excellent travel health sites on the Internet. From the Lonely Planet home page there are links to the WHO (World Health Organization) and the US Centers for Disease Control & Prevention at www.lonelyplanet.com/web links/wlheal.htm.

Other Preparations Make sure you're healthy before you start travelling. If you are going on a long trip make sure your teeth are OK. If you wear glasses take a spare pair and your prescription.

If you require any medication take an adequate supply, as it may not be available locally. Take part of the packaging showing the generic name, which will make getting replacements easier. It's a good idea to have a legible prescription or letter from your doctor to show that you legally use the medication to avoid any problems.

Basic Rules

Food Remember the old colonial adage that says: 'If you can cook it, boil it or peel it you can eat it...otherwise forget it'. Vegetables and fruit should be washed with purified water or peeled where possible. Beware of ice cream that is sold in the street or anywhere it might have been melted and refrozen; if there's any doubt (eg, a power cut in the last day or two), steer well clear. Shellfish such as mussels, oysters and clams should be avoided as well as undercooked meat, particularly in the form of mince. Steaming does not make shellfish safe for eating.

If a place looks clean and well run and the vendor also looks clean and healthy, then the food is probably safe. In general, places that are packed with travellers or locals will be fine, while empty restaurants may be questionable. The food in busy restaurants is cooked and eaten quite quickly with little standing around and is probably not reheated.

Water The number one rule is *be careful of the water* and especially of ice. If you don't know for certain that the water is safe, assume the worst. Reputable brands of bottled water or soft drinks are generally fine, although in some places bottles may be refilled with tap water. Only use water from containers with a serrated seal – not tops or corks. Take care with fruit juice, particularly if water may have been added. Milk should be treated with suspicion as it is often unpasteurised, though boiled milk is fine if it is kept hygienically. Tea or coffee should also be OK, since the water should have been boiled.

Water Purification The simplest way of purifying water is to boil it thoroughly. Vigorous boiling should be satisfactory. Consider purchasing a water filter for a long trip. There are two main kinds of filter. Total filters take out all parasites, bacteria and viruses and make water safe to drink. They are often expensive, but they can be more cost effective than buying bottled water. Simple filters (which can even be a nylon

mesh bag) take out dirt and larger foreign bodies from the water so that chemical solutions work much more effectively; if water is dirty, chemical solutions may not work at all.

Medical Kit Check List

Following is a list of items you should consider including in your medical kit – consult your pharmacist for brands available in your country.

☐ **Aspirin or paracetamol (acetaminophen in the USA)** – for pain or fever
☐ **Antihistamine** – for allergies, eg, hay fever; to ease the itch from insect bites or stings; and to prevent motion sickness
☐ **Cold and flu tablets, throat lozenges and nasal decongestant**
☐ **Multivitamins** – consider for long trips, when dietary vitamin intake may be inadequate
☐ **Antibiotics** – consider including these if you're travelling well off the beaten track; see your doctor, as they must be prescribed, and carry the prescription with you
☐ **Loperamide or diphenoxylate** – 'blockers' for diarrhoea
☐ **Prochlorperazine or metaclopramide** – for nausea and vomiting
☐ **Rehydration mixture** – to prevent dehydration, which may occur, for example, during bouts of diarrhoea; particularly important when travelling with children
☐ **Insect repellent, sunscreen, lip balm and eye drops**
☐ **Calamine lotion, sting relief spray or aloe vera** – to ease irritation from sunburn and insect bites or stings
☐ **Antifungal cream or powder** – for fungal skin infections and thrush
☐ **Antiseptic (such as povidone-iodine)** – for cuts and grazes
☐ **Bandages, Band-Aids (plasters) and other wound dressings**
☐ **Water purification tablets or iodine**
☐ **Scissors, tweezers and a thermometer** – note that mercury thermometers are prohibited by airlines
☐ **Sterile kit** – in case you need injections in a country or area with medical hygiene problems; discuss with your doctor

Nutrition

If your diet is poor or limited in variety, if you're travelling hard and fast and therefore missing meals or if you simply lose your appetite, you can soon start to lose weight and place your health at risk.

Make sure your diet is well balanced. Cooked eggs, tofu, beans, lentils (dhal in Sri Lanka) and nuts are all safe ways to get protein. Fruit you can peel (bananas, oranges or mandarins, for example) is usually safe and a good source of vitamins. Melons can harbour bacteria in their flesh and are best avoided. Try to eat plenty of grains (including rice) and bread. Remember that although food is generally safer if it is cooked well, overcooked food loses much of its nutritional value. If your diet isn't well balanced or if your food intake is insufficient, it's a good idea to take vitamin and iron pills.

In hot climates make sure you drink enough and don't rely on feeling thirsty to indicate when you should drink. Not needing to urinate or voiding small amounts of very dark yellow urine is a danger sign. Always carry a water bottle with you on long trips. Excessive sweating can lead to loss of salt and therefore muscle cramping. Salt tablets are not a good idea as a preventative, but in places where salt is not used much, adding salt to food can help.

It's important when buying a filter to read the specifications, so that you know exactly what it removes from the water and what it doesn't. Simple filtering will not remove all dangerous organisms, so if you cannot boil water it should be treated chemically. Chlorine tablets will kill many pathogens, but not some parasites such as giardia and amoebic cysts. Iodine is more effective in purifying water and is available in tablet form. Follow the directions carefully and remember that too much iodine can be harmful.

Medical Problems & Treatment

Self-diagnosis and treatment can be risky, so you should always seek medical help. An embassy, consulate or five-star hotel can usually recommend a local doctor or clinic.

Although we do give drug dosages in this section, they are for emergency use only. Correct diagnosis is vital. In this section we have used the generic names for medications – check with a pharmacist for brands available locally.

Note that antibiotics should ideally be administered only under medical supervision. Take only the recommended dose at the prescribed intervals and use the whole course, even if the illness seems to be cured earlier. Stop immediately if there are any serious reactions and don't use the antibiotic at all if you are unsure that you have the correct one. Some people are allergic to commonly prescribed antibiotics such as penicillin; carry this information (eg, on a bracelet) when travelling.

Environmental Hazards

Heat Exhaustion Dehydration and salt deficiency can cause heat exhaustion. Take time to acclimatise to high temperatures, drink sufficient liquids and do not do anything too physically demanding.

Salt deficiency is characterised by fatigue, lethargy, headaches, giddiness and muscle cramps; salt tablets may help, but adding extra salt to your food is better.

Anhidrotic heat exhaustion is a rare form of heat exhaustion that is caused by an inability to sweat. It tends to affect people who have been in a hot climate for some time, rather than newcomers. It can progress to heatstroke. Treatment involves removal to a cooler climate.

Heatstroke This serious, occasionally fatal, condition can occur if the body's heat-regulating mechanism breaks down and the body temperature rises to dangerous levels. Long, continuous periods of exposure to high temperatures and insufficient fluids can leave you vulnerable to heatstroke.

The symptoms are feeling unwell, not sweating very much (or at all) and a high body temperature (39°C to 41°C or 102°F to 106°F). Where sweating has ceased, the skin becomes flushed and red. Severe, throbbing headaches and lack of coordination will also occur, and the sufferer may be

Pottering around the workshop

Mother and daughter, Pettah bazaar

Musician in the Temple of the Tooth, Kandy

Washing up at Colombo's bustling Pettah bazaar

DALLAS STRIBLEY

The urban face of Sri Lanka: a vibrant scene of daily life in the streets of Colombo

DALLAS STRIBLEY

Shops and billboards, Pettah bazaar

ANDERS BLOMQVIST

Artificial flowers for sale, Pettah bazaar

confused or aggressive. Eventually the victim will become delirious or convulse. Hospitalisation is essential, but in the interim get victims out of the sun, remove their clothing, cover them with a wet sheet or towel and then fan continually. Give fluids if they are conscious.

Jet Lag When a person travels by air across more than three time zones (each time zone usually represents a one-hour time difference) jet lag is experienced. It occurs because many of the functions of the human body (such as temperature, pulse rate and emptying of the bladder and bowels) are regulated by internal 24-hour cycles. When we travel long distances rapidly, our bodies take time to adjust to the 'new time' of our destination, and we may experience fatigue, disorientation, insomnia, anxiety, impaired concentration and loss of appetite. These effects will usually be gone within three days of arrival, but to minimise the impact of jet lag:

• Rest for a couple of days prior to departure.
• Try to select flight schedules that minimise sleep deprivation; arriving late in the day means you can go to sleep soon after you arrive. For very long flights, try to organise a stopover.
• Avoid excessive eating (which bloats the stomach) and alcohol (which causes dehydration) during the flight. Instead, drink plenty of non-carbonated, nonalcoholic drinks such as fruit juice or water.
• Avoid smoking.
• Make yourself comfortable by wearing loose-fitting clothes and perhaps bringing an eye mask and ear plugs to help you sleep.
• Try to sleep at the appropriate time for the time zone you are travelling to.

Motion Sickness Eating lightly before and during a trip will reduce the chances of motion sickness. If you are prone to motion sickness try to find a place that minimises movement – near the wing on aircraft, close to midships on boats and near the centre on buses. Fresh air usually helps; reading and cigarette smoke don't. Commercial motion-sickness preparations, which can cause drowsiness, have to be taken before the trip commences.

Ginger (available in capsule form) and peppermint (including mint-flavoured sweets) are natural preventatives.

Prickly Heat Excessive perspiration trapped under the skin causes an itchy rash called prickly heat. It usually strikes people who have just arrived in a hot climate. Keeping cool, bathing often, drying the skin and using a mild talcum or prickly heat powder or resorting to air-conditioning may help.

Sunburn In tropical Sri Lanka you can get sunburnt surprisingly quickly, even through cloud. Use sunscreen, a hat and apply a barrier cream for your nose and lips. Calamine lotion or a commercial after-sun preparation are good for mild sunburn. Protect your eyes with good quality sunglasses, particularly if you will be near water or sand.

Infectious Diseases

Diarrhoea Simple things such as a change of water, food or climate can all cause a mild bout of diarrhoea, but a few rushed toilet trips with no other symptoms is not indicative of a major problem.

Dehydration is the main danger with any diarrhoea, particularly in children or the elderly as dehydration can occur quite quickly. Under all circumstances *fluid replacement*

Everyday Health

Normal body temperature is about 37°C (98.6°F); more than 2°C (4°F) higher indicates a high fever. The normal adult pulse rate is 60 to 100 per minute (children 80 to 100, babies 100 to 140). As a general rule the pulse increases about 20 beats per minute for each 1°C (2°F) rise in fever.

Respiration (breathing) rate is also an indicator of illness. Count the number of breaths per minute; between 12 and 20 is normal for adults and older children (up to 30 for younger children, 40 for babies). People with a high fever or serious respiratory illness breathe more quickly than normal. More than 40 shallow breaths a minute may indicate pneumonia.

▲ ▲ ▲ ▲ ▲ ▲ ▲ ▲

(at least equal to the volume being lost) is the most important thing to remember. Weak black tea with a little sugar, soda water or soft drinks allowed to go flat and diluted 50% with clean water are all good. With severe diarrhoea a rehydrating solution is preferable to replace minerals and salts lost. Commercially available oral rehydration salts (ORS) are very useful; add them to boiled or bottled water. In an emergency you can make up a solution of six teaspoons of sugar and a half teaspoon of salt to a litre of boiled or bottled water. You need to drink at least the same volume of fluid that you are losing in bowel movements and vomiting. Urine is the best guide to the adequacy of replacement – if you have small amounts of concentrated urine, you need to drink more. Keep drinking small amounts often. Stick to a bland diet as you recover.

Gut-paralysing drugs such as loperamide or diphenoxylate can be used to bring relief from the symptoms, although they do not actually cure the problem. Only use these drugs if you do not have access to toilets, eg, if you *must* travel. Note that these drugs are not recommended for children under 12 years.

In certain situations, antibiotics may be required, such as with diarrhoea with blood or mucus (dysentery), any diarrhoea with fever, profuse watery diarrhoea, persistent diarrhoea not improving after 48 hours, and severe diarrhoea. These suggest a more serious cause of diarrhoea; in these situations gut-paralysing drugs should be avoided.

In these situations, a stool test may be necessary to diagnose what bug is causing your diarrhoea, so you should seek medical help urgently. Where this is not possible the recommended drugs for bacterial diarrhoea (the most likely cause of severe diarrhoea in travellers) are norfloxacin 400mg twice daily for three days or ciprofloxacin 500mg twice daily for five days. These are not recommended for children or pregnant women. The drug of choice for children would be co-trimoxazole with dosage dependent on weight. A five-day course is given. Ampicillin or amoxycillin may be given in pregnancy, but medical care is necessary.

Two other causes of persistent diarrhoea in travellers are giardiasis and amoebic dysentery.

Giardiasis is caused by a common parasite, *Giardia lamblia*. Symptoms include stomach cramps, nausea, a bloated stomach, watery, foul-smelling diarrhoea and frequent gas. Giardiasis can appear several weeks after you have been exposed to the parasite. The symptoms may disappear for a few days and then return; this can go on for several weeks.

Amoebic dysentery, caused by the protozoan *Entamoeba histolytica*, is characterised by a gradual onset of low-grade diarrhoea, often with blood and mucus. Cramping abdominal pain and vomiting are less likely than in other types of diarrhoea, and fever may not be present. It will persist until treated and can recur and cause other health problems.

You should seek medical advice if you think you have giardiasis or amoebic dysentery, but where this is not possible, tinidazole or metronidazole are the recommended drugs. Treatment is a 2g single dose of tinidazole or 250mg of metronidazole three times daily for five to 10 days.

Fungal Infections Fungal infections occur more commonly in hot weather and are usually found on the scalp, between the toes (athlete's foot) or fingers, in the groin and on the body (ringworm). You get ringworm (which is a fungal infection, not a worm) from infected animals or other people. Moisture encourages these infections.

To prevent fungal infections wear loose, comfortable clothes, avoid artificial fibres, wash frequently and dry yourself carefully. If you do get an infection, wash the infected area at least daily with a disinfectant or medicated soap and water, and rinse and dry well. Apply an antifungal cream or powder such as tolnaftate. Try to expose the infected area to air or sunlight as much as possible and wash all towels and underwear in hot water, change them often and let them dry in the sun.

Hepatitis Hepatitis is a general term for inflammation of the liver. It is a fairly common disease worldwide. There are several viruses that cause hepatitis, which differ in the way that they are transmitted. The symptoms are similar in all forms of the illness, and include fever, chills, headache, fatigue, feelings of weakness and aches and pains, followed by loss of appetite, nausea, vomiting, abdominal pain, dark urine, light-coloured faeces, jaundiced (yellow) skin and yellowing of the whites of the eyes. People who have had hepatitis should avoid alcohol for some time after the illness, as the liver needs time to recover.

Hepatitis A is transmitted by contaminated food and drinking water. You should seek medical advice, but there is not much you can do apart from resting, drinking lots of fluids, eating lightly and avoiding fatty foods. Hepatitis E is transmitted in the same way as hepatitis A; it can be particularly serious in pregnant women.

There are almost 300 million chronic carriers of hepatitis B in the world. It is spread through contact with infected blood, blood products or body fluids, for example, through sexual contact, unsterilised needles and blood transfusions, or contact with blood via small breaks in the skin. Other risk situations include having a shave, tattoo or body piercing with contaminated equipment. The symptoms of hepatitis B may be more severe than type A and the disease can lead to long-term problems such as chronic liver damage, liver cancer or a long term carrier state. Hepatitis C and D are spread in the same way as hepatitis B and can also lead to long-term complications.

There are vaccines against hepatitis A and B, but there are currently no vaccines against the other types of hepatitis. Following the basic rules about food and water (hepatitis A and E) and avoiding risk situations (hepatitis B, C and D) are important preventative measures.

HIV & AIDS Infection with the human immunodeficiency virus (HIV) may lead to acquired immune deficiency syndrome (AIDS), which is a fatal disease. Any exposure to blood, blood products or body fluids may put the individual at risk. The disease is often transmitted through sexual contact or dirty needles – vaccinations, acupuncture, tattooing and body piercing can be potentially as dangerous as intravenous drug use. HIV/AIDS can also be spread through infected blood transfusions. If you do need an injection, ask to see the syringe unwrapped in front of you, or take a needle and syringe pack with you. Fear of HIV infection should never preclude treatment for serious medical conditions.

The number of AIDS cases in Sri Lanka is estimated at 275, while HIV carrier estimates range from 6000 to 8000 people. Although these figures are low compared with other Asian countries, awareness about the issues of HIV/AIDS is poor among Sri Lankans. An added concern is that around 50% of the reported cases of HIV carriers are Sri Lankans who have returned from working overseas.

Intestinal Worms These parasites are most common in rural, tropical areas. Different worms have different ways of infecting people. Some may be ingested on food such as undercooked meat (eg, tapeworms) and some enter through your skin (eg, hookworms). Infestations may not show up for some time, and although they are generally not serious, if left untreated some can cause severe health problems later. Consider having a stool test when you return home to check for these and determine the appropriate treatment.

Sexually Transmitted Diseases HIV/AIDS and hepatitis B can be transmitted through sexual contact – see the relevant sections earlier for more details. Other STDs include gonorrhoea, herpes and syphilis; sores, blisters or rashes around the genitals and discharges or pain when urinating are common symptoms. In some STDs, such as wart virus or chlamydia, symptoms may be less marked or not observed at all, especially in women. Chlamydia infection can cause infertility in men and women before any symptoms have been noticed. Syphilis symptoms eventually disappear completely but the disease continues and can cause severe problems in later years. While abstinence from sexual contact is the only 100% effective prevention, using condoms is also effective. The treatment of gonorrhoea and syphilis is with antibiotics. The different sexually transmitted diseases each require specific antibiotics.

Typhoid Typhoid fever is a dangerous gut infection caused by contaminated water and food. Medical help must be sought.

In its early stages sufferers may feel they have a bad cold or flu on the way, as early symptoms include a headache, body aches and a fever that rises a little each day until it is around 40°C (104°F) or more. The victim's pulse is often slow relative to the degree of fever present – unlike a normal fever where the pulse increases. The victim may also suffer from vomiting, abdominal pain, diarrhoea or constipation.

In the second week the high fever and slow pulse continue and a few pink spots may appear on the body; trembling, delirium, weakness, weight loss and dehydration may occur. Complications such as pneumonia, perforated bowel or meningitis may occur.

Insect-Borne Diseases

Filariasis, leishmaniasis, Lyme disease and typhus are all insect-borne diseases, but they do not pose a great risk to travellers. For more information on them see Less Common Diseases at the end of this Health section.

Dengue Fever This viral disease is transmitted by mosquitoes and is fast becoming one of the top public health problems in the tropical world. In the year 2000, Sri Lanka had over 40 deaths due to the disease and over 7000 suspected cases. Unlike the malaria mosquito, the *Aedes aegypti* mosquito, which transmits the dengue virus, is most active during the day, and is found mainly in urban areas, in and around human dwellings.

Signs and symptoms of dengue fever include a sudden onset of high fever, headache, joint and muscle pains (hence its old name, 'breakbone fever') and nausea and vomiting. A rash of small red spots sometimes appears three to four days after the onset of fever. In the early phase of illness, dengue may be mistaken for other infectious diseases, including malaria and influenza. Minor bleeding such as nose bleeds may occur in the course of the illness, but this does not necessarily mean that you have progressed to the potentially fatal dengue haemorrhagic fever (DHF). This is a severe illness, characterised by heavy bleeding, which is thought to be a result of a second infection, due to a different strain (there are four major strains) and it usually affects residents of the country rather than travellers. Recovery even from simple dengue fever may be prolonged, with tiredness often lasting for several weeks.

You should seek medical attention as soon as possible if you think you may be infected. A blood test can exclude malaria and indicate the possibility of dengue fever. There is no specific treatment for dengue. Aspirin should be avoided: it increases the risk of haemorrhaging. There is no vaccine against dengue fever. The best prevention is to avoid mosquito bites at all times by covering up and using insect repellents containing the compound DEET and mosquito nets – see Malaria later in this section for more advice on avoiding mosquito bites.

Japanese B Encephalitis This viral infection of the brain is transmitted by mosquitoes. Most cases occur in rural areas as the virus exists in pigs and wading birds. Symptoms include fever, headache and sensitivity to light, drowsiness, confusion and other signs of brain dysfunction. Hospitalisation is needed for correct diagnosis and treatment. There is a high mortality rate among those who have symptoms; of those who survive many are intellectually disabled.

Malaria This serious and potentially fatal disease is spread by mosquito bites. If you are travelling in endemic areas it is extremely important to avoid mosquito bites and to take tablets to prevent this disease. Symptoms range from fever, chills and sweating, headache, diarrhoea and abdominal pains to a vague feeling of ill-health. Seek medical help immediately if malaria is suspected. Without treatment, malaria can rapidly become more serious.

If medical care is not available, malaria tablets can be used for treatment. You need to use a malaria tablet that is different from the one you were taking when you contracted malaria. The standard treatment dose of mefloquine is two 250mg tablets and a further two, six hours later. For Fansidar, it's a single dose of three tablets. If you were previously taking mefloquine and cannot obtain Fansidar, then other alternatives are Malarone (atovaquone-proguanil; four tablets once daily for three days), halofantrine (three doses of two 250mg tablets every six hours) or quinine sulphate (600mg every six hours). There is a greater risk of side effects with these dosages than in normal use if used with mefloquine, so medical advice is preferable. Be aware also that halofantrine is no longer recommended by the WHO as emergency stand-by treatment, because of its side effects, and should only be used if no other drugs are available.

Travellers are advised to prevent mosquito bites at all times. The main messages are:

- Wear light-coloured clothing.
- Wear long trousers and long-sleeved shirts.
- Use mosquito repellents containing the compound DEET on exposed areas (prolonged overuse of DEET may be harmful, especially to children, but its use is certainly considered preferable to being bitten by mosquitoes that transmit disease).
- Avoid perfumes or aftershave.
- Use a mosquito net impregnated with mosquito repellent (permethrin) – it may be worth taking your own.
- Impregnating clothes with permethrin will effectively deter mosquitoes and other insects.

Cuts, Bites & Stings
See Less Common Diseases for details of rabies, which is passed through animal bites.

Bedbugs & Lice Bedbugs live in various places, but particularly in dirty mattresses and bedding, and are evidenced by spots of blood on bedclothes or on the wall. Bedbugs leave itchy bites in neat rows.

Calamine lotion or a sting-relief spray may help.

All lice cause itching and discomfort. They make themselves at home in your hair (head lice), your clothing (body lice) or in your pubic hair (crabs). You catch lice through direct contact with infected people or by sharing combs, clothing and the like. Powder or shampoo treatment will kill the lice and infected clothing should then be washed in very hot, soapy water and left in the sun to dry.

Bites & Stings Bee and wasp stings are usually painful rather than dangerous. However, in people who are allergic to them severe breathing difficulties may occur and require urgent medical care. Calamine lotion or a sting-relief spray will give relief, and ice packs will reduce the pain and swelling. There are some spiders with dangerous bites but antivenins are usually available. Scorpion stings are notoriously painful and in some parts of Asia can actually be fatal. Scorpions often shelter in shoes or clothing.

There are various fish and other sea creatures that can sting or bite dangerously or which are dangerous to eat – seek local advice.

Cuts & Scratches Wash well and treat any cut with an antiseptic such as povidone-iodine. Where possible avoid bandages and Band-Aids, which can keep wounds wet. Coral cuts are notoriously slow to heal and if they are not adequately cleaned, small pieces of coral can become embedded in the wound.

Jellyfish Avoid contact with these sea creatures, which have stinging tentacles – seek local advice. Dousing in vinegar will deactivate any stingers that have not 'fired'. Calamine lotion, antihistamines and analgesics may reduce the reaction and relieve the pain.

Leeches & Ticks Leeches may be present in damp rainforest conditions particularly in the Sinharaja Forest Reserve; they attach themselves to your skin to suck your blood.

Trekkers often get them on their legs or in their boots. Salt or a lighted cigarette end will make them fall off. Do not pull them off, as the bite is then more likely to become infected. Clean and apply pressure if the point of attachment is bleeding. An insect repellent may keep them away.

You should always check all over your body if you have been walking through a potentially tick-infested area as ticks can cause skin infections and other more serious diseases. If a tick is found attached, press down around the tick's head with tweezers, grab the head and gently pull upwards. Avoid pulling the rear of the body as this may squeeze the tick's gut contents through the attached mouth parts into the skin, increasing the risk of infection and disease. Smearing chemicals on the tick will not make it let go and is not recommended.

Snakes There are five species of venomous snakes in Sri Lanka, and these are relatively commonly spotted, especially in the dry zone area around Anuradhapura and Polonnaruwa. Be careful when wandering around the ancient ruins. To minimise your chances of being bitten always wear boots, socks and long trousers when walking through undergrowth where snakes may be present. Don't put your hands into holes and crevices, and be careful when collecting firewood.

Snake bites do not cause instantaneous death and antivenins are usually available. Immediately wrap the bitten limb tightly, as you would for a sprained ankle, and then attach a splint to immobilise it. Keep the victim still and seek medical help, if possible with the dead snake for identification. Don't attempt to catch the snake if there is a possibility of being bitten again. Tourniquets and sucking out the poison are now comprehensively discredited.

Women's Health
Gynaecological Problems Antibiotic use, synthetic underwear, sweating and contraceptive pills can lead to fungal vaginal infections, especially when travelling in hot climates. Thrush or vaginal candidiasis is characterised by a rash, itch and discharge.

Nystatin, miconazole or clotrimazole pessaries are the usual treatment, but some people use a more traditional remedy involving vinegar or lemon juice douches, or yogurt. Maintaining good personal hygiene and wearing loose-fitting clothes and cotton underwear may help prevent these infections.

Sexually transmitted diseases are a major cause of vaginal problems. Symptoms include a smelly discharge, painful intercourse and sometimes a burning sensation when urinating. Medical attention should be sought and male sexual partners must also be treated. For more details see the section on Sexually Transmitted Diseases earlier. Besides abstinence, the best thing is to practise safer sex using condoms.

Pregnancy It is not advisable to travel to some places while pregnant: Some vaccinations used to prevent serious diseases are not advisable during pregnancy. In addition, some diseases are much more serious for the mother (and may increase the risk of a stillborn child) in pregnancy (eg, malaria).

Most miscarriages occur during the first three months of pregnancy. Miscarriage is not uncommon and can occasionally lead to severe bleeding. The last three months should also be spent within reasonable distance of good medical care. A baby born as early as 24 weeks stands a chance of survival, but only in a good modern hospital. Pregnant women should avoid all unnecessary medication, although vaccinations and malarial prophylactics should still be taken where needed. Additional care should be taken to prevent illness and particular attention should be paid to diet and nutrition. Alcohol and nicotine, for example, should be avoided.

Less Common Diseases
The following diseases pose a small risk to travellers, and so are only mentioned in passing. Seek medical advice if you think you may have any of these diseases.

Cholera This is the worst of the watery diarrhoeas and if you suspect infection, medical help should be sought. Outbreaks of cholera are generally widely reported, so you can avoid such problem areas. Fluid replacement is the most vital treatment – the risk of dehydration is severe as it is possible to lose up to 20L a day. If there is a delay in getting to hospital, then begin taking tetracycline. The adult dose is 250mg four times daily. It is not recommended for children under nine years or for pregnant women. Tetracycline may help shorten the illness, but adequate fluids are required to save lives.

Filariasis This is a mosquito-transmitted parasitic infection found in many parts of Asia. Possible symptoms include fever, pain and swelling of the lymph glands; inflammation of lymph drainage areas; swelling of a limb or the scrotum; skin rashes; and blindness. Treatment is available to eliminate the parasites from the body, but some of the damage already caused may not be reversible. Medical advice should be obtained if the infection is suspected.

Leishmaniasis This is a group of parasitic diseases transmitted by sandflies, which are found in Sri Lanka. Cutaneous leishmaniasis affects the skin tissue causing ulceration and disfigurement, and visceral leishmaniasis affects the internal organs. Seek medical advice, as laboratory testing is required for diagnosis and correct treatment. Avoiding sandfly bites is the best precaution. Bites are usually painless, itchy and yet another reason to cover up and apply repellent.

Lyme Disease This is a tick-transmitted infection that may be acquired throughout Asia. The illness usually begins with a spreading rash at the site of the tick bite and is accompanied by fever, headache, extreme fatigue, aching joints and muscles and mild neck stiffness. If untreated, these symptoms usually subside over several weeks but over subsequent weeks or months disorders of the nervous system, heart and joints may develop. Treatment works best early in the illness. Medical help should be sought.

Rabies This fatal viral infection is found in many countries. Many animals can be infected (such as dogs, cats, bats and monkeys) and it is their saliva that is infectious. Any bite, scratch or even lick from an animal should be cleaned immediately and thoroughly. Scrub with soap and running water, and then apply alcohol or iodine solution. Medical help should be sought promptly to receive a course of injections to prevent the onset of symptoms and death.

Tetanus This disease is caused by a germ that lives in soil and in the faeces of horses and other animals. It enters the body via breaks in the skin. The first symptom may be discomfort in swallowing, or stiffening of the jaw and neck; this is followed by painful convulsions of the jaw and whole body. The disease can be fatal. It can be prevented by vaccination.

Tuberculosis TB is a bacterial infection usually transmitted from person to person by coughing, but may be transmitted through consumption of unpasteurised milk. Milk that has been boiled is safe to drink, and the souring of milk to make yogurt or cheese also kills the bacilli. Travellers are usually not at great risk as close household contact with the infected person is usually required before the disease is passed on. You may need to have a TB test before you travel as this can help diagnose the disease later if you become ill.

Typhus This disease is spread by ticks, mites or lice. It begins with fever, chills, headache and muscle pains followed a few days later by a body rash. There is often a large painful sore at the site of the bite and nearby lymph nodes are swollen and painful. Typhus can be treated under medical supervision. Seek local advice on areas where ticks pose a danger and always check your skin carefully for ticks after walking in a danger area such as a tropical forest. An insect repellent can help, and walkers in tick-infested areas should consider having their boots and trousers impregnated with benzyl benzoate and dibutylphthalate.

WOMEN TRAVELLERS

The more modestly you dress, the less unwanted attention you will attract. Covering your legs and your shoulders helps you blend in more effectively. No matter what you wear though, you should expect to be stared at. Some women find wearing sunglasses in city centres helps them avoid eye contact, and the ensuing unwanted interaction. You may also want to wear a wedding ring. But you may not completely avoid some of the pests who like to latch onto or follow foreign women. The more remote places, in particular, are where a woman alone may have to cope with some annoyances. Lone women travellers may be hassled walking around at night.

Avoid lonely beaches or anywhere you may be caught out alone. Stray hands on crowded buses are something else to watch out for. The sight of foreign women (although this isn't an experience exclusive to foreign women) seems to make a few men masturbate on the spot. Fortunately, such behaviour rarely escalates to anything more threatening. However don't imagine travelling in Sri Lanka is one long hassle. Such upleasant incidents are the exception not the rule.

Supermarkets in the main cities (eg, Keells and Cargills) sell toiletries, including tampons and pads. Stock up, as tampons can be hard to find in towns and villages; pads are easy to find, even in villages.

Organisations

There are several organisations that provide counselling, emergency accommodation and other assistance to women, others publish magazines and conduct research. The following places are good starting points:

The Centre for Women's Research (Cenwor; ☎/fax 01-502828) 225/4 Kirula Rd, Havelock Town (Col 5). The centre primarily researches the status of women in Sri Lanka, but also lobbies, runs training programs and more. It has a good library.
Web site: www.cenwor.lk

The Women's Education & Research Centre (WERC; ☎ 01-595296) 58 Dharmarama Rd, Wellawata (Col 6). This centre keeps up-to-date clippings on matters affecting women in Sri Lanka and has a library.

GAY & LESBIAN TRAVELLERS

Male homosexual activity is illegal in Sri Lanka (there is no law against female homosexuality) and the subject is not openly discussed. There have been some convictions in recent years so it would be prudent not to flaunt your sexuality. Probably the best way to tap into the local gay scene is via with Internet. Check out the Sri Lankan Gay Friends' Web site at www.geocities.com/sri lankangay/ which has information as well as a schedule of gay and lesbian activities.

Companions on a Journey (☎ 075-331988, ✉ coj@sri.lanka.net) is an organisation for the gay and lesbian community based in Colombo. It provides a drop-in centre, a library, film screenings, health-related advice and more. It also lobbies for legislative changes. Companions on a Journey can also be contacted by writing to PO Box 48, Wattala, Sri Lanka.

DISABLED TRAVELLERS

Sri Lanka is a challenge for disabled travellers. If you have restricted mobility you may find it difficult, if not impossible, to get around on public transport; for example, buses and trains don't have facilities for wheelchairs. Moving around towns and cities can also be difficult for those in a wheelchair or the visually impaired because of the continual roadworks and crummy roads (don't expect many footpaths). Think about hiring a car and driver as a practical and convenient alternative to public transport, and if possible travel with a strong, able-bodied person. See the Getting Around chapter, under Car for general information and Organised Tours for details on organisations that can help you get a car and driver together.

Apart from top-end places, accommodation is generally not geared for wheelchairs. However, many places would be able to provide disabled travellers with rooms and bathrooms that are accessible without stairs. It might take a bit of time to find places in each destination with the right facilities, but is possible. Medical facilities outside Colombo are limited.

The ever-obliging Sri Lankans are always ready to assist disabled travellers. A hearing-impaired traveller noted her trip had been thoroughly enjoyable and hassle-free – thanks to Sri Lankans' willingness to always lend a hand.

Organisations

The Royal Association for Disability and Rehabilitation (Radar; ☎ 020-7250 3222), 12 City Forum, 250 City Rd, London, England EC1V 8AF, is a useful point of contact if you are thinking of travelling to Sri Lanka. Check out Radar's Web site at www.radar.org.uk.

The Sri Lanka Federation of the Visually Handicapped (☎/fax 01-437768, ⓔslfvh@ mail.ewisl.com) at 74 Church St, Slave Island (Col 2) may also be able to provide advice.

TRAVEL WITH CHILDREN

Sri Lankans adore children, and places to stay and eat cater for children as a matter of course. Hotels and guesthouses invariably have triple rooms, and extra beds are routinely supplied on demand. Evening meal times are often rather late – around 7.30 pm – so you may have to make arrangements for children to be fed earlier. Check whether you are to be charged extra for this service.

If you have a very young child, one dilemma is whether to bring a backpack carrier or a pram. Opinion seems divided on this – if you can, bring both. One reader, who opted for a pram, decided this was the best choice because a backpack would have been too sweaty in the tropical heat. However, prams have to contend with uneven footpaths and often no footpaths at all.

Sri Lankan food tends to be spicy, and chillies are liberally used. However, it's perfectly feasible to have spice-free food anywhere you go. Rice is the staple, and you can usually get steamed or boiled vegetables, eggs and plain fried fish. Fruit is widely available: pineapples, oranges, bananas and so on. Remember that fruit you can peel yourself is safest. Water should be boiled *and* filtered. Be wary of cordials and ice in drinks. Bottled water is available everywhere and is perfectly safe. A healthy drink is the water from a king coconut – it's cheap and for sale everywhere in Sri Lanka. Coca-Cola, Fanta and Sprite are found in even the smallest villages. In Colombo, all the major fast-food chains are represented, including McDonald's. The Deli Market in the World Trade Centre in Colombo has a special children's menu.

It's important to be sun-conscious in this tropical country. Children should wear hats when they are outside, and should have their skin covered. Bring a good sunblock with you as well; most suncreams available in Sri Lanka are unsuitable for children. Children should wear something on their feet to prevent them from picking up parasites.

Pharmaceutical supplies, as well as imported baby food and disposable nappies (diapers), are available at Keells and Cargills supermarkets, however, they can be relatively expensive.

Never allow children to play with stray animals. Dogs, cats and even monkeys may harbour all sorts of parasites and diseases – rabies being the most deadly. Check with your doctor before you leave home to ensure all vaccinations are up to date, and bring a reasonably good medical kit with you. See the Health section earlier in this chapter for details.

Travelling on public transport is OK on trains (1st class is obviously more comfortable) but is not OK on buses. Buses are horribly overcrowded and the driving is dangerous. A better option is to hire a car and driver. Reputable hire-car companies provide safety child seats free of charge.

There aren't a great many attractions dedicated solely to children, although a favourite for kids is the elephant orphanage near Kandy. There are various turtle hatcheries along the coast, and in Tangalla you can see the turtles come up to the beach to lay their eggs (although this is a night-time trip). A safari in one of the national parks would also appeal to children. All top-end hotels have swimming pools (often in really magnificent settings) and, of course, Sri Lanka is famous for its beaches.

DANGERS & ANNOYANCES
Ethnic Tensions

Areas in the north and east of Sri Lanka are unsafe to visit due to ongoing conflict. See the boxed text 'Is it Safe?' in the Introduction.

Scams

Sri Lanka's tourism industry provides an income to many, from the owner of a fancy hotel to the three-wheeler who dropped you at the door. At the top of the financial pyramid the money pours in seemingly endlessly; for the folks down the bottom, commissions are the name of the game. Touts, or as they like to call themselves 'friends' or 'guides', lurk around bus and train stations with the intention of taking you to a hotel or guesthouse of their choice. (The place you want to stay in, you see, is closed, a festering fleapit, overpriced etc.) If you stay at the hotel of their choice, the tout will gain a commission, sometimes up to 30% of your bill. This will either be subsidised by an increase in charges to you, or the hotelier will make do with less money. Many travellers like going with a tout, as often you get better deals and you don't have the headache of tramping the streets. This is OK provided the hotelier forks out the tout's commission. Others always prefer to find their own accommodation. Some travellers get paranoid and rude. Saying you have a reservation, whether true or not, is often a good ploy if you want to avoid touts.

The airport is prime scam-breeding ground for tourists fresh off the plane. You may be approached with stories designed to make you sign up for a tour on the spot. See the boxed text 'Warning' in the Colombo chapter for more details.

Restaurants also play the commission game: Your guide just received a kickback for the lunch you ate. Relax. It makes sense for the guide to take you somewhere where the food's good, and the cleanliness and standard of restaurants tends to increase with picky tourists regularly traipsing through. Gem shops, handicraft stalls, in fact most businesses connected to the tourist industry, have some kind of commission system set up and this can really disenchant some visitors.

Just remember: this is how many make a living – you can help out, or you can spend your money elsewhere. Either way, don't get hung up on beating the commission racket.

Theft

Always guard against theft in Sri Lanka, whether you're on the move or staying in a guesthouse or hotel. Pickpockets are active on crowded buses, notably in Colombo along Galle Rd. They often work together – one to jostle you and the other to pick your pocket or slit your bag with a knife, often as you board the bus. All you can do is try to keep a little space around you and hold tight to what you're carrying. It's often unwise to sleep with your windows open. Even if the windows have bars, thieves may use long poles with hooks on the end to lift out your goods.

One thieves' trick reported by a number of travellers is to take the bottom one or two of a block of travellers cheques, so that you don't notice anything missing until later.

If you do get robbed go to the police – you won't get your money back but passports and tickets are often jettisoned later. One Australian actually got her passport back from her embassy after the pickpockets dropped it in a mailbox!

Traffic

The standard of some Sri Lankan driving – above all, by drivers of private buses – poses a real danger. It seems to be acceptable for a bus, car or truck to overtake in the face of oncoming smaller road-users – who sometimes simply have to get off the road or risk getting hit. To announce that they are overtaking, or want to overtake, drivers use a series of blasts on loud, shrill horns. If you're walking or cycling along any kind of main road make sure you keep all your senses on alert in every direction – even (or especially) if you're walking on the side of oncoming traffic, when you could be collected from behind by a crazed overtaker.

Drugs

Drug use, mainly marijuana and even heroin, is on the increase in tourist centres such as Hikkaduwa and Unawatuna. Dabbling is a very perilous risk; you can expect to end up in jail if you are caught dealing or using anything illegal.

BUSINESS HOURS

The working week in offices is usually from 8.30 am to 4.30 pm weekdays. Some businesses also open until about 1 pm on Saturday. Shops normally open from 10 am to about 7 pm weekdays, and until 3 pm on Saturday. Businesses run by Muslims may take an extended lunch break on Friday so that staff can attend Friday prayers. Banks are generally open from 9 am to 3 pm on weekdays, although some banks are open on Saturday.

PUBLIC HOLIDAYS & SPECIAL EVENTS

Sri Lanka has many Buddhist, Hindu, Christian and Muslim festivals, and around 26 public holidays a year. A full five-day working week is a rarity! Many of the holidays are based on the lunar calendar so the dates vary from year to year according to the Gregorian calendar: See Poya later in this section to help you work out the *poya* (full moon) holiday dates for each year. The tourist board publishes an annual *Current Events Calendar* on its Web site at www.lanka.net/ctb. The main festivals are listed following.

The Muslim festivals Id-ul-Fitr (the end of Ramadan, 16 December 2001), Id-ul-Adha (the Hajj festival, 23 February 2002) and Milad-un-Nabi (Mohammed's birthday, 23 May 2002) vary, subject to the sighting of the moon.

January

Duruthu Perahera Held on the full-moon day in January at the Kelaniya Temple in Colombo and second in importance only to the huge Kandy perahera, this festival celebrates a visit by the Buddha to Sri Lanka.

Thai Pongal This is a Hindu harvest festival, held on 14 or 15 January, to honour the Sun God.

February

National Day National Day (4 February) celebrates independence from Britain and features parades, dances and national games all over the country.

Navam Perahera Navam Perahera was first celebrated in 1979, but is already one of Sri Lanka's biggest peraheras. Held on the February full moon around Viharamahadevi Park and Beira Lake in Colombo, it starts from the Gangaramaya Temple. About 50 elephants take part: this is now bigger than the Kelaniya Perahera.

February/March

Maha Sivarathri In late February or early March the Hindu festival of Maha Sivarathri commemorates the marriage of Shiva to Parvati.

March/April

Easter The Christian Good Friday holiday usually falls in April, but can fall in late March. An Easter passion play is performed on the island of Duwa, off Negombo.

Sinhalese & Tamil New Year Both New Year's Eve on 13 April and New Year's Day on 14 April are holidays. This is an occasion for hospitality, and it also coincides with the end of the harvest season and marks the start of the southwest monsoon. See the boxed text 'Celebrating New Year Sri Lankan Style' later in this section for more information.

May

May Day As in other parts of the world, May Day (1 May) is a holiday.

Vesak This two-day holiday – full-moon day and the day after – commemorates the birth, enlightenment and death of Lord Buddha. Villages are decorated with huge panels showing scenes from the Buddha's life, and puppet shows and open-air theatre performances take place. Temples are crowded with devotees bringing flowers and offerings. The high point is the lighting of countless paper lanterns and oil lamps that turn the island into a fairyland. The Adam's Peak pilgrimage season ends at Vesak.

National Heroes' Day Although not a public holiday, 22 May is a day honouring soldiers who have died in the ethnic conflict.

June

Poson Poya The Poson full-moon day in June is a celebration of the bringing of Buddhism to Sri Lanka by Ashoka's son Mahinda. Anuradhapura and Mihintale, where Mahinda met and converted the Sinhalese king, are the main sites for this celebration. On this day thousands of white-clad pilgrims climb the stairs to the summit of Mihintale.

July/August

Kandy Esala Perahera The Kandy Esala Perahera, the most important and spectacular festival in Sri Lanka, is the climax of 10 days and nights of increasingly frenetic activity in Kandy. It's held during the month of Esala (July/August), ending on the Nikini full moon. This great procession honours the Sacred Tooth Relic of Kandy. Thousands of dancers, drummers and temple chieftains take part in the parade, which also features 50 or more magnificently decorated elephants including the most splendid of them all, the mighty Maligawa Tusker, which carries the golden relic casket. Smaller peraheras are held at other locations around the island.

Hindu Vel This festival is held in Colombo. The gilded chariot of Skanda, the God of War, complete with his *vel* (trident), is ceremonially hauled from a temple in Sea St, Pettah, to another at Bambalapitiya.

Kataragama Another important Hindu festival is held at Kataragama, where devotees put themselves through the whole gamut of ritual masochism. Some thrust skewers through their tongues and cheeks, others tow heavy carts or suspend weights from hooks piercing their skin. The grand finale is the fire-walking ceremonies, as the devotees walk barefoot across beds of red-hot embers. A pilgrimage from Batticaloa to Kataragama takes place.

Other Hindu Festivals Several Hindu festivals are held in the Jaffna area in July and August. Munneswaram Temple, 5km east of Chilaw, hosts a major festival in August, when devotees test their faith by walking on red-hot coals.

October/November

Deepavali The Hindu festival of lights takes place in late October or early November. Thousands of flickering oil lamps celebrate the triumph of good over evil and the return of Rama after his period of exile. Lakshmi, the goddess of wealth, is usually worshiped on the third day of the festival.

December

Adam's Peak The pilgrimage season, when pilgrims (and the odd tourist) climb Adam's Peak, starts in December.

Unduvap Poya This full-moon day commemorates Sangamitta, Ashoka's daughter, who accompanied her brother Mahinda to Sri Lanka and brought a sapling from the sacred Bodhi Tree. The tree grown from that sapling still stands in Anuradhapura today.

Christmas Day (25 December) The celebration of Christ's birth is a holiday.

Poya

Every poya or full-moon day is a holiday. Especially if it falls on a Friday or Monday, poya causes people to swarm all over the island and accommodation, buses and trains fill up. No alcohol is supposed to be sold in hotels, restaurants, bars or stores on poya days, and some establishments close. If you're likely to be thirsty, stock up in advance! Many hotels and guesthouses discreetly provide their needy guests with a bottle of beer 'under the table'.

The poya days in 2002 are 28 January, 27 February, 28 March, 27 April, 26 May, 24 June, 24 July, 22 August, 21 September, 21 October, 20 November, 12 December. In 2003 they are 18 January, 16 February, 18 March, 16 April, 16 May, 14 June, 13 July, 12 August, 10 September, 10 October, 9 November, 8 December.

ACTIVITIES
Surfing

The best surf beach is at Arugam Bay on the east coast. This destination has been off limits at times because of fighting in the surrounding districts, but at the time of writing keen surfers were returning. Surf is up from April to September. Hikkaduwa is another long-time favourite for international surfers, and the point at Midigama farther down the west coast another good, if more isolated, spot. The best time to surf here is from November to April.

You can hire surfboards and boogie boards, wetties and anything else you'll need from shops beside the beaches. You can also buy second-hand gear.

Diving & Snorkelling

There is OK-quality scuba diving, with coral and interesting shipwrecks to be seen at several spots along the west coast such as Hikkaduwa and Tangalla; once again, the east coast and the Basses in the south are perhaps better, but are off limits for now. Pigeon Island off Nilaveli (north of Trincomalee) is a fine place to go snorkelling. Diving shops can be found in Colombo and in the major west coast

Celebrating the New Year Sri Lankan Style

When the sun moves from Pisces, the last zodiac sign in its cycle, to Aries, Sinhalese Buddhist and Tamil Hindu Sri Lankans celebrate their new year. Astrologically determined auspicious moments set the time for significant tasks, including the lighting of the hearth to cook *kiri bath* (milk rice), bathing and the anointing of oil, the first business transaction and the first meal of the new year. There are also auspicious colours to be worn and directions to face, all to help ensure good fortune for the year ahead.

Falling on April 14, this is the time when the harvest ends and the fruit trees produce bounteous crops. The festival brings the country to a standstill for almost a week after a hectic preparation. Public transport is packed on the eve of new year as everyone returns to their parental homes for the celebration. Bread supplies are scarce for a week – bakeries and businesses close down to allow staff to travel home for a few days.

The rituals begin with cleaning the house and lighting the oil lamp. The pounding of the *raban*, a large drum played by several women, sounds the dawning of the new year. The lighting of the hearth is the first ceremonial act for the new year, and even women who are not especially devoted to astrology ensure they light the fire to heat the new pot filled with milk. Families constantly watch the clock, assisted by countdowns on state television, until it is time to take the first meal for the new year. And just in case you missed it, a shrill chorus of firecrackers reminds everyone that the moment has arrived.

After the other rituals are performed, the family visits friends or joins the games being played in the village, and children ride high on swings hanging from a nearby mango or jackfruit tree.

Special *aurudu* (new year) food is enjoyed during the following days. The ubiquitous plantains (bananas) are a staple, and special additions are *kaung* (a small oil cake) and *kokis* (a light, crisp sweetmeat of Dutch origin).

Family members exchange gifts after eating at the appointed time, usually clothes (a sari for mother, a shirt or sarong for father and clothing 'kits' for the children) and give sweetmeats or fruit to neighbours. Aurudu sales and markets give Sri Lankans the opportunity to shop for bargains of all sorts.

Aurudu has become deeply embedded in the culture of Sinhalese Buddhist and Tamil Hindu Sri Lankans. It is not celebrated by Buddhists or Hindus anywhere else in the world, evidence of the shared cultural heritage of the Sinhalese and Tamil people of the island. Many expat Sri Lankans return to their homeland at this time of year to share the new year and holiday season with their family and friends. The wealthier expats often avoid the heat and humidity of the southern premonsoonal season by escaping to the cooler hills around Nuwara Eliya. Accommodation prices here soar at this time of year – if you can find a room at all. The elite flock here for 'the season' and spend the days playing golf and tennis, horse riding or motor racing in the annual hill climb, and partying at night.

Brigitte Ellemor

resorts. They hire and sell gear, including snorkelling equipment. PADI courses are available, as well as dives for beginners and experienced people. You can snorkel at Hikkaduwa, Unawatuna, Mirissa and at Polhena near Matara.

Along the west coast, the best time to dive and snorkel is generally from November to April. The seas are calmest from April to September along the east coast.

Windsurfing
Top-end hotels in the main west-coast beach resorts are the only places that rent windsurfers. Bentota is the best spot to windsurf, and several outfits there hire out equipment and provide lessons.

White-Water Rafting, Canoeing & Boating

White-water rafting can be done at a few places, notably on the river near Kitulgala in the Hill Country (it's the place where *Bridge on the River Kwai* was filmed). Adventure Sports Lanka arranges trips here and in a few other places (see the Getting Around chapter for contact details). Canoeing trips can also be arranged through this company, although there are other options as well. Ging Oya Lodge north of Negombo has canoes for guests (the lodge is on the river) – see the Around Negombo entry in the West Coast chapter.

Boat or catamaran trips for sight seeing, twitching or fishing are becoming popular. You can organise excursions in Negombo, Bentota and Weligama. See the West Coast and The South chapters for details.

Cycling

Mountain biking is quite rare in Sri Lanka, although it's a great place for it. If you want to tour by mountain bike you should bring your own gear and be prepared to be self-sufficient. Adventure Sports Lanka, Connaissance de Ceylan and Walkers Tours arrange mountain biking excursions (see Organised Tours in the Getting Around chapter for contact details). Adventure Sports Lanka also sells parts and can help you plan your trip.

Hiking

Hiking is gaining popularity in Sri Lanka. There isn't an organised hiking industry as there is in India, and it's usually a matter of striking out on your own. For details see the the Hill Country chapter. Adam's Peak provides an opportunity for a good, stiff hike up Sri Lanka's most sacred mountain with stunning views as a reward.

Golf

There is an excellent course at Nuwara Eliya and another good course near Kandy (see the Hill Country chapter for details). The Royal Colombo Golf Club also has a decent course, the Ridgeway Golf Links. For more details, see under Golf in the Colombo chapter.

COURSES
Meditation

Kandy has meditation places that are open to foreigners (see Kandy in the Hill Country chapter for details).

Diving

Several outfits run PADI courses for divers (see the Colombo and West Coast chapters).

Language

You can learn Sinhala in Colombo through the British Council, but this is really only an option for expats (see the Colombo chapter).

WORK

To become a resident in Sri Lanka with the right to work you need to make a substantial investment in a project approved by the Board of Investment. The other option is to go to Sri Lanka as an employee or contract worker for a company that can make the necessary arrangements, or as a volunteer.

Volunteer Work

Earthwatch has a project that focuses on 32 groups of macaque monkeys that have been studied for more than 30 years in Polonnaruwa. If you are interested in volunteering contact Earthwatch International (☎ 978-461 0081), 3 Clock Tower Place, Suite 100, Maynard, Massachusetts 01754, USA. Check out the Web site at www.earthwatch.org.

There are about half a dozen major volunteer agencies that operate in Sri Lanka (Peace Corps closed down their program in 1998 due to security concerns):

Australian Volunteers International (☎ 03-9279 1788, fax 9419 4280) 71 Argyle St (PO Box 350), Fitzroy, Melbourne, 3065. This organisation runs the Australian Volunteers Abroad program and several other international volunteer schemes throughout Asia, the Middle East, Africa, Latin America and the Pacific, and in remote Aboriginal communities in Australia. At the time of writing there were 15 volunteers in Sri Lanka working in a range of fields including environmental science, community health (including people with disabilities, HIV/AIDS), vocational training, working with displaced people and women's development. Web site: www.ozvol.org.au

Volunteer Life Beats Travelling

There was no-one to meet me after midnight at the airport arrivals area – a bus stop was as close as nonauthorised visitors could get to the terminal. The next night, power workers started a four-day strike leaving homes without fans and water (if they had electric water pumps). Soon after, the government imposed power cuts of up to eight hours a day in an effort to make what little hydroelectricity was left last until the monsoon brought rains and the potential for more power. *Ayubowan!* Welcome to Sri Lanka!

During later months, a couple of bombs blasted Colombo targets killing dozens of people, a national Parliamentarian was assassinated and a curfew was imposed to limit violence during local government elections. Tropical paradise? I think not.

At home in my bed-sit flat, I handwashed clothes on the floor of the shower for 18 months and made do without the essentials of the West – a fridge, TV and stereo. Outside, I travelled in crazily driven buses crammed full like sardine cans.

But for every negative or confusing experience, there was an equally delightful interaction. The family at the general store who understood my charade-like request for candles during the power strike became friendly greeters whom I visited if I needed cheering up. My landlady-neighbour delivered the auspicious dish *kiri bath* (milk rice) on the first day of each month. When visiting friends without washrooms I enjoyed bathing in the garden at their private wells, and the excitement of the national cricket team winning an international tournament was never far away. Most touching were the invitations to witness the cycle of life events and the rituals attached to birth, adolescent rites of passage, marriage and death.

Living and working as a volunteer in another country is one of the best ways to experience life as it really is for citizens of the country. The opportunity provides unique challenges and rewards, and allows you to move beyond the sometimes superficial encounters and observations of a traveller. If visiting a place renders it part of your consciousness forever, then living in a country for a year or more means it is indelibly marked on your mind and heart. However, the longer-term experience often raises as many questions as it answers, and I doubt I will ever understand Sri Lanka's politics and the intractable ethnic conflict.

Australian Volunteers International (formerly the Overseas Service Bureau), the agency that coordinates the Australian volunteer program, has placed 150 people in one-year, two-year or longer-term jobs in Sri Lanka since 1980. Volunteers are placed with organisations who request their help and they go with the attitude that they are not experts with solutions to every problem, but that they have much to learn from the culture in which they will live and work. The contribution they have made to workplaces and the transfer of skills are important, but even more so are the relationships built, insights gained and goodwill generated. My work, writing and publishing a newsletter in English for a public sector youth services agency, is being continued by a Sri Lankan employee, and I learnt as much as I taught and received as much as I gave during my time in Sri Lanka.

Living and working in the 'Third World' brings the inescapable realisation that although life is physically demanding and a struggle for most of the world's people, people generally meet the difficulties with resourcefulness and make the most of available opportunities. Like me, Sri Lankans also endured verbal and sometimes physical harassment, the frustration of working in a public sector bureaucracy, and the physical limitations and emotional trauma of living in a country at war with itself; but they generally don't have the freedom or opportunity to catch a flight home.

Brigitte Ellemor

Japan International Cooperation Agency & Japan Overseas Cooperation Volunteers (☎ 03-535 25311) 6–13F Shinjuku Maynds tower 2-1-1 Yoyogi, Shibuya-ku, Tokyo. This organisation has a large variety of programs on offer.
Web site: www.jica.go.jp/Index.html

Project Trust (☎ 01-8792 30444) Hebridean Centre, Isle of Coll, Argyll, Scotland PA78 6TE. Project Trust sends students all over the world to volunteer for 11 months in the gap year between A levels and university. The students are sent in pairs (usually of the same sex). There are eight projects in Sri Lanka to choose from.
Web site: www.projecttrust.org.uk

United Nations Volunteers (☎ 228-815 2000, fax 815 2001) Box 260 111, D-53153 Bonn, Germany. This organisation has lists of smaller volunteer organisations in Sri Lanka and it also organises volunteers.
Web site: www.unv.org

Voluntary Service Overseas (VSO; ☎ 020-8780 7500) 317 Putney Bridge Rd, London SW15 2PN UK. At the time of writing, VSO had 33 volunteers in Sri Lanka. VSO also has offices in Canada (Ottawa Web site: www.vso can.com) and the Netherlands (Utrecht Web site: www.vso.nl).
Web site: www.vso.org.uk

ACCOMMODATION

Sri Lanka has a good range of accommodation options, from five-star resorts to a room in a family home, but it doesn't cater well for shoestring travellers. Unlike India, for example, which is crawling with cheap-as-chips options, only a handful of places in the country have dormitory-style accommodation. The only other option for lone travellers is single rooms, and they're often miserable shoeboxes or cost the same amount as double rooms. Dorms are also a great place to meet people, so without them it can be difficult to hook up with fellow travellers. Still, Sri Lanka is perfectly set up for starry-eyed couples, groups and lone travellers with a bit of cash to splash. See the preceding Dangers & Annoyances section for information on scams, as this is an important aspect of the accommodation scene.

Prices for accommodation in Sri Lanka are very seasonal, particularly along the beach strips on the west coast. The prices

The Accommodation Basics

To save boring repetition in our Places to Stay listings, we've left out facilities common to most hotel/guesthouse rooms in Sri Lanka; attached bathrooms, mozzie repellent facilities (net or electric 'mat') and fans. For example, most rooms in Sri Lanka have bathrooms – where rooms have shared bathrooms we've stated so. Similarly, most rooms have mozzie nets and fans. Again, if we don't mention them don't worry – if there are no mozzie facilities (either a net or an electric 'mat') or a fan we'll say so.

Finally, all hill-country budget accommodation has hot water. Few budget places elsewhere in the country, ie, west coast, ancient cities, east coast, have hot water – if you don't read it, you won't have it. All top-end hotels and most mid-range hotels in Sri Lanka have hot water.

▲ ▲ ▲ ▲ ▲ ▲ ▲ ▲ ▲

quoted in this guide are generally high-season rates, and you can often find spectacular bargains in the low season. The 'season', and its prices, has a more or less official starting date – 15 December on the west and south coasts, 1 April on the east – and the monsoon may have ended well before the season starts. Of course, you can often bargain prices down at any time of the year.

Many places have a variety of rooms at different prices, and it's often worth asking, after staff have shown you their first room or quoted you their first price, if there are any cheaper rooms available. If there are more than two of you, some places have three- or four-person rooms, which brings the cost per person well down.

In Sri Lanka, the cost of accommodation is routinely quoted with and without meals. Prices quoted in this book are room only – ie, with no meals – unless otherwise stated. Generally you can get a range of prices from room only to bed and breakfast (B&B), half board (room plus breakfast and one main meal) and full board (breakfast, lunch and dinner). All places to stay listed in this book serve meals, unless otherwise stated.

Tackling the Taxes

In Sri Lanka, a 10% service charge is applied to accommodation. There is also a Goods and Services Tax (GST) of 12.5%. How this is applied is a bit of a mystery, but generally only top-end places and some upper-mid-range places actually add it to the bill. We have included both the service charge and the GST, where applicable, in all hotel prices quoted throughout this book.

▲ ▲ ▲ ▲ ▲ ▲ ▲ ▲ ▲

Most room prices in this book are quoted in rupees, but some are in US dollars if a hotel quotes them that way – which some do to ensure that they get the same number of dollars whatever the fluctuations in the rupee-dollar exchange rate.

Reservations

For resthouses contact the Ceylon Hotels Corporation (☎ 01-503497, fax 503504) at 411 Galle Rd, Bampalapitiya (Col 4). Guesthouses and hotels are in big demand during April (around the time of the Sinhalese and Tamil New Year) in Nuwara Eliya, and in Kandy during the perahera (generally July/August). It would certainly pay to book well ahead if you plan to be in these places at these times. Always confirm your reservation. If you want to stay in a national park you can book up to a month ahead (see Accommodation in National Parks following for details).

National Parks

The Department of Wildlife Conservation (☎ 01-694241, fax 698556), 18 Gregory's Rd, Cinnamon Gardens (Col 7) is open from 9.15 am to 4 pm Monday to Saturday. It has bungalows, each accommodating up to 10 adults and two children, in five national parks: Yala West (Ruhuna), Uda Walawe, Wasgomuwa, Gal Oya and Horton Plains. It costs US$24 per person per night in a bungalow, and a whopping US$30 'service charge' per trip. You must bring your own dry rations, kerosene and linen. Camp sites cost US$6 per site per day, plus US$5 'service charge' per trip. Students and chil-dren six to 12 years of age are half price (kiddies under six are free). On top of these costs, there is a US$12 park entry fee.

The Wildlife Trust (☎/fax 01-502271) maintains bungalows in national parks, and offers some 'nature' tours; see the small shop at the Department of Wildlife Conservation for information. Companies such as Connaissance de Ceylan and Adventure Travel Lanka also arrange trips to parks (see Organised Tours in the Getting Around chapter for contact details).

Guesthouses

You'll find some very cheap places to stay in this category, plus some in the mid-range bracket and even the occasional top-end place. Sometimes a guesthouse will rent just a couple of rooms, like the English B&B establishments; other times guest-houses are like small hotels. It's a good idea to pin down exactly what you're getting for your money, or be prepared in some places for an unpleasant surprise when you find out how many cups of tea you've had and how much each of them has cost you!

Apart from the low cost, the 'meeting people' aspect is the big plus of guesthouse accommodation. If you're after privacy, stick to the guesthouses with a separate guest annexe; some guesthouses have separate entrances for guests, others require you to tip-toe through the lounge after a night on the town.

Resthouses

Originally established by the Dutch for travelling government officials, then developed into a network of wayside inns by the British, resthouses now mostly function as small mid-range hotels. They're found all over the country, including in little out of the way towns (where they may be the only regular accommodation) as well as in the tourist centres. Many of the more popular ones now come under the wing of the government-sponsored Ceylon Hotels Corporation, which has a booking office in the arrivals hall at the airport in Katunayake and another at 411 Galle Rd, Bampalapitiya in Colombo 4 (☎ 01-503497, fax 503504). In the main December

Common Courtesies at Guesthouses

Most of the places listed in the budget and mid-range price brackets are family homes with rooms to let. They are not hotels with 24-hour lobbies and room service. As such, you should observe a few simple courtesies:

- Many guesthouses have only a few rooms to let; sometimes just one or two. Rather than simply turning up hoping for the best, telephone first to see if a room is available.
- If you intend arriving at your destination late at night or very early in the morning, contact the guesthouse where you intend to stay and ask whether it's convenient for you to turn up at an unusual hour. A few guesthouse owners reported having people arrive at all sorts of hours of the night (sometimes straight from the airport), demanding a room – and getting angry when they were told there were no rooms available. Most guesthouse owners are accommodating, but don't appreciate being woken up by unannounced arrivals.
- If you've just arrived and have nowhere to stay – and it's 1 am or some other unearthly hour – consider a hotel room for one night: you can make other arrangements in the morning.

to March tourist season, it's often worth booking ahead as tour groups tend to fill up resthouses quickly. We have also received some complaints from disgruntled travellers about reservations not being honoured, or of having to move rooms, or check out altogether, because preference was given to groups at some more popular resthouses, so bear that in mind.

Although they vary widely in standards and prices (those run by the Ceylon Hotels Corporation are usually the best maintained), many resthouses offer the most pleasant and well-kept accommodation in town – old fashioned, with big rooms, and are usually very well situated. Wherever you go, you'll find that resthouses enjoy the view from the highest hill, are along the best stretch of beach or in some other way have grabbed the best position. Prices in resthouses vary from the lower-middle price range to the bottom end of the upper price range. A double costs anywhere from US$12 up to US$36.

Hotels

The borderline between lower-price hotels and upper-range guesthouses is a blurred one, and not least in name since some 'hotels' are really guesthouses, while other small hotels may call themselves inns, lodges, villas and so on. You'll rarely find a double in a hotel for less than Rs 800. There are places going all the way up the price scale, as far as US$120 and above. For Rs 1200 you will usually get a spacious and clean double.

The larger hotels are of two basic types: modern resort hotels and older colonial-style places. The latter type definitely has the edge when it comes to atmosphere, and the facilities are often just as good. The newer places pride themselves on luxury facilities such as tennis courts, windsurfing instruction, nightclubs and prime beach, riverside or hill-top sites, and are mostly geared to package tourists. Resort-hotel doubles on the west coast go from around US$35 up to US$100 plus, while the colonial-type places in the upper bracket rarely cost much over US$55.

Tea Estate Bungalows

Difficult to track down, but generally worth the effort, are the small number of bungalows available for rent on working tea estates. Generally they are not widely advertised and the best ones become known through word of mouth within the local and expat communities. See the Haputale section of the Hill Country chapter for one booking service and the Bandarawela section for another. The Ceylon Tourist Board should also be able to assist.

FOOD

Sri Lanka is not generally thought to have one of the great Asian cuisines, but the food is enjoyable. The staple meal is rice and curry, with all sorts of variations. In Colombo you have a wide array of cuisines from which to choose. In places such as Hikkaduwa you can get all the usual travellers stand-bys (pizza, french fries, and so on). Sri Lanka rates right up there with the best places in South-East Asia when it comes to finding the knock-out best of tropical fruits.

Food preparation seems to take a long time in Sri Lanka: Rice and curry can take up to 1½ hours to prepare. To save you banging your cutlery and tearing up your serviette in frustration, get into the habit of pre-ordering your meal. Peruse the menu during the day, order, turn up at the allocated time, and everyone should be happy.

In Sri Lanka, a 10% service charge is applied to food; there is also a GST of 12.5%. As with accommodation, how this is applied is a bit of a mystery, but generally only top-end restaurants and some upper-mid-range places actually add it to the bill. We have included both the service charge and the GST, where applicable, in all food prices quoted throughout this book.

See the special section 'Cuisine of Sri Lanka' for descriptions on the taste sensations awaiting you.

ENTERTAINMENT
Cinemas

Hollywood blockbusters are screened in English in Colombo, though they're likely to be has-beens by the time they hit Sri Lanka's shores. See Entertainment in the Colombo chapter for details of venues. Art-house films (in English and European languages) are shown at cultural centres such as the British Council and the Alliance Française in Colombo and Kandy. See Entertainment in the Colombo chapter and in the Kandy section of the Hill Country chapter for details. Ubiquitous billboards confront you with Sri Lankan–made and Indian-made films that show in cinemas everywhere.

Discos & Nightclubs

Sri Lanka isn't a clubber's paradise, though you will find some clubs in Colombo and a few in resort areas such as Negombo, Bentota and Hikkaduwa. Kandy has a casino called the Lake Club. Most places are centred around top-end hotels, and will fleece your wallet. See Entertainment in the Colombo chapter for details on venues there.

Theatre, Classical Music & Galleries

Theatre of European heritage, for example, Shakespeare, is focussed around cultural centres such as the British Council and Alliance Française, both found in Colombo and Kandy, and the Goethe Institut in Colombo. Colombo is where most things happen. Theatre that is written and directed by Sri Lankans is often shown at the Lionel Wendt Gallery & Theatre – ring ahead to find out if it's in English or Sinhala. The Lumbini Theatre shows Sinhala theatre. Lionel Wendt and the cultural centres are the main venues for classical music (Western and Eastern), though top-end hotels have occasional performances. If you're into art, there are often exhibitions at the Lionel Wendt, the National Art Gallery or at the 'in' cafes in Colombo.

[Continued on page 90]

FOOD

Sri Lanka boasts a unique cuisine, shaped by the fruit and vegetables found in its abundant garden, and by recipes brought by traders and invaders – Indians, Arabs, Malays, Moors, Portuguese, Dutch and English have all left their mark on the Sri Lankan diet.

If you plan to eat at restaurants, remember that food takes a long time to prepare in Sri Lanka. To prevent angst and tears, get into the habit of pre-ordering your meal. When you order, arrange a time to come back, then turn up at the allocated time; that way everyone should be happy.

Rice & Curry

Like many other aspects of Sri Lankan life, the food is closely related to that of India. However, Sri Lankan rice and curry (not curry and rice – you get much more rice than curry) has many variations from its Indian counterpart. Curries in Sri Lanka can be very hot indeed but adjustments will often be made to suit sensitive Western palates. If you find you have taken a mouthful of something that is simply too hot, relief does not come from a gulp of cold water: That's like throwing fuel on a fire. Far better is a fork of rice, or better still some cooling yogurt or curd (buffalo yogurt), or even cucumber. Another surprisingly effective strategy is to sprinkle plain grated coconut over the curry. That's what those side dishes are for. Of course, if the curry is not hot enough the solution to that is there too – simply add some **pol sambol**, a red-hot side dish made with grated coconut, chilli and spice. Sambol is the general name used to describe any spicy-hot dish.

Sri Lankan rice and curry usually includes a variety of small curry dishes – vegetable, meat or fish. Chicken and fish or dried fish are popular, and beef and mutton are also available. Vegetarians won't have trouble finding tasty food – vegetable curries are made from banana (ash plantain), banana flower, breadfruit, jackfruit, mangoes, potatoes, beans and pumpkins, to name just a few. An accompaniment of **mallung** (shredded green leaves with spices, lightly stir-fried) is common, and the meal would not be complete without **parripu** (red lentil dhal) or another pulse curry.

The usual Indian curry varieties are also available, including south Indian vegetarian **thali**, or the delicate north Indian **biryani**. From the northern Jaffna region comes **kool**, a boiled, fried and dried-in-the-sun vegetable combination.

The spices used to bring out the flavours of Sri Lankan curry are all made locally. It was spices, particularly cinnamon, that first brought Europeans to the island. The essential ingredients in most curries are chilli powder and fresh chillies, turmeric, cinnamon quills, curry powder, curry leaves, pandanus leaves, garlic, coconut milk and sometimes crushed 'Maldive fish' – dried sprats.

Inset: Sri Lanka boasts many varieties of banana. (photo by Christine Niven)

GREG ELMS

Disappointingly, and despite the amount of it eaten in Sri Lanka, the rice is often bland. There's even one variety that has a musty smell and tastes just like cardboard. Try the delicious partly hulled red rice instead.

Fish & Seafood

Coastal towns have excellent fish (often served with chips and salad); prawns are also widespread, and in Hikkaduwa, Unawatuna and Tangalla, to name but a few places, you can find delicious crab. In the south of the island a popular dish is **ambul thiyal**, a pickle usually made from tuna, which is literally translated as 'sour fish curry'.

Other Specialities

Unique Sri Lankan foods include **hoppers**, which are usually a breakfast or evening snack. A regular hopper is rather like a small, bowl-shaped pancake skilfully fried over a high flame (sometimes served with an egg fried into the middle or with honey and yogurt). **String hoppers** are tangled little circles of steamed noodles; used as a curry dip instead of rice they make a tasty and filling meal at breakfast or lunch.

A popular breakfast among Sri Lankans is fresh bread dipped in dhal or a curry with a thin gravy or **hodhi**.

Another rice substitute is **pittu**, a mixture of flour and grated coconut steamed in a bamboo mould so that it comes out shaped like a cylinder.

Lamprai, a popular dish of Dutch origin, is made of rice boiled in meat stock, then added to vegetables and meat and slowly baked in a banana-leaf wrapping.

At lunchtime you can dine lightly on a plate of **short eats**. This is the local term for a selection of 'Chinese' rolls (though they're not really like Chinese spring rolls), meat and vegetable patties called cutlets, pastries, **vadai** (made with lentils or flour) and other snacks that are placed in the middle of the table. You eat

Right: Red-hot chillies are an integral part of Sri Lankan cuisine

as many as you feel like and the bill is added up according to how many are left.

A filling snack, which crops up mainly in streetside huts, is the **rotty**, a small parcel of anything you fancy wrapped up in a sort of elasticated, doughy pancake. Fillings can range from chilli and onion to bacon and egg. A rotty chopped up and mixed with vegetables (or meat or egg) is called a **kotthu rotty**. You'll soon become attuned to the chop-chop sounds of the kotthu rotty maker at the local hotel in the evening.

Lunch Packets

Office workers, and indeed anyone wanting a filling, tasty and quick meal at lunch, generally go for lunch packets. These are parcels of rice and curry sold at street corners and on footpaths all over the country between about 11 am and 2 pm. Usually what you'll find inside a lunch packet is a generous portion of steamed or boiled rice, a piece of curried chicken, fish or beef (if you're vegetarian you'll get an egg instead), a portion of curried vegetables and a sambol. At Rs 45 to 90, they're about the best-value meal you can get in Sri Lanka.

Desserts & Sweets

The Sri Lankans also have lots of ideas for desserts, including **wattalappam**, a Malay-originated egg pudding, vaguely caramel-like in taste. Curd and honey, or curd and treacle known as **kiri peni**, is good at any time of day. Curd is yogurt made from buffalo milk – it's rich and tasty. If you buy it to take away, it comes in a shallow clay pot complete with a handy carrying rope that is so attractive you'll hate to throw it away. The treacle, called **kitul**, is really syrup from the kitul palm. If it's boiled and set to form hard blocks you have **jaggery**, an all-purpose Sri Lankan candy or sweetener.

Like Indians, Sri Lankans waste no opportunity to indulge their sweet tooth – sweets are known as **rasa-kavili**. You could try **kavun**, spiced flour and treacle batter-cake fried in coconut oil, or **aluva**, which is rice flour, treacle and cashew-nut fudge. Coconut milk, jaggery and cashew nuts give you the dark and delicious **kalu dodol**. **Kiri bath** is a dessert of rice cooked in milk. It's served at weddings and is traditionally the first solid food fed to babies. But it's also enjoyed as a tasty dish with a sambol or jaggery.

Fruit

Sri Lanka has a wide variety of delicious fruits. Melons, passion fruit, avocados and guavas (particularly the little pink variety which are like crispy pears) are among some of the fruits to be discovered and enjoyed. Or try the sweet red bananas or a papaya (pawpaw) with a dash of lime for a delicious way to start the day. **Wood-apples**, a hard, wooden-shelled fruit, are used to make a delicious

GREG ELMS

drink, a creamy dessert topping or a uniquely Sri Lankan jam. The infamous **durian**, in season from July to September, comes under its own category; this big, green, spiky-skinned fruit smells – but doesn't taste – like a blocked sewer. The **rambutan**, related to the lychee, is so sought after that growers must guard their trees keenly to prevent eager poachers. During rambutan season from July to September, stalls spring up along the Kandy Rd at Nittambuwa and on the Old Kandy Rd at Kaduwela.

The flavour of the **mangosteen** has been described as a combination of strawberries and grapes. Queen Victoria is said to have been so keen to sample one of these fruits that she offered a considerable prize to anyone who brought one back to her from the tropics. Mangosteens are in season from July through to September, and if there are any to be found you'll see them for sale on the roadside at Kalutara, on the west coast south of Colombo.

The ubiquitous **mango** comes in a variety of shapes and tastes, although generally in the green-skinned, peach-textured variety. The mangoes from Jaffna are considered by some to be the best.

The **jackfruit**, the world's largest fruit, may be eaten fresh or cooked, and the seeds may also be cooked as a curry. The fruit breaks up into hundreds of bright orange-yellow segments that have a slightly rubbery texture.

ETIQUETTE OF EATING

Sri Lankans say that it's only by eating with the fingers that you can fully enjoy the flavour combinations from the different curries – and it's true. To eat Sri Lankan-style, start by ladling a heap of rice onto your plate, followed by the desired quantities of the different curries. Then delve the ends of the fingers of your right hand in and mix things up a bit to mingle the flavours. With the aid of your

Right: Coconut flesh has many uses in Sri Lankan cuisine, while the liquid makes a refreshing drink.

thumb you then mix a mouthful-sized wad of food. With the same finger-ends, slightly cupped, push the food into your mouth with the thumb. Try not to let the food pass the middle knuckles on your fingers. A finger bowl will appear for you to wash your fingers when you have finished.

DRINKS

As in most parts of Asia, you're advised not to drink water in Sri Lanka unless you're certain that it has been thoroughly boiled. Of course you've got no way of telling if this has really been done when a restaurant assures you that it has. You'll get awfully thirsty at times, so what are the safe substitutes?

Non-Alcoholic Drinks

Sri Lanka is famous for its tea, though much of the best stuff is exported. Most Sri Lankans drink a concoction called 'milk tea' – tea, hot milk and sugar are mixed together before being poured into the cup.

Coffee is a lottery, and you will rarely win. The local version of coffee tastes nothing like coffee, but instant coffee is available. Colombo is the only place you can get a really good espresso, unless you're staying in a top-end hotel.

Lime juice is excellent but unfortunately is made with the questionable water (unless you specifically ask for soda water). Coca-Cola and other well-known soft drinks are widely available in Sri Lanka. A 300ml bottle of Coca-Cola costs around Rs 15 (depend-

ing on where you buy it). Elephant House is the most widespread of the Sri Lankan soft drinks; try the tart ginger beer (Rs 15).

A refreshing, natural option is **thambili** (king coconut), the orange-coloured drinking coconut for sale at stalls and shops for about Rs 10.

Alcoholic Drinks

The Royal Pilsner beers produced by Nuwara Eliya Breweries are more palatable than Lion Lager or any of the other local variations – all will serve the purpose, though none will win any prizes. Beer, at around Rs 110 a bottle, is an expensive drink by Sri Lankan standards. You can buy all manner of imported grog too. Note that alcohol cannot be sold on the monthly *poya* (full moon) holiday.

Sri Lanka also has two extremely popular local varieties of intoxicating beverages. **Toddy** is a natural drink, a bit like cider, produced from coconut palms. Getting the tree to produce toddy is a very specialised operation performed by people known as 'toddy tappers' (for more information see the boxed text '101 Uses for a Coconut' in the Facts about Sri Lanka chapter).

Fermented and refined toddy becomes **arrack**. It's produced in a variety of grades and qualities, some of which are real firewater. Proceed with caution! Kalutara, 40km south of Colombo on the road to Bentota and Hikkaduwa, is the toddy and arrack capital of Sri Lanka. Annually Sri Lanka produces five million gallons of toddy and 7½ million bottles of arrack. With a soft-drink mixer (ginger ale is good) arrack is very pleasant.

MICK WELDON

[Continued from page 83]

Apart from the British Council and Alliance Française in Kandy, there is little happening outside Colombo.

Traditional Music & Dance

Traditional music and dance is an important, though fading, part of Sri Lankan culture. The dances for tourists are usually sanitised snapshots of various types blended into one performance. Still, it's worthwhile seeing. The Lionel Wendt Gallery & Theatre in Colombo holds occasional performances, as do top-end hotels in major resorts and in Colombo. The School of Dance at Ambalangoda (see the West Coast chapter for details) has irregular performances that are worth catching. Dancing and drumming is also performed nightly at several venues in Kandy (see that section in the Hill Country chapter for details).

Pubs & Bars

Sri Lankans who drink alcohol tend to do it at home or in seedy venues. The few pubs and bars that do exist tend to be congregated around tourist haunts. Many are attached to top-end hotels, with top-end prices, and often have a cheesy 'British' or 'German' theme and imported ales. Women travellers seeking a bar will feel most comfortable in these places. The resort towns such as Hikkaduwa and Negombo have a handful of bopping drinking holes. In other places you're more likely to find yourself drinking at a restaurant or, perish the thought, in your hotel room. Some of the colonial mansions-cum-hotels have lovely wide verandas, perfect for a sunset beer.

The Cricket-Crazy Nation

The nation stops when Sri Lanka is playing cricket. War and poverty are all but forgotten as radio and television dials tune in to 'the match'. Workers take leave from their workplaces for the day or afternoon, transistor radios reveal the score in the corner of the office, crowds gather around television screens in the Singer stores, radios blare on buses with coverage in Sinhala, Tamil and English. Almost everyone follows the game – discussion is not limited to boys and men. And when the game's over and Sri Lanka's won, fire crackers sound around the neighbourhood.

Ever since their historic 1996 World Cup victory in Lahore, Pakistan, Sri Lanka's cricketers have become national heroes, shopping centre stars, advertising icons, the idols of would-be cricketers and the pin-ups of teenage girls. The winners were feted like kings when they returned. They received from the equally cricket-crazy government valuable gifts of land, cash and import-duty exemption on vehicles. Advertising contracts earn big bucks for the sportsmen, who add their names, faces and signatures to products ranging from milk powder to textured vegetable protein and electrical goods.

During its rise to fame in the 1996 World Cup the Sri Lankan team revolutionised the way batting teams started their innings. The previous respectable run target of 60 from the first 15 overs was smashed as key openers Sanath Jayasuriya and Romesh Kaluwitharana hit their way into the record books. Jayasuriya won Most Valuable Player for the series and broke three records in one innings during a tournament in Singapore: the fastest one-day century (100 off 48 balls); the most number of sixes in an innings (11); and the highest number of runs in one over (29).

Political commentators say cricket has the appeal and power to transcend Sri Lanka's ethnic conflict. The only Tamil player in the 1999 squad, controversial off-spinner Muttiah Muralitharan, is equally applauded and defended in the 'chucking' controversy by Sinhalese and Tamil fans. Voters for 'Murali' in the 1998 Man of the Year contest run by the English weekly *Midweek Mirror* argued that his sporting feats helped build 'unity in diversity' among Sri Lankans.

Introduced to cricket by the British when they colonised the island in the 18th century, visits by teams from England and Australia during their sea voyages en route to Ashes series also encouraged the local competition.

SPECTATOR SPORTS

Although Sri Lankans play volleyball, netball, soccer, tennis and a few other sports, the most popular is cricket. Radio commentaries of big games are broadcast down streets, boys play the game on the roadside or in forest clearings, and Sri Lankans whose knowledge of English is otherwise limited can tell you 'First innings, two hundred and twelve, eight wickets, declared'. See the boxed text 'The Cricket-Crazy Nation' for an insight into Sri Lanka's obsession with cricket and its love-hate relationship with the national team.

It's usually easy to see a big match – the main international stadium is the Premadasa Stadium at Kettarama (Col 10), with other venues including the Sinhalese Sports Club (SSC) in Cinnamon Gardens (Col 7) and ovals at Moratuwa, Borella (Sara Stadium), Kandy, Dambulla and Galle. You can buy tickets for matches at the Board for Cricketing Control office next to SSC (see the Colombo chapter for details). You can catch a club match or international game at almost any time of year. Check the local newspapers to find out what's coming up.

One entirely sedentary sport enjoyed by large numbers of Sri Lankans is betting – on British horse and dog racing! With racing in Sri Lanka frowned upon by the Buddhist establishment, you'll see people in hole-in-the-wall betting shops throughout the land avidly studying the day's runners and riders from Aintree, Ascot and Hackney. Commentaries on the races are beamed over from Britain starting at about 6 pm. This passion is one reason for the mushrooming of satellite dishes in Sri Lankan towns.

The Cricket-Crazy Nation

The game has gained unrivalled popularity among 'the masses'. You'll see people playing some sort of match everywhere – adults on Sunday at certain known gathering places and children anywhere, any day, with almost any objects sufficing for a bat and ball. However, although there are a handful of players in the current national squad from outside the schools of urban Colombo, the game remains the preserve of the well-resourced schools. Cricket gear is expensive – it costs at least Rs 14,000 to fit out a batsman – and so the game of 'softball' cricket played with a tennis ball has evolved for those who can't afford the protective equipment.

But the national team's dream ended with the 1999 World Cup in the UK, when Sri Lanka failed to make it through to the second round of the event. The previously adoring fans turned on their heroes, with claims that 'cricket is dead' and calls for captain Ranatunga's resignation and a clean-up of the game's administration. Ranatunga did step down and was replaced by Jayasuriya. Even though international match-fixing scandal of 2000 didn't really touch the Sri Lankan team and further reduce its standing, it is yet to regain the heights of its 1996 glory.

Brigitte Ellemor

SHOPPING

Sri Lanka has a wide variety of attractive handicrafts on sale. Laksala, a government-run store, is found in most cities and tourist towns. Each store has a good collection of items from all over the country and its stock is generally of reasonable quality, moderately priced, and each item has fixed price tags. There are other handicraft outlets in Colombo; see that chapter for details. Street stalls can be found in touristy areas, but you'll need to bargain – expect the vendor to start the bidding at two to three times the value of the article.

Masks

Sri Lankan masks are a popular collector's item for visitors. They're carved at a number of places, principally along the south-west coast, and are sold all over the island, but Ambalangoda, near Hikkaduwa, is the mask-carving centre. You can visit several of the showroom-workshops here.

Touristy or not, the masks are remarkably well made, good value and look very nice on the wall back home. They're available from key-ring size for a few rupees up to big, high-quality masks for over Rs 2000. See the boxed text 'Sri Lanka's Dances & Masks' for more information.

Batik

The Indonesian art of batik making is a relatively new development in Sri Lanka but

Colourful, carved *kolam* masks produced in Ambalangoda are a popular souvenir.

one that has been taken to with alacrity. You'll see a wide variety of batiks made and sold around the island. Some of the best and most original are the batik pictures made by Upali Jayakody in Kandy, and Fresco Batiks on the Peradeniya road outside Kandy. 'Kandy batiks were very poor compared with the superb ones at the batik village of Mahawewa beyond Negombo', wrote a visitor. Batik pictures start from about Rs 200, and go up to well over Rs 1000. Batik is also used for a variety of clothing items.

Leather

You can find some very low-priced and good-quality leatherwork – particularly bags and cases. Look in the leatherwork shops and shoe shops around Fort (Col 1). The bazaar on Olcott Mawatha, beside Fort Station, is cheaper than Laksala for similar-quality goods. The Leather Collection in Colombo is a more upmarket place to shop. Hikkaduwa is also a good place for leather bags.

Gems

Sri Lanka's famous gemstones remain an important and interesting facet of the economy. Initially gems were found mainly around Ratnapura, which remains one of the most important areas for gemming, but gems are now also found in many other localities.

There are countless showrooms and private gem dealers all over the country. In Ratnapura everybody and their brother is a spare-time gem dealer! See the Colombo chapter for details on recommended shops. At the State Gem Corporation's testing laboratory (☎ 01-576144) tourists can get any stone tested free; you can get a certificate for Rs 340. It has its own showroom next door, too. The only snag with the testing service is that it's not always easy, or practical, to 'borrow' a stone to take it in for testing before you buy it. However, one reader wrote that a reputable dealer, at least in Colombo, would accompany you to the State Gem Corporation for a testing.

There have been letters from readers who have had Sri Lankans try to sell them large amounts of gems with the promise that they can be resold for a big profit in other countries. Strict export regulations are apparently given as the reason why the Sri Lankans can't trade the stones themselves. Galle seems to be the epicentre of this sort of activity – our advice is to be extremely careful. Even if it is legal, the only people who make money on that sort of deal are usually those who really know what they are about. For more information see the boxed text 'Gems' under Ratnapura in the Hill Country chapter.

Other Souvenirs

There are countless other purchases waiting to tempt your travellers cheques out of your moneybelt. The ubiquitous coconut shell is carved into all manner of souvenirs and useful items. Like the Thais and Burmese, Sri Lankans also make lacquerware items such as bowls and ashtrays – layers of lacquer are built up on a light framework, usually of bamboo strips. Kandy is a centre for jewellery and brassware, both antique and modern. There are some nice chunky silver bracelets, as well as some rather dull stuff. The brass suns and moons are attractive, or you could try a hefty brass elephant-head door-knocker for size.

Coir (rope fibre made from coconut husks) is made into baskets, bags, mats and other items. Weligama on the south coast turns out some attractive lacework. The usual travellers-style clothes are available, particularly in Hikkaduwa. The quality is often low, but the prices are even lower. Colombo is the best place to buy brand-name, export clothing.

Tortoiseshell and ivory are best left on the backs of turtles or in the tusks of elephants, especially as Sri Lanka's unique subspecies of elephant is threatened by illegal hunting. Avoid ebony, from which many wooden elephants are carved, to preserve these hardwood trees, which are endangered.

If you are planning to take some tea home with you, check either before you leave on your trip or with your embassy in Sri Lanka regarding import controls. If you are taking tea into Australia, for example, ordinary commercial packets are OK, but if you have tea in rattan boxes or tea that is flavoured it may be subject to quarantine.

Cargills in Fort (Col 1) will pack items in cardboard or wooden boxes – they do a good job at reasonable prices.

Getting There & Away

AIR
Airports & Airlines
The only international airport in Sri Lanka is the Bandaranaike International Airport at Katunayake, 30km north of Colombo. The terminal has 24-hour money changing facilities. The bank counters on arrival give good rates, but count the money carefully. In the arrival halls you'll find a Ceylon Tourist Board information desk (open 24 hours) and booking desks for hotels, guesthouses and the Ceylon Hotels Corporation, which runs several rest houses. There are also bank counters in the departures lounge, but the rates are not very good. There are a few duty-free shops and a cafeteria in the departures lounge, but prices are high.

Charter flights and commercial domestic flights leave from Ratmalana airport, south of Colombo. For information on airlines servicing Sri Lanka, see Getting There & Away in the Colombo chapter.

Buying Tickets
The plane ticket will probably be the most expensive item in your budget, and buying it can be an intimidating business. There is likely to be a multitude of airlines and travel agencies hoping to separate you from your money and it is always worth putting aside a few hours to research the current state of the market.

Start early because some of the cheapest tickets have to be bought months in advance and some popular flights sell out quickly. Look at the ads in newspapers and magazines (not forgetting the Sri Lankan press) and watch out for special offers. You should then phone around travel agencies for bargains. (Airlines can supply information on routes and timetables; however, except at times of inter-airline war they do not supply the cheapest tickets.) Find out the fare, the route, the duration of the journey and any restrictions on the ticket (see Restrictions in the boxed text 'Air Travel Glossary' in this chapter). You may discover that those impossibly

cheap flights are 'fully booked, but we have another one that costs a bit more...' or that the flight is on an airline notorious for its poor safety standards and leaves you in the world's least favourite airport mid-journey for 14 hours.

The other thing you can do is surf the Internet. Many airlines, whether providing full service or 'no-frills' service, offer some excellent fares to Web surfers. They may sell seats by auction or simply cut prices to reflect the reduced cost of selling electronically. Many travel agencies around the world have Web sites, providing a quick and easy way to compare prices. This is a good place to start before negotiating with your favourite travel agency.

The days when some travel agencies would routinely fleece travellers by running off with their money are, happily, almost over. Paying by credit card generally offers protection, as most card issuers provide refunds if you can prove you didn't get what you paid for. Similar protection can be obtained by buying a ticket from a bonded agency, such as one covered by the Air Travel Organisers' Licensing (ATOL) scheme in the UK. Agents who accept cash only should hand over the tickets straight away rather than tell you to 'come back tomorrow'. After you've made a booking or paid your deposit, call the airline and confirm that the booking was actually made. It's generally not advisable to send money (even cheques) through the post unless the agency is very well established.

You may decide to pay more than the rock-bottom fare and opt for the safety of a better-known travel agency. Firms such as STA Travel, which has offices worldwide, Council Travel in the USA and Usit Campus (formerly Campus Travel) in the UK are not going to disappear overnight and they do offer good prices to most destinations.

Once you have your ticket, write down its number, together with the flight number and other details, and keep the information separate from your ticket. If the ticket is lost or stolen, this will help you get a replacement. It's sensible to buy travel insurance as early as possible. For more information, see Travel Insurance under Visas & Documents in the Facts for the Visitor chapter.

Use the fares quoted in this book as a guide only. They're approximate and based on rates advertised by travel agencies at the time of research. Quoted air fares don't necessarily constitute a recommendation for the carrier.

Colombo is not as good as some other Asian centres for cheap flights and you may be better off booking your onward tickets before you leave home. For details on travel agencies in Colombo see Organised Tours in the Getting Around chapter.

Travellers with Special Needs

If you have special needs of any sort – you've broken a leg, you're vegetarian, you're taking the baby or you're terrified of flying – you should let the airline know as soon as possible so that it can make arrangements accordingly. You should remind it when you reconfirm your booking (at least 72 hours before departure) and again when you check in at the airport. It may also be worth ringing round the different airlines before you make your booking to find out how they can handle your particular needs.

If you are travelling in a wheelchair, most international airports can provide an escort from check-in to plane where needed. Ramps, lifts and facilities for disabled people, such as toilets and phones, are generally available. There are passable facilities at Bandaranaike International Airport.

Guide dogs for the blind will often have to travel in a specially pressurised baggage compartment with other animals; smaller guide dogs may be admitted to the cabin. Deaf travellers can ask for airport and in-flight announcements to be written down for them.

Airlines usually allow babies up to two years of age to fly for 10% of the adult fare, although a few may allow them to travel free of charge. Reputable international airlines usually provide nappies (diapers), tissues, talcum powder and all the other paraphernalia needed to keep babies clean, dry and half-happy. For children between the ages of two and 12, the fare on international flights is generally 50% of the regular fare or 67% of a discounted fare.

Departure Tax

The departure tax is Rs 500, payable at the airport on departure.

The UK

Airline ticket discounters are known as bucket shops in the UK. Despite the somewhat disreputable connotations of the term, there is nothing under-the-counter about them. Advertisements for many travel agencies appear in the travel pages of weekend broadsheets such as the *Independent* and the *Sunday Times*. Look out for the free magazines, such as *TNT,* that are widely available in London, especially outside the main train and underground stations.

For students or travellers under 26, popular travel agencies in the UK include STA Travel and Usit Campus. Both sell tickets to

Air Travel Glossary

Alliances Many of the world's leading airlines are now intimately involved with each other, sharing everything from reservations systems and check-in to aircraft and frequent-flyer schemes. Opponents say that alliances restrict competition. Whatever the arguments, there is no doubt that big alliances are the way of the future.

Check-In Airlines ask you to check in a certain time ahead of the flight departure – it's usually three hours in Colombo, rather than one or two hours on international flights from other places. If you fail to check in on time and the flight is overbooked, the airline can cancel your booking and give your seat to somebody else.

Courier Fares Businesses often need to send urgent documents or freight securely and quickly. Courier companies hire people to accompany the package through customs and, in return, offer a discount ticket which is sometimes a bargain. However, you may have to surrender all your baggage allowance and take only carry-on luggage.

Fares Airlines traditionally offer 1st class (coded F), business class (coded J) and economy class (coded Y) tickets. These days there are so many promotional and discounted fares available that few passengers pay full fare.

Lost Tickets If you lose your airline ticket, an airline will usually treat it like a travellers cheque and, after inquiries, issue you with another one. Legally, however, an airline is entitled to treat it like cash and if you lose it then it's gone forever. Take very good care of your tickets.

Onward Tickets An entry requirement for many countries is that you have a ticket out of the country. If you're unsure of your next move, the easiest solution is to buy the cheapest onward ticket to a neighbouring country or a ticket from a reliable airline which can later be refunded if you do not use it.

Open-Jaw Tickets These are return tickets where you fly out to one place but return from another. If available, this can save you backtracking to your arrival point.

Overbooking Since every flight has some passengers who fail to show up, airlines often book more passengers than they have seats. Usually excess passengers make up for the no-shows, but occasionally somebody gets 'bumped' onto the next available flight. Guess who it is most likely to be? The passengers who check in late. If you do get 'bumped', you are normally offered some form of compensation.

Reconfirmation Some airlines require you to reconfirm your flight at least 72 hours prior to departure. Check your travel documents to see if this is the case. SriLankan Airlines automatically reallocates your seat if you haven't reconfirmed.

Restrictions Discounted tickets often have various restrictions on them – such as needing to be paid for in advance and incurring a penalty to be altered or cancelled. Others are restrictions on the minimum and maximum period you must be away.

Round-the-World Tickets RTW tickets give you a limited period (usually a year) in which to circumnavigate the globe. You can go anywhere the carrying airlines go, as long as you don't backtrack. The number of stopovers or total number of separate flights is decided before you set off and they usually cost a bit more than a basic return flight.

Ticketless Travel Airlines are gradually waking up to the realisation that paper tickets are unnecessary encumbrances. On simple one-way or return trips, reservations details can be held on computer and the passenger merely shows ID to claim their seat.

Transferred Tickets Airline tickets cannot be transferred from one person to another. Travellers may try to sell the return half of their ticket, but officials can ask you to prove that you are the person named on the ticket. On an international flight, tickets are compared with passports.

all travellers, but cater especially to young people and students. STA Travel (☎ 0870-160 0599; northern call centre ☎ 0161-830 4713) has an office at 86 Old Brompton Rd, London SW7 3LQ, as well as many other offices in the UK. Visit its Web site at www.statravel.co.uk. Usit Campus (☎ 0870-240 1010), 52 Grosvenor Gardens, London SW1W OAG, has branches throughout the UK. Check its Web site at www.usitcampus.com for details.

Other recommended travel agencies in the UK include:

Bridge the World (☎ 020-7734 7447) 4 Regent Place, Regent Street, London W1R 5FB
Flightbookers (☎ 020-7757 2000) 177–178 Tottenham Court Rd, London W1P 9LF
Trailfinders (☎ 020-7938 3939) 194 Kensington High St, London W8 7RG

At the time of research, both Emirates and SriLankan Airlines were offering the cheapest fares from the UK to Sri Lanka. Fares from London to Sri Lanka start at UK£350/540 one way/return in the low season (roughly April to June), going up to UK£470/725 in the high season (around July, August and December). SriLankan Airlines has eight direct flights a week on the London-Colombo route, and the same number going the other way. If you wish to stop over in India, expect fares to start at about £540.

Continental Europe

SriLankan Airlines has two weekly flights between Stockholm and Colombo (via Dubai). It also has three weekly direct flights from Rome and Milan. From Switzerland, there are three weekly flights from Zurich to Colombo. Swissair also has direct Zurich-Colombo flights for about Sfr 1390 return.

Germany SriLankan Airlines has two Berlin-Colombo (via Dubai) flights a week. There are three weekly direct flights between Frankfurt and Colombo. SriLankan Airlines also has flights to/from Munich. Flights from Frankfurt to Colombo with

Emirates or SriLankan Airlines cost around DM 1550 in the high season.

France France has a network of student travel agencies which can supply discount tickets to travellers of all ages. OTU Voyages (☎ 01 40 29 12 12) has a central Paris office at 39 Ave Georges Bernanos (5e) and another 42 offices around the country. Its Web address is www.otu.fr. Nouvelles Frontières (☎ 08 03 33 33 33), 5 Ave de l'Opéra (1er) is another popular agency. Visit its Web site at www.nouvelles-frontieres.com.

SriLankan Airlines has three Paris-Colombo flights every week. Return flights from Paris to Colombo range from 6500FF to 8800FF.

The Netherlands In Amsterdam, NBBS is a popular travel agency. Check out its Web site at www.budgetair.nl. Expect to pay from Gl2000 to Gl6000 for a return Amsterdam-Colombo flight.

Australia

STA Travel and Flight Centre are major dealers in cheap air fares. Flight Centre's Web site, www.flightcentre.com.au, regularly advertises cheap flights. Check for other travel agency ads in the *Yellow Pages* and newspapers. SriLankan Airlines has direct flights from Colombo to Sydney.

The low season for flights to Sri Lanka from Australia is from 5 February to 3 March and from 12 October to 16 November. At the time of research, Cathay Pacific Airlines had the cheapest fares from the east coast, with low-season flights for A$927/1305 one way/return and high-season flights for A$1196/1415. Fares from the west coast range from A$870/1125 in the low season to A$1064/1285 one way/return in the high season.

If you want to stop over in Sri Lanka en route to another Asian destination expect to pay from A$1350 in the low season and A$1450 in the high season for return fares. Fares to Europe via Colombo with SriLankan Airlines or Malaysia Airlines start at about A$1090/1840 one way/return in the low season.

New Zealand

The *New Zealand Herald* has a travel section with travel agency ads. Flight Centre (☎ 09-309 6171) has a large central office in Auckland at National Bank Towers (corner Queen and Darby Sts) and many branches throughout the country. Its Web site is at www.flightcentre.com/nz. STA Travel (☎ 0800 874 773) also has heaps of offices; call to find out the closest branch to you or check out the Web site at www.statravel.com.au.

An Auckland-Colombo return flight with Singapore Airlines should cost around NZ$1464.

Asia

STA Travel has branches in Hong Kong, Tokyo, Singapore, Bangkok and Kuala Lumpur. A Tokyo-Colombo flight with Japan Airlines or Singapore Airlines costs about ¥195,000. With Singapore Airlines, you'll pay around S$2200 for a Singapore-Colombo flight.

From India, fares for a one-way flight between Thiruvananthapuram (Trivandrum) to Colombo start at around US$57. One-way fares from Delhi to Colombo are about US$320, Chennai (Madras) to Colombo US$85 and Mumbai (Bombay) to Colombo US$220. Please note that passenger service charges are now payable on air tickets bought in India for both domestic and international flights.

SriLankan Airlines has several weekly flights from Colombo to Malé in the Maldives for Rs 3800/7600 one way/return.

The USA

The *New York Times,* the *LA Times,* the *Chicago Tribune* and the *San Francisco Examiner* all have weekly travel sections in which you'll find any number of travel agency ads. Council Travel has offices in major cities nationwide. Visit the Web site at www.ciee.org. STA Travel, another major ticket seller, also has many offices; its Web site is at www.statravel.com. Ticket Planet, a leading ticket consolidator (discount travel agency) in the USA, is recommended. Visit Ticket Planet's Web site at www.ticketplanet.com.

The high season for flights from the USA to Sri Lanka is 12 June to 12 August and again from December to January. The low season runs from March to around mid-May and from September to November. A return New York–Colombo flight with SriLankan Airlines costs around US$2620 in the low season and US$3150 in the high season. From Los Angeles, you'll pay US$1420 for a Singapore Airlines flight in the low season and US$2295 in high season.

Canada

The *Globe & Mail,* the *Toronto Star,* the *Montreal Gazette* and the *Vancouver Sun* carry travel agency ads and are good places to look for cheap fares. Travel CUTS (☎ 800-667 2887) is Canada's national student travel agency and has offices in all major cities. Its Web site is at www.travelcuts.com.

Return fares from Vancouver to Colombo (via Hong Kong) cost C$3140 with Cathay Pacific Airways or C$3200 with SriLankan Airlines. Swissair flies from Montreal to Colombo for C$3900 return.

Africa

Fares from Johannesburg to Colombo, flying with SriLankan Airlines or South African Airlines, start at R12,000 return.

SEA

Due to the ongoing ethnic conflict, there is no longer a ferry service running between Rameswaram in South India and Talaimannar in Sri Lanka and there are no plans for its resumption in the near future.

A handful of cruise liners voyaging around India and the Maldives, or on longer cruises from Singapore to Dubai, dock in Colombo. Some cruises start at Colombo and travel via Malaysia and Singapore, ending up in Indonesia. The cruising season is from October to May and cruises last about 12 to 16 days. Two cruise-related Web sites worth a look are www.value-cruise.com and www.planacruise.com.

ORGANISED TOURS

The majority of visitors to Sri Lanka come on package tours (mainly from Europe, especially Germany). On some holiday packages it's possible to stay on at your own expense for a few days or weeks. Some of the European package deals are significantly cheaper than the normal economy return fares. The cheaper the package, however, the less flexibility you are likely to have. It's something to consider when booking. You should also inquire about cancellation fees.

See Organised Tours in the Getting Around chapter for a list of companies that specialise in package trips and tours around Sri Lanka.

Getting Around

Domestic flights between Jaffna and Colombo have resumed – although it's not safe to go to Jaffna – but no other domestic flights are available. Public transport is therefore a choice between buses and trains. Both are cheap. Trains can be crowded, but its nothing compared with the seemingly endless numbers of passengers that squash into most buses. Trains are a bit slower than buses, but a seat on a train is preferable to standing on a bus. Even standing on a train is better than standing on a bus, come to that. Pricewise, an ordinary bus fare is usually between the 2nd- and 3rd-class fares on a train.

All public transport gets particularly crowded around *poya* (full moon) holidays and their nearest weekends, so try to avoid travelling then if you can.

BUS

There are two main kinds of bus in Sri Lanka – Central Transport Board (CTB) buses (part owned by the state, part privatised) and private buses. CTB buses are often bright yellow or white, and ply most long-distance and local routes. Private buses range from modern, quite large coaches used on intercity express runs to decrepit old minibuses that limp along some city streets or on short runs between towns and villages. Private air-con intercity buses cover all the major routes; for long-distance travel they are by far the most comfortable.

Reservations

In theory it's possible to reserve a seat on a CTB bus, but in practice it never happens. On buses and trains certain seats are reserved for women. Like the 'smoking prohibited' sign, this injunction is completely ignored; it's first come, first served. On the other hand the first two seats are always reserved for 'clergy' (Buddhist monks) and this is never ignored – a pregnant woman would probably have to stand if a strapping teenage monk hopped on! If you want to

Warning

The price of diesel and petrol in Sri Lanka continues to rise. In January 2001, for example, diesel rose from Rs 21.50 to 39 per litre. These price hikes will obviously push up bus fares and car hire costs. The prices quoted in this book were correct at the time of our research.

guarantee a seat, you'll need to board the bus at the beginning of its journey; get to the bus station at least 30 minutes before it leaves and grab your spot.

Costs

In most cases private bus companies run services parallel to CTB services. Intercity express buses are about twice the price of the CTB buses plying the same route, but are more than twice as comfortable, and are usually faster. Fares, for both CTB buses or private buses, are very cheap. A trip from Kollupitiya to Bambalapitiya in Colombo, for example, costs Rs 3. The journey between Kandy and Colombo costs Rs 35 on a CTB bus and Rs 63 on an air-con intercity express. The fare is written on the ticket.

All buses have unbelievably small luggage compartments and they rarely have storage on the roof. To overcome this problem, Sri Lankans have developed a delightful system whereby a seated person will rest a standing person's bag on their lap. If you have a large pack, don't get any ideas – buy an extra ticket for your bag. If you have a surfboard and you're not too precious about it, you can slip it under the seats. Otherwise, you'll need to buy an extra ticket – and stick with the large buses.

TRAIN

Train travel is a great way to see Sri Lanka. Although the trains are reasonably slow, the distances are short so there are few overnight or all-day ordeals to contend with. Generally a train ride is a more relaxed experience than a bus ride, although trains can be packed at weekends and public holidays.

There are three train lines of most importance to travellers. One goes from Colombo down the west coast to Aluthgama, Hikkaduwa, Galle and Matara. The second goes east from Colombo into the hill country, through Kandy, Nanu Oya (the station for Nuwara Eliya), Haputale and Ella to Badulla. The third line goes north from Colombo to Anuradhapura. A branch line to Trincomalee on the east coast runs off the Anuradhapura line; there is another branch heading south to Polonnaruwa.

If you intend travelling from the south coast to the hills, eg, from Galle to Kandy via Colombo, remember that trains to Colombo from the coast are often late. It may be better to take an express bus to Colombo and catch the train from there.

Train services to Trincomalee and Batticaloa on the east coast and running from Anuradhapura to Talaimannar, Jaffna and Kankesanturai in the north are subject to the security situation.

There's a helpful information desk (No 10) at Fort station, Colombo 1. JF Tours & Travels, a private company that organises steam-train trips (see Organised Tours later in this chapter), has a branch office (☎ 01-440048) at Fort station, Colombo 1. It's open from 9 am to 4.30 pm Monday to Saturday. Staff are helpful and can provide information on timetables and routes even if you are not interested in taking a tour.

Be a little cautious of thieves on trains, particularly at night. Seemingly innocuous objects can also be a threat:

One friend of ours had his hand out the window; it came crashing down and he broke three fingers and needed a number of stitches…after this incident we saw a couple more windows fall down, but luckily no limbs were hanging out.

Sophie Hutchinson (England)

Classes

There are three classes on Sri Lankan trains. Third class is dirt-cheap but invariably crowded and you generally sit on benches (if you're lucky), although night mail trains have sleepers with fold-down benches. Second class has padded seats and sometimes the fans work, plus it's generally less crowded. There are no 2nd-class sleeping berths, only sleepers (fold-down beds in a compartment shared with others). First class comes in three varieties: air-con coaches, observation saloons (with air-con and large windows for viewing the scenery) and sleeping berths (also air-con).

Reservations

You can reserve places on 1st-class coaches and on intercity expresses. It is essential to book for the observation saloons (the booking fee is Rs 50) as these carriages often fill up. The best seats to book are Nos 11, 12, 23 and 24, as these have a full window view. The other seats are also comfy, but the view is little better than in 2nd or 3rd class – you may as well save your money. Note that if you're prone to motion sickness, the seats in the observation saloons face towards the end of the train, so in effect you'll be travelling backwards. Reservations cost Rs 25 for 2nd-class seats and Rs 20 for 3rd-class seats.

Reservations can be made at stations up to 10 days before departure or you may book a return ticket up to 14 days before departure (to do this you must know the date you intend returning – tickets are not open-dated).

If you are travelling more than 80km you can break your journey at any intermediate station for 24 hours without a penalty. However, you must make fresh reservations for seats on the next leg of the journey.

Costs

The cost of train travel roughly averages Rs 1.50 a kilometre, less over long distances. The intercity express from Kandy to Colombo costs Rs 172 in 1st class (plus a Rs 50 reservation fee for the observation saloon), Rs 72 in second class. A return 1st-class ticket from Kandy to Colombo costs Rs 208 (plus Rs 50 reservation fee for the observation saloon). From Colombo to Matara costs Rs 211 in 1st class (plus Rs 50 reservation fee), Rs 157 in 2nd class.

CAR & MOTORCYCLE

Self-drive car hire is becoming more popular in Sri Lanka, but it is more common to rent a car with a driver for a day trip or a few days' tour. If you're on a relatively short visit to Sri Lanka on a mid-range budget, the costs can be quite reasonable.

Motorcycling is a reasonable alternative for intrepid travellers. Distances are relatively short and some of the roads are simply a motorcyclist's delight. The exceptions include the busy Colombo-Galle road, especially between Hikkaduwa and Matara, where the appalling driving, particularly by bus drivers, makes motorcycling downright dangerous. There are a number of places that rent motorcycles in Hikkaduwa and at least one in Kandy. In addition to a cash deposit you must provide your passport number and leave your airline ticket as security.

Road Rules & Conditions

The speed limit for cars and motorcycles is 56km/h in built-up areas and 72km/h in rural areas. Driving is on the left-hand side of the road as in the UK and Australia. The Automobile Association of Ceylon can supply information on road conditions and answer other driving queries. It also sells a booklet called *The Highway Code* for Rs 15. This gives a rundown on the road rules and all the signs you will encounter.

Although you may see a number of accidents during your time on the road, driving seems fairly safe provided you take care. You have to watch out for sudden crazed manoeuvres by other road users, particularly bus drivers. Whenever you meet oncoming traffic you'll have to slow right down; often the roads are not wide enough and each vehicle will have to pull over part way. Also watch out for the unpredictable behaviour of pedestrians and cyclists.

Apart from the Colombo-Negombo, Colombo-Kandy and Colombo-Galle roads, which are crowded, traffic is usually reasonably light. But don't travel at any great speed, because the roads are narrow and potholed and there is often much pedestrian, bicycle and animal traffic to navigate around.

Punctures seem to be a way of life – the roads are hard on tyres, which are not always in first-class condition. But every little village seems to have a puncture-repair specialist who will do an excellent, though rather time-consuming, job using decidedly primitive equipment.

Rental

Car & Driver You can find taxi drivers who will happily become your chauffeur for a day or more in all the main tourist centres. Guesthouse owners will probably be able to put you in touch with a driver, or you can ask at travel agencies or big hotels. The Galle Face Hotel in Colombo (see the Colombo chapter for contact details), for example, has a good travel desk where you can arrange drivers and cars for a day or a few weeks.

The advantages of being driven rather than taking public transport include door-to-door travel, stops of your own choosing, easy baggage handling and greater comfort and speed. You also have a ready-made guide. And you don't have the responsibilities that go with driving yourself, such as looking after the vehicle and avoiding the dangers on the road. The biggest drawback of going by car (with or without a driver), even if the cost is not a consideration, is that you lose most of the day-to-day contact with Sri Lankan life and people that public transport always provides.

Expect to pay about Rs 19 per kilometre, including petrol/diesel. If you want an aircon vehicle, you'll pay around Rs 24 per kilometre, including petrol/diesel. When you begin negotiating, make sure you spell out that the rate includes petrol/diesel and waiting time (and air-con if you want it). Drivers will usually expect you to pay for their lunch, though you may want to organise an upfront fee of about Rs 150. Most drivers will expect a tip of around 10%, though of course it's up to you. Make all payments at the end of the journey.

Self-Drive Mackinnons Travels and Quickshaws Tours are the two main companies offering self-drive cars. (See Organised Tours later in this chapter for contact details.) Mackinnons is the agent for Avis. Quickshaws has self-drive air-con cars from Rs 1400 (including insurance and the first 100km); there is a Rs 10 charge for each kilometre in excess of 100km. Avis has air-con cars from Rs 3700 per day (including insurance) for unlimited mileage. There's a minimum age of 18 with Avis and 25 with Quickshaws, and a maximum age of 65 with both companies. Generally you're not allowed to take the car into national parks, wildlife sanctuaries or jungle, or along other unmade roads. For information on driving licences and other documentation, see the Facts for the Visitor chapter.

BICYCLE

Keen cyclists will probably find Sri Lanka a joy, apart from the uphill sections of the hill country and the terrifying Colombo-Galle road. If you're heading south along the coast, you may want to catch a train as far as Beruwela and then start riding – this way you'll avoid the traffic crush in Colombo. Adventure Sports Lanka in Colombo stocks many mountain bike parts, V- and cantilever-brake blocks, and 26 and 27 inch and 700C tyres. It also has maps and can suggest cycling routes to avoid traffic. See Organised Tours later in this chapter for contact details.

Bringing Your Own Bicycle

Bringing your own bicycle to explore Sri Lanka is quite a different story from hiring one when you get there:

As a cyclist I would recommend Sri Lanka because its size means it can easily be covered in six weeks or so. The usual advantages that a cyclist has in mobility and independence are emphasised when you look at crowded trains and minibuses.

There are disadvantages. Number one is the state of the roads, which ranges from very poor to appalling, especially around the monsoon period. I was able to go on flooded roads that no four-wheeled transport could use, but this required a combination of wading, swimming, wheeling the bike along handy railway lines and, when necessary, hiring a canoe! It all adds to the interest.

I would recommend bringing a good supply of spare tyres and tubes as these can suffer excessively from the poor road surfaces. The normal size bicycle tyre in Sri Lanka is 28 by 1½ inches. Some imported 27-inch tyres for our 10-speed bikes were available but only in a few shops in Colombo and at high prices.

I recommend a good lock when your bike is out of sight or else constant vigilance, particularly in small villages. Early starts are essential due to the heat. The distances you cover will be limited by the state of the roads and a large amount of 'eyes down' cycling will be necessary. Bring lots of sunblock.

Ian Anderson, England

We found that from Hikkaduwa to Colombo the traffic was too busy to enjoy riding, which implies getting involved with the Sri Lankan railway bureaucracy. Every part of the bicycle has to be described on the travel documents (even bells, lights and padlocks). Therefore you should deliver the bicycle at least half an hour before the departure of the train.

Gilles Rubens, the Netherlands

One traveller suggests getting your bicycle to the station even earlier if you are departing from Colombo's Fort train station:

In Fort train station, Colombo, you should bring your bicycle two hours before the journey. You have to pay about twice the 2nd-class fare to take your bike on the train.

Jan Galesloot

Hire bicycles with gears are an exception and you'll find that that most range from merely adequate to desperately uncomfortable. Always check the brakes on any bike you are offered before you put your money down.

HITCHING

Hitching is never entirely safe in any country in the world, and we don't recommend it. Travellers who decide to hitch should understand that they are taking a small but potentially serious risk. People who do choose to hitch will be safer if they travel in pairs and let someone know where they are planning to go.

LOCAL TRANSPORT

Many Sri Lankan towns are small enough to walk around. In larger towns, you can get around by bus, taxi or three-wheeler.

Bus

Buses go to most places including villages outside main towns. Their signboards are usually in Sinhala, so you'll have to ask which is the right bus. Fares are low, eg, the trip from Galle to Unawatuna (15 minutes, 5km) is usually Rs 5.

Taxi

Sri Lankan taxis are often vans. They're common in all the sizeable towns and even some villages will be able to dig up a taxi from somewhere. Only a few are metered, and even then it is advisable to agree on the fare before you get in, as you never know how fast a meter will tick over. Radio cabs are available in Kandy and Colombo; see those chapters for fare details.

Three-Wheeler

These vehicles – known in other parts of Asia as *tuk-tuks, bajajs* or autorickshaws – are everywhere. Turn a corner and you'll find one. To avoid hassles, agree on the fare before you get in. Some keen drivers will offer to take you to the moon; check the distance of your journey with a map before you embark on a potentially hellish ride, as it's no fun being in a three-wheeler for more

than half an hour. As a rule of thumb, a three-wheeler should cost about Rs 20 per kilometre. Three-wheelers and taxis waiting outside tourist hotels and similar places expect higher than usual fares.

ORGANISED TOURS

Competition is fierce between the travel agents and tour companies in Sri Lanka. Most would like to organise everything, some do specialised tours (eg, steam-train trips and wildlife safaris) and others can't organise anything. Word of mouth is the best way to find out which operators are good; ask fellow travellers about their experiences. You can organise everything before you leave home, or once you hit the island. For example, you can organise a tour to Yala West (Ruhuna) National Park from Colombo or Hikkaduwa, or you can wait until you reach Tissamaharama, where every second guesthouse can put together a half-day tour or more for you.

Listed below is a small selection of what's on offer.

Adventure Sports Lanka (☎ 074-713334, fax 01-577951) 1/1 Deanston House, 337 Galle Rd, Colombo 3. Arranges outdoor adventure activities ranging from white-water rafting, scuba diving and mountain biking to gentle walks through Sinharaja
Web site: www.adventureslanka.com

Aitken Spence Travels (☎ 01-308308, fax 436382) 305 Vauxhall St, Colombo 2. One of the biggest tour operators in Sri Lanka, Aitken Spence organises standard and 'Nature Trail' tour packages, hires cars and drivers and books hotels.
Web site: www.aitkenspencetravels.com

A Baur & Co (Travel) Ltd (☎ 01-320551, fax 448493) 5 Upper Chatham Street, Colombo 1. This outfit specialises in bird-watching tours.
Web site: www.baurs.com

Connaissance de Ceylan (☎ 01-698346, fax 685555) 58 Dudley Senanayake Mawatha, Colombo 8. Another big player, Connaissance runs several upmarket hotels and organises 'Buddhist trails', adventure tours such as mountain biking and white-water rafting, and more.
Web site: www.connaissanceceylan.com

George Steuarts Travel (☎ 01-342426, fax 430156, ⓔ g.s.travels@lanka.ccom.lk) 45 Janadhipathi Mawatha, Colombo 1. This established company books outbound travel and local tours.

George Travel (☎ 01-422345, fax 423099) 2nd floor, Ex-Servicemen's Bldg, Bristol St, Colombo 1. Popular with budget travellers for years, George Travel is still going strong.

Jetwing Travels (☎ 01-345700, fax 345725) 46/26 Navam Mawatha, Colombo 2. Yet another of the biggest operators, Jetwing has a large chain of upmarket hotels and organises tours within Sri Lanka and to the Maldives. Web site: www.jetwing.net

JF Tours & Travels (☎ 01-589402, fax 580507, ⓔ jft@slt.lk) 189 Bauddhaloka Mawatha, Colombo 4. This company specialises in steam-train tours, which can be tailored to suit groups. A typical two-day excursion between Colombo and Kandy costs about US$260 per person (a minimum of 30 people is needed; accommodation in Kandy, food and a visit to the Pinnewala Elephant Orphanage are included).

Mackinnons Travels (☎ 01-448065, fax 440881) 4 Leyden Bastian Rd, Colombo 1. A member of John Keells Hotels, Mackinnons organises tours, accommodation, flights, car hire (it's the agent for Avis) and even weddings. Web site: www.mackinnonstravels.com

Quickshaws Tours (☎ 01-583133, fax 587613) 3 Kalinga Place, Colombo 5. This company organises standard tours but specialises in personalised tours with a car and driver. Web site: www.quickshaws.com

Walkers Tours (☎ 01-421101, fax 439026) 130 Glennie St, Colombo 2. Walkers offers a range of activities, from golfing and weddings to mountain biking. You can also customise your own holiday. Web site: www.walkerstours.com

Woodlands Network (☎/fax 057-22735, ⓔ haas@ sltnet.lk) 30/6 Esplanade Rd, Bandarawela. With Woodlands you can compose your own ecotourism itinerary. The possibilities range from viewing projects aimed at wildlife conservation or making an abandoned tea estate productive, to joining a fishing community in Negombo.

Colombo

☎ 01

With a handful of foibles and a fair dash of merits, Colombo's odorous crush will either instantly repel or draw you in by its charms, the juxtaposition of religion and power, and the overt political climate – it's a microcosm of Sri Lanka. If you're only on a short trip to Sri Lanka, you may wish to pass Colombo by, but if you've time – at least two days – wander around Fort (the centre), Cinnamon Gardens and Pettah.

Colombo is the political, economic and cultural centre of Sri Lanka, so if you need to extend your entry permit, or perhaps buy a flight ticket, you'll find yourself here.

If staying in the hustle and bustle of central Colombo doesn't appeal, a short train ride will drop you along the restaurant-lined beachfront of Mt Lavinia; from here you can take day trips to the city centre.

Or if you would prefer to totally give the city a miss you can travel from the airport (30km north of Colombo at Katunayake) by taxi to another destination the same day.

HISTORY

Colombo's history can be traced back to at least the 5th century, when it was a way station for sea trade between the East and the West. Colombo was a small port with the bustling market area of Pettah beside it, and Kotte, on the south-east fringe of Colombo, was the capital of a major Sinhalese kingdom (until the 1870s Galle had been the largest port in the country). During the 8th century Arab traders settled near the port and in 1505, the Portuguese arrived. By the mid-17th century the Dutch had taken over, growing cinnamon in the area now known as 'Cinnamon Gardens', but it wasn't until the British arrived that the town became a city and the city, in 1815, was proclaimed the capital of Ceylon.

In the 1870s the breakwaters were built and 'Fort' was created by flooding surrounding wetlands. Colombo remained the capital under British rule and through to

Highlights

- Chewing, sipping and slurping your way through the huge variety of food on offer
- Elbowing your way through the street stalls at Pettah, squeezing into this and buying that at the city's plentiful shopping malls
- Relishing peaceful Viharamahadevi Park after navigating the darting three-wheelers and the jungle of streets
- Gossiping with locals during a sunset promenade along the beach at Mt Lavinia or on Galle Face Green
- Visiting Hindu *kovils* (temples) during the Thai Pongal festival or watching elephants and dancers parade during the Gangaramaya Temple Navam Perahera

▲ ▲ ▲ ▲ ▲ ▲ ▲ ▲

independence. A new parliament (designed by Sri Lankan architect Geoffrey Bawa) was built in Kotte in 1982. Today, Kotte goes under the name Sri Jayawardenepura-Kotte, and is really just a suburb of Colombo. Gradually, businesses may relocate to the surrounds of parliament as a result of the security measures at Fort.

Colombo continues to spread north and south along the coast as people (some of whome are refugees from the north and east of the island) move here to work.

Colombo was never Sri Lanka's tourism trophy, even before the ethnic problems, but it was at least a stopover point for the many leisure cruises passing by, and tourists would spend a day or two in the city, using it as a base for day trips. A handful of cruise ships still stop at the city, but the problems have severely dented its image.

ORIENTATION

Colombo is broken up into 15 postal code areas; these areas are also sometimes used to identify specific areas, ie, Pettah is also often referred to as Colombo 11 and Slave

Island is referred to as Colombo 2. Once you've got a few directions down, you'll find it relatively easy to find your way around Colombo. From the visitor's point of view, it's virtually a long coastal strip extending 10km or 12km south from the central area, Fort (Col 1). The spine of this strip is Galle Rd – which eventually leaves Colombo far behind and ends up in Galle. If you head straight inland from Fort you quickly come to Pettah (Col 11). Colombo's main train station, Fort, is actually in Pettah, as are the main bus stations – all 10 or 15 minutes' walk from Fort itself.

Travelling south down Galle Rd from Fort you come to Galle Face Green. Inland from here is Slave Island (Col 2), which isn't really an island at all since only two of its three sides are surrounded by water (though it really was used for keeping slaves in the Dutch era). The Galle Face Green area and neighbouring Kollupitiya are Colombo 3. Next along are Bambalapitiya (Col 4) and Wellawatta (Col 6), followed by Dehiwala and the old beach resort Mt Lavinia, which aren't officially part of Colombo but are definitely within its urban sprawl.

Finding addresses along Galle Rd is slightly complicated by the street numbers starting again each time you move into a new district. Thus there will be a 100 Galle Rd in Colombo 3, in Colombo 4, in Colombo 6, in Dehiwala and in Mt Lavinia.

If you turn inland (east) from Kollupitiya along Dharmapala Mawatha or Ananda Coomaraswamy Mawatha, you'll soon find yourself in Cinnamon Gardens (Col 7) – home of the art gallery, museum, university, Viharamahadevi Park (the city's biggest), the most exclusive residential quarters and many embassies.

Some Colombo streets have both an old name and a new name; we've adopted the name most commonly used. The road running through Viharamahadevi Park is called Ananda Coomaraswamy Mawatha and Green Path; and RA de Mel Mawatha, which runs parallel to Galle Rd for a few kilometres, is also still known as Duplication Rd. Some alternative names are given in brackets in this chapter.

Colombo's Suburb Codes

zone	suburb
Colombo 1	Fort
Colombo 2	Slave Island
Colombo 3	Kollupitiya
Colombo 4	Bambalapitiya
Colombo 5	Havelock Town
Colombo 6	Wellawatta
Colombo 7	Cinnamon Gardens
Colombo 8	Borella
Colombo 9	Dematagoda
Colombo 10	Maradana
Colombo 11	Pettah
Colombo 12	Hulftsdorp
Colombo 13	Kotahena
Colombo 14	Grandpass
Colombo 15	Mutwal

Maps

If you're going to be spending any time in Colombo, the *A-Z Street Guide* (Rs 350) will come in handy. This 90-page guide extends as far south as Dehiwala and Mt Lavinia and also covers Kandy, Nuwara Eliya, Anuradhapura, Polonnaruwa and Galle. It includes information on Colombo's suburban and inner-city buses, and carries a list of both old and new street names. The *A-Z* is available from bookshops such as Vijitha Yapa (there's one on the ground floor of Unity Plaza, Bambalapitiya) and Lake House, as well as from hotel bookshops.

INFORMATION

Hands on Colombo by Peter Kamps and published by InvestCreative Products (Colombo) is packed with useful information for residents and tourists. It includes listings for hotels, restaurants, jewellers, antique dealers etc. Updated annually, it's available from Lake House and Vijitha Yapa bookshops as well as top-end hotel bookshops.

The Linc is a freebie magazine with information for expats living in Colombo. It has a mixed bag of classifieds, too many ads, a helpful calendar of events, and more; you can pick it up in the Alliance Française.

COLOMBO

COLOMBO

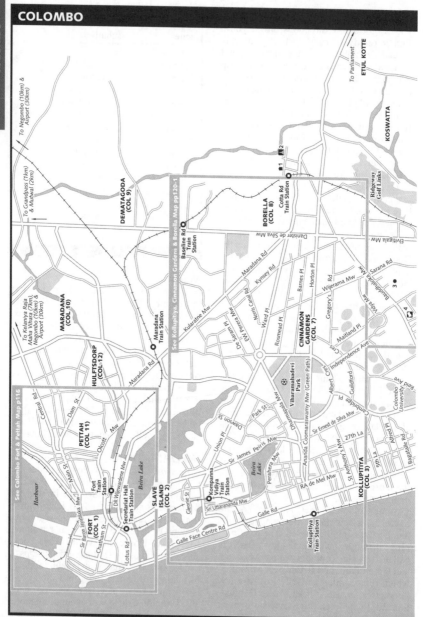

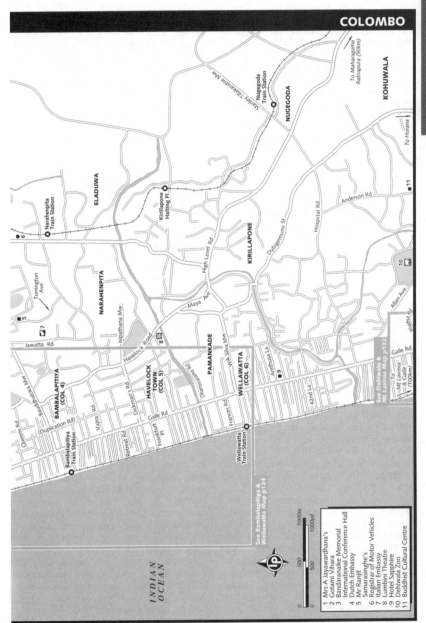

KOHUWALA

To Maharagama
Ratnapura (90km)

NUGEGODA

Nugegoda
Train Station

Stanley Tilakaratne Mw

To Horana

ELADUWA

Kirillapone
Halting Pl

Anderson Rd

11

KIRILLAPONE

Hospital Rd

Dutugemunu St

High Level Rd

Narahenpita
Train Station

6

Torrington
Ave

NARAHENPITA

7

5

Isipathana Mw

Maya Ave

Jawatta Rd

Havelock Road

PAMANKADE

WA Silva Mw

Allan Ave

Washa Rd

10

8

Dhammaram Rd

Arethusa La

Galle Rd

9

Baudhaloka Mw

BAMBALAPITIYA
(COL 4)

Queens Rd

(Duplication Rd)

Vajira Rd

Dickman's Rd

HAVELOCK
TOWN
(COL 5)

Frances Rd

WELLAWATTA
(COL 6)

42nd La

See Dehiwala &
Mt Lavinia Map p132

To
Mt Lavinia
& Galle
(100km)

Bambalapitiya
Train Station

Retreat Rd

Frankfurt
Pl

Galle Rd

Wellawatta
Train Station

See Bambalapitiya &
Wellawatta Map p124

INDIAN
OCEAN

1000m

1000yd

0   500

0   500

1 Mrs A Jayawardhana's
2 Gotami Vihara
3 Bandaranaike Memorial
    International Conference Hall
4 Dutch Embassy
5 Mr Ranjit
6 Samarasinghe's
7 Registrar of Motor Vehicles
8 Italian Embassy
9 Lumbini Theatre
10 Hotel Sapphire
11 Dehiwala Zoo
    Buddhist Cultural Centre

Tourist Offices

The Ceylon Tourist Board has information desks at the airport (☎ 252411), open 24 hours, and at its head office (☎ 437571, fax 440001, ℮ ctb_dm@sri.lanka.net) at 80 Galle Rd, Kollupitiya (Col 3), near the Lanka Oberoi hotel. The tourist office covers not just Colombo but the whole island, and staff can help with hotel bookings as well as answer queries and hand out the accommodation guide and leaflets. (You can also grab great posters for a dirt-cheap Rs 25 each.) The Galle Rd office is open from 9 am to 4.45 pm Monday to Friday, until 12.30 pm Saturday.

At Fort station, there is a Tourist Information Office (☎ 440048), in fact a branch office of JF Tours. It is open from 9 am to 4.30 pm Monday to Saturday, and can help with timetables, itineraries and bookings.

The Tourist Police (☎ 433342) are at the Fort police station, Bank of Ceylon Mawatha, Fort (Col 1).

Money

Most of the main banks are in Fort. There are also several bank branches in the arrivals hall at the airport (open 24 hours). There are a couple of exchange offices open outside normal banking hours. One of these is the Bank of Ceylon Bureau de Change (☎ 422730) on York St, Fort, just down from the Grand Oriental Hotel, which is open from 9 am to 6 pm Monday to Friday and until 4 pm Saturday and Sunday. You can get cash advances on Visa cards here. Thomas Cook (☎ 445971), 15 Sir Baron Jayatilaka Mawatha, Fort, also sells and exchanges travellers cheques. It's open from 8.30 am to 5 pm Monday to Friday and 10 am to 12.30 pm Saturday. American Express (☎ 682787), 104 Dharmapala Mawatha, Cinnamon Gardens (Col 7), is open from 9 am to 5 pm. Check out the Web site at www.americanexpress.com.

There are plenty of moneychangers in Fort, particularly in and around Chatham St and Mudalige Mawatha. Their rates (cash only) are a little higher than you would get in a bank. You can change cash or travellers cheques at reduced rates in the main hotels.

You can get cash advances on Visa and MasterCard credit cards at the HongKong & Shanghai Bank and the Hatton National Bank. If you are carrying any other sort of credit card you should check whether it's viable in Sri Lanka, and with which bank, before you leave home.

The following banks' head offices change travellers cheques:

Bank of Ceylon (☎ 446790) 4 Bank of Ceylon Mawatha, Fort, Col 1
Hatton National Bank (☎ 421885) 10 RA de Mel Mawatha, Kollupitiya, Col 3
HongKong & Shanghai Bank (☎ 325435) 24 Sir Baron Jayatilaka Mawatha, Fort, Col 1
People's Bank (☎ 327841) 74 Chittampalam Gardiner Mawatha, Slave Island, Col 2
Seylan Bank (☎ 437901) 33 Sir Baron Jayatilaka Mawatha, Fort, Col 1
Standard Chartered Grindlays Bank (☎ 446150) 37 York St, Fort, Col 1
State Bank of India (☎ 326133) 16 Sir Baron Jayatilaka Mawatha, Fort, Col 1

ATMs in Colombo There's a Standard Chartered Grindlays Bank ATM at 37 York St, Fort (Col 1), as well as in Colombo 3, 4 and 6. HongKong & Shanghai Bank has an ATM at 24 Sir Baron Jayatilaka Mawatha, Fort (Col 1), as well as in Colombo 2, 3, 4, 6, 8 and in Mt Lavinia (see maps). These ATMs accept Visa and MasterCard.

Post

Colombo's main post office is on DR Wijewardene Mawatha in Fort. It's open from 7 am to 6 pm Monday to Saturday. Poste restante holds mail for two months, and accepts parcels and telegrams as well as letters – call ☎ 441427 to ask if there's anything awaiting you. Stamp collectors may want to visit the philatelic bureau (turn right at the inquiry counter and go down the stairs; it's on your left just past the telegram counter).

If you are sending home anything of particular value you should consider using a courier service. Reliable couriers include Ace Cargo (TNT; ☎ 445331) at 315 Vauxhall St, Slave Island (Col 2); DHL Keells (☎ 338060) at 130 Glennie St, Slave Island

(Col 2); and Mountain Hawk Express (Federal Express; ☎ 577055) at 300 Galle Rd, Kollupitiya (Col 3). See the Post & Communications section in the Facts for the Visitor chapter.

Telephone & Fax

The telephone area code for calls to Colombo is ☎ 01.

International phone calls from the main post office are operator-connected, with a wait of half an hour or so. (You can make collect calls – reverse charge – from here.) With operator-assisted calls you are charged for a minimum of three minutes and per minute after that.

If you don't want to wait, you can use the card-operated IDD telephones, of which there are many in Colombo. The main post office sells Sri Lanka Telecom phonecards in Rs 250, Rs 500 and Rs 800 denominations – calls from these card phones are slighter cheaper than those from the private card-phone booths. The only drawback is that these phones are only located in some post offices. You'll probably find it more convenient to use one of the yellow Lanka Pay or Tritel booths. You could also use one of the numerous (but more expensive) private communication bureaus (you can usually send faxes from these places as well). All five-star hotels have business centres that offer a range of communications services, from email and fax to telephone. However, they are relatively expensive. See the Post & Communications section in the Facts for the Visitor chapter for more information.

Cellphones are becoming increasingly common. The following companies offer various packages, Celltel probably having the most extensive coverage:

Celltel (☎ 541541) 164 Union Place, Slave
  Island, Col 2
  Web site: www.celltelnet.lk
Dialog GSM (☎ 678678) 502 RA de Mel
  Mawatha, Kollupitiya, Col 3
  Web site: www.dialog.lk
Mobitel (☎ 330550) 108 WAD Ramanayake
  Mawatha, Bambalapitiya, Col 4
  Web site: www.mobitellanka.com

Email & Internet Access

Places offering Internet services are popping up throughout the city – look out for private communication bureaus. There are also many Internet cafes along Galle Rd – the largest and most convenient is Cafe@internet (☎ 074-521902, e info@isplanka.lk) at 491 Galle Rd, near Barefoot. Charges are in half-hour slots with a Rs 10 discount for each additional half hour; the first half hour is Rs 95, the second Rs 85 and so on. There are weekly, monthly and yearly memberships that carry discounts. Cafe@internet is open from 9 am to 2 am daily. In Bambalapitiya try Lanka Internet or World@net, in Wellawatta head to Infotech Internet. Closer towards Fort at Kollupitiya, you'll find Berty's Cyber Cafe (☎ 574110, e bertyw@ hotmail.com) at 380 Galle Rd. Berty's is open from 9 am to 9 pm daily except Sunday.

In Fort try the Nisalka Agency Post Office (☎ 454435) near the entrance to the World Trade Centre, at 126 York St. You can use the Internet between 7 am and 6.30 pm daily. Rainbow Travels at 113 Chatham St, Fort, also has Internet facilities.

You can use email services at the business centres in top-end hotels, but prices are considerably more than in the centres mentioned here.

Travel Agencies

Colombo's many travel agencies can help organise a tour, car hire or whatever you're after. See Organised Tours in the Getting Around chapter for contact details.

Photographic Supplies & Repairs

In Fort, head to Millers (☎ 329151) for purchasing print and slide film. Kodachrome 100 ASA (36 exposures) costs Rs 195 – check the use-by date before you buy. Millers also develops film for Rs 9 per print. It takes two days to process print film and three days for transparency film. A cheaper and faster option is Fujifilm (☎ 575771) at 303 Galle Rd, Kollupitiya (Col 3). Processing costs Rs 7.90 per print for 24-hour processing or Rs 12 per print for one-hour processing. Slide film costs Rs 300 per roll for 24-hour processing and mounting.

For camera repairs Photoflex (☎ 587824) at 451/2 1st Floor, Galle Rd, Kollupitiya (Col 3) has been recommended.

Bookshops

Colombo is well serviced with bookshops, and books and periodicals in English are easily obtained. Two of the largest stockists are Vijitha Yapa and Lake House, but there are many smaller places. Top-end hotels also have bookshops where you'll find up-to-date foreign magazines and newspapers (though prices are generally higher than you would pay elsewhere).

The Barefoot Bookshop (☎ 502467, fax 576936, e barefoot@eureka.lk), 704 Galle Rd, Kollupitiya (Col 3), is better known for textiles than for books, but the bookshop downstairs is excellent. There's a good range of quality books on local and foreign art, architecture, culture, travel and literature plus a range of up-to-date periodicals. You'll also find a few lovely books on Sri Lanka that are impossible to obtain elsewhere.

Bibliomania (☎ 432881), 32 Hospital St, Fort (Col 1), is jam-packed with a vast selection of second-hand fiction (from around Rs 75) and a mixed bag of periodicals, educational books and more. Most are in English.

Bookland (☎ 565248, e bookland@ sri.lanka.net), 432 Galle Rd, Kollupitiya (Col 3), offers the usual range of books about Sri Lanka plus other English titles and magazines.

Buddhist Cultural Centre (☎ 734256, fax 736737, e bcc@sri.lanka.net), 125 Anderson Rd, Nedimala, Dehiwala, has a wide range of books about Buddhism in English.

Lake House Bookshop (☎ 432105, e bookshop@sri.lanka.net), 100 Chittampalam Gardiner Mawatha, Slave Island (Col 2), carries an extensive range of books on Sri Lanka and on other subjects. Current foreign and local periodicals and foreign newspapers are also stocked. There are also branches in Colombo 3 and Dehiwala.

The Taprobane Bookshop (☎ 502491, e taprobane@eureka.lk), 720 Galle Rd, Kollupitiya (Col 3), has a decent selection of books but does not have a large range of books specifically about Sri Lanka.

The Vijitha Yapa Bookshop (☎ 596960, e vijiyapa@sri.lanka.net), 392 Galle Rd, Kollupitiya (Col 3), has a few branches around town with a good, well-presented selection of books and periodicals and, in the basement of the Unity Plaza outlet in Bambalapitiya (Col 4), a multimedia collection. Foreign magazines and newspapers are also stocked.

Libraries

The Colombo Public Library (☎ 696156) on Marcus Fernando Mawatha, in Cinnamon Gardens (Col 7), is at the west end of Viharamahadevi Park, and has a reference section and a wide selection of foreign periodicals. It's open from 8 am to 7 pm daily (except Wednesday and holidays). You pay Rs 11.25 to enter.

The National Library of Sri Lanka (☎ 698847, fax 685201) at 14 Independence Ave, Cinnamon Gardens (Col 7) is open from 9 am to 5 pm, Tuesday to Saturday. However, you need to be a member to use it and as it's a reference library only, you can't borrow books. It has a valuable collection of *ola* (palm leaf) manuscripts. There is a permanent exhibition housed in the former study of respected author Martin Wickramasinghe.

If you are seriously interested in human rights or women's studies in Sri Lanka, try the International Centre for Ethnic Studies (☎ 685085, fax 698048, e ices_cmb@sri .lanka.net) at 2 Kynsey Terrace, Borella (Col 8). The centre has books, periodicals and newspapers, and sells its own publications. Because it's air-conditioned, it's a delightfully cool place to browse. It's open from 9 am to 5 pm Monday to Friday.

There is a small reference library beside the National Museum open to readers from 9 am to 5 pm daily, except Sunday and public holidays. You must fill out an application form; it costs Rs 150 to register per year. Short-term users may apply to the librarian directly. The library has a sizeable collection of works, particularly in relation to history and culture.

For libraries attached to cultural centres, see the following section.

Cultural Centres

The Alliance Française (☎ 694162, fax 688735) at 11 Barnes Place, Cinnamon Gardens (Col 7), just east of Viharamahadevi Park, hosts seminars and shows films at 6 pm on Wednesday and 3 pm on Friday. You may read the newspapers and magazines and watch videos in the library (open from 9 am to 6 pm Tuesday to Friday, until 3 pm Saturday) for free. To borrow you'll need to pay a deposit of Rs 250 per item.

The American Information Resource Center (☎ 332725, fax 437662) at 44 Galle Rd, Kollupitiya (Col 3) also puts on films, seminars and so on. You'll need to take out a temporary membership for Rs 50 per day, or an annual membership for Rs 500, to access the library's facilities (including Internet). It's open from 10 am to 5 pm weekdays. Cable news is usually screened in the periodical room at 3.30 pm. You can read the newspapers for free. Their Web site is www.usembassy.state .gov/srilanka.

The British Council (☎ 581171, fax 587079) at 49 Alfred House Gardens, Kollupitiya (Col 3) is just inland off RA de Mel Mawatha. It puts on regular free cultural events including films (usually Friday and Saturday), exhibitions, concerts and lectures. It has a library, open from 9 am to 6 pm Tuesday to Saturday, but you must take out an annual membership – Rs 750 per year or Rs 3000 for video membership. You may look at the newspapers even if you're not a member, and it's a pleasant air-con place to rest and catch up on news. Visit the Web site at www.britcoun.org/srilanka.

The Goethe Institut (☎ 694562, fax 693351), at 39 Gregory's Rd, Cinnamon Gardens (Col 7), offers German language courses, screens German films and puts on music concerts, seminars and more. The library is open from 9.30 am to 6 pm Monday to Thursday, until 12.30 pm Saturday. You'll need to pay an annual fee of Rs 300 if you want to borrow books. Check out the Web site at www.goethe.de/su/col.

The Japan-Sri Lanka Cultural Friendship Association (☎ 699279) at 21 Gregory's Rd, Cinnamon Gardens (Col 7), doesn't seem to organise many events but check out the Web site to see what's on (www.mofa .go.jp/embjapan/srilanka).

Current listings for events such as concerts, plays and lectures are published in *The Linc* and are often posted at cafes and hotels frequented by foreigners.

Laundry

The cheapest place to regenerate your crusty clothes is at the laundry in the YWCA at Union Place, Slave Island (Col 2). It's open from 8.30 am to 4.30 pm. The Laundromat (☎ 582766), at 126 Reid Ave, Bambalapitiya (Col 4), charges around Rs 42 for the full works on a T-shirt, Rs 73 for a dress. Five-star hotels offer laundry and dry cleaning services, but they're pricey.

Left Luggage

There is a left-luggage facility at Fort train station (as you approach the station from the main road, it's on the extreme left of the building in the room labelled 'cloakroom'). It's open from 5 am to 9 pm daily and charges Rs 10 a bag per day.

Medical Services

If you have to go to hospital, the private sector is likely to offer better care. Nawaloka Hospital (☎ 544444, fax 439393) at 23 Sri Saugathodaya Mawatha (off Union Place), Slave Island (Col 2), has emergency care and an English-speaking doctor available 24 hours. As an outpatient, except for the initial (and free) consultation, you must pay to see a specialist so bring cash with you (for non-Sri Lankans it could cost anywhere from Rs 550 to 800 per visit).

The main public hospital, Colombo General (☎ 691111) on EW Perera Mawatha, Borella (Col 8), has few in-patient facilities. Its accident ward is on Ward Place at De Soysa (Lipton) Circus, Cinnamon Gardens (Col 7). The state-run pharmacy Osu Sala (☎ 694716) at 255 Union Place, Slave Island (Col 2), is open 24 hours. Other hospitals, clinics and pharmacies are listed in *Travel Lanka*.

Emergency

Here are a few phone numbers you hopefully won't need:

Accident Service	☎ 691111
Fire	☎ 422222
Police	☎ 433333
Red Cross	
Society Ambulance	☎ 691905, 694487
Tourist Police	☎ 433342

Dangers & Annoyances

Bombs Unfortunately Colombo continues
to be the target of terrorism. In October
1997 a bomb exploded near the World
Trade Centre killing 12 people and injuring
dozens more, including 34 foreigners. Security in the Fort's business district has
been tightened and most roads are closed to
vehicles; some are off-limits to pedestrians.
Due to the increased security measures, suicide bombing (whereby a bomb is attached
to the terrorist who then proceeds, by foot,
to the target) seems to have become the latest mode of terrorism. In January 2000, a
suicide bomber killed herself and 12 others
and wounded up to 28 people in an explo-
sion outside the prime minister's office in
Kollupitya. Later that year, eight people
were killed and 21 injured during a bomb
blast outside the Eye Hospital at De Soysa
(Lipton) Circus, Cinnamon Gardens. Contact your embassy for the latest news and
advice. Unless that advice is to the contrary,
avoid public gatherings and unnecessary
trips into the Fort and Pettah areas.

Bus Travel Women may find riding the
buses extremely trying at times. Ordinary
buses are so packed that sometimes it's impossible to avoid bodily contact with other
passengers. If a sleazebag is making a con-
certed effort to invade your space, such as it
is, you have a few options: Put your bag up
as a shield; move to another part of the bus
if you can; or if things are unbearable, get
off and catch another bus. In Colombo buses
are so frequent that you don't generally have
to wait long for one that's less crowded.

If you are touched or groped, shout
'*Epaa!*' (Don't!), grab the perpetrator's arm

and draw attention to them; humiliation
seems to be effective (and it offers sweet,
satisfying revenge).

Crime While violence towards foreigners
is almost unheard of, it would be wise to
take precautions to avoid the possibility of
making yourself a target. Make sure you always tell someone reliable where you are
going and when to expect you back.

Women in particular are urged to take
care at night. Even couples should be very
wary about walking along lonely beach
areas, such as those near Mt Lavinia, after
dark. Solo women should be cautious taking taxis and three-wheelers at night; if, as
occasionally happens, your taxi turns up
with two men inside, call another. Travellers should avoid taking three-wheelers
between the airport and Colombo at night.

Pickpockets Pickpockets are active on
public transport. Never get on a bus or train
with your shoulder bag unzipped – in fact,
don't even walk down the road with it in
that state. If you are carrying valuables such
as a passport, travellers cheques or reasonably large amounts of cash, you are urged to
keep these things in a moneybelt or a pouch
under your clothes (in other words, out of
sight and out of reach). Bum bags, although
handy for the user, are far too conspicuous.

Touts Colombo has its share of touts and
con artists. Fort train station is a favourite
hang-out and touts here are particularly
skilful and persuasive – you have been
warned. You will likely be approached at
some stage by someone who, after striking
up a conversation, asks for a donation for a
school for the blind or some such cause –
these people are invariably con artists.

Traffic Colombo's vehicles are seemingly
driven by maniacs. Bus drivers delight in
weaving in and out of the traffic, three-
wheelers dart around suicidally, taxis rush
from one job to the next and private vehicles
jockey and toot for road space. Never assume, as a mere pedestrian, that you have
right of way, even on the yellow crossings.

If you do manage to get part of the way across the yellow stripes, don't assume that all traffic will stop; some seem to use the opportunity of a stationary vehicle to overtake, crossing or no crossing. Be alert until you reach the other side safely. When alighting from a bus, always check that the way is clear between the bus and the footpath.

FORT

During the European eras 'Fort' was indeed a fort. Today it's the commercial centre of Sri Lanka, where modern marble and glass structures contrast with such venerable institutions as Cargills and Millers, with their wood panelling, brass fittings and display cases. The entire Fort area is subject to strict security, which has curtailed vehicle access to most of it and pedestrian access to some of it. Fort can be eerily quiet in spots, though vendors still line the Cargills side of York St, selling everything from fluorescent alarm clocks to padded bras.

A good landmark in Fort is the **clock tower** at the junction of Chatham St and Janadhipathi Mawatha (once Queen St), which was originally a lighthouse. Other sights in Fort include the heavily fortified **president's residence** (which the president moved back into in late 2000). There's a busy **port** (also off limits) and the large white dagoba of **Sambodhi Chaitiya** perched about 20m off the ground on stilts – a major landmark for those approaching by sea.

In York St you can see traffic police on horseback from about 4 pm on weekdays.

PETTAH

Adjacent to Fort, and immediately inland from it, is Pettah, one of the oldest districts in Colombo and the city's bustling bazaar area. You name it, and some shop or street stall will be selling it in Pettah – each street seems to have its own speciality. Pettah also harbours many religious buildings – see Places of Worship later in this chapter. Colombo's bus and train stations are on the east and south fringes of Pettah.

The **Dutch Period Museum** (☎ 448466) at 95 Prince St, Pettah has been used as the Dutch town hall, a residence, an orphanage,

a hospital, a police station and a post office. Now restored to its former glory, with a pleasant garden-courtyard, it's open from 9 am to 5 pm Saturday to Thursday. Entry is Rs 55, Rs 30 for children; there's also a Rs 135 camera charge.

GALLE FACE GREEN

Immediately south of Fort is Galle Face Green. 'Green' is an exaggeration – it's a brown expanse of bare earth begging for returfing. Still, it's a popular rendezvous spot; on weekdays it's dotted with joggers, kite flyers and strollers, and on weekends (especially Sunday evenings) food vendors gather to feed the hordes. Facing each other at opposite ends of the 'green' are the delightful old Galle Face Hotel and the Ceylon Intercontinental skyscraper.

GALLE ROAD

Galle Rd – the 'backbone' of Colombo – is noisy, choked with pollution and, not surprisingly, no fun to walk along. Hold your breath and launch in – you'll find some yummy restaurants, shopping centres brimming with goodies and, near the northern end, the Indian and British high commissions, the US embassy and the prime minister's official residence **Temple Trees**.

CINNAMON GARDENS

Cinnamon Gardens (Col 7), 4km to 5km south of Fort and 1km to 3km inland, is Colombo's ritziest address, full of overgrown residences and embassies. A century ago it was covered in cinnamon plantations. Today, as well as elegant tree-lined streets and the posh mansions of the wealthy and powerful, it contains the city's biggest park, several sports grounds and a cluster of museums and galleries.

Viharamahadevi Park

This is Colombo's biggest park, originally called Victoria Park but renamed in the 1950s after King Dutugemunu. It's notable for its superb flowering trees in March, April and early May. Cutting across the middle of the park is the broad avenue Ananda Coomaraswamy Mawatha (Green

COLOMBO FORT & PETTAH

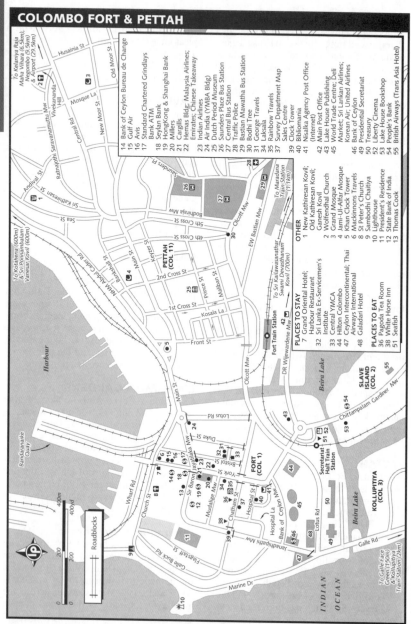

14 Bank of Ceylon Bureau de Change
15 Gulf Air
16 Avis
17 Standard Chartered Grindlays
   Bank ATM
18 Seylan Bank
19 HongKong & Shanghai Bank
20 Millers
21 Cargills
22 Hemas Bldg; Malaysia Airlines;
   Emirates; Chinese Takeaway
23 Indian Airlines
24 Air India (YMBA Bldg)
25 Dutch Period Museum
26 Saunders Place Bus Station
27 Central Bus Station
28 Traffic Police
29 Bastian Mawatha Bus Station
30 Bodhi Tree
31 George Travels
34 Laksala
35 Rainbow Travels
37 Survey Department Map
   Sales Centre
39 Clock Tower
40 Bibliomania
41 Nisalka Agency Post Office
   (Internet)
42 Main Post Office
43 Lake House Publishing
45 World Trade Centre; Deli
   Market; Sri Lankan Airlines;
   Korean Air; United Airlines
46 Bank of Ceylon
49 Presidential Secretariat
50 Treasury
52 Liberty Cinema
53 Lake House Bookshop
54 People's Bank
55 British Airways (Trans Asia Hotel)

OTHER
1 New Kathiresan Kovil;
  Old Kathiresan Kovil;
  Ganesh Kovil
2 Wolfendhal Church
3 Grand Mosque
4 Jami-Ul-Affar Mosque
5 Khan Clock Tower
6 Mackinnons Travels
8 St Peter's Church
9 Sambodhi Chaitya
10 Lighthouse
11 President's Residence
12 State Bank of India
13 Thomas Cook

PLACES TO STAY
7 Grand Oriental Hotel;
  Harbour Restaurant
32 Sri Lanka Ex-Servicemen's
   Institute
33 Central YMCA
44 Hilton Colombo
47 Ceylon Intercontinental; Thai
   Airways International
48 Galadari Hotel

PLACES TO EAT
36 Pagoda Tea Room
38 White Horse Inn
51 Seafish

Path). Colombo's white-domed **Town Hall** or 'white house' overlooks the park from the north-east. Working elephants sometimes spend the night in the park, happily chomping on palm branches.

DEHIWALA ZOO

By Asian standards the zoo (☎ 712751) at Dehiwala, 10km south of Fort, treats its animals well – though the big cats and monkeys are still rather squalidly housed. The major attraction is the elephant show at 5.15 pm, when elephants troop on stage in true trunk-to-tail fashion and perform a series of feats of elephantine agility. While very impressive, this is, of course, far from natural behaviour for the elephants. You may want to consider whether you really want to support it.

The zoo has a wide collection of other creatures, including a fine range of birds and an aquarium. It's open from 8.30 am to 6 pm daily; entry for foreigners is Rs 150 (half price for children). There is also a charge for bringing in a camera. You can get there on a No 118 bus from the Dehiwala train station.

NATIONAL MUSEUM

Housed in a fine colonial-era building on Albert Crescent, just south of Viharamahadevi Park, the museum (☎ 694767) has a good collection of ancient royal regalia, Sinhalese artwork (carvings, sculptures and so on), antique furniture and china, and ola manuscripts. There are fascinating reproductions of English paintings of Ceylon from 1848 to 1850, and an excellent collection of antique demon masks.

Admission is Rs 55 for adults and Rs 30 for children under 12 years (Rs 5 for foreign residents) and it's open from 9 am to 5 pm daily except Friday. You are not allowed to take photos. You can get there on a No 138 bus from Fort station.

Behind the National Museum you'll find an extensive collection of dusty stuffed creatures at the **Natural History Museum** (☎ 691399). It's open from 9 am to 5 pm daily except Friday; entry is Rs 35 for adults, Rs 20 for children.

OTHER MUSEUMS & GALLERIES

The **Bandaranaike Museum** in the Bandaranaike Memorial International Conference Hall (☎ 696364) on Bauddhaloka Mawatha, Cinnamon Gardens (Col 7), tells of the life, times and assassination of the 1950s' prime minister SWRD Bandaranaike. It's open from 9 am to 4 pm daily except Monday and *poya* (full moon) days.

The **Dutch Period Museum** is worth a visit (see Pettah earlier in this chapter).

The **National Art Gallery** (☎ 693965) is at 106 Ananda Coomaraswamy Mawatha (Green Path), opposite Viharamahadevi Park. It's open from 9 am to 5 pm daily except poya days. The permanent collection is mostly portraits, but there are also some temporary exhibitions of Sri Lankan artists.

The stylish **Lionel Wendt Centre** (☎ 695794) at 18 Guildford Crescent, Cinnamon Gardens (Col 7) has contemporary art and craft exhibitions, musical performances, and stages the occasional sale of antiques and other items.

Art galleries are becoming a popular attraction at the cafes springing up in Colombo, for example Paradise Road's **The Gallery** at 2 Alfred House Gardens, Kollupitiya (Col 3) and **The Commons** at 74A Dharmapala Mawatha, Cinnamon Gardens, (Col 7). Barefoot, the popular textiles sales outlet at 704 Galle Rd, Kollupitiya (Col 3), has exhibitions in **Gallery 706**, downstairs next to the Garden 706 Cafe.

PLACES OF WORSHIP
Buddhist Temples

Colombo is a relatively young city so there are no great religious monuments of any age. The most important Buddhist centre is the **Kelaniya Raja Maha Vihara** 7km east of Fort, a short distance off the Kandy road. The Buddha is reputed to have preached here on a visit to Sri Lanka over 2000 years ago. The temple later constructed on the spot was destroyed by Indian invaders, restored, destroyed again by the Portuguese, and restored again in the 18th and 19th centuries. The dagoba, which is unusual in being hollow, is the focus of the Duruthu

Perahera in January each year. There is a very fine reclining Buddha image here. To reach the temple take bus No 235 from in front of the traffic police station just north-east of the Bastian Mawatha bus station.

Other important Buddhist centres in Colombo include the **Gangaramaya Temple** at Sri Jinaratana Rd, Slave Island (Col 2), near Beira Lake. It has two resident temple elephants and is the focus of the Navam Perahera on the poya day in February each year (for more information see Public Holidays & Special Events in the Facts for the Visitor chapter). For Rs 80 you can tour the temple, library and 'museum' and view the extraordinarily eclectic array of gifts presented by devotees and well-wishers over the years. Perhaps the most surprising sight is the collection of antique cars, one of which is apparently in full working order.

Isipathanaramaya Temple in Havelock Town has particularly beautiful frescoes.

The **Vajiraramaya Temple** on Vajira Rd, Bambalapitiya is a centre of Buddhist learning from where monks have taken the Buddha's message to countries in the West. The modern **Gotami Vihara** at Borella (Col 8), 6km south-east of the centre near Cotta Rd train station, has some impressive murals of the life of the Buddha.

Hindu Temples

Hindu temples, known as *kovils* in Sri Lanka, are numerous. On Sea St, the gold-smiths' street in Pettah, the **New Kathiresan kovil** and the **Old Kathiresan kovil**, which are dedicated to the war god Skanda, are the starting point for the annual Hindu Vel Festival (see Public Holidays & Special Events in the Facts for the Visitor chapter), when the huge Vel chariot is dragged to kovils on Galle Rd in Bambalapitiya. There is also a temple to Ganesh here.

In Kotahena, 600m north-east of Fort, you'll find the **Sri Ponnambalam Vanesar Kovil**, which is built of south Indian granite. Many other kovils are blessed with some equally unpronounceable names. The **Sri Kailawasanathar Swami Devasthanam**, reportedly the oldest Hindu temple in Colombo, has shrines to Shiva and Ganesh

and is at Captain's Gardens, off DR Wije-wardena Mawatha, Maradana (Col 10). The huge **Sri Shiva Subramania Swami Kovil** is on Kew Rd, Slave Island (Col 2) and the **Sri Muthumariamman Kovil** is on Kotahena St, Kotahena (Col 13).

During the harvest festival of Thai Pongal (held in January) devotees flock to these temples, which become even more colourful and lively.

Mosques

The **Grand Mosque**, on New Moor St in Pettah, is the most important of Colombo's many mosques. In Pettah you'll also find the decorative 1909 **Jami-Ul-Alfar Mosque**, on the corner of 2nd Cross and Bankshall Sts, with its candy-striped red-and-white brickwork. There are many mosques in Slave Island, dating from the British days when it was the site for a Malay regiment.

Churches

The 1749 **Wolfendhal Church** on Wolfen-dhal Lane in Pettah is Colombo's oldest Dutch church, and still holds services – in English and Tamil – on Sunday morning. Its floor is made of tombstones from a Dutch church in Fort, moved here in 1813. The 1842 **St Andrew's Scots Kirk** has been lost by the bonny Highlands to Galle Rd, Kollupitiya (Col 3). **St Peter's Church** near the Grand Oriental Hotel in Fort was converted from the Dutch governor's banquet hall and first used as a church in 1804.

AYURVEDA & MASSAGE

Siddhalepa Hospital (☎ 738622) at 106A Templers Rd Mt Lavinia is a good place to go for a proper Ayurvedic massage. Massages last an hour and 10 minutes and involve a head and body oil massage followed by a herbal bath. The whole lot costs Rs 1800 – you must book. Ayurvedic treatments are available for those who seek them; a consultation costs Rs 400.

For a relaxing massage try the Ratne Health Clinic (☎ 584694) at 13 Adam's Ave, Bambalapitiya (Col 4). The masseurs use reflexology and accupressure – a 45-minute session costs Rs 1000. The clinic is open from 9 am to 7 pm daily – book ahead. There's no sign but you'll find the clinic hiding round the bend of Adam's Ave.

GOLF
The Royal Colombo Golf Club (☎ 695431, fax 687592, **e** colombo.golf@lanka.ccom .lk) has an 18-hole golf course at the Ridge-way Golf Links, Borella (Col 8) that predates the one in Nuwara Eliya by 10 years. Visitors are welcome but ring in advance to let them know when you're coming. A day on the course costs Rs 1225 Monday to Friday and Rs 2450 on weekends and public holidays. A one-week membership costs Rs 6125. You can hire a set of clubs for Rs 600 and a cart (there are no caddies) for Rs 25. There is, however, a dress code: Sports shoes and socks and a shirt with a collar must be worn (no T-shirts). You may wear shorts, but not short shorts. There is a shop that sells all sorts of gear as well as golf balls – at a price.

JOGGING
The Hash House Harriers (☎ 581675) 27 Elibank Rd, Havelock Town (Col 5), holds a men-only run every Monday at 5.30 pm. The Hash House Harriettes (☎ 574573) holds a mixed at 5.30 pm every Wednesday. They both organise runs through the countryside as well as Colombo; there are regular long runs over the weekend.

SWIMMING & DIVING
The only Colombo beach where you'd consider swimming is Mt Lavinia, a somewhat faded resort area 11km south of Fort – and even that's borderline, with a severe undertow at times and some foul waterways issuing into the ocean not too far north.

Visitors can use the pools at several top-end Colombo hotels for a fee. One of the nicest spots is the **outdoor saltwater pool** right by the seafront at the Galle Face Hotel, which costs Rs 200 for nonguests (you must bring your own towel). A dip in the magnificently positioned Mt Lavinia Hotel pool costs Rs 300 and includes access to the hotel's private stretch of beach.

Many shipwrecks are available to divers near Colombo. You could try Underwater

Safaris (☎ 694012, **e** scuba@eureka.lk) 25C Barnes Place, Cinnamon Gardens (Col 7), which runs PADI courses (open water with a group of four costs US$475) and organises sea dives and snorkelling trips. You can buy fins, masks and snorkels (divers are expected to supply their own) at the Underwater Safaris dive shop.

COURSES
Buddhism & Meditation
The best place for inquiries about courses available in Colombo is the Buddhist Cultural Centre (☎ 734256, fax 736737) at 125 Anderson Rd, Nedimala, Dehiwala, though a reader has said they're not too helpful. You may be better off heading to Kandy (see the Hill Country chapter) which has a greater variety of options.

Diving & Snorkelling
Underwater Safaris runs PADI diving and snorkelling courses. See the Swimming & Diving section for details.

Languages
The British Council runs Sinhala classes for beginners as well as advanced students. The classes (morning or evening) run for 2½ months (40 hours) and cost Rs 11,000. Lessons in English, French and German are available from the British Council, Alliance Française and the Goethe Institut respectively. See Cultural Centres earlier in this chapter for contact details.

SPECIAL EVENTS
The Duruthu Perahera is held on the full-moon day in January at the Kelaniya Raja Maha Vihara. The Navam Perahera on the February full moon is led by 50 elephants; it starts from the Gangaramaya Temple and is held around Viharamahadevi Park and Beira Lake. During the Hindu Vel, the gilded chariot of Skanda, the God of War, is ceremonially hauled from the Kathiresan kovils in Sea St, Pettah, to a kovil at Bambalapitiya.

See Places of Worship earlier in this chapter for details about the temples. For festivals outside Colombo, see Public Holidays & Special Events in Facts for the Visitor.

KOLLUPITIYA, CINNAMON GARDENS & BORELLA

PLACES TO STAY
2 Hotel Nippon
4 Taj Samudra Hotel; Ports of Call; Swissair
5 Galle Face Hotel; Sea Spray
8 Holiday Inn
12 Hilton JAIC Tower; HongKong & Shanghai Bank ATM
18 YWCA International Guesthouse
20 Mrs Swarna Jayaratne's
21 Mrs Chitrangi de Fonseka's
38 Crescat Residencies
39 Lanka Oberoi Hotel
41 YWCA National Headquarters
44 Mrs D Peiris
49 A Wayfarer's Inn
52 Parisare
85 Hotel Renuka; Palmyrah Restaurant
94 Mrs Padmini Nanayakkara's

PLACES TO EAT
7 The Bavarian Bar
13 Pizza Hut
33 Don Stanley's Restaurant & Supper Club
40 Crescat Boulevard; Keells
57 Le Palace
64 Don's Cafe
65 Summer Gardens
74 The Commons
75 Eastern Dragon Halal Restaurant
84 Amaravathi
93 Chesa Swiss

OTHER
1 Sri Shiva Subramania Swami Kovil
3 Hatton National Bank
6 Air France
9 Automobile Association of Ceylon
10 Nawaloka Hospital
11 Celltel
14 AOM French Airlines
15 Aitken Spence Travels
16 Ace Cargo (TNT)
17 Singapore Airlines
19 Pakistan High Commission
22 Colombo General Hospital & Accident Service
23 Odel Unlimited; Delifrance
24 Clocktower
25 Dewata-gaha Mosque
26 Baptist Church
27 Osu Sala
28 Post Office
29 Town Hall
30 Paradise Road; Paradise Road Cafe
31 KLM Royal Dutch Airlines
32 Sampath Bank

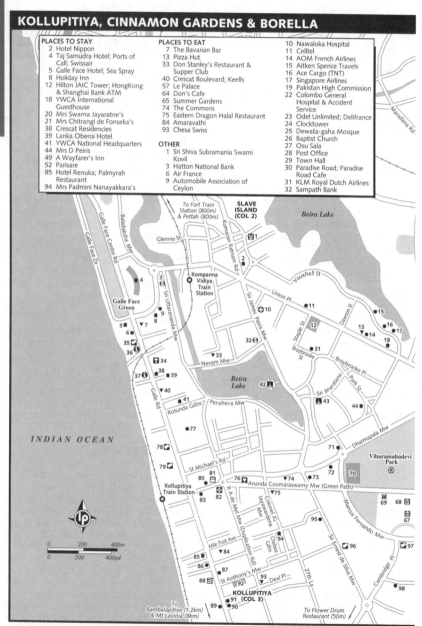

KOLLUPITIYA, CINNAMON GARDENS & BORELLA

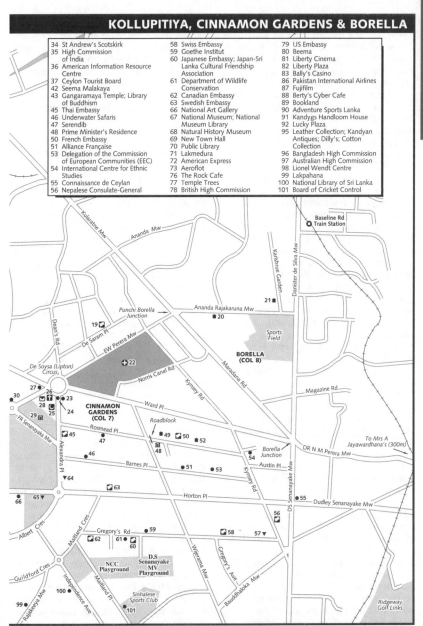

34 St Andrew's Scotskirk
35 High Commission of India
36 American Information Resource Centre
37 Ceylon Tourist Board
42 Seema Malakaya
43 Gangaramaya Temple; Library of Buddhism
45 Thai Embassy
46 Underwater Safaris
47 Serendib
48 Prime Minister's Residence
50 French Embassy
51 Alliance Française
53 Delegation of the Commission of European Communities (EEC)
54 International Centre for Ethnic Studies
55 Connaissance de Ceylan
56 Nepalese Consulate-General

58 Swiss Embassy
59 Goethe Institut
60 Japanese Embassy; Japan-Sri Lanka Cultural Friendship Association
61 Department of Wildlife Conservation
62 Canadian Embassy
63 Swedish Embassy
66 National Art Gallery
67 National Museum; National Museum Library
68 Natural History Museum
69 New Town Hall
70 Public Library
71 Lakmedura
72 American Express
73 Aeroflot
76 The Rock Cafe
77 Temple Trees
78 British High Commission

79 US Embassy
80 Beema
81 Liberty Cinema
82 Liberty Plaza
83 Bally's Casino
86 Pakistan International Airlines
87 Fujifilm
88 Berty's Cyber Cafe
89 Bookland
90 Adventure Sports Lanka
91 Kandygs Handloom House
92 Lucky Plaza
95 Leather Collection; Kandyan Antiques; Dilly's; Cotton Collection
96 Bangladesh High Commission
97 Australian High Commission
98 Lionel Wendt Centre
99 Lakpahana
100 National Library of Sri Lanka
101 Board of Cricket Control

PLACES TO STAY

Colombo has a limited range of accommodation: Some cheapies are forlorn and overpriced, there's only a handful of mid-range places, and then there's so many top-end options you won't know where to start.

Colombo doesn't have 'cheap' or 'midrange' areas staked out like many other cities in the world, so instead you need to work out what kind of area (eg, ritzy, commercial, colourful) you'd like to stay in.

If you head to Fort you're right in the heart of the city's commercial centre (which isn't as noisy as it sounds since security measures have sucked out a lot of its life) and here you'll find the businesses and large hotels as well as their fancy restaurants and nightclubs. Slave Island has hectic streets, a heavy police presence and small dwellings jammed in between office blocks.

Kollupitiya covers Galle Face Green, the ritziest stretch of Galle Rd with the highest security. The other chunk of Kollupitiya follows noisy Galle Rd south, and is lined with larger shops, restaurants and businesses; inland, expensive dwellings mix with the commercial.

Moving into Bambalapitiya, Galle Rd starts losing some of its gloss, the buildings are smaller, footpaths are busier, and shops abound.

By Wellawatta, Galle Rd has lost all pretentiousness. Here, small shops and elbowing shoppers vie for space, and even the odd cow wends its way through the traffic. It's one of the most colourful parts of Colombo.

Cinnamon Gardens has posh houses, stately public buildings and lots of embassies – it's a green area.

Borella and Maradana are a bit out of the way but, although the area doesn't hold much obvious interest, you can get an idea of what it's like living in a suburb of Colombo.

Dehiwala's beachfront is a shabby but quiet spot, as is sleepy Mt Lavinia, with a beachfront lined with restaurants. This is the perfect spot to avoid busy Colombo and, with Fort's skyline at the end of the beach, you'll feel like you're close to the action.

Unless stated otherwise, you'll find all budget places listed do not have hot water but do have bathrooms, fans, meals, nets or electric mosquito 'mats'. Mid-range places have bathrooms, hot water, nets or mosquito 'mats', and most have air-con too. The top-bracket hotels in Colombo typically have elegant, spacious public areas, large swimming pools, shops, gyms, several restaurants and air-conditioning.

PLACES TO STAY – BUDGET & MID-RANGE
Fort (Col 1)

The busy, friendly **Central YMCA** (☎ 325252, fax 436263, 39 Bristol St) has cramped 16-bed dorms (men only) for Rs 125 a bed. There are no lockers so you'll have to chain up your gear or risk it. Small dim singles/doubles with fan and shared bathroom go for Rs 300/400; with no fan you'll pay Rs 175/200. With fan and private bathroom you'll pay Rs 650. There's a Rs 5 daily membership charge. Billiard tables, a gym and other facilities are available (for a fee). The busy cafeteria will feed you for under Rs 100.

Only for the desperate, **Sri Lanka Ex-Servicemen's Institute** (☎ 422650), virtually next door, has rickety bunks in a grim 10-bed dorm for Rs 185. The coffin-like rooms are exorbitant at Rs 375/800. Solo women travellers would not feel comfortable here.

Slave Island (Col 2)

Mrs D Peiris has a small guesthouse (☎ 328350, 62/2 Park St) that's close to Viharamahadevi Park. She's a helpful host, which is just as well since her rooms are depressing and the shared bathroom is awful. At least it's cheap (for this area) at Rs 500/600; try bargaining. To get there from Fort station take a No 138 bus and get off at the town hall stop. From Dharmapala Mawatha, this place is a couple of minutes' walk up Park St on your left.

The **YWCA International Guesthouse** (☎ 324181, 393 Union Place) is a rambling colonial mansion set in large grounds, 2km inland from Galle Rd. It has 20 basic rooms for Rs 500/730 if you want a shared bathroom or Rs 850/1250 with private bathroom; rates include breakfast. Both men and women are welcome. You can resurrect your stinky gear at the laundry.

Hotel Nippon (☎ 431887, fax 332603, 123 Kumaran Ratnam Rd) has a promising colonial exterior hiding 32 gloomy rooms. At least the first-floor rooms have a balcony, hot water and air-con – at Rs 1570 for a single or double, they're decent value. Rooms with fan and hot water cost Rs 1275.

Kollupitiya (Col 3)

The clean *YWCA National Headquarters (☎ 323498, fax 434575, e natywca@sltnet.lk, 7 Rotunda Gardens)* has basic, though a little dark, rooms for Rs 900/1500 including breakfast. Men can stay in these rooms if they're travelling with a female companion. For rooms with shared bathroom (women only) you'll pay Rs 300/600. The rooms surround a leafy courtyard. There's a cheap cafeteria that's open from Monday to Saturday for breakfast, lunch and dinner. (The lunch buffet is only Rs 120.)

Mrs Padmini Nanayakkara's (☎/fax 573095, 20 Chelsea Gardens) has colonial furnishings and a pretty little garden. The two rooms – neither are spotless, but both are charming – have their own entrances. The upstairs room costs Rs 750/850, the downstairs Rs 750/950; rates include a scrumptious breakfast. Mrs Nanayakkara speaks fluent French. This is a popular place so book ahead.

Hotel Renuka (☎ 573598, fax 574137, e renukaht@panlanka.net, 328 Galle Rd) has 80 air-con rooms for US$55/60. The spotless rooms are a little dated though most have bathrooms and TV. The hotel's restaurant, Palmyrah, is well known for superb Sri Lankan food (see Places to Eat, later in this chapter).

Bambalapitiya (Col 4)

Mrs D Bandara's (☎ 582646, 24 Castle Lane) has a dim room for Rs 350/400 or Rs 500/550 if you use the kitchen. The bathroom's a bit scary, but there's a small sitting area attached and a separate entrance. Phone in advance to book; turning up unannounced when it's occupied is not welcomed.

Mrs Marie Barbara Settupathy (☎ 587 964, fax 502080, e jbs@slt.lk, 23/2 Shrubbery Gardens) has five clean and tidy rooms for Rs 750/850 including breakfast. There's a sitting area with a TV and a minuscule pebble courtyard, but the place lacks character. Apart from breakfast, no other meals are served.

Wellawatta (Col 6)

Chanuka Guest House (☎ 585883, 29 Frances Rd) has five rooms for Rs 440/550. Rooms with hot water go for Rs 770 for a single or double. Although the rooms are without charm – and the building's ugly – the owners are friendly and the rooms are very clean. The only meal served is breakfast (Rs 120).

Hotel Sapphire (☎ 583306, fax 585455, e sapphire@slt.lk, 371 Galle Rd) has 40 air-con rooms for US$50/60. The large, clean rooms have a fridge, TV and phone and an overwhelming 1970s feel. The front rooms are noisy.

Cinnamon Gardens (Col 7)

If you're heading to the guesthouses along Rosmead Place, ask the driver to take you via the Kynsey Rd entrance; the approach from the other end of the street is blocked as the prime minister's residence is at that end of the road.

Parisare (☎ 694749, e sunsep@sltnet.lk, 97/1 Rosmead Place) is a superb example of modern architecture. It's designed with minimum definition between the homely, comfy indoor and the leafy outdoor spaces. There are two rooms upstairs for Rs 550/1100. The deluxe room downstairs with a four-poster bed, ensuite and private garden costs Rs 650/1350. All rooms have hot water. Parisare is very popular – book ahead.

Nearby, and almost next to the prime minister's residence, is *A Wayfarer's Inn (☎ 693936, fax 686288, e wayfarer@slt.lk, 77 Rosmead Place)*. Clean, quaint rooms cost from Rs 1000 to 1700 (with air-con); rates include an English breakfast. There's

COLOMBO

BAMBALAPITIYA & WELLAWATTA

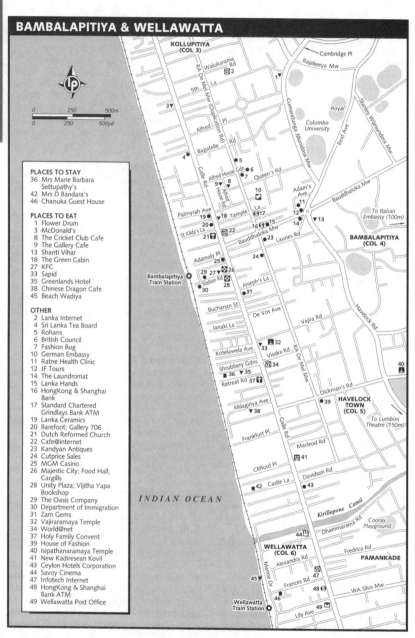

PLACES TO STAY
36 Mrs Marie Barbara
   Settupathy's
42 Mrs D Bandara's
46 Chanuka Guest House

PLACES TO EAT
1 Flower Drum
3 McDonald's
8 The Cricket Club Cafe
9 The Gallery Cafe
13 Shanti Vihar
18 The Green Cabin
27 KFC
33 Sapid
35 Greenlands Hotel
38 Chinese Dragon Cafe
45 Beach Wadiya

OTHER
2 Lanka Internet
4 Sri Lanka Tea Board
5 Rohans
6 British Council
7 Fashion Bug
10 German Embassy
11 Ratne Health Clinic
12 JF Tours
14 The Laundromat
15 Lanka Hands
16 HongKong & Shanghai
   Bank
17 Standard Chartered
   Grindlays Bank ATM
19 Lanka Ceramics
20 Barefoot; Gallery 706
21 Dutch Reformed Church
22 Cafe@internet
23 Kandyan Antiques
24 Cutprice Sales
25 MGM Casino
26 Majestic City; Food Hall;
   Cargills
28 Unity Plaza; Vijitha Yapa
   Bookshop
29 The Oasis Company
30 Department of Immigration
31 Zam Gems
32 Vajiraramaya Temple
34 World@net
37 Holy Family Convent
39 House of Fashion
40 Isipathanaramaya Temple
41 New Kadiresean Kovil
43 Ceylon Hotels Corporation
44 Savoy Cinema
47 Infotech Internet
48 HongKong & Shanghai
   Bank ATM
49 Wellawatta Post Office

a leafy garden, hot water, a guest sitting room and kitchen (with a washing machine!) and even a grand piano you can play to torment fellow guests.

Mr Ranjit Samarasinghe's guesthouse (*☎/fax 502403, ☏ ranjitksam@hotmail.com, 53/19 Torrington Ave*) has three homely rooms (two with private bathroom) at Rs 1050/1500 – it's Rs 500 extra for air-con. One room has a telephone, writing desk and bar fridge. The house is modern and airy with a small leafy courtyard. Ask about the modern bungalow retreat on the leafy outskirts of Colombo.

Borella (Col 8) & Maradana (Col 10)

Mrs A Jayawardhana's (*☎ 693820, 42 Kuruppu Rd*) is an unpretentious family home with a large garden, dogs and three tidy rooms for Rs 500/700. Two rooms share a bathroom. This place is a bit out of the way but is still reasonably serviced by public transport: If you catch a bus from Fort (bus No 168, 174 or 177, Rs 5) get off at Cotta Rd train station. A three-wheeler from Fort will cost about Rs 150 – tell the driver to head to the Gateway International School. If you ring, the family may be able to arrange to pick you up from the bus or train stations.

Mrs Swarna Jayaratne's guesthouse (*☎ 695665, fax 687707, ☏ indcom@sltnet .lk, 70 Ananda Rajakaruna Mawatha*) has two clean singles/doubles for Rs 500/ 750 (plus Rs 100 for hot water) with a common bathroom. There's a guest sitting area (with TV), a balcony and a small patch of lawn. To get here catch bus No 103 or 171 (Rs 3.50 from Fort train station) and get off at Punchi Borella Junction.

Mrs Chitrangi de Fonseka's guesthouse (*☎/fax 697919, 7 Karlshrue Garden*) is a modern, spotless home bubbling over with endearing eccentricity. The three good-sized rooms – each costing US$40 – have TV, hot water, air-con and laptop and phone connection. There's a fax and even a karaoke machine. Try your frothing skills on the cappuccino machine in the fully equipped guest kitchen or sip your freshly squeezed juice in the leafy courtyard. Bus No 103 or 171 from Fort will take you nearby (see the directions to Mrs Swarna Jayaratne's place in previous listing).

Dehiwala & Mt Lavinia

Big John Guest House (*☎ 715027, fax 580108, 47 Albert Place, Dehiwala*) has 10 sparkling new rooms (no nets) for Rs 600/ 700. You could eat off the tiled restaurant floor if you wanted, but you'll be too busy marvelling at the 'shaving foam' ceiling. To get there a three-wheeler from Fort should cost about Rs 250, although you can always catch a south-bound bus down Galle Rd.

The *Blue Seas Guest House* (*☎ 716298, 9/6 De Saram Rd, Mt Lavinia*) has 12 clean, simple and spacious rooms (some with balconies) for Rs 600/800 including breakfast, which is the only meal provided. There's a large sitting room decked out with colonial furniture, and a garden.

The *Tropic Inn* (*☎ 738653, fax 344657, 6 College Ave, Mt Lavinia*) has 16 spotless rooms in a simple, stylish building. There's an internal courtyard and many of the rooms have a balcony – all rooms have hot water. You'll pay Rs 900/1000 or Rs 1200/1400 with air-con. Rates include breakfast.

The motel-like *Ivory Inn* (*☎ 715006, 21 Barnes Ave, Mt Lavinia*) has 21 clean, no-frills rooms with balconies. Rooms cost Rs 1000/1100 including breakfast – some have a view to the sea. There's a garden and a huge undercover restaurant.

Mr & Mrs Shanti Perera's (*☎ 716272, 3 De Saram Rd, Mt Lavinia*) is just off Beach Rd. There is a nice tropical garden. The three clean rooms cost Rs 1040/1200. You can negotiate for long stays.

Opposite Tropic Inn is *Mr Lyn Mendis'* (*☎/fax 732446, ☏ ranmal@bigfoot.com, 11 College Ave, Mt Lavinia*) a popular and friendly guesthouse with rooms for Rs 1000/ 1350 including breakfast – add Rs 400 for air-con. The rooms each have a separate entrance and hot water. There's a light-filled guest sitting area and a kitchen complete with a stove and fridge.

The *Cottage Gardens* (*☎ 713059, 42–48 College Ave, Mt Lavinia*) offers three self-contained bungalows each equipped with cooking facilities and fridge, set in a small garden, for Rs 1320.

Haus Chandra (☎ *732755, fax 733173, 37 Beach Rd, Mt Lavinia*) has buildings on both sides of the road; the reception is located on the right-hand side as you face the beach. Air-con rooms with bathroom, TV, telephone and fridge cost US$32/42 including breakfast; some can be a bit cramped so check them out before you book in. The suites have antique furnishings, carpets, and a fully equipped kitchen; they cost US$65 for bed and breakfast. The pool's barely big enough for one person.

Airport Area

The Bandaranaike International Airport is at at Katunayake, 30km north of the city. Transport there from the city, and indeed from elsewhere in Sri Lanka, isn't difficult. The cheapest accommodation near the airport is at Negombo, about 10km north (see the West Coast chapter). At any time of the day or night it's easy to jump in a taxi and head to Colombo for Rs 900, but if you're desperate to stay near to the airport there are some cheapies closeby.

Try the day rooms at the airport (Rs 700 for 24 hours). Ask at the tourist office in the arrivals lounge for information.

Five minutes' drive from the airport the *Hotel Goodwood Plaza* (☎ *252356, fax 252562*) and the *Orient Pearl Hotel* (☎ *252563, fax 252562*) are side by side on Canada Friendship Rd. The hotels share their management, a pool, casino and 80 faded but clean rooms for Rs 2235/2500.

PLACES TO STAY – TOP END
Fort (Col 1)

A top hotel of an older generation is the *Grand Oriental Hotel* (☎ *320391–2, fax 447640,* e *goh@sltnet.lk, 2 York St*), formerly the Taprobane, opposite the harbour. Don't be fooled by the colonial facade though; inside, the 62 air-con rooms have been stripped of original features. The spotless, tiled and slightly box-like rooms cost US$40/60 or US$80 for a suite. There are superb views from its 4th-floor Harbour

Restaurant, but it lacks the open spaces that make some other top hotels appealing.

The *Galadari Hotel* (☎ *544544, fax 449875,* e *galadari@sri.lanka.net, 64 Lotus Rd*) has rooms starting at US$75. It's not as posh as the Hilton, but it's got almost as many facilities as well as great views.

The *Ceylon Intercontinental* (☎ *421221, fax 447326,* e *colombo@interconti.com, 48 Janadhipathi Mawatha*) is beautifully located facing the sea on one side and the north end of Galle Face Green on another. Rooms cost US$80 and US$105 for suites. They're very comfortable but, like many of their competitors, disappointingly small for the money.

The *Hilton Colombo* (☎ *544644, fax 544657,* e *info_colombo@hilton.com*) on Lotus Rd has plush rooms. Rates start at a staggering US$200/230 for a standard room, go to US$260/280 for an executive room or, if you're begging to pay more, there are executive 'plus' rooms for an extra US$30. A nonsmokers floor is available on request. With seven restaurants, four bars, a disco, a 24-hour business centre, a gym and even a masseur at hand, you needn't step out the door. There is a direct entrance into the World Trade Centre next door.

Slave Island (Col 2)

For a top-end apartment, try the 34-floor *Hilton JAIC Tower* (☎ *300613, fax 075-344648,* e *towers@itmin.com, 200 Union Place*), with 175 apartments. Two-bedroom fully furnished apartments cost from US$2520 and three-bedroom apartments cost from US$2990 per month. Amenities include parking for guests, a tennis court, pool, squash court, gym and private restaurant and bar. There is a good, modern shopping arcade on the ground floor with restaurants and other services, including a 24-hour ATM.

Kollupitiya (Col 3)

For a hotel with more character than any of the other top enders, the 1864 *Galle Face Hotel* (☎ *541010–6, fax 541072,* e *gfhrsvn@itmin.com, 2 Kollupitiya Rd*) is at the south end of Galle Face Green. It was the superior establishment during the British colonial era and still has loads of colonial charm. There are boards listing famous people who've stayed there, so you'll know you have at least one thing in common with Bo Derek, Yuri Gagarin, Prince Philip and John D Rockefeller. The air-con rooms range from US$65 (there are a few budget rooms for US$55); a suite costs from US$80 to US$195. The cheaper rooms look a bit moth-eaten so check before you book in; the more expensive ones are spacious with views. Have an evening drink on the terrace overlooking the ocean or try the oceanside restaurant Sea Spray (see Places to Eat, later). The Galle Face Hotel has a helpful travel desk on the veranda to the left of the main entrance that nonguests can use.

The **Holiday Inn** (☎ 422001–9, fax 447977, e holiday@sri.lanka.net, 30 Sir Mohamed Macan Markar Mawatha) has 100 spotless rooms at US$75/85. A step down from other top-end hotels, this hotel has all mod cons, but is smaller and simpler.

The **Taj Samudra Hotel** (☎ 446622, fax 446348, e taj@sri.lanka.net, 25 Galle Face Centre Rd) has rooms at US$150/160 with pool views, or US$160/170 with a sea view, plus more expensive rooms with balconies. There are some particularly elegant public areas and a large, well-tended garden.

The **Lanka Oberoi** (☎ 437437, fax 449280, e lkoberoi.bc@netgate.mega.lk, 77 Steuart Place) is, despite its address, actually on Galle Rd a short distance from Galle Face Green. Rooms start at US$170/190. Externally it's a bland tower block, but internally it's a hollow atrium hotel with gigantic batik banners hanging from the top to the bottom of the airy lobbies.

If you're interested in renting an apartment, **Crescat Residencies** (☎ 075-530686, fax 516134, e cresales@sri.lanka.net, 75 Galle Rd) is next to the Lanka Oberoi and is a couple of minutes from the upmarket Crescat Boulevard shopping centre. It has fully and semifurnished luxury apartments with basement parking from US$1500 for one bedroom or US$1600 for two bedrooms per month. Residents may use the swimming pool and squash courts at the Lanka Oberoi and are entitled to discounts for food, drink and laundry at the hotel.

Mt Lavinia

The **Berjaya Mount Royal Beach Hotel** (☎ 739610–5, fax 733030, e berjaya@slt.lk, 36 College Ave) has air-con rooms at US$85/100. It sits on a prime position beside the beach and although the comfy rooms have all the mod cons, they are a little dated and we've received a complaint about the service. Still it's a cheaper option, for a room of similar standard, than the Mt Lavinia Hotel.

The magnificently marbled **Mt Lavinia Hotel** (☎ 715221–7, fax 738228, e lavinia2@sltnet.lk, 100 Hotel Rd), once the flashy residence of the British governor, is on the waterfront and is very close to Mt Lavinia train station. There's a private sandy beach, elephant rides on Sunday and a beautifully positioned pool and terrace where you can have meals. The rooms range from US$50/60 in the colonial relic governor's wing to US$125/135 in the more modern (air-con) bay wing.

Airport Area

The Bandaranaike International Airport is 30km north of Colombo. At any time of the day or night there are plenty of taxis at the airport willing to take you to Colombo (Rs 900) or anywhere else in Sri Lanka for that matter. However, there are several top-end options close to the airport, and others dotted between Colombo and the airport.

The **Tamarind Tree** (☎ 253802, fax 254298, e tamarind@eureka.lk, Yatyana Miniwangoda), 7km east of the airport, has air-con rooms for US$70 as well as fully contained cabanas (US$75) dotted through the garden. This spot is popular with foreign residents who commute daily to work in Colombo or the airport.

The **Pegasus Reef Hotel** (☎ 930205/8, fax 930254, e pegasus@pan.net, Santha Maria Mawatha, Hendala, Wattala) is 24km from the airport and 12km from Colombo. It has spotless, simple air-con rooms with beach frontage for US$68/83.

A taxi to the airport will cost around Rs 900; it'll cost Rs 700 to Colombo.

On the main Colombo-Negombo road and 2km south of the airport, you'll find the lagoon-side ***Airport Garden Hotel*** *(☎ 252950, fax 252953, ℮ agh@slt.lk, 234–238 Negombo Rd, Seeduwa)*. The marbled foyer looks like something from the Gulf States. The air-con rooms are comfy, spotless and overpriced at US$92/105.

PLACES TO EAT

Colombo has the best selection of restaurants in Sri Lanka. In addition to good Sri Lankan food you will find German, Swiss, French, Italian, Lebanese, Indian, Japanese, Chinese, Korean and even Mongolian cuisine. Junk-food junkies will find Pizza Hut, KFC and McDonald's. Some of the best restaurants can be found in the five-star hotels; the all-you-can-eat buffets are generally good value even if you're on a budget. Trendy cafes are all the rage, especially with young professionals and students. They are a good place to see how some Sri Lankans live and the good coffee, good food, good music and occasional art exhibition they provide can be a welcome refuge for homesick expats and those just seeking time out.

But for some of the cheapest and tastiest food, it's hard to beat ***lunch packets***. Sold between about 11 am and 2 pm on street corners and footpaths all over the city, they generally cost between Rs 45 and Rs 65. A lunch packet consists of rice and curry; usually boiled rice with vegetables, with fish or chicken as optional extras. Restaurants will also prepare your meal for you to take away if that's what you want; ask for a parcel.

Fort (Col 1)

For the self-caterers, ***Cargills*** has a food city in its Fort store.

For cheap, tasty food head to the ***Central YMCA*** *(☎ 325252, 39 Bristol St)* during lunch hours only.

The ***Pagoda Tea Room*** *(☎ 323086, 105 Chatham St)* is one of the oldest eating establishments in Fort and the service is graciously old fashioned. There's a variety of

Asian and Western food. Basic rice and curry is Rs 60, there are different lunch specials daily (on Friday you'll get mixed fried rice, sweet-and-sour prawns and shredded beef) for Rs 130 or short eats such as bacon pie for Rs 22. It is open from 8.30 am to 5.30 pm Monday to Friday, until 1.30 pm on Saturday. Incidentally, former Duran Duran fans may once have seen the Pagoda Tea Room in one of their heroes' videos.

At the ***White Horse Inn*** *(☎ 342005, 51 Chatham St)* the toasted cheese sandwiches (Rs 100) are melt-in-the-mouth quality. It's open from 10 am to 2.30 pm and 5 to 11 pm Sunday to Thursday, and 10 am to 2.30 pm and 5 pm to 3 am on Friday and Saturday.

The ***Deli Market*** on the 3rd floor of the World Trade Centre is very popular with business types. It's open from 8 am to 11 pm Monday to Thursday, 8 am to midnight Friday and Saturday and 11 am to 11 pm Sunday and holidays. The eating area is spotless and has air-con – plus you get a good view of the treasury building. There are eight kiosks serving more than 180 dishes. You can choose espresso, beer, hot chocolate or fruit juice at one counter and cakes, sandwiches and sundaes at another. Or try the mains, including the Indian 'dinner deal' from Rs 200 or a Chinese 'dinner deal' from Rs 320. Australian T-bone steak costs Rs 550, garlic prawns go for Rs 380 or you can make up your own pizza (Rs 340). There are kids meals for Rs 210.

The ***Harbour Restaurant*** at the Grand Oriental Hotel is worth visiting just for its superb harbour views. Fortunately there's also tasty food and decent prices. You can gorge on the lunch buffet (Rs 225) only on weekdays; the dinner buffet (Rs 450) is available daily. Otherwise, spaghetti bolognaise costs Rs 200, or for a meat fix, chew on their steak for Rs 350.

More upmarket dining can be had at any of the Hilton's restaurants. ***Il Ponte*** is open for lunch and dinner; it's light and airy with a range of Italian and continental dishes, imported wines and beers and a good salad bar. For excellent Sri Lankan food try the ***Curry Leaf*** restaurant. It has a garden setting aimed at recreating the atmosphere of a traditional village. In addition to all sorts of local specialities, there is an *arrack* bar. It's only open for dinner and the buffet costs Rs 680. The *Moghul Ghar* restaurant specialises in Pakistani halal cuisine, *Ginza Hohsen* serves sushi and other Japanese fare (with all-imported ingredients), with mains from Rs 920 to 1225; for good Chinese food try the *Emperor's Wok*.

Slave Island (Col 2)

Pizza Hut (☎ 305305, 323 Union Place) has air-con and all the ubiquitous features of a chain restaurant – plastic ferns, sparkling tiles, cheesy smiles – to make you feel at home. Try a 'Meal Deal' for two (Rs 400): a regular-sized pan pizza, drinks, and garlic bread or fries. French fries cost Rs 65, spaghetti bolognaise Rs 165 and lasagne Rs 220. It's open from 11 am to 10 pm Monday to Thursday and 11 am to 11 pm Friday to Sunday (and on public holidays). There's another Pizza Hut on Galle Rd in Dehiwala.

A few doors down, next to the Hilton JAIC Tower, is a *KFC* outlet.

Just south of Fort, *Seafish (☎ 326915, 15 Chittampalam Gardiner Mawatha)* has excellent seafood. It's open from 11.30 am to 2.30 pm and 6 to 11 pm daily. Most main courses cost up to Rs 300 – sweet-and-sour prawns costs Rs 360.

The posh *Don Stanley's Restaurant & Supper Club (☎ 074-719192, 42 Navam Mawatha)* is on the 15th floor of the DHPL building. One of the great attractions here is the view: Take the street-side glass elevator up to the restaurant for a bird's-eye peak at the extraordinary pea-green Beira Lake. There's a lunch buffet for Rs 480 and an a la carte menu for dinner – splash out on the seafood paella (Rs 600). Ring ahead to reserve a window-side table.

Kollupitiya (Col 3)

Self-Catering & Cafes A supermarket popular with expats is *Keells* at Liberty Plaza. Self-caterers should head to *Beema* near Liberty Plaza on the 2nd floor of the big market building. It's an indoor marketplace with fruit, vegetables and a good range of imported foods at very competitive prices.

The Gallery Cafe (☎ 582162, 2 Alfred House Rd) contains what used to be an office belonging to Sri Lanka's most famous architect, Geoffrey Bawa. Entry is through a series of colonnaded courtyards featuring ornamental pools; from the outer latticed gate you can gaze right through to the inner courtyard via a series of similarly latticed gates that frame, right at the end, a large terracotta storage jar. Paradise Road has a shop in the outer courtyard.

Exhibitions of paintings and photography are featured in this courtyard as well as further inside. The lounge bar is where Bawa's old office used to be and his desk is still there. The open-air cafe area looks over a pebbled courtyard and is open from 10 am to 11 pm daily. Main meals cost from Rs 420 to 1100. As a cheaper option, come for an afternoon coffee (Rs 115). It's definitely one of the places to be seen in Colombo but more importantly, it's a stunning spot and a terrific retreat from the bustle of Colombo.

Garden 706 Cafe (☎ 580708, 704 Galle Rd), located on the lower level of the well-known Barefoot shop, is set in a pretty courtyard next to the gallery and bookshop. Prices are moderate. It's open from 9.30 am to 6.30 pm daily.

Restaurants YWCA National Headquarters has a busy *cafeteria* offering a wide variety of dirt-cheap eats.

McDonald's (498 Galle Rd) has standard grub for junk-food desperados: Regular hamburgers cost Rs 50, a Big Mac Rs 120 and coffee Rs 30.

Crescat Boulevard, a couple of minutes from the Lanka Oberoi Hotel, has a good food hall downstairs (there is also a Keells supermarket here). You have a choice of Sri Lankan, Chinese, Indian and international food (Pizza Hut and The Cricket Club Cafe have outlets here). Service is efficient, the surroundings are clean (with clean toilets nearby), it's air-conditioned and the prices are moderate (Rs 170 for rice and curry). It's open from 10 am.

Eastern Dragon Halal Restaurant (☎ 576276, 52 Ananda Coomaraswamy

Mawatha) has good halal food and take-away services. It's open from 11 am to 3 pm and 6.30 to 11 pm. Fish coriander soup costs Rs 140 and mains – try their 'soggy' noodles – start at Rs 150.

Amaravathi (☎ 577418, 2 Mile Post Ave), near Hotel Renuka, has air-con, attentive service and scrumptious south Indian food for very reasonable prices. Thalis from Rs 105 are served at lunch (from 11 am to 3 pm), but there is a wide selection of other dishes: chicken biryani Rs 150, vegetable korma Rs 100, or for a special treat try the brain *masala* for Rs 120.

The spotless *Flower Drum (☎ 574811, 29 Cumaratunga Munidasa Mawatha)* is a dark air-con eatery that is well known for good Chinese food. It's open for lunch from 11.30 am to 3 pm and for dinner from 6.30 to 11 pm. There's home delivery too. The soups cost around Rs 200 and mains cost from Rs 220.

Lurking in a nondescript kitchen a chef is whipping up some of the finest Sri Lankan curries in Colombo. Salivating? Head to the *Palmyrah Restaurant (☎ 573598)* in the basement of Hotel Renuka. Rice and chicken curry costs Rs 240 and the chef's good with other cuisines – spaghetti bolognaise, for example, costs Rs 300.

The *Ports of Call* coffee shop in the Taj Samudra Hotel does a good breakfast buffet for Rs 550.

One of the most popular places to meet, drink and eat is *The Cricket Club Cafe (☎ 501384, 34 Queens Rd)*. In an older-style bungalow with a garden and veranda and air-con, the setting is very pleasant. But what really sets this place apart from all others is, as the name suggests, its cricketing theme: The place is packed with cricket memorabilia, and replays of notable matches are screened continuously. There are menus for both snacks and meals – and a special children's menu. Options range from potato wedges for Rs 125 and club sandwiches for Rs 155 to crab for Rs 495. There's a good bar and an excellent selection of beer and wine. It's open from 11 am to 11 pm daily.

The Bavarian Bar (☎ 421577, 11 Galle Face Court), opposite the Galle Face Hotel,

does all things German. It's open from noon to 2.30 pm and 6 to 11 pm daily (except Sunday, when it's only open at night). Main meat dishes are around Rs 450. You may wish to make your visit coincide with the happy hour (7 to 8 pm) to sample the draught German beer and German wines.

The Galle Face Hotel has a quaint oceanside restaurant called *Sea Spray (☎ 541010)* that serves Sri Lankan and Western-style food. The daily buffets cost Rs 490 for lunch or Rs 700 for dinner. Meals include the 'Seafood Symphony' for Rs 490 and a vegetable lasagne for Rs 250. The veranda is a great place for having a sunset drink, though with Lion lager at Rs 200, you're paying for the privilege.

Chesa Swiss (☎ 573433, 3 Deal Place) serves good Swiss food. It's simple, spotless and the service is attentive. It's open from 7 to 11 pm Tuesday to Sunday. Soup (for example, carrot and ginger) starts at Rs 180, mains start at Rs 300 (sliced venison in Cognac-pepper sauce costs Rs 1000). A good selection of imported wines and beers is available.

Bambalapitiya (Col 4)

A good spot for a cheap but reasonable-quality lunch is the food hall in the basement of *Majestic City*. And there's plenty of choice, including Malay, Chinese, Sri Lankan, Western-style fast food (including pizza and fried chicken) and Indian. There's air-con, so it's pleasantly cool, and there's a play area for young children next to the eating area. Majestic City also has *KFC* and a good *Cargills* on the ground floor.

The *Greenlands Hotel (☎ 585592, 3A Shrubbery Gardens)*, despite its ward-like interior whips up mean, fresh south Indian food. There's an air-con section and a busy, clean canteen area. The prices are so low you won't mind that you may have to beg to be served: Superb rice and curry costs Rs 55, masala dosa Rs 40 and *iddli* (south Indian rice dumpling) Rs 13. It's open from 8 am to 10 pm daily.

The Green Cabin (☎ 588811, 453 Galle Rd) is a bit of an institution in the restaurant trade and still serves good food at very reasonable prices. The lunch-time buffet (Rs 130 for vegetarian) is excellent value – the mango curry, if it's on, is very good. For a snack, try the vegetable pastries (Rs 12) or the fish-and-egg pies (Rs 32).

Sapid (☎ *500441, 2A Vajira Rd)* is open from 11 am to 11 pm daily. It has good Sri Lankan food from Rs 100 to 300 for mains. It's air-conditioned and has some pleasantly breezy upstairs rooms.

There's a cheap *Chinese takeaway* outlet at ground level (with meals for around Rs 100); there's another at the Hemas Building, York St, Fort.

The *Chinese Dragon Cafe* (☎ *503637, 11 Milagiriya Ave)* is an old mansion serving inexpensive rice and noodle dishes. It's open from 11 am to 3 pm and 6 to 11 pm daily. Starters cost around Rs 100, mains are around the Rs 200 mark. Heed the sign 'Complaints Welcome at Reception' but save your breath if you want to complain that the restaurant doesn't serve or allow alcohol on the premises.

Havelock Town (Col 5)

Shanti Vihar (☎ *580224, 3 Havelock Rd)* is popular with locals and foreigners because of its deliciously spicy vegetarian food for very reasonable prices. It's a basic, well-worn eatery, though there is a fancier air-con section. The menu's south Indian offerings are especially good: masala dosa for Rs 42, *curd vadai* (a deep fried lentil or flour patty with yogurt) for Rs 18, Madras thalis for Rs 80 (lunch only) and special thalis for Rs 125. Shanti Vihar also has a home-delivery service.

Wellawatta (Col 6)

Beach Wadiya (☎ *588568, 2 Station Ave)* is a beach hut at the bottom of Station Rd, near the Wellawatta train station. It's a popular spot for seafood, but the main drawcard is the photoboards of people – many famous (ie, cricketers), others drunk, some both – who have visited the restaurant. Crab with vegetables costs Rs 370, prawns cost Rs 370 and fried fish is Rs 190. The last order is at 10.15 pm. It might pay to book, as this place gets busy.

Cinnamon Gardens (Col 7)

Cafes The *Paradise Road Cafe* (☎ *686043, 213 Dharmapala Mawatha)*, part of the shop of the same name, serves great coffee for Rs 90, milkshakes for Rs 140, cakes and light meals – quiche for Rs 80, spaghetti from Rs 140 – in an airy veranda-style atmosphere upstairs. It's open from 10 am to 7 pm daily.

Delifrance (☎ *553354, 5 Alexandra Place, De Soysa [Lipton] Circus)* open from 10 am to 7 pm daily (until 3 pm Sunday). This busy cafe is on the ground floor of the very popular Odel Unlimited store and is delighted to siphon off your shopping change. Delicious sweet pastries go for Rs 75, real coffees cost Rs 100.

A trendy crowd frequents *The Commons* (☎ *574384, 74/A Dharmapala Mawatha)*, which is part garden, part gallery and part open-lounge cafe (with large, soft sofas). Open from 8 am to 8 pm weekdays (and until 10 pm Friday), it's a perfect spot to take a break. There's a good selection for the sweet-toothed, with fudge brownies or waffles for Rs 180 and a delicious 'brunch' (from 11 am to 8 pm Saturday, noon to 6 pm Sunday) that features pancakes, bacon and syrup for Rs 300. Sandwiches cost Rs 185 and a coffee fix costs Rs 135.

Restaurants In a leafy spot with outdoor tables sheltered with palm thatch is the *Summer Gardens* (☎ *678019, 110 Ananda Coomaraswamy Mawatha)*. It's open from 10 am till around 11 pm. Rice dishes start at Rs 70, curries are Rs 55 and seafood is from Rs 140. You can also get ice cream (Rs 35) and crème caramel (Rs 40). You won't write home about the food, but the atmosphere is pleasant, the service is attentive and the prices are cheap. Bring mosquito protection with you (which unfortunately won't protect you from the toilets).

Owned by Don of Don Stanley's restaurant in Slave Island (Col 2), *Don's Cafe* (☎ *686486, 69 Alexandra Place)* has an air-con seating area and an outdoor spot overlooking the street. Mains, such as burgers, go for around Rs 350. It's open from 11 am to 3 pm and 7 to 11 pm weekdays, and 11 am to 11 pm on the weekends. Treat yourself to the chocolate fudge in the deli downstairs.

Le Palace (☎ *695920, 79 Gregory's Rd*) in a beautiful old mansion in one of Colombo's most exclusive streets is run by a French chef, and the pastries and bakery products are first class. It's open from 7 am to midnight daily. A pot of Italian coffee costs Rs 90, mouth-watering desserts start at Rs 175 (tiramisu costs Rs 365) and French wines start at Rs 950 – corkage is an outrageous Rs 375. Mains range from Rs 460 (eg, Thai chicken) to 725 (eg, baked crab). If your budget's tight you can always come during the day and enjoy a pastry for Rs 75. If you are coming here by taxi or three-wheeler ask the driver to take you via the Kynsey Rd entrance; there are many schools in this street, which means much of it is closed to traffic.

Dehiwala & Mt Lavinia

There are many places to eat and drink along Mt Lavinia's beachfront; it's a great place to watch the sun set and to 'people watch'. Note that some restaurants have limited menus on weekdays, as most local tourists come on the weekend.

The Big Apple (☎ *074-200599, 21 Hill St, Dehiwala*) is an air-con complex of Chinese, Sri Lankan and Indian restaurants as well as a rooftop beer garden; all are open from 7.30 to 11.30 pm. The *Rajasthan Indian Restaurant* has good meals for around Rs 220, tandoori chicken for Rs 440 and lots of vegetarian dishes from Rs 110. The *Shandong Chinese Restaurant* has rice and noodle dishes from Rs 85, chicken from Rs 140 and prawns from Rs 220.

The *Happening Restaurant* (☎ *074-204351, 43/A1 Beach Rd, Mt Lavinia*) isn't happening, but it does have cheap tasty food. Try the vegetable noodles for Rs 125 or the chicken with cashew nuts for Rs 180.

Try the *Catamaran Beach Restaurant* (☎ *724400, 23 College Ave, Mt Lavinia*) for similar fare at similar prices.

Fisherman's Villa (☎ *074-202821, 43/19 College Ave, Mt Lavinia*) is a posh, beachfront place with great food and service. With seafood dishes you have to order a minimum

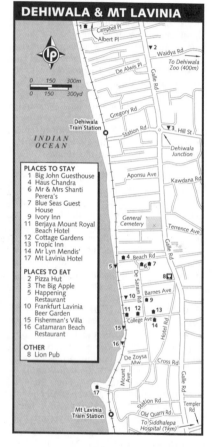

DEHIWALA & MT LAVINIA

INDIAN OCEAN

0   150   300m
0   150   300yd

Dehiwala Train Station

Mt Lavinia Train Station

To Dehiwala Zoo (400m)

To Siddhalepa Hospital (1km)

PLACES TO STAY
1 Big John Guesthouse
4 Haus Chandra
6 Mr & Mrs Shanti Perera's
7 Blue Seas Guest House
9 Ivory Inn
11 Berjaya Mount Royal Beach Hotel
12 Cottage Gardens
13 Tropic Inn
14 Mr Lyn Mendis'
17 Mt Lavinia Hotel

PLACES TO EAT
2 Pizza Hut
3 The Big Apple
5 Happening Restaurant
10 Frankfurt Lavinia Beer Garden
15 Fisherman's Villa
16 Catamaran Beach Restaurant

OTHER
8 Lion Pub

of 300g so the prices can be high (jumbo prawns with herbs and mustard costs Rs 920), but there are cheaper meals, eg, fish satay with fries for Rs 220 and fish and chips for Rs 250. The restaurant is open from 11 am to 11 pm daily. There is a children's play area open from 3 to 7 pm.

The Frankfurt Lavinia Beer Garden (☎ *716034, 34/8A, De Saram Rd, Mt Lavinia*) serves German speciality food in a leafy garden setting. Home-made sausages cost Rs 370 – most mains are around this price. It's open from 11 am to 2.30 pm and 6 pm to midnight (food orders until 10.30 pm).

The food is excellent at the *Mt Lavinia Hotel* (see Places to Stay, earlier), as it should be for US$15 per dinner, but some have complained about sloppy service and a lack of attention to detail.

ENTERTAINMENT
Pubs & Bars

The *Sri Lanka Ex-Servicemen's Institute* *(29 Bristol St, Fort, Col 1)* bar serves local Lion lager for Rs 80 a bottle, which is about the cheapest you'll buy it anywhere – but you're not paying for atmosphere.

A pleasant place to stop for a beer is the cool, airy *White Horse Inn* *(☎ 342005, 51 Chatham St, Fort, Col 1)*. Local beer costs Rs 45 and imported ale from Rs 150.

For a 24-hour venue try *The Rock Cafe* *(☎ 565986, 41–43 Ananda Coomaraswamy Mawatha, Cinnamon Gardens, Col 7)*. It's decorated with all kinds of music industry memorabilia. There is seating in the garden, on the balconies and inside. There's live music Wednesday, Friday and Saturday nights or you can shake the food down (or up) in the nightclub in the basement. Unfortunately the food is only for the intoxicated – tasteless burgers (Rs 200) and minuscule salads (Rs 210).

The *Saxophone Jazz Club (46B Galle Rd, Kollupitiya, Col 3)* has been recommended by a reader for live music including, not surprisingly, jazz.

The *Rhythum & Blues Bar* on Duplication Rd in Kollupitya (Col 3), near the Atlantic Club, has been highly recommended. It has live music on Friday and Saturday nights, and billiard tables.

Step through the tacky lion's mouth into the *Lion Pub* at Mt Lavinia. It has a leafy beer garden.

All of the top hotels have bars. Spruce up and head to the colonial-styled *Echelon* at the Hilton Hotel. It has a billiard table, darts and occasionally bingo. The Hilton also has a karaoke bar open from 8 pm if you like embarrassing yourself. The *bar* at the Galle Face Hotel is very pleasant.

Some good places to drink are also good places to eat so they've been listed under Places to Eat earlier. Try *The Cricket Club Cafe* in Queens Rd, Kollupitiya (Col 3) or the *Deli Market* in the World Trade Centre, Fort (Col 1). For German booze head to *The Bavarian Bar* for Happy Hour (7 to 8 pm) *(11 Galle Face Court, Kollupitiya, Col 3)* or *The Frankfurt Lavinia Beer Garden (34/8A, De Saram Rd)* in Mt Lavinia, where Lion lager costs Rs 135, Carlsberg is Rs 140 and Heineken is Rs 170. In Dehiwala, *The Big Apple (21 Hill St)* has a rooftop beer garden open from 7.30 to 11.30 pm.

Nightclubs

Most of Colombo's nightlife centres on the top hotels. All clubs have a cover charge of a few hundred rupees and are open daily (on poya days no drinks can be sold). Dress is smart casual. Things only really get going at about 10 pm and continue through to 6 am. Most have theme nights. Some choices include the *Blue Elephant* (at the Hilton), *The Library* at the Trans Asia *(Chittampalam Gardinia Mawatha, Slave Island, Col 2)*, *Cascades* (Lanka Oberoi Hotel) and *Colombo 2000* (Galadari Hotel). Other possibilities include *Legends*, on the 5th floor at Majestic City (open from 6 pm daily), and the *Cyclone Music Bar (29 Maitland Place, Cinnamon Gardens, Col 7)*, which has live music from 8 pm to 4 am.

Casinos

Most casinos are along the strip of Galle Rd that runs between Majestic City in Bambalapitiya and Kollupitiya (the signs outside say 'foreigners only'). The casinos have all sorts of incentives with which to lure punters, including free meals and drinks, free transport to and from the casino and so on. Most are open 24 hours. They include *Bally's Casino (☎ 573497, 14 Dharmapala Mawatha, Kollupitiya, Col 3)* near Liberty Plaza, and the *MGM Casino (☎ 502268, 772 Galle Rd, Bambalapitiya, Col 4)* near Majestic City. These casinos are run by the same management.

Cinemas

Colombo's most modern cinema is on Level 4 of *Majestic City*. Another older cinema, *Liberty Cinema*, is opposite Liberty Plaza.

Shows run in the morning and evening (usually starting at 6.30 pm). The Majestic City cinema runs old blockbuster films. The foreign cultural centres show arthouse films; for what's on see *Travel Lanka* and *The Linc*.

Theatre

The **Lionel Wendt Centre** (☎ 695794, 18 Guilford Crescent, Cinnamon Gardens, Col 7) sometimes puts on theatre. The foreign cultural centres, for example, the British Council, also host shows. These are advertised in periodicals such as *Travel Lanka* and *The Linc* and at cafes and hotels frequented by expats. The **Lumbini Theatre** (Havelock Rd, Havelock Town, Col 5) hosts Sinhala theatre.

SPECTATOR SPORTS

The top spectator sport in Sri Lanka is, without a doubt, cricket. You can buy tickets for major games from the **Sri Lanka Board for Cricket Control** (☎ 681601, e toc@itmin.com, 35 Maitland Place, Col 7) next to the Sinhalese Sports Club.

See the Spectator Sports section in the Facts for the Visitor chapter for more information about spectator sports.

SHOPPING
Handicrafts

Colombo is a good place to shop for handicrafts. The longest established place is the government-run Laksala in Fort (Col 1). Here you'll find two floors showcasing all manner of traditional Sri Lankan crafts, including batik and wood carving. The decent prices are clearly marked so there's no need to bargain.

Lanka Hands at 135 Bauddhaloka Mawatha, Bambalapitiya (Col 4), has a good variety of local crafts including jewellery, brightly painted wooden toys and puzzles, cane and basketry, drums, brasswork and more. Prices are reasonable. The store is open from 9.30 am to 6.30 pm daily. Lakpahana, 21 Rajakeeya Mawatha, Cinnamon Gardens (Col 7), also has a good range from which to choose, including lacework, jewellery, batik, tea and masks.

Hand-Loom Fabrics

Barefoot, 704 Galle Rd, Kollupitiya (Col 3), is very popular, especially among expats, for its bright hand-loomed textiles fashioned into bedspreads, cushions and serviettes (or you can buy by the metre). You'll also find irresistible soft toys, lampshades, textile-covered notebooks and albums, and a large selection of stylish, simple clothing downstairs. The items are quite pricey but of uniformly good quality.

Another place for fabrics is The Oasis Company at 18 Station Rd, Bambalapitiya (Col 4). Here you'll find similar fare to Barefoot but some of the textiles are block-printed; there are carpets too. Kandygs Handloom House at 333 Galle Rd, Kollupitiya (Col 3) has a selection of hand-painted cotton and jute bed spreads, wall hangings, rugs and more.

Clothing

Sri Lanka is a major garment manufacturer and all manner of clothing, from beach wear to warm padded jackets, is easy to find in Colombo. Many of the items are Western-style clothes – you'd be able to find them in department stores all over the world – while others, fortunately, you'll only find here. Either way, clothing is decently priced and you should be able to forage yourself plenty of bargains.

Shop with the glamorous at Odel Unlimited at 5 Alexandra Place, Cinnamon Gardens (Col 7). It's open from 10 am to 7 pm daily except Sunday, when it closes at 3 pm. You'll find everything from homeware, designer-label clothing and sports wear to banana soap.

Levi's, in Liberty Plaza, stocks Levi's jeans, as its name suggests. Cotton Collection, at 40 Sir Ernest de Silva Mawatha, Cinnamon Gardens (Col 7), is a good place to shop for T-shirts, jackets, children's clothing and summer dresses. Next door, Dilly's has stylish dresses made with delicate (read pricey) fabrics. Closeby, Leather Collection has heaps of fashionable women's sandals and handbags.

You'll find many clothing stores along RA de Mel Mawatha. House of Fashion has a popular store close to Dickman's Rd; Fashion Bug and Rohan's are chaotic stores popular with locals – they're much cheaper than Odel Unlimited.

Collectibles

Serendib at 36 1/1 Rosmead Place, Cinnamon Gardens (Col 7), sells sculpture, paintings, rare Sri Lankan maps, prints, books, antique furniture and porcelain. You will find similar wares at Paradise Road at 213 Dharmapala Mawatha, Colombo 7.

Paradise Road's other outlets (Gallery Cafe, Hilton JAIC Tower shopping mall, Trans Asia shopping gallery) sell selected delectable collectibles; it's a good place to look for small gifts to take home. Kandyan Antiques at 36 Sir Ernest de Silva Mawatha, Cinnamon Gardens (Col 7) and 106 Bauddhaloka Mawatha, Bambalapitiya (Col 4) has heaps of items – some junky, others funky – though they're not prepared to bargain much. Under the dust at Cutprice Sales, 20 RA de Mel Mawatha, Bambalapitiya (Col 4), you'll find oddities, colonial furniture, lampshades and more. If you're into antique jewellery, a reader has recommended the shops along Chatham St in Fort.

Tea

Sri Lankan tea comes in all sorts of interesting packages and all sorts of flavours. You can export up to 3kg of tea duty free. Mlesna Tea Centre, at Majestic City, Liberty Plaza, Crescat Boulevard and the Hilton, is a well-known outlet for quality products. The Sri Lanka Tea Board at 574 Galle Rd, Kollupitiya (Col 3), also has a good selection.

Gems

You'll find gem dealers along Galle Rd, RA de Mel Mawatha and in Sea St, Pettah (Col 11). The State Gem Corporation has its free testing centre on the 2nd floor, 310 Galle Rd. It's open from 9.30 am to 12.30 pm and 1 to 5.30 pm Monday to Friday. Zam Gems, popular with foreigners, has a gem and jewellery showroom at 81 Galle Rd, Bambalapitiya (Col 4) and outlets in the Lanka Oberoi Hotel, Trans Asia Hotel and the Hilton. Check out its Web site at www.zamgems.com. There's also Stone 'n' String in Kollupitiya (Col 3) at 275 RA de Mel Mawatha and Crescat Boulevard; Ceylinco Gem & Jewellery Salon at 15A Alfred Place, Kollupitiya (Col 3); and The Bullion Exchange at 521 Galle Rd, Bambalapitiya, Col 4).

Other Items

Select a dinner set from the exported quality porcelain at Lanka Ceramics, 696 Galle Rd, Kollupitya (Col 3). Or if you're after something different, the doll houses from Eclar Toys (☎ 671925) at 36/10–1/1 Rosmead Place, Cinnamon Gardens (Col 7) are particularly noteworthy. You must call to make an appointment if you wish to buy a house. Check out the Web site at www.eclartoys.com.

See Shopping in the Facts for the Visitor chapter for information on other good buys.

GETTING THERE & AWAY

Colombo is the gateway to Sri Lanka from abroad, and is also the centre of the island's bus and rail networks. See the Getting Around chapter for general information on buses and trains.

You may find leaving Colombo by train is easier than by bus, though trains are usually less frequent and a little more expensive than bus services. There's more order at the train station than at the bus stations, and often less overcrowding on board.

Information on transport to/from particular towns and cities is given in the relevant regional sections.

Air

The international airport is at Katunayake, 30km north of the city and 2km east of the Colombo-Negombo road. The airport is subject to heavy security. Information on flights in and out of Colombo is given in the Getting There & Away chapter.

For arrivals, departures and other airport information, call ☎ 073-5555 or ☎ 073-2677. Don't forget to save Rs 500 for the departure tax.

For details on accommodation near the airport see the Airport Area listings under Places to Stay earlier in this chapter.

For information about transport to/from the airport (including to/from Negombo and farther afield), see the Getting Around section following.

Airline offices in Colombo include:

Aeroflot (☎ 671201) 7A Sir Ernest de Silva Mawatha, Cinnamon Gardens, Col 7
Air France (☎ 327605) 2 Galle Face Hotel Shopping Village, Galle Rd, Kollupitiya, Col 3
Air India (☎ 325832) YMBA Bldg, 108 Sir Baron Jayatilaka Mawatha, Fort, Col 1
AOM French Airlines (☎ 435597) 323 Union Place, Slave Island, Col 2
Bangladesh Airlines (☎ 565391) 4 Mile Post Ave, Kollupitiya, Col 3
British Airways (☎ 320231) Trans Asia Hotel, 115 Chittampalam Gardiner Mawatha, Slave Island, Col 2
Canadian Airlines (☎ 348100) 11A York St, Fort Col 1
Cathay Pacific Airways (☎ 334145–7) 186 Vauxhall St, Slave Island, Col 2
Emirates (☎ 300200) 9th floor, Hemas Bldg, 75 Braybrooke Place, Slave Island, Col 2
Gulf Air (☎ 434662) 11 York St, Fort, Col 1
Indian Airlines (☎ 326844) 4 Bristol St, Fort, Col 1
Japan Airlines (☎ 300315) 6th floor, EML Bldg, 61 WAD Ramanayake Mawatha, Slave Island, Col 2
KLM Royal Dutch Airlines (☎ 439747) GSA Carsons Airline Services, 29 Braybrooke St, Slave Island, Col 2
Korean Air (☎ 449773) 7th floor, East Tower, World Trade Centre, Echelon Square, Fort, Col 1
Lufthansa (☎ 300501) EML Bldg, WAD Ramanayake Mawatha, Slave Island, Col 2
Malaysia Airlines (☎ 342291) Hemas Bldg, 81 York St, Fort, Col 1
Pakistan International Airlines (☎ 573475) 342 Galle Rd, Kollupitiya, Col 3
Royal Nepal Airlines (☎ 565391) 4 Mile Post Ave, Kollupitiya, Col 3
Singapore Airlines (☎ 300741) 315 Vauxhall St, Slave Island, Col 2
SriLankan Airlines (☎ 073-5555, reconfirmation ☎ 073-5500) 22–01 East Tower, World Trade Centre, Echelon Square, Fort, Col 1
Swissair (☎ 435403) Taj Samudra Hotel Shopping Arcade, 25 Galle Face Centre Rd, Kollupitiya, Col 3
Thai Airways International (☎ 438050) Ceylon Intercontinental Hotel, 48 Janadhipathi Mawatha, Fort, Col 1
United Airlines (☎ 346026) United Holidays, 06–02 East Tower, World Trade Centre, Echelon Square, Fort, Col 1

Bus

Colombo has three main bus stations, or rather yards, all on the south edge of Pettah, a few minutes' walk east of Fort train station. The most important, and the most chaotic, is the Bastian Mawatha station, where you catch buses to, among other places, Kandy, Nuwara Eliya, Trincomalee, Ambalangoda, Hikkaduwa, Galle, Matara, Tangalla, Kataragama and the airport (No 187). The buses to Negombo, Ratnapura, Kurunegala, Haputale, Badulla, Anuradhapura and Polonnaruwa leave from the Saunders Place station. The Central Bus Station on Olcott Mawatha is where many suburban buses start and stop, and is quite orderly. The stations have information kiosks, but always double check anything they tell you.

Train

The main train station, Colombo Fort, is within walking distance of the city centre. See the 'Main Trains from Fort' boxed text for details of services.

A tourist information office (☎ 440048), which is actually a branch office of JF Tours, is located at the front of the station. It's open from 9 am to 4.30 pm Monday to Saturday and the staff can tell you most of what you need to know about schedules, booking and so on. Or you could try the helpful information desk (at desk No 10) at the station. Keep your cool: Fort station is crawling with touts waiting to hook you up with their 'uncle's' hotel down the coast.

GETTING AROUND
To/From the Airport

Taxis and buses are the most convenient forms of transport to and from the airport.

If you're arriving in the dead of the night it's best to book a room and let the hotel or guesthouse know what time you'll be arriving. They should be able to organise a driver to pick you up from the airport, though it's easy enough to jump in a taxi.

If you want to take a bus, walk to the end of the platform and turn right. Cross the road and you'll see a sign indicating where the airport bus stops (it's not far from the toilet and restaurant). It's an air-con bus:

Main Trains from Fort

destination	departure time	fare (Rs) 3rd	2nd	1st class	approx duration (hrs)
Anuradhapura	5.45 am, 2.05 pm	42	116	277	8
Anuradhapura *Intercity Express*	3.55 pm	-	115	250	4½
Badulla *Podi Menike* via Kandy	5.55 am	60	165.50	339*	9
Badulla *Udarata Menike* via Peradeniya Junction, not Kandy	9.45 am	60	165.50	339*	9
Badulla *Night Mail*	7.40, 10 pm	60	165.50	289	9
Kandy *Intercity Express* via Peradeniya	7 am, 3.35 pm	-	72	122*	2½
Kandy via Rambukkana for elephant orphanage	10.30 am, 12.40 pm 4.55, 5.55, 7.40 pm	25	68.50	-	3
Matara via Bentota, Hikkaduwa, Galle	7, 9, 10.15 am, 2.05**, 4, 5 pm	33	89	-	4
Negombo	4.30, 5.20, 6, 8.25, 9.25 am, 1.45, 2.45, 5.20, 5.35, 5.38, 6.20 pm	11	26	-	2
Polonnaruwa	6.10, 10.05 am	53.50	147	331	6 to 9
Trincomalee	6.10, 10.05 am	61	168	-	8

* First-class observation saloon fare includes a booking fee of Rs 50
** On Saturday only 3rd class is available

The first departure is at 4.30 am and there are departures approximately every half hour till 11 pm. The fare to Colombo is Rs 25 – the bus terminates in Pettah (Col 11) at the Bastian Mawatha bus station. There is no bus directly to Negombo from the airport but you can catch the air-con bus to Katunayake junction (Rs 6) from where you can catch a Negombo-bound bus (Rs 15 for an intercity express). Buses from Negombo head to the airport every 15 minutes from about 5 am to 9 pm. The trip takes about 45 minutes. Buses to the airport from Colombo (Bus No 187, Rs 25) depart from the Bastian Mawatha station during daylight hours.

It's possible, although not particularly convenient, to catch a commuter train to Colombo: The station is near the turn-off from the main road, but is a bit of a hike (500m) from the terminal. This is inadvisable after dark.

If you want a taxi, head to the Ceylon Tourist Board's information desk (open 24 hours), in the first arrivals hall after you exit through customs, and find out the latest fixed rates. At the time of writing a one-way fare was Rs 900 (40 minutes to 1½ hours) to Colombo; Rs 500 (20 minutes) to Negombo; and Rs 2700 (two to three hours) to Kandy. Armed with this information, after you've exited the second arrivals hall full of hotel and hire-car agencies (see the boxed text 'Warning' later in this chapter), you'll be pounced on by an army of taxi drivers – take your pick, as you know what to pay. Taxis *to* the airport cost: Rs 1200 from Colombo, Rs 550 from Negombo and Rs 3000 from Kandy.

Avoid taking a three-wheeler between the airport and Colombo; it's a long, miserable journey and you'll be sucking in exhaust fumes all the way. Three-wheeler fares to/from Negombo should be around Rs 350 (30 minutes). Three-wheelers may not pick up passengers from the terminal but you can pick one up on the road outside the airport. If you are going to the airport late at night you are advised not to take a three-wheeler. Unaccompanied women in particular should not do this; the road is long and lonely. To be safe, take a taxi instead.

Bus

The *A-Z Street Guide* (see Maps under Orientation earlier in this chapter) has useful information on bus routes, as does *Travel Lanka*. CTB and private buses operate parallel services. A timetable is not necessary – the buses can hardly be described as running to one. Buses going

down Galle Rd from Fort or Pettah, include Nos 100, 101 and 400 and can be picked up at the Central Bus Station. While there are supposedly fixed fares on buses, you may come across minor variations in price. From Fort to Dehiwala down Galle Rd should be about Rs 6.

Private semiluxury and luxury buses are a recent addition to the Galle Rd service. There is no apparent timetable, and they are far fewer than the regular buses. Sometimes they have a sign in English in the front window. Generally they have curtains and soft seats. The fare is about twice that for ordinary buses, but still a bargain, really.

Women may want to check out Bus Travel under Dangers & Annoyances earlier in this chapter.

Train

You can use the train for reaching the suburbs dotted along Galle Rd – Kollupitiya, Bambalapitiya, Wellawatta, Dehiwala and Mt Lavinia – and avoid the smog, noise and hassle of bus travel. Timetables are clearly marked at the stations though if you just turn up you shouldn't have to wait long. If you board the train at Fort train station, double check it stops all stations or you may end up speeding to Galle before you'd planned to. Train fares are fixed and usually marginally lower than bus fares.

Taxi

Some taxis are metered but often the driver won't use the meter and you must bargain for the fare – do this *before* you get in. A taxi from Fort train station to the Galle Face Hotel (a little over 2km) should be about Rs 100, and to Mt Lavinia should cost around Rs 450.

A less-fraught alternative is using one of Colombo's radio cab companies, the best-known being Quick Radio Cabs (☎ 588588), also known as Kangaroo Cabs, and GNTC (☎ 688688). Both have air-con cars with electronic meters and charge Rs 40 per kilometre. There is a discount of 40% for a 60km-plus return trip.

Three-Wheelers

Everywhere you look you'll see a three-wheeler. As a rule of thumb, you should pay about Rs 25 per kilometre – you must bargain for the fare *before* you get in. You can expect to pay Rs 70 from Fort train station to Fort clock tower (or from the clock tower to the Galle Face Hotel), Rs 200 from Fort to Bambalapitiya and Rs 350 from Fort to Mt Lavinia. You'll often get a better price hailing a three-wheeler on the street than using one that's waiting outside a hotel or sitting at a three-wheeler stand. Don't take a three-wheeler to the airport late at night (see To/From the Airport earlier in this section).

West Coast

The west coast is Sri Lanka's tan-seekers, tourists and touts haunt, with long strips of palm-lined beaches, clear water and an abundance of touristy pleasures: outdoor restaurants, tasty food, buzzing bars...

This chapter covers Puttalam and Chilaw, two towns of minimal interest but often used as stopovers between Anuradhapura (part of the ancient cities) and Colombo; Negombo (about 36km north of Colombo, close to the international airport); and the area south of Colombo including Kalutara, Beruwela, Bentota, Aluthgama, Induruwa, Ahungala, Ambalangoda and Hikkaduwa.

The west coast is at its best from around December to March. From May to August the south-west monsoon makes it less palatable than being in the east. Most accommodation is concentrated in a few touristy towns along the coast, but there are also many small guesthouses and hotels scattered in secluded spots between the larger centres.

Anywhere on this coast you have to watch out for dangerous currents, undertows and rip tides. These may be more likely with the bigger seas in the wet season from April/May to October/November, but you should take care at any time of year. Watch where other people are swimming and if in any doubt keep asking reliable people; see the boxed text 'Safe Swimming' for tips. Pollution is another deterrent to swimming in some places – the farther you are from town centres, and from Colombo, the better.

PUTTALAM & AROUND
☎ 032

Puttalam has little to interest tourists (or anyone for that matter), but you may pass through if you're travelling from Anuradhapura to Colombo, or vice versa. The turn-off to Talawila and Kalpitiya is nearby. There's a well-preserved Dutch fort dating from 1670, and St Peter's Kirk, with a gabled entrance and distinctive Dutch columns, as well as an old graveyard. At **Talawila**, there's a Roman Catholic shrine to St Anne.

> ### Highlights
>
> - Bicycling along Negombo's Dutch canals; breaking for lunch at a beachside restaurant
> - Lolling on the beach, lapping up the sun, living it up at Bentota
> - Surfing the surf or busting the boogie board, and maybe doing some diving at Hikkaduwa
> - Watching the *kolam* dancers strut their stuff at Ambalangoda; buying a grotesque devil dancer's mask there (and wishing you hadn't)

The church features satinwood pillars and is pleasantly situated on the seafront. Thousands of pilgrims come here in March and July when the major festivals to St Anne are held. The festivals include huge processions, healing services and a fair.

The small fishing village of Kalpitiya is the home of many refugees – it has seen much unrest and some violence over the years and it's off limits from time to time. There's no accommodation. Check with your embassy before venturing up there; even when it's accessible, there are many roadblocks.

In Puttalam, there is a ***resthouse (☎/fax 65299)*** near the council park. The basic rooms cost Rs 1000 per single or double, add Rs 800 for air-con. An alternative is the ***Senatilake Guest Inn (☎ 65403, 81A Kurunegala Rd)***, which has eight reasonable rooms from Rs 550 to 1350 for a room with air-con.

The road between Puttalam and Chilaw is terrible at the best of times, and often impassable during wet weather.

WILPATTU NATIONAL PARK

Wilpattu, 26km north of Puttalam and covering 1085 sq km, is Sri Lanka's largest park, and used to be the most visited until the ethnic violence closed it in 1985. There has been intermittent talk of a reopening,

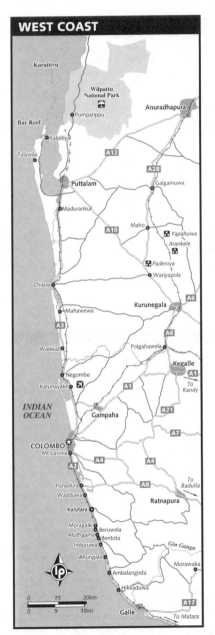

WEST COAST

but nothing is definite. It is probably the best spot in Sri Lanka to see leopards. The park also has less glamorous residents: sloth bears, deer, many species of birds and more.

CHILAW
☎ 032

Chilaw has little going for it except a lively market, its strong Roman Catholic flavour and a rather interesting Hindu temple, **Munneswaram**, 5km to the east of the town. The temple is an important centre of pilgrimage. There are three shrines at this complex, the central one being to Shiva. A major festival occurs in August, when devotees test their faith by walking on red-hot coals. About 12km to the north of Chilaw is another important temple, **Udappuwa**. This seaside structure also features a complex of three temples. A colourful festival featuring fire-walking is held here in August.

There's very little accommodation in Chilaw. The *resthouse (☎/fax 22299)* has 16 overpriced rooms (singles and doubles cost the same): Rs 750 for no frills, Rs 1000 for rooms with views, and Rs 1250 for air-con. Rice and curry costs Rs 220. The *New Hawaii Hotel*, opposite the bus station, has delicious food for just Rs 40 for rice and curry or Rs 80 for fried rice.

Chilaw is easily visited on a day trip from Negombo (expect to pay around Rs 1500 for the taxi). Buses also run frequently along this route. You may find that the pretty scenery along this coastal road – fishing villages, toddy tappers and coconut palms – is the best part of the trip. Alternatively, there are frequent buses between Kurunegala and Chilaw.

NEGOMBO
☎ 031

Negombo's beach is a disappointment compared with Hikkaduwa and other fine beaches in the country such as Mirissa, Tangalla or Nilaveli (on the east coast). It is long, but often narrow and grubby. One of the better stretches of this beach is in the Browns Beach Hotel area – and with the sea rarely clean enough for a swim, outsiders can use the good pool at this hotel for a fee.

Safe Swimming

Every year drownings occur off Sri Lanka's beaches. If you aren't an experienced swimmer or surfer it's easy to underestimate the dangers – or even be totally unaware of them. There are few full-time life-saving patrols as there are in places such as Australia, so there's usually no-one to jump in and rescue you. A few common sense rules should be observed:

• Don't swim out of your depth. If you are a poor swimmer, always stay in the shallows.
• Don't stay in the water until you are exhausted.
• Never go swimming under the influence of alcohol or drugs.
• Supervise children at *all* times.
• Watch out for currents. Water brought onto the beach by waves is sucked back to sea and this current can be strong enough to drag you out with it. This type of current is called a rip. The bigger the surf, the stronger the rip. Rips in rough surf can sometimes be seen as calm patches in the disturbed water. However, inexperienced people are not good at picking where the currents are and how strong they might be. It would pay to check with someone reliable before venturing into the water. If you do get caught in a rip, swim *across* the current if you can – *not* against it. If it's too strong for you to do this, keep afloat and raise a hand so someone onshore can see that you are in distress. A rip eventually weakens. The important thing is not to panic.
• Exercise caution when there is surf.
• Beware of coral. Coming into contact with coral can be painful for the swimmer and fatal for the coral. Always check with someone reliable if you suspect the area you're about to swim in may have coral.
• Never dive into the water. Hazards may be lurking under the surface or the water may not be as deep as it looks. It pays to be cautious.

Negombo town, bustling and historically interesting, the lagoon islands to its south and the many canals make for good exploring, but some visitors may prefer to chill out at the beachside restaurants, shops and bars.

The Dutch captured the town from the Portuguese in 1640, lost it again the same year, then captured it again in 1644. The British then took it from them in 1796 without a struggle. Negombo was one of the most important sources of cinnamon during the Dutch era, and there are still reminders of the European days.

Negombo has a reputation for gay prostitution, and Sri Lankans think of it as their AIDS capital, although the recorded number of AIDS cases in Sri Lanka is relatively low.

Orientation & Information

Many people make Negombo their last stop in Sri Lanka before flying out, as it's conveniently close to Colombo's Bandaranaike International Airport at Katunayake.

The busy centre of Negombo lies to the west of the bus and train stations. In the centre of town you'll find the post office, a Bank of Ceylon and a Vijitha Yapa Bookshop with English-language novels and magazines. Internet facilities are sprinkled around the hotels; try Prinku Tours at 49 Lewis Place or, further north, Sobana Communications.

Most places to stay in Negombo line the main road that heads north from the town centre, running almost parallel to the beach and on to Waikkal, Mahawewa, Chilaw and beyond. Closer to town the road is called Lewis Place, then Sea St. Here you'll find laid-back, cheap accommodation. Continue 1km north and the name changes to Porutota Rd; the prices increase, the hotels have multiplied (as have the room rates) and the streets are alive with souvenir shops by day and bars by night. Most top-end places are up this end of the beach strip and in Waikkal (see Around Negombo later in this chapter).

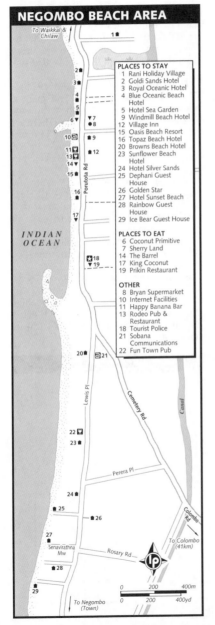

NEGOMBO BEACH AREA

To Waikkal &
Chilaw

INDIAN
OCEAN

PLACES TO STAY
1 Rani Holiday Village
2 Goldi Sands Hotel
3 Royal Oceanic Hotel
4 Blue Oceanic Beach Hotel
5 Hotel Sea Garden
9 Windmill Beach Hotel
12 Village Inn
15 Oasis Beach Resort
16 Topaz Beach Hotel
20 Browns Beach Hotel
23 Sunflower Beach Hotel
24 Hotel Silver Sands
25 Dephani Guest House
26 Golden Star
27 Hotel Sunset Beach
28 Rainbow Guest House
29 Ice Bear Guest House

PLACES TO EAT
6 Coconut Primitive
7 Sherry Land
14 The Barrel
17 King Coconut
19 Prikin Restaurant

OTHER
8 Bryan Supermarket
10 Internet Facilities
11 Happy Banana Bar
13 Rodeo Pub & Restaurant
18 Tourist Police
21 Sobana Communications
22 Fun Town Pub

Porutota Rd

Lewis Pl

Cemetery Rd

Canal

Perera Pl

Colombo Rd

To Colombo
(41km)

Senavirathna Mw

Rosary Rd

To Negombo
(Town)

0   200   400m
0   200   400yd

WEST COAST

Things to See

Close to the seafront near the lagoon mouth are the ruins of the old **Dutch fort** with its fine gateway inscribed with the date 1678. Also here is a green where cricket matches are a big attraction.

Several old Dutch buildings are still in use, including the **lagoon resthouse** on Custom House Rd. The Dutch also revealed their love of **canals** here as nowhere else in Sri Lanka. Canals extend from Negombo all the way south to Colombo and north to Puttalam; a total of over 120km. You can easily hire a bicycle in Negombo from various hotels and ride the canal-side paths for some distance.

Each day, the people of Negombo – the Karavas, fisherfolk of Indian descent – take their *oruvas* (outrigger canoes) and go out in search of the fish for which Negombo is well known. They're a fine sight as they sweep home into the lagoon after a fishing trip. Fish auctions on the beach and fish sales in the market near the fort are common – the shark catch is brought in to the beach in the early afternoon. The catch is not all from the open sea: Negombo is at the northern end of a lagoon that is well known for its lobsters, crabs and prawns. If you're hanging around the markets you won't have to wait long before you're invited to go out on an oruva or another kind of vessel. Expect to pay around Rs 500 per boat per hour. A **Fishers' Festival** is held here in late July.

Negombo is dotted with churches – so successfully were the Karavas converted to Catholicism that today the town is often known as 'little Rome'. **St Mary's Church** in the town centre has very good ceiling paintings by a local artist. The **Angurukaramulla Temple**, east of town, with its 6m-long reclining Buddha is also worth seeing. A three-wheeler from Lewis Place should cost Rs 250 for the return trip. The island of **Duwa**, joined to Negombo by the lagoon bridge, is famed for its Easter passion play.

Small villages dot the coast to the north and south, and these can be reached by bicycle. Across the lagoon bridge there's a second fish market. If you can stagger out of bed at 6 am, it's a good place to watch the fishing boats returning with their catches.

The road over the lagoon bridge continues along a small coastal road between lagoon and ocean almost all the way to Colombo.

Places to Stay – Budget & Mid-Range

Town & Airport Towards the airport is *Mr Srilal Fernando's* (☎ 22481, 67 Parakrama Rd, Kurana). The six clean singles/doubles go for Rs 450/550. The family will pick you up or drop you off at the airport or Kurana bus stop. Ring to find out how much (if anything) they charge for this. You can also take a Colombo-Negombo bus (No 240; get off at the RAC Motors Kurana bus stop and walk east 1km from the main road).

If you're desperate for air-con but lacking cash, the *New Rest House* (☎ 22299, 14 Circular Rd) in town has grungy cheap air-con rooms for Rs 950/1050. What it lacks in cleanliness, it makes up for in fading colonial charm.

Lewis Place Area The *Rainbow Guest House* (☎ 22082, 3 Carron Place) has five clean, quaint rooms at Rs 450/550, but they adjoin a function hall, so it could be noisy on the night of a wedding reception.

Golden Star (☎ 38689, 104 Lewis Place) has 12 clean singles or doubles, charging Rs 500 for the small rooms or Rs 1000 for rooms with a balcony. There are views from the rooftop and the family that runs the place is superfriendly.

Hotel Silver Sands (☎ 22880, 229 Lewis Place) looks like it would feel more at home in Morocco with its arched walkways and central courtyard garden. There's a restaurant fronting the beach. The 15 rooms have their own balcony or patio for Rs 500 to 880 for singles or doubles. Bicycle hire is Rs 75 per day.

The *Dephani Guest House* (☎ 34359, fax 38225, 189/15 Lewis Place) has 12 clean spacious rooms, some with colonial-style furnishings. Downstairs rooms cost Rs 550, or upstairs rooms with balcony cost Rs 850. There's a pretty garden opening onto the beach and a restaurant that, unfortunately, serves terrible food.

Sunflower Beach Hotel (☎/fax 38154, 289 Lewis Place) is a circular building with wedge-shaped rooms costing Rs 1800/2000. The rooms are clean, though dated, and there's a swimming pool (Rs 150 for nonguests).

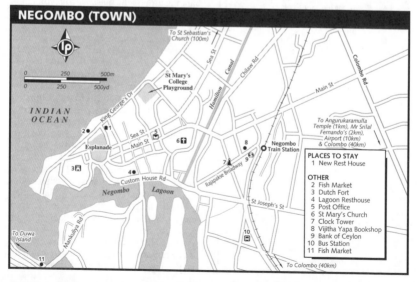

NEGOMBO (TOWN)

INDIAN OCEAN

To St Sebastian's Church (100m)

St Mary's College Playground

To Angurukaramulla Temple (1km), Mr Srilal Fernando's (2km), Airport (10km) & Colombo (40km)

Negombo Train Station

Negombo Lagoon

To Duwa Island

To Colombo (40km)

PLACES TO STAY
1 New Rest House

OTHER
2 Fish Market
3 Dutch Fort
4 Lagoon Resthouse
5 Post Office
6 St Mary's Church
7 Clock Tower
8 Vijitha Yapa Bookshop
9 Bank of Ceylon
10 Bus Station
11 Fish Market

Ice Bear Guest House (☎/fax 33862, [e] *GAHicebear@aol.com, 103/2 Lewis Place)* is a gorgeous traditional villa set in a leafy garden opening onto the beach. There are five homely rooms; four of them cost Rs 1800 each for a single or double, while the air-con room costs Rs 2300.

Jetwing's *Hotel Sunset Beach (☎ 22350, fax 074-870623, 5 Senavirathna Mawatha)* has a scrap of lawn and a beachfront pool. The rooms, all of which have sea views, are US$33 to US$40 for singles or doubles. It's a sparkling white, busy place but it is lacking in character.

Porutota Rd Area The *Village Inn (20A Porutota Rd)* has three 'rooms', which are in reality spacious, comfortable, clean three-room suites each with a big double bed and sitting/dressing rooms. They're great value at Rs 600 per 'room'.

Windmill Beach Hotel (☎ 79572, fax 79323, [e] priyan1@lanka.ccom.lk), which is virtually next door to the Village Inn, has bare singles/doubles for Rs 700/800; air-con costs an addional Rs 500. It's good value for the area and there's a quaint garden restaurant.

The *Oasis Beach Resort (☎ 79526, fax 79022, 31 Porutota Rd)* is terrifyingly ugly, but it does have cheap, though slightly musty-smelling, air-con rooms for Rs 1650/1750 and the added bonus of a swimming pool.

Topaz Beach Hotel (☎ 79265, fax 075-310329, 21 Porutota Rd) has air-con rooms for Rs 1400/2000. Some rooms are a little grimy – the air-con rooms are OK value, but don't get sucked into staying in the standard rooms.

Rani Holiday Village (☎ 074-870718, fax 031-79289, 154/9 Porutota Rd, Palangathurai, Kochchikade) has modern self-contained villas in a garden setting. A double-room villa with hot water and a kitchen (with fridge) costs Rs 2200 a day for doubles. Villas (without a kitchen) cost Rs 1900 a day for singles, and a villa with two bedrooms costs Rs 3800 a day. Discounts are available for long stayers.

Close to the Village Inn, you'll find *Hotel Sea Garden (☎ 22150, fax 79999,* [e] *jethot@sri.lanka.net)*, another one of Jetwing's hotels. The rooms are clean but without air-con; some have balconies directly looking on to the beach while others towards the back of the hotel are cramped. Rooms cost a rip-off Rs 2800 for singles/ doubles during the high season, but they're good value at other times. Guests have free use of the pool at the nearby Blue Oceanic Beach Hotel (see Places to Stay – Top End following).

Places to Stay – Top End

Goldi Sands Hotel (☎ 79021, fax 79227, [e] *goldi@eureka.lk)* is a no-frills hotel with friendly staff and air-con rooms for US$37/43. The clean rooms have a balcony and garden or beach views. There's also a pool (Rs 115 for nonguests).

The busy *Browns Beach Hotel (☎ 22031/2, fax 24303, [e] ashmres@lanka .ccom.lk, 175 Lewis Place)* has spotless air-con rooms with sea views (great showers) and a balcony for US$62/80. There's a private beach area, heaps of facilities and a lunch buffet (Rs 500) and live music on Sunday.

Jetwing's *Royal Oceanic Hotel (☎ 790 003, fax 79999, [e] jethot@sri.lanka.net)* has air-con rooms from US$56 to US$105 for a lavish suite. The spacious rooms have polished floorboards, a balcony and handicraft decorations. There's a pool and a beach disco on Friday and Saturday nights.

Blue Oceanic Beach Hotel (☎ 79000-3, [e] *jethot@sri.lanka.net)* is also managed by Jetwing. The air-con rooms cost US$105 for a single or double – it's grossly overpriced.

Places to Eat & Drink

For a cheap feed, join the locals for the delicious *kotthu rotty* (rotty chopped up with vegetables, eggs or meat) at the Hotel Sea Garden; it costs Rs 20 to 50. The chef starts cooking in the early evenings.

Coconut Primitive (☎ 79706, 55 Porutota Rd) has a laid-back, undercover restaurant beside the beach. Vegetarian meals cost around Rs 240, pizza costs Rs 230 and you can wash it all down with a beer for Rs 140.

It's open from 8 am to midnight, and there's usually music in the evening.

King Coconut (11 Porutota Rd) is a lively, popular spot beside the beach. You can just have a drink (Carlsberg Rs 130, Lion Lager Rs 110), a snack (eg, French fries) or a meal. There's a proper pizza oven (pizzas from Rs 190), as well as a good range of seafood (baked crab Rs 260) and the ubiquitous rice and curry (Rs 250). It's open from 8 am to midnight.

At *The Barrel (☎ 077-347563, 33 Porutota Rd)* you'll enjoy delicious food such as devilled fish at Rs 180 or fried rice for Rs 120, all in a beachfront setting. If you indulge on a very long lunch you can join the busy bar crowd for a sunset beer (Rs 130).

The *Prikin Restaurant (10 Porutota Rd)* has cooks trained under a chef from Beijing who concoct good Chinese, Sri Lankan and Western-style dishes. The service can be slow, but the sweet-and-sour dishes (between Rs 270 and Rs 380) are delicious and there's an undercover eating area.

Although *Sherry Land (☎ 78618, 74 Porutota Rd)* lacks a beachfront spot, it makes up for it by having a pretty garden setting (bring insect repellent), attentive service and tasty food. Rice and curry is Rs 165 and prawn dishes cost around Rs 260.

For a late night drink, try the *Fun Town Pub (295 Lewis Place)* with its cheap beer (Lion for Rs 90, Carlsberg for Rs 110) and loud Western music. The *Happy Banana Bar* and *Rodeo Pub & Restaurant*, both on Porutota Rd, also kick on to the small hours.

The major hotels are good places for stuff-your-face buffets: the Browns Beach Hotel's lunch buffet has been recommended. Prices are around Rs 500.

Getting There & Away

Bus & Train Private and Ceylon Transport Board (CTB) buses as well as intercity express buses run between Colombo (Saunders Place, Pettah) and Negombo every 20 minutes or so (Rs 10 for a CTB bus, No 240; Rs 25 for an express). The first bus goes at 5 am, the last leaves at 10.30 pm. The trip takes about an hour by express bus. Long queues form at Negombo bus station

on weekend evenings as day-trippers return to the capital. There are also trains for Rs 15 (3rd class), but they're slower (two hours) and rarer than the buses.

Buses to Kandy start at 5.30 am and run on the half hour until 7.30 am, while afternoon buses leave at 1.30, 2.30 and sometimes 3.45 pm. CTB buses cost Rs 35 (four hours), express buses charge Rs 80 (three hours).

Taxi You can get a taxi between Negombo and Colombo for about Rs 1600. Any hotel, guesthouse or travel agent will arrange a taxi for you.

Getting Around

To/From the Airport One of Negombo's most useful roles is as a transit point to/from the Bandaranaike International Airport at Katunayake, and airport transport is cheaper from Negombo than from Colombo. Private and CTB buses (Rs 6, both are bus No 270) run every 15 minutes from about 5 am to 9 pm. The trip takes about 45 minutes. A taxi costs about Rs 400 from the bus station (south-east of town) and Rs 500 from Lewis Place; the trip takes about 20 minutes. A three-wheeler is about half those prices.

Bus & Three-Wheeler To get from the bus station to Lewis Place or Porutota Rd, catch a Kochchikade-bound bus. A three-wheeler will cost about Rs 100 to the middle of Lewis Place from either the bus or train station.

Bicycle A rented bicycle is good for a leisurely look around Negombo, along the canals or over the lagoon bridge to the islands. Many guesthouses rent bicycles for Rs 100 a day.

AROUND NEGOMBO
☎ 031

North of Negombo, houses are dotted among jungle, palm trees and farmland. At Waikkal, 12km north of Negombo, there's a handful of top-end hotels. These are isolated options: perfect for travellers seeking quiet respite, and a nightmare for those wanting to kick up in the bars of Negombo. The sea, in these parts, is lined by a rocky embankment, so there are no beaches to speak of.

About 15km to the north of Negombo, at Wilagedera, Gonawilla, is the **Netherlands Welcome Village** (☎ 99785, e fhp@eureka.lk). Some 100 traditional Dutch houses were built here in 1996 with funding initiated by a Dutch expat. The inhabitants are elderly homeless people gathered from all over Sri Lanka. There's no entrance fee, but donations are welcome. It's open from 8 am to 4.30 pm daily. From Negombo, a three-wheeler should cost Rs 800 for the return trip.

Thirty kilometres north along the coast from Negombo is **Mahawewa**, a village renowned for its batiks.

Places to Stay

Ging Oya Lodge (☎ 77822, fax 01-252587, e gingoya@sri.lanka.net) oozes charm with handicraft decorations and colonial furnishings – it's run by a Belgian expat. Air-con cabanas cost US$40 for singles or doubles. There are 10 cabanas (all spotless), plus a pool, bar, restaurant and playroom (table tennis, darts etc). Ging Oya is on the river, a 10-minute walk from the beach. Canoes and kayaks are available to guests free of charge.

Club Hotel Dolphin (☎ 33129, fax 01-253504, e dolphin@slt.lk) has 73 rooms and 50 cottages with air-con for US$45/55 for singles/doubles. There's a gigantic pool and a palm-studded lawn, but the hotel looks a little weather beaten.

Ranweli Holiday Village (☎ 22136, fax 77358, e ranweli@sri.lanka.net) has air-con rooms for US$60 a single/double. Most of the rooms are in separate bungalows with a small lounge, balcony and lagoon or sea views. The hotel promotes itself as an 'eco-friendly resort' and offers activities such as meditation and bird and flora spotting.

KALUTARA & WADDUWA
☎ 034

Kalutara, 42km south of Colombo, was once an important spice-trading centre controlled at various times by the Portuguese, Dutch and British. Today it has a reputation for fine **basketware** (visit Basket Hall) and also for the best mangosteens on the island.

Immediately south of the Kalu Ganga bridge on the main road is the **Gangatilaka Vihara**, which has a hollow dagoba (Buddhist shrine) with an interesting painted interior. By the roadside there's a small shrine and bodhi tree where drivers often stop to make offerings to ensure a safe journey. Wadduwa is 8km north of Kalutara.

Places to Stay

Kalutara and Wadduwa have beaches and a number of mid-range and top-end places to stay. But there's little to halt the individual traveller en route to more laid-back beach spots farther south.

Hibiscus Beach Hotel (☎ 22704-6, fax 22405, e ashmres@lanka.ccom.lk, Mahawaskaduwa, Kalutara North) is nothing fancy. Its basic singles/doubles (without air-con) cost US$30/43. The hotel is right on the beachfront.

Tangerine Beach Hotel (☎ 22982/3, fax 26794, e tanbch@sltnet.lk, de Abrew Rd, Waskaduwa, Kalutara North) is a busy and friendly place with homely air-con rooms from US$52/55. Ducks also enjoy the hotel's hospitality by inhabiting the pools in the garden.

LTI Sindbad (☎ 26537, fax 26530, St Sebastian's Rd, Katukurunda) has a great location on a spit, with one side on the beach and the other on the river. It's a creation of Geoffrey Bawa (Sri Lanka's eminent architect). The colourful rooms start at US$55/68; add US$12 for air-con.

Golden Sun Resort (☎ 28484, fax 28485, e ashmres@aitkenspence.lk, Kudawaskaduwa, Kalutara North) has spacious air-con rooms starting from US$75/85. There's a large beachside pool and a sandy garden.

The *Villa Ocean View* (☎ 32463, fax 074-299699, e villaocn@sltnet.lk, 200/1 Molligodawatte Rd, Wadduwa) resembles a minicity, with just as many facilities. It offers full-board rates (US$80/120) only for its large air-con rooms.

The Blue Water (☎ 038-35067, fax 95708, e bluewater@eureka.lk, Thalpitiya, Wadduwa) is an elegant hotel designed by Geoffrey Bawa. The chic air-con rooms start at US$120. Facilities include squash, tennis and a health club.

Royal Palms Hotel (☎ *28113-7, fax 28112,* e *tangerinetours@eureka.lk, de Abrew Rd, Kalutara North)* has immaculate air-con rooms, two executive suites and two royal suites. Rooms start at US$122/127. It has a simply stunning garden and an even more stunning swimming pool.

The respected Ayurvedic hospital at Mt Lavinia, Siddhalepa, runs the *Siddhalepa Ayurveda Health Resort* (☎ *96967, fax 96971,* e *siddalep@slt.lk)* at Wadduwa. It offers everything from stress relief to detoxification. Seven-day packages including treatment, all meals and accommodation cost US$1060/US$1880.

BERUWELA & MORAGALLE
☎ 034

Beruwela, 58km to the south of Colombo, together with Bentota farther south, has been developed into Sri Lanka's chief area of package-tour resorts. It has a long string of mid-range and top-end hotels along its fine beach, where locals address foreigners initially in German. There's little to attract independent travellers here. Moragalle is technically slightly north of Beruwela, but it's practically merged with it.

The first recorded Muslim settlement of the island took place at Beruwela in AD 1024. The Kechimalai Mosque, on a headland north of the hotel strip, is said to be built on the site of the landing and is the focus for a major festival at the end of Ramadan.

Places to Stay

The tourist hotels are all very much aimed at the package groups that come to Sri Lanka to escape from the European winter. All the hotels have various facilities including tennis and water sports. Some have Ayurvedic health centres.

Places to Stay – Budget & Mid-Range

Hotel Berlin Bear (☎ *76525, Maradana Rd, Beruwela)* has 10 basic but OK singles/doubles for Rs 580/630. It has a great beachside position, but the building has

seen better days and the pool has been taken over by slime.

Blue Lagoon Hotel (☎/*fax 76062, Galle Rd, Moragalle)* has dark but clean rooms for Rs 880/1100. Although it's nothing flash the rooms are good value given the location. Try the beachfront restaurant's mouthwatering devilled fish (Rs 230) and cheese toast (Rs 80).

Hotel Sumadal (☎ *76404, fax 76374, 61 Maradana Rd, Beruwela)* is in a lagoonside spot with an airy restaurant, 16 decent rooms for Rs 1250/1520 and hot water! Half of the rooms have a balcony overlooking the lagoon.

Ypsylon Guest House (☎ *76132, fax 76334,* e *ypsylon@slt.lk, Moragalle)* is the pick of these cheapies. It has clean rooms, a pool and a prime beachfront position. Rooms with hot water cost Rs 1500/1710 – for the room with air-con add Rs 350. The restaurant has good food, serving meals such as fish fillets (Rs 300) and baked veggies (Rs 200). The guest house also has a diving school with a German instructor.

Muthumuni Ayurveda Resort (☎ *76766, fax 76072, 16 Galle Rd, Moragalle)* has a pool, a riverside garden and large rooms for Rs 1650/2100 (add Rs 500 for air-con). A full-body massage costs Rs 1425, though two weeks of treatment costs a very scary Rs 60,000. The restaurant serves good food.

Places to Stay – Top End

Barberyn Reef Hotel (☎ *76036, fax 76037,* e *barbrese@slt.lk, Moragalle)* has more character than most of the other 'top enders'. The Barberyn's rooms start at US$40/65 for singles/doubles, including all meals (no room-only rates), plus an optional Ayurvedic cure supplement for a staggering US$230. There's no pool but it's on the waterfront.

Tropical Villas Hotel (☎ *76157, fax 01-345729,* e *tropvilla@eureka.lk, Moragalle)* on Galle Rd, has air-con rooms for US$86 for singles or doubles. There is no direct access to the beach and no pool but the rooms are stylish; each has a separate lounge, and they are set around a quiet, leafy garden.

I Do...Want to Marry in Sri Lanka

Tying the knot, getting hitched – whatever you call it, Sri Lanka is a hot destination for starry-eyed couples on their way to the altar. The palm-lined beaches and sunsets on balmy evenings seem conducive to matrimonial bliss, while also helping to kick start that saucy first wedding night!

Never slow to spot opportunity when it knocks, travel agents are clamouring to send you down the aisle in this pretty isle. There is a plethora of options ranging from simple design-your-own weddings to lavish, quasi-traditional Sri Lankan events complete with traditional wedding attire, dancers and drummers. You can arrive at your wedding on caparisoned elephants, with girls in white sprinkling frangipani flowers along the path, or you can choose to have a sandy beachside wedding, a Kandyan-style function, or one with touches of ancient tradition. The options are endless. A typical package includes airfares, accommodation, transfers, licence and legal fees, foreign-language translation, Foreign Ministry documentation, a wedding cake and outfits for the couple. Optional extras include video coverage of the event and firecrackers – the only limit is your imagination (and your budget). Connaissance de Ceylan and Walkers Tours organise weddings (for contact details see Organised tours in the Getting Around chapter), but you'll also find many travel agencies in your own country that are ready and willing to help.

▲ ▲ ▲ ▲ ▲ ▲ ▲ ▲ ▲ ▲ ▲ ▲ ▲ ▲ ▲ ▲ ▲

WEST COAST

Neptune Hotel (☎ 76031, fax 76033, e ashmres@aitkenspence.lk, Moragalle) has swish rooms starting at US$100/134. It is covered on Aitken Spence's Web site at www.aitkenspence.com.

Club Palm Garden (☎ 76039, fax 76038, e palmgdn@eureka.lk, Moragalle) is a mishmash package-tourist metropolis. Its huge rooms cost US$135/170 (full board only), which is pricey for what you get.

Riverina Hotel (☎ 76044, fax 76047, e riverina@eureka.lk, Moragalle) next door, with 192 rooms for US$100/125, is slightly better.

Getting There & Away
Beruwela is on the main Colombo to Matara railway line. See the Getting There & Away section under Bentota, Aluthgama & Induruwa following for details on getting to Beruwela and Moragalle.

BENTOTA, ALUTHGAMA & INDURUWA
☎ 034
Like Beruwela, Bentota is dominated by big package hotels, but it also has a number of smaller places catering to independent travellers. There are more such places in Aluthgama, a small town on the main road between Beruwela and Bentota.

Aluthgama has a raucous fish market, local shops and the main train station that services the whole resort area. Induruwa doesn't really have a centre – it's spread out along the coast.

Orientation & Information
Just south of the town centre of Aluthgama, the main road crosses the Bentota River into Bentota where, on its seaward side, there's the Bentota resort centre with a post office, a Bank of Ceylon, a tourist office, tourist shops and a few restaurants, all near the little-used Bentota train station. From the bridge, the river turns to flow north, parallel to the coast, for a few hundred metres, divided from the sea only by a narrow spit of land on which are built some of Bentota's top hotels (they're reachable only from the beach or by boat across the river). The river mouth is the dividing line between Bentota and Beruwela. Induruwa is 5km south of Bentota.

There are Internet facilities in the big hotels and others are sprinkled throughout the towns. Ironically, the cheapest deal you'll get is at the Taj Exotica.

Things to See
In addition to **beaches** that are as fine as Beruwela's, Bentota, like Aluthgama enjoys

the beautiful calm waters of the **Bentota River**, good for water sports. A few kilometres inland, on the south bank of the river, is the **Galapota Temple**, said to date from the 12th century. To reach it, take the side road to your left, 500m after crossing the bridge. It's signposted.

Fine beaches continue several kilometres south from Bentota. Induruwa has a small cluster of places to stay on a lovely, quiet length of beach, at the north end of which is one of the **turtle hatcheries** that you can visit in this area.

Ten kilometres inland from Bentota is the pretty **Brief Garden**. It used to be the home of Bevis Bawa, older brother of renowned Sri Lankan architect Geoffrey Bawa. Bawa's house is the highlight and the artwork on display is eclectic, including a piece from one-time house guest, Australian artist Donald Friend. The garden itself covers two hectares and is beautiful, though in places a little unkempt. Entry is Rs 125 and the garden (☎ 70462) is open from 8 am to 5 pm daily. To get there, follow the road south from Aluthgama to Matagama Rd and turn inland from there to the village of Dharga. From here there are periodic yellow signs saying 'Brief', but as everyone knows this place, it's easy enough to ask directions. You do need your own transport though – a three-wheeler from Aluthgama should cost about Rs 500 and a taxi about Rs 700 return.

Activities

The attraction of this part of the coast is the huge variety of fish (including large specimens such as barracuda), which seem unperturbed by the presence of divers. There are several **diving** outfits in Bentota and Aluthgama. For example, at Eden Roc Divers (☎ 75017, fax 75228) at the Hotel Nilwala, Aluthgama, a one-tank dive with a group, including boat hire costs US$18 with your own equipment and US$24 with equipment hired from the centre. A PADI open-water course costs US$250, while an advanced course costs US$180. Ypsylon Guest House (see Places to Stay – Budget &

Mid-Range in the Beruwela & Moragalle section earlier in this chapter) also has a diving centre. Major hotels at Bentota and Aluthgama can provide details of other diving outfits in the vicinity.

It's important to be aware of the impact of snorkelling and diving on the environment. See the boxed text 'Responsible Diving & Snorkelling' later in this chapter.

This area has plenty of opportunities for other water sports. If you'd like to try **windsurfing, water-skiing, deep-sea fishing** or virtually anything else watery, try the Fun Surf Centre (☎ 071-765029) at River Ave, Aluthgama.

Boat trips along the Bentota River are becoming popular. Most trips go for three hours and charge Rs 350 per person with a minimum of five people per boat. The farther you go upstream the better it gets; you're likely to see water monitors and some bird species. If you're closer to town you'll be avoiding rubbish and waterborne touts with trained monkeys. Make sure your boat driver doesn't get too close to the wildlife.

Places to Stay – Budget & Mid-Range

Bentota The *Hotel Susantha* (☎ 75324, *Holiday Resort Rd)* has clean, moderately sized rooms (some of which are bungalows) in a garden setting for Rs 850/950 per single/double. There's a restaurant that serves reasonably priced Western and Eastern food. It's only a short walk over the train tracks to the beach.

Palm Villa (☎/fax 70752) behind the Taj Exotica (and across the train tracks), has 14 clean rooms for Rs 1000/1200 including breakfast. Two air-con rooms (Rs 1600 each) are available. Some rooms have balcony views over the garden. It's a short walk to the beach.

Ayubowan (☎/fax 75913, **e** info@ ayubowan.ch, 171 Galle Rd, Bentota South) also isn't right beside the beach but the four large spotless bungalows are set in pretty gardens. There's also tasty food: beef with cashews (Rs 330) and Swiss-German meals. Rooms cost Rs 1500/1700 (B&B).

Aluthgama The *Terrena Lodge (☎/fax 074-289015, River Ave)* has a pretty garden leading down to a riverside seating area. The colourful, clean, slightly small rooms cost Rs 1250/1350 for B&B. You should book ahead.

Hotel Hemadan (☎/fax 75320, 25 River Ave) has 10 large, clean rooms starting from Rs 1480/1670 – more if there's a balcony. It's pricey for the standard of the rooms (no air-con) but there's a leafy courtyard and prime river viewing and it's popular with travellers.

Waterfall Garden (☎ 074-289355, 45 River Ave) also has a riverside setting. It's run by a German couple. Only half board is available and guests must book for at least three days. Rooms cost Rs 14,000/24,000 for one week. The rooms here are sparkling white and each one has a double waterbed and a porch.

Induruwa The *Long Beach Cottage (☎/fax 75773, e hanjayas@sltnet.lk, 550 Galle Rd)*, 200m north of Induruwa train station, has five clean, quaint rooms (three upstairs with shared balcony, and two downstairs) for Rs 550/660. This place has heaps going for it – a pretty sandy garden fronting on to the beach, welcoming hosts, good value rooms – but the food is bland and mozzies are a nuisance. The owners will arrange free transport from the Bentota or Aluthgama train stations if you ring.

Little Rock Cabanas (☎/fax 70184, 712 Galle Rd, Yalagama) is about 1km south of Long Beach Cottage along Galle Rd. It has two quaint timber treehouse-cabanas complete with balcony. Single or double occupancy costs Rs 1050, with discounts for people staying a month or longer. Little Rock is run by a German–Sri Lankan couple. It's right on the beach and they can also organise pony rides.

Emerald Bay Hotel (☎/fax 75363, e serenlti@sri.lanka.net), 500m south along Galle Rd, has clean, simple rooms for Rs 1750/2000 (no air-con). Each room has a porch looking on to the beach – there's also a pool (Rs 100 for nonguests).

Places to Stay – Top End

Bentota The *Hotel Serendib (☎ 75248, fax 75313, e serendib@slt.lk)* has 90 air-con singles/doubles for US$67/85. The rooms are a bit small, but each has a balcony or terrace, and the hotel's right on the beach.

Lihiniya Surf Hotel (☎ 75126, fax 75486) has air-con rooms for US$75/80 including breakfast. The rooms are clean though bland and it's also right on the beach. It's popular with British tour groups.

The *Bentota Beach Hotel (☎ 75176, fax 01-439046)* has 133 spotless rooms for US$99/124. It's right on the beach and every room has beach views from a balcony or terrace.

For a touch of colonial style there are two beautiful old villas, near the main hotel area. Train tracks run through their gardens though, so the rattle of the trains may be a problem.

About 1.5km south of town down the main road is the turn-off to *Club Villa (☎/fax 75312, 138/15 Galle Rd)*, a spacious, elegant 19th-century Dutch-style villa with a big coconut grove garden and a pool, all within a two-minute walk from the beach. The 17 rooms cost US$80 for a single or double (no air-con).

Next door to Club Villa is *The Villa (☎ 75311, fax 074-287007, e reservation@thevilla.eureka.net)*, a stunning 19th-century villa also done up in traditional style, but with discreet modern touches. Rooms are large and clean. There's also a tiny swimming pool. A single/double is US$145 and a suite US$210.

The most luxurious hotel here is arguably the *Taj Exotica (☎ 75650, fax 751 60, e exotica@sri.lanka.net)*, which is near the Bentota Beach Hotel. Rooms cost from US$160/180 for a standard to US$185/200 for 'superior' sea-view rooms. Some readers have complained of shoddy service.

Aluthgama Beruwela is so close to this area that some of the top-end hotels listed under that heading could equally suffice for Aluthgama.

Hotel Ceysands (☎ 75073, fax 75395) has a prime position, with the river on one side and the beach on the other: You arrive and leave by boat. Its clean air-con rooms go for US$99/111.

Web site: www.keells.com/hotels

Induruwa The *Induruwa Beach Resort* (☎ 75445, fax 75583, ℮ inbeachr@sltnet.lk, Kaikawala) has large, air-con rooms for US$64/68 including breakfast. There's a pool (Rs 125 for nonguests), a billiard table and more. Each room has all the mod-cons (television, minibar etc), which you'll enjoy if you don't mind the beige colour theme.

Saman Villas (☎ 75435, fax 75433, ℮ samanvil@sri.lanka.net, Aturuwella) is outrageously expensive and absolutely divine. The luxury suites start from US$188 though rates vary greatly depending on when you want to visit. There's a Japanese-style garden, great views and a superbly sited pool. The plush chalets have a private garden, a CD player, satellite television – need we say more?

Places to Eat

There is a number of eating places near the main hotel complex at Bentota. Restaurants tend to come and go and the best strategy is to ask other travellers for their recommendations. Prices are relatively uniform and generally mid-range. If you want all-you-can-eat buffets, head to the top-end hotels.

The restaurant at the *Hotel Susantha* serves reasonable Eastern and Western food including fried fish, roast chicken with vegetables, and rice and curry for moderate prices, as well as a variety of snacks.

Golden Grill has a pleasant spot beside the river, near the Bank of Ceylon, with pasta (Rs 200), sweet and sour prawns (Rs 260) and more.

Aida Restaurant & Bar with river views, is on the main road opposite the resort complex. Choose grilled prawns with garlic butter, steaks, and rice and curry at prices similar to the Golden Grill.

Getting There & Away

Bentota and Beruwela are on the main Colombo to Matara railway line, but Aluthgama, the town sandwiched between them, is the station to go to as many trains do not make stops at the smaller stations at Bentota and Beruwela. Aluthgama has five or six express trains (1½ to two hours) daily to/from Colombo (Rs 12.50 in 3rd class and Rs 34 in 2nd class), and a similar number to/from Hikkaduwa, Galle and Matara. Avoid the other, slower trains.

When you get off the train you'll hear the usual boring tales from the touts that the hotel of your choice is 'closed', 'fried' and/or 'putrid'. Just ignore them. A three-wheeler to Bentota should cost Rs 200, and to Induruwa (eg, Little Rock Cabanas) should cost around Rs 300.

Aluthgama is also the best place to pick up a bus when you're leaving, although there's no trouble getting off a bus at Bentota or Beruwela when you arrive.

AHUNGALA

Ahungala is 9km north of Ambalangoda. The only place to stay is the top-end *Triton Hotel* (☎ 09-64041, fax 64046, ℮ ashm res@lanka.ccom.lk). There are plush air-con rooms for US$85/124. Check its Web site at www.aitkenspence.com/triton.

AMBALANGODA
☎ 09

South of Bentota the road and railway run close to the continuously beautiful coast. Ambalangoda, 86km from Colombo, is a fair-sized town, but its touristy neighbour, Hikkaduwa, overshadows it as a destination. It does, however, have a beautiful sweep of sandy beach to its north, some famous **mask carvers**, whom you will find concentrated on the northern edge of town, and a bustling fish market.

MH Mettananda at 142 Patabendimulla, on the Colombo road about 500m north of the train and bus stations, is among the good mask carvers here. Another 300m towards Colombo, two sons of the famous mask carver Ariyapala each have a shop on either side of an intersection. In both shops there is a **mask museum** (entry free, but a donation is appreciated), but the Ariyapala mask-carving studio on the south side of the intersection has the better museum. A

The School of Dance

It's Saturday morning and the young students at the Ambalangoda School of Dance are being put through their paces. In the beginners' class, students bend and stretch to the sound of a drum. In a neighbouring room two older girls are following the movements of their dance teacher. They twirl and stamp to the rhythm of a song sung by a woman seated nearby. The dance over, the teacher congratulates the girls. It's an impressive effort for youngsters who've only had one class a week for less than a year.

The School of Dance, which specialises in teaching the southern forms of dance such as *kolam* (masked dance-drama) and devil dancing as well as south Indian dance, is tucked away behind a wall across the road from two major carving studios. There's a sign out front, but it's easy to miss. The school is sponsored by the Ministry of Foreign Affairs and the German government, and is run by Bandu Wijesuriya, himself a descendant of a long line of famous mask carvers. Anyone can join the classes: There's a minimal fee of Rs 50 per class for foreigners or Rs 75 per month for Sri Lankans. About 300 students are currently enrolled.

The school has many videos including a three-hour tape of southern dances with kolam performances. You may view these if you arrange to do so in advance. The school also puts on the occasional public performance – ring to find out the schedule; tickets cost around Rs 100.

Dance isn't the only art form taught at the school. Bandu Wijesuriya will teach anyone interested how to carve and paint masks, as well as traditional drumming and singing. He's also planning to open a hostel so foreign students can stay on site. For more information contact the school in person or ring ☎ 58948 or fax 58750.

former carver from this workshop has set up his own venture (Southland Masks) nearby at 353 Main St (near the Sumudu Tourist Guest House). The quality here is also good.

For **batiks**, check out those made by Dudley Silva at 53 Elpitiya Rd (there's a signpost a little past MH Mettananda's shop as you are heading towards the centre of town). **Handwoven cotton** is another of Ambalangoda's crafts.

You can also see traditional Sri Lankan dance in Ambalangoda (see the boxed text 'The School of Dance').

The Bank of Ceylon is on Main St. Go one block west from the train station, then turn right (north) and it's about 200m along.

Places to Stay & Eat

Most places are north of the centre – keep in mind that Main St is one block west of the main road.

The *Sumudu Tourist Guest House* (☎ 58832, 418 Main St, Patabendimulla), about 500m north of the Bank of Ceylon, past the post office, is a large, cool, old-style house run by a friendly family. There are six pleasant, clean rooms ranging from

Rs 600 to 700 for singles and Rs 1200 to 1400 for doubles. Meals are available. It's a 10-minute walk to the beach; a three-wheeler to/from the bus station should cost Rs 60.

Shangrela (☎ 58342, fax 59421, 38 Sea Beach Rd) is a modern, spotless place with 23 rooms. It's often used for wedding receptions so it may be noisy. Rooms in the modern wing cost Rs 800/1100 for singles/doubles and there are a few rooms in the original building for Rs 500. Or splurge on the air-con room for Rs 1500. It's right opposite the beach and meals are available.

The *resthouse* (☎ 58299) is about 300m south of the centre of town along Main St. The depressing rooms are overpriced (from Rs 800/900). But there's a reasonable restaurant so you may just want to stop for a bite to eat and a dip in the natural swimming hole beside the resthouse.

About halfway between Ambalangoda and Hikkaduwa, *Piya Nivasa* (☎ 58146) is on the main road, opposite the beach, at Akurala. If you like old-style houses, you'll love this white mansion. The six clean rooms are great value at Rs 300/350.

You can eat your meals in the family's sitting room. From Ambalangoda bus or train stations a three-wheeler should cost around Rs 200. Otherwise you can catch a Hikkaduwa-bound bus and ask the driver to let you off at the doorstep (there's no sign so look carefully for the name plaque on the house).

Go one block west from the train station to Main St, then turn right (north). After about 200m, beside the Bank of Ceylon on the right, is the *Chinese Hotel Restaurant*. Alight the rickety stairs to this fan-cooled scruffy cafeteria. Forget your surrounds, there's good food to be had. Rice and vegetable curry is Rs 55, fried prawns with soya beans are Rs 160 and chicken fried rice is Rs 95.

Getting There & Away

Ambalangoda is on the main road and railway line from Colombo to Hikkaduwa, Galle and the south. The fares from Colombo are Rs 20 by CTB bus, Rs 17.50/47.50 in 3rd/2nd class on the train. Frequent buses come through en route to/from Hikkaduwa (Rs 6.50).

HIKKADUWA & AROUND
☎ 09

Hikkaduwa, 98km south of Colombo, has long been among the most popular of Sri Lanka's beach spots. It's the variety that attracts people – accommodation ranges from a handful of top-end hotels to heaps of laid-back guesthouses stacked full of backpackers. Add to this an equally varied selection of restaurants, bars and cafes and you've got a busy, fun town. Hikkaduwa has swallowed the villages south of it and it's three or four kilometres long – spread out on either side of the road and along the beach.

There's an equally varied choice of beach and sea – coral for snorkellers, waves for board and body surfers, and good wide strips of sand, backed by cafes, if you just want to sit back and relax.

During the May to October monsoon season, many places close and the water can get quite rough.

Orientation

Services such as the train and bus stations, banks, post office and non-tourist-oriented shops congregate in the northern end of Hikkaduwa proper, which was the original settlement. Farther south is where the first tourist hotels, guesthouses and restaurants opened up, but this area now seems overdeveloped and a bit shabby compared with Wewala and Narigama, farther south again (around 2km from the stations), where most independent travellers stay. These areas are more relaxed and spread out, and have better beaches than Hikkaduwa proper. South of Narigama the waters tend to be rougher and less safe for bathing – but there are even more guesthouses scattered along the beach and road through Thiranagama and Patuwata, even as far as Dodanduwa, almost halfway to Galle.

Information

Money You can change money or travellers cheques at three banks in Hikkaduwa. The People's Bank, the Commercial Bank and the Bank of Ceylon are open 9 am to 3 pm Monday to Friday. The Bank of Ceylon also offers a safe-deposit service for tourists at a cost of Rs 550 a week. There are various moneychangers along Galle Rd that are open daily, but make sure you know the bank exchange rate beforehand, and count your money after every transaction.

Post & Communications The main post office is on the Baddegama Rd, a five-minute walk inland from the bus station. It's open from 8 am to 7 pm Monday to Saturday and 8 to 10 am Sunday. As it's a one-hour wait for an operator-connected call at the main post office, you're better off using one of the many IDD telephone bureaus in Hikkaduwa's main street. There are several places to use the Internet. Try Sri Lanka Travels & Tours at 371 Galle Rd or Tandem Guest House at 465 Galle Rd.

Books You can borrow books in numerous European languages from tourist libraries on Galle Rd. There's usually a small fee (Rs 75) per read for the book itself plus a

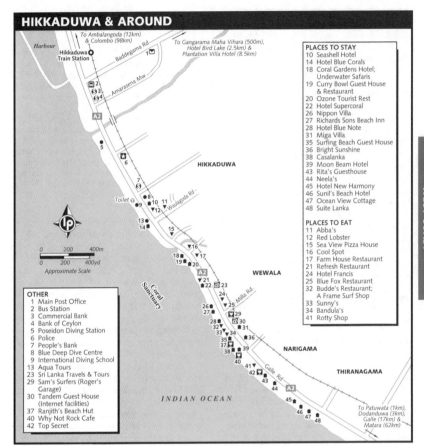

HIKKADUWA & AROUND

PLACES TO STAY
10 Seashell Hotel
14 Hotel Blue Corals
18 Coral Gardens Hotel;
   Underwater Safaris
19 Curry Bowl Guest House
   & Restaurant
20 Ozone Tourist Rest
22 Hotel Supercoral
26 Nippon Villa
27 Richards Sons Beach Inn
28 Hotel Blue Note
31 Miga Villa
35 Surfing Beach Guest House
36 Bright Sunshine
38 Casalanka
39 Moon Beam Hotel
43 Rita's Guesthouse
44 Neela's
45 Hotel New Harmony
46 Sunil's Beach Hotel
47 Ocean View Cottage
48 Suite Lanka

PLACES TO EAT
11 Abba's
12 Red Lobster
15 Sea View Pizza House
16 Cool Spot
17 Farm House Restaurant
21 Refresh Restaurant
24 Hotel Francis
25 Blue Fox Restaurant
32 Budde's Restaurant;
   A Frame Surf Shop
33 Sunny's
34 Bandula's
41 Rotty Shop

OTHER
1 Main Post Office
2 Bus Station
3 Commercial Bank
4 Bank of Ceylon
5 Poseidon Diving Station
6 Police
7 People's Bank
8 Blue Deep Dive Centre
9 International Diving School
13 Aqua Tours
23 Sri Lanka Travels & Tours
29 Sam's Surfers (Roger's Garage)
30 Tandem Guest House (Internet facilities)
37 Ranjith's Beach Hut
40 Why Not Rock Cafe
42 Top Secret

Map labels: To Ambalangoda (12km) & Colombo (98km); Harbour; Hikkaduwa Train Station; Baddegama Rd; To Gangarama Maha Vihara (500m), Hotel Bird Lake (2.5km) & Plantation Villa Hotel (8.5km); Amarasena Mw; A2; HIKKADUWA; Toilet; Waulagoda Rd; Coral Sanctuary; WEWALA; Milla Rd; NARIGAMA; Galle Rd; THIRANAGAMA; INDIAN OCEAN; To Patuwata (1km), Dodanduwa (3km), Galle (17km) & Matara (62km)

Scale: 0 200 400m / 0 200 400yd / Approximate Scale

---

deposit (Rs 200), which is refunded on the safe return of the book.

Coral Sanctuary

Hikkaduwa's 'coral sanctuary', stretching out from the string of 'Coral' hotels (see under Places to Stay later in this section) to a group of rocks a couple of hundred metres offshore, is a large, shallow area enclosed by a reef – fishing and spear fishing are banned. You can swim out to the rocks from the Coral Gardens Hotel, where the reef runs straight out from the shore. The water over the reef is never more than three or four me-

tres deep. Many visitors have been disappointed with the coral and the lack of fish. In many places the coral has died directly due to being disturbed or broken. At least in the sanctuary the coral isn't being torn up and burnt to make lime for building, as is happening elsewhere at Hikkaduwa – with the consequence that the beach is being eroded in places.

If you do decide to visit the reef you can rent a mask, snorkel and fins from the dive centres listed under Scuba Diving later. Most places hire a set out for around Rs 50 an hour or Rs 200 a day.

Saving the Beaches

Hikkaduwa was one of the earliest tourism hotspots in Sri Lanka. But over the years it has also suffered as a result of its popularity. Recently a group of local journalists formed an organisation that they hope will bring the issues Hikkaduwa faces to a wider audience and therefore prompt some sort of positive action.

Proposals so far centre on traffic (moving the main road inland and the main hotels away from the beach), coral (stricter controls on poaching and vandalism), garbage disposal (instituting a better garbage collection system) and touts (clearing the beach of all unlicensed operators).

The Southern Province United Media Association (☎ 09-60816) at 141 Main St, Ambalangoda, hopes that through newspapers and other media it can spread the message and gain support for the preservation not only of Hikkaduwa but all at-risk beach places on this part of the west coast.

There are also two or three enterprises that will take you out in a glass-bottom boat to see the coral for around Rs 300 for four people for 30 minutes. However, these boats have caused damage to the reef, especially at low tide, and we even heard from one unhappy pair of snorkellers who complained of nearly being run over by a glass-bottom boat. We do not recommend going by boat; the best way to see the reef is with a snorkel. Check out the boxed text 'Responsible Diving & Snorkelling'.

Scuba Diving

The season runs from November to April. All offer PADI courses for similar prices: open-water for US$320, advanced for US$220, plus a selection of dives such as wreck dives, night dives and dives for those who just want to try diving out.

Blue Deep (☎/fax 074-383190). This centre runs PADI courses, CMAS courses and discovery courses (US$34, equipment included). There's a good restaurant here.

The International Diving School (☎/fax 57436). This school runs PADI courses and two-dive discovery courses (US$40). It rents snorkelling equipment for Rs 50 an hour. There are also deep-sea fishing trips for US$50 for four hours.

Poseidon Diving Station (☎ 77294, fax 76607, e poseidon@visual.lk). Poseidon has PADI dive courses. There is also a small shop with equipment for sale.

Underwater Safaris (☎ 01-694012, e scuba@eureka.lk). Operating as Scuba Safari from the Coral Gardens Hotel, this outfit has a range of PADI courses (from US$245), discovery dives (US$35) and specialist programs including a photography diver session. Fins, masks and snorkels can be hired for US$14 a day.

Surf & Beach

A short distance south of the coral reef, at Wewala, there's good surf for board riders; international surfers flock here. The best time to surf is from November to April.

At Narigama the beach widens out into a fine strip for sunbathing with, in places, good waves for body surfing. Some of the guesthouses and beach cafes rent out surfboards and boogie boards. The A Frame Surf Shop beside Budde's Restaurant, for example, rents out surfboards and boogie boards for Rs 150 per hour.

Beware of the sharp coral in places. If you are unfamiliar with surfing, or with this beach in particular, ask someone reliable about which spots to avoid. As with anywhere on this west coast, take care in the water at Hikkaduwa – the currents can be tricky and there are no life-saving facilities. There have been drownings. See the boxed text 'Safe Swimming' earlier in this chapter for some useful hints.

Inland Attractions

Life at Hikkaduwa isn't only sea and sand, although it may often feel that way. There are countless **shops** along the road selling Sri Lankan goodies: masks, gems, jewellery, batik and antiques. There are also clothes shops making all the usual travellers' gear: skirts, light cotton trousers and so on. Unfortunately a lot of traffic – notably, of course, private buses – screams through Hikkaduwa far too fast, which

Responsible Diving & Snorkelling

Sri Lanka is a wonderful place for diving and snorkelling. But it is important to observe a few simple rules to minimise your impact, and help preserve the reefs' ecology and beauty:

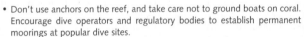

- Don't use anchors on the reef, and take care not to ground boats on coral. Encourage dive operators and regulatory bodies to establish permanent moorings at popular dive sites.
- Avoid touching living marine organisms with your body or dragging equipment across the reef. Polyps are damaged even by gentle contact. Never stand on corals, even if they look solid and robust. If you must hold onto the reef, only touch exposed rock or dead coral.
- Be conscious of your fins. Even without contact the surge from heavy fin strokes near the reef can damage delicate organisms. When treading water in shallow reef areas, avoid kicking up clouds of sand. Settling sand can easily smother the reef's delicate organisms.
- Practise and maintain proper buoyancy control. Major damage can be done by divers descending too fast and colliding with the reef. Make sure you're correctly weighted and that your weight belt is positioned so that you stay horizontal in the water. If you have not dived for a while, have a practice dive in a pool before taking to the reef. Be aware that buoyancy can change over the period of an extended trip; initially you may breathe harder and need more weight, but a few days later you may breathe more easily and need less weight.
- Take great care in underwater caves. Spend as little time within them as possible as your air bubbles may be caught beneath the roof and leave previously submerged organisms high and dry. Take turns to inspect the interior of a small cave to lessen the chances of damaging contact.
- Resist the temptation to collect or buy corals or shells. Aside from the ecological damage, taking home marine souvenirs depletes the beauty of a site and spoils the enjoyment of others. The same goes for marine archaeological sites (mainly shipwrecks). Respect their integrity; some sites are even protected from looting by law.
- Ensure that you take home all your rubbish and any litter you may find. Plastics in particular are a serious threat to marine life. Turtles can mistake plastic for jellyfish and eat it.
- Resist the temptation to feed fish. You may disturb their normal eating habits, encourage aggressive behaviour or feed them food that is detrimental to their health.
- Minimise your disturbance of marine animals. In particular, do not ride on the backs of turtles as this causes them great anxiety. Similarly, discourage your boat driver from circling around turtles, which also puts them under stress.

Safety Guidelines for Diving & Snorkelling

Before embarking on a scuba-diving, skin-diving or snorkelling trip, careful consideration should be given to having a safe, as well as an enjoyable, experience. You should:

- Possess a current diving certification card from a recognised scuba diving instructional agency.
- Be sure you are healthy and feel comfortable diving (if scuba diving).
- Obtain reliable information about physical and environmental conditions at the dive site (eg, from a reputable local dive operator).
- Be aware of local laws, regulations and etiquette about marine life and the environment.
- Dive only at sites within your realm of experience; if available, engage the services of a competent, professionally trained dive instructor or dive master.
- Be aware that underwater conditions vary significantly from one region, or even site, to another. Seasonal changes can significantly alter any site and dive conditions. These differences influence the way divers dress for a dive and what diving techniques they use.
- Ask about the environmental characteristics that can affect your diving and how locally trained divers deal with these considerations.

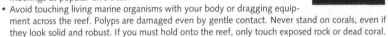

makes walking or cycling along the road an unpleasant, sometimes dangerous, activity.

To leave the beach scene, just walk or cycle along any of the minor roads heading inland. They lead to a calmer, completely different, rural world. Just up Baddegama Rd from the bus station is **Gangarama Maha Vihara**. This is an interesting Buddhist temple which has lots of popular educational paintings (the work of one man over nearly a decade). The monks are happy to show you around, but please show respect by not turning up in beachwear; cover your legs and shoulders and remove your hat and shoes before entering the temple area. After 2km there's a **lake** with a lot of bird life. Boat tours can be organised from beside the lake.

Places to Stay – Budget & Mid-Range

Virtually all of Hikkaduwa's places to stay are strung out along the main road. The best way to find something to suit is simply to wander down the road and look at a variety of rooms. All bottom-end prices can be bargained over. Those given here are what you'd expect to pay in the high season; out of season the same room may go for half the quoted price. For lower prices, ask for rooms with shared bathroom – or look on the 'jungle side' of the road. Prices also vary according to which stretch of the strip you're on – down the Narigama end, where the sands are wider, room rates tend to get higher. In high season, the best-value, smaller places fill up quickly; you may need to make a booking a few days ahead.

The places that follow are just a cross-section of the wide choice along the strip, starting in Hikkaduwa proper and moving south. If mosquitoes are in season you'll probably find fewer of them on the beach side of the road.

Hikkaduwa Generally the beach is narrower and less attractive and the buildings are closer together, up this northern end, though there are some good-value places to be found.

Seashell Hotel (☎ 77898) has seven bargain singles/doubles for Rs 380/420. The rooms are small, clean, quiet and set around a tiny pebble courtyard.

Ozone Tourist Rest (☎ 074-383008, 374 Galle Rd) lacks personality, but you can't complain about its dirt-cheap basic rooms at Rs 450 for a single or double. It's right on the beach.

Curry Bowl Guest House & Restaurant (☎ 77201, fax 77339, e kishans@pan .lk, 368 Galle Rd) has a popular restaurant as well as good-value accommodation. Singles or doubles, in a refurbished old-style house, start from Rs 400 for a clean room; with air-con you'll pay Rs 1100.

Away from the beach altogether, at Pathan, 2.5km inland along the Baddegama Rd from the Hikkaduwa bus station, you'll find the lovely *Hotel Bird Lake* (☎ 77018). It's an older-style place, surrounded by gardens and near the lake (which is rich with bird life). The eight basic rooms (with balcony) cost Rs 500/1000 each. A meal of rice and curry costs Rs 120. Bicycle rental costs Rs 75 a day, or you can hire a canoe to paddle out onto the lake. To get here, a three-wheeler from Hikkaduwa should cost about Rs 70 one way.

About 8.5km from Hikkaduwa, at Halpatota, Baddegama, is the *Plantation Villa Hotel* (☎ 52405, fax 01-587454). This is a beautiful tea-plantation bungalow in lovely, peaceful grounds (it's right in the St Mary's tea estate). Basic rooms cost US$20 with breakfast. You can arrange to have Sri Lankan cooking classes here if you wish.

Wewala The beach is steep and thin but this area has the best surf spots.

The *Surfing Beach Guest House* (☎ 77008, 522 Galle Rd) has 12 rooms ranging from Rs 300 (with shared bathroom) to 800 (with private bathroom). It's a bit of a doss house but it has prime viewing over one of Hikkaduwa's top surfing spots.

Richards Sons Beach Inn (☎ 77184), has a huge garden and is a prime piece of beachfront real estate. The small, but clean rooms cost Rs 600 for singles or doubles. There's no food available.

Miga Villa (☎/fax 075-451559) is an attractive older house set in pretty gardens.

The clean rooms cost about Rs 500 but as it's mainly geared towards wedding receptions it may be noisy; ask for the rooms near the pond. There's no food available.

Bright Sunshine (☎ *074-383113, 501 Galle Rd*) has six clean and airy rooms for Rs 400/600. Although there's no garden and it's not beside the beach, the owners are delightful and very keen to please.

There are 11 rooms at *Casalanka* (☎/fax *074-383002*). The downstairs rooms (Rs 500) are nothing flash but they look onto a bare garden. The upstairs rooms (Rs 1200) have hot water – a luxury for Hikkaduwa!

Hotel Blue Note (☎/fax *77016, 424 Galle Rd*) has bungalows set around a sandy garden. The rooms are clean, though nothing special, but the drawcard for some may be the hotel's sitting room, complete with satellite television. Singles or doubles cost Rs 1260.

Moon Beam Hotel (☎ *075-450657, 548/1 Galle Rd*) has 12 sparkling clean rooms with hot water. Rooms cost Rs 1100/1540. Don't bother paying the Rs 100 extra for an upstairs room – they're the same as the rooms downstairs.

Nippon Villa (☎ *074-383149, fax 77103, 412 Galle Rd*) has rooms for Rs 1350/1650 (B&B) with hot water. There's a small courtyard, and the rooms are clean but they're slightly overpriced.

Narigama & Thiranagama This end of the beach is wider and better for swimming and sunbathing. It's crowded with hotels and restaurants, but it's still pleasant.

Hotel New Harmony (☎ *76559*) has 13 large rooms, with tables, for Rs 650/750. There are heaps of comfy sun lounges on the sand.

Family-run *Neela's* (☎/fax *074-383166, 634 Galle Rd*) has eight rooms for Rs 750 per single/double and two dirt-cheap cabanas for Rs 150 each. The rooms are clean, but nothing special; the cabanas are a little dark, but comfortable. The food is delicious.

Rita's Guesthouse (☎ *77496*) has nine basic rooms and a sandy, palm-treed garden. Doubles or singles cost Rs 1000 for upstairs rooms, or Rs 700 for the downstairs rooms.

Sunil's Beach Hotel (☎ *77186, fax 77187*) has a fenced garden surrounding a small pool (nonguests can swim in the pool for Rs 140). Each large, clean room has a balcony and costs Rs 1500/2000; add Rs 600 for air-con.

If you like plenty of space, head to the *Ocean View Cottage* (☎ *77237*) with its three mini-apartments. Each has a large bedroom, lounge, fridge and veranda; with air-con you'll pay Rs 2400, without air-con costs Rs 1800. There's a huge garden leading down to the beach. Galle Rd is nearby though, so it may be a bit noisy.

Places to Stay – Top End
There are a few top-end places overlooking the coral sanctuary – and just to ensure that you get them nicely confused, they nearly all have 'coral' in their names.

Hotel Supercoral (☎ *074-383385, fax 074-383384*, e *supercor@pan.lk*) has spacious, light rooms for US$25/30; air-con costs another US$10. There's a pool (Rs 150 for nonguests) and a huge beachside garden, but the outside of the building looks like it needs a holiday.

Hotel Blue Corals (☎ *77679, fax 074-383128*, e *bluecora@eureka.lk*) is a busy, leafy hotel with a pool and 42 rooms. Air-con rooms cost US$50/60 with breakfast.

Suite Lanka (☎/fax *77136, Narigama*) is a small, friendly hotel with fan-only rooms for US$35/40 and air-con rooms for US$55/60; rates include breakfast. There's a tiny pool, a garish restaurant and a shaded garden lining the beachfront.

Coral Gardens Hotel (☎ *77023, fax 77189*) is nothing special, but it's the poshest hotel in town. The air-con rooms have views, but no balcony, and cost US$75/112. There's an Ayurvedic centre, a pool and most other facilities you'd expect for this price.

Places to Eat
Hikkaduwa has all the usual travellers stand-bys: the ubiquitous banana pancakes, rotty and all manner of things homesick foreigners crave for (French fries, pizza, good coffee, cake etc). Hikkaduwa's main speciality is, naturally, seafood. Baked crab,

served with salad, French fries or ginger sauce, is a must. There are a few stores selling imported foods that you can stock up on before heading farther afield.

The stand-by for travellers with late-night hunger pangs is the *Rotty Shop* in Narigama, which offers super-cheap stomach fillers (such as chocolate-banana-honey rotty) for under Rs 40 from 7 am till the wee hours of the morning. For other cheapies, *Bandula's* all-you-can-eat rice, vegie and fish curry for Rs 80 will stuff you up (you must order by 3 pm), while *Sunny's* has top value breakfasts for Rs 110.

Budde's Restaurant, right beside the sand, has tomato jaffles for Rs 25, grilled fish and chips for Rs 165 and more tasty good-value treats. Dog lovers will love Budde's pet.

Sea View Pizza House has superb pizzas, and decent pastas and seafood for around the Rs 200 mark.

The *Cool Spot* is one of Hikkaduwa's original places; it's been here since the 1970s (and it looks it). The food is still very good, inexpensive, and the menu surprisingly varied. Garlic prawns, salad and chips costs Rs 260. The veranda is the best place to sit.

Curry Bowl Guest House & Restaurant (368 Galle Rd) hasn't got the best setting (it's a bit noisy) but it does have tasteful decor and the food is good. Curry and rice costs Rs 110, grilled tuna Rs 140.

Hotel Francis (☎ 77019, 389 Galle Rd) has a large uninviting seating area, but it does good, well-priced Chinese. Try the chop suey with cashew nuts (Rs 135), sweet and sour prawns (Rs 160) or splash out on the full crab (Rs 610).

Abbas's (Waulagoda Rd) serves good Western food with many German items on the menu – as well as Sri Lankan fare. The restaurant is upstairs; it's pleasantly cool and removed from the noise of the main road. The prices are reasonable: steaks from Rs 230, fish and chips Rs 220. There's a pub (Kings) with music downstairs.

Red Lobster (273 Galle Rd) is a friendly place set back from the road. Tasty dishes include devilled fish (Rs 135) and baked crab (Rs 370). Best known as a dive centre, *Blue Deep* has a good attached restaurant, serving fish from Rs 225 and prawns from Rs 200, plus rice and noodle dishes.

The *Farm House Restaurant (☎ 77082, 341 Galle Rd)* has decent food and cold Lion beer (Rs 90). The rice and curry is a bit of a rip-off as each curry is charged separately – cheaper options include grilled calamari with chips (Rs 200) or seafood spaghetti (Rs 250).

Blue Fox Restaurant (☎ 77029, 397 Galle Rd) has a great first-floor spot perfect for people-watching on the street below. It's a vibrant, busy place with decent prices but the food is average and it's understaffed. Fried prawns cost Rs 210, rice and curry Rs 80 (ask for Sri Lankan–style curry if you like it hot; otherwise they'll assume that you, like most tourists, don't want chilli and other hot spices added).

If you feel like splurging head to *Refresh Restaurant (☎ 77810, 384 Galle Rd)* with its simple, modern decor – it's a pleasant spot, especially in the evening. Prices are rather higher here than at some other places (devilled prawns for Rs 320, baked crab for Rs 750), but it gets rave reviews.

Entertainment

Hikkaduwa's nightlife is clustered around Narigama. Down here you'll find a stack of choices including the buzzing *Why Not Rock Cafe* and *Top Secret*. Top Secret is usually a bar but on Saturday nights you can kick your feet in the sand to live music. The band churns out the fodder (reggae cover songs) but with an entry fee of Rs 50, decently priced local beers (Rs 120) and plenty of atmosphere, you can't complain.

At the laid-back *Sam's Surfers (Roger's Garage) (403 Galle Rd)* there are showings of recent movies every night at 7.30 pm, or you may prefer to shoot some pool (three games for Rs 100), or swill a beer with a cheap bite to eat (Rs 90 rice and curry).

Abbas's (Waulagoda Rd) has an indoor bar with music until late. *Ranjith's Beach Hut*, which is basic, opens at 7 am daily and serves Rs 100 beer until the last punter staggers home.

Getting There & Away

Bus There are frequent buses from Colombo, both private (from the Bastian Mawatha bus station) and CTB. The express buses are best (Rs 60, two to 2½ hours). Buses to Galle or beyond will take you through Hikkaduwa and drop you somewhere south of the bus station if you know where you're headed. Buses also operate frequently to nearby Ambalangoda and Galle (both Rs 6.50). When leaving Hikkaduwa, you stand more chance of a seat if you start at the bus station.

Train Trains on this route can get very crowded – and also attract a number of touts who try to latch on to you at Colombo Fort station or on the train. Avoid the really slow trains that stop everywhere. The rail schedules seem subject to change, so it's best to check at the station.

Normal express trains to Colombo leave at 7.05, 8.05 (intercity express), 9.20 and 11.05 am, and 3.05 and 6.35 pm. The fare is Rs 20/55 in 3rd/2nd class. The intercity express costs Rs 55 to Colombo, and the trip takes two hours as opposed to the 2½ hours on a normal express.

Trains to Matara via Galle leave at 9.05 and 11.05 am and 12.45, 4.27, 6 and 8.20 pm. The fare to Galle is Rs 4/11 in 3rd/2nd class.

The Kandy direct express leaves at 3.05 pm (Rs 44.50/122.50 in 3rd/2nd class, 5½ hours). The express train to Vavuniya (for Anuradhapura) leaves at 11.05 am.

Taxi Most Hikkaduwa taxis are small minibuses able to hold eight or so passengers, so they can be relatively cheap if there's a group of you. Most gather in front of the top-end hotels. Some fares include: Galle Rs 800, Unawatuna Rs 900 to 1000, Colombo or Tangalla Rs 1700, Banaranaike International Airport Rs 2200 and Kandy Rs 5500.

Motorcycle Motorcycles are readily available for rent in Hikkaduwa, both for local use and farther afield. A traveller has recommended Sri Lanka Travels & Tours (☎ 77354, ℮ slttours@mail.ewisl.net) at 371 Galle Rd. A 125cc machine costs around Rs 400 a day, while a 250cc is Rs 500. You can usually get a discount of about 10% if you take the bike for several days or a week. Of course you have to add the cost of petrol. Some of the operators offer insurance (costing 10% of the hire rate), but you should still check the bike out thoroughly before agreeing on a deal.

Getting Around

A three-wheeler costs about Rs 70 from the train or bus station to Wewala or Narigama. Once you're settled in, a bicycle is a nice way to get around and it's easy to hire a bike here for Rs 100 to 150 a day.

The South

The south is different from the west coast: here the towns are less touristy, there are still beautiful beaches ringed with palm trees, but the resorts have petered out. There are plenty of nature spots too, so your visit should include a safari in one of the wildlife parks, or a night watch for turtles. Then there's the pretty fort of Galle – Sri Lanka's most historically interesting town. But overwhelmingly this area offers calm respite, with lazy afternoons on a beach lounge, many tasty brunches and snorkel-clad dips in the clear water. The coast is at its best from November to April.

The south starts at Galle, then heads around the coast to lovely Unawatuna, on to Weligama, sleepy Mirissa and bustling Matara. The coast road continues to Tangalla, where you might see sea turtles, and then on to Hambantota, where you can base yourself for visits Bundala National Park. The road then heads north to Tissamaharama, a busy town that's a perfect base for a visit to the coastal village of Kirinda or a safari into Yala West (Ruhuna) National Park. Continuing north, you'll find Kataragama, one of the two most important pilgrimage site in Sri Lanka.

You have to watch out for dangerous currents, undertows and rip tides anywhere on this coast. These may be more likely with the bigger seas in the wet season from April/May to October/November, but you should take care at any time of year. Watch where other people are swimming and if in any doubt keep asking around (see the boxed text 'Safe Swimming' in the West Coast chapter for some useful hints). Pollution is another deterrent to swimming in some places – the farther you are from town centres the better.

GALLE
☎ 09 • pop 85,000
The port of Galle (pronounced gaar-le), Sri Lanka's fourth-biggest town, is 115km south of Colombo and 17km south-east of

Highlights
• Taking a stroll with the locals at sunset around Galle Fort's historic ramparts
• Waiting, hoping, wishing for the turtles to come in at Rekawa – they *will* come
• Boozing into the night at a beach bar in Unawatuna after a day of snorkelling and pigging out at the beach restaurants
• Reading a favourite book, counting sand grains – whiling away time at sleepy Mirissa
• Searching for the elusive leopard on a safari in Yala West (Ruhuna) National Park
• Watching the feisty religious rituals at Kataragama

Hikkaduwa. Galle is Sri Lanka's most historically interesting living city. Although Anuradhapura and Polonnaruwa are much older, they are effectively dead cities – the modern towns are quite divorced from the ancient ruins. Until the construction of breakwaters at Colombo harbour was completed in the late 19th century, Galle was the major port in Sri Lanka and still handles shipping – and cruising yachts – today.

Historians believe Galle may be the Tarshish of Biblical times – where King Solomon obtained gems, spices and peacocks – but it became prominent only with the arrival of the Europeans. In 1505 a Portuguese fleet bound for the Maldives was blown off course and took shelter in the harbour at dusk. It is said that, on hearing a cock (*galo* in Portuguese) crowing, they gave the town its name. Another story is that the name is derived from the Sinhala *gala* (rock), of which the harbour has plenty. In 1589, during one of their periodic squabbles with the kingdom of Kandy, the Portuguese built a small fort, which they named Santa Cruz. Later they extended it with a series of bastions and walls, but the

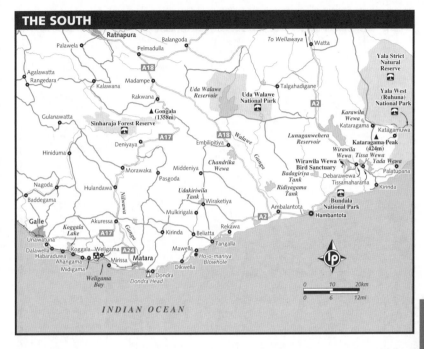

THE SOUTH

Dutch, who took Galle in 1640, destroyed most traces of the Portuguese presence.

In 1663 the Dutch built the 36-hectare fort (which is now a World Heritage site), occupying most of the promontory that forms the older part of Galle. By the time Galle passed into British hands in 1796, commercial interest was turning to Colombo, and old Galle has scarcely altered since. It's delightfully quiet and easy-going, with a real sense of being steeped in history.

Unfortunately Galle has a bad reputation for rip-offs and con artists. Travellers report being told things such as the Fort is closed (a ridiculous suggestion), or that there are no buses to Unawatuna (equally ridiculous), or being offered tours to see crocodiles (actually water monitors beside the canal on Havelock Place). Generally the real aim is to get you into gem shops. There you may be charged absurdly high prices or sold fakes, or asked to buy gems and re-sell them for a profit in other countries – the kind of activity that even a gem expert would think twice about doing.

Galle is an easy day trip from Hikkaduwa or Unawatuna, but there are a variety of places to stay if you want to soak up more of the atmosphere.

Orientation & Information

The old town, or Fort, occupies most of a south-pointing promontory. Around where the promontory meets the 'mainland' is the centre of the new town, with the bus and train stations, shops and banks. The main post office is near the market on the Matara road. TG Communications, at Pedlar St, Fort, has fax, IDD and Internet facilities.

The Fort Walls

One of the most pleasant strolls you can take in town is the circuit of the Fort walls at dusk. As the daytime heat fades away you can, in an easy hour or two, walk almost the complete circuit of the Fort along

THE SOUTH

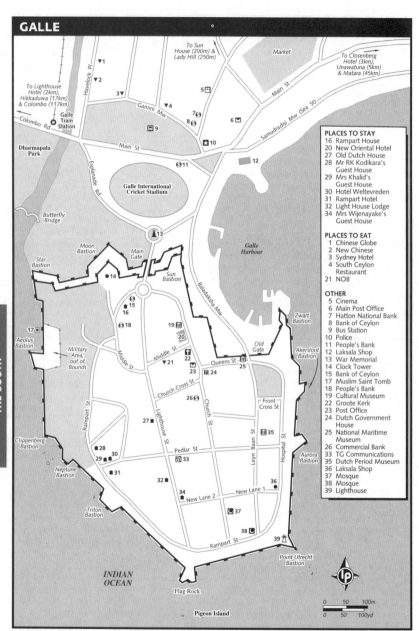

GALLE

PLACES TO STAY
16 Rampart House
20 New Oriental Hotel
27 Old Dutch House
28 Mr RK Kodikara's
   Guest House
29 Mrs Khalid's
   Guest House
30 Hotel Weltevreden
31 Rampart Hotel
32 Light House Lodge
34 Mrs Wijenayake's
   Guest House

PLACES TO EAT
1 Chinese Globe
2 New Chinese
3 Sydney Hotel
4 South Ceylon
   Restaurant
21 NOB

OTHER
5 Cinema
6 Main Post Office
7 Hatton National Bank
8 Bank of Ceylon
9 Bus Station
10 Police
11 People's Bank
12 Laksala Shop
13 War Memorial
14 Clock Tower
15 Bank of Ceylon
17 Muslim Saint Tomb
18 People's Bank
19 Cultural Museum
22 Groote Kerk
23 Post Office
24 Dutch Government
   House
25 National Maritime
   Museum
26 Commercial Bank
33 TG Communications
35 Dutch Period Museum
36 Mosque
37 Mosque
38 Mosque
39 Lighthouse

the top of the wall. Only once – between Aurora Bastion and the Old Gate – is it necessary to leave the wall (part of the area between the Star and Aeolus Bastions is an off-limits military compound and you must descend from the walls here).

The **main gate** in the northern stretch of the wall is a comparatively recent addition – it was built by the British in 1873 to handle the heavier flow of traffic into the old city. This part of the wall, the most heavily fortified because it faced the land, was originally built by the Portuguese with a moat, and was then substantially enlarged by the Dutch, who in 1667 split it into separate Star, Moon and Sun Bastions.

Following the Fort wall clockwise you soon come to the **Old Gate**. On its outer side the British coat of arms tops the entrance. Inside, the letters VOC, standing for the Dutch East India Company, are inscribed in the stone, flanked by two lions and topped by a cock, with the date 1669. The National Maritime Museum (see Inside the Fort following) is housed in the walls, and is entered via the Old Gate. Just beyond the gate is the Zwart Bastion, or Black Fort, thought to be Portuguese-built and the oldest of the Fort bastions. Today it houses a police station.

The eastern section of the wall ends at the **Point Utrecht Bastion**, close to the powder magazine and topped by the 18m-high lighthouse, which was built in 1938. The lighthouse keeper may magically materialise when visitors arrive and, for a few rupees, show you up to the top.

Flag Rock, at the end of the next stretch of wall, was once a Portuguese bastion. From there the Dutch signalled approaching ships to warn them of dangerous rocks – hence its name Flag Rock. Musket shots were fired from Pigeon Island, close to the rock, to further alert ships to the danger. On the **Triton Bastion** there used to be a windmill that drew up sea water, which was sprayed from carts to keep the dust down on the city streets. This stretch of the wall is a great place to be at sunset. There's a series of other bastions, as well as the tomb of a Muslim saint, before you arrive back at your starting point.

Inside the Fort

Most of the older buildings within the Fort date from the Dutch era. Many of the streets still bear their Dutch names, or are direct translations – thus Mohrische Kramer Straat became the Street of the Moorish Traders and Rope Walk St has become Leyn Baan St. The Dutch also built an intricate sewer system that was flushed out daily by the tide. With true colonial efficiency, the Dutch then bred musk rats in the sewers, which were exported for their musk oil.

The **Dutch Period Museum**, in a well-restored Dutch house at 31–39 Leyn Baan St, is not really a museum as many of the exhibits have price tags and there's also a gem shop attached. It's a junkyard of colonial artefacts, including collections of antique typewriters, VOC china, spectacles, jewellery and so on. In the courtyard is a well, and on the veranda around the well there are gem polishers and cutters at work, and an elderly woman busily making lace in the traditional way. The deft movements required to make the intricate lace patterns are all done from memory. It's open 10 am to 6 pm daily, except for Friday when it's closed from noon to 2 pm; admission is free.

The **National Maritime Museum** (open 9 am to 5 pm Saturday to Wednesday; entry Rs 55) is inside the thick, solid walls of former storehouses. The dusty exhibits are poorly displayed, but have a certain kitsch appeal: fibreglass whales, pickled sea creatures, models of catamarans. Fishermen from this area once made pilgrimages to Kataragama in the hope that by doing so they could increase their catches. There's a small exhibit on this subject.

The **National Museum** (open 9 am to 5 pm Tuesday to Saturday; entry Rs 35) is next to the New Oriental Hotel, near the main gate. It's rather disappointing, with poorly displayed exhibits.

The **New Oriental Hotel** was built in 1684 to house the Dutch governor and officers. It became a hotel in 1863. The maps and prints on its walls reveal much about the town's history. You can imbibe the colonial atmosphere over a lime soda on its airy veranda. The Groote Kerk, or Great

Church, nearby, was originally built in 1640, but the present run-down church dates from 1752–55. Its floor is paved with gravestones from the old Dutch cemetery.

Near the church are a 1701 bell tower and the old **Dutch Government House** which was being renovated into a promising restaurant at the time of writing. Over the doorway a slab bears the date 1683 and the figure of a cock.

Places to Stay – Budget

If you're short on rupees, there are *railway retiring rooms* at Galle train station available on a 24-hour basis – the single costs Rs 170 and the doubles cost Rs 340. The rooms are clean enough, but there's no food.

Light House Lodge (☎ 075-450514, 62B Lighthouse St) has superfriendly owners, which is just as well since its rooms (at Rs 300 to 350 for singles, Rs 400 to 450 for doubles) will give you the unsettling experience of feeling like you're sleeping in a shoebox. The two rooms at the front of the building are the best; the small sunny balcony is another redeeming feature. Cheap food (Rs 80 for breakfast) is available.

Hotel Weltevreden (☎ 22650, e piyas en2@sltnet.lk, 104 Pedlar St) has seven clean rooms. Singles with shared bathroom cost Rs 400 and doubles with bathroom cost Rs 550. The rooms surround a leafy courtyard and there's a pretty garden out the back. The welcoming host will be happy to make your meals (Rs 150 for breakfast).

The *Old Dutch House* (46 Lighthouse St) was a lovely small colonial house but it's now shabby and overpriced and the service can be apathetic. The eight rooms have good bathrooms but the rooms themselves are grimy and dark. A single/double costs Rs 350/600 – there's no food available here. Each room is named after a former Dutch governor or officer and the walls are decorated with interesting if occasionally gruesome historical snippets (such as a 17th-century eyewitness account of the execution – by elephant – of a Dutch soldier).

Mrs Wijenayake's Guest House (☎ 34663, e thalith@sri.lanka.net, 65 Lighthouse St), also called Beach Haven, is a modern home with six clean and tidy guestrooms. The cheaper rooms (from Rs 330 a single or double) are in the family home, and the larger and more expensive ones (Rs 770) are in a separate section, upstairs at the back. There's ample living space, a kitchen to use, and the family is very welcoming. Good meals are available, including breakfast for Rs 150.

Mr RK Kodikara's Guest House (☎ 22351, 29 Rampart St) is a charming ramshackle mansion overlooking the ramparts, with a bare patch of garden out the front. The four clean, simple rooms downstairs cost from Rs 450/600. The two value-for-money rooms upstairs (with views over the ramparts) cost Rs 880 a single or double; each has a small private roof garden and overgrown beds. Meals are available.

Rampart House (☎ 34448, 3 Rampart St) is a large, 1970s home owned by Dr Stanley Ladduwahetty, who lets two large rooms for Rs 720 a single or double. One room has a small study attached, and the other has a small balcony and hot water. Breakfast costs Rs 125. It's not signposted.

Mrs Khalid's Guest House (☎ 34907, 106 Pedlar St) is a modern, homely place with three spotless guestrooms – two with bathroom, and one without. The rooms cost Rs 400 to 1000 and there's a small grassed courtyard. Mrs Khalid's cooking gets rave reviews; it costs Rs 150 for breakfast and Rs 200 for vegie rice and curry.

Rampart Hotel (☎ 074-380103, fax 09-42794, 31 Rampart St) has two colonial-style rooms for Rs 1500 with bathroom, although they are nothing special. You won't get personal or attentive service – the hotel is geared towards being a lunch stop for tour groups, and there's also a lucrative gem shop attached. The food is pricey, but good.

Places to Stay – Mid-Range & Top End

The *Closenberg Hotel* (☎/fax 32241, 11 Closenberg Rd), built as a 19th-century P&O captain's residence in the heyday of British mercantile supremacy, sits out on a promontory with views over Galle beach and the Fort. The 21 rooms have colonial wooden furniture, with 16 of them in a modern wing with balconies overlooking the beach. Rooms cost US$37/55 – add US$5 for air-con. It should cost Rs 120 to get there in a three-wheeler from the bus or train stations.

The *Lady Hill* (☎ 44322, fax 34844, **e** la dyhill@diamond.lanka.net, 29 Upper Dickson Rd) has spotless, modern rooms with balconies that let you enjoy one of the highest views in Galle. Rooms with all the modcons cost $US50 a single or double. There's a rooftop bar/restaurant and a small pool.

New Oriental Hotel (☎/fax 34591, 10 Church St, Fort) is a grand old place with rooms that, although worn around the edges, exude the atmosphere of a bygone era. The standard rooms at US$49/55 are a rip-off – they're a bit rough and most have a makeshift bathroom built inside the room. The huge suite rooms at US$73/85 however, pick up the standard, and the colonial furnishings, complete with four-poster bed and claw-foot baths, are gorgeous. The pretty garden hides a pool (Rs 150 for nonguests to use).

The *Sun House* (☎/fax 22624, **e** sun house@sri.lanka.net, 18 Upper Dickson Rd) is a gracious old villa built in the 1860s that's been renovated with superb taste. As the villa is on a hilltop, you have wonderful views towards the Fort on one side and the port on the other. There's a large, well-kept garden and a small pool. Tours can be arranged. The food here is excellent, as is the hospitality offered by the hosts. The delightful cinnamon suite will cost you US$220, the garden room US$160 and the standard rooms US$100. At the time of writing the Sun House owners were renovating another villa nearby, which will have three luxury suites. They also manage the house on Taprobane island (see under Weligama, later in this chapter) and Seenimodera, a beautiful four-bedroom villa beside the beach at Tangalla.

Lighthouse Hotel (☎ 23744, fax 24021, **e** lighthousehotel@lanka.com.lk, Dadella) occupies a prime position on the seafront, 2km before you reach the Fort, coming from Colombo. It was designed by Sri Lanka's most famous architect, Geoffrey Bawa. It beautifully blends Dutch colonial style with modern design, but the rooms are outrageously overpriced at US$240 with air-con for a single or double.

Places to Eat

See under Places to Stay for some of the best places to eat, including *Mrs Khalid's Guest House* (where nonguests can dine, if they book ahead). The *Closenberg Hotel* has a pretty, grassed terrace with views over Galle beach – it's a great spot for breakfast (Rs 200) or lunch. The *New Oriental Hotel* is worth visiting even if you're not staying. You could try their breakfast (Rs 230), rice and curry (Rs 240) or just have a beer (Rs 130). *Rampart Hotel* has delicious food – seating is on a wide, wooden balcony that overlooks the ramparts. Vegie chop suey costs Rs 190 and fried prawns cost Rs 330.

There are not many other eateries in the Fort but you could try *NOB* (3 Middle St). It's old-fashioned and a little worn, but it does decent rice and curry (for Rs 80 to 140) at lunch time and snacks at other times. It's open 7.30 am to 6.30 pm daily.

Outside the Fort, opposite the bus station, is the *South Ceylon Restaurant*, above the South Ceylon Bakery. The food is tasty and this place is cheap and friendly. Nearby is the *Sydney Hotel* where Rs 40 buys you a lunch-time rice and meat curry.

Around the corner are more eateries, including *Chinese Globe* (38 Havelock Place) and the *New Chinese* (14 Havelock Place). The food – Western, Chinese and Sri Lankan – is very reasonable (mains are from around Rs 120 to 220) and filling.

Getting There & Away

Bus There are plenty of CTB and private buses running up and down this busy coastal strip. The bus fare to Colombo is Rs 35 for a CTB bus and Rs 65 for an intercity express (every 15 minutes or so between 4.30 am and 10 pm; three hours); to Hikkaduwa it costs Rs 10; Unawatuna Rs 5; and Matara Rs 13. There are buses to destinations as far afield as Tangalla (Rs 25 with CTB, two hours), Tissamaharama (Rs 45 with CTB), Kataragama, Wellawaya (leaves at 5.20 am, Rs 125 for the intercity express, five hours), Ella (via Deniyaya), and Deniyaya (change at Akuressa).

Train Normal express trains to Colombo Fort leave at 6.45, 7.40 (intercity express), 9.05 and 10.40 am (express to Anuradhapura from Matara), and 2.05, 2.45 and 6.05 pm. Fares include Colombo Rs 23.50/64.50 3nd/2rd class and Hikkaduwa Rs 4/11 3nd/2rd class.

Trains to Matara leave regularly: the expresses run at 10.15 and 11.45 am, and 1.25, 6.35 and 8.55 pm (Rs 9/24.50 in 3nd/2rd class). The direct train to Kandy leaves at 2.45 pm (Rs 48/133 in 3nd/2rd class). There is no 1st class and there are no sleepers.

Three-Wheeler A three-wheeler from Galle to Unawatuna will cost Rs 90 to 120.

UNAWATUNA
☎ 09

Five kilometres south-east of Galle is Unawatuna, a wide, curving bay with a picturesque sweep of golden beach. Swimming is safe thanks to the reef that protects the beach, and, unlike Hikkaduwa, Unawatuna does not have a dangerously busy road running right through it. These factors have made Unawatuna popular with travellers and locals. Unfortunately, Unawatuna isn't immune to the problems associated with popularity. On public holidays in particular, Unawatuna can get very crowded. Petty crime and drugs have become issues in recent years and travellers are urged to take particular care with their possessions, especially on the beach. Overall, though, Unawatuna is less hectic than Hikkaduwa – a pleasant place to while away time.

Information
The post office is out of town, but there's an informal postal agency along The Strand. There are Internet facilities in the South Ceylon Restaurant, at Bravo Tours near the Unawatuna Beach Resort and also at Neptune Bay Guest House. There are no banks in Unawatuna.

Things to See & Do
You can hire **snorkelling** equipment from some of the beachfront places (or borrow it from guesthouses) to explore the reef a short distance out from the west end of the beach. There are several interesting **wreck dives** around Galle. Seahorse Diving (☎/fax 83 733, ⓔ krohuna@gmx.net), on the main road near the Sun 'n' Sea guesthouse, can arrange dives. One dive costs US$30 and five dives cost US$125 (no equipment). Snorkeling (including boat) costs US$22 per person and snorkel hire costs Rs 165 per hour. See the boxed text 'Responsible Diving & Snorkelling' under Hikkaduwa in the West Coast chapter for advice.

You can take some interesting **walks** over the rocks rising from the west end of the beach or along the tracks back past the Strand guesthouse and up the hill. The rocky outcrop on the west end of the beach is called **Rumassala** and is known for its medicinal herbs – which are protected. The temple right on the promontory is fenced off, but you may walk the short distance up to the dagoba on top of the hill and to Jungle Beach on the other side.

It's an easy day trip to see the large **lake** near Koggala (see Things to See & Do in the Unawatuna to Weligama section later in this chapter).

Places to Stay
Unawatuna is chock full of places to stay. Listed below is just a small sample of some of the better places. There is only one top-end place, and even it's on a modest scale. You can save a lot of money by staying a few minutes' walk from the beach, instead of right on it. Prices given here are for high season (from November/December to about March) – out of season you can get a third or so off most prices.

The Strand Area Many places to stay in Unawatuna are dotted along and near The Strand, the track that leaves the main road just north of the 122km marker. It wiggles along behind the beach, before changing its name to Yaddehimulla Rd and heading north.

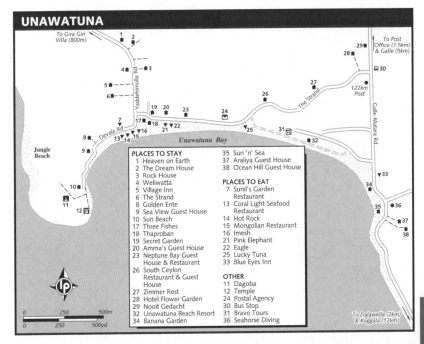

UNAWATUNA

To Gira Giri Villa (800m)

To Post Office (1.5km) & Galle (5km)

122km Post

Yaddehimulla Rd

Devala Rd

The Strand

Galle-Matara Rd

Jungle Beach

Unawatuna Bay

PLACES TO STAY
1 Heaven on Earth
2 The Dream House
3 Rock House
4 Weliwatta
5 Village Inn
6 The Strand
8 Golden Ente
9 Sea View Guest House
10 Sun Beach
17 Three Fishes
18 Thaproban
19 Secret Garden
20 Amma's Guest House
23 Neptune Bay Guest House & Restaurant
26 South Ceylon Restaurant & Guest House
27 Zimmer Rest
28 Hotel Flower Garden
29 Nooit Gedacht
32 Unawatuna Beach Resort
34 Banana Garden

35 Sun 'n' Sea
37 Araliya Guest House
38 Ocean Hill Guest House

PLACES TO EAT
7 Sunil's Garden Restaurant
13 Coral Light Seafood Restaurant
14 Hot Rock
15 Mongolian Restaurant
16 Imesh
21 Pink Elephant
22 Eagle
25 Lucky Tuna
33 Blue Eyes Inn

OTHER
11 Dagoba
12 Temple
24 Postal Agency
30 Bus Stop
31 Bravo Tours
36 Seahorse Diving

0   250   500m
0   250   500yd

To Dalawella (2km) & Koggala (12km)

The *South Ceylon Restaurant & Guest House* (☎ 45863) has four bare rooms with a shared bathroom for Rs 250. The food is vegetarian and is very good.

Zimmer Rest (☎ 074-380366) has seven rooms; two with shared bathroom and five with private bathroom. Rooms cost from Rs 300 to 700 for a single or double. The large, clean rooms in the modern wing have hot water and cost Rs 700. There's a large garden, friendly service and free tea.

Hotel Flower Garden (☎ 25286, fax 074 384311) has 17 cabanas for Rs 700 each with their own cutesy flower garden. Rooms inside the main, modern house cost Rs 800 to 1500 with hot water. Bicycles are supplied free to guests.

Amma's Guest House (☎ 25332) has 10 rooms that cost Rs 400 for singles and Rs 600 to 700 for doubles. Although the rooms here are nothing special, they're clean and there's a large communal balcony and veranda.

Neptune Bay Guest House & Restaurant (☎/fax 34014, e neptunbay@eureka .lk) has three singles for Rs 600 and 13 doubles from Rs 700 to 1500. There's a new wing with clean but small rooms. The older wing's rooms are clean too, but all are uninspiring. Some rooms have balconies that face the sea. There's a tour office (with Internet facilities) onsite and a restaurant.

Thaproban (☎/fax 074-381722, e pres hand@hotmail.com) has seven clean rooms, five with hot water. Singles or doubles cost from Rs 700 to 2500; the more expensive rooms look into the beach. There's a small sandy spot beside the beach and a restaurant. This place is always busy so the rooms are now verging on being overpriced.

Farther towards the western end of the beach is *Three Fishes* (☎ 41857), a low-key guesthouse with a colonial ambience. There are five rooms, two single bungalows for Rs 800 (good value, but with shared bathroom) and three double rooms for Rs 1400. There's a jungle-like garden beside the beach and shaded verandas.

Just before you get to the turn-off to Unawatuna from Galle, on the Galle-Matara Rd, you'll find the *Nooit Gedacht* (☎/fax 23449), a 1735 Dutch colonial mansion with a small pool and a large garden. The rooms in the old part of the house cost Rs 1400 with bathroom and four-poster beds. There's a four-bed room for Rs 3000 that fronts onto the pool. The best room is upstairs and costs Rs 2000/2500. Rooms in the new block cost Rs 1000/1500 with bathroom. All rooms have hot water and some have air-con.

The *Secret Garden*, near Three Fishes on the landward side of the road, is very secret indeed; entry is through a discreet door in the garden wall. There are four bedrooms in this pleasant, old-style place. The entire house costs US$185 a night (including a kitchen) or you can rent the bedrooms for US$50 to US$70 each. There are four cute bungalows for US$25 a single or double, dotted throughout the gorgeous garden. There's also a meditation pagoda. Bookings can be made through Three Fishes (☎ 41857).

The top-end *Unawatuna Beach Resort* (☎ 24028, fax 32247, e ubr@sri.lanka.net) is one of the first places you reach if you walk along the village beach from the main road. The rooms are modern and spacious and have a balcony. There's also a pool (nonguests pay Rs 200). Rates for half board (no room-only rates) are from US$55 to US$80 for singles and US$73 to US$110 for doubles (the more expensive rooms have sea views and air-con).

Yaddehimulla & Devala Rds Devala Rd runs off Yaddehimulla Rd towards the west end of the beach. Laid-back *Sun Beach* (☎ 42284) on Devala Rd has two rooms, each with a balcony, in a wooden shack right on the beach. If you like your comforts you'll hate Sun Beach: there's no electricity and no shower (you use a container) – but it's dirt-cheap at Rs 200/400 per single/ double. Book ahead.

Golden Ente (☎ 074-381228) is a small, modern block with a palm-tree-studded lawn. The nine basic rooms each have their own balcony or veranda. It's good value with singles at Rs 350 to 450 and doubles at Rs 400 to 700. Book ahead.

Heaven on Earth on Yaddehimulla Rd has four rooms, two with bathroom and two without. The rooms are clean, quaint and the host is superfriendly. Rooms cost Rs 350/400. To top it off there's a pretty, leafy garden.

Village Inn (☎/fax 25375) has an assortment of rooms spread over five buildings. It's run by a hospitable family. The clean basic rooms cost from Rs 350 to 900 for singles and doubles. This place gets good reviews.

The Strand (☎/fax 24358, e strand_u@ sltnet.lk) is an attractive early-20th-century house set in pretty gardens. The six charming rooms cost from Rs 500 to 1250. There is a modern apartment (four beds) for Rs 1750.

Weliwatta (☎/fax 42891) is an old house with loads of charm, a small garden and an airy sitting area. The five clean rooms cost Rs 600/700.

Rock House (☎ 24948, 213a Yaddehimulla Rd) has four buildings with 14 rooms. Singles cost from Rs 300 to 700. Clean doubles range from Rs 450 to 900 (for a huge spotless upstairs room with its own veranda and fridge). This place gets mixed reviews. Next door, relatives have another *Rock House* (☎ 24949) with similar rooms for Rs 500 to 700 a single or double; the cheapest rooms have a small balcony.

Sea View Guest House (☎ 24376, fax 23649) on Devela Rd is another of Unawatuna's longest-running guesthouses. It has expanded to 24 comfortable rooms spread over four buildings. There's a large garden, but the service is a bit impersonal. Rooms cost Rs 900 to 2100 for a double (with hot water) and Rs 500 for the one single.

Gira Giri Villa (☎ 074-380948, fax 09-53387) is at the extreme north end of Yaddehimulla Rd, about a five-minute walk by shortcut from Unawatuna beach. It's a colonial-style place with three double bedrooms, a veranda with planters' chairs and a walled garden. Steps at the rear of the property lead to a spot where you can get good views of Galle and the harbour. Rooms cost Rs 1200 per single or double. At the time of writing a new building with two rooms was being built.

The Dream House (☎ *074-380018, fax 380019*) is a delightful Italian-run guesthouse with four rooms with colonial ambience and four-poster beds. Rooms with hot water cost US$34 including breakfast. There is a good restaurant with Italian food.

Along the Main Road Up an inland track, the friendly *Araliya Guest House* (☎ *83706, fax 074-380365*) has 10 clean rooms facing a pretty garden from Rs 550 to 650 for singles and Rs 660 to 880 for doubles; rates include breakfast.

Ocean Hill Guest House (☎ *24827*) has wonderful views, perched as it is on the hillside across the road from the beach. Large spotless upstairs rooms (with views) cost Rs 600/1000 per single/double; rooms without views cost Rs 500/800. The hosts are very welcoming and there's a small garden.

Banana Garden (☎/*fax 074-381089*) has nine rooms including four quirky wooden shacks on the beach. The rooms at the back are on the main road and they may be noisy, so stick to the huts (with balconies) on the beach. Singles or doubles cost from Rs 700 to 900. Book ahead.

Sun 'n' Sea (☎ *83200, fax 83399*) is on a good spot of beach – clean and uncrowded – and has great views of the bay and a leafy garden. There are 10 rooms from Rs 1300; add Rs 200 for air-con and hot water.

Places to Eat

All places to stay provide meals, and the home-cooked food can be very good indeed. Eating places along the beachfront are numerous, all offer seafood and often there is not a lot to distinguish one from the other. As they tend to come and go, the best strategy is to ask fellow travellers for their recommendations. A few of the possibilities are listed following.

The *Eagle* is a no-frills beach hut with dirt-cheap, decent food. Breakfast is Rs 75 and jumbo prawns are ridiculously cheap at Rs 130. Closeby, the *Pink Elephant* beach hut also has tasty food at low prices. Prawns with chips and salad costs Rs 185; breakfast costs Rs 85.

South Ceylon Restaurant (☎ *45863*) has a comfy, airy setting, but even better is the delicious vegetarian food. This place offers a refreshing change. The choice includes vegetable juices from Rs 80, muesli with fruit and curd (Rs 85), salads (from Rs 60) and a selection of evening meals (order early) such as lasagne and enchiladas. There's soya milk, tofu and vegan food, and if you want to write home about it, there are Internet facilities as well.

Imesh has good banana fritters. Prawns with chips and salad costs Rs 150, and breakfast is Rs 85.

Sunil's Garden is back from the beach, but it's ringed by a leafy garden and the service is friendly and attentive. Fish with chips and salad costs Rs 170, and calamari with chips and salad or vegetables costs Rs 200. There's always music playing and it's a good spot for 'people watching' and a beer.

Thaproban (see Places to Stay) is popular. Here you can get fresh fruit juices (from Rs 45), pizza (from Rs 165), noodle and rice dishes (from Rs 90), banana fritters, and so on. Beer (Lion Lager) costs Rs 120 and imported wine is also available. There's music as well.

Hot Rock near Three Fishes is popular and the prices are reasonable. There is a good selection of seafood (around Rs 250) as well as rice and noodle dishes and jaffles.

Lucky Tuna has live music on Tuesday nights during the season (don't get too excited, though), and regular barbecues – pop by to check the program. However, some tunas aren't so lucky: grilled tuna and chips costs Rs 200.

Also worth trying is the *Mongolian Restaurant* on the beach. Vegetarian dishes start at Rs 60, and there's also calamari for Rs 180 as well as a selection of rice and noodle dishes.

THE SOUTH

Coral Light Seafood Restaurant next door has good fried fish and chips for Rs 165, sweet and sour fish with rice for Rs 150, devilled crab and chips for Rs 450 and the usual noodle and rice dishes.

Blue Eyes Inn along the Galle-Matara Rd, near the Banana Garden, is spotless and efficient. It does pasta from Rs 175, sweet and sour from Rs 275, garlic prawns for Rs 250, and the intriguingly named Buddhist fasting food (fried vegetables with hot garlic sauce) for Rs 140.

A good place to go for Italian coffee and Italian food is *The Dream House* (see Places to Stay). The coffee costs Rs 100 and mains range from Rs 250 to 950. There's a pleasant veranda where you can sit and relax, and attentive service.

The *Unawatuna Beach Resort* does good buffets, though there's not a great selection of Sri Lankan dishes.

Getting There & Away

You'll hardly notice Unawatuna from the main coastal road, so make sure you don't miss the stop if you're coming by bus. It's only 10 or 15 minutes east from Galle to Unawatuna – take any bus heading that way (Rs 5). From Colombo, a Matara-bound bus is the best bet. Leaving Unawatuna, probably the easiest place to get a bus to stop is near the few shops along Galle-Matara Rd, north of The Strand junction. A taxi to the international airport from Unawatuna costs Rs 2500 and a three-wheeler to Galle costs from Rs 90 to 120 one way.

UNAWATUNA TO WELIGAMA
☎ 09

Beyond Unawatuna the road runs close to the coast for most of the 23km to Weligama, and beyond. There are numerous beautiful stretches of beach and picturesque coves in this area, as well as a number of attractive, secluded places to stay.

Along this part of the coast you will see stilt fishermen if the tides are running right (often around 5.30 to 6 pm). Each fisherman has a pole firmly embedded in the sea bottom, close to the shore. When the sea and fish are flowing in the right direction, the fishermen perch on their poles and cast their lines out. Stilt positions are passed down from father to son and are highly coveted. The fishermen expect payment if you take photographs of them.

Things to See & Do

Just before Koggala there's a WWII airstrip, beside which a small road turns inland to a large **lake** that is alive with bird life, and dotted with islands. It also provides many prawns (you've probably just eaten some). You can take a **catamaran** ride on the lake for Rs 250 per person per hour. There's also the Ananda **spice garden** to visit if you long to cure your bad breath or sunburn, or perhaps you'd like to taste the herbal wine. Both the catamaran and spice garden are managed by the same people and it's best to book ahead on ☎ 83805. The return trip (including waiting time) by three-wheeler from Unawatuna should cost Rs 400.

Near the Hotel Horizon at Koggala, a little inland from the road and railway line (a sign will direct you), there's the **Martin Wickramasinghe Folk Art Museum**. The museum, named after the respected Sinhalese author, is open from 9 am to 5 pm daily; entry is Rs 15. It's a surprisingly large place. The exhibits are extensive, interesting and well displayed. Information is in English and Sinhala. Included among the exhibits is a good section on dance (costumes and instruments), puppets, kolam masks, kitchen utensils and carriages (including one built to be pulled by an elephant). Martin Wickramasinghe's house (and the one in which he was born) is open to the public and is well worth a visit. There is plenty of memorabilia from his life, and some interesting history on the area. All the other houses in this area were demolished in WWII to make way for an airbase. However, this house was left alone. The entire area is beautifully kept and the gardens are peaceful and cool.

Just beyond Koggala the Kataluwa Purwarama temple, with some recently restored murals, is well worth a visit. The turn-off for it is in Kataluwa – you'll see the signs on the inland side of the road.

Stilt fishermen, often seen between Unawatuna and Weligama, only take to their poles when the sea and fish are flowing in the right direction.

Continue a couple of kilometres inland – ask for directions. A friendly monk will open the building and explain the murals to you if you ask. Some of the jataka (episodes from the Buddha's lives) scenes painted here are said to be 200 years old. Note the European figures in their 19th-century attire – you can't help but notice the punishments metered out to sinners.

Soon after the 138km post, at **Midigama**, is a small point with a little beach and good surf when the waves are right. It's a low-key, relaxed place where some surfers and a few others find cheap rooms and meals with local families.

Places to Stay & Eat

Dalawella As you leave Unawatuna, you head into Dalawella, which has a thin, clean beach – some stay here as a quieter option to staying in Unawatuna. First up is *Sun*

Shine Inn (☎ 074-380667, fax 09-83225, e sunshine@sltnet.lk). It's on the inland side of the road and it charges Rs 750 for clean rooms of reasonable size and Rs 1150 with air-con. There's car parking and the service is very friendly. Some rooms have small balconies. Good food is available.

Just east of the 124km post, *Shanthi Guest House (☎/fax 83550)* has six cabanas and six rooms. Rates range from Rs 550 to 1100 for cabanas/rooms. Some are spotless, others are a little grubby, but it's a popular place and there's a garden. There are stilt fishermen on your doorstep.

Two doors east, the *Sri Gemunu Guest House (☎ 83202, fax 074-380078, e susi@ sltnet.lk)* has 21 rooms, a pleasant garden and sea frontage. Rooms cost Rs 2100/2400 for singles/doubles in the new building (with hot water) and Rs 1650/2000 in the old. These rates are for high season half board – it has cheaper room-only rates off season.

A few hundred metres on, *Beach Cottage Wijaya (☎ 83610, fax 074-381659)* has 10 rooms and seven cabanas. Rooms cost from Rs 350 to 600 for singles and Rs 400 to 800 for doubles. Cabanas cost Rs 1200 for singles or doubles. All rates include breakfast. There's a sandy palm-treed garden, all rooms are clean and the hosts are friendly.

Koggala & Habaraduwa Koggala is little more than a few, large beachfront hotels for package tourists, but it has a fine stretch of beach.

Koggala Beach Hotel (☎ 83244, fax 83260) has a pretty pool, an Ayurvedic centre and all the facilities you'd expect in a top-end hotel. All the rooms have sea views (US$43 for single or double).

Hotel Horizon (☎ 83229, fax 83299, e confifi@eureka.lk) has rooms and cabanas for US$110/135. All the rooms have air-con, there's a large garden, an Ayurvedic centre and more. The staff are friendly here too.

Ahangama The *Hotel Club Lanka (☎/fax 83361)* on the beach at Ahangama has clean, comfy rooms for US$22/33, full board only

THE SOUTH

(no air-con). The rooms have simple but stylish furnishings, most have sea views. There's a pool and grassy gardens.

Just after the 137km post you'll find *Villa Gaetano* (☎ *83234, fax 82099*). There are 13 clean large rooms from Rs 600 to 700 per room. The three rooms upstairs at the front have balconies and views, but all the rooms are good value. The place is right on the beach.

Midigama At *Hot Tuna* (☎ *83411*) the friendly family home has five slightly dark, but OK-quality rooms. Three rooms share a bathroom (Rs 250); the two rooms with private bathroom cost Rs 300.

Right beside the train tracks near Midigama train station, *Subodanee* (☎/*fax 83383*) has 13 rooms, all with shared bathroom. It's a messy, colourful family-run hang-out – it'll frighten some and charm others. Singles (no fans) cost Rs 200 and doubles range from Rs 300 to 450. Surfboard rental here costs Rs 150 per day and bicycle rental costs Rs 100.

Sugath's House in front of Midigama train station has no sign, but it's easy to find. It's a superfriendly family home with five rooms, all with shared bathroom. Although a bit grubby, the dirt-cheap rooms only cost Rs 100 per person. There are mosquito nets but you'll have to arm wrestle for the lone fan.

At the 139km post, *Hiltens Beach Resort* (☎ *041-50156*) on the seaward side of the main road makes a mockery of the word 'resort', let alone 'Hilten'. It has seven rooms, all with bathroom. The rooms are small, and some are a bit smelly, but all are great value at Rs 400 per single or double. It has a plum position overlooking the point and there's a pretty garden.

At the 140km post is a country house built in colonial style. The Austrian-owned *Villa Samsara* (☎/*fax 51144*) has four spotless rooms with hot water, all furnished in English/Dutch colonial style. They cost US$55 per room (for two people). There's a large tranquil sitting area, and a palm-studded lawn that fronts onto the beach.

Getting There & Away

There are frequent buses along this stretch of coast connecting Galle, Unawatuna, Weligama, Matara and other points. Bus No 350 from Galle costs Rs 8 to Midigama, although there are any number of other buses plying this route. The main train stations are at Talpe and Ahangama. Some trains originating from Colombo stop at these stations. Only a few local trains stop at the lesser stations such as Midigama.

WELIGAMA
☎ 041

About 30km east of Galle, the town of Weligama (which means Sandy Village) has a fine sandy sweep of bay – just as its name might suggest. It's a busy fishing town, and as there are not many things to do, it's not a popular haunt for travellers.

Very close to the shore, so close in fact that you could walk out to it at low tide, is a tiny island known as **Taprobane**. It looks like an ideal artist's or writer's retreat, which indeed it once was: the novelist Paul Bowles wrote *The Spider's House* here in the 1950s. The island was once owned by the French Count de Maunay. It's possible to rent the whole house here (a stunning place) – which also gives you exclusive use of the island. Contact the Sun House in Galle (see Places to Stay in the Galle section earlier in this chapter for details).

Orientation & Information

The main road divides to go through Weligama, with one branch running along the coast, and the other running parallel through the town centre, a short distance inland. The bus station and Bank of Ceylon are in the middle of town. To reach the centre from the coast road, turn inland 500m east of Taprobane.

Things to See & Do

Scenic though the bay is, Weligama beach is close to the main road and none too clean in the vicinity of the town centre. It's primarily a fishing village and **catamarans** line the west end of the bay. You could organise an hour-long ride in one – expect to pay Rs 500 per catamaran – by approaching a fisherman along the beach. **Snorkelling** at Weligama is good, or you can scuba dive. Try the dive centre at the Bay Beach Hotel (☎ 50201, **e** bbasdive@sltnet.lk). It runs PADI courses as well as excursions such as wreck dives. Prices are comparable to those of other dive centres in Hikkaduwa and elsewhere.

Turning inland, off the inland road west of the centre, takes you over the railway line to a small park with a large **rock-carved figure** known as the Kustaraja. It's been variously described as a king who was mysteriously cured of leprosy, or as Avalokitesvara, a disciple of the Buddha. Nearby there's a temple with a large modern standing Buddha.

Weligama is famous for its **lacework**.

Places to Stay

At the time of writing, *Raja's Guesthouse* (☎ 51750) was building on a new spot, right beside the beach. The four rooms, each with a small terrace, will cost a supercheap Rs 300/350 for singles/doubles including breakfast.

The smaller *resthouse* (☎ 51286) has four basic rooms and a small garden out the front. It's nothing special, but the rooms are decently priced at Rs 500 per single or double.

Greenpeace Inn (☎ 071-215082) is a short walk back from the beach. It's a friendly, family-run venture with six quaintly decorated rooms for Rs 400/500. The place is packed with pot plants and fish ponds.

The friendly *Sam's Holiday Cabanas* (☎ 50803, 484 New By Pass Rd) has a pretty garden beside a relatively secluded beach. The name is a bit of a misnomer because there are no cabanas, only rooms. The rooms are clean, but the bathrooms are a bit grotty. Rooms cost Rs 450/550. It's a pleasant, unhurried place with good food (fish costs Rs 250).

Chez Frank (☎ 50584, 158 Kapparatota Rd) is a spotless place with eight rooms in a garden setting for Rs 450/650. There is a

good restaurant here, as well as bicycle and motorbike hire.

Jaga Bay Resort (☎/fax 50033, Palena), some 2.5km on the main road before Mirissa, is a very pleasant spot on the seaward side of the road. There are 17 rooms. Double rooms range from Rs 650 (with cold water) to Rs 850 (with hot water and a sea view); single rooms cost Rs 100 less.

The attractive *Weligama Bay Inn* (☎ 50299), run by Ceylon Hotels Corporation, has a wide veranda, pleasant green gardens and a fine view across the beach. There are eight sizeable rooms here at Rs 1100/1300.

Crystal Villa (☎ 50635, fax 735031) is a modern place facing the sea offering four rooms (three with air-con) and two bungalows (without air-con). Rooms are clean, airy and cost US$25/35 (without air-con), the bungalows cost US$45 each. Rates are for half board. This place has a swimming pool.

Bay Beach Hotel (☎/fax 50201) has air-con rooms, an attractive swimming pool and extensive gardens. The plain rooms cost US$36/40.

Places to Eat

Given that there's no real restaurant scene in Weligama, you may end up eating at the place where you are staying. *Sam's Holiday Cabanas* has good food (it's best to book ahead).

If you continue on the road past Chez Frank for a couple of hundred metres, you'll find *Keerthi's Seafood Restaurant* (☎ 51172). It's a small, simple hut beside the owner's house. Keerthi is a seafood supplier, so you know the catch will be fresh – it's also tasty and reasonably priced at Rs 180 for rice and fish, and Rs 180 for calamari.

Getting There & Away

Weligama is on the train line from Colombo to Matara. The journey from Colombo takes about three to 3½ hours. There are also frequent buses in both directions along the coast.

MIRISSA
☎ 041

Sleepy Mirissa, 4km south-east of Weligama on the Matara road, has a headland dividing its small fishing harbour from its beautiful curve of sandy beach with calm, clear waters. The places to stay line the beach. Mirissa is becoming very popular as travellers seek out quieter alternatives to Unawatuna and Hikkaduwa.

Things to See & Do
The water is crystal clear so it's perfect for **snorkelling**. Ask your guesthouse if they have gear to hire out or lend. The rocky outcrop to the east of the bay, Parrot Rock, is the perfect place to watch the sunset, and it's also a popular fishing spot.

There are pleasant **walks** around Mirissa. One passes through cinnamon plantations to the small **Kandavahari temple**, where you'll often see peacocks. The headland is a good spot to view Weligama Bay. About 6km inland, there's a **snake farm** with an Ayurvedic practitioner. Ask your guesthouse for details of getting to these spots.

Places to Stay & Eat
Places to stay are listed in order from west (the end closest to Weligama) to east.

Paradise Beach Club (*☎/fax 50380, e mirissa@sltnet.lk*) has small but clean bungalows and four rooms set in lovely landscaped gardens. Both the bungalows and rooms cost Rs 1500/2000 for singles/doubles, half board – add Rs 350 for aircon. There's a pool (nonguests pay Rs 100) and a busy beachfront restaurant (main meals cost around Rs 300).

Central Beach Inn (*☎ 51699*) has six rooms at Rs 400/450 plus two cabanas for Rs 550/700 each. The rooms are small, simple and a little bit grubby, but each has a small veranda, and there's a restaurant hut on the beach.

Ocean Moon (*☎ 52328*) has five cabanas and four rooms set in a lawn fronting on to the beach. The clean cabanas have verandas and cost from Rs 770 to 880. The simple and clean rooms go for Rs 400 a single or double. There's a small restaurant.

Amarasinghe's (*☎ 51204*) is not on the beach, but is a pleasant, leafy spot. Amarasinghe will be a familiar name to those who have enjoyed the hospitality of the manager's brother in Haputale. The guesthouse is signposted on the main road. Turn off at the petrol station and travel down that road for 60m until you come to another signed turn-off. There are six basic (but slightly dull) rooms; two with bathroom at Rs 250/350, and four with shared bathroom at Rs 200. Meals are available.

Mount Garden (*☎ 51079*) is signposted and is on an inland road near the end of Mirissa. It's a superfriendly family home, set back from the beach. The four clean rooms cost Rs 300/400. At the time of writing the family was building a new place, with 10 guestrooms (Rs 500/600), closer to the beach. Meals are available.

Almost opposite the road heading to Mount Garden, *Giragala Village* (*☎ 50496, e nissanka.g@lycosmail.com*) is on a stunning spot that fronts on to Parrot Rock. There's a huge, palm-treed lawn with hammocks, a small restaurant and, to top it all off, the seven rooms only cost from Rs 200 to 550 for singles or doubles. If you're staying here you can use the snorkelling gear for free.

Getting There & Away
The bus fare from Weligama is Rs 4; a three-wheeler is Rs 120. To Matara costs Rs 20 in an air-con bus or Rs 6 in a CTB bus; a three-wheeler will cost Rs 220. If you're heading to Colombo, it's better to catch a bus to Matara and change as many buses will be full by the time they pass through Mirissa.

MATARA
☎ 041 • pop 40,000

Matara, 160km from Colombo, is at the end of the southern railway line. It's Sri Lanka's eighth-biggest town, and is a busy, sprawling mass set beside a grubby, long beach. However, it has some colourful areas and scenes including the odd goat weaving through traffic, and there are a handful of historic elements you may be interested in.

Information

The post office is in the old part of town, to the south of the Nilwala Ganga. Mighty Vision Computer Systems at 171 Anagarika Dharmapala Mawatha has Internet facilities from 9 am to 5.30 pm daily. There's a Vijitha Yapa bookshop on the eastern end of the same street.

Things to See & Do

Matara has a fine Dutch fort, called the **Star Fort** (see the boxed text 'Star Fort'), and a **Dutch rampart** that occupies the width of the promontory that separates the Nilwala Ganga from the sea. Built in the 18th century to protect the Dutch East India Company's administrative buildings, the rampart provides the boundary for much of old Matara, which is quiet and picturesque. Its structure is a little peculiar, as it was to be a fort but cost cutting at the time dictated otherwise. The Star Fort is about 350m from the main rampart gate, across the river.

If you're interested in batik, drop into **Jez Look Batiks** at 12 St Yehiya Mawatha or **Art Batiks** at 58/6 Udyana Rd. It's worth walking along the east end of Kumarathunga Mawatha, where anything and everything is for sale.

Polhena, a quiet suburb (it used to be a village) 3km towards Colombo, has a good coral reef that you can snorkel to.

Places to Stay

Matara has quite a few places to stay, but most are shabby and overpriced. Many travellers stay in the leafy suburb of Polhena, south-west of the centre.

Matara About 200m from the bus station, you'll find Matara's *Rest House* (☎/fax 22299), which is beautifully situated right by the beach. It's said to be built on a site where captured elephants were corralled. The rooms are large, comfortable and clean, and cost from Rs 620 to 750 for singles and

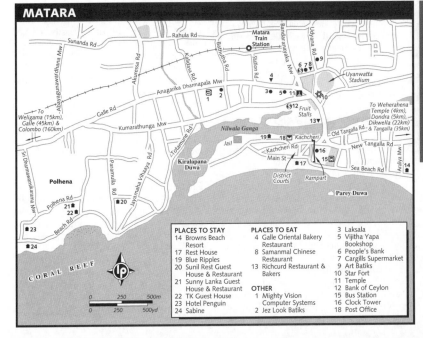

MATARA

THE SOUTH

PLACES TO STAY	PLACES TO EAT	3 Laksala
14 Browns Beach	4 Galle Oriental Bakery	5 Vijitha Yapa
Resort	Restaurant	Bookshop
17 Rest House	8 Samanmal Chinese	6 People's Bank
19 Blue Ripples	Restaurant	7 Cargills Supermarket
20 Sunil Rest Guest	13 Richcurd Restaurant &	9 Art Batiks
House & Restaurant	Bakers	10 Star Fort
21 Sunny Lanka Guest		11 Temple
House & Restaurant	OTHER	12 Bank of Ceylon
22 TK Guest House	1 Mighty Vision	15 Bus Station
23 Hotel Penguin	Computer Systems	16 Clock Tower
24 Sabine	2 Jez Look Batiks	18 Post Office

Star Fort

The attractive little Star Fort at Matara was built by the Dutch to compensate for deficiencies in the fortification built on the seaward side of the river. The fortification, a rampart in fact – although it was supposed to have been a fort – was built to protect the VOC's (Dutch East India Company's) administrative buildings. As this area was open to attack on the river side, a new, more secure defensive structure was called for. The Star Fort was completed in 1763 (within about three years of its first being mooted); the date is embossed over the main gate along with the VOC insignia and the coat of arms of the governor responsible for constructing the building. If you look carefully, you can see the slots that once secured the drawbridge beams.

The fort was designed to accommodate 12 big cannons, but today only seven of the embrasures remain. The fort is surrounded by a mosquito-infested moat. Inside there's a model replica of the fort, a well, and what remains of the original quarters. There are also two eerie prisoners' quarters. A guide will show you around the fort, for a tip.

The Star Fort fulfilled its purpose as an administrative building, and was never attacked. It represents the last major defensive construction by the VOC in Sri Lanka.

Rs 800 to 920 for doubles. There's a large garden and a decent restaurant.

Blue Ripples (☎ 22058, 38 Wilfred Gunasekera Mawatha) is a friendly and peaceful place in a shady, riverside garden. Two rooms with cute balconies are set right by the river, another two a little way back. Each costs Rs 350/375 for singles/doubles. Discounts are available. Book ahead.

Browns Beach Resort (☎ 26298) is on a bleak stretch of Sea Beach Rd and an uninviting stretch of beach, but it's one of the few places with air-con (Rs 1200 per single/double) and the rooms are spotless.

Polhena In a prime spot on the beach, *Sabine (☎ 27951, Beach Rd)* is a small house with four rooms. It's rough around the edges, but is friendly and cheap. The going rates are Rs 175 for singles and Rs 200 to 300 for doubles. There's a small garden, and there are also hammocks and cheap eats.

The *Hotel Penguin (☎ 078-511090, Sri Dharmawansikarama Mawatha)*, a short way inland from Sabine, has bungalows set in a pretty garden. The five clean rooms cost Rs 350 for singles and Rs 350 to 500 for doubles. It has welcoming hosts, leafy surrounds and cheap food, although there's no breakfast. Note also that there are no mozzie nets.

The *TK Guest House (☎ 22603)* has 11 roomy, clean rooms and a pleasant, large grassed garden. Rooms cost Rs 450 for singles and from Rs 400 to 550 for doubles. You can hire snorkelling gear from Titus, who frequents the guesthouse in search of custom.

Sunny Lanka Guest House & Restaurant (☎ 23504, 93 Polhena Rd) has five rooms for Rs 350/450. This is a friendly, relaxed and clean place, and it has good food too. You can rent scuba and snorkelling gear as well as bicycles.

Sunil Rest Guest House & Restaurant (☎ 21983, 16/3 A, 2nd Cross Rd) has three basic rooms in one house and three more in another house nearby. Singles cost Rs 250 and doubles cost from Rs 300 to 600. There's a kitchen here, and Sunil hires out motorbikes and snorkelling gear. Guests can use his bicycles for free.

Places to Eat

The *Rest House* at Matara has a pleasant setting and it serves a range of decent meals. You can get breakfast there for around Rs 80, sandwiches from Rs 90, and mains from Rs 150 to 200.

The old-fashioned *Richcurd Restaurant & Bakers*, along the roadside just north of the bridge, is worth a try for dirt-cheap rice and fish curry (Rs 25) at lunch time. Some well-stocked fruit stalls can be found nearby.

The popular *Galle Oriental Bakery Restaurant* along Anagarika Dharmapala Mawatha does rice and vegie curry for Rs 36 (lunch time only) as well as cakes and tasty short eats.

Samanmal Chinese Restaurant (64 Udyana Rd), next to Cargills supermarket, is a dark den but serves good food that is accompanied with boppy music. Try the sweet-and-sour fish (Rs 135), fried prawns with veggies (Rs 165) or just sip a beer (Rs 85).

Getting There & Away

CTB buses travel to/from Colombo and intermediate coastal points half-hourly, on average, throughout the day. Colombo is a 3½- to four-hour trip (Rs 33). The one-hour trip east to Tangalla is Rs 12. Intercity expresses leave regularly; prices include to Galle for Rs 55 and to Colombo for Rs 80. There are also direct buses up to Ratnapura and the hill country. If you miss the direct ones you can get to Wellawaya and take a connection from there if you don't leave it too late in the day.

Matara is at the end of the railway line from Colombo. Trains head to Colombo at 5.40, 7.25 and 9.10 am, and 1.15 and 4.50 pm (Rs 33/90/157 in 3rd/2nd/1st class). The express train to Vavuniya (for Anuradhapura) leaves at 9.10 am. The 1.15 pm train to Kandy costs Rs 57/157 in 3rd/2nd class; the trip takes seven hours, although delays are not uncommon.

Getting Around

Polhena is a short ride by bus No 350, 356 or 260 from Matara bus station, but there's only a handful of buses right to the beach each day. Otherwise you'll have to get off at the junction of Galle and Sri Dharmawansikarama Rds and walk a kilometre or so to the beach. To reach the beach with the reef, turn left at the T-junction 500m south of the main road, then right at the next junction.

A three-wheeler from the Matara train station to Polhena should cost Rs 100, while from the bus station at Matara it should be Rs 120.

MATARA TO TANGALLA

At Meddawatte, on the main road a few kilometres east of Matara, is the impressive Ruhuna University campus. There are several other places of interest just off the 35km of road from Matara to Tangalla, including two superb examples of what one visitor labelled 'neo-Buddhist kitsch'.

Weherahena Temple

Just as you leave Matara, a turn inland will take you to the gaudy Weherahena Temple, where an artificial cave is decorated with about 200 comic-book-like scenes from the Buddha's life. There's also a huge Buddha figure here. You can get here on bus No 349, or a three-wheeler will charge Rs 200 from Matara's bus station. There's no entry fee as such, but you may be asked for a donation.

At the time of the late November/early December full moon, a *perahera* (procession) is held at the temple to celebrate the anniversary of its founding. During the evening there's a big procession of dancers and elephants, which come from all the surrounding villages. There's also a smaller 'preview' procession the day before.

Dondra

About 5km south-east of Matara you come to the town of Dondra. Travel south from here for 1.2km and you'll reach the lighthouse at the southernmost point of Sri Lanka. Unfortunately the lighthouse isn't open to the public and staring at it through the fence can be rather disappointing. At least you can console yourself with a drink at the nearby *Lighthouse Restaurant (Hammana Rd)*, which is exquisitely sited (it's signposted about 250m from the lighthouse itself). Food is reasonably priced and quite OK: prawns in hot garlic sauce cost Rs 220, noodle and rice dishes start at Rs 70, fish starts at Rs 190, and vegetable dishes start at Rs 110.

A CTB bus from Matara (Rs 5) will drop you in the centre of Dondra. From there you could three-wheel it to the lighthouse and/or restaurant if you don't feel like walking.

THE SOUTH

Wewurukannala Vihara

If the Weherahena Temple is 'Marvel Comics meets Lord Buddha', then here it's Walt Disney who runs into him. At the town of Dikwella, 22km from Matara, a road turns inland towards Beliatta. About 1.5km along you come to a 50m-high seated Buddha figure – the largest in Sri Lanka. Entry is Rs 25; it's Rs 50 extra for a camera and Rs 100 for a video.

The temple has three parts. The oldest is about 250 years old but is of no particular interest. The next part, a real hall of horrors, has life-size models of demons and sinners shown in graphic, gory detail. Punishments for those who've strayed from the path include being dunked in boiling cauldrons, sawn in half, disembowelled and so on. Finally there's the gigantic seated figure that was constructed in the 1960s. As if to prove that it really is as high as an eight-storey building, what should be right behind it but an eight-storey building? You can climb up inside and peer right into the Buddha's head. The walls of the backing building have been painted with hundreds of comic-strip representations of events in the Buddha's lives. There's one other thing to see here, an interesting clock in the adjoining building, made by a prisoner about 70 years ago.

Mawella

About 6km beyond Dikwella, near the 186km marker, a road heads off for 1.1km to the (sometimes) spectacular **Ho-o-maniya blowhole** on the coast. During the southwest monsoon (June is the best time) high seas can force water 23m up through a natural chimney in the rocks and then spout out up to 18m in the air. At other times the blowhole is disappointing – don't bother going.

Places to Stay & Eat

Manahara Beach Cottage & Cabanas (*☎/fax 047-40585*) near the 189km post and about 6km west of Tangalla, has six clean, roomy cabanas, and three good rooms. The cabanas and rooms cost Rs 1500/2200 for singles/doubles with half board (no room-only rates). There's a large leafy garden, a pool and beach frontage. It's a quiet spot.

The Italian-built *Dickwella Village Resort* (*☎ 041-55271/2, fax 55410,* *e dickwella@ mail.ewisl.net*) stands on a headland on the Matara side of Dikwella. There are non air-con rooms that cost US$70/90 for full board (no room-only rates). There is a diving school (nonguests are welcome); two dives including gear cost US$40, and PADI courses are available from US$350. See the boxed text 'Responsible Diving & Snorkelling' in the Hikkaduwa section of the West Coast chapter for advice on safe diving. You can also go windsurfing, snorkelling and fishing, and if these don't appeal there is tennis, volleyball and minigolf. There are two bars, and there is a restaurant.

For those who are looking for something special and can afford the price tag, there's *Claughton* (*☎ 01-509134*), 11km west of Tangalla and 400m off the main road (look for the sign that says Nilwella). This beautiful villa has a distinctly Mediterranean flavour. When you approach it, you look straight through the elevated entrance to the sea. The garden runs down to a secluded beach and there's a fine swimming pool. The house can be rented by the room (there's one double and two twin-bed rooms, all with their own bathrooms) or in its entirety (US$375 per day for up to six people, full board).

TANGALLA
☎ 047

Situated 195km from Colombo, Tangalla (also spelt Tangalle, Tengale and Tengalla but usually pronounced ten-gol) is one of the nicest spots along the coast, particularly if you just want somewhere to laze and soak up the sun. The town itself is an easy-going place with several reminders of Dutch days, including the Rest House, which was once home for the Dutch administrators.

Tangalla's series of bays are the modern attraction. To the north-east of the Rest House the long white sands of Medaketiya Beach shimmer away into the distance, while to the west is a whole series of smaller bays. But beware: Some of the beaches, including Medaketiya, shelve off very steeply, and the resulting waves make them dangerous for

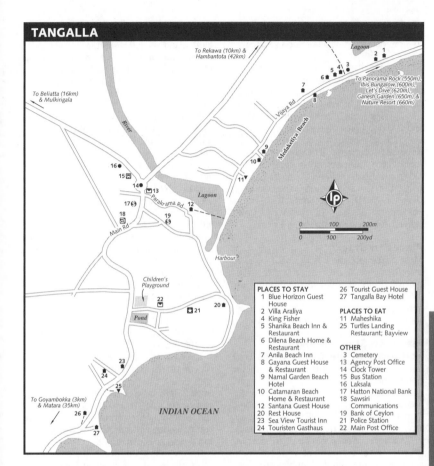

TANGALLA

To Rekawa (10km) &
Hambantota (42km)

Lagoon

To Panorama Rock (550m),
Ibis Bungalow (600m),
Let's Dive (620m),
Ganesh Garden (650m) &
Nature Resort (660m)

To Beliatta (16km)
& Mulkirigala

River

Vijaya Rd

Medaketiya Beach

Lagoon

Parakrama Rd

Main Rd

Harbour

Children's
Playground

Pond

To Goyambokka (3km)
& Matara (35km)

INDIAN OCEAN

0   100   200m
0   100   200yd

PLACES TO STAY
1 Blue Horizon Guest
   House
2 Villa Araliya
4 King Fisher
5 Shanika Beach Inn &
   Restaurant
6 Dilena Beach Home &
   Restaurant
7 Anila Beach Inn
8 Gayana Guest House
   & Restaurant
9 Namal Garden Beach
   Hotel
10 Catamaran Beach
   Home & Restaurant
12 Santana Guest House
20 Rest House
23 Sea View Tourist Inn
24 Touristen Gasthaus

26 Tourist Guest House
27 Tangalla Bay Hotel

PLACES TO EAT
11 Maheshika
25 Turtles Landing
   Restaurant; Bayview

OTHER
3 Cemetery
13 Agency Post Office
14 Clock Tower
15 Bus Station
16 Laksala
17 Hatton National Bank
18 Sawsiri
   Communications
19 Bank of Ceylon
21 Police Station
22 Main Post Office

THE SOUTH

swimmers if there's any sort of wind or tidal current. See the boxed text 'Safe Swimming' in the West Coast chapter for advice.

The bay, just on the town side of the Tangalla Bay Hotel, is probably the most sheltered, although right beside the Rest House is a tiny bay that is very shallow and generally calm and is popular with snorkellers. By the Palm Paradise Cabanas, south-west of the Tangalla Bay Hotel, is a picturesque and fairly secluded bay popular with seekers of an overall suntan. It's also far enough from the town to minimise worries about the cleanliness of the water.

Information
The Hatton National Bank (open 9 am to 3 pm Monday to Friday) changes most travellers cheques and gives cash advances on Visa, MasterCard and American Express (AmEx) credit cards. The Bank of Ceylon, open the same hours, provides cash advances on Visa and AmEx, but not MasterCard.

There is an agency post office opposite the main bus stand, which is open from 7 am to 6 pm daily. Local and international calls can be made from here. The main post office is near the Rest House. You can use the Internet at Sawsiri Communications on Main

Rd. It's open from 8 am to 6 pm weekdays, to 5 pm on Saturday, and to noon Sunday.

Scuba Diving

Scuba diving can be arranged at Let's Dive (☎ 077-902073, fax 40401), 1.5km along the beach road, north-east of the centre of town. Trips include a night dive (US$35) and PADI courses (open-water beginner is US$325, advanced is US$210). There are discounts for groups. The dive sites are at reefs where you see plenty of coral and myriad tropical fish including coral fish, angel fish, puffer fish and more. See the boxed text 'Responsible Diving & Snorkelling' in the Hikkaduwa section in the West Coast chapter for advice on diving safely.

Places to Stay

Most accommodation is in small, relaxed travellers guesthouses with just a few simple rooms, typically with bathroom, fan, mosquito net, but no hot water. Prices given here are for the high season: they drop, sometimes considerably, at other times.

Places to Stay – Budget

North-East of the Centre If you head north-east from the bus station over the bridge, then take the first road on the right, you'll find yourself travelling towards Medaketiya, the long beach stretching about 3km north-east of Tangalla's town centre. Several guesthouses dot the beachfront track.

Catamaran Beach Home & Restaurant (☎ 40446) has three rooms with bathroom and one without. Singles/doubles are cheap at Rs 275/390, which is just as well since they're shabby, forlorn and you'll probably be sharing the room with wildlife. The host is friendly, but bargain for a better deal.

Namal Garden Beach Hotel (☎ 40352) fronting right on to the beach has 16 sizeable rooms at Rs 440/660. The top-floor rooms have a private balcony, the ground-floor rooms are depressing; all are grotty, though the bathrooms are OK and some rooms have great views over the sea.

Dilena Beach Home & Restaurant (☎ 42240) has two clean, quaint rooms in a friendly family home for Rs 350 each. It's right across from the beach. There's a sandy garden and a small restaurant.

Shanika Beach Inn & Restaurant (☎ 42079), next door to Dilena, has six rooms for Rs 300/350. The rooms are clean, though a little dark, but they're OK value for money.

King Fisher (☎ 40817) has seven clean rooms, four with bathroom and three without. Rooms cost from Rs 250 to 600. The cute single room upstairs is good value (though the shared bathroom is a bit frightening). It's a friendly, busy family home.

Blue Horizon Guest House (☎/fax 40721) has two rooms downstairs and a room upstairs with its own sea-view balcony. The clean rooms cost from Rs 330 to 550. If you like views, welcoming hosts and value for money, you'll love this place. Three new rooms were under construction at the time of writing.

Anila Beach Inn (☎ 40446) has six rooms from Rs 350 to 880. The rooms are large and clean and two have balconies but you'll need to BYO personality, as there's little in this place. You can hire bicycles for Rs 100 per day.

Gayana Guest House & Restaurant (☎ 40659, fax 40477) has 15 rooms, eight with beach frontage, seven out the back, and a restaurant right on the beach. Rooms cost from Rs 550 to 1100 – they're spotless and simple, but nothing special. Here you're paying extra for the beachfront spot and the popular restaurant.

If you follow the beach there are even more places; all are wedged between the beach and the lagoon (you can organise catamaran trips on the lagoon). An alternative route to this area is via the Hambantota road – they are signposted. A three-wheeler from the bus station to these places should cost around Rs 70.

The *Panorama Rock* (☎/fax 40458) on the beach has four clean bungalows in a garden setting for Rs 450/650. With a welcoming host, a small restaurant beside the beach, the lagoon nearby and regular barbecues, you won't want to leave.

Ibis Bungalow has nine roomy, spotless cabanas spread throughout a large garden.

There are two types of cabanas: the smaller ones are especially good value at Rs 550 and the larger ones cost Rs 1100. There's a small pond and the hosts are very welcoming.

South of the Centre The *Santana Guest House* (☎ 40419, 55 Parakrama Rd), in the town centre, has five plain rooms. A single with shared bathroom costs Rs 250 and doubles with bathroom cost Rs 350. The friendly owner – who not only likes but looks like Carlos Santana – has added a rickety little restaurant on stilts out over the lagoon with a bamboo bridge leading to the beach.

Ten to 15 minutes' walk in the Matara direction from the bus station, the *Sea View Tourist Inn* is a quiet and friendly family home with four rooms. A double with bathroom costs Rs 350 and a single with a shared bathroom costs Rs 220. The food here is inexpensive.

The *Touristen Gasthaus* (☎/fax 40370) farther along has a leafy garden and spotless rooms – three upstairs and three downstairs – for Rs 500/650. One of the rooms here has a balcony and a kitchen, which is particularly good value.

The modern *Tourist Guest House* (☎ 40389), opposite the big Tangalla Bay Hotel, is near the main road so it may be a bit noisy. It has eight spotless rooms, hot water, IDD facilities, and some sea-facing balconies, for Rs 330 to 880 (singles) or Rs 440 to 1250 (doubles). You can hire bicycles for Rs 125 a day. The owners will pick you up for free from the bus station if you telephone, or you can catch a three-wheeler here for Rs 50.

Places to Stay – Mid-Range
North-East of the Centre The gorgeous *Villa Araliya* (☎/fax 42163) is an old-style place with colonial furniture and a garden (complete with a friendly Jack Russell terrier). There are two bungalows, each with large inviting verandas and enticing four-poster beds, for Rs 1200. The room inside the house costs Rs 1000. The food is delicious, but is only for guests. Book ahead.

Ganesh Garden (☎ 40844, fax 40401) has four bungalows with another two new ones on the way. The bungalows (Rs 700/1000), each of which has a veranda, are dotted throughout a garden (with hammocks) and there's a hut restaurant beside the beach. The host is friendly, there are board games and regular barbecues. To summarise, this place oozes potential for laid-back times.

Nature Resort (☎/fax 40844) has large, spotless bungalows for US$37 a single or double, a billiard table and a pool (nonguests pay Rs 100). It's a relaxed place with a garden and a quiet, beachfront location.

South of the Centre The *Rest House* (☎ 40299) is pleasantly situated on the promontory above the harbour. It's one of the oldest resthouses in the country, originally built, as a plate on the front steps indicates, by the Dutch in 1774. Unfortunately it has retained few original features, and even less charm. The rooms are modern, bare and not worth Rs 800/1100 (which includes breakfast).

The *Tangalla Bay Hotel* (☎ 433754, fax 449548) is a 1970s monstrosity built to look like a boat. It's kitsch and dated in an endearing kind of way. It has certainly got a great location right on a promontory, the service is attentive and there is a swimming pool (nonguests Rs 100). Don't be tempted to use the beach, which has very dangerous currents. Rooms cost US$26/30.

If you continue for 3km along the Matara road, you'll come to a signposted turn-off at Goyambokka, and a road lined with a few guesthouses, most with cabanas. This is a quiet, leafy area with a clean secluded beach. You can catch any Matara-bound bus to drop you at the turn-off (Rs 4). A three-wheeler from Tangalla bus station should cost Rs 100.

About 400m up the track you'll come to *Calm Garden Cabanas* (☎ 40523). It's a family-run affair, back from the beach, and there's a large lawn garden. The three clean cabanas cost Rs 660/1000 each, including breakfast. Other meals are available.

THE SOUTH

Nearby, *Palm Paradise Cabanas* (☎/fax 40338, e ppc@vinet.lk) has large, clean, wooden cabanas scattered around a secluded beachside palm grove. They're solidly built on stilts and all have their own sleeping/living area, bathroom and breezy veranda. The beach is safe for swimming. There's an open-air bar (you can get South African, Californian and French wines) and a good restaurant. Rooms cost US$25 to US$30 for a single, and US$30 to US$35 for a double (for half board, no room-only rates).

Further on, the *Goyambokka Guest House* (☎/fax 40838) has four small, spotless rooms (no mozzie nets) for Rs 1000/1200 including breakfast. It's away from the beach, but there's a pretty garden and a small veranda.

Butterflies Cabana has two basic cabanas for Rs 800 including breakfast. It's a no-frills, family-run place set back from the beachfront.

Rocky Point Beach Bungalows (☎ 40834, fax 40994) is a popular spot with great views, a large garden, three bungalows and four rooms. Rooms cost Rs 1200/1400 and bungalows Rs 1300/1600; these rates include breakfast, but are a little overpriced. There's a restaurant (with board games) that overlooks a small beach.

Places to Eat

As you'd expect from the number of fishing boats, there's good seafood to be found in Tangalla.

Maheshika is a low-key beach hut lit by kerosene lamps. The tasty food starts from Rs 30 for soups, vegetarian meals from Rs 80, rice and curry from Rs 110, and fish and chips for Rs 220. It's a small place so it may pay to place your order during the day.

Of the places to stay, the restaurants at *Panorama Rock* and *Ganesh Garden*, at the far end of the beach, also have good, inexpensive food. The *Gayana Guest House & Restaurant* does good food too, for decent prices.

Turtles Landing Restaurant and *Bayview* are two hut restaurants beside the beach, south of town and overlooking a bay covered with bobbing fishing boats. It's a pretty setting, but don't worry, you're paying for it: both restaurants have tasty, similar fare and inflated prices, with fish and chips for Rs 270 and tiger prawns for Rs 560.

Getting There & Away

There are no trains to Tangalla – the railway terminates at Matara – but there are plenty of buses. To get to Galle (Rs 60), catch the intercity express bound for Colombo. The express all the way to Colombo costs Rs 90 and leaves approximately every half-hour, between 6 am and midnight. There are hourly buses to Wellawaya (from 6 am to 3 pm) for Rs 40; an intercity express costs Rs 80. Buses to Tissamaharama cost Rs 25 and leave regularly; to both Hambantota and Matara it costs Rs 13.

MULKIRIGALA

Mulkirigala rock temple, about 16km north of Tangalla, has a little of Dambulla and Sigiriya about it. Steps lead up to a series of cleft-like caves in the huge rock. As with Dambulla, the caves shelter large reclining Buddhas, together with wall paintings and other smaller sitting and standing figures. You can then continue on your barefoot way to a dagoba perched on the very top of the rock, where there's a fine view over the surrounding country. There is a Buddhist school for young monks nearby.

Manuscripts discovered here in a monastic library by a British official in 1826 were uses as sthe basis for scholars translating the *Mahavamsa* from the Pali script. You will be asked for a Rs 150 donation to enter.

Getting There & Away

Mulkirigala can be reached from Tangalla either via Beliatta or Wiraketiya. Take a Middeniya bus (make sure that it actully goes via Beliatta) and ask to be let off at the Mulkirigala junction. Otherwise, take a bus just to Beliatta and then another on to the Mulkirigala junction. You can even get there by bicycle from Tangalla – some guesthouses hire them – although it's a rather rough ride at times. A three-wheeler from Tangalla costs about Rs 500 for a return trip.

Saving the Turtles

It's close to midnight at Rekawa, a small fishing village some 10km east of Tangalla. A few tourists stand on the darkened beach, scanning the ocean. They've come to see marine turtles, familiar but endangered visitors to this part of the coast. It's November and only one lonely turtle heaves itself out of the water to lay its eggs this night. But between January and July, the peak laying season, as many as 17 turtles may make their slow, deliberate journey up the beach. Hidden beneath the sand at any time of the year are many nests, each harbouring a clutch of incubating eggs. At any time the tiny hatchlings may burst forth and scuttle down to the sea.

The nightly ritual is repeated year round without interference from poachers or predators, thanks to the efforts of a nongovernment organisation known as the Turtle Conservation Project (TCP; ☎/fax 047-40581, e turtle@panlanka.net) located at 73 Hambantota Rd, Tangalla.

The TCP is not a hatchery. Instead its staff employ local people as nest protectors. This ensures that the eggs lie undisturbed until they hatch naturally, at night. The hatchlings are free to scamper towards the ocean as soon as they emerge from their nests, as nature intended. In its first two days of life a hatchling's overriding instinct is to swim – and swim. This allows it to get well away from the shore, and out of reach of land-based predators.

The TCP arranges turtle watches for interested visitors and the money earned from these goes towards paying the nest protectors – usually local fisherfolk. The turtle watches start at the TCP's Rekawa office at 7 pm every night (a turtle watch ticket costs Rs 300; children and students pay Rs 200). However, at the time of writing the TCP's funding had dried up. The Department of Wildlife is taking over the turtle watches (same time and prices) until the TCP's new grant is finalised.

If you have experience in this sort of conservation work, you may apply to become a volunteer with the TCP, although a commitment of at least six months is required.

There are a few guidelines you should observe if you wish to join a turtle watch:

- Wear dark clothing. Light coloured clothing can be seen by turtles and may disturb them.
- As a courtesy to the local people here, women should wear long skirts/dresses or trousers – at least something that covers your legs – and tops that cover the shoulders.
- Cameras with flash are not allowed as the bright light disturbs the turtles.
- If you bring a torch (flashlight), don't use it while on the beach for the same reason.
- Never go onto the beach without a TCP research officer.
- Arrive on time.

Rekawa Beach is a 20-minute drive from Tangalla. Take the turn-off at the Netolpitiya Junction (from the Hambantota Rd). A three-wheeler driver will take you there and back and wait for you for about Rs 600. The Rekawa office is instantly recognisable: it has turtles painted on the walls.

TAMSIN WILSON

The olive Ridley turtle is one of five species of marine turtle found in the seas surrounding Sri Lanka.

HAMBANTOTA
☎ 047

Between Tangalla and Hambantota, 237km from Colombo, you move from a wet zone into a dry zone, which continues right across Yala West (Ruhuna) National Park.

Hambantota is a bustling town with little going for it, although there are some magnificent sweeps of beach both east and west of the small promontory in the town. A large collection of outrigger fishing boats is often beached on the sands.

Hambantota has a high proportion of Malay Muslims, many of whom speak Malay as well as Tamil and Sinhala. A major industry in Hambantota is the production of salt by the age-old method of evaporating sea water from shallow salt pans. You will see these pans alongside the road on the east side of Hambantota as you turn inland from the coast. Between Hambantota and Tissamaharama there are a number of roadside stalls selling delicious curd and honey or treacle – definitely worth a stop if you can manage it.

There is a Bank of Ceylon here, which is a good place to change travellers cheques. It's open until 3 pm. The bank is almost opposite the resthouse.

Bundala National Park

Bundala National Park (see the boxed text 'Bundala') stretches nearly 20km along a coastal strip starting just east of Hambantota. The main road east passes along Bundala's northern boundary. Bundala is famous for its bird life, and you may see the occasional elephant. It's also good for crocodile-spotting – and it's less visited than Yala. A four hour, five person jeep trip to Bundala from Hambantota should cost about Rs 2000. Entry costs US$6.50 (including taxes, and a tracker).

Hambantota has a number of touts angling to take travellers to the Bundala or Yala West National Parks, but the most reliable places to organise a trip to these places include the Peacock Beach Hotel, the Sunshine Tourist Rest and the Resthouse. See the boxed text 'Snagging the Perfect Safari Tout' later in this chapter for tips on getting a driver. There's little advantage in going to Yala from Hambantota rather than from Tissamaharama.

Places to Stay & Eat

Mr Hassim's guesthouse (☎ 20569, 33 Terrace St) has rooms from Rs 250 to 400 but all the rooms, except the one at the front, are a bit depressing. Still keen? To get there, walk 100m from the bus station along Main St (towards Tissamaharama), and turn up the track on your left.

Bundala

Bundala National Park is an important wetland sanctuary. Within its 62-sq-km area shelter at least 149 species of bird and a small population of elephants (between 25 and 60 depending on the season). It's a winter home to the greater flamingo (Phoenicopterus ruber); up to 2000 have been recorded here at any one time. Many other birds make extraordinary journeys from Siberia and the Rann of Kutch in India to winter here, arriving between August and April. In addition to elephants, Bundala also provides sanctuary to leopards, sloth bears, civet cats and giant squirrels. Between October and January four of Sri Lanka's five species of marine turtle (olive Ridley, green turtle, leathery, hawksbill, loggerhead) visit the coast to lay their eggs. Marsh and estuarine crocodiles are also found in Bundala.

There are two camp sites in the park. For information contact the Wildlife Department (☎ 01-694241, fax 698556) at 18 Gregory's Rd, Cinnamon Gardens, Colombo 7.

▲ ▲ ▲ ▲ ▲ ▲ ▲ ▲ ▲

Sunshine Tourist Rest (☎ 20129, 47 Main St), a five-minute walk from the bus station in the Tissamaharama direction, has five singles/doubles for Rs 350/400 with shared bathroom and two rooms for Rs 450/500 with private bathroom. The place is rather dull, but Mrs Nihar, the manager, is an excellent cook. The traffic noise quietens down after about 8 pm.

It's worth paying extra, if you can manage it, to stay at the pick of the cheapies, *Hambantota Resthouse* (☎/fax 20299). It's nicely situated on top of the promontory overlooking the town and beach, about 300m south of the bus station. The rooms are large, clean and most have good views. Rooms cost from US$22/25. The food is good.

About 7km along the main road before you reach Hambantota from Colombo is the *Oasis Hotel* (☎/fax 20650) in Sisilasagama, which is a spotless, modern place with a swimming pool and large grounds. The air-con rooms cost US$48 a single or double.

You'll find the **Peacock Beach Hotel** (☎ 20377, fax 20690, e peacock@sltnet.lk) about 600m along the road to Tissamaharama. It's a bit worn, but there are large air-con rooms for US$50 a single or double, plus a fine swimming pool that nonguests can use for Rs 200.

Getting There & Away

Hambantota is about six hours from Colombo by bus. The intercity express costs Rs 110. To get to Tissamaharama costs Rs 15 and takes an hour; to get to Tangalla costs Rs 13 for the 1¼-hour trip. There are also a few buses between Hambantota and Ratnapura via Embilipitiya (which cost about Rs 40, 3½ hours), as well as others heading north to Wellawaya and the hill country.

TISSAMAHARAMA
☎ 047

Tissamaharama, often called Tissa, is a busy town surrounded by rice paddies

that are dotted with temples. Yala West (Ruhuna) National Park (see that section later in this chapter) is the main reason most visitors come to Tissa, so it's something of a cowboy town with 'safari' touts lurking at guesthouses and bus stops, and everybody else trying to get their cut of the safari business too.

Orientation & Information

If you're coming via Hambantota or Wellawaya you'll pass the village of Deberawewa (look out for the clock tower), about 2km from Tissa itself. Ignore the signs announcing 'Tissamaharama' as you enter it and the accommodation touts who board buses and advise travellers to get off because 'this is Tissa'. Tissa itself is the best place to organise a Yala trip.

Money The Bank of Ceylon and Hatton National Bank are on Main Rd. They are open from 9 am to 3 pm Monday to Friday.

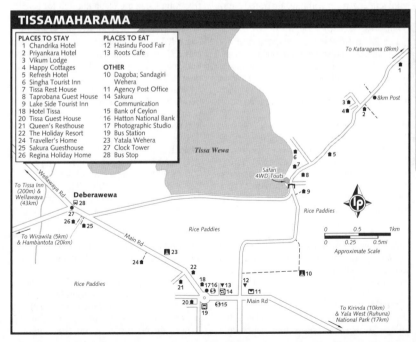

TISSAMAHARAMA

PLACES TO STAY
1 Chandrika Hotel
2 Priyankara Hotel
3 Vikum Lodge
4 Happy Cottages
5 Refresh Hotel
6 Singha Tourist Inn
7 Tissa Rest House
8 Taprobana Guest House
9 Lake Side Tourist Inn
18 Hotel Tissa
20 Tissa Guest House
21 Queen's Resthouse
22 The Holiday Resort
24 Traveller's Home
25 Sakura Guesthouse
26 Regina Holiday Home

PLACES TO EAT
12 Hasindu Food Fair
13 Roots Cafe

OTHER
10 Dagoba; Sandagiri Wehera
11 Agency Post Office
14 Sakura Communication
15 Bank of Ceylon
16 Hatton National Bank
17 Photographic Studio
19 Bus Station
23 Yatala Wehera
27 Clock Tower
28 Bus Stop

To Kataragama (8km)

8km Post

THE SOUTH

Tissa Wewa

Safari 4WD Touts

To Tissa Inn (200m) & Wellawaya (43km)

Wellawaya Rd

Deberawewa

To Wirawila (5km) & Hambantota (20km)

Main Rd

Rice Paddies

Rice Paddies

Rice Paddies

Main Rd

0   0.5   1km
0   0.25   0.5mi
Approximate Scale

To Kirinda (10km) & Yala West (Ruhuna) National Park (17km)

Post & Communications There is an agency post office along the Main Rd. If you want to make IDD calls or use the Internet try Sakura Communication in Main Rd, open from 7 am to 11 pm daily.

Tissa Wewa & Dagobas

The tank in Tissa, the Tissa Wewa, is thought to date from the 3rd century BC. There are several ancient dagobas in the Tissa area. The large white restored dagoba between Tissa town centre and the tank is credited to Kavantissa, a king of the ancient southern kingdom of Ruhunu, centred on Tissamaharama. Next to the dagoba is a statue of Queen Viharamahadevi.

According to legend, Viharamahadevi landed at Kirinda, about 10km south of Tissa, after being sent to sea by her father King Kelanitissa as a penance for his killing of a monk. The daughter landed unharmed and subsequently married Kavantissa. Their son, Dutugemunu, was the Sinhalese hero who, starting from Ruhunu, liberated Anuradhapura from Indian invaders in the 2nd century BC.

The Sandagiri Wehera, a dagoba near the Tissa dagoba, is also credited to Kavantissa. By the Tissa-Deberawewa road is Yatala Wehera, built 2300 years ago by King Yatala Tissa, who fled Anuradhapura after a palace plot and founded the Ruhunu kingdom.

Wirawila Wewa

Between the northern and southern turn-offs to Tissamaharama, the Hambantota to Wellawaya road runs on a causeway across the large Wirawila Wewa. This extensive sheet of water forms the **Wirawila Wewa Bird Sanctuary**. The best time for bird-watching is early morning. From Hambantota or Tissamaharama you can get a bus to Wirawila junction on the south side of the tank and walk north; from Tissa you can go to Pandegamu on the north side and walk south. You may also spot a few crocodiles, monkeys or (west of the tank) elephants.

Kirinda

On the coast, about 10km south of Tissa, the village of Kirinda has a fine beach and a small Buddhist shrine on the rocks. Kirinda was used as a land base by Arthur C Clarke's party when diving for the Great Basses wreck (see Clarke's *The Treasure of the Reef*). The Great and Little Basses reefs have some of the most spectacular scuba diving around Sri Lanka, but only on rare occasions are conditions suitable for diving; in recent times it has been off limits for security reasons anyway. For much of the year fierce currents sweep across the reefs. A lighthouse was erected on the Great Basses in 1860.

The *Kirinda Beach Resort (☎ 23405)* has two unpretentious rooms for Rs 400 each. It's just a hop, skip and a jump away from the cliff-top Kirinda temple complex that overlooks the wild Yala coast.

There is a bus from Tissa to Kirinda every half-hour or so (Rs 9).

Places to Stay

Tissamaharama Although it's nothing special, *The Holiday Resort (☎ 37228)* has five rooms that are clean enough for Rs 500 (no mosquito nets).

The *Queen's Resthouse (☎ 37264)* off Main Rd is an eclectic mess – some might call it ugly. Still, the seven rooms are clean but basic, and cost Rs 550/700 for a single/double, or Rs 900 for air-con.

Near the bus station is a pleasant family home, the *Tissa Guest House (☎ 37057)*, with four spotless guest rooms for Rs 700 to 800 a single or double. Meals are available. The owners run the photographic studio on Main Rd, opposite the bus station.

Hotel Tissa (☎ 37104) has rooms for Rs 450 to 900 for singles and Rs 800 to 1500 (with air-con) for doubles. The nine rooms are a mixed bag: some rooms are bland, others are squeaky-clean – all enjoy a garden setting. The owner, Tissa, is helpful and knowledgeable about wildlife. He runs an overnight camping safari into Yala for Rs 14,766 (for two people). You can also hire bicycles here for Rs 150 a day.

Most of Tissa's accommodation is near the Tissa Wewa, about 1.5km from the centre of Tissa, and on or near the road to Kataragama. It's easy enough to get into town by bus (Rs 4) or by three-wheeler (Rs 60) from this area.

Taprobana Guest House (☎ 37372) has grotty, noisy but supercheap rooms from Rs 250.

Singha Tourist Inn (☎ 37090) is a no-frills place with a palm-studded lawn reaching down to the lake's edge. It has 10 basic rooms (some are a bit dark) for Rs 600.

Vikum Lodge (☎ 37585), signposted opposite the Priyankara Hotel, is a modern, friendly, family-run place set in a nice garden. It has 10 spotless rooms for Rs 500 per single, from Rs 800 to 950 for a double.

Happy Cottages (☎ 37085), behind Vikum Lodge, has three modern, clean cottages, each with three bedrooms (one with shared bathroom). You can rent an entire cottage for Rs 2000 or a room for Rs 750; these rates include breakfast. There's a fully equipped kitchen available to guests (for a fee).

Lake Side Tourist Inn (☎ 37216) has rooms for Rs 950 – add Rs 200 for hot water and Rs 400 for air-con. Some rooms have views to the lake, some are dark dens, so check out the room before you book in. There is a bar and restaurant. This place is quite popular with groups.

Refresh Hotel (☎ 37357) has four colourful, stylish rooms facing a small courtyard. Rooms cost Rs 1150/1400 – add Rs 700 for air-con. The restaurant's food is delicious.

Chandrika Hotel (☎/fax 37143), about 2km farther towards Kataragama, has 13 rooms with fan only and seven with air-con. Rooms start at Rs 1200/1400 – add Rs 400 for air-con. It's a clean, quiet place and the rooms face onto a courtyard-style garden.

Priyankara Hotel (☎ 37206, fax 37326) is a modern place with rooms with hot water for Rs 1650/1950 – add Rs 500 for air-con. Each room has a small balcony with views over rice paddies. At the time of writing, a pool was under construction.

The *Tissa Rest House (☎ 37299, fax 37201)* is delightfully situated right on the banks of the Tissa Wewa. It has comfortable rooms, a pool and a pleasant open-air restaurant and bar, but it's not cheap at US$30/37 (with hot water) – add US$12 for air-con. There is a buffet at lunch time. This place is the number one choice for groups, so it pays to book ahead.

Deberawewa The *Tissa Inn (☎ 37233, fax 37080, **e** tissainn@cga.lk, Wellawaya Rd, Polgahawela)*, 1.5km along the northern road from the Deberawewa clock tower, has 11 clean rooms for Rs 550/660. There's a restaurant here, and there are also Internet facilities.

Heading towards Tissa you'll find a small road leading to the friendly, family-run *Regina Holiday Home (☎ 37159)*. It has six clean and spacious rooms for Rs 330 to 450 for the older rooms, and Rs 750 for the newer ones. There's a good-sized garden out the back. Bicycles are available for hire.

On the opposite side of the creek, the friendly *Sakura Guesthouse (☎ 37198)* is a traditional family home set in spacious, quiet grounds. There are three (somewhat grubby) rooms for Rs 440 plus two clean 'cottages' that sleep three for Rs 750. If you ring ahead, the family will pick you up (for free) from the bus station in Tissa or Deberawewa. A three-wheeler from the Tissa bus station will cost Rs 60.

About half-way along the main road between Tissa and Deberawewa is *Traveller's Home (☎ 37958, fax 37080)*, surrounded by rice paddies. It has two rooms with private bathroom (Rs 300/400), and one with shared bathroom (Rs 250/300). It gets rave reviews, and the hosts are unbelievably friendly.

Places to Eat
In the centre of town, *Hasindu Food Fair* has cheap rice and curry (Rs 70) – it's tasty and very spicy. *Roots Cafe* also has delicious rice and curry for Rs 110 to 165, and lunch and dinner packets for Rs 70. It's a relaxed place, and a good spot to have a chat and a beer (Rs 100).

Of the places to stay, *Refresh Hotel* is a stylish restaurant with tasty food. Pasta costs around Rs 320, vegetable fried noodles go for Rs 155 and there are heaps of choices of pizza. The *Tissa Rest House* has a good buffet at lunch time for Rs 300 to 475.

Getting There & Away
A CTB bus from Colombo to Tissa costs about Rs 48 and takes six to seven hours, while an air-con bus costs Rs 115 and takes about half an hour less. To Hambantota

THE SOUTH

costs Rs 15 (one hour). Only a few buses go direct to the hill country, and if you can't get one you'll need to change at Wirawila junction (Rs 6) and/or Wellawaya (Rs 21). From Tissa you can reach Kirinda (Rs 9) by bus, but not Yala West (Ruhuna) National Park.

YALA WEST (RUHUNA) NATIONAL PARK

Yala West (Ruhuna) National Park combines a strict nature reserve and a national park that brings the total protected area to 126,786 hectares. It is divided into five

blocks with the most visited being block one (14,101 hectares). Block one, also known as Yala West, was originally a reserve for hunters, and was given over to conservation in 1938.

Yala West is a mixture of scrub, plains, brackish lagoons and rocky outcrops. Elephants are among the better-known inhabitants of the park (the best time to see them is from January to August), but there is also a small population of leopards (best seen in January). You'd be lucky to see a leopard, but you'll probably spot sambar deer, spotted deer, wild boar, crocodiles,

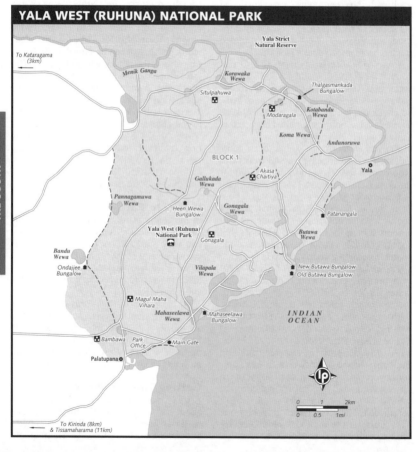

YALA WEST (RUHUNA) NATIONAL PARK

THE SOUTH

wild buffaloes and monkeys. You may also see sloth bears, jackals, mongooses, pangolins and porcupines.

Around 130 species of birds have been recorded at Yala, many of which are visitors escaping the northern winter. These birds include white-winged black terns, curlews and pintails. Locals include jungle fowl, hornbills and orioles.

Also inside the park are the remains of a once-thriving community, whose size can, in part, be gauged by the extent of its agricultural activities. A monastic settlement (Situlpahuwa) appears to have housed about 12,000 inhabitants. Now restored, it's an important centre of pilgrimage. A 1st century BC *vihara* (the Magul Maha Vihara) and a 2nd century BC *chetiya* (shrine) also point to a well-established community that is believed to have been part of the Ruhunu kingdom.

Some people are disappointed by Yala. It's not in the same league as Africa's safari parks and, with so many people visiting, it can at times seem uncomfortably overcrowded, with a dozen or so jeeps all searching the same small area where elephants are thought to be. There is no limit to the

---

Snagging the Perfect Safari Tout

If you decide to go on a safari you're not going to have far to look to find someone willing to take you – for a price. In fact you probably had trouble getting off the bus past the hopefuls waiting with open arms. Guides generally drive the 4WD, (hopefully) offering titbits of wildlife information along the way. You may be told you need a driver *and* a guide, but this is not the case – you'll always have to hire a 'tracker' once you enter the park anyway. This tracker and your guide-driver should be enough.

But choosing a good guide from a dud is a challenge, and in this game it's (unfortunately) often true that you get what you pay for. Guides who know their stuff (and charge accordingly) know where the animals are and when/how to find them. Other guides splutter fumes into the air as they zoom around the park hoping, wishing and praying to find wildlife.

Here are some tips to help you spend your money wisely:

- It goes without saying that you should chat to other travellers for recommendations. If you don't like chatting, you'll find many travellers write about the safari they did in guestbooks. Bear in mind that people often write to compliment, but rarely to complain.
- Ask the guide how regularly his tours see elephants, or leopards, for example. If beads of sweat appear on his forehead when he says 'every tour' you'll know it's time to walk on.
- Check the vehicle and ask the driver to turn it on; some are potentially lethal rust buckets that sound like lawn mowers – not conducive to wildlife spotting.
- Make sure the driver has a pair of binoculars. You may also want to see if he supplies wildlife identification books.
- Finally, as you'll always have to hire a tracker (who should know his stuff), you may decide to go cheap with the guide-driver and hope you get a good tracker. Good luck.

MICK WELDON

number of jeeps allowed in at one time. But everyone with some kind of interest in wildlife is likely to find it well worthwhile as part of a longer trip to this region of Sri Lanka.

There really is no best time to visit, though if you visit between October and December you're guaranteed to see a lot of bird life, deer and crocodiles – anything else will be a bonus. Whatever the season, dawn and dusk are the best times of day to witness animals. If it's raining, you'll still see some wildlife but if you've time, hold off until the weather clears.

The park is open from 6.30 am to 6.30 pm daily, but is closed from 1 September to 15 October every year. Tickets can be bought at the park office near the entrance, which is near Palatupana. Entry costs US$12 for foreigners, children aged from six to 12 are half-price, and those aged under six are free. It costs Rs 135 to take a jeep into the park, and Rs 100 for a car, although most people will use a tour company or safari operator to get into the park (Rs 1500 to 2200 for the entire jeep for half a day). You will also have to pay a US$6 'service charge' for a compulsory tracker at the park.

There are six **bungalows** and one **camp site** in the park, which can be booked from Colombo through the Department of

Kataragama Puja

Kataragama hums with activity at the time of *pujas* (offerings or prayers). Devotees laden with offerings move lightly, barefoot, up the temple steps. From inside comes the sharp sound of breaking coconuts as worshippers begin their devotions. It's just after six in the evening, not long now to the evening puja. A queue snakes round the shrine's inner walls; the people stand patiently, clutching plates heaped with fruit and flowers and decorated with brilliant red garlands made only for Skanda, son of Shiva and the god of war and wisdom, for whom the main shrine in Kataragama is dedicated. It is said that Skanda rested on the mountain at Kataragama after defeating an army of demons.

A murmur ripples through the crowd. The temple elephant is making its ponderous way through the north gate and across the courtyard to the first of three shrines. Aloft in its trunk it holds a single lotus flower. The mahout taps the elephant gently on the shoulder and it kneels, placing the lotus before a statue of the Buddha. The elephant heaves itself off its knees and turns towards the next shrine, dedicated to Ganesh. The performance is repeated and the elephant is rewarded with a few bananas. It moves towards the final shrine, the Maha Devale. The crowd parts silently and the elephant glides gracefully through, unperturbed. It kneels. A sigh rises from the crowd. The shrine doors are about to be flung open to admit the worshippers and their gifts.

This gentle rhythm is broken only for the annual festival that is held on the Esala *poya* (full moon), usually in late July or early August. This is a time of feverish activity at Kataragama. Elephants parade, drummers drum. Vows are made and favours sought by devotees who demonstrate their sincerity by performing extraordinary acts of penance and self-mortification: some swing from hooks that pierce their skin, others roll half naked over the hot sands near the temple. A few perform the act of walking on beds of red-hot cinders – treading the flowers, as its called. The fire-walkers fast, meditate and pray, bathe in the Menik Ganga and then worship at the Maha Devale before facing their ordeal. Then, fortified by their faith, the fire-walkers step out onto the glowing path while the audience cries out encouragement. The next morning the festival officially ends with a water-cutting ceremony (said to evoke rain for the harvests) in the Menik Ganga.

The Kataragama shrine is ancient. Legend has it that it was built by King Dutugemunu in the 2nd century BC, but it is apparently even older than this. There is an old pilgrimage route to Kataragama that starts in Jaffna and runs down the east coast, passing through Yala. Because of the war, this route is sadly too risky to undertake. But pilgrims still make the trek up the mountain. At dusk you can see the lights from the shrine on the mountain from the precincts of the Kataragama shrine.

Hanging out at the beach, Sri Lankan style

A series of small bays adds to the charm of Tangalla on Sri Lanka's south coast.

A great beach and good diving opportunities make Hikkaduwa on the west coast a popular destination.

A fisherman's work is never done...

Fishing from the shore of a tank

A fine balance: stilt fisherman at sunset

It's a big 'un! Fishermen haul in the nets at Hikkaduwa on the west coast.

Wildlife Conservation (☎ 01-694241, fax 698556) at 18 Gregory's Rd, Cinnamon Gardens (Col 7). You must bring all of your own provisions.

Close to the entrance to Yala West, 28km from Tissa, on a rather desolate stretch of coast at Amaduwa, is the well-run *Yala Safari Beach Hotel* (☎/fax 20471, e *jethot@ sri.lanka.net*), which has rooms at US$85 a single or double, or US$110 with air-con.

You'll need to organise a safari from Tissamaharama (or even Hambantota) to get to Yala. If you have your own transport it'll have to be a 4WD.

KATARAGAMA
☎ 047

Fifteen kilometres north of Tissa is Kataragama. Along with Adam's Peak, this is the most important religious pilgrimage site in Sri Lanka. It is a holy place for Buddhists, Muslims and Hindus, and across the Menik Ganga from the small residential part of the town is a sprawling religious complex containing buildings of all three religions. Many believe that King Dutugemunu built a shrine to the Kataragama Deviyo (the resident god) here in the 2nd century BC, and the Buddhist Kirivehera dagoba dates back to the 1st century BC.

The most important shrine is the Maha Devale, which supposedly contains the lance of the six-faced, 12-armed Hindu war god, Skanda, who is identical here with the Kataragama Deviyo. Followers of all three religions make offerings here at the three daily pujas (offerings or prayers) at 4.30 and 10.30 am, and 6.30 pm (no 4.30 am offering on Saturday). See the boxed text 'Kataragama Puja' for a description of this interesting event. The neighbouring shrines are dedicated to Buddha and Ganesh (remover of obstacles and champion of intellectual pursuits). Remember to remove your shoes and hat before entering the shrine area.

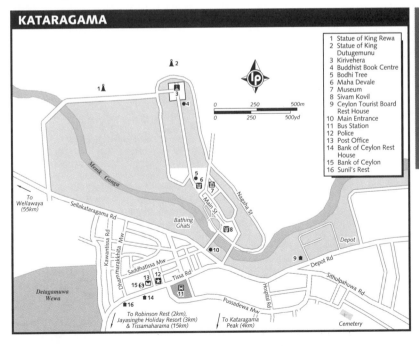

KATARAGAMA

1 Statue of King Rewa
2 Statue of King Dutugemunu
3 Kirivehera
4 Buddhist Book Centre
5 Bodhi Tree
6 Maha Devale
7 Museum
8 Sivam Kovil
9 Ceylon Tourist Board Rest House
10 Main Entrance
11 Bus Station
12 Police
13 Post Office
14 Bank of Ceylon Rest House
15 Bank of Ceylon
16 Sunil's Rest

THE SOUTH

In July and August the predominantly Hindu Kataragama Festival draws thousands of devotees who make the pilgrimage over a two-week period.

Apart from festival time, the town is busiest with pilgrims at weekends and on *poya* (full moon) days. At other times it can feel like a ghost town. If you're staying in Tissamaharama you may just want to visit on a day trip.

Places to Stay & Eat

The *Bank of Ceylon Rest House (☎ 01-544315)* is an airy, well-run place where each of the 22 basic rooms cost Rs 530. Some rooms have views to Kataragama Peak and others overlook the town. You're supposed to reserve your room here from Colombo, but there are often on-the-spot vacancies so it is worth asking. Book in for the vegetarian food, ie, rice and curry (Rs 90).

The *Ceylon Tourist Board Rest House (☎ 35227)* is just off the Situlpahuwa Rd. From the bus station, head along the main road and take the first fork on your left. There are very clean rooms for Rs 680 for a single or double. Guests are entitled to one free dinner (vegetarian only) each. The food is tasty, cheap and spicy.

Sunil's Rest (☎ 35300), a clean, family-run place, has three rooms and a pleasant garden. Rooms cost Rs 660 for a single or double.

About 2km out of town on the road to Tissamaharama you'll find *Robinson Rest (☎ 35175)* with basic rooms for Rs 800. It hasn't got much going for it, but it's OK for a night. Meals are served here.

A farther 1km along is the *Jayasinghe Holiday Resort (☎ 35146, 32A Detagamuwa).* It has a pool (which nonguests may use for Rs 100) and 25 clean, plain rooms for Rs 1100 with fan and Rs 1650 with air-con. Meals are available.

Getting There & Away

Buses from Tissamaharama are fairly frequent; the fare is Rs 9 for a normal bus and Rs 20 for an air-con express (in fact, the Colombo bus). There are some direct buses to Colombo, and places on the south coast. The intercity express to Colombo costs Rs 135 (you can pick up the same bus in Tissa). If you want to go to the hill country (Ella, Nuwara Eliya, Kandy) you must change at Wellawaya.

The Hill Country

The hill country in the centre of Sri Lanka is totally different from anywhere else on the island. The altitude dispels the often sticky heat of the coastal regions or the dry air of the central and northern plains, producing a cool, perpetual spring. Everything is green and lush, and much of the region is carpeted with the glowing green of the tea plantations.

The kingdom of Kandy resisted European takeover for over 300 years after the coastal regions had succumbed, and the city of Kandy remains the Sinhalese cultural and spiritual centre. Since the 19th century there has been a large population of Tamils in the hill country, brought from India by the British to labour on the tea estates.

The hill country is a relaxed area, where it's very easy to find the days just drifting by. Higher up into the hills are many towns that are worth a visit, and an abundance of walks and climbs, refreshing waterfalls and historic sites.

COLOMBO TO KANDY

The **Henerathgoda Botanic Gardens** near Gampaha, off the Colombo-Kandy road about 30km north-west of Colombo, are overshadowed by the better-known Peradeniya Botanic Gardens near Kandy. However, it was at Henerathgoda that the first rubber trees planted in Asia were carefully grown and their potential proved – some of those original rubber trees are still in the gardens today.

Some 47km from Colombo is the village of Pasyala where there's a turn-off leading to the **Pasgama** tourism village (☎ 033-85183) about 1.5km from the main road. This privately owned venture is an attempt to bring to life a pre-1940 settlement showcasing craftspeople and other features of traditional village life. Some enjoy this place, while others may see it as corny, crafty (excuse the pun) commercialism – few will be delighted by the entry fee of US$11 for tourists. There's a shop selling handicrafts.

About 3km farther towards Kandy from Pasyala is **Cadjugama**, a village famous for its cashew nuts. Stalls line the road and brightly clad cashew nut sellers beckon passing motorists. More villages specialising in various products can be found along this road. At the 48km post is **Radawaduwa**, where all sorts of cane items are woven and displayed for sale at roadside stalls.

Kegalle, 77km from Colombo, is the nearest town to the Pinnewala Elephant Orphanage. A little farther towards Kandy, you can see **Utuwankandu**, a prominent rocky hill, from which the 19th-century Robin Hood–style highwayman, Saradiel, preyed on travellers until he was caught and executed by the British. At Kadugannawa, just after the road and railway make their most scenic climbs – with views south-west to the large **Bible Rock** – is a tall pillar in memory of Captain Dawson, the English engineer who built the Colombo-Kandy road in 1826.

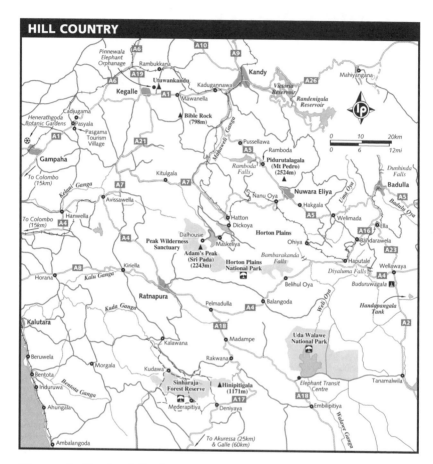

HILL COUNTRY

Pinnewala Elephant Orphanage

The government-run Pinnewala Elephant Orphanage (☎ 035-65284) near Kegalle, which was set up to save abandoned or orphaned wild elephants, is the most popular jumbo attraction in Sri Lanka. And with good reason, for nowhere else except at *peraheras* (processions) are you likely to see so many elephants at close quarters. The elephants are controlled by their mahouts (keepers), who ensure they feed at the right times and don't endanger anyone, but otherwise the elephants roam freely around the sanctuary area.

There are 63 young elephants and some are surprisingly small; this must be one of the few places where an elephant can step on your foot and you might walk away with a smile! Bathing times for the babies are from 10 am to noon and from 2 to 4 pm, with meal times at 9.15 am, 1.15 and 5 pm. Most of the elephants become working elephants once they are grown up. Occasionally, one of the older female elephants produces a baby to add to the herd.

There's a cafe and some shops selling snacks, camera film, elephant T-shirts, elephant toys, elephant burgers (only joking), and so on with the elephant merchandising. The orphanage is open from 8.30 am to 5.45 pm daily and entry costs Rs 150 for adults (half price for children under 12) and Rs 20 for foreigners resident in Sri Lanka. There's a charge of Rs 200 per video camera; ordinary cameras are free. Should you need to change money, outside the orphanage is a Hatton National Bank, open weekdays.

Near the Pinnewala Elephant Orphanage are a couple of **spice gardens**. You can turn up unannounced and a guide will show you around, explaining their uses and growth habits. A tip will be expected, and more often than not, you'll end your tour at the garden's shop. Here you'll find a plethora of potions and lotions: cures for obesity, flatulence and baldness, to name a few. You'll also be able to buy packets of the spices. It's a good idea to shop around in local markets to get an idea of prices before you get carried away; the salespeople in these gardens are generally good at their jobs.

Around 2.5km down the road (by the 3km post), on the way back to Kandy, is another elephant sanctuary and bathing spot, **The Millennium Elephant Foundation** (☎ 035-65377, e elefound@sltnet.lk). This place is far less crowded than the elephant orphanage. There are six elephants including Lakshmi and her calf, Puja, and a small 'museum' with background on the life cycle and habits of elephants. The river is just inside the entrance and the elephants are often bathing here. Entry costs Rs 200 and includes an elephant ride (if you wish). It's open from 8 am to 5 pm daily. You can sponsor an elephant too.

Getting There & Away The orphanage is on a minor road, quite passable for cars and buses, a few kilometres north of the Colombo-Kandy road. The turn-off is just out of Kegalle on the Kandy side. You can reach the orphanage by bus, train and bus, or car (en route between Colombo and Kandy), either as an outing from Kandy, or even as an outing from Colombo – though that's twice as far. From Kandy you can take a private bus or Ceylon Transport Board (CTB) bus No 662 to Kegalle (Rs 10)

– get off before Kegalle at Karandupona junction. From the junction catch the bus No 681 (Rs 7) going from Kegalle to Rambukkana and get off at Pinnewala. It's about an hour from Kandy to the junction, and 10 minutes from the junction to Pinnewala. There are also numerous buses between Colombo and Kegalle.

Rambukkana station on the Colombo-Kandy railway is about 3km north of the orphanage. From Rambukkana get a bus going towards Kegalle. Trains leave Kandy at 6.45 am (arriving at Rambukkana station at 8 am), 10.30 am (arriving at noon) and 3.40 pm (arriving at 4.40 pm). Trains for Kandy leave at 12.45 and 2.45 pm.

KANDY
☎ 08 • pop 120,000
Kandy is only 115km inland from Colombo, but it is climatically a world away due to its 500m altitude. This is Sri Lanka's second-biggest city, and the easy-going 'capital' of the hill country. Kandy was also the capital of the last Sinhalese kingdom, which fell to the British in 1815 after defying the Portuguese and Dutch for three centuries.

Kandy is particularly well known for the great Kandy Esala Perahera (see the 'Kandy Esala Perahera' boxed text later in this chapter) held over 10 days leading up to the Nikini *poya* (full moon) at the end of month of Esala (July–August), but it has enough attractions to justify a visit at any time of year.

The town, and the countryside around it, is lush and green and there are many pleasant walks both from the town or farther afield. The town centre, close to Kandy's picturesque lake set in a bowl of hills, is a delightful jumble of old shops, antique and gemstone specialists, a bustling market and a good selection of hotels, guesthouses and restaurants. As night falls the city becomes eerily quiet; women travellers may find it sleazy, especially in the back streets.

Locally Kandy is known either as Maha Nuwara (Great City) or just Nuwara (City), which is what some conductors on Kandy-bound buses call out.

Orientation

The focus of Kandy is its lake, with the Temple of the Tooth (Dalada Maligawa) on its north side. The city centre is immediately north and west of the lake, with the clock tower a handy reference point. The train station, market and the various bus stands are just a short walk from the lake. The city spreads into the surrounding hills, where many of the places to stay are perched, looking down on the town.

Maps The *Colombo A-Z Street Guide*, available at bookshops such as Vijitha Yapa, has one of the most detailed maps of Kandy. The tourist office has maps as well, but these tend to be a bit dodgy. Nelles Verlag has a reasonable map of Kandy.

Information

Tourist Office Housed on Palace Square, beside the Olde Empire Hotel, the Ceylon Tourist Board office (☎ 222661) is helpful for transport and things to do in the Kandy area, and also has some information on places to stay. It's open from 9 am to 4.45 pm Monday to Friday (closed 1 to 1.30 pm for lunch).

Cultural Triangle Office The office where you can buy round-trip tickets that cover many of the sites of the ancient cities is located in a white building across the road from the tourist office. It's open from 9 am to 4 pm daily (closed 12.30 to 1.30 pm for lunch). Books are available for sale (see Bookshops later in this section) though they're often out of stock.

Within Kandy the round ticket covers the four Hindu *devales* or shrines (Kataragama, Natha, Pattini, Vishnu), two monasteries (Asgiriya, Malwatte), the National Museum and the Archaeological Museum. It is customary to make a donation (usually Rs 30 and upwards) at the devales and monasteries, though you are unlikely to be asked to produce a triangle ticket. The National Museum costs Rs 55 to enter without a triangle ticket, although the Archaeological Museum insists on one. See later in this section for more details on these places.

Money Most of the banks are on Dalada Vidiya. The Hatton National Bank is open from 9 am to 3 pm Monday to Friday (MasterCard and Visa cash withdrawals available); the People's Bank from 8.30 am to 3 pm Monday to Friday, and 9 am to 3.30 pm on Saturday; and the Bank of Ceylon from 8.30 am to 3 pm Monday to Friday (Visa, but not MasterCard, cash withdrawals available). Visa and MasterCard holders may make cash withdrawals at the ATMs at Standard Chartered Grindlays, 7 Temple St, and HongKong & Shanghai Bank, 27 Cross St.

Post & Communications The main post office is over the road from the train station and is open from 7 am to 9 pm Monday to Friday and 8 am to 8 pm on Saturday for stamp sales, telephone calls and telegrams. Post restante is open from 9 am to 5 pm Monday to Saturday. Staff will arrange to have mail forwarded to you in Kandy if you decide to stay for a few weeks. International operator-connected calls (including collect calls – reverse charges) mean at least a two-hour wait although you can book a call a day or more in advance – and if you have a private telephone number, you can arrange to have the call transferred there. A phonecard or a private bureau may be more convenient if you want to make a call in a hurry.

There are a few smaller, more central post offices including one next door to the Olde Empire Hotel. There are numerous private communications bureaus in town.

For super fast and cheap Internet access, Koffeepot (☎ 234341, e admin@koffeepot.com) at 36 Dalada Vidiya has knocked its competitors out of the race. It's open from 8 am to 8 pm daily, there are heaps of computers, attentive service and also cappuccino (Rs 90).

Up the other end of town you'll find Webster Internet Cafe (☎ 074-475267, e webster@kandyan.net) at Kande Veediya (Hill St), near the British Council. It's open from 8.30 am to 6 pm weekdays and 9 am to 5 pm on weekends. There are eight computers with Internet access, faxes (Rs 140 per minute to New Zealand and Australia and Rs 165 per minute to the USA, UK and continental Europe), and you can make international calls (Rs 120 per minute to New Zealand and Australia, Rs 135 per minute to the USA, Rs 165 to the UK and continental Europe).

Internet Resources Check out the Kandy Web site (www.kandycity.org) with historical information, details about accommodation, things to see and do and more.

Bookshops The good Vijitha Yapa bookshop chain has an outlet at 5 Kotugodelle Vidiya (near the Seetha agency post office) where you can buy periodicals, newspapers (including foreign ones) and assorted fiction and nonfiction.

Mark Bookshop at 15 1/1 Dalada Vidiya has a good selection of books about Sri Lanka, as well as fiction and nonfiction. It's pokey, but the staff are very helpful.

The Cultural Triangle ticket office opposite the tourist office has a selection of books for sale on the ancient cities, Kandy (*Kandy*, by Dr Anuradha Seneviratna, is an informative guide to the temples and monuments of the city; Rs 85), and also on traditional dance (Rs 120). Available here is *The Cultural Triangle*, published by Unesco and the Central Cultural Fund, which provides good background on the ancient sites and monuments, but which isn't cheap at Rs 1950; a slimmer but less comprehensive volume is available for Rs 900.

If you're interested in books on Buddhism, visit the friendly folks at the Buddhist Publication Society towards the east end of the lake.

Libraries & Cultural Centres At the British Council (☎ 234634, fax 222410, e bckandy@britcoun.lk), which is at 178 DS Senanayake Vidiya (formerly Trincomalee St), there's a library with back copies of British newspapers, cassettes and videos; sometimes it has film nights, exhibitions and plays. Nonmembers may read newspapers (but only on presentation of a passport). You may use the reference section occasionally for free, but if you want to peruse it on a regular basis, you will have to pay Rs 150 per month. The library is open from 9.30 am to 5 pm Tuesday to Saturday. Visit the Web site (www.british council.lk).

Alliance Française (☎ 224432) to the south-west of town at 412 Peradeniya Rd has film nights (the films are in French but frequently with English subtitles), as well as books and periodicals. Good coffee is available. It's open from 8.30 am to 6 pm Monday to Saturday. Nonmembers are welcome to browse in the library (membership, and therefore borrowing rights, costs Rs 500).

The Hindu Cultural Centre (☎ 222940) nearby at 348 Peradeniya Rd has a small library and occasionally holds performances of traditional dancing. Inquire at the centre for the current program.

Laundry Queen's Laundry, beside Laksala, is open from 8 am to 6 pm Monday to Saturday, but in this town, smelling good doesn't come cheap: having a T-shirt cleaned costs Rs 50, a skirt Rs 60.

Medical Services If you need a doctor in Kandy, the Lakeside Adventist Hospital (☎ 223466), which is at 40 Sangaraja Mawatha, offers good, efficient service.

Dangers & Annoyances Women may want to avoid the back streets at night as some Kandyans are sleazebags.

Touts are particularly numerous around the train station and the lake. They'll hound you with Kandyan dance tickets, ghastly necklaces and wobbly headed elephant figurines. See Dangers & Annoyances in the Facts for the Visitor chapter for advice on how to deal with touts.

Kandy Lake

Kandy Lake, a lovely centrepiece to the town, was created in 1807 by Sri Wickrama Rajasinha, the last ruler of the kingdom of Kandy. Several small-scale local chiefs who protested because their people objected to labouring on the project were put to death at stakes in the lake bed. The island in the centre was used as Sri Wickrama Rajasinha's personal harem – to which he crossed on a barge. Later the British used it as an ammunition store, adding the fortress-style parapet around the perimeter of the lake.

An evening stroll around the perimeter is a must. Traffic is banned from the north side up to the Temple of the Tooth for security reasons so this area is the quietest. From the west end of the lake you can take short cruises on small motorboats (Rs 450 per boat for 20 minutes). On the south shore, in front of the Malwatte Vihara (Buddhist monastery), there's a circular enclosure, which is the monks' bathhouse.

Temple of the Tooth (Dalada Maligawa)

Near the lake, the Temple of the Tooth houses Sri Lanka's most important Buddhist relic – a sacred tooth of the Buddha. The temple sustained damage when a bomb was detonated near the main entrance in early 1998. At the time of writing scaffolding still covered parts of the relic chamber.

The tooth was said to have been snatched from the flames of the Buddha's funeral pyre in 543 BC, and was smuggled into the island during the 4th century AD, hidden in the hair of a princess. At first it was taken to Anuradhapura, but with the ups and downs of Sri Lankan history it moved from place to place before eventually ending at Kandy. For a short period from 1283 it was actually carried back to India by an invading army, but was then brought back again by King Parakramabahu III.

Gradually, the tooth came to assume more and more importance. In the 16th century the Portuguese, in one of their worst spoilsport moods, seized what they claimed was the tooth, took it away and burnt it with Catholic fervour in Goa. 'Not so' is the Sinhalese rejoinder; they were fobbed off with a replica and the real incisor remained safe.

The present Temple of the Tooth was constructed mainly under Kandyan kings from 1687 to 1707 and 1747 to 1782. It is an imposing pink-painted structure, surrounded by a deep moat. The octagonal tower in the moat was built by Sri Wickrama Rajasinha and used to house an important collection of *ola* (palm-leaf) manuscripts. However, this section of the temple was heavily damaged

in the 1998 bomb blast. The eye-catching gilded roof over the relic chamber was added by President Premadasa.

The temple has a constant flow of worshippers and flocks of tourists. It's open from 6 am to 4 pm daily, with *pujas* (offerings or prayers) held at 6 and 10 am, and 6 pm. Entry costs Rs 100, Rs 50 extra for a camera and Rs 250 for a video. Shorts are not acceptable attire (you should cover your legs and your shoulders) and it is required that you remove your shoes (which are kept by shoe minders near the entrance). The security at the temple's entry points, which has been fairly rigorous for some time, was tightened following the bomb attack in early 1998. You have to pass through two bag and body searches before the place where you leave your shoes. There is another bag and body search once you're in the temple.

Drums beat throughout the pujas while the heavily guarded room housing the tooth is open to devotees and tourists. Of course you don't actually see the tooth – just a gold casket said to contain a series of smaller and smaller caskets and eventually the tooth itself. Or perhaps a replica – nobody seems too sure. The casket is behind a window and two decidedly mean-looking monks stand heavily on either side.

To see the stuffed remains of the Maligawa Tusker who died in 1988 (see the boxed text 'Kandy Esala Perahera', following), take a left after ascending the first steps up to the temple, after passing security.

Around the Temple of the Tooth

The **National Museum** beside the Temple of the Tooth, once the quarters for Kandyan royal concubines, houses royal regalia and reminders of pre-European Sinhalese life. It has a copy of the 1815 agreement handing over the Kandyan provinces to British rule. This document announces:

...the cruelties and oppressions of the Malabar ruler, in the arbitrary and unjust infliction of bodily tortures and pains of death without trial, and sometimes without accusation or the possibility of a crime, and in the general contempt and contravention of all civil rights, have become flagrant, enormous and intolerable.

Kandy Esala Perahera

The big night of the year in Kandy is the culmination of 10 days of increasingly frenetic activity. A *perahera* is a parade or procession, and Kandy's is held to honour the sacred tooth enshrined in the Temple of the Tooth (Dalada Maligawa). It runs for 10 days in the full-moon month of Esala (July–August), ending on the Nikini poya (full moon).

The first six nights are relatively low-key; on the seventh things start to take off as the route lengthens, the procession becomes more and more splendid and accommodation prices go right through the roof.

The procession is actually a combination of five separate peraheras. Four come from the four Kandy *devales* – shrines to deities who protect the island and are also devotees and servants of the Buddha: Natha is a Buddha-to-be of special importance to Kandy; Vishnu is the guardian of Sri Lanka and an indicator of the intermingling of Hindu and Buddhist beliefs since he is also one of the three great Hindu gods; the third and fourth peraheras are from the devales to Skanda, the god of war and victory, and Pattini, the goddess of chastity. The fifth and most splendid perahera is that of the Dalada Maligawa itself.

The procession is led by thousands of Kandyan dancers and drummers beating thousands of drums, leaping with unbounded energy, cracking whips and waving colourful banners. Then come long processions of elephants – 50 or more of them. The brilliantly caparisoned Maligawa Tusker is the most splendid of them all – decorated from trunk to toe, he carries a huge canopy that shelters, on the final night, a replica of the sacred relic cask. A carpet-way of white linen is laid in front of the elephant so that he does not step in the dirt. In 1988 the old Maligawa Tusker died after 50 years of faithful service, and was replaced by a Thai-born youngster specially trained for the task. You can view the stuffed remains of the elder in the Temple of the Tooth.

The Kandy Esala Perahera is the most magnificent annual spectacle in Sri Lanka, and one of the most famous in Asia. It has been an annual event for many centuries and is described by Robert Knox in his 1681 book *An Historical Relation of Ceylon*. There is also a smaller procession on the full-moon day in June, and special peraheras may be put on for important occasions. It's essential to arrive early for roadside seats for the perahera – by 2 pm for the final night. Earlier in the week you can get seats about halfway back in the stands quite cheaply.

There's a daylight procession on the first day of the Nikini full-moon month which marks the end of the Kandy Esala Perahera.

Scores of elephants robed in glittering cloaks parade around Kandy during the Esala Perahera.

THE HILL COUNTRY

Sri Wickrama Rajasinha was therefore declared, 'by the habitual violation of the chief and most sacred duties of a sovereign', to be 'fallen and deposed from office of king' and 'the dominion of the Kandyan provinces' was 'vested in the sovereign of the British Empire'.

The audience hall, notable for the tall pillars supporting its roof, was the site for the convention of Kandyan chiefs that ceded the kingdom to Britain in 1815.

The museum is open from 9 am to 5 pm daily except Friday and Saturday. Admission is Rs 55 (Rs 30 for children under 12). It's Rs 135 extra if you want to take photos.

The National Museum, along with the less-interesting Archaeological Museum behind the temple, four devales and two monasteries – but not the Temple of the Tooth itself – together make up one of Sri Lanka's Cultural Triangle sites. You can buy a Cultural Triangle round ticket at the office across the road from the tourist office (see Information earlier in this section).

The **British Garrison cemetery** is behind the National Museum. There are nearly 200 gravesites lovingly taken care of by the 'Friends' of the cemetery. The caretaker is more than happy to show you around and provide information about many of the graves. It's open daily except Sunday. A donation is appreciated.

Monasteries

Kandy's principal Buddhist *viharas* (monasteries) have considerable importance – the high priests of the two best-known monasteries, Malwatte and Asgiriya, are the most important in Sri Lanka. The priests also play an important role in the administration and operation of the Temple of the Tooth. The **Malwatte Vihara** is directly across the lake from the Temple of the Tooth, while the **Asgiriya** is on the hill off Wariyapola Sri Sumanga Mawatha to the north-west of the town centre, and has a large reclining Buddha image.

Elephants

Elephants can be seen frequently in and around Kandy. Working elephants might be spotted anywhere, and you may catch the Temple of the Tooth elephant chained up along the lakeside near the temple. (See also Elephants in Around Kandy later for information about the River Side Elephant Park.)

From Kandy it's a fairly easy trip to the Pinnewala Elephant Orphanage (see the Colombo to Kandy section earlier).

Scenic Walks

There are many walks almost in the centre of Kandy, such as up to the **Royal Palace Park**, also constructed by Sri Wickrama Rajasinha, overlooking the lake. It's open from 8.30 am to 4.30 pm, and entry costs Rs 22.50. Farther up the hill on Rajapihilla Mawatha there are even better views over the lake, the town and the surrounding hills, which disappear in a series of gentle ranges stretching far into the distance. If you're in the mood for a longer walk, there are also a couple of paths, along from Rajapihilla Mawatha, that head up into the hills.

Looming over Kandy, the huge concrete **Bohiravokanda Buddha statue** can be reached by walking 20 minutes uphill from the police station on Peradeniya Rd. Entry costs Rs 100. Save your sweat and money – there are no views from the top and the statue is (ho hum) unremarkable.

Udawattakelle Sanctuary North of the lake, you can take a longer stroll around this cool and pleasant forest close to the heart of Kandy. There are lots of huge trees, much bird and insect life and many monkeys, but visitors are advised to be careful in this woodland if they're alone. Muggers are rare in Sri Lanka but not unknown, and single women should take care. The odd leech is likely to accompany you after rain. Entry to the sanctuary (open from 8 am to 6 pm) is overpriced at Rs 250. You enter through the gate, which you reach by turning right after the post office on DS Senanayake Vidiya (there's a sign at the junction). There are clear paths, but it's worth paying attention to the map at the entrance.

Ayurveda

At the time of writing there were no places in the centre of Kandy worth recommending, so you may have to splurge at the Ayurvedic treatment centre at Le Kandyan Resorts (☎ 233521). A body oil massage and steam bath (1½ hours) costs Rs 1970. The steam bath is *very* hot, so if you've got high blood pressure you should be careful – maybe opt for the herbal bath. A facial treatment (oil massage, sandalwood mask, steam) costs Rs 570 for 30 minutes. Although Le Kandyan Resorts is a bit far from town, you can relax around the pool after the treatment with a drink, and make an afternoon (or morning) of it. A three-wheeler from Kandy should cost Rs 650 return.

Meditation

Visitors can learn or practise meditation and study Buddhism at several places in the Kandy area. Ask at the Buddhist Publication Society (☎/fax 237283) by the lake for details about courses. It's open from 8.30 am to 4 pm weekdays, to noon on Saturday. Many centres offer free courses, but they'd obviously appreciate a donation. Give what you'd normally be paying per day for food and accommodation in Sri Lanka.

Nillambe Meditation Centre (☎ 225471), near Nillambe Bungalow Junction, can be reached by bus (catch a Delthota bus via Galaha and get off at Office Junction; the trip takes about an hour). It's a pretty spot, with great views, and is popular with foreigners. There's a daily set schedule of meditation classes – visitors not intending to learn meditation are not encouraged. You can stay for Rs 300 a day (including food), and although blankets are supplied you may wish to bring a sleeping bag. There's no electricity, so bring a torch (flashlight). There's a large library of books and a tape library here. To reach Nillambe from the Office Junction you have a steep 3km walk (or a three-wheeler may be at the junction to take you for Rs 150) through tea plantations. A taxi to/from Kandy costs Rs 650.

Nillambe runs another centre on the outskirts of Kandy, the **Lewella Meditation Centre** (☎ 225471) at 150 Dharmashoka Mawatha, Lewella. There is no set program, so it's more of a retreat for experienced meditators (male only).

At Ampitiya, near Kandy, the **Sri Jemieson International Meditation Centre** (☎ 225057) on Samadhi Mawatha only runs (free) set meditation programs – if you turn up when a program isn't on you'll have to practise meditation unsupervised; ring first to find out the situation. At the time of writing five rooms were being built; until they're finished you can't stay on the premises – women are not allowed to stay overnight at all. To get there, catch a Talatu Oya bus from the clock tower bus stop (Rs 5). Look for the sign on the right-hand side of the road about 3km along the Ampitiya– Talatu Oya road. There's a 1.2km walk up a winding track to the centre.

The **Dhamma Kuta Vipassana Meditation Centre** (☎ 070-800057, [e] dhamma@ sltnet.lk) at Mowbray, Hindagala, is in the hills and has superb views. It offers free 10-day courses following the SN Goenka system; you must book into one of the courses, you can't just turn up. There's dorm accommodation with separate male and female quarters. Take a Mahakanda-bound bus from the clock tower bus stop in Kandy and get off at the last stop. There's a small sign at the bottom of the track to the centre. It's a steep 4km walk, or you can catch a three-wheeler for Rs 150. A taxi to/from Kandy should cost Rs 500.

At the time of writing, the new **Paramita International Buddhist Society** in Kandy was due to open soon. Ask at the Buddhist Publication Society for details.

Swimming

Close to the centre of town, the Hotel Suisse charges Rs 150 (including a towel) for nonguests to use the pool, in a garden setting. Queens Hotel also has a good pool (Rs 150) and a pretty garden. There are some stunningly positioned pools around Kandy including: the Hotel Thilanka (Rs 122), on a terrace looking down on the lake; at Hotel Hilltop (Rs 100); and at Le Kandyan Resorts (Rs 100), from whose terrace you get great views over the countryside.

Snooker

The Hotel Suisse has a large, well-kept snooker table where you can play billiards or snooker for Rs 100 per half hour.

Golf

The Victoria International Golf Club (☎/fax 070-800249, e victoriagolf@kandy.ccom .lk), 20km from Kandy (towards the Victoria Reservoir) has 207 hectares with water frontage. It's an 18-hole course; green fees are Rs 1800 on weekdays or Rs 2200 on weekends. Golf club rental is Rs 575 a day and a caddie costs Rs 150 a day.

Places to Stay

Kandy has heaps of good guesthouses. In the middle and top brackets there are some lovely, luxurious houses and an increasing number of good hotels. Many places are set on the hills surrounding the town – in some cases 3km or more from the centre – but they are worth the effort of reaching because of their outstanding locations and views.

At the time of the Kandy Esala Perahera, room prices in Kandy treble, quadruple, or even worse; you can't find a room at all. If you're intent on coming to see the perahera, booking far ahead may secure you a more reasonable price.

Kandy has numerous touts and it's impossible to avoid them completely. They are very persuasive and determined. A favourite haunt for touts is the train station. They generally have a well-rehearsed stock of stories about guesthouses they don't want you to patronise (presumably because those guesthouses won't pay them commission). Take these stories with several large grains of salt.

It's impossible to list all the places to stay in Kandy. The following is just a selection. The Ceylon Tourist Board office in Kandy can help you find places as well.

Places to Stay – Budget

North & West of the Lake The *Burmese Rest* is part of a Buddhist monastery and has six large rooms (no fans) for Rs 150/300 per single/double. The shared bathroom is pretty grim. You are welcome to drink as much tea as you want, but there are no meals. If you ask permission, you may use the kitchen to prepare your own food (vegetarian only).

Olde Empire Hotel (☎ 224284, 21 Temple St) has simple, clean rooms with well-kept shared bathrooms. Some of the rooms at the back are a little dingy but there's a gorgeous balcony crammed with colonial-style furniture at the front, overlooking the lake. Rooms cost up to Rs 360/440. There's a good, dirt-cheap restaurant here.

Anagarika Dharmapala Mawatha, which goes up the hill past the Temple of the Tooth, leads to a number of popular guesthouses on the edge of the town. Bus Nos 654, 655 and 698 (or just ask for 'Sangamitta Mawatha' at the clock tower bus stand) will get you to this area and beyond. There's a handful of small places on Sangamitta Mawatha, the road up to the left off Anagarika Dharmapala Mawatha at the top of the hill. There are also places to the right on Dharmaraja Rd and Louis Pieris Mawatha.

Green Woods (☎ 232970, 34A Sangamitta Mawatha) is a quiet, friendly house with a jungle atmosphere that is located on the edge of the Udawattakelle Sanctuary (you'll share the balcony with monkeys). Pleasant rooms cost Rs 440/550 – there's one room with hot water. Breakfast is Rs 150 and rice and curry Rs 250. The food is excellent.

Next door is the *Little Nest*, which costs Rs 250 per person with breakfast and dinner included. The rooms are dingy, there are no fans, and the bathroom isn't for the faint-hearted. But don't despair! The food's delicious, the hosts are welcoming and the price is right.

The *Travellers Nest* (☎ 222633, 117/4 Anagarika Dharmapala Mawatha), slightly to the left off the road a few hundred metres after Sangamitta Mawatha, caters for a variety of budgets. At the shoestring end there are dorm beds (with three beds to a dorm) for Rs 250. Rooms with hot water cost Rs 500/600. It's a bit sterile though, and the staff here won't make you feel particularly welcome.

At 18 First Lane, Dharmaraja Rd (turn right off Anagarika Dharmapala Mawatha a

KANDY

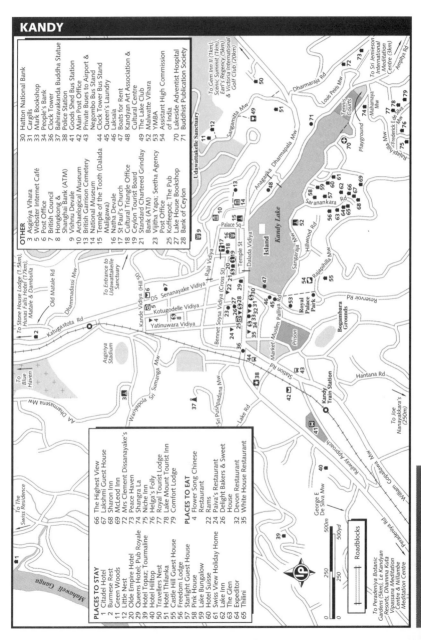

fraction past Sangamitta Mawatha) you'll find friendly **Mrs Clement Dissanayake's** (☎ 225468). There are five double rooms ranging from Rs 500 to 660. The most expensive room has hot water. A single costs Rs 400. Breakfast costs Rs 150 and rice and curry with dessert Rs 250. The food is very good. If you phone from the main post office when you arrive in Kandy, they'll come and pick you up for free.

Peace Haven (☎ 232584, 47/10 Louis Pieris Mawatha) has four rooms, two with hot water, costing from Rs 400 to 600. The rooms are clean, there are kitchen facilities (for Rs 100 more), a communal balcony and a bare sitting area.

South of the Lake Saranankara Rd is jam-packed with decent value (and extremely competitive) guesthouses. The places up towards the top of the road have views.

Pink House (15 Saranankara Rd) has six rooms with shared bathroom for Rs 200/300 and one with bathroom for Rs 450. It's a quaint old rambling house, but wins no prizes for cleanliness. The owners are very friendly and helpful.

Next door to the Pink House is the **Starlight Guest House** (☎ 233573) with hot water in each of its six rooms, which cost Rs 550; the two family cottages cost Rs 1000 for four people. It's a clean place, but is a bit sterile. The food is good.

Farther up on the other side of the road the **Freedom Lodge** (☎ 223506, **e** freedom omega@yahoo.com, 30 Saranankara Rd) has three spotless, bright rooms, all with hot water. The two downstairs doubles cost Rs 620 and Rs 675 and the double upstairs, with a balcony, costs Rs 730. There's a small garden and the hosts are very welcoming.

The Glen (☎ 235342, 58 Saranankara Rd) has clean, homely rooms, two with shared bathroom (Rs 400) and one with a bathroom (Rs 450). The couple here are friendly and there's also a pretty garden.

Expeditor (☎/fax 238316, **e** expeditor kandy@hotmail.com, 58A Saranankara Rd) is a low-key spot with good food, hot water, Internet facilities, clean rooms (Rs 450/720)

and charming hosts. You can arrange off-the-beaten-track tours here. It's a popular place so book ahead.

The **Thilini** guesthouse (☎ 224975, 60 Saranankara Rd) has two clean enough rooms in a family home for Rs 300 and Rs 350. It's a friendly place with good food (the owner used to cook for Peace Corps workers, who still visit from time to time).

Lakshmi Guest House (☎ 222154, 57 Saranankara Rd) has a large dash of old-fashioned charm – it's a shame little effort is put in to welcome guests. The clean rooms cost from Rs 400 to 500. No food is served.

The road that skirts the south side of the lake is Sangaraja Mawatha. A lane, just one street along from Saranankara Rd, leads to two more places. **Lake Bungalow** (☎ 222075, 22/2B Sangaraja Mawatha) has three quaint, basic rooms in a colonial-style main house as well as two apartments (each with three bedrooms) in the modern annexe next door. All rooms are clean with hot water – the newer rooms have a balcony and a communal kitchen. There's a small garden. Rooms cost from Rs 440 to Rs 880 or Rs 2500 for an apartment. **Swiss View Holiday Home** (☎ 223246, 32/40 Sangaraja Mawatha) is a friendly place with four clean rooms for Rs 440/660 (with hot water). The food is reportedly good.

Mcleod Inn (☎ 222832, 65A Rajapihilla Mawatha) has stunning views from the shared balcony and from rooms Nos 2 and 6. The spotless rooms have hot water and cost Rs 550/650.

Lake Mount Tourist Inn (☎ 233204, fax 235522, **e** hirokow@sltnet.lk, 195A Rajapihilla Mawatha) is clinical and tidy. There are a variety of rooms, with and without bathroom, at prices ranging from Rs 440 to 1100. All rooms have hot water.

Follow Louis Peiris Mawatha or Sangaraja Mawatha to the end, and near the tennis courts you will find Mahamaya Mawatha. The **Shangra La** (☎ 222218, **e** shang@slt.lk, 2 Mahamaya Mawatha) has a bit of a noisy spot near the main road but the rooms are clean and set in a garden. There's a kitchen you can use, a sitting area and hot water. Rooms cost Rs 550/620.

Places to Stay – Mid-Range

Lake Inn (☎ *222208, fax 232343,* e *mat sui@slt.lk, 43 Saranankara Rd)* has eight rooms with hot water for Rs 825/1100 including breakfast. The rooms are clean though a little sterile, but there's a colourful restaurant with decently priced food (dinner costs from Rs 165 to Rs 200).

The Highest View (☎ *233778, 129/3 Saranankara Rd)* has rooms for Rs 1650. You'd expect a lot for this price (including, of course, the highest view) – you'll get a spotless, slightly sterile room with hot water and a balcony with good views. Rooms without a balcony cost the same. The tea here gets rave reviews.

At the top of the road *Sharon Inn* (☎ *222416, fax 225665,* e *sharon@ sltnet.lk, 59 Saranankara Rd)* is famous. It has a mixed bag of rooms: reasonably clean rooms in the older annexe cost Rs 720; spotless standard rooms have a balcony and cost Rs 1100; and the top rooms with the best views cost Rs 1320 and Rs 1450. There's a rooftop garden with great views, Internet facilities, and hot water in every room. The dinner buffet (8 pm) gets mixed reviews.

There are several good middle-range guesthouses along Rajapihilla Mawatha, which is high above the south side of the lake. All have good views.

Overlooking the lake from the slopes to its south is the *Castle Hill Guest House* (☎/fax *224376, 22 Rajapihilla Mawatha),* a top-end guesthouse with four rooms, all with bathroom, for Rs 1500 to 1800. It's good for a luxury stop and the view from the lovely garden is stunning. One visitor commented that the immense rooms, Art Deco–like furniture, French doors to the gardens and stylised flower arrangements conjure up images of hotel stage-sets from a Fred Astaire movie.

Niche Inn (☎ *222466, 68 Rajapihilla Mawatha)* is a colonial-era bungalow with superb views of the lake from a lovely garden. The four rooms (with bathroom) cost Rs 1000/1650, the sole room with shared bathroom costs Rs 850/1100. The rooms are bland, but clean and each has hot water.

Royal Tourist Lodge (☎ *222534, fax 233364, 93 Rajapihilla Mawatha)* looks like it's come straight from a *Flintstones* cartoon. If you're not already scared away, the two clean rooms cost Rs 1100 and Rs 1375 with private balcony and hot water. Meals are available, but you must order in advance.

The *Comfort Lodge* (☎ *074-473707,* e *comfort@sri.lanka.net, 197 Rajapihilla Mawatha)* has six modern rooms with all the mod cons, including hot water, TV, telephone, that you wouldn't expect at Rs 1430/1650. There's a large sitting area, a roof garden, cooking facilities and to top it all off, a friendly host.

Places to Stay – Top End

Kandy has a couple of hotels in colonial-era style, as well as several modern luxury places.

Queens Hotel (☎ *233290, fax 232079,* e *queens@kandy.ccom.lk),* right in the centre of town and minutes from the Temple of the Tooth, is an older-style airy place with a pretty garden and a clean pool. The large rooms have polished floorboards, old-style furniture (bedspreads your grandmother would love), and modern bathrooms. Rooms cost US$30/40 – add US$10 for air-con. It can get a bit noisy here during the day, so go for the quieter rooms that overlook the pool.

The *Hotel Hilltop* (☎ *224162, fax 232459,* e *hilltop@slt.lk, 200/21 Bahirawa-kanda)* is a five-minute walk up to the right off Peradeniya Rd. It has colourful rooms, great views over the town and surrounding hills, and a peaceful garden with a good-sized, clean swimming pool. Rooms cost US$37/49.

Hotel Thilanka (☎ *232429, fax 225497,* e *thilanka@ids.lk, 3 Sangamitta Mawatha)* is a pleasant place amid trees and overlooking the lake. Rooms cost US$38/50 – add US$11 for air-con. Avoid the rooms at the front of the building over the kitchens; there's a constant stream of noisy cars and coaches right outside. There's a pleasant terrace bar and a good restaurant (huge buffets with both Eastern and Western food), plus a pool with a great view over the town and lake. The numerous wall hangings, masks, batiks and interesting furniture give this place a bit more character than most.

Eccentric *Helga's Folly* (☎ 074-474314, e chalet@sltnet.lk, 32 Fedrick E de Silva Mawatha), off Rajapihilla Mawatha, is crammed with palatial furnishings, puffed with comfy cushions and partially lit by wax-dripping candelabras. It'll be a realisation of a decadent medieval dream, or the makings of your nightmare. Either way, you'll pay US$60 per plush room (no aircon) and US$196 for a suite (no air-con). There's a pool surrounded by fairies (we kid you not), and a restaurant where merely curious nonguests can eat. Lunch or dinner costs US$12. Book ahead.

In Anniewatte, way up on top of a hill overlooking the town from the west, about 2km up from Peradeniya Rd, the *Hotel Topaz* (☎ 232326, fax 232073, e topaz@ eureka.lk) has 77 boring rooms (36 air-con). Singles and doubles cost US$69 – add US$11 for air-con. This hotel has superb views, a pool and you can even play tennis under floodlights. Owned by the same company, the *Tourmaline* on the hill below is similar but pricier. Forget it – the Topaz is better value for money.

The Swiss Residence (☎ 074-479055, fax 479057, 23 Bahirawakanda) is set against a steep hillside to the north-west of town. It's modern and brisk with attentive service and a small pool. Spotless rooms cost US$70.

To the south of the lake the old-style *Hotel Suisse* (☎ 233025, fax 232083, e suisse@ kandy.ccom.lk, 30 Sangaraja Mawatha) has air-con rooms at US$68/75. It's secluded and quiet, but not too far to stroll around the lake to the town centre. There are spacious public areas, including a snooker room, and a fine garden and swimming pool.

Places to Eat

Many people eat in their guesthouses, where some of Kandy's tastiest food is to be had and where you can also enjoy some of the local specialities, particularly at poya. There are a number of popular cheap places in central Kandy but they all seem to yo-yo between acceptable and absolutely awful. Most of them are along Dalada Vidiya, or in the back streets to the north.

The *Delight Bakers & Sweet House* has reasonable bread, pastries, cakes and short eats, and dozens of sweets waiting to march out the door.

Olde Empire, at the Olde Empire Hotel between Queen's Hotel and the Temple of the Tooth, has locals elbowing to get in (well, very nearly) for the delicious spicy rice and curry for Rs 68 and lunch packets for Rs 40.

Stylish on the outside, ugly on the inside, *Devon Restaurant* (☎ 224537) has a food court on the 1st floor open from 10 am to 9 pm. It's impossible to charm the surly staff, but the food is cheap, eatable and filling: fried rice (Rs 45), beef curry (Rs 25) and so on.

Down the street, the *White House Restaurant* (☎ 223393) is tacky but cheap. It has snacks, drinks and ice cream, or you can fill up on their meals such as mixed fried rice (Rs 110), chicken fried noodles (Rs 95) and sweet and sour chicken (Rs 145).

Paiva's Restaurant (☎ 234493, 37 Yatinuwara Vidiya) has a north Indian menu, a Chinese menu and a bakery. You can sit in the airy, busy section downstairs, or you can go upstairs to the office-like surrounds. The food is good and ranges from dosas (Rs 18) to Chinese mains (from Rs 115 to 335). There's also rice and curry costing from Rs 55 to 85 at lunch time.

Rams (☎ 236143, Bennet Soysa Vidiya, also known as Cross St) serves excellent south Indian food in a gaudy, colourful setting. A vegetarian thali costs Rs 200, *vadai* Rs 38 and samosas Rs 110. Plain rice costs a ridiculous Rs 110, as does a large bottle of water. It's open from 7.30 am to about 10 pm.

The Pub (☎ 324868) has delicious food at reasonable prices. Spaghetti carbonara costs Rs 260 and a nicoise salad costs Rs 160. You'll find it above the Koffeepot Internet cafe along Dalada Vidiya St, west of the Bank of Ceylon. There's also booze served here.

At the top end of Kotugodelle Vidiya is a posh surprise: the *Flower Song Chinese Restaurant*, a clean, air-con place that even

Your cuppa begins here: Tea, a legacy of colonial times, remains one of Sri Lanka's main exports.

ANDERS BLOMQVIST

Old traditions die hard. Tea is still picked by hand and gathered in baskets worn on the pickers' backs.

DALLAS STRIBLEY

The brightly hued saris of Tamil tea pickers add a distinctive splash of colour to the landscape.

ERIC L WHEATER

ANDERS BLOMQVIST

The hurly-burly of a busy Kandy street seems a world away from the laid-back beaches of the coasts.

ANDERS BLOMQVIST

You better get a lawyer, son! Legal offices in Kandy.

CHRIS MELLOR

Kandy, Sri Lanka's second-largest city, is nestled high up in the hill country beside a picturesque lake.

has a substantial wine list. Mains range from Rs 330 to Rs 470. Apart from this place, if you want to splash out there's little to choose from except at the hotels (Hotel Suisse's food has been recommended).

Entertainment
Pubs/Bars Thankfully this quiet town has been injected with a new night-time venue, the originally named *The Pub*. It's a busy, comfy place with music, an overgrown TV screen and a balcony packed with cane chairs (see Places to Eat earlier in this section).

The *Pub Royale* beside the Queens Hotel is a large, airy bar with an old-fashioned flavour. It's a place for a quiet drink, and a cheap one too at Rs 100 for a Lion.

The top hotels all have bars, but be careful of the cost of the drinks. You can buy beer to take away at Cargills.

Kandyan Dancers & Drummers The famed Kandyan dancers are not principally a theatrical performance, but you can see them go through their athletic routines each night at four locales around Kandy. The *Kandy Lake Club,* 300m up Sangamitta Mawatha, starts its show at 7 pm (Rs 250). It's very popular; the finale is a display of fire-walking. The front seats are usually reserved for groups and if you want to get good seats, turn up at least 20 minutes early. The Kandy Lake Club is also a casino. Beware of the price of drinks. There are also shows in the *Kandyan Art Association & Cultural Centre*, the *Red Cross Building* next door and at the *YMBA* (Young Men's Buddhist Association), all of which charge Rs 250 and start at 5.45 pm.

You can also hear Kandyan drummers every day at the Temple of the Tooth and the other temples surrounding it – their drumming signals the start and finish of the daily pujas.

Spectator Sport
If you're a rugby fan and you're in Kandy between May and September, you can take in a game or two at the Nittawella rugby grounds (near the Stone House Lodge, see Places to Stay in the Around Kandy section).

Check with the tourist office for details on who's playing when.

Shopping
The Kandyan Art Association & Cultural Centre beside the lake has a good selection of local lacquerwork, brassware and other craft items, and there are some craftspeople working on the spot.

There's a government-run Laksala arts and crafts shop to the west of the lake with cheaper prices than the Art Association & Cultural Centre, but it has nothing on the big Laksala in Colombo.

Central Kandy has a number of shops selling antique jewellery, silver belts and other items. Peradeniya Rd has many of these shops as well as a Fashion Bug outlet for clothing. You can also buy crafts in and around the colourful main market on Station Rd. Kandy also has a number of batik manufacturers; some of the best and most original are the batik pictures made by Upali Jayakody and by Fresco Batiks on the Peradeniya road outside Kandy.

Getting There & Away
Bus Kandy has one main bus station (the manic Goods Shed) and a series of bus stops near the clock tower. It can be hard to work out which one to head to. A rule of thumb worth following is that the Goods Shed bus station has long distance buses, ie, to Colombo, Polonnaruwa, Nuwara Eliya, while local buses, ie, Peradeniya, Ampitiya, Matale, Kegalle leave from near the clock tower. However, just to complicate things further some private intercity-express buses (to the airport, Negombo and Colombo for example) leave from Station Rd between the clock tower and the train station. If you're still confused, ask a passer-by.

Colombo CTB buses run from the Goods Shed bus station. The first of the ordinary buses pulls out at 3 am. They then run every half hour till 8.30 pm (Rs 35, 3½ hours). There are also intercity non air-con buses (Rs 53, three hours), and air-con intercity express buses (Rs 63, 2½ to three hours), both of which start at about 5 am

Main Trains from Kandy

Tickets can be bought and reserved (up to 10 days in advance) at counter No 1, which is open from 5.30 am to 5.30 pm daily. If you cancel less than six hours before departure, you will be subject to a Rs 75 fee.

Four seats in the 1st-class observation saloon are available from Kandy and should be booked a week ahead. (The other observation seats are reserved for passengers from Colombo.) If you want to break your journey between Kandy and Ella or beyond you can, but you must use your ticket within 24 hours.

destination	departure time	fare (Rs)			approx duration (hrs)
		3rd	2nd	1st class	
Badulla _Podi Menike_	8.55 am	38	104	281.50*	7½
Bandarawela _Podi Menike_	8.55 am	31	85.50	249*	6
Colombo _Intercity Express_	6.30 am, 3 pm	-	72	122*	2½
Colombo via Rambukkana (for Pinnewala Elephant Orphanage)	6.45, 10.30 am, 3.40, 4.50 pm	25	68.50	-	3
Ella _Podi Menike_	8.55 am	33.50	97	261*	6½
Haputale _Podi Menike_	8.55 am	28.50	79	237*	5½
Hatton _Podi Menike_	8.55 am	13.50	37.50	166*	2½
Matale	5.45, 7.15, 10.05 am, 2.35, 5.20, 6.55 pm	6	-	-	1½
Matara via Bentota, Galle	5.25 am	57	157	-	6
Nanu Oya (for Nuwara Eliya) _Podi Menike_	8.55 am	20.50	56.50	197.50*	4

* The 1st-class observation saloon includes a booking fee of Rs 50.

▲▲▲▲▲▲▲▲▲▲▲▲▲▲

and leave when full throughout the day. The express and ordinary buses leave from stand No 1.

Private buses leave from Station Rd (also known as SWRD Bandaranaike Mawatha). Private air-con intercity buses start running at about 4 am and continue every 25 minutes or so till 9.30 pm. They take around 2½ to three hours to reach Colombo. Tickets cost Rs 90.

Tickets for both CTB and private buses can be bought on the buses themselves.

International Airport & Negombo Private intercity express buses to the international airport and Negombo leave from the Station Rd bus stand. CTB buses leave from the Goods Shed. The first intercity bus departs at about 6.30 am and the last at about

5.30 pm. They tend to leave when full, every 20 to 30 minutes. The fare for the three to 3½ hours journey is Rs 35 for the CTB bus and Rs 75 for the air-con express bus.

Nuwara Eliya & Hatton CTB and private buses go to Nuwara Eliya and then on to Hatton. They leave from the Goods Shed bus station. The CTB buses start running at about 5.30 am, leaving when full throughout the day until about 4.30 pm. The one-way fare to Nuwara Eliya is Rs 47. There are also private air-con buses that operate on the same basis except the last bus leaves at 5.30 pm; to Nuwara Eliya costs Rs 70.

Haputale & Ella For these destinations, change at Nuwara Eliya.

Anuradhapura & Dambulla Buses to Anuradhapura also leave from Goods Shed bus station. Air-con intercity buses start running at about 5.30 am and go approximately every hour until 6.30 pm. The trip takes three hours and costs Rs 80. Ordinary buses take about half an hour longer and cost Rs 35. You can also catch one of the air-con Anuradhapura-bound buses to Dambulla, but you must pay the full amount (Rs 80) regardless.

Polonnaruwa Air-con buses to Polonnaruwa leave the Goods Shed bus station from about 5.30 am and go approximately every hour until 6.30 pm. Tickets cost Rs 80 – the journey takes three hours. The ordinary bus takes about half an hour longer and costs Rs 39.

Sigiriya There's a CTB bus to Sigiriya from the Goods Shed bus station at 8 am (it returns at 3 pm); Rs 32. See the Sigiriya section in the Ancient Cities chapter for more details.

Trincomalee About seven buses to Trincomalee leave the Goods Shed between 6.30 am and 1.15 pm. Ordinary buses cost Rs 45 and air-con intercity buses cost Rs 90.

Other Destinations Bus No 594 to Matale (Rs 25, intercity express; Rs 11, CTB) leaves

from beside the central clock tower. CTB buses to Kegalle and Kurunegala (Rs 24, intercity express) stop at clock tower bus stops.

Taxi It's easy to get long-distance taxis to or from Kandy (see Getting Around, following). To the international airport costs about Rs 3000 and to Colombo about Rs 2600.

Many taxi drivers hang around outside the entrance to the Temple of the Tooth waiting for work. Your guesthouse or hotel can organise taxi tours but you'll probably get a cheaper deal if you organise it through these chaps. You could do a day trip to Sigiriya (via Dambulla) for example, or even just visit the three temples and the botanic gardens (see Around Kandy later in this chapter). For a whole van, expect to pay about Rs 2500 a day, which includes driver and fuel.

Getting Around

Bus Buses to outlying parts of Kandy and nearby towns such as Peradeniya, Ampitiya, Matale and Kegalle leave from near the clock tower.

Bicycle & Motorbike You can hire a 125cc motorbike from Malik (☎ 072-222687, ℮ matsui@slt.lk). It costs Rs 750 per day or Rs 650 per day for five days. This includes a helmet and insurance – but double check. You can also hire bicycles for Rs 150 per day, and Malik takes tours around the island (he's fluent in French).

Taxi Radio Cabs (☎ 233322), with metered air-con taxis, are a comfortable alternative to three-wheelers. However, be aware that you may have to wait some time for your cab, especially if it's raining and demand is heavy. Settle on a price before you start your journey with taxis (vans) that are not metered.

Three-Wheeler It costs about Rs 80 to take a three-wheeler from the train station to the Pink House, Sharon Inn, Hotel Suisse and other places towards the east end of the lake, Rs 120 or so to places a bit farther out such as the Travellers Nest or Green Woods.

AROUND KANDY

☎ 08

There are a few things worth seeing around Kandy that can be done in a morning or afternoon trip or, if you're not in a rush, you could take the day.

Peradeniya Botanic Gardens

The Peradeniya Botanic Gardens are 6km out of Kandy towards Colombo. Before the British came this was a royal pleasure garden: Today it's the largest botanic garden in Sri Lanka, covering 60 hectares and bounded on three sides by a loop of the Mahaweli Ganga. It's beautiful and well worth a visit.

There's a fine collection of orchids and a stately avenue of royal palms planted in 1950. A major attraction is the giant Javan fig tree on the great lawn – it covers 1600 sq metres. There's an avenue of cannon ball trees and another of cabbage palms. Don't miss the avenue of double coconut palms or coco de mer – each coconut weights from 10kg to 20kg. The spice garden allows you to see nutmeg, cinnamon, cloves and more without the hassle of a salesperson breathing down your neck. The snake creeper closeby is also well worth seeing. Then there are the giant bamboo and Assam rubber trees, and who could resist wanting to hunt down the sausage tree? You can easily spend a whole day wandering around the gardens.

The *Royal Gardens Cafeteria*, about 500m to the left of the entrance, has a good buffet lunch for Rs 300 or you can choose a la carte (but the service is sometimes slow). Those on a budget can always take a picnic.

At the entrance you can buy a copy of *Illustrated Guide, Royal Botanic Gardens*, which has a map and suggested walks through the garden. There are other books available too – all decently priced. The gardens are open from 8 am to 5.45 pm daily, and admission is Rs 150 and Rs 75 for students and children under 12. Bus No 654 from the clock tower bus stop in Kandy will take you to the gardens for Rs 4.50. A three-wheeler from the centre of Kandy to the gardens will set you back about Rs 400 (return trip) and a van will cost Rs 500.

A Temple Loop from Kandy

Visiting some of the many temples around Kandy gives you a chance to see a little rural life as well as observe Sri Lankan culture. This particularly pleasant loop will take you to three temples and back via the botanic gardens. There's quite a bit of walking involved so if you're not in the mood you could narrow down your visit to one or two of the temples listed or take a taxi trip to all three; expect to pay about Rs 1400

The first stop is the **Embekka Devale**, for which you need catch bus No 643 (to Vatadeniya via Embekka) from near the clock tower. The buses only run about once an hour and the village of Embekka is about seven twisting and turning kilometres beyond the botanic gardens. From the village you've got a pleasant countryside stroll of about 1km to the temple, built in the 14th century. Its carved wooden pillars, thought to have come from a royal audience hall in the city, are said to be the finest in the Kandy area. The carvings include swans, double-headed eagles, wrestling men and dancing women. A miniature version of the Kandy Esala Perahera is held here in September. It costs Rs 100 to enter the temple.

From here to the **Lankatilake Temple** is a 1.5km stroll along a path through the rice paddies until you see the blue temple loom up on the left. From Kandy you can go directly to the Lankatilake Temple on bus No 666 or take a Kiribathkumbara or Pilimatalawa bus from the same stop as the Embekka buses. It's a Buddhist and Hindu temple with fine views of the countryside. There's a Buddha image, Kandy-period paintings, rock-face inscriptions and stone elephant figures. A festival is held here in August. Entry costs Rs 100.

It's a farther 3km walk from here to the **Gadaladeniya Temple**, or you can catch a bus (No 644, among others, will take you there). Built on a rocky outcrop, covered with small rock pools, the temple is reached by a series of steps cut directly into the rock. This Buddhist temple with a Hindu annexe dates from a similar period to the Lankatilake Temple and the Embekka Devale. A moonstone marks the entrance to the

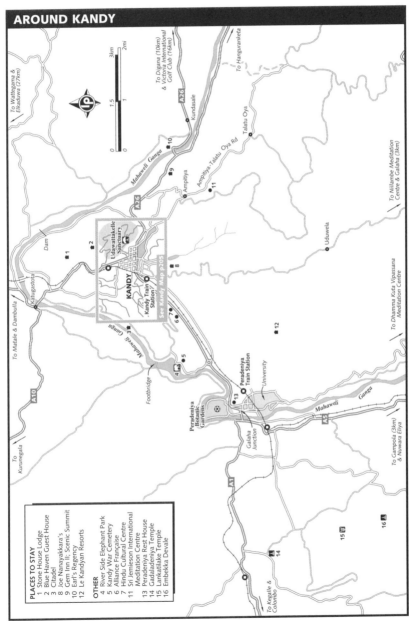

AROUND KANDY

3km
2mi

To Wattegama &
Elkaduwa (27km)

To Matale & Dambulla

To Kurunegala

To Kegalle &
Colombo

To Kegalle &
Colombo

To Digana (10km)
& Victoria International
Golf Club (16km)

To Hanguranketa

To Nillambe Meditation
Centre & Galaha (3km)

To Dhamma Kuta Vipassana
Meditation Centre

To Gampola (3km)
& Nuwara Eliya

Mahaweli Ganga

Kundasale

Talatu Oya

Ampitiya

Ampitiya-Talatu Oya Rd

Uduwela

Udawattakelle
Sanctuary

KANDY

Kandy Train
Station

See Kandy Map p205

Mahaweli Ganga

Katugastota

Dam

Mahaweli Ganga

Footbridge

Peradeniya
Botanic
Gardens

Peradeniya
Train Station

University

Galaha
Junction

Mahaweli Ganga

PLACES TO STAY
1 Stone House Lodge
2 Blue Haven Guest House
3 Citadel
8 Joe Nanayakkara's
9 Gem Inn II; Scenic Summit
10 Earl's Regency
12 Le Kandyan Resorts

OTHER
4 River Side Elephant Park
5 Kandy War Cemetery
6 Alliance Française
7 Hindu Cultural Centre
11 Sri Jemieson International
   Meditation Centre
13 Peradeniya Rest House
14 Gadaladeniya Temple
15 Lankatilake Temple
16 Embekka Devale

PERADENIYA BOTANIC GARDENS

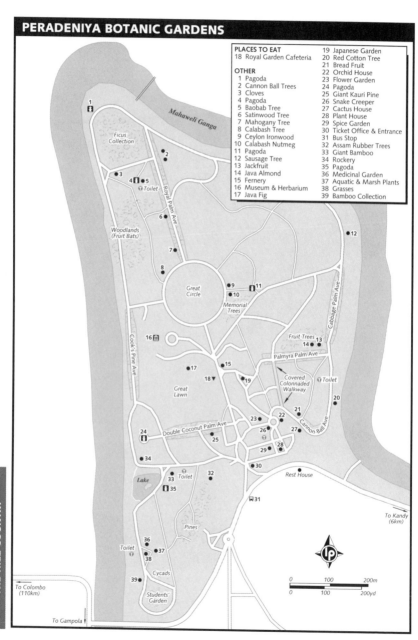

PLACES TO EAT
18 Royal Garden Cafeteria

OTHER
1 Pagoda
2 Cannon Ball Trees
3 Cloves
4 Pagoda
5 Baobab Tree
6 Satinwood Tree
7 Mahogany Tree
8 Calabash Tree
9 Ceylon Ironwood
10 Calabash Nutmeg
11 Pagoda
12 Sausage Tree
13 Jackfruit
14 Java Almond
15 Fernery
16 Museum & Herbarium
17 Java Fig
19 Japanese Garden
20 Red Cotton Tree
21 Bread Fruit
22 Orchid House
23 Flower Garden
24 Pagoda
25 Giant Kauri Pine
26 Snake Creeper
27 Cactus House
28 Plant House
29 Spice Garden
30 Ticket Office & Entrance
31 Bus Stop
32 Assam Rubber Trees
33 Giant Bamboo
34 Rockery
35 Pagoda
36 Medicinal Garden
37 Aquatic & Marsh Plants
38 Grasses
39 Bamboo Collection

main shrine. A resident artist will be happy to show you around. Entry is Rs 100.

From Gadaladeniya Temple the main Colombo-Kandy road is less than 2km away; you reach it close to the 105km marker. It's a pleasant stroll, and from the main road almost any bus will take you to the Peradeniya Botanic Gardens or on into Kandy.

Elephants

The **River Side Elephant Park** has anywhere from three to seven elephants. They knock off work at around noon and bathe in the river south-west of Kandy, near the War Cemetery on Deveni Rajasinghe Mawatha. There's an entry fee of Rs 150, Rs 1000 if you want a ride. It's open from 7.30 am to 4.30 pm daily.

Places to Stay

If you want quiet days spent wandering along shaded tracks, with views of rolling hills, then stay just out of Kandy. It's always easy to get into town should you want to – a taxi or three-wheeler is never far away.

Places to Stay – Budget & Mid-Range

Gem Inn II (☎ 224239, 102/90 Hewaheta Rd, Talwatta) is about 2.5km south-east of the town centre, perched on a hillside with wonderful views over the Mahaweli Ganga and the Knuckles Range. Clean, simple rooms cost from Rs 440 to Rs 850; most have their own balcony. There's a large garden and good food.

Just before Gem Inn II is the well-run *Scenic Summit (☎ 232636, e sherard@ kandy.ccom.lk, 102/95A Hewaheta Rd)*. This place also has great views over the Mahaweli, and the owners are very helpful. There are eight spotless rooms with hot water for Rs 1700/2000 a single/double (no air-con). To get to these places catch a No 654 or No 621 from the clock tower bus stop in Kandy (Rs 3.50). The steep track is up to the right off Hewaheta Rd, just before the Kandy municipal limit sign. Follow it around its first hairpin, but at the second hairpin continue straight on: You'll see Scenic Summit on the right, and Gem Inn II is the house at the end.

On the other side of the Udawattakelle Sanctuary is *Blue Haven Guest House (☎/fax 232453, e bluehaven@kandyan .net, 30/2 Poorna La)*. Each of the five rooms has florid floral decor, hot water and a large, airy balcony overlooking the jungle setting. Rooms cost from Rs 330 to 720.

At *Joe Nanayakkara's (☎ 234767, 29 Gemunu Mawatha, Public Servants Housing Scheme, Hantana Place)* there are good views over the town and surrounding hills. Mr and Mrs Nanayakkara are a friendly, lively pair only too happy to impart their knowledge of Sri Lankan life. Homely double rooms in a building separate from the main house cost Rs 500. Go up Hospital Rd (off Station Rd) past the space-capsule-like former Hantana Hotel, then take the first road up to the left and keep left until you reach the house, about 1km from Station Rd. An Uduwela bus from near the clock tower will take you some of the way, or a three-wheeler will cost Rs 80. Once there, you'll be shown a short cut that will have you down in town in 10 minutes.

Places to Stay – Top End

Stone House Lodge (☎ 232769, fax 232 517, e stonehse@sltnet.lk, 42 Nittawella Rd) is about 3km north of the train station. There's a lovely garden and the lodge itself is tastefully furnished, spacious and charming. There are four rooms (no air-con); US$62 for 'garden' rooms, US$64 for 'master' rooms. The place is very well kept – it's an excellent retreat. Meals are served. To get there catch an Akurana-bound bus from the clock tower bus stop (ask to be let out at the rugby field); a three-wheeler should cost no more than Rs 200.

Citadel (☎ 234365/6, fax 232085, e htl res@keels.com, 124 Srimath Kuda Ratwatte Mawatha) is 5km west of the town centre and is a large, modern hotel built beside the Mahaweli Ganga. The air-con rooms cost US$75/85. All rooms have balconies overlooking the river. The swimming pool is worth a visit. A taxi from Kandy will cost Rs 350.

Hunas Falls Hotel (☎ 476402, fax 071-735134, e jethot@sri.lanka.net) is a hotel with one of the most spectacular settings. It's 27km out of Kandy, high up in a tea estate at Elkaduwa. Rooms with air-con cost US$110; there are all the mod cons including a swimming pool, tennis court, a well-stocked fish pool above the Hunas waterfalls and plenty of walks in the surrounding hills.

Peeking from the top of the hills is the luxury hotel *Le Kandyan Resorts* (☎ 233521/2, fax 233948, e *lekandy@sltnet.lk*) at Heerassagala, Peradeniya. The air-con rooms, decorated with Kandyan craftwork, cost US$95. There's an inviting pool with superb views that nonguests may use for Rs 100 and a well-equipped Ayurvedic centre, which is also open to nonguests.

A recent comer to the top-end market, *Earl's Regency* (☎ 422122, fax 422133, e *erhotel@sltnet.lk*) at Kundasale, has all the mod cons, great views and immaculate rooms – all stylishly packaged. The air-con rooms have a slick black bathroom, polished floorboards and most have a balcony – all for US$110/122.

EAST OF KANDY

Most travellers from Kandy go west to Colombo, north to the ancient cities or south to the rest of the hill country. It's also possible to go east to Mahiyangana, beyond which you will find Badulla on the southeast edge of the hill country and Monaragala on the way to Arugam Bay, the Gal Oya National Park and, farther north, Batticaloa on the east coast.

The Buddha is supposed to have preached at **Mahiyangana** and there's a *dagoba* (Buddhist monument) here to mark the spot. On the way from Kandy are a series of bends, where the road winds hair-raisingly down from the hill country to the dry-zone plains, through 18 hairpins. From the top you have a magnificent view of the Mahaweli Development Project – but don't attempt the trip if you're of a nervous disposition or familiar with the maintenance standards on Sri Lankan buses! On the way up you worry about overheating, on the way down you worry about the brakes. You usually pass at least one jeep or truck that didn't make it and lies in the jungle beneath.

Travellers from Mahiyangana to Monaragala may need to change buses at Bibile.

ADAM'S PEAK

Whether it is Adam's Peak (the place where Adam first set foot on earth after being cast out of heaven), Sri Pada (Sacred Footprint) or Samanalakande (Butterfly Mountain, where butterflies go to die), Adam's Peak is a beautiful and fascinating place. Not all faiths believe the huge 'footprint' on the top of the 2224m peak to be that of Adam – some claim it to be that of the Buddha, of St Thomas the early apostle of India or even of Lord Shiva.

Whichever legend you care to believe, the fact remains that it has been a pilgrimage centre for over 1000 years. King Parakramabahu and King Nissanka Malla of Polonnaruwa provided *ambalamas* (resting places) up the mountain to shelter the weary pilgrims.

Today the pilgrimage season begins on poya day in December and runs until the Vesak festival in May. The busiest time is January and February. At other times the temple on the summit is unused, and between May and October the peak is obscured by cloud for much of the time. During the season a steady stream of pilgrims (and the odd tourist) makes the climb up the countless steps to the top from the small settlement of Dalhousie, 33km by road south-west of the tea town of Hatton, which is on the Colombo-Kandy-Nuwara Eliya railway and road. The route is iluminated in season by a string of lights, which look very pretty as they snake up the mountainside. Out of season you can still do the walk, you'll just need a torch (flashlight). Many pilgrims prefer to make the longer, much more tiring – but equally well-marked and lit – seven-hour climb from Ratnapura via the Carney Estate, because of the greater merit thus gained.

It's not only the sacred footprint that pilgrims seek. As the first rays of dawn light up the holy mountain you're treated to an extremely fine view – the hill country rises to the east, while to the west the land slopes away to the sea. Colombo, 65km away, is easily visible on a clear day. It's little wonder that English author John Stills described the peak as 'one of the vastest and most reverenced cathedrals of the human race'.

Interesting as the ascent is, and beautiful as the dawn is, Adam's Peak saves its *pièce de résistance* for a few minutes after dawn. The sun casts a perfect shadow of the peak onto the misty clouds down towards the coast. As the sun rises higher this eerie triangular shadow races back towards the peak, eventually disappearing into its base. As you scramble back down the countless stairs to the bottom you can reflect on how much easier the ascent is today than it was in the 19th century – as described in a Victorian guidebook to Sri Lanka (then Ceylon):

...others struggle upwards unaided, until, fainting by the way, they are considerately carried with all haste in their swooning condition to the summit and forced into an attitude of worship at the shrine to secure the full benefits of their pilgrimage before death should supervene; others never reach the top at all, but perish from cold and fatigue; and there have been many instances of pilgrims losing their lives by being blown over precipices or falling from giddiness induced by a thoughtless retrospect when surmounting especially dangerous cliffs.

The Climb

You can start the 7km climb from Dalhousie (del-**house**) soon after dark – in which case you'll need at least a good sleeping bag to keep you warm overnight at the top – or you can wait till the early hours of the morning. The climb is up steps most of the way, and with plenty of rest stops you'll get to the top in 2½ to four hours. A 2 am start will easily get you there before dawn, which is usually around 6 or 6.30 am.

From the car park the slope is gradual for the first half hour or so. You pass under an entrance arch then by the Japan-Sri Lanka Friendship Dagoba, the construction of which started in 1976. From here the path gets steeper and steeper until it is simply a continuous flight of stairs. There are tea houses for rest and refreshment all the way to the top, some of which are open through the night. A handful are open out of season.

Since it can get pretty cold and windy on top, there's no sense in getting to the top too long before the dawn and then having to sit around shivering. Bring warm clothes in any case, including something extra to put on when you get to the summit, and bring plenty of water with you. Some pilgrims wait until after sunrise for the priests to make a morning offering – 'Buddha's breakfast' as one irreverent witness put it.

One traveller wrote that at holiday times, climbing the peak can be much more time consuming: 'I climbed it on a full-moon holiday – along with 20,000 pilgrims – and it took 11 hours'. Another wrote: 'Why all the emphasis on rushing up in the dark? The walk up, with stops to wash in the stream, to take tea with the Japanese monks at the beautiful Peace Pagoda, and rest and chat at the *chai* (tea) shops, was as good as the time spent on the top – on Christmas morning'.

Women shouldn't make the ascent alone out of season; between June and November, when the pathway isn't illuminated and there are few people around, travellers are urged to go up in pairs, at least. If you are travelling alone, try to organise for someone to climb with you through your guesthouse. Expect to pay around Rs 500.

Leeches may be about. A popular method of deterring these unpleasant little beasties is an Ayurvedic balm produced by Siddhalepa Hospital. From the way climbers enthusiastically smear it on one would think it does for leeches what garlic does for vampires. It only costs a few rupees and is available in Dalhousie and indeed throughout Sri Lanka.

Remember to stretch your leg muscles before and after the climb, or you'll be limping for the next few days.

Places to Stay & Eat

The area surrounding Adam's Peak has a handful of places to stay. Dalhousie is the best place to start the climb, and it also has the best budget accommodation in the area. Head to Dickoya for mid-range choices. Maskeliya or Hatton hold little interest.

Dalhousie Out of season you may be dumped by the bus in the bare main square, but during the season the buses stop near the beginning of the walk.

In the pilgrimage season there are a few tea shops, some of which stay open all night, where you can get something to eat, buy provisions for the climb, or get a place to sleep (before you start the climb).

About 1.5km before you get to the place where the buses stop are two guesthouses (on your left as you approach Adam's Peak). They are the **Wathsala Inn** (☎ 052-77427) and **Sri Pale** (☎ 01-617345). The modern Wathsala Inn has 14 rooms with hot water. It has great views. Most rooms are clean enough, however the ones on the ground floor are crusty. It's overpriced at Rs 600/720 for singles/doubles and the hosts can be pushy. There's a restaurant here. The friendly hosts aren't pushy at Sri Pale, which is just as well since their four rooms are worn and forlorn (Rs 330/440).

The following two places are near the beginning of the climb. To find the **Green House** (☎ 051-23956) take the left-hand path when you reach the large, yellow 'Adam's Peak' sign. You can see it up ahead – and yes, this place is painted green. There are clean rooms at Rs 220 for tiny rooms and Rs 440 for larger rooms. A huge breakfast, dinner and a snack before the walk will cost Rs 300 per person. There's a pretty garden and the host will prepare a herbal 'bath' for you after the walk if you ask. If you take the right-hand path at the sign, you will shortly reach the friendly **Yellow House** (☎/fax 051-23958) set in a pretty garden. It's a pleasant, homely place with five clean, sizeable rooms all with hot water and bathrooms. Rooms cost Rs 330/440. Breakfast costs Rs 170 and dinner costs around Rs 200.

Maskeliya The **Aneetha Inn** (☎ 052-77122, 64 Old Post Office Rd) is on the lakeshore near the Tamil School. The four rooms are clean enough – all have an OK shared bathroom and cost Rs 250/300. The town is nothing special, and neither is Aneetha Inn, so push on if you can.

Dickoya About 7km from Hatton towards Maskeliya are two old plantation homes converted into hotels. **Lower Glencairn** (☎ 051-22342) is below the main road. It's rather jaded and shabby, but the garden is nice, as are the views. No meals are served. Rooms cost Rs 735/980 – which is a lot.

Upper Glencairn (☎ 051-22348, fax 01-447845) is in better shape and meals are available. It's a grand old place, built in 1906, surrounded by pretty gardens. The area around it is still a working tea estate. Rooms cost Rs 980. If you have your own transport it is possible to do Adam's Peak from Dickoya.

Hatton The **Ajantha Guest House** (☎ 051-22337) is a seven-minute walk from the train station (it's signposted on Main St) in the Ratnapura direction. It has simple rooms for Rs 500/660 with hot water. Meals are available.

Getting There & Away

Reaching the base of Adam's Peak is quite simple, and if you're making a night ascent you've got all day to arrive. Buses run to Dalhousie from Kandy (from the Nuwara Eliya bus stand), Nuwara Eliya and Colombo in the pilgrimage season. Otherwise, you need to get first to Hatton or to Maskeliya (which is about 20km along the road from Hatton to Dalhousie).

There are buses from Colombo, Kandy (three hours) or Nuwara Eliya to Hatton. There are also some direct buses from Nuwara Eliya and even Colombo to Maskeliya, which enables you to avoid stopping in Hatton if you wish.

Also, there are buses from Hatton to Dalhousie via Maskeliya every half hour in the pilgrimage season (private bus Rs 30, CTB Rs 22; two hours). Otherwise you have to take one bus from Hatton to Maskeliya (Rs 10.50, last departure about 7.30 pm), then another to Dalhousie (Rs 10, last departure about 8.30 pm). There are usually hotel touts on, in, above and beside the bus when it terminates at Dalhousie.

The *Podi Menike* train from Colombo and Kandy and the *Udarata Menike* from Colombo (not via Kandy) reach Hatton at 11.28 am and 2.14 pm respectively. The

Podi Menike in the other direction passes through Haputale and Nanu Oya, reaching Hatton about 2.12 pm. Main trains to Kandy leave at 2.12 *(Podi Menike)* and 10.48 pm. Trains from to Nanu Oya (for Nuwara Eliya) leave at 7.26, 11.28 am *(Podi Menike)*, 2.14, 4.20 pm.

A taxi from Hatton to Dalhousie should cost Rs 600. If you're really running late, taxis from Nuwara Eliya will take you to Hatton or Dalhousie.

KANDY TO NUWARA ELIYA

The 80km of road from Kandy to Nuwara Eliya is an ascent of nearly 1400m but you start to climb seriously only after about halfway.

At Pussellawa, 45km from Kandy, there's a well-positioned *resthouse (☎ 08-478397)* with three rooms and also fine views. Singles/doubles are Rs 1320. A little farther up the road you can look down to the large **Kothmale Reservoir**, created as part of the Mahaweli Development Project, and partly blamed by some locals for unusual climatic conditions in recent years.

About 58km from Kandy are the Ramboda Falls, and nearby is the *Ramboda Falls Hotel (☎/fax 052-59582)*, which is down a very steep driveway to your right. The view you get of the falls from here is quite marvellous and there's a restaurant with a pleasant veranda to view them from. The food has been recommended: rice and curry costs Rs 300. There are five clean rooms for US$21.

About 15km before Nuwara Eliya, the **Labookellie high-grown tea factory** is a convenient factory to visit as it's right on the roadside and they'll willingly show you around. It's open from 7 am to 7 pm daily. You can buy boxes of good tea cheaply here – Rs 100 for 200g – and enjoy a cup of tea with a slice of their good chocolate cake (Rs 30 for tea and cake). It's possible to arrange *accommodation* on an estate bungalow (cook provided) for about Rs 2200 a night.

Closer to Nuwara Eliya there are roadside stalls overflowing with all manner of vegetables, a legacy of Samuel Baker who first visited the area in 1846 and decided it would make a pleasant summer retreat. He introduced vegetables here, and they're still grown in abundance today. Also grown in abundance are flowers, which are transported to Colombo and abroad. Along the steep approach to Nuwara Eliya you'll come across children selling flowers by the roadside. If you don't buy their wares, they hurtle down a path to meet you at each hairpin turn until (hopefully) you'll fork out some cash.

NUWARA ELIYA

☎ 052

At 1889m Nuwara Eliya (pronounced nu-**rel**-iya, meaning 'City of Light') was the favourite hill station of the British, who kitted it up like a misplaced British village. The old pink-brick post office, the English-country-house-like Hill Club with its hunting pictures, mounted fish and hunting trophies, and the 18-hole golf course (said to be one of the finest in Asia) all cry out 'England'.

Nuwara Eliya has a fair assortment of other country-style houses with large gardens – many now turned over to vegetables to make this one of Sri Lanka's main market gardening centres. There's a well-kept **central park** that comes alive with flowers around March to May and August to September.

Gregory's Lake just south of the town is encircled by a variety of walking paths. It has been earmarked for renovation (not before time). The trout hatcheries are still maintained and, all in all, a retired tea planter would feel absolutely at home here. Come prepared for the evening cool – Nuwara Eliya is much higher than Kandy. In January and February you may find yourself needing to sleep with two blankets and all your clothes on.

The town is in the middle of the tea-growing country and there are occasional outbreaks of tension between Sinhalese and Tamils. The destruction caused during the 1983 riots has been patched up and is now invisible to anyone unaware of what the place looked like previously.

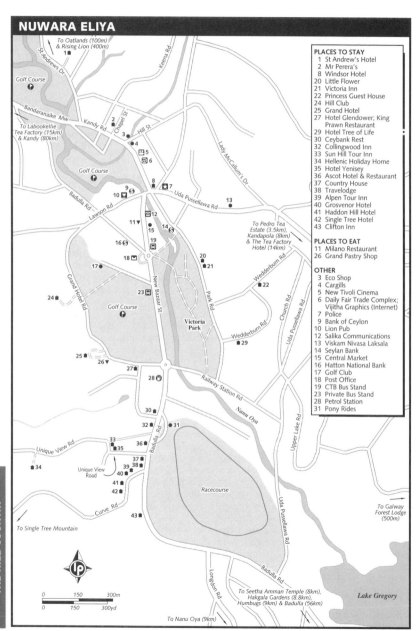

NUWARA ELIYA

PLACES TO STAY
1   St Andrew's Hotel
2   Mr Perera's
8   Windsor Hotel
20 Little Flower
21 Victoria Inn
22 Princess Guest House
24 Hill Club
25 Grand Hotel
27 Hotel Glendower; King
    Prawn Restaurant
29 Hotel Tree of Life
30 Ceybank Rest
32 Collingwood Inn
33 Sun Hill Tour Inn
34 Hellenic Holiday Home
35 Hotel Yenisey
36 Ascot Hotel & Restaurant
37 Country House
38 Travelodge
39 Alpen Tour Inn
40 Grosvenor Hotel
41 Haddon Hill Hotel
42 Single Tree Hotel
43 Clifton Inn

PLACES TO EAT
11 Milano Restaurant
26 Grand Pastry Shop

OTHER
3   Eco Shop
4   Cargills
5   New Tivoli Cinema
6   Daily Fair Trade Complex;
    Vijitha Graphics (Internet)
7   Police
9   Bank of Ceylon
10 Lion Pub
12 Salika Communications
13 Viskam Nivasa Laksala
14 Seylan Bank
15 Central Market
16 Hatton National Bank
17 Golf Club
18 Post Office
19 CTB Bus Stand
23 Private Bus Stand
28 Petrol Station
31 Pony Rides

To Oatlands (100m)
& Rising Lion (400m)

Golf Course

Bandaranaike Mw

To Labookellie
Tea Factory (15km)
& Kandy (80km)

Golf Course

St Andrew's Dr

Keena Rd

Kandy Rd

Chapel St

Hill St

Lady McCallum's Dr

Badulla Rd

Lawson Rd

Uda Pussellawa Rd

To Pedro Tea
Estate (3.5km),
Kandapola (8km)
& The Tea Factory
Hotel (14km)

Wedderburn Rd

Grand Hotel Rd

Golf Course

New Bazaar St

Park Rd

Victoria
Park

Wedderburn Rd

Church Rd

Uda Pussellawa Rd

Railway Station Rd

Nanu Oya

Upper Lake Rd

Unique View Rd

Unique View
Road

Badulla Rd

Curve Rd

Racecourse

Uda Pussellawa Rd

To Galway
Forest Lodge
(500m)

To Single Tree Mountain

Longdon Rd

Badulla Rd

To Seetha Amman Temple (8km),
Hakgala Gardens (8.8km),
Humbugs (9km) & Badulla (56km)

Lake Gregory

To Nanu Oya (9km)

0   150   300m
0   150   300yd

THE HILL COUNTRY

Nuwara Eliya is the 'in place' for Sri Lankan socialites to be during April, around the Sinhalese and Tamil New Year. At that time of year the cost of accommodation – if you can find any – goes through the roof. Horse races are held on the picturesque semi-derelict racecourse then too.

The town has an abundance of touts, who work overtime in search of rake-offs from the local guesthouses. You'll very likely be approached by at least some of them when you step off the train at Nanu Oya (the train station for Nuwara Eliya) or emerge from the bus station.

Orientation

The CTB bus station is opposite the pink-brick post office. North along New Bazaar St is the central market and a collection of cheap eateries. At the top of the street is the Windsor Hotel and nearby is the Bank of Ceylon. If you veer left into Kandy Rd, you will come to Cargills (you can see the golf course on your left) and a little past Cargills is St Andrew's Drive. If you head south from the bus stand along New Bazaar St, you will pass Victoria Park on your left and enter Badulla Rd – many of the cheaper guesthouses are clustered nearby.

Information

Money The Bank of Ceylon just off New Bazaar St is open from 9 am to 3 pm Monday to Friday. You can get cash advances on Visa cards here. The Seylan Bank in Park Rd is open from 9 am to 4 pm Monday to Friday and to 12 pm on Saturday. The Hatton National Bank is open from 9 am to 3 pm Monday to Friday. You can cash travellers cheques at both these banks, but you can't get cash advances on credit cards. On the weekends you can also change travellers cheques at the Grand Hotel. Alpen Tour Inn (see Places to Stay later in this section) plans to have daily money exchange facilities.

Post & Communications The post office is open for stamp sales and telephone calls from 7 am to 8 pm Monday to Saturday (closed Sunday and public holidays). You can send faxes and make international calls from Salika Communications (open from 7.30 am to 9 pm daily).

For Internet facilities head to Vijitha Graphics at 28 Daily Fair Trade Complex, Kandy Rd. It's open from 9 am to 5.30 pm daily, except *some* Mondays.

Things to See

If you're keen to see where a good, strong cuppa comes from, head to the **Pedro Tea Estate** factory about 3.5km from Nuwara Eliya on the way to Kandapola. Factory tours, at a dirt-cheap Rs 25 per person, run for half an hour from 8.30 am to 12.30 pm and again from 2 to 5 pm. There's a pleasant tea house overlooking the plantations where you can have a tea break; boxes of tea cost Rs 100 each. A three-wheeler from Nuwara Eliya should cost Rs 400 return, including waiting time. On the way out you'll pass Hawa Eliya, which is where the Lion brewery is (alas, no tours). A side road takes you up to what's locally known as **Lovers Leap** (there are various stories as to who the lovers actually were). From here you get a good view of the countryside.

Hakgala Gardens were originally a plantation of cinchona, from which the anti-malarial drug quinine is extracted. Later the gardens were used for experiments in acclimatising temperate-zone plants to life in the tropics, and were run by the same family for three generations until the 1940s. Today Hakgala is a delightful garden of over 27 hectares, famed for its roses and ferns, 9.6km out of Nuwara Eliya (and about 200m lower) on the road to Welimada and Bandarawela. Legend has it that Hanuman, the monkey god, was sent by Rama to the Himalaya to find a particular medicinal herb. He forgot which herb he was sent for and decided to bring a chunk of the Himalaya back in his jaw, hoping the herb was growing on it. The gardens grow on a rock called Hakgala, which means 'jaw-rock'.

The Hakgala Gardens are a Rs 6 bus ride from Nuwara Eliya (take a Welimada-bound bus), and there's a Rs 150 admission charge (Rs 75 for students). The gardens are open from 7.30 am to 5 pm daily.

THE HILL COUNTRY

Tea

Tea remains a cornerstone of the Sri Lankan economy and a major export. However, there are concerns that many plantations are degrading through insufficient care. The quality of Ceylon tea has also declined after growers turned to lower-grade bushes in the late 1980s, in response to a world tea slump that drastically cut the profits of high-grade tea.

Tea came to Sri Lanka as an emergency substitute for coffee when the extensive coffee plantations were all but destroyed by a devastating disease in the 19th century. The first Sri Lankan tea was grown in 1867 at the Loolecondera estate, a little south-east of Kandy, by one James Taylor. Today the hill country is virtually one big tea plantation, for tea needs a warm climate, altitude and sloping terrain – a perfect description of the Sri Lankan hill country.

Tea grows on a bush; if not cut back it can grow up to 10m high. Tea bushes are pruned back to about one metre in height and squads of Tamil tea pluckers (all women) move through the rows of bushes picking the leaves and buds. These are then 'withered' (de-moisturised by blowing air at a fixed temperature through them) either in the old-fashioned multistorey tea factories, where the leaves are spread out on hessian mats, or in modern mechanised troughs. The partly dried leaves are then crushed, which starts a fermentation process. The art in tea production comes in knowing when to stop the fermentation, by 'firing' the tea to produce the final, brown-black leaf. Tours of tea plantations and factories are readily available all over Sri Lanka.

There is a large number of types and varieties of teas, which are graded both by size (from cheap 'dust' through fannings and broken grades to 'leaf' tea) and by quality (with names such as flowery, pekoe or souchong). Tea is further categorised into low-grown, mid-grown or high-grown. The low-grown teas (under 600m) grow strongly and are high in 'body' but low in 'flavour'. The high-grown teas (over 1200m) grow more slowly and are renowned for their subtle flavour. Mid-grown tea is something between the two. Regular commercial teas are usually made by blending various types – a bit of this for flavour, a bit of that for body.

Unfortunately, as in India, Sri Lanka may grow some very fine tea but most of the best is exported. Only in a small number of hotels, guesthouses and restaurants will you get a quality cup. But you can buy fine teas from plantations or shops to take home with you.

On the way out to Hakgala Gardens, near the 83km post, stop off to see the colourful Hindu **Seetha Amman Temple**. It's said to mark the spot where Sita was held captive by the demon king Rawana, where she prayed daily for Rama to come and rescue her. On the rock face across the stream are a number of circular depressions said to be the footprints of Rawana's elephant.

Pidurutalagala, or Mt Pedro as is also known, is the highest mountain in Sri Lanka at 2524m, rising immediately to the north of the town. It is topped by the island's main TV transmitter and because of this is now out of bounds to the public. In days gone by it was possible to walk up Pidurutalagala along well-marked paths, a journey that took less than two hours.

An alternative walk is to go to **Single Tree Mountain**. To get there, walk out of Nuwara Eliya on Queen Elizabeth Rd, go up Haddon Hill Rd as far as the communications tower (about 45 minutes) and then take the left-hand path. You should get to the top of Single Tree in about 10 minutes.

Activities
The Grand Hotel, St Andrew's Hotel and Hotel Glendower all have snooker rooms; nonguests can usually play for around Rs 150 per hour. You can take pony rides on the racecourse or up into the hills.

Golf The golf course (☎/fax 22835), which spreads north from Grand Hotel Rd, is beautifully kept. You may become a temporary member by paying Rs 100 a day. Green fees are Rs 1245 (Monday to Friday), Rs 1520 (Saturday, Sunday and public holidays) and Rs 530 for six holes Monday to Friday after 3.30 pm. The fee for seven consecutive weekdays is Rs 6955. Practice tees (including clubs, balls and caddie) cost Rs 690 for up to three hours. You can hire golf clubs for Rs 300 a day and golf shoes for Rs 100 a day. Caddie fees are Rs 150 for 10 or fewer holes and Rs 175 for 11 to 18 holes (caddies are compulsory). A half-hour lesson costs Rs 100. There's a dress code: shirt with collar and slacks or shorts (of a decent length), socks and shoes. Presumably women golfers can wear what they usually wear on a golf course. The club has a bar, dining room, badminton hall and billiard room, plus a few twin-bed rooms with bathroom.

Tennis There are tennis courts at the Hill Club for Rs 225 per hour per person (including balls and racquet hire).

Organised Tours
Nuwara Eliya touts and guesthouse hosts will do their best to persuade you to do a day trip by car or jeep to Horton Plains and World's End. The standard price for up to five passengers is Rs 1600. The road is better than it used to be and the trip takes about 1½ hours one way. But you can do the trip cheaply by public transport if you're really keen, and you could also do it from Haputale. For more information see the Horton Plains & World's End section later in this chapter.

Places to Stay
Nuwara Eliya is not a great place for cheap accommodation, although prices in many places come down during the quieter times of the year. During the 'season', around the Sinhalese and Tamil New Year in April, rooms are three to five times their normal price. Prices also increase during long-weekend holidays and in August when tourists on package tours descend from abroad.

You'll need blankets to keep warm at night at almost any time of year, owing to the altitude. All places to stay *claim* to have hot water, but in many places you have to

wait for it to heat up, and only a handful have a 24-hour hot water service. It's worth double checking the hot water situation before you book in. Another way of keeping warm is to get a fire lit in your room, for which you'll be asked to pay Rs 100 or more. Make sure the room has ventilation or an open window, or you may get carbon monoxide poisoning (which can be fatal), especially if coal heaters are used.

Places to Stay – Budget & Mid-Range
South End of Town A large number of good-value guesthouses are along or tucked in behind Badulla Rd.

Ascot Hotel & Restaurant (☎ 22708, 120 Badulla Rd) is a soulless place with an uninviting dirt front yard. How many times a day will you shower? If you answered twice you'll pay Rs 440/715 a single/double, if you answered once you'll pay Rs 440/600 – if you're a masochist you can have a cold shower and a dirt-cheap room for Rs 380. The owners are very friendly.

Charming *Clifton Inn (☎ 22471, 154 Badulla Rd)* is on the edge of town with views over tea plantations. It's a bit worn and rough around the edges, but there's a quaint sitting area and old-style furniture. The rooms in the annexe (Rs 600) aren't as nice as the rooms inside the house (Rs 720).

The *Travelodge (☎ 22733)* is an old-fashioned colonial bungalow that has seen better days. The rooms cost from Rs 550 to 770 – bargaining is invited! Some of the rooms have new bathrooms and all the rooms have older-style furnishings.

Single Tree Hotel (☎ 23009, 1/8 Haddon Hill Rd) is tiles, tiles and more tiles – rather like a hospital ward. Spotless rooms cost from Rs 440 to 820. The rooms upstairs are best. There's a cable TV.

Country House (☎ 22368, fax 01-917088, 126 Badulla Rd) has decor like grandma's old country house. It might be a bit noisy since it's near the main road, but the hosts are welcoming and the rooms are certainly comfy; you'll be tucked in bed for Rs 550/880.

[Continued on page 226]

THE HILL COUNTRY

Birds of Sri Lanka

A tropical climate, long isolation from the Asian mainland and a diversity of habitats have helped endow Sri Lanka with an astonishing abundance of bird life. There are over 400 bird species, of which 26 are endemic (unique to Sri Lanka), while others are found only in Sri Lanka and adjacent southern India. Of the estimated 198 migrant birds, most of which stay from August to April, the waders (sandpipers, plovers etc) are the long-distance champions, making an annual journey from their breeding grounds in the Arctic tundra.

Reference books on Sri Lanka's birds include *A Selection of the Birds of Sri Lanka* by John & Judy Banks, a slim, well-illustrated book perfect for amateur twitchers. *A Photographic Guide to Birds of Sri Lanka* by Gehan de Silva Wijeyeratne, Deepal Warakagoda and TSU de Zylva, recently published, is a notch above. It's pocket-sized and jam-packed with colour photos. *A Field Guide to the Birds of Sri Lanka* by John Harrison is a hardback with colour illustrations. It's a bit pricey and heavy but it's one of the best field guides available.

Cities, Towns & Villages

Food scraps and flower gardens around dwellings attract insects, which in turn attract many birds. The call of the black house crow *(Corvus splendens)* is probably the first bird sound you'll hear. Like the common myna and house sparrow, this species is ubiquitous around settlements. The common swallow *(Hirundo rustica)* can be seen chasing insects over virtually any open space, while Loten's sunbirds *(Nectarinia lotenia)*, little birds with iridescent plumage and a sharp down-curved bill, are often seen flitting in flower gardens. The black-headed oriole *(Oriolus xanthornus)* has a bright yellow back and belly, a black head, orange beak and yellow-and-black wings. It usually hides in the treetops; its frequent singing is a giveaway. Some species are so accustomed to human settlement that they are rarely found far away, eg, house swifts *(Apus affinis)*, which nest under eaves.

Best Bird-Watching Spots You'll see many species at Viharamahadevi Park in central Colombo. Try the beautiful Peradeniya Botanic Gardens near Kandy. Sigiriya village is also home to dozens of species.

The Countryside

A surprising variety of birds can be seen on rice paddies, in open wooded areas and by the roadside. These birds are often lured by the insects that crops and livestock attract. The shiny black drongos *(Dicrurus macrocercus)* have a forked tail; noisy and ostentatious, they're often seen swooping after flying insects. Tiny black palm swifts *(Cypsiurus balasiensis)* sweep low over the fields chasing prey, while white cattle egrets *(Bubulcus ibis)*, whose breeding plumage is actually fawn-coloured, pluck lice from water buffalo. Egrets also flock around farmers as they plough. Brahminy kites *(Haliastur indus)* may be spotted flying overhead. Adults of this species have a white head and chest and chestnut-brown wings and belly. Green bee-eaters *(Merops orientalis)* are often seen in pairs, perched low to the ground or flitting around catching flying insects. You can identify this bird by the black stripe on each side of its head, its aqua-coloured throat and chin, the orange on the back of its head, and its green wings. The Ceylon junglefowl *(Gallus lafayettii)*, an endemic relative of the domestic chicken, is widespread in remote areas but rarely found near settlements.

Best Bird-Watching Spots Most of these species are easily spotted from the comfort of a bus seat.

Wetlands, Waterways & Tanks

In the dry regions, bodies of water and their fringe vegetation provide an important habitat for many birds. You can't miss the clumsy-looking painted stork *(Mycteria leucocephala)*, with its distinctive orange face and pink rump feathers. Great egrets *(Casmerodius albus)*, huge white birds with yellow beaks, pick off fish with deadly precision, while spoonbills *(Platalea leucorodia)* swish their peculiar flattened bills from side to side, snapping up small creatures.

Green bee-eater *(Merops orientalis)*

Kingfisher *(Alcedo atthis)*

House crow *(Corvus splendens)*

Brahminy kite *(Haliastur indus)*

MICHAEL AW

DAVID TIPLING

DAVID TIPLING

DAVID TIPLING

Indian darter *(Anhinga melanogaster)*

Pheasant-tailed jacana *(Hydrophasianus chirurgus)*

Spoonbill *(Platalea leucorodia)*

Painted stork *(Mycteria leucocephala)*

Little cormorant *(Phalacrocorax niger)*

Birds of Sri Lanka

Little cormorants (*Phalacrocorax niger*) are regularly seen in large flocks. The little cormorant is smaller and less heavily built than the Indian cormorant (*Phalacrocorax fuscicollis*), and it has a shorter neck and beak. Both birds are dark brown to black and are often seen with wings outstretched to dry. Keep an eye out for the Indian darter (*Anhinga melanogaster*), which has a lanky brown neck and spears fish underwater with its dagger-like bill. It is also known as the snake bird because of its peculiar habit of swimming like a snake.

The common kingfisher (*Alcedo atthis*), with striking blue plumage and a tan belly and flank, is often seen skimming the water or watching for fish from a high vantage point.

The dark-brown-and-white pheasant-tailed jacana (*Hydrophasianus chirurgus*) trots across lily pads on incredibly long, slender toes. Its long tail feathers are shed after the breeding season.

The famous greater flamingos (*Phoenicopterus ruber*) have short bent beaks, spindly legs and white-and-pink plumage. They are mostly found in Bundala National Park.

Best Bird-Watching Spots Virtually any tank or large body of water is host to a selection of water birds. Try the tanks at Anuradhapura and Polonnaruwa. Bundala and Yala West (Ruhuna) National Parks are also particularly good spots.

Best Bird-Watching Times Water birds are active for most of the day. Although morning is always the best time to go bird-watching, you will see noisy flocks of birds preparing to roost in the evening.

Rainforests & Jungle

Most of Sri Lanka's endemic birds are found in the rainforests of the hill zone. A walk in the forest can be eerily quiet until you encounter a feeding party, and then all hell breaks loose! Birds of many species travel in flocks, foraging for bark and leaves in the forest canopy and among the leaf litter of the forest floor. You'll probably see noisy orange-billed babblers (*Turdoides rufescens*), which have brown plumage and orange beaks (hence their name). Then there's the Ceylon paradise flycatcher (*Terpsiphone paradisi ceylonensis*), which has a distinctive chestnut-coloured back and tail, white chest and black-crested head. The male of this species has a long, showy tail. You may also see the black Ceylon crested drongo (*Dicrurus paradiseus ceylonicus*) with its deeply forked tail and noisy chattering, or if you are lucky, the beautiful blue-and-chestnut Ceylon blue magpie (*Urocissa ornata*). Noisy flocks of blossom-headed parakeets (*Psittacula cyanocephala*) are often seen flying between patches of forest in the lower hills.

Best Bird-Watching Spots Sinharaja Forest Reserve contains many endemic species, while others are found at Horton Plains National Park. Udawattakelle Sanctuary is also rewarding.

Best Bird-Watching Times Get there early – at first light, if possible – because birds that are active at dawn may be quiet for the rest of the day.

Tips for Bird-Watchers

- Visit a variety of habitats – rainforest, water bodies of the dry zone, and urban parks – to see the full diversity of bird life in Sri Lanka.
- February to March is the best time for bird-watching – you miss the monsoons and the migrant birds are still visiting.
- A pair of binoculars is an invaluable tool to help with identification. Small models can be bought cheaply duty-free and they don't weigh much.
- Consider taking a tour with a specialist if you're keen to see the endemic species and achieve a healthy bird-watching tally. See Organised Tours in the Getting Around chapter for details.

THE HILL COUNTRY

[Continued from page 223]

Sun Hill Tour Inn (☎ 22878, fax 052-23770, 18 Unique View Rd) has modern, clean but box-like rooms from Rs 660 to 820. There are also fancy deluxe rooms for Rs 1200/1650. There's a rooftop restaurant, laundry facilities and a small pub.

Hotel Yenisey (☎ 34000, 16B Unique View Rd) has five clean, reasonably sized rooms for Rs 660/820. The staff is friendly and the bathrooms are immaculate, but the rooms are a bit dark and gloomy. The attempt to liven up the decor with mounted trophies has, not surprisingly, missed the mark.

Haddon Hill Hotel (☎ 23500) has little character, but does have spotless, modern rooms and a bare living area. Some of the rooms have a small balcony. Rooms cost from Rs 600 to 920.

Collingwood Inn (☎ 23550, 112 Badulla Rd) is a charming colonial-era home with polished teak floors, antique furniture and a large and pretty garden. The rooms are clean and the bathrooms modern – the rooms upstairs at the front are best. You'll pay from Rs 920 to 1160 per room. Service is given with a smile, but you may have to beg for extra blankets. The food is awful.

Ceybank Rest (☎ 23053, fax 01-447845) was once the mansion of a British governor. It's now owned and managed by the Bank of Ceylon. The rooms cost Rs 1000/1470, 'some in the 'new' wing, others in the 'old' wing. The older rooms have a colonial flavour, while some of the 'new' rooms are smelly and damp (avoid the ones on the ground floor). This place is OK, but the staff are apathetic.

Grosvenor Hotel (☎ 22307, 6 Haddon Hill Rd) is another colonial place. The rooms are clean and spacious – some have a small balcony with views. There's a large old-style restaurant and friendly staff. Rooms cost Rs 1100/1320. Apparently another 20 rooms will be built soon.

Hellenic Holiday Home (☎/fax 34437, 49/1 Unique View Rd) has superb views and 10 modern, carpet-clad rooms for Rs 1320/1650. The rooms are clean and you could eat off the bathroom floor – don't bother, there's a tiled restaurant with great views. A three-wheeler from the bus station should cost Rs 100.

Hotel Glendower (☎ 22501, fax 22749, 5 Grand Hotel Rd) is a renovated colonial house with sizeable, squeaky-clean rooms at Rs 1550. There's a pretty garden, a large lounge with soft couches, a bar and a snooker table. This place gets rave reviews.

At the time of writing **Alpen Tour Inn** (☎ 23500, fax 34500, 4 Haddon Hill Rd) was a building site. By the time you read this it *should* have 24 modern, new rooms (all with a bathroom), a huge family suite in the attic and a large restaurant. Rooms will cost from Rs 1530 to 3000. Money exchange and Internet facilities are planned. The family that owns the Alpen Tour Inn also owns the nearby Single Tree and Haddon Hill hotels, as well as Collingwood Inn and, across the valley, Victoria Inn.

East End of Town The **Victoria Inn** (☎ 22321, 15/4 Park Rd) has reasonable rooms from Rs 400 to 660 – the cheaper rooms have a decent shared bathroom. It's opposite Victoria Park so it's a quiet spot.

Next door **Little Flower** (☎ 34897, 22 Park Rd) has an assortment of spotless, modern rooms. The two apartments on the top floor have two bedrooms each at Rs 2200. Rooms cost Rs 550/1100. There's a roof-top restaurant with great views over the park.

Charming **Princess Guest House** (☎ 436527, fax 439197, e frutvege@sri.lanka.net, 12 Wedderburn Rd) is a building of venerable age set in an enclave of colonial houses of various styles. This place, one of Nuwara Eliya's original hotels, has a mixed bag of quaint, old-fashioned rooms – some even have bay windows. Spacious, if a little tired, rooms go for Rs 1050/1100.

Hotel Tree of Life (☎ 23684, fax 23127, 2 Wedderburn Rd) is a pleasant place in an old-style bungalow. There is a lovely garden and an Ayurveda centre (full treatment costs Rs 2000). Clean rooms with modern facilities cost Rs 1600/2000 (two rooms have shared bathroom but they cost the same as the rooms with a bathroom).

North End of Town The friendly *Mr Perera's (9 Chapel St)* has three no-frills rooms costing from Rs 150 to 400. Tea is on the house, but the hosts don't usually provide food. This is one of the few family run places in town. The house is unsigned – look for the Millennium Restaurant on Kandy Rd. Chapel St is opposite.

Take a step back in time at *Oatlands (☎ 22572, 124 St Andrew's Drive)*, just behind St Andrew's Hotel. This spacious, immaculate old British bungalow oozes charm: a pretty parlour with lace curtains, the flower garden with pleasant views and even breakfast with waffles with syrup (Rs 270). Unfortunately the old-world charm comes with modern prices at Rs 1650/2200. A three-wheeler from the bus station should cost Rs 60.

Farther on, past Oatlands, is the overly decorated *Rising Lion (☎ 22083, 3 Sri Piyatissapura)*. Rooms cost from Rs 660 to 1100. All rooms are basic and clean, the more expensive ones have a minimalist approach to furnishings and good views. If you ring ahead, the guys will pick you up from the bus station for free, or from the train station for Rs 150.

Hakgala Just beyond the Hakgala Botanic Gardens entrance, *Humbugs (☎/fax 22709, e humbugs@sltnet.lk)* is a pleasant small restaurant/snack bar with a modern chalet at the back where you can get a room for Rs 770 with hot water, a pine double bed and floor-to-ceiling windows that look out on a stunning view. If you like you can take your shower in a waterfall at the bottom of the garden. The cafe has rice and curry (Rs 60) and yummy strawberries and cream (Rs 77).

Places to Stay – Top End

Windsor Hotel (☎ 22554, fax 22889, 2 Kandy Rd) looks jaded from the outside and is not much better within. The clean, but tired rooms cost US$37/43, but it's right in the heart of town and the staff are friendly.

Galway Forest Lodge (☎ 23728, fax 22978, 89 Upper Lake Rd, Havelock Drive) is about 2km south-east of town. This is a get-away-from-it-all place that's good for people interested in bird-watching. The clean slightly dated rooms cost US$44/50 including breakfast.

Hill Club (☎ 22653, fax 22654, e hill club@eureka.lk) positively revels in its colonial heritage. Once a preserve of the British male, the Hill Club now admits both Sri Lankans and women, but remains very much in the colonial tradition. There is a ladies lounge (next to the dining room) and the nearby ladies restroom has a full-length mirror, dressing tables and lamps. Temporary members are welcome to help keep the tills ringing (Rs 60 a day).

The Hill Club is well looked after. In the reading room you can sink back into old-fashioned leather armchairs while a waiter brings you a drink. Mounted trophies still glare down from the walls. In the evening someone will carefully turn down your bed and, if you wish, place a hot water bottle between the sheets. Tennis courts are available to guests (and nonguests). The lawns and gardens are immaculate.

The rooms don't have as much charm as the rest of the place but they're clean and the bathrooms are modern and spotless. Rooms facing the back cost US$49; rooms facing the gardens cost US$62; suites cost from US$86 to US$110. Dinner is an experience in itself (see Places to Eat & Drink later in this section).

The *Grand Hotel (☎ 22881-7, fax 22265, e tangerinetours@eureka.lk)*, right by the golf course, has remnants of old English style, including an ostentatious facade, immaculate lawns, a reading lounge and a wood-panelled billiard room. However, the rooms have lost most of their original features, and cost US$53/55 in the old wing and US$74/76 in the new. The Grand Hotel is now popular with European tour groups.

St Andrew's Hotel (☎ 22445, fax 23153, 10 St Andrew's Drive), in the north of the town on a rise overlooking the golf course, resembles a 19th-century Scottish manse. It has terraced lawns with white cast-iron garden furniture. The immaculate rooms cost US$74.

The Tea Factory Hotel (☎ 23600, fax 070-522105, e ashmres@aitkenspence.lk) at Kandapola, 14km east of Nuwara Eliya, is a beautifully renovated tea factory that overlooks a still-working tea estate (tea from the estate is on sale at the hotel). The generator in the basement is fired up in the evening and other bits and pieces of factory machinery are on display. The views from the hotel and the walks around it are very pleasant and there's plenty of information available from the front desk on what to see and do. There are billiard tables, but beginners be warned: A tear in the cloth will cost you Rs 10,000. The luxurious rooms cost US$67/92.

Places to Eat & Drink

Guesthouses and hotels are probably your best bet when it comes to eating and drinking in Nuwara Eliya, as most places in the town centre aren't particularly inspiring.

The Grand has a *pastry shop* near the Hotel Glendower, which is good for filled rolls, tasty mini pizzas, fried things and cold drinks – all around Rs 30 each.

The *Lion Pub* on Lawson St, open from 11 am to 2 pm and 5 to 10 pm daily, is a decent place for a cold beer. Lion lager costs Rs 68, Carlsberg Rs 73, Guinness stout Rs 78 and Lion draught Rs 35 (per mug). You can sit outside under umbrellas.

Milano Restaurant (94 New Bazaar St), has delicious Chinese mains starting from Rs 150, soups start at Rs 70. It's dim and uninviting but the waiters are friendly. It's open from 8 am to 10 pm daily. The upstairs toilet is most off-putting.

Good Chinese food can also be had at the stylish Hotel Glendower's *King Prawn Restaurant*. Try the sweet-and-sour pork (Rs 275), vegetable fried rice (Rs 220) or stuff your face with the lunch-time buffet for Rs 450.

Dinner at the *Hill Club* is an experience that shouldn't be missed. The delicious five-course set menu is served promptly at 8 pm (US$12). You can also order off the a la carte menu and spend considerably less (eg, fish and chips for Rs 220, curried vegie burger for Rs 200) but you still have to eat

at 8 pm. There's a wine list, but check the prices before ordering. Corkage at Rs 375 may put you off... The whole thing is carried off with delightful panache: white-gloved waiters, candles, flowers on every table, and linen tablecloths and serviettes. Men must wear a collar and tie (they'll lend you one) and a jacket. Women seem to get away with fairly casual attire, but some turn up in evening wear. After-dinner drinks and coffee can be served in the reading room (there's sometimes a fire in the grate), although there is also a mixed bar. Despite sounding like pretentiousness at its worst, the Hill Club is a welcoming place – laid-back with excellent service. If you're not staying the night here, you'll have to pay a Rs 60 'temporary joining' fee.

There's a restaurant and bar at *The Tea Factory Hotel*; the food is good (lunch buffet for Rs 900 or mains for around Rs 250). Even if you're not staying here, The Tea Factory Hotel is a worthwhile place to visit for a meal, a snack or a drink. (A taxi there and back will cost Rs 750.) It's a good place to get away from it all, and you can work up an appetite by going for a walk in the surrounding tea estate. (See Places to Stay – Top End for contact details.)

Shopping

The Eco Shop, near Cargills, sells handicrafts (embroidery, weaving, ceramics) as well as jams and preserves. Profits go back to the rural community.

Viskum Nivasa Laksala, the Small Industries Department saleroom 300m from the Windsor Hotel, is also worth a visit.

Along New Bazaar St you can pick up padded jackets and other warm clothing (sometimes good brand name garments) at some pretty reasonable prices – although expect to bargain.

Getting There & Away

Bus The bus trip from Kandy is about four hours and costs around Rs 55 in a CTB bus and Rs 70 in a private intercity express bus. It's a spectacular climb and is covered by several buses each day. There are also buses to/from Colombo (Rs 95 for CTB buses, six hours; Rs 135 for air-con expresses). For Haputale you usually have to change at Welimada (Rs 13). To get to Bandarawela you will also have to change at Welimada. For Matara on the south coast, an intercity express bus is scheduled to leave at 8.15 am and costs Rs 150, the CTB bus costs Rs 90.

Train Nuwara Eliya does not have its own train station, but is served by Nanu Oya, about 9km along the road towards Hatton and Colombo. Buses *always* meet the main trains (Rs 10 to Nuwara Eliya), so take care you are not sucked in by touts. You can always take a taxi yourself from the station, and there are many of these (Rs 250).

The 5.55 am *Podi Menike* from Colombo (via Kandy) reaches Nanu Oya at 1 pm. The 9.45 am *Udarata Menike* from Colombo – but not via Kandy – reaches Nanu Oya at about 3.40 pm. Fares to Badulla cost Rs 18/49/85 in 3rd/2nd/1st class. Going west, the *Udarata Menike* to Colombo – but not Kandy – leaves Nanu Oya at 9.35 am; the *Podi Menike* leaves at 12.55 pm, reaching Kandy about 5 pm before continuing on to

Colombo. Fares to Kandy cost Rs 20.50/56.50/197.50 in 3rd/2nd/1st class. The 1st-class fare includes a booking fee of Rs 50 for the observation carriage.

HORTON PLAINS & WORLD'S END

The Horton Plains form an undulating plateau more than 2000m high, about 20km south of Nuwara Eliya and 20km west of Haputale. They consist mainly of grasslands interspersed with patches of forest with some unusual high-altitude vegetation. Sri Lanka's second- and third-highest mountains – Kirigalpotta (2395m) and Totapola (2359m) – rise from Horton Plains.

The plains are a beautiful, silent, strange world with some excellent walks. The most famous and stunning feature is World's End, where the southern Horton Plains come suddenly to an end and drop almost straight down for 700m. It's one of the most awesome sights in Sri Lanka, but unfortunately the view is often obscured by mist, particularly during the rainy season, from April to September. Dawn or very early morning usually offers the best chance of a glimpse of this scenic wonder which, if you

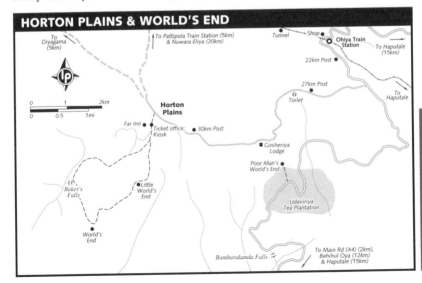

can afford it, is a good reason to spend the previous night on the plains rather than arrive later in the day on a day trip. In the evening Horton Plains gets cool – you'll need long trousers and a sweater.

Farr Inn is a convenient central landmark on the plains, reachable by road from Ohiya or Nuwara Eliya or by two or three hours walking from the Ohiya train station. There are plans to turn Farr Inn into a visitors centre. The ticket office, at the start of the track from Farr Inn to World's End, is open from 6 am to 4 pm. Tickets cost US$12 for adults, US$6 for children (six to 12 years) and students (with ID). It's free for kiddies under six. Foreigners with resident visas pay Rs 20. If you're not doing the walk to World's End you don't need to pay the park fees.

Flora & Fauna
Vegetation includes a type of tufty grass called *Crosypogon* and bog moss (spagnum), which grows in the marshy areas. Flowering plants include *Aristea ekloni*, which has tiny blue flowers, and *Exacum macranthum*, which is similar. The main canopy tree of the montane forest is the umbrella-shaped, gnarled, white-blossomed *keena (Callophylum)*. Another notable species is *Rhododendron zelanicum*, which has blood-red blossoms. The purple-leafed *Strobilanthes* blossoms once every five years, and then dies.

Herds of elephants used to roam the plains but most of them were shot by colonial hunters. The last few elephants departed in the first half of the 20th century. But there are still a few leopards, and any droppings you see containing animal fur are likely to be leopard droppings. The shaggy bear-monkey (or purple-faced langur) is sometimes seen in the forest on the road up from Ohiya, and occasionally in the woods around World's End (its call is a wheezy grunt). Sambar emerge from the forest onto the edge of the grasslands around Farr Inn in the evening.

The plains are very popular with birdwatchers. Endemics include the yellow eared bulbul, the fantailed warbler, the ashy headed babbler, the Ceylon hill white eye, the Ceylon blackbird, the Ceylon white-eyed arrenga, the dusky blue flycatcher and the Ceylon blue magpie. Birds of prey include the mountain hawk eagle.

There are three varieties of lizards here including the horned lizard.

Walks
Walking is the most worthwhile way to get onto the plains (see under Getting There & Away for more information). The walk to World's End is about 4km, but the trail loops back to Baker's Falls (2km) from where you can walk to the entrance (another 3.5km); the round trip is 9.5km and usually takes around three hours. Be aware that after about 10 am the mist usually comes down – and it's thick. All you can expect to see from World's End after this time is a swirling white wall, something that disappoints many. Although the ticket gate is open from 6 am you can actually start walking earlier and pay on the way out. Try to avoid doing this walk on Sunday and public holidays when it's crowded and noisy.

Wear strong and comfortable walking shoes, a hat and sunglasses. Bring sunscreen (you can really get burnt up here) and lots of water – as well as something to eat. The weather can change very quickly on the plains – one minute it can be sunny and clear, the next chilly and misty. Bring warm clothing just in case. Don't drop litter along the track; there's already enough of it around. Resist the temptation to blaze your own trail; with so many people trudging around this area, sticking to the well-trodden paths will help minimise the damage. There are no toilets en route to World's End though there are toilets on the road coming up to Farr Inn from Ohiya train station.

The walk to World's End incurs pricey park fees. An alternative is what's been dubbed Poor Man's World's End. The track that used to start near Giniheriya Lodge is now closed. The lengthy alternative is to head towards Udaviriya Tea Plantation from the signed turn-off you'll see as you head up to Farr Inn from the Ohiya train station. This road continues to Belihul Oya.

Responsible Hiking

Sri Lanka offers plenty of scope for great hiking. The hill country especially has popular trails such as World's End as well as relatively little-known ones that are rewarding to explore. One of the pleasures of hiking is enjoying pristine surroundings, unsullied by rubbish, noisy groups and other unwelcome intrusions. The popularity of hiking is placing great pressure on the natural environment. Please consider the following tips when hiking and help preserve the ecology and beauty of the area.

Rubbish

• Carry out all your rubbish. If you've carried it in, you can carry it out. Don't overlook those easily forgotten items, such as silver paper, orange peel, cigarette butts and plastic wrappers. Empty packaging weighs very little anyway and should be stored in a dedicated rubbish bag. Make an effort to carry out rubbish left by others.
• Never bury your rubbish: digging disturbs soil and ground cover and encourages erosion. Buried rubbish will more than likely be dug up by animals, who may be injured or poisoned by it. It may also take years to decompose, especially at high altitudes.
• Minimise the waste you must carry out by taking minimal packaging and taking no more food than you will need. If you can't buy in bulk, unpack small-portion packages and combine their contents in one container before your trip. Take reusable containers or stuff sacks.
• Don't rely on bought water in plastic bottles. Disposal of these bottles creates major problems. Use iodine drops or purification tablets instead.
• Sanitary napkins, tampons and condoms should also be carried out despite the inconvenience. They burn and decompose poorly.

Human Waste Disposal

• Contamination of water sources by human faeces can lead to the transmission of hepatitis, typhoid and intestinal parasites such as *Giardia*, amoebas and roundworms. It can cause severe health risks not only to members of your party, but also to local residents and wildlife.
• Where there is a toilet, please use it. Where there is none, bury your waste. Dig a small hole 15cm (6 inches) deep and at least 100m (320 feet) from any watercourse. Consider carrying a lightweight trowel for this purpose. Cover the waste with soil and a rock. Use toilet paper sparingly and bury it with the waste.

Washing

• Don't use detergents or toothpaste in or near watercourses, even if they are biodegradable.
• For personal washing, use biodegradable soap and a water container (or even a lightweight, portable basin) at least 50m (160 feet) away from the watercourse. Disperse the waste water widely to allow the soil to filter it fully before it finally makes it back to the watercourse.
• Wash cooking utensils 50m (160 feet) from watercourses using a scourer or sand instead of detergent.

Erosion

• Hillsides and mountain slopes, especially at high altitudes, are prone to erosion. It is important to stick to existing tracks and avoid short cuts that bypass a switchback. If you blaze a new trail straight down a slope, it will turn into a watercourse with the next heavy rainfall and eventually cause soil loss and deep scarring.
• If a well-used track passes through a mud patch, walk through the mud: walking around the edge will increase the size of the patch.
• Avoid removing the plant life that keeps topsoils in place.

It's more than 13km to the part of the plantation where you cut through to head up to Poor Man's World's End; you'll have to ask directions from the tea pickers. Guestbooks in travellers haunts in Haputale are good sources for innovative ways to see the plains without being slugged with hefty entry fees, although of course you follow the advice at your own risk.

Places to Stay & Eat
There are two basic Wildlife Conservation Department bungalows where you can stay: *Giniheriya Lodge*, which used to be known as Anderson Lodge, and *Mahaeliya Lodge*. There are 10 beds in each. It costs US$12 a day park entry, US$24 per person per night in a bungalow, US$2 per person for linen hire and a whopping US$30 'service charge' per trip. You must bring all of your own dry rations and kerosene. The lodges only open up when people are staying, and you must book ahead through the Department of Wildlife Conservation (☎ 01-694241, fax 698556), 18 Gregory's Rd, Cinnamon Gardens, Colombo 7.

There are two *camp sites* (signposted near the start of the World's End track). There is water at the sites but nothing else; you must bring everything you need. As you are inside the World's End park, you are obliged to pay a US$12 daily park entry fee plus the site fee (US$6 per day, plus US$5 service charge per trip). For information and booking contact the Department of Wildlife Conservation (see Giniheriya and Mahaeliya Lodges, previously).

Opposite the Ohiya train station the first small *shop* you come to has a clean room out the back for Rs 500 if you're desperate. It also sells delicious dahl and bread (Rs 26), biscuits, lollies and so on if you want to fill up before the hike up to Farr Inn. The food at the *kiosk* near Farr Inn is twice the price.

Getting There & Away
Train & Foot Given that the mist comes down at World's End at around 10 am, you'll want to get there at least by 9.30 am. Despite what jeep operators might tell you,

it is possible to get to World's End – in time – by taking public transport. An option for keen, early risers is to take a day trip from Nuwara Eliya by rail. If you catch the 2.55 am train (the night mail from Colombo) from Nanu Oya you should be at Ohiya at 3.48 am. The walk from Ohiya to Farr Inn is an enjoyable, easy 11.2km, or 2½ to 3½ hours, by road – you'll need a torch (flashlight). Then you've got another 1½ hours to World's End. It's a slog but it is doable. You'll need about two hours for the walk back down towards Ohiya to catch the 8.36 pm night mail train back to Nanu Oya. You'll sleep well.

Alternatively, you can come from Haputale, but you won't reach World's End by 10 am. The 7.55 am train from Haputale (Rs 4 in 3rd class) reaches Ohiya at 8.35 am. From Ohiya you can return to Haputale on the 4.36 pm train (sometimes it's late). You could also catch a taxi from Ohiya train station all the way to Farr Inn (see under taxi following).

There used to be a shortcut from the railway tunnel (near Ohiya train station) to Farr Inn, which is now closed. The trip up the main road is a pretty walk with great views and you can be sure you won't get lost. Near the 27km post you'll find a toilet block.

You can also walk to Farr Inn from Pattipola, the next train station north of Ohiya (a walk of about 10km along a jeep track), or from Belihul Oya on the Ratnapura-Haputale road, about four hours downhill from the plains (see the Belihul Oya section later in this chapter).

Taxi If you don't feel like walking up the road to Farr Inn, there is often a taxi waiting at the Ohiya train station. From there Farr Inn should cost about Rs 900 return, including waiting time. It's 11.2km, or 40 minutes.

It takes about 1½ hours to get from Haputale to Farr Inn by road (Rs 1500 return in a taxi). From Ohiya, the road rises in twists and turns through forest before emerging on the open plains. It's a pleasant journey (the road's in good condition) and on the way through the forest you may catch sight of monkeys.

You can also get to Farr Inn from Nuwara Eliya. The road has been much improved in recent times and the trip takes about 1½ hours one way. A taxi costs about Rs 1600 return.

There is a 4WD road that goes past the Bambarakanda Falls (the road signposted on the main road between Haputale and Belihul Oya) and emerges near Ohiya train station. It's pretty rough and it would probably be impassable in wet weather.

BELIHUL OYA

Belihul Oya isn't a town as such, but a pretty hillside region worth passing through on your way to/from the hill country – it's 35km from Haputale and 57km from Ratnapura. From here you can walk up to Horton Plains, a very strenuous undertaking; going the other way is much less work and takes about four hours.

About 11km from Belihul Oya in the direction of Haputale, near the village of Kalupahana, are the **Bambarakanda Falls**. (Ask the bus driver to let you off at Kalupahana.) At 240m, they're the highest in Sri Lanka. March and April are the best months for viewing the falls; at other times the water flow may be reduced to a disappointing trickle. There's a trail from here to Horton Plains as well, although it's pretty challenging.

Places to Stay & Eat

The exquisitely situated *Rest House* (☎/fax 045-80199) is perched beside a stream that rushes down from Horton Plains. There's a restaurant and a lounge packed with comfy chairs near a natural rock pool – feel like a dip? The clean rooms (no nets) cost US$33.

River View (☎ 045-80222, fax 80223) has three cottages set in a lush, terraced garden beside the stream the resthouse shares. Each spotless single/double (with crisp white sheets) costs US$20/27 for half board. There's a restaurant beside the road.

About 17km along the road to Haputale you'll find *World's End Lodge* (☎ 071-730015, ⓔ welodge@itmin.com, Lower

Ohiya, Haldumulla). The sign to the Lodge is near the 177km post; from here there's a 4km path up to the hotel. You will be rewarded by superb views, a pool, tasty cooking and attentive service. The clean rooms cost Rs 1100 per person for full board (no room-only rates). A taxi from Haputale will cost about Rs 600. Alternatively, if you are coming from Haputale or Belihul Oya by bus, get off at Halatuthan Junction. If you can find a taxi it'll take you to the lodge for a rip-off Rs 400. A better option is to organise a ride with the hosts. You must book ahead for this place.

HAPUTALE
☎ 057

The village of Haputale is perched right at the southern edge of the hill country. It lies along a ridge with the land falling away steeply on both sides. As you come in from Bandarawela to the north, the road rises up to the ridge, crosses the railway, dips down the main street – then suddenly sails off into space! Actually it makes a sharp right turn at the edge of town and runs along just beneath the ridge, but at first glance it looks as if it simply disappears into thin air. On a clear day you can see all the way to the south coast from this ridge, and at night the Hambantota lighthouse may be visible.

Like many places in the hill country the legacies of the British planters live on. There are the tea estates, which cling to the hillsides, and the old plantation bungalows, some of which have lovely gardens. There's also a pretty little Anglican church (St Andrew's) on the Bandarawela road. The headstones in the well-kept cemetery make for interesting reading.

Haputale is a pleasant place with some good cheap accommodation, and makes a good base for visiting Horton Plains, exploring other places in the area, or just taking pleasant walks in cool mountain air.

Information

The town isn't too small to have a Bank of Ceylon branch, open Monday to Friday from 9 am to 2.30 pm. You can change money, travellers cheques and get cash advances on Visa cards.

The agency post office is in the centre of town. Amarasinghe Guest House is the only place with Internet facilities (see Places to Stay & Eat later in this section).

Dambatenne Tea Factory

A few tea factories in this area are happy to have visitors. The factory built in 1890 by Sir Thomas Lipton, 11km from Haputale, is popular and easily accessible. There is a Rs 180 entry fee, but for this you get a tour around the whole works. On an average day a tea picker would bring in around 15kg of tea leaves to the factory (and earn around Rs 125); in the high season up to 20,000kg comes into the factory from the fields each day. The leaves then go through a process of drying, rolling, chopping and sieving before being graded. Ten thousand kilograms of leaves yields about 2500kg of tea.

A bus (a service for the estate workers) goes from the town to the factory and back again about every 25 minutes (Rs 7). Alternatively a taxi there and back will cost about Rs 300. If you are fit and energetic this is a great walk, with wonderful views.

Diyaluma Falls

Heading towards Wellawaya, you'll pass the 170m-high Diyaluma Falls, one of Sri Lanka's highest waterfalls, just 5km beyond the town of Koslanda. By bus, take a Wellawaya service from Haputale and get off at Diyaluma (1¼ hours). The falls leap over a cliff face and fall in one clear drop to a pool below – very picturesque and clearly visible from the road.

If you're energetic you can climb up to the beautiful rock pools and a series of mini-falls at the top of the main fall. Walk about 500m down the road from the bottom of the falls and take the estate track that turns sharply back up to the left. From there it's about 20 minutes' walk to a small rubber factory, where you strike off left uphill. The track is very indistinct, although there are some white arrows on the rocks – if you're lucky, people in the rubber factory will shout if they see you taking the wrong turn! At the top the path forks: the right branch (more distinct) leads to the pools above the main falls, the left fork down to the top of the main falls. The pools above the second set of falls are good for a cool swim.

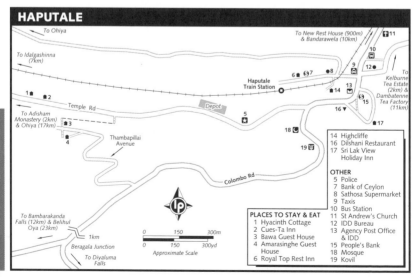

HAPUTALE

To Ohiya
To Idalgashinna (7km)
To New Rest House (900m) & Bandarawela (10km)
11
10
9
12
6 7 8
Haputale Train Station
To Kelburne Tea Estate (2km) & Dambatenne Tea Factory (11km)
13
14
1 2
Temple Rd
Depot
5
15
16
To Adisham Monastery (2km) & Ohiya (17km)
3
4
Thambapillai Avenue
17
18
Colombo Rd
19
To Bambarakanda Falls (12km) & Belihul Oya (23km)
Beragala Junction
To Diyaluma Falls
1km
0   150   300m
0   150   300yd
Approximate Scale

14 Highcliffe
16 Dilshani Restaurant
17 Sri Lak View Holiday Inn

OTHER
5 Police
7 Bank of Ceylon
8 Sathosa Supermarket
9 Taxis
10 Bus Station
11 St Andrew's Church
12 IDD Bureau
13 Agency Post Office & IDD
15 People's Bank
18 Mosque
19 Kovil

PLACES TO STAY & EAT
1 Hyacinth Cottage
2 Cues-Ta Inn
3 Bawa Guest House
4 Amarasinghe Guest House
6 Royal Top Rest Inn

THE HILL COUNTRY

Adisham Monastery

Adisham is a Benedictine monastery about an hour's walk from Haputale. To get there follow Temple Rd until you reach the sign at the Adisham turn-off. The monastery is an old British planter's house that some claim is a replica of the planter's Yorkshire house and others say is a Canterbury one. It's open to visitors from 9 am to noon and 2 pm to 4.30 pm Saturday and Sunday; entry costs Rs 50. There's a small shop selling produce from the monastery's garden. There's lots of stonework around here – walls, steps, terracing – all done by hand. Inside, visitors are allowed to see the living room and library, and occasionally a couple more rooms. There's a sign at the main gate that reads 'Silence is Golden'; you should respect this by keeping your chatter down during your visit here. Bus No 327 from Haputale will get you most of the way to Adisham. A taxi will charge Rs 150 return, including waiting time.

Before you reach Adisham you pass by **Tangamalai**, a bird sanctuary and nature reserve.

Other Attractions

If you can't get enough of the views, take the train to **Idalgashinna** train station, 8km along the railway west of Haputale. You can walk back beside the train tracks enjoying a spectacular view since the land falls away steeply for a great distance on both sides.

Near the Dambatenne Tea Factory the **Lipton's Seat** lookout has some exclaiming that it rivals the views from World's End, without the World's End price tag. To see for yourself, take the signed narrow paved road, and climb about 7km through tea plantations to the lookout. From the tea factory, the ascent should take about 2½ hours.

Places to Stay & Eat

The ***Bawa Guest House*** (☎ 68260, 32 Thambapillai Ave), run by a friendly Muslim family, is a basic house nestled on the hillside. There are five cosy rooms with tolerable shared bathrooms in the original building, and two rooms with bathroom, in the newer building next door. Singles cost Rs 220 with doubles from Rs 275 to Rs 440. Breakfast is Rs 100 and rice and curry is Rs 160.

The ***Amarasinghe Guest House*** (☎ 68 175, e agh777@sltnet.lk, Thambapillai Ave) is a neat, white house with a front garden. There are two rooms in a separate block for Rs 440 and four modern spotless rooms (with balconies) in the house for Rs 660. There's also a family room/dorm. The food is very good. Mr Amarasinghe is a helpful host (he will pick you up for free from the train station if you ring) and can supply maps of the area, has Internet facilities and keeps a guestbook that has some interesting comments and advice. If you're arriving by foot to the Bawa Guest House or Amarasinghe Guest House follow Temple Rd until you see a yellow Amarasinghe Guest House sign to the south, just off the side of the road. Go down the first flight of stairs and head along the path (past the mangy truck) for about 250m. You'll come to Bawa first, a further flight of steps will take you in the back way to Amarasinghe Guest House.

Cues-Ta Inn (☎ 68110, 118 Temple Rd) has five basic but clean enough rooms for Rs 330/440. Each room has a small balcony, and the large sitting room has superb views over tea plantations. The hosts are welcoming, but this spot may be a bit noisy as the train tracks are closeby.

Hyacinth Cottage (☎ 68283) has a handful of dank, musty rooms with shared bathrooms – the dorm is a converted garage beside the road! But if you wanted cheap and cheerful you've got it: rooms cost Rs 220/330 and a dorm bed costs Rs 175. The shared toilets and showers are clean enough (hot water is available), the food is good, and Mrs Daniel (the host) is friendly.

Royal Top Rest Inn (☎ 68178, 22 Station Rd) is a modern, friendly place with pleasant views and clean rooms for Rs 330/550 with bathroom and Rs 330/440 with spotless shared bathroom. There's a restaurant, a small outdoor area and a little sunny shared balcony.

Highcliffe (☎ 68096, 15 Station Rd) was one of the first budget travellers stops in town, and it sure looks it. Rooms are basic, a little dark, but cheap at Rs 275/440. There's a bar if you need to be drunk to stay here.

The *Sri Lak View Holiday Inn (☎ 68125, fax 68291, Sherwood Rd)* is a modern, squeaky-clean spot with seven rooms and four more on the way. Rooms cost from Rs 500 to 820. The more expensive rooms have a skinny balcony with superb views. The lawn hasn't a blade of grass out of place, the tiles shine, the host smiles. If you call you'll get picked up from the train station for free.

The *New Resthouse (☎ 68099)* is about 1km along the Bandarawela Rd (Rs 60 in a taxi). The rooms are clean, clinical and clearly overpriced at Rs 760/1000.

Dilshani Restaurant (27 Colombo Rd) is a small lunch-time spot with the added bonus of superb views. Rice and curry costs Rs 70, short eats sell for around Rs 15.

For a taste of the good life treat yourself to a night or three, or longer, at the *Kelburne Tea Estate (☎ 01-573382, fax 573253, e kelburne@eureka.lk)*, about 2km from the Haputale train station. Three estate bungalows have been made available to visitors, complete with staff (including a cook) and all the trimmings. There's one bungalow with two bedrooms (Aerie, Rs 5000) and two smaller bungalows (Wild Flower and Rose, Rs 4500 each). Wild Flower and Rose each contain three bedrooms with bathroom. Linen and firewood – and staff – are included in the price, but food is extra (when you book you can specify exactly what you want and they will provide it). You can only stay here if you book ahead, which you must do in Colombo on (see above).

There are a few basic local *eateries* around the town centre where you can get short eats, rice and curry etc cheaper than in the guesthouses. There's also a *Sathosa Supermarket*, tucked away near the abandoned Old Resthouse, if you want to buy your own supplies.

Getting There & Away

Bus There are direct buses to Nuwara Eliya at 7 am and 2 pm, but if you miss these buses you'll have to change at Welimada (which has a resthouse on the north-east side of town). Haputale-Welimada and We-

limada–Nuwara Eliya both cost Rs 10. To/from Bandarawela there are frequent buses for Rs 7 that run into the early evening. There are also express buses to Colombo (Rs 100, 5½ hours).

Usually for the south coast you have to change at Wellawaya, 1½ hours down the hill from Haputale. The last bus from Haputale to Wellawaya is at about 5 pm.

Train Haputale is on the Colombo-Badulla line, so you can travel direct by train to/from Kandy or Nanu Oya (the station for Nuwara Eliya). It's 8½ to nine hours from Colombo, 5½ hours from Kandy, 1½ hours from Nanu Oya, 40 minutes from Ohiya, half an hour on to Bandarawela and two hours on to Badulla.

The daily departures in the Badulla direction are at 4.28, 6.48 and 11.45 am, and 1, 2.32 *(Podi Menike)* and 5.13 pm *(Udarata Menike)*. In the Colombo direction depart at 7.55 *(Udarata Menike)* and 11.12 am *(Podi Menike)* and 3.11, 7.57 (night mail) and 9.24 pm. The *Udarata Menike* doesn't go to Kandy.

Fares to/from Haputale in 3rd/2nd/1st class include the following: Colombo Rs 51/140.50/296; Kandy Rs 28.50/79/237; and Nanu Oya Rs 8.50/23.50/90.50. To Ohiya (leaving Haputale at 7.55 am) it's Rs 4/10/67.50; to Badulla, it's Rs 9.50/25.50 (3rd/2nd class). The 1st-class observation carriage includes a booking fee of Rs 50.

BANDARAWELA
☎ 057

Bandarawela, 10km north of Haputale but noticeably warmer at only 1230m, is a busy market town that is a good base for exploring the surrounding area. On each Sunday morning there is a lively market.

Orientation & Information

The focal point of town is the busy junction just north of the train station. From here Haputale Rd goes south-west; Welimada Rd heads north-west then, turns fairly sharply left by a mosque; and Badulla Rd, with the main bus and taxi stands, heads downhill to the east.

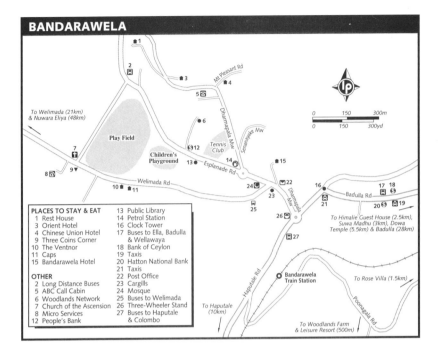

BANDARAWELA

To Welimada (21km)
& Nuwara Eliya (48km)

Play Field

Children's
Playground

Tennis
Club

Mt Pleasant Rd

Dharmapala Mw

Senanayake Mw

Welimada Rd

Esplanade Rd

Badulla Rd

Dharmapala Mw

To Himalie Guest House (2.5km),
Suwa Madhu (3km), Dowa
Temple (5.5km) & Badulla (28km)

To Rose Villa (1.5km)

Bandarawela
Train Station

Haputale Rd

Poonagala Rd

To Haputale
(10km)

To Woodlands Farm
& Leisure Resort (500m)

0   150   300m
0   150   300yd

PLACES TO STAY & EAT
1 Rest House
3 Orient Hotel
4 Chinese Union Hotel
9 Three Coins Corner
10 The Ventnor
11 Caps
15 Bandarawela Hotel

OTHER
2 Long Distance Buses
5 ABC Call Cabin
6 Woodlands Network
7 Church of the Ascension
8 Micro Services
12 People's Bank
13 Public Library
14 Petrol Station
16 Clock Tower
17 Buses to Ella, Badulla
   & Wellawaya
18 Bank of Ceylon
19 Taxis
20 Hatton National Bank
21 Taxis
22 Post Office
23 Cargills
24 Mosque
25 Buses to Welimada
26 Three-Wheeler Stand
27 Buses to Haputale
   & Colombo

Woodlands Network A good source of information on walks and things to see and do in and around Bandarawela and beyond is Woodlands Network (☎/fax 22735, ℮ haas@ sltnet.lk), 30/6 Esplanade Rd. This is a small, local initiative run by a team headed by Sarojinie Ellawela. The network trains local people to act as guides (they are certified by the tourist board) and will help you arrange visits to or accommodation on nearby tea estates (including a visit to an organic tea estate), take you on jungle walks, and more. Woodlands Network is tirelessly researching the tourism potential of the region and is always well informed on what's new and interesting. The Network has also developed an eco-tourism circuit. You can get in contact with them before you leave home to plan your Sri Lankan visit around a less conventional program. For example, you could view a wildlife conservation project, join a fishing community in Negombo, or see a project that's endeavouring to make an abandoned tea estate productive again. You can also see places not normally accessible to visitors such as forest hermitages. Homestays can be arranged in some cases through the Network.

Woodlands Network has helped set up an information centre at nearby Welimada – itself an unremarkable little town, but whose surrounding countryside is rich in sites related to the Rama-Sita legend. Contact Woodlands Network for the information centre's details.

Money The Hatton National Bank, which is on Badulla Rd, gives cash advances on Visa and MasterCard. There's a Bank of Ceylon nearby, and a People's Bank near Woodlands Network.

Post & Communications The main post office, near the Bandarawela Hotel, is open from 7 am to 9 pm daily, except Sunday. For telephone calls try the ABC Call Cabin at the foot of the road that leads to the rest-house. You can send emails from Micro Services, which is off Welimada Rd.

Dowa Temple

About 6km out of Bandarawela on the road to Badulla, the little Dowa Temple is pleasantly situated close to a stream on the right-hand side of the road, with a beautiful 4m-high standing Buddha cut in low relief into the rock face below the road. The temple is easy to miss so ask the bus conductor to tell you when to get off.

Ayurveda

About 3.5km from Bandarawela on the Badulla road is an Ayurvedic treatment centre called Suwa Madhu (☎/fax 22504). It's a large, plush place catering to tourists. The 1½ hour program includes a 45-minute oil massage, steam and herbal sauna for Rs 2000. It's open from 8 am to 8 pm daily. If you're interested in an Ayurvedic treatment without the tourist-trap prices, the Woodlands Network (see Orientation & Information) can point you in the right direction.

Places to Stay & Eat

The *Chinese Union Hotel* (☎ 22502, 8 Mt Pleasant Rd) is an old-fashioned place with four clean rooms for Rs 330/550 and one room with a shared bathroom for less. There's a small bazaar/junk yard inside the front door selling everything and anything – don't let it frighten you away.

Along Welimada Rd are two guesthouses in former colonial-era bungalows. *Caps* (☎ 31115, 21 Welimada Rd) charges Rs 720/820 for singles/doubles with hot water or Rs 385/500 without. The rooms are drab, moth-eaten, and lacking mozzie nets, but there's a pretty garden and a rooftop spot with perfect views over the hills. Its long-time friend next door, *The Ventnor* (☎ 22511), is shamelessly overpriced. Quaint, but fading-fast rooms cost Rs 1400/1900 including breakfast. Try bargaining.

Those seeking something longer term – or just something different – might like to check out the *Woodlands Farm & Leisure Resort* (☎ 22426, Marlodge Lane), a small farm about 1km from the train station, off Poonagala Rd. The six basic rooms (in a former colonial bungalow) cost Rs 500/700. Cheap meals are supplied.

Himalie Guest House (☎ 22362) is an old-fashioned place set on a hill surrounded by an attractive garden and a tea plantation. The OK rooms cost Rs 820 per person including breakfast. It's about 3km out of town towards Badulla; a three-wheeler will cost about Rs 80.

The *Rest House* (☎ 22299, fax 22718) has nine rooms for Rs 620/1220. The five clean bland, rooms in the newer wing have a balcony with a view over the town. There are two decent family rooms in the older wing for Rs 1850. There's a pretty garden and friendly service – it's a quiet spot.

The *Bandarawela Hotel* (☎ 22501, fax 22834, e ashmres@aitkenspence.lk, 14 Welimada Rd) is the poshest place in town. This former tea planters' club is a large chalet-style building still kitted out with the furniture and fittings of a bygone era – vast easy chairs to sink into in the lounge, and bathrooms with lots of hot water in spacious rooms at US$31/43. There is a little courtyard garden with tortoises. Groups stay here so it pays to book ahead. There is a restaurant and bar.

Orient Hotel (☎ 22407, fax 32532, 10 Dharmapala Mawatha) has had a personality bypass, but at least the modernish, clean rooms have views over the town. Rooms cost US$34/37. There's a restaurant, where dinner costs US$8, and a billiard room.

The *Rose Villa* (☎ 22329, fax 22712, e loshan@sltnet.lk) is off Poonagala Rd, 2km from Bandarawela. This is a haven for peace and quiet; all vegetables served here are home grown and organic. It's a family home, crammed with decorations. Spotless rooms with breakfast and a main meal included cost a pricey US$50/100. You must book ahead.

The *Three Coins Corner* is a shack with tasty lunch-time rice and curry from Rs 40. Other eateries are near the bus stops, but none of them are too flash, so you may want to eat in your guesthouse.

Getting There & Away

Bus To get to Nuwara Eliya catch a bus to Welimada (Rs 9) and another from there to Nuwara Eliya (Rs 10) – there are buses to Nuwara Eliya from Welimada every 10 to 15 minutes. There are regular buses between Bandarawela and Haputale (Rs 7), Ella (Rs 8) and also Badulla (Rs 10). Long-distance services include runs to Colombo (Rs 150, six hours), Tissamaharama, Tangalla and Galle. Change at Wellawaya for buses to Tissa or the south coast.

Train Bandarawela is on the Colombo-Badulla railway. Main trains to Colombo (via Haputale) leave at 7.26 am (*Udarata Menike*) and 10.42 am (*Podi Menike*, via Kandy), and 7.17 and 8.45 pm. Main trains to Badulla (via Ella) leave at 4.58 and 7.15 am, and 12.30, 2.15, 3 and 5.40 pm.

Taxi A taxi to Ella will cost Rs 400.

ELLA
☎ 057
Sri Lanka is liberally endowed with beautiful views, and Ella has one of the best. The sleepy town is nestled in a valley peering straight through Ella Gap to the coastal plain nearly 1000m below, and over to the coast where, on a clear night, you can see the Kirinda lighthouse. As if views weren't enough, Ella is surrounded by hills perfect for walks through tea plantations to temples and waterfalls.

Information
There's a post office in the centre of town but for banking you'll need to head to Bandarawela. Rodrigo Communications, also in town, has Internet and IDD facilities.

Places to Stay
Touts at Ella are persistent – you may be approached on the train with tales that the hotel of your choice is too expensive, closed down, or rat-infested. All places listed have meals, hot water and bathrooms unless stated otherwise.

Beauty Mount Tourist Inn (☎ 077-618386) is an unpretentious little place with four rooms and a bungalow. The dirt-cheap rooms cost Rs 150 for singles, Rs 200 to Rs 350 for doubles and the bungalow (with a private veranda) costs Rs 750. The rooms are clean enough and the food is cheap.

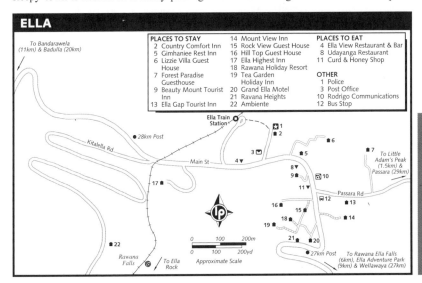

ELLA

PLACES TO STAY
2 Country Comfort Inn
5 Gimhaniee Rest Inn
6 Lizzie Villa Guest House
7 Forest Paradise Guesthouse
9 Beauty Mount Tourist Inn
13 Ella Gap Tourist Inn
14 Mount View Inn
15 Rock View Guest House
16 Hill Top Guest House
17 Ella Highest Inn
18 Rawana Holiday Resort
19 Tea Garden Holiday Inn
20 Grand Ella Motel
21 Ravana Heights
22 Ambiente

PLACES TO EAT
4 Ella View Restaurant & Bar
8 Udayanga Restaurant
11 Curd & Honey Shop

OTHER
1 Police
3 Post Office
10 Rodrigo Communications
12 Bus Stop

To Bandarawela (11km) & Badulla (20km)

Ella Train Station

28km Post
Kitalella Rd
Main St
To Little Adam's Peak (1.5km) & Passara (29km)
Passara Rd
Rawana Falls
To Ella Rock
27km Post
To Rawana Ella Falls (6km), Ella Adventure Park (9km) & Wellawaya (27km)

0   100   200m
0   100   200yd
Approximate Scale

Ella Highest Inn (☎ 23308) is set in a tea plantation. It's a hike up the track from the main road, but it's worth it – you'll get great views of the hilly countryside. The three rooms are boring and basic, but cheap at Rs 250/300.

The *Mount View Inn* (☎ 23292), despite its name, hasn't any views but it does have three basic, clean rooms in a super-friendly family home. Rooms cost from Rs 330 to 440.

Gimhaniee Rest Inn (☎ 22127) on the main road also doesn't have any views but it's clean and surprisingly quiet considering its location. Rooms cost Rs 380/550, cheaper without hot water.

Rock View Guest House (☎ 22661) is a large old house with views over the main road to Ella Gap. The clean but slightly worn rooms cost Rs 660 and are set around a large living area.

The *Forest Paradise Guesthouse* (☎/fax 23507) has four clean rooms with four poster beds for Rs 660/770 including breakfast. It's in a quiet setting and some of the rooms have a private veranda with views into the forest.

Hill Top Guest House (☎ 30080) has rooms downstairs with verandas surrounded by garden, for Rs 440/660, while the upstairs rooms share a balcony with superb views of Ella Gap and cost Rs 550/880. The rooms are clean, large and the friendly family cooks tasty food.

Lizzie Villa Guest House (☎ 23243) is signposted on the main road; the track to this place is about 60m long. Lizzie's is one of the longest-running establishments at Ella. Rooms cost from Rs 390 to 990. The more expensive rooms are spotless, but they're a bit pricey considering this place has no views. There's a spice garden.

Tea Garden Holiday Inn (☎ 22915) has eight rooms with three more on the way. Rooms cost from Rs 400 to 1100. The cheaper rooms are clean but a bit small; the more expensive rooms (spotless) share a roomy balcony. There's also a leafy communal balcony with pleasant views to the small Rawana Falls (and decent views through Ella Gap), friendly hosts and good food.

Rawana Holiday Resort (☎ 072-264338) is near the Tea Garden Holiday Inn. The clean, basic rooms line a veranda with OK views – the hosts are friendly. The price of singles/doubles is Rs 615/920.

Near the junction is the *Ella Gap Tourist Inn* (☎ 22628) which has a range of clean rooms from Rs 720 to 1375. There's a large homely restaurant and a lovely leafy garden.

The *Ambiente* (☎ 055-31666, fax 31667, e kanta@telenett.net, Kitalella Rd) is at the top of a hill and it enjoys magnificent views, great service and spotless rooms. There are a variety of rooms, with and without bathrooms, from Rs 1000 to 1500. Good news travels fast, and at the time of writing four new rooms were under construction. A three-wheeler from here to the train station should cost Rs 60.

Country Comfort Inn (☎ 23132, fax 01-716349, e countrycomfortella@yahoo.com) has an older building with a new annexe. The place is well run, clean and the gardens are immaculate. The rooms in the new wing have all the mod cons for Rs 2200/2750. The older-style rooms have more character and cost from around Rs 550 to 920. Rates are negotiable – go for it!

Opposite the 27km post on the Ella-Wellawaya road, *Ravana Heights* (☎/fax 31182) has three super-clean rooms for Rs 1600/1760. It's a stylish, modern home with great service and friendly owners. There's a veranda and a pretty garden – guests and nonguests can avail themselves of the various excursions organised by the hosts.

Grand Ella Motel (☎/fax 22636), formerly the Ella Resthouse, has great views from the front lawn right through Ella Gap. The large, new rooms cost US$61 – each has a balcony. At the time of writing some older rooms (at US$33) were left untouched, but these were due to be renovated.

Ella Adventure Park (☎ 87263, 01-739243, e jith1@sri.lanka.net) is 9km out of Ella on the Wellawaya road. This modern top-end place is different to the usual cardboard-cut-out hotel. It has log furniture, natural toned decor, stone features and a quiet bush setting. All this style doesn't come cheap though – rooms costs from US$80.

Is it the footprint of Adam, Buddha or Shiva? The revered Adam's Peak keeps its secret.

The dramatically plunging cliffs of World's End

The lush, verdant landscape of the hill country

Dawn heralds a spectacular view at Adam's Peak.

Concrete Buddha, Kandy

Thuparama Dagoba

An intricately carved guardstone at the ruins of Polonnaruwa

The magnificent carved ornamental staircase at the ancient rock fortress city of Yapahuwa

Management organises paragliding, canoeing, rock climbing, abseiling, camping and more (nonguests welcome).

Places to Eat

The shack-like **Curd & Honey shop** has good, cheap food. Rice and curry, fried rice and noodle dishes all cost Rs 55. Then try the delicious curd for Rs 15 – add lashings of kitul (palm syrup).

Udayanga Restaurant has tasty rice and curry for Rs 90, as well as Western-style dishes from Rs 110. The owner is very friendly, and this place is simple and clean.

Clad with 1970s grass matting, **Ella View Restaurant & Bar** has food that is not worth writing home about, but this is a good place to have a quiet drink. If you're a solo women traveller you may get annoyed by stares.

Getting There & Away

Bus & Taxi The road to Ella diverges from the Bandarawela-Badulla road about 9km out of Bandarawela. Buses to Matara stop at Ella from about 6.30 am, and then around every hour until about 2.30 pm (CTB bus costs Rs 60, intercity express Rs 150). The buses are likely to be quite full by the time they reach Ella, though the buses around noon are usually less busy. You can always catch a bus to Wellawaya (Rs 16), though, and change there for the south, or for Monaragala (for Arugam Bay).

If you wish to go to Kandy you must change at Badulla. Alternatively you could go to Wellawaya, catch the intercity to Nuwara Eliya and then change again for Kandy (see the Wellawaya section later in this chapter). Buses to Bandarawela cost Rs 8 and are fairly frequent. There are infrequent buses to Badulla, although you can always get a bus to Bandarawela and change there for Badulla. It costs Rs 350 to go by taxi to Bandarawela from Ella. Intercity express buses leave from Bandarawela, Wellawaya and Badulla.

Train Ella is an hour from both Haputale and Badulla on the Colombo-Badulla railway. The stretch from Haputale (through Bandarawela) is particularly lovely. About 10km north of Ella at Demodara the line performs a complete loop around a hillside and tunnels under itself at a level 30m lower. Ella's train station is quaint, and the fares and timetables well posted. Trains to Colombo depart at 6.52 (Udarata Menike), and 10.07 am (Podi Menike) (these two trains have an observation car that should be booked ahead), and 6.44 and 8.13 pm (Rs 154.50 in 2nd class); to Kandy at 10.07 am and 1.07 and 6.44 pm (Rs 97 in 2nd class); to Badulla at 5.28 and 7.55 am, and 1.02, 2.45, 3.28 (Podi Menike) and 6.09 pm (Udarata Menike, Rs 12 in 2nd class).

The Colombo-bound trains generally stop at Bandarawela (Rs 7.50 in 2nd class), Haputale (Rs 14), Ohiya (for Horton Plains, Rs 23), Nanu Oya (for Nuwara Eliya, Rs 37), Kandy (Rs 97), and Hatton (for Adam's Peak, Rs 55).

AROUND ELLA

Some people like to visit the **Dowa Temple** from Ella. (For more information see that entry under Bandarawela earlier in this chapter.) Others might want to visit a tea factory. **Uva Halpewaththa tea factory** runs tours. To get there catch a bus to Bandarawela, get off at the Kumbawela junction and flag a bus going to Badulla. Get off just after the 27km post, near the Halpe temple. From here you've got a 2km walk to the factory. A three-wheeler from Ella will charge Rs 100 return.

Ella is also a great base for keen walkers to explore the surrounding countryside – the views can be spectacular. It would be inadvisable for women to head off alone; it's best to go with a companion or two.

The **Rawana Ella Falls** are about 6km down Ella Gap towards Wellawaya. The water comes leaping down the mountainside in what is claimed to be the wildest-looking fall in Sri Lanka, although some travellers aren't impressed. There are vendors selling food and trinkets and the invariable array of 'guides' wanting to point out 'the waterfall'. Buses from Ella cost Rs 6 and a three-wheeler will charge Rs 25 return including waiting time.

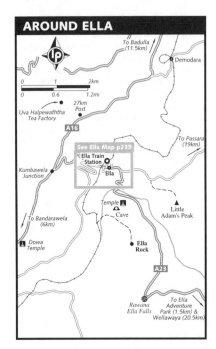

AROUND ELLA

this path passes through a tea estate. The walk takes about 45 minutes each way.

Ella Rock is more demanding, and you'll pass by the small **Rawana Falls** on your way. Head along the railway tracks (towards Bandarawela) for about 2.5km until you come to the metal bridge; here you'll see the falls. Continue along the tracks to just before the 166¼km sign where you'll see a path heading to the left. Follow this over a creek, turn left, continue around a volleyball court, pass some houses and you'll soon come to a woodland. The track continues to the top of the rock where you'll be rewarded with stunning views. The walk takes about two hours each way.

BADULLA
☎ 055

Standing at an altitude of about 680m, Badulla marks the south-east extremity of the hill country and is a gateway to the east coast. It's one of Sri Lanka's oldest towns. The Portuguese occupied it briefly, then torched it upon leaving. For the British it was an important social centre, although there is little evidence of that today. If you are a history buff, though, it's interesting to take a look through St Mark's Church and peruse the old headstones. Inside the church is a plaque to the elephant hunter Major Rogers, who was killed by lightning. The railway through the hill country from Colombo and Kandy terminates here.

Information
The post office is near the bus station. A Bank of Ceylon, open from 8.30 am to 2.30 pm daily, is along its namesake, Bank Rd. Opposite you'll see the sign to Cybrain Computer Systems, at 40/1 Bank Rd. It has cheap Internet access.

Dunhinda Falls
Five kilometres out of Badulla you'll find the 60m-high Dunhinda Falls – said to be the most awe-inspiring in Sri Lanka. The best time of the year to see them is June and July but they're worth a visit anytime. It's a good spot for a picnic, but watch out for the monkeys who'll grab your food if you're

Farther up the road and to your left as you approach Ella, a side road takes you to a little **temple** and a **cave** that is associated with the Sita-Rama story. You may visit the temple, which is part of a monastery, but remember to remove your shoes and hat and to cover your legs and arms. Just before the temple, in a cleft in the mountain that rises to Ella Rock is a cave said to be the very one in which the king of Lanka held Sita captive. Boys often materialise to show you where the track up to the cave starts, but the track is steep, overgrown and slippery. Most find the cave itself to be a disappointment.

A gentle walk will take you to what is locally dubbed **little Adam's Peak**. Go down the Passara road until you get to the plant shop on your right, just past the 1km post. Follow the track that is on your left as you face the garden shop. Little Adam's Peak is the biggest hill on your right. Take the second path that turns off to your right and follow that to the top of the hill. Some of

not looking! Bus No 314 leaves Badulla around every half hour (Rs 10) and will take you close to the falls. From the bus stop it's about 1km along a clearly defined, sometimes rocky, path. As it can be a bit of a scramble, wear suitable shoes. There's a good observation spot at the end of the path and you can see a lower falls on the walk. There are many cold drink and snack places both on the main road and along the trail. Avoid public holidays and weekends, when the place can get packed. Entry is Rs 10 (Rs 2 for locals). A three-wheeler from town will charge Rs 300 for the return trip.

Places to Stay & Eat

Friendly *Wijedasa Soysa's* place (☎ 22105, 5/2 Mailagastenne) is a five-minute walk from the train station. From the station, walk a minute or so along the track (in the opposite direction to Kandy) to where the road intersects it (alternatively, you can take the road), then turn right. Follow this road for two minutes to a junction dominated by the large Cooperative Union Office building with 'COOP' on its gate. Turn left along this road, you'll pass a house with 'No 19, MA Subian' on its gate. At the top of the road are two houses; the guesthouse is on

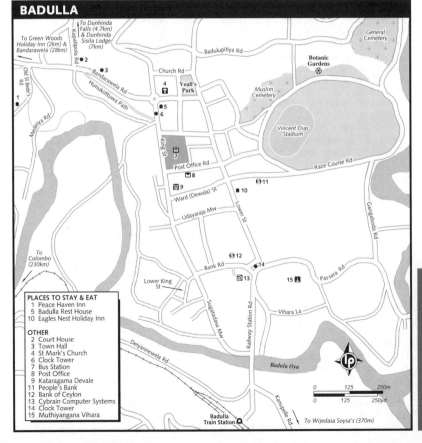

BADULLA

To Dunhinda Falls (4.7km) & Dunhinda Sisila Lodge (7km)

To Green Woods Holiday Inn (2km) & Bandarawela (28km)

Old St Bede's Rd
Medriya Rd
Kapatipola Rd
Bandarawela Rd
Hunukottuwa Path
Badulupitiya Rd
Church Rd
Veall's Park
King St
Post Office Rd
Ward (Dewala) St
Udayaraja Mw
Lower St
Race Course Rd
Gangaboda Rd
Muslim Cemetery
Botanic Gardens
General Cemetery
Vincent Dias Stadium

To Colombo (230km)

Bank Rd
Lower King St
Sugatadasa Mw
Railway Station Rd
Passara Rd
Vihara La
Deiyannewela Rd
Badulu Oya
Kanupelle Rd

Badulla Train Station
To Wijedasa Soysa's (370km)

0   125   250m
0   125   250yd

PLACES TO STAY & EAT
1 Peace Haven Inn
5 Badulla Rest House
10 Eagles Nest Holiday Inn

OTHER
2 Court House
3 Town Hall
4 St Mark's Church
6 Clock Tower
7 Bus Station
8 Post Office
9 Kataragama Devale
11 People's Bank
12 Bank of Ceylon
13 Cybrain Computer Systems
14 Clock Tower
15 Muthiyangana Vihara

the right. There are three basic singles/doubles for Rs 160/315 (two with an OK shared bathroom).

Eagles Nest Holiday Inn (☎ 22841, 159 Lower St) is a no-frills place with quaint rooms set around a courtyard. Rooms cost Rs 330/550.

Near the falls the modern *Dunhinda Sisila Lodge (☎ 31302, fax 23423)* has four rooms that have a coat of grime for Rs 400/550. However, the bathrooms are spotless. There's a natural swimming hole closeby. To find it, follow the Dunhinda Falls road past the falls for a farther 2.3km.

Peace Haven Inn (☎ 22523, 18 Old St Bedes Rd) is a bit out of town near some rice paddies. It's a modern place (some might call it ugly) with a pretty, leafy garden looking out to the countryside. Clean, large rooms cost Rs 480/600 – the two rooms with hot water cost Rs 660. Meals are available; rice and curry costs from Rs 150. A three-wheeler from the bus station will cost about Rs 40, or Rs 70 from the train station.

Green Woods Holiday Inn (☎ 31358) is about 3km from the centre of town, on Bandarawela Rd. It's a modern, spotless place with ceiling-to-floor windows looking out to the countryside. The rooms – all with hot water – cost Rs 550/610. There are no mozzie nets available, and the rooms by the road are a bit noisy.

The *Badulla Rest House (☎ 22299)* has a great location smack in the centre of town, but it may be a bit noisy. Basic, fading rooms cost Rs 540/620. There's a grassy courtyard garden, and meals are available; the rice and curry lunch is good.

Getting There & Away

Bus Buses run approximately every 30 to 40 minutes to Nuwara Eliya (private bus Rs 26; first bus 6 am, last bus 4.30 pm); Bandarawela (private bus Rs 15; every 20 minutes from 6.30 am until 4.30 pm); Ella (private bus Rs 18; about every 2½ hours, first bus 6 am, last bus 5.45 pm); Colombo (intercity express Rs 150; first bus 7.30 am and last bus 10 pm); Kandy (CTB and private intercity buses, Rs 60 and Rs 100

respectively; from 5.30 am until 2 pm); Matara and then on to Galle (one daily at 6.30 am, CTB bus Rs 56.50); and Monaragala (CTB bus Rs 20; every hour between 5.30 am and 5.45 pm).

Train The main daily services to Colombo leave Badulla at 5.55 (the *Udarata Menike*, not to Kandy) and 9.10 am (*Podi Menike* via Kandy), and 5.45 and 7.15 pm (the latter is a slow train). The *Podi Menike* has a 1st-class observation car for which you pay an additional Rs 50. The 5.45 pm has sleeping accommodation. Fares are Rs 60/165.50/289 in 3rd/2nd/1st class.

WELLAWAYA
☎ 055

By Wellawaya you have left the hill country and descended to the plains. Apart from the nearby Buduruwagala carvings, there's not much of interest in the area, Wellawaya being just a small crossroads town. Roads run north up past the Rawana Ella Falls and through the spectacular Ella Gap to Ella and the hill country, south to Tissamaharama and the coast at Hambantota, east through Monaragala to Arugam Bay on the coast, and west through Ratnapura to Colombo with a branch up to Haputale in the hill country. There's a Bank of Ceylon near the bus station.

Buduruwagala

About 5km south of Wellawaya a side road branches west off the road to Tissa to the rock-cut **Buddha figures** of Buduruwagala. A small signpost points the way along a 4km road.

Buduruwagala means Buddha *(Budu)*, images *(ruva)* of stone *(gala)*. The figures are thought to date from around the 10th century AD, and are of the Mahayana Buddhist school, which enjoyed a brief heyday in Sri Lanka. The gigantic standing Buddha still bears traces of its original stuccoed robe and a long streak of orange suggests it was once brightly painted. The central of the three figures to the Buddha's right is thought to be the Buddhist mythological figure, the Bodhisattva Avalokitesvara.

To the left of this white-painted figure is a female figure in the 'thrice bent' posture, who is thought to be his consort, Tara. The three figures on the Buddha's left appear to an inexpert eye to be of a rather different style. One of them is holding up the hourglass-shaped Tibetan thunderbolt symbol known as a *dorje* – an unusual example of the Tantric side of Buddhism in Sri Lanka. One of them is said to be Maitreya, the future Buddha, while another is Vishnu. Several of the figures hold up their right hands with two fingers bent down to the palm – a beckoning gesture.

Entry is Rs 100. You may find yourself accompanied by a guide who will expect a tip.

A three-wheeler from Wellawaya will cost about Rs 150 return and a taxi Rs 250 to 300 return.

Elephants

About 9km along the road to Tissa you'll find a turn-off to the Handapangala Tank. Elephants come here from Yala (Ruhuna) National Park to raid the plantations of the nearby sugar factory. As you can imagine the factory owners aren't thrilled by the feasting, and it's also not a safe situation for the nearby villagers. The jumbos are regularly 'shooed' back to Yala, but the sweet cane is too inviting and the cool water of the tank provides the perfect after-lunch bath – in the distance you can see elephants at the water's edge. A three-wheeler will cost Rs 400 for the return trip from Wellawaya. Really the only time to see the elephants is between 4 and 6 pm, despite what the three-wheeling dealers will tell you.

Places to Stay & Eat

About 3km along the road to Tissa to the left you'll see *The Little Rose (101 Tissa Rd)* surrounded by rice paddies. It has four basic singles/doubles for Rs 250/350, cheap food (Rs 75 for breakfast) and a jolly, welcoming family.

If you take the Old Ella Rd from the central crossroads in the middle of Wellawaya to where it merges with the New Ella Rd running north to Ella, and then continue a little farther, you reach *Saranga Holiday Inn (☎ 74891)*. It has rooms for Rs 600 or Rs 820 with air-con. It's reasonably clean and friendly but the ornate curtains may scare you.

A little farther out, *Wellawaya Inn Rest House (☎ 74899)*, has basic but reasonably clean rooms with bathroom for Rs 660.

Getting There & Away

Wellawaya is a major staging point between the hill country and the south and east coasts. If you can't find a through bus you can usually find a connection in Wellawaya – but don't leave it too late in the day. Buses to Haputale start running at around 5 am and the last bus leaves at about 5.30 pm (Rs 15). There are regular buses to Monaragala (Rs 16, one hour) with the last bus leaving about 6.30 pm. Buses to Ella run approximately every half hour (Rs 14, last bus 6 pm). If you want to go to Kandy you must catch a bus to Nuwara Eliya and change there. For Tissamaharama you must change at Pannegamanuwa Junction. There are also buses to Tangalla (Rs 35, three hours), Colombo (intercity express Rs 150, seven hours) and Nuwara Eliya (intercity express Rs 80, only one bus at 10 am).

KITULGALA
☎ 036

South-west of Kandy, Kitulgala's main claim to fame is that it was here that David Lean filmed his epic tale, *Bridge on the River Kwai*. You can walk down a paved pathway to the site where the filming took place along the banks of the Kelaniya Ganga. The pathway is signposted on the main road, about 1km from the Plantation Hotel in the direction of Adam's Peak. It is virtually impossible to head down the path without attracting an entourage of 'guides' (including a few claiming to have been extras in the movie), who of course will expect a consideration for their trouble. There's nothing left to see, but if you know the film you can recognise some of the places.

Kitulgala's second claim to fame is **white-water rafting**. You can organise this through the Plantation Hotel (see later in this section) but it's better to organise it before you get here (see Organised Tours in the Getting Around chapter for the contact details of companies that organise rafting). The Kelaniya Ganga has good **swimming** spots – a popular hole is beside Plantation Hotel.

The dining room of the *Rest House (☎/fax 87528)* is a veritable shrine to the David Lean epic; black-and-white photos of the stars grace the walls with accompanying text explaining what's what. The resthouse was around when filming occurred so can claim to be part of the history of the epic's production.

Avoid the lunch-time buffet – it costs a ridiculous US$7.50 a head. The rooms are clean, large and each has a veranda facing the river. Singles or doubles cost US$33.

Farther towards Adam's Peak, *Plantation Hotel (☎ 87575, fax 87574, Kalukohutenna)* is a great place to stay. Stylish rooms with air-con cost US$33/40. There's a terrific lunch-time buffet (Rs 350) served in the restaurant beside the river. A video of *Bridge on the River Kwai* runs on an endless loop in the main eating area. This place is popular with groups, so book ahead.

Gems

Ratnapura is the gem centre of Sri Lanka; every second person you meet on the street is likely to whisper that they have the bargain of your lifetime wrapped up in their pocket. If you're no expert on gemstones the bargain is 100% likely to be on their side of the line, not yours.

Gems are still found by an ancient and traditional mining method. Gem miners look for seams of *illama*, a gravel-bearing stratum likely to hold gemstones. It's usually found in lowland areas – along valley bottoms, riverbeds and other, usually very damp, places. On the Colombo-Ratnapura road you'll see countless gem-mining operations in paddy fields beside the road, but there are many more off in the hills and fields all around.

Gem mining is a cooperative effort: You need someone to dig out the illama, someone to work the pump to keep water out of the pit or tunnel, someone to wash the muddy gravel, and an expert to search through the pebbles for the stone that may make all their fortunes. If a stone is found, the profit is divided between all the members of the coop, from the person who supplies the finances to the one up to his neck in mud and water, clad only in a tiny loincloth known as an *amudes*. Children are sometimes sent down the shafts. The mines can be vertical or horizontal depending on which way the illama runs.

It's a peculiarity of Sri Lankan gemming that a variety of stones is almost always found in the same pit. A stone's value depends on a number of factors including rarity, hardness and beauty. Gems are still cut and polished by hand, although modern methods are also coming into use. Some stones are cut and faceted *(en cabochon)*, while others are simply polished. The division between precious and semiprecious stones is purely arbitrary – there is no clear definition of what makes one stone a precious stone and another only semiprecious. Some of the more popular types of stone are listed here.

Corundrums

This group includes sapphires and rubies, both precious stones and second only to the diamond in hardness. The best and most valuable rubies are red and are not found in Sri Lanka in commercial deposits. You will, however, see pink rubies, which are also correctly called pink sapphires. Rubies and sapphires are the same kind of stone, with gradations of colour depending on the precise proportions of the chemicals in their make-up. Star rubies and star sapphires are a feature of the Ratnapura gem industry. The stone is duller than others of their type, but under a light you can see a starburst appear on the stone. Other sapphires can be yellow, orange, white and, most valuable, blue. Beware of people trying to pass off pink or blue spinels as sapphires. You can often find corundrums containing 'silk': minute inclusions that give the stone a star effect, particularly with a single

It's easy enough to have a quick stop at Kitulgala even if you are travelling by bus. If you're coming from Ratnapura, you'll have to change at Avissawella; catch the bus to Hatton and get off at Kitulgala (Rs 22). When you're over Kitulgala, flag a bus to Hatton from the main road (Rs 25).

RATNAPURA
☎ 045

Busy Ratnapura (City of Gems) is 100km south-east of Colombo – if gems aren't your thing, you may want to pass Ratnapura by.

However, the scenery around Ratnapura is pretty and this is reputed to be the best place for views of Adam's Peak, since here you view the mountain from below while from the Hatton side you're looking at it from about the same level. Ratnapura is also the starting point for the classic (read hard) trekking route up Adam's Peak via Gilimale and Carney Estate.

There is beautiful scenery in abundance from Ratnapura to Haputale, which makes this an interesting alternative route to or from the hill country; you skirt round the

---

Gems

light source. In 1998 an 880-carat blue sapphire (the size of a chicken egg) was found here. If cut properly, the stone was estimated to be worth more than US$1 million. Sri Lanka has produced three of the world's largest blue sapphires, including the Star of India (displayed at the New York Museum of Natural History).

Chrysoberyl
Cat's-eye and Alexandrite are the best known in this group. Cat's-eyes, with their cat-like ray known as *chatoyancy*, vary from green through a honey colour to brown; look for translucence and the clarity and glow of the single ray. Alexandrite is valued for its colour change under natural and artificial light. One rip-off to watch for is tourmalines, which are far less valuable, being sold as cat's-eyes.

Beryl
The best known stone in this group, the emerald, is not found in Sri Lanka. The aquamarine, which is found here, is quite reasonably priced since it is not as hard or lustrous as other stones.

Zircon
The appearance of a zircon can approach that of a diamond, although it is a comparatively soft stone. Zircon comes in a variety of colours, from yellow through orange to brown and green.

Quartz
This stone can vary from transparent to opaque, and is usually quite well priced. Quartz can also vary widely in colour, from purple amethyst to brown smoky quartz, right through to yellow or orange citron quartz.

Feldspar
The moonstone is Sri Lanka's special gem. Usually a smooth, grey colour, it can also be found with a slight shade of blue although this colouring is rarer.

Other
Spinels These are fairly common in Sri Lanka but are also quite hard and rather attractive. They come in a variety of colours and can be transparent or opaque.
Garnets A sort of poor person's ruby; light-brown garnets are often used in rings in Sri Lanka.
Topaz The Topaz is not found in Sri Lanka – if someone offers it to you it'll probably be quartz.

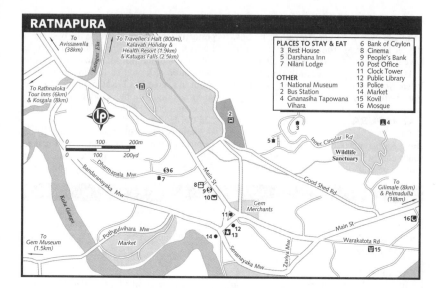

RATNAPURA

PLACES TO STAY & EAT
3 Rest House
5 Darshana Inn
7 Nilani Lodge

OTHER
1 National Museum
2 Bus Station
4 Gnanasiha Tapowana Vihara

6 Bank of Ceylon
8 Cinema
9 People's Bank
10 Post Office
11 Clock Tower
12 Public Library
13 Police
14 Market
15 Kovil
16 Mosque

southern edge of the hill country and then ascend into the hills at Haputale.

Things to see & Do

The **National Museum** (☎ 22451) is open from 9 am to 5 pm Saturday to Wednesday. Entry is Rs 35 for adults, Rs 25 for children and Rs 135 for your camera. On display are the fossil remains of various animals (rhinos, elephants) discovered in gem pits. There are items of local culture as well, including gems, fabrics and jewellery.

There's a **Gem Museum** on Pothgulvihara Mawatha, Getangama (it's signposted from the main street where the clock tower is); it's open from 9 am to 4 pm daily; entry is free. There's a good display of gems as well as information on mining and polishing. A return three-wheeler trip from the centre of town should cost Rs 100 (including waiting time).

There aren't any **gem mines** catering for tourist visits but if you're interested in seeing one your guesthouse or hotel should be able to organise something. You can also watch gem merchants selling their wares in the area north-east of the clock tower.

There are less arduous walks than Adam's Peak much closer to town, even right from

the resthouse. Three kilometres north of town are the **Katugas Falls**, which are quite pleasant but are crowded on Sunday and public holidays. There's a full-size replica of the **Aukana Buddha** at the Gnanasiha Tapowana Vihara, on top of a hill overlooking the town; you can walk to it through a wildlife sanctuary.

About 8km from town, at Kosgala, are some **caves**.

You can also use Ratnapura as a base for a day trip to Sinharaja Forest Reserve. Expect to pay around Rs 3000 (up to four people). You'll also be offered trips to Uda Walawe National Park (see later in this chapter) for Rs 4000 but it's really too long a journey to do in a day.

Places to Stay & Eat

Darshana Inn (☎ 22674, 68/5 Inner Circular Rd, also called Rest House Rd) is just a bit lower than the Rest House. The rooms are dark, grim and none too cheap at Rs 600, although the hosts are friendly. The well-stocked bar is popular with local men and it can get a bit noisy at night, although it closes at 10.30 pm. It's only an option for the desperate.

Travellers Halt (☎ 23092, 30 Outer Circular Rd), in the direction of Polhengoda Village, just over 1km out of town, has six singles/doubles (with two more in the making) for Rs 550/660 – add Rs 400 for air-con. The rooms are clean and pleasant, but the balcony is caged in and management can be a bit pushy (it offers tours). A three-wheeler from the bus station should cost Rs 50.

Ratnapura's *Rest House* (☎ 22299) has the best site in town, right on top of the hill that dominates Ratnapura. From up here you can overlook the town and surrounding countryside, well above the noise and heat down below (the bus station is right at the foot of this hill). The rooms have seen better days, but supposedly renovations are on the way so by the time you read this the rooms may be worth the Rs 1100. Still, the place has heaps of charm with its spacious veranda (perfect for an evening beer) and a small grassy garden.

The concrete-block-like *Nilani Lodge* (☎ 22170, e hashani@sltnet.lk, 21 Dharmapala Mawatha) has rooms with hot water for Rs 1100/1200, cheaper with cold water. The rooms are clean but the carpets are a bit grotty; each has a small balcony with OK views.

Kalavati Holiday & Health Resort (☎ 22465, fax 23657, Polhengoda Village) is 2.5km from the Ratnapura bus station. There is an extensive herb garden and the place itself is kitted out with antique furniture. Kalavati offers a 30-minute health treatment that involves an oil massage, a 'gum wash', 'fermentation', and 'medicinal smoke'. Intrigued by the possibilities? Find out what it's about for Rs 1870. The basic rooms cost from Rs 1250 to 1360 – add Rs 200 for air-con. A three-wheeler from the bus station will cost Rs 75.

Rathnaloka Tour Inns (☎/fax 22455, e ratnaloka@eureka.lk, Kosgala/Kahangama) is an upmarket place 6km from town. It's an eyesore, but there's a large garden, an inviting pool and attentive service. Rooms cost US$30 and have air-con and hot water – there are also deluxe rooms for US$43. There is a good restaurant here. A taxi from Ratnapura should cost Rs 500.

The most popular place for a bite to eat is the *Rest House*, which does rice and curry as well as other dishes for reasonable prices. *Kalavati Holiday and Health Resort* also has good food and quite an extensive menu. There are several places in and near Main St that serve reasonable rice and curries for low prices.

Getting There & Away

There are heaps of intercity buses to long-distance destinations such as Colombo (Rs 55) as well as CTB buses (Rs 27). Any bus coming from Colombo is likely to be jam-packed. For Hatton or Nuwara Eliya, you'll have to catch a bus to Avissawella (Rs 11.50) and change there. For Haputale, Ella and Badulla you'll probably have to catch a bus to Balangoda (Rs 17.50) and change there. The CTB bus to Embilipitiya (for Uda Welawe) costs Rs 27. To get to Galle you must change at Matara.

SINHARAJA FOREST RESERVE

Sinharaja, the last major, undisturbed area of rainforest in Sri Lanka, is some 30km south of Ratnapura. There are several entry points, but the most relevant to travellers is either via Kudawa in the north-west or via Mederapitiya (from Deniyaya) in the south-east.

History

Sinharaja (literally Lion King) comprises some 18,899 hectares of natural and modified forest. Legend has it that the area was once the preserve of kings and some colonial records refer to it as Rajasinghe Forest. But no-one knows for sure how it came upon its name. The area first entered European records when the Portuguese detailed all the villages in the area, plus their timber and fruit trees, for tax collection purposes. The Dutch mapped the area and the British continued surveying the region, partly for commercial reasons (to assess its potential for coffee and timber) and partly for scientific study.

In 1840 it became Crown land and from that time efforts were made to preserve at least some of it. In the 1930s John Baker mounted a three-month expedition to record

THE HILL COUNTRY

the forest's flora and fauna, the first systematic study ever done here. However, in 1971 loggers moved in and began what was called selective logging. Replanting involved replacing the logged native hardwoods with mahogany (which does not occur naturally here). Logging roads and trails snaked into the forest and a woodchip mill was built. Conservationists, including the Wildlife Nature and Protection Society of Sri Lanka, lobbied hard for an end to the destruction. In 1977 a newly elected government called a halt to all logging; the machinery was dismantled and taken out of the forest, the roads gradually grew over and Sinharaja was saved. In 1989 it was made a Unesco World Heritage site.

Sinharaja Today
Conservation work is an ongoing activity, and finding the right balance between the needs of locals and the requirements of conservationists is sometimes difficult. There are 22 villages around the forest and locals enter it to tap *kitul* palms for sap (to make *jaggery*, a hard brown sweet) – this is allowed to a limited degree – and to collect wood and leaves for fuel and for construction. Rattan collection is of more concern as the demand for raw cane is high. Medicinal plants are collected during specific seasons, although this is not of concern to conservationists.

Unfortunately the area is subject to damage by gem miners, whose abandoned open pits pose dangers to humans and animals and cause erosion. There is some poaching of wild animals such as sambar, mouse deer, wild boar and purple-faced langur.

Flora
Sinharaja has a wild profusion of flora, which is still being studied. The canopy trees reach heights of up to 45m, with the next layer down topping about 30m. The vegetation below the canopy is not thick and impenetrable, as rumour sometimes has it. Nearly all the sub-canopy trees found here are rare or endangered. More than 65% of the 217 types of trees and woody climbers endemic to Sri Lanka's rainforest are found in Sinharaja.

Fauna
Mammals Of the animals that inhabit Sinharaja, the largest carnivore is the leopard. Seldom seen, the leopard's presence can usually only be gauged by droppings and tracks. Even rarer are rusty spotted cats and fishing cats. In the past, elephants commonly browsed around the edges of the forest, but drifted elsewhere when logging began in the 1970s. Sambar, barking deer and wild boar can be found on the forest floor. Purple-faced langur, which live in groups of 10 to 14, are fairly common, although you are more likely to see the branches and leaves shaking as they move through the trees and hear their territorial calls than to actually catch sight of the monkeys themselves.

Shrews and squirrels are among smaller mammals found in the forest. There are three kinds of squirrel: the flame-striped jungle squirrel, the dusky-striped jungle squirrel and the western giant squirrel. Porcupines and pangolins waddle around the forest floor, although you seldom see them. Six species of bat have been recorded here. Civets and mongooses are nocturnal, though you may glimpse see the occasional mongoose darting through the foliage during the day.

Reptiles There are 45 species of reptiles here, 21 of which are endemic. Venomous snakes include the green-pit viper, which inhabits trees, the hump-nosed viper and the krait, which lives on the forest floor. One of the most frequently found amphibians is the wrinkled frog, whose croaking is often heard at night. The sharp-nosed tree frog lays its eggs underneath cardamom leaves that overhang streams; the tadpoles drop straight into the water when they hatch.

Insects There is little information about insects and butterflies in Sinharaja. However, one butterfly you are likely to see is the black-and-white tree nymph, which lives in the forest canopy. Look out for giant millipedes.

Bird Life There is a wealth of bird life: 147 species have been recorded with 18 of Sri Lanka's 20 endemic species being seen here.

Orientation & Information

Sinharaja is bordered by streams and rivers: Napala Dola in the north, Gin Ganga in the south, and Kalukandawa Ela and the Pitakele Ganga in the west. An old foot track that goes past the Beverley Estate marks the eastern border. The land decreases in elevation towards the west. The east has the highest peak in the forest, which is Hinipitigala (1171m).

Sinharaja receives between 3500mm and 5000mm of rain annually, with a minimum in the driest months (August to September, January to early April) of 50mm. The drier months are the best times to visit. There's little seasonal variation in the temperature (it averages about 24°C inside the forest itself, with humidity at about 87%).

Sinharaja has leeches in abundance. It would be most unusual to walk through this forest and not attract one or more of these unpleasant little critters. Never pull a leech off; its head may stay in the wound and cause infection. Leeches will drop off if you sprinkle them with salt or salt water, or burn them with a match or cigarette end. They'll also drop off once they've gorged themselves on your blood, but most people just want to get rid of the thing as quickly as possible. The wound they leave behind will probably bleed for some time, but as long as you disinfect it properly it will heal quickly.

You need a permit to enter the forest. The main ticket office is at the Forest Department at Kudawa. You can apply in advance in Colombo or just turn up here and pay. It costs Rs 250 a day (Rs 50 for a foreigner with a resident visa); it's half that price for children under 12. A guide is compulsory and costs Rs 100 a day. If you wish to stay overnight in the park you need permission from the Forestry Department in Galle. The department offers basic dormlike accommodation; see Places to Stay & Eat, following.

Deniyaya

Deniyaya is the closest base for visiting Sinharaja if coming from the south or east.

The entrance is near Mederapitiya via Pallegama (10km from Deniyaya). There is a path that follows the northern bank of the Gin Ganga, which flows along the park's southern border.

Tickets to the forest reserve must be bought at Deodawa, which is 5km from Deniyaya on the Matara road.

Places to Stay & Eat

Accommodation at or near Sinharaja is very limited and basic.

Kudawa & the North-West The Forest Department at Kudawa offers only basic *accommodation* at Rs 250 a person per bed. There is one four-bed room and two six-bed rooms, both with bunk beds and a bathroom. Apparently you also pay for the beds that are not occupied, so one person occupying the four-bed room pays Rs 1000, although this seems a bit tough but you may be able to negotiate a better deal. Electric lighting costs Rs 30 per hour, a bed sheet costs Rs 10 and a pillow case Rs 5. You must bring your own food and there is also a charge for using the cooking facilities.

Martin Wijesinghe's place, right on the park's boundary near Kuduwa, is much more congenial. It's about 4km from the ticket office. You contact Martin by telegram in advance at the Weddagala post office (☎ 045-55256) or by letter (Forest View, Kudawa, Weddagala). Martin has basic accommodation (three double rooms in the house with shared bathroom and a bunkhouse that can sleep about 10). Martin is an expert on Sinharaja, having worked as a ranger here for years, and is a mine of information. He has no set price for the accommodation, but you should pay at least Rs 450 a night including breakfast.

You can get a good rice and curry meal here – vegetarian, as there is no fridge – but if you are coming with your own vehicle it would be a courtesy to bring your own vegetables (and if you want chicken, bring a frozen one from Kalawana, 16km from Kudawa). The family will cook it all for you.

At Ingiriya, a crossroads for those coming from the west coast in the direction of

Ratnapura, is the ***Ingiriya Citizens Rest*** (☎ *034-69315*). This is a good place for a bite (rice and curry costs Rs 200) and a drink (beer's available). Accommodation if you need it goes for Rs 800 (rooms are clean and have bathroom).

Deniyaya You can save a lot of hassle by arranging your trip through Palitha Ratnayaka at the ***Sinharaja Rest*** (☎ *041-73368, Temple Rd*). Palitha is a certified guide and very knowledgeable about the forest. His enthusiastic leadership is popular with travellers. You can stay at his home for Rs 500 a double with bathroom. It's fairly basic, but is clean and friendly, and there's loads of information on Sinharaja and good home cooking. A trip to Sinharaja with Palitha costs Rs 500 per person per day (plus the Rs 250 entry). Nonguests can take his tours too. It's possible to stay overnight at the park, but you'll need to allow for a delay of two or three days while the permits are applied for at Galle.

Deniyaya also has a ***Rest House*** (☎ *041-73600)*, which has rooms for Rs 550. The views are great; like most resthouses this place has a plum position, in this case, overlooking the town and the countryside. The large rooms are a bit rundown, but they're quaint. It's worthwhile coming for the food or a drink even if you don't stay here.

Getting There & Away
Kudawa There are buses from Ratnapura to Kalawana (Rs 40 for an express). There are buses from Colombo to Weddagala (4km before Kudawa) and there are about four buses daily from Weddagala to Kudawa. As usual, if you are coming from Colombo or Ratnapura by bus, start as early as you can.

Deniyaya There are several buses to Galle (CTB Rs 60), although you can always catch one of the more frequent buses to Akuressa (Rs 15) and change there. Many buses pass through Akuressa.

There's an intercity express bus to Colombo (Rs 130, 5½ hours); if you want a CTB bus you're better off going to Akuressa

or Pelmadulla and changing. For Ella and Nuwara Eliya you must catch a bus to Pelmadulla and change there.

For Ratnapura there are buses from 6.45 am and approximately every hour until the afternoon (CTB Rs 60).

If you have a car, the road through the Hayes tea estate north of Deniyaya, en route to Madampe and Balangoda (for Belihul Oya, Haputale or Ratnapura) is very scenic.

SOUTH OF RATNAPURA
At Pelmadulla, between Ratnapura and Haputale, a road splits off to the south, leading to the coast at Galle, Matara or Hambantota. The Galle and Matara branch goes through a southern spur of the hill (and tea) country.

Pelmadulla
Most travellers pass through this town en route north or south. The bus station is right in the centre of town. There are intercity express buses to Badulla starting at 5.45 am and running approximately every hour till about 6.30 pm. The trip takes 4½ hours and costs Rs 65. This is the bus you catch to get to places such as Haputale, Bandarawela and Ella. The Colombo to Monaragala (for Arugam Bay) bus also stops here, although it's a lot less frequent. There are intercity express buses to Colombo between 3.30 am and 8.30 pm every half hour (Rs 40). To get to Galle you must change at Deniyaya. Frequent buses run to Ratnapura (Rs 10.50).

Embilipitiya
Embilipitiya is a good base for tours to Uda Walawe National Park (it's 21km south of the ticket office). It's a small, hectic town that services the nearby rice-growing area. The bus station is in the centre of town on the main road.

Sarathchandra Rest (☎ *047-30044)* is on the main road, about 200m south of the bus station, opposite the People's Bank. It has an assortment of clean rooms: Rs 430 will get you the basics; Rs 920 and you've got hot water; and Rs 1250 for hot water and air-con. It's a friendly, well-run spot. They offer Uda Walawe tours for Rs 1500 per half day (maximum six people).

Continue about 600m south along the main road and you'll see the turn-off to *Centauria Tourist Hotel* (☎ 047-30514, fax 30104) in a rambling garden beside a lake. The rooms cost Rs 1210 or Rs 1485 for air-con. The bathrooms are a bit neglected, but they have hot water. A three-wheeler from the bus station costs Rs 50. Tours to Uda Walawe can be arranged from here: A jeep for a half-day safari costs Rs 1750.

Getting There & Away Buses leave regularly for most destinations from, or near, the bus station. There are CTB buses to Tangalla (Rs 18.50), Matara (Rs 29), and Ratnapura (Rs 22); the intercity buses cost about twice as much. Colombo intercity buses leave every half hour (Rs 105).

UDA WALAWE NATIONAL PARK
The entrance to Uda Walawe National Park, or Udawalawa, is about 12km east from the turn-off on the Ratnapura-Hambantota road, and 21km from Embilipitiya. For adults entry costs US$12 per day; students and children from six to 12 are half price (under six is free). If you select a jeep from one of the many gathered outside the gate, you can expect to pay Rs 1200 for a half day for up to eight people (see the boxed text 'Snagging the Perfect Safari Tout' in The South chapter). There's a Rs 112 charge for an 'open hood' (any excuse to fleece you), Rs 135 to take a jeep into the park, and Rs 100 for a car. You will also have to pay a US$6 'service charge' for a compulsory tracker. The park is open from 6 am, and visitors have to be out by 6.30 pm. Last tickets are usually sold at about 5 pm.

The park's 30,821 hectares include a large reservoir (the Uda Walawe Tank) which is fed by the Walawe Ganga.

Flora & Fauna
Apart from stands of teak near the river, there's little forest owing to extensive slash-and-burn farming. The tall pohon grass, which grows in place of the forest, can make wildlife-watching difficult except during dry months. In the dry weather 30km of track in the park is passable for cars.

There are about 500 elephants in the park in herds of up to 100. This is a good place to see elephants, because there's an elephant-proof fence around the perimeter of the park, preventing elephants from getting out and cattle (and humans) from getting in. The best time to see elephants is from 6.30 to 10 am and again from 4 to 6.30 pm. The best places for spotting elephants are by the river and the various streams and reservoirs.

Other creatures that call Uda Walawe home are sambar deer, wild buffaloes (their numbers have been boosted by tame buffaloes), mongooses, bandicoots, foxes, water monitor lizards, crocodiles, sloth bears and the occasional leopard. There are 30 varieties of snakes and a wealth of bird life; northern migrants join the residents between November and April.

Elephant Transit Centre
About 5km east of the Ratnapura-Hambantota road turn-off there's an Elephant Transit Centre. Heading east from the intersection, you'll pass a turn-off on your right to the Walawa Safari Village (see Places to Stay, following). Continue on towards Uda Walawe past the People's Bank until you'll see a sign to the Centre (not in English) on a turn-off to the left. It's not this road, but the previous road heading to the left – why? Who knows! Head up this road for about 500m and you'll find the centre. Orphaned and sick elephants are cared for until they are able to return safely to the park. At the time of writing there were 28 tiny elephants. The babies are fed by Forestry Department staff at 6 and 9 am, noon, and 3 and 6 pm. Unlike at the more famous elephant orphanage near Kandy, these youngsters are fed not with bottles, but through plastic hosing with funnels attached. When they're not being fed you can watch them (for free) roaming around, actually in a part of Uda Walawe. When they are being fed you'll be stung Rs 1200 for adults, half that for children.

Places to Stay
The *Walawa Safari Village* (☎ 047-33201, fax 01-591223, RB Canal Rd) is 3km south

of a small junction on the road to Uda Walawe – you'll see the sign – and 10km from the park entrance. Clean and basic singles/doubles in a garden setting cost Rs 1500/1800 including breakfast – add Rs 500 for air-con. Trips to the park from here cost a reasonable Rs 1200 per half day (up to eight people).

If you want to stay in the park there are three *bungalows* and two *camp sites* within the park. You must book ahead at the Department of Wildlife Conservation (☎ 01-694241, fax 698556), 18 Gregory's Rd, Cinnamon Gardens (Col 7). For more details, see Accommodation in the Facts for the Visitor chapter.

Getting There & Away

Most people prefer to take a tour organised by their guesthouse or hotel. While this saves stuffing about, if you are counting every rupee you can organise a 4WD from one of the drivers eagerly waiting at the gate of Uda Walawe.

If you're staying at Embilipitiya, catch a bus heading to Tanamalwila (CTB Rs 25, intercity express Rs 50) and ask to be dropped at the gate to the park.

The Ancient Cities

The ancient cities region of Sri Lanka lies north of the hill country, in one of the driest parts of the island. During the golden age of Sinhalese civilisation, the Sinhalese overcame continual harassment from invading south Indian forces to build two great cities (Anuradhapura and Polonnaruwa) and create many other magnificent reminders of the strength of their Buddhist culture, only to abandon them all. For almost a thousand years the jungle did its best to reclaim them, but major archaeological excavations over the past century have partially restored their past glory.

Apart from the 1985 Anuradhapura massacre, the civil war has not reached the main ancient city sites, though killings have sometimes come alarmingly close to Polonnaruwa. Outlying sites such as Medirigiriya or Dimbulagala may be borderline.

Kandy (see the Hill Country chapter) is a good starting point for a visit to the ancient city region.

The Sri Lankan government and the United Nations Educational, Scientific and Cultural Organisation (Unesco) are carrying out a number of restoration projects within the area of the ancient cities region known as the 'cultural triangle'. This is the area formed by the old Sinhalese capitals of Kandy, Anuradhapura and Polonnaruwa. You will need a ticket if you want to visit a site here (see the boxed text 'Cultural Triangle Tickets' for more details).

MATALE
☎ 066

This small, busy town 24km north of Kandy is encircled by hills. The town's pleasant park includes a monument to the leaders of the 1848 Matale Rebellion – one of the less-famous contributions to history's Year of Revolutions! Not far north of the bus stop for Kandy is an interesting Hindu temple, the **Sri Muthumariamman Thevasthanam**. A priest will show you the five enormous, colourful 'cars', which are

---

Highlights

- Pausing to catch your breath by the saucy frescoes as you clamber up the Sigiriya rock fortress
- Sweating up Yapahuwa's steps to compare your Rs 10 note with the lion's head
- Bicycling through the dappled shade around Polonnaruwa's ancient sites and spending time at the serene, enchanting Gal Vihara
- Counting the Buddhas at Dambulla's beautiful cave temples
- Witnessing pilgrim offerings at the sacred bodhi tree at Anuradhapura

---

ceremonial chariots that people pull along during an annual festival. You'll need to buy a ticket for Rs 25.

Matale Heritage Centre

About 2km north of Matale, the Matale Heritage Centre (☎ 22 404), at 33 Sir Richard Aluwihare Mawatha, is fostering some of the best handicraft in Sri Lanka. From small beginnings, some 110 people, mostly women, are now engaged in turning out a range of quality handicrafts, from batik to embroidery, and carpentry to brass work. The driving force behind the centre is Ena de Silva who started the venture back in 1984 as part of an attempt to foster self-employment. You can order meals at the centre's big house for groups of 10 or more by phone (but order at least two days in advance). The cost is Rs 450 per person for rice and curry plus dessert. The centre doesn't have a direct sales outlet, but you may order goods if you wish. The same people run Aluwihare Kitchens (see Places to Stay & Eat later) by the main road near the turn-off leading to the centre. A three-wheeler from Matale will cost about Rs 250 return plus waiting time, while a bus will cost Rs 3.

ANCIENT CITIES

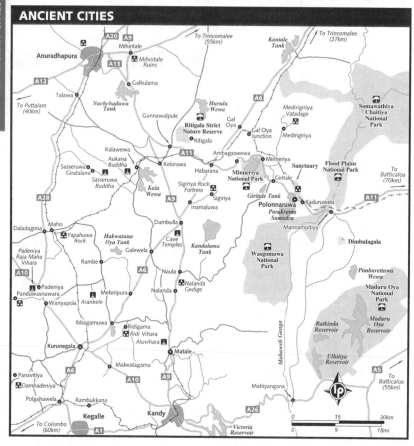

Aluvihara

The rock monastery of Aluvihara is beside the Kandy-Dambulla road, 3km north of Matale. The monastery caves are situated among rocks that have fallen from the mountains, high above the valley. It's an extremely picturesque setting. Some of the caves have fine frescoes; there are two reclining Buddha images and one cave is dedicated to Buddhagosa, the Indian Pali scholar who is supposed to have spent several years here. It is said that the doctrines of the Buddha were first recorded here, in Pali script, around the 1st century BC. The

monks today inscribe Buddhist scriptures in *ola* (palm leaf) books. You can see their workshop, in return for which you will be asked for a Rs 50 'donation'.

One of the monastic caves contains a horror chamber. Entry costs Rs 1. It's money well spent if you're considering straying from the straight and narrow – the gaudy statues of devils and sinners show the various forms of punishment handed out in the afterlife. One scene shows a sexual sinner with his skull cut open and his brains being ladled out by two demons. Another exhibit shows the gory drawing and quartering of a

Cultural Triangle Tickets

If you intend visiting sites within the Cultural Triangle, you need to buy either a round ticket that covers most of the major sites, or individual tickets at the sites themselves. Currently a round ticket costs US$32.50 (payable in the rupee equivalent) and covers the following: Anuradhapura, Polonnaruwa, Sigiriya, Ritigala, Medirigiriya and Nalanda, plus a few sites in Kandy (but *not* the Temple of the Tooth). (Dambulla is not included in the ticket and costs Rs 300 per person.) The ticket is valid for 60 days from the date of purchase, and you must start using your ticket within 14 days of purchasing it. The ticket entitles you to one day's entry only – if you wish to spend a second day at any site, you pay the full day's fee. If paid for individually, the sites cost US$15 each (Anuradhapura, Polonnaruwa, Sigiriya), US$8 (Medirigiriya) and US$5 (Ritigala, Nalanda). If you are only visiting one or two sites it isn't worth getting a round ticket. All foreign nationals and even foreigners with resident visas must pay the full amount. There are no student discounts on the round ticket, though sometimes you can get half-price individual site tickets if you sweet talk the ticket seller. Children under 12 years are charged half price, while those under six get in for free.

Round tickets can be bought at the Anuradhapura, Polonnaruwa and Nalanda ticket offices. You can also buy them at the Cultural Triangle office (☎ 08-234257), near the tourist office in Kandy, and from the Cultural Triangle Fund main office (☎ 01-500733, fax 500731) at 212/1 Bauddhaloka Mawatha, Cinnamon Gardens (Col 7) – if you can get through the security at either end of the street (bring your passport).

For details of which sites the round ticket covers in Kandy, see Information in the Kandy section of The Hill Country chapter.

prostitute. A three-wheeler from Matale will cost about Rs 280 return plus waiting time, and a bus will cost Rs 3.50.

There are many **spice gardens** and several **batik showrooms** along the road between Matale and Aluvihara. The various treats you can expect on a tour of the gardens include milkless cocoa tea sweetened with vanilla and banana, and various creams and potions claimed to make your hair shinier or to cure your flatulence. Prices at some spice garden shops can be a little on the high side, so check in a market before you set out so that you have something to compare prices with.

Places to Stay & Eat

Although *Aluwihare Kitchens* (☎ 22343, 833 Dambulla Rd) has gone overboard with the colour scheme, the rooms are clean and inviting. Rooms cost from Rs 400 to 550 (no hot water). The hosts are friendly and the food is good (rice and curry from Rs 165). You must book ahead for accommodation. You'll find it 2km north of Matale near the turn-off to the Matale Heritage Centre.

The *Rest House* (☎ 22299) has a garden setting and is south of the town centre, in between the lower and upper roads from Kandy. Clean singles/doubles (with hot water) cost Rs 675/900, or Rs 1200 for an air-con single or double. The food is cheap and OK – rice and curry costs Rs 100.

The *Clover Grange Hotel* (☎ 31144, fax 30406, 95 King St), west of the centre of town, is a gorgeous colonial house with six quaint and clean rooms with hot water for Rs 1300. The restaurant serves good food such as vegie chop suey for Rs 185 and chicken fried rice for Rs 225.

Just to the south of the Rest House (it is signposted on the main road) is the modern *Rock House* (☎ 23239, 17/16A Hulangamuwa Rd), set in a pretty garden. There are seven spotless, reasonably large rooms but considering they don't have hot water (and they're nothing special) they're a bit overpriced at Rs 1320 for a single or double.

Getting There & Away

Bus No 594 to Matale (Rs 25 by intercity express, Rs 11 by CTB) leaves from beside the central clock tower in Kandy. Dambulla or Anuradhapura buses from Kandy or Matale will drop you at Aluvihara or at the spice gardens. There are also a number of daily trains that make the journey between Matale and Kandy (Rs 6, 1½ hours).

NALANDA
☎ 066

There is an 8th-century *gedige* (temple) at Nalanda, 25km north of Matale and only 20km before Dambulla. It is a rare example of mixed Buddhist and Hindu architecture, though to some eyes it looks oddly like a Mexican Mayan temple! It has a couple of Tantric carvings with sexual subjects, but before you get too excited, be aware that the carvings are weather beaten – some people are disappointed. The entrance fee is overpriced at US$5 for foreigners, or 'free' as part of the Cultural Triangle round ticket (see the boxed text for details).

The site is beside a tank 1km east of the main road – a sign marks the turn-off near the 49km post.

Anuradhapura buses from Kandy or Matale will drop you at the turn-off to the Nalanda gedige. An intercity express bus going from Nalanda to Kandy costs Rs 80, and the CTB bus costs Rs 16.

Places to Stay & Eat
The *Rest House* (☎ 46199) is a colonial-era place set in leafy gardens, 100m north of the turn-off to the gedige. The six rooms (Rs 600) are clean enough, but the bathrooms are not for the faint-hearted.

The *Country Side Hotel* (☎/fax 46241, 📧 *countryside@nascarmail.net*) is on the main road, 3km south of the gedige. It has clean cottages dotted throughout an attractive garden, and slightly worn rooms with hot water in the main building. Rooms cost Rs 750/1000, including breakfast. The restaurant serves tasty but pricey food such as rice and curry (Rs 330) and fish and chips (Rs 320).

DAMBULLA
☎ 066

Dambulla is a barren town with little going for it except the cave temples. You can visit it as a day trip on public transport from Kandy, or travel through on your way to/from Sigiriya. The accommodation is decent though, if you do decide to stay the night.

Cave Temples
The beautiful cave temples of Dambulla are 100m to 150m above the road in the southern part of Dambulla. The hike up to the temples begins along a vast, sloping rock face (steps have been built over the steepest bits). The temples are open from 7.30 am to 7 pm. This site isn't on the Cultural Triangle round ticket so you must buy a ticket (Rs 300). The ticket office is in the building near the monstrous Buddha, and your receipt is checked at the entrance to the temples. Photography is prohibited inside the caves. There are superb views over the surrounding countryside from the level of the caves. Sigiriya, 22km away, is clearly visible to the north-east.

The caves' history is thought to date back to around the 1st century BC when King Valagambahu, driven out of Anuradhapura, took refuge here. When he regained his throne, he had the interior of the caves carved into magnificent rock temples. Later kings made further improvements, including King Nissanka Malla who had the caves' interiors gilded, earning the place the name Ran Giri (Golden Rock).

There are five separate caves containing about 150 Buddha images. As dusk draws in, hundreds of swallows swoop and dart around the cave entrance.

Cave I (Devaraja Viharaya) The first cave has a 15m-long reclining Buddha. Ananda, the Buddha's most loyal disciple, is depicted nearby. There are other seated Buddhas as well as a statue of Vishnu, for which the cave is named.

Cave II (Maharaja Vihara) This cave is arguably the most spectacular. It measures some 52m from east to west and 23m from the entrance to the back wall. The highest point of the ceiling is 7m. This cave's is named after the two statues of kings it contains. There is a painted wooden statue of Valagamba (Vattajamini Ahhaya) on the left

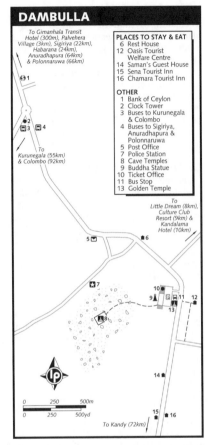

DAMBULLA

To Gimanhala Transit
Hotel (300m), Palvehera
Village (3km), Sigiriya (22km),
Habarana (24km),
Anuradhapura (64km)
& Polonnaruwa (66km)

To
Kurunegala (55km)
& Colombo (92km)

To
Little Dream (8km),
Culture Club
Resort (9km) &
Kandalama
Hotel (10km)

To Kandy (72km)

PLACES TO STAY & EAT
6 Rest House
12 Oasis Tourist
Welfare Centre
14 Saman's Guest House
15 Sena Tourist Inn
16 Chamara Tourist Inn

OTHER
1 Bank of Ceylon
2 Clock Tower
3 Buses to Kurunegala
& Colombo
4 Buses to Sigiriya,
Anuradhapura &
Polonnaruwa
5 Post Office
7 Police Station
8 Cave Temples
9 Buddha Statue
10 Ticket Office
11 Bus Stop
13 Golden Temple

0 250 500m
0 250 500yd

the 18th century by King Kirti Sri Raja-singhe of Kandy, one of the last of the Kandyan monarchs. This cave too is filled with Buddhas and frescoes.

Cave IV (Pachima Viharaya) This relatively small cave is not, as its name (which translates as 'Western Cave') suggests, the cave farthermost to the west – that label belongs to Cave V. The central Buddha figure is seated under a *makara torana*, with its hands in *dhyana mudra* (a meditative pose in which the hands are cupped). The small dagoba (Buddhist monument) in the centre was broken into by thieves who believed that it contained jewellery belonging to Queen Somawathie.

Cave V (Devana Alut Viharaya) This newer cave was once used as a storehouse, but it's now called Second New Temple. It features a reclining Buddha. Hindu deities including Kataragama and Vishnu are also present.

Places to Stay & Eat

Saman's Guest House *(☎ 84412)* has reasonably clean singles/doubles lining a central hallway for Rs 200/300. The food is very good.

Almost directly opposite the entrance to the cave temple car park is the cheap-and-cheerful ***Oasis Tourist Welfare Centre*** *(☎ 84388)*. It's hot, rough (the nets have more tears than legitimate holes) and all rooms share an OK-quality bathroom. Rooms cost Rs 250/300. Dorm beds cost Rs 100. The food is cheap too.

The ***Sena Tourist Inn*** *(☎ 84421)* has six basic rooms in a friendly family house for Rs 300/400.

The ***Little Dream*** *(☎ 072-618871)* has little going for it in terms of amenities – no hot water, no electricity – but it's a hit with some because of the laid-back, guitar-strumming hosts and the lakeside spot. There are six rooms (none with great sound insulation) for Rs 300/400. It's about 8km along the road to Culture Club Resort – a three-wheeler from town will cost Rs 150.

as you enter and another farther inside of Kirti Sri Nissankamalla. The cave's main Buddha statue, which appears to have once been covered in gold leaf, is situated under a *makara torana* (ornamental archway), with the right hand raised in *abhaya mudra*. Hindu deities are also represented. Of particular note are the brilliantly coloured frescoes depicting scenes relating to the arrival of Buddhism in Sri Lanka, meritorious deeds done by kings and great battles.

Cave III (Maha Alut Viharaya) This cave, the New Great Temple, was built in

The ***Chamara Tourist Inn*** (☎ 84488) is a relaxed place with five clean basic rooms for Rs 600/825.

The Dambulla ***Rest House*** (☎ 22299, fax 32911) has four large, clean and overpriced rooms for Rs 1100.

About 800m beyond the Colombo junction, on the north edge of town, is the good-value ***Gimanhala Transit Hotel*** (☎ 84864, fax 84817) with eight rooms with air-con at Rs 1400/1750. The staff are helpful, the food is good and there is also a swimming pool (Rs 100 for nonguests to use).

Three kilometres north of Dambulla (at Bullagala Junction) and just off the main road is a modern place, ***Palvehera Village*** (☎ 84281). Here you'll find 10 spotless, bare rooms with hot water for Rs 1850/2200, cheaper without air-con. The restaurant serves good food too – it's a nice place to stop for a bite to eat, even if you're not staying there.

For those with cash to splash, there are two top-end places several kilometres east of Dambulla. Following the Kandalama road for about 3km from Dambulla you will come to a turn-off (signposted) where you veer left for another 6km or so, via the Kandalama tank wall, to reach the ***Culture Club Resort*** (☎ 31822, fax 31932, ℮ cdchm@eureka.lk). There is another turn-off to this place farther north, on the main road nearer Sigiriya, which is 4km from the club, but the road is in poor condition. At the resort you will find a huge, airy complex consisting of air-con bungalows set in beautiful gardens. Stylish single or double rooms cost US$95 and the facilities include a swimming pool, two restaurants, an Ayurvedic health centre and, just what you need, a palm reader. The hotel will arrange transport to wherever you want to go; the return trip by van to Dambulla costs Rs 750.

If you continue along the Kandalama road another couple of kilometres past the turn-off to the Culture Club Resort and turn left onto an unpaved road (it's signposted), you'll eventually come to the ***Kandalama Hotel*** (☎ 84100, fax 84109, ℮ ashmeres@aitkenspence.lk). The hotel

overlooks the Kandalama Tank. If you're interested in modern architecture, this place will set your heart racing. It's a huge establishment – 1km from end to end, with 162 air-con rooms – but the design beautifully complements the landscape thanks to the vision of Geoffrey Bawa, Sri Lanka's best-known architect. It's primarily a luxury nature retreat and rooms with all the mod cons start at US$68/93. Once again, transport to anywhere can be arranged from the hotel.

Getting There & Away

Dambulla is 72km north of Kandy on the road to Anuradhapura. The Colombo-to-Trincomalee road meets this road 2km north of the cave temple, then splits off from it a couple of kilometres farther north, leading also to Sigiriya and Polonnaruwa. Because Dambulla is on so many major routes, plenty of buses pass through it with varying frequency. However, the nearest train station is at Habarana, 24km to the north.

It takes 1½ hours to get to Polonnaruwa (Rs 18, 66km), two hours to get to Anuradhapura (Rs 20, 64km), and two hours to get to Kandy (Rs 30). There are buses to Sigiriya (Rs 10, 40 minutes) roughly on the hour from 7 am, but less often in the afternoon. Beware of touts, who will tell you otherwise in order to get you into a three-wheeler. It takes four hours to get to Colombo (Rs 50 for the CTB bus, and Rs 120 for the intercity express).

You can flag buses plying this busy route to go between the two parts of Dambulla, or a three-wheeler should cost Rs 20.

SIGIRIYA
☎ 066

The spectacular rock fortress of Sigiriya (pronounced See-gir-iya), 22km north-east of Dambulla, is among Sri Lanka's major attractions. In AD 473 King Dhatusena of Anuradhapura was overthrown and, so one legend goes, walled-in alive by Kasyapa, his son by a palace consort. Moggallana, Dhatusena's son by his true queen, fled to India swearing revenge, so Kasyapa, fearing an invasion, decided to build an impregnable fortress on the huge rock of Sigiriya. When the long-expected invasion finally came in 491, Kasyapa didn't just skulk in his stronghold, but rode out at the head of his army on an elephant. Attempting to out-flank his half-brother, Kasyapa took a wrong turn and became bogged in a swamp. He was deserted by his troops and took his own life.

Sigiriya later became a monastic refuge but eventually fell into disrepair, and was only rediscovered by archaeologists during the British colonial era. To describe Sigiriya as merely a fortress does it no justice. Atop the 200m-high rock (377m above sea level) Kasyapa built a wet-season palace – a kind of 5th-century penthouse. It is hard to imagine Sigiriya at the height of its glory, but it must have been something akin to a European chateau plonked on top of Australia's Uluru (Ayers Rock)!

If you would like to find out more about Sigiriya, including the many points of inter-est on the route up the rock, try to find a copy of the booklet by RH de Silva called *Sigiriya*, published by the Department of Archaeology in Colombo (1976).

Tickets are sold at the entrance between 7.30 am and 6 pm for US$15 for adults and half-price for children between six and 12. Cultural Triangle round tickets are not sold here, but entry is free if you already have one. You can also buy tickets from the Rest House in the village (see Places to Stay). Dozens of hopeful guides hang around the entrances to the site; most expect to get about Rs 350 for the trip up and down the rock. However, on a relatively busy day – or at least when there are two or more groups visiting – a guide is hardly necessary as the commentaries given to the tour groups are generally audible.

An early or late ascent of the rock avoids the main crowds and the fierce midday heat. Allow at least two hours for the return trip, more on very busy days. Bring plenty

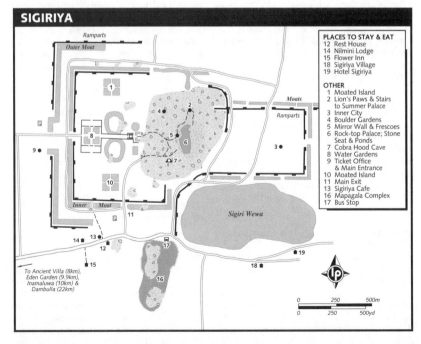

SIGIRIYA

PLACES TO STAY & EAT
12 Rest House
14 Nilmini Lodge
15 Flower Inn
18 Sigiriya Village
19 Hotel Sigiriya

OTHER
1 Moated Island
2 Lion's Paws & Stairs to Summer Palace
3 Inner City
4 Boulder Gardens
5 Mirror Wall & Frescoes
6 Rock-top Palace; Stone Seat & Ponds
7 Cobra Hood Cave
8 Water Gardens
9 Ticket Office & Main Entrance
10 Moated Island
11 Main Exit
13 Sigiriya Cafe
16 Mapagala Complex
17 Bus Stop

Ramparts
Outer Moat
Moats
Ramparts
Inner Moat
Sigiri Wewa

To Ancient Villa (8km), Eden Garden (9.9km), Inamaluwa (10km) & Dambulla (22km)

0   250   500m
0   250   500yd

of water with you and wear a hat (as it's often too windy near the summit to carry an umbrella). Drinks are available at stalls near the lion's paws, but they cost about twice the usual amount.

Sigiriya is a pleasant, leafy village teeming with wildlife. Once the sun sets it does become very dark – if you want to explore at night you'll need a torch (flashlight). And behind the sleepy facade lies a bunch of bored touts – at night women may not feel comfortable wandering about, and even during the day these chaps can be annoying.

Water Gardens

The usual approach to the rock is through the western (and most elaborate) gate. This takes you through Kasyapa's beautiful water gardens, which extend from the western foot of the rock with royal bathing pools, little moated islands with pavilions that acted as dry-season palaces, and trees framing the approach to the rock. The rock rises sheer and mysterious from the jungle. A switchback series of steps leads up through the boulders at its foot to the western face, then ascends it steeply.

Cobra Hood Cave

This rocky projection earned its name because the overhang resembles a fully opened cobra's hood. Generally you will pass by this cave after descending the rock on your way to the south gate and the car park. Below the drip ledge is a 2nd-century-BC inscription that indicates it belonged to Chief Naguli, who would have donated it to a monk. The plastered interior of the cave was once embellished with floral and animal paintings.

Frescoes – The Sigiriya Damsels

About half way up the rock there is a modern spiral stairway that leads up from the main route to a long, sheltered gallery in the sheer rock face.

In this niche there is a series of paintings of beautiful women, which is similar in style to the rock paintings at Ajanta in India. These 5th-century pin-ups are the only non-religious old paintings to be seen in Sri Lanka. Although there may have been as many as 500 portraits at one time, only 22 remain today – several were badly damaged by a vandal in 1967. Today security is quite tight on the approach to this section of the rock. Protected from the sun in the sheltered gallery, the paintings remain in remarkably good condition, their colours still glowing. They're at their best in the late afternoon light. You are not allowed to use flash photography at this site.

Mirror Wall with Graffiti

Beyond the fresco gallery the pathway clings to the sheer side of the rock and is protected on the outside by a 3m-high wall.

This wall was coated with a mirror-smooth glaze upon which visitors of a thousand years ago felt impelled to note their impressions of the women in the gallery above. The graffiti were inscribed principally between the 7th and 11th centuries, and 685 of them have been deciphered and published in a two volume edition, *Sigiri Graffiti*, by Dr S Paranavitana (Oxford University Press, 1956). They are of great interest to scholars for their evidence of the development of the Sinhalese language and script.

One typical graffito reads:

The ladies who wear golden chains on their breasts beckon me. As I have seen the resplendent ladies, heaven appears to me as not good.

Another, by a female scribbler, reads:

A deer-eyed young woman of the mountain side arouses anger in my mind. In her hand she had taken a string of pearls and in her looks she has assumed rivalry with us.

Lion's Paws

At the northern end of the rock the narrow pathway emerges on to the large platform from which the rock derives its name – the lion rock, Sigiriya. In 1898 HCP Bell, the British archaeologist responsible for an enormous amount of discovery in Sri Lanka, found two enormous lion paws when excavating here. At one time a gigantic brick lion sat at this end of the rock and the final ascent to the top commenced with a stairway which led between the lion's paws and into its mouth!

The lion has since disappeared, apart from the first steps and the paws. To reach the top means clambering up across a series of grooves cut into the rock face. Fortunately there is a stout metal handrail, but vertigo sufferers are strongly advised not to look down.

The Summit

The top of the rock covers 1.6 hectares, and at one time must have been completely covered with buildings, only the foundations of which remain today. The design of this rock-top palace, and the magnificent views it commands even today, make one think that Sigiriya must have been much more of a palace than fortress. A pond scooped out of the solid rock measures 27m by 21m. It looks for all the world like a modern swimming pool, although it may have been used merely for water storage.

A smooth slab of flat stone, often referred to as the king's stone throne, faces the rising sun. You can sit here and gaze across the surrounding jungle as Kasyapa probably did over 1500 years ago.

Mapagala Complex

There is evidence these large rocks, located to the south of the fortress, were once part of Sigiriya's outer defensive network.

Places to Stay & Eat

There are two guesthouses virtually opposite one another just before you reach the resthouse. The *Nilmini Lodge* (☎ 33313) has a couple of rooms with private bathroom (Rs 400), and a couple with shared bathroom (Rs 350). The rooms are a bit grubby, but the family is friendly and the food good. Rice and curry costs Rs 225. The *Flower Inn*, on the same side as the resthouse and down a path, is run by such a friendly family with such a pretty garden that you can excuse the bland cooking and the dodgy ceiling in one of the three

rooms. The quaint rooms cost from Rs 450 to 600.

The *Rest House* (☎/fax 31899) has an unbeatable location about 400m from the side of the rock. There are 17 big, clean rooms for US$33 a single or double, add US$8.50 for air-con. As this place is particularly popular, you should book in advance. There's a large, airy restaurant with friendly, but slow service. You can buy tickets to the rock here.

If you don't mind staying a little farther away from the entrance, there are two places near the junction of the road leading to Sigiriya village. A popular place at Galakotuwa, 2km from the junction, is *Ancient Villa* (☎ 85322). There are three clean cabanas and two bungalows in a roomy, grassed setting for Rs 670/770 for a single/double. Meals are available (breakfast costs Rs 100). It's a quiet spot that's good for nature lovers. There are buses to the village for Rs 4 or you can catch a three-wheeler (Rs 125).

Eden Garden (☎/fax 84635) is 100m from the junction, at Inamaluwa. Despite the ugly facade, this is a good spot – large, clean rooms overlook a well-kept garden and cost Rs 1500/1750 (add Rs 500 for air-con). There's also a pool. You can easily get to the rock by three-wheeler (Rs 150) or by bus (Rs 5).

Sigiriya's two upper-bracket hotels are close together about 1km beyond the resthouse, separated only by their extensive gardens. The first you reach is *Sigiriya Village* (☎/fax 31803, ⓔ sales.svhl@lanka .ccom.lk); the second is *Hotel Sigiriya* (☎/fax 84811, ⓔ serendib@serendib.lanka .net). Both are modern and fairly well designed. The Hotel Sigiriya has splendid views of the rock from its dining room and pool, while at the Sigiriya Village the rooms and grounds are a bit bigger, and the layout is a bit airier. Rooms at the Village are US$67 a night (there is a US$12 air-con supplement) and at the Hotel US$49/55 (plus a US$12 air-conditioning supplement). Both hotels have good breakfast, lunch and dinner buffets for about Rs 375, Rs 400 and Rs 550, respectively.

Getting There & Away

Sigiriya is about 10km east of the main road between Dambulla and Habarana. The turn-off is at Inamaluwa. There are buses from Dambulla about hourly in the morning from 7 am (Rs 10, 40 minutes), but they are less often in the afternoon. The last bus back to Dambulla leaves at 6.30 pm (but double check this). There's a direct CTB bus to Sigiriya from Kandy (Goods Shed bus station) at 8 am that returns at noon (Rs 32 one way, three hours). The paved road does not continue beyond Sigiriya, so if you want to head north you'll have to go to the junction and catch one of the many buses plying the main highway, or change at Dambulla.

POLONNARUWA

☎ 027

It was the south Indian Chola dynasty that first made its capital at Polonnaruwa, after conquering Anuradhapura in the late 10th century AD. Polonnaruwa was a more strategic place to guard against any rebellion from the Ruhunu Sinhalese kingdom in the south-east. It also, apparently, had fewer mosquitoes! When Vijayabahu I, the Sinhalese king, drove the Cholas off the island in 1070, he kept Polonnaruwa as his capital.

King Parakramabahu I (r. 1153–86) raised Polonnaruwa to its heights, erecting huge buildings, planning beautiful parks and, as a crowning achievement, creating a 2400 hectare tank – so large that it was named the Parakrama Samudra (Sea of Parakrama). The present lake incorporates three older tanks, so it may not be the actual tank he created.

Parakramabahu I was followed by King Nissanka Malla (r. 1187–96), who succeeded in virtually bankrupting the kingdom through his attempts to match his predecessors' achievements. By the early 13th century, Polonnaruwa was beginning to prove as susceptible to Indian invasion as Anuradhapura, and despite another century of efforts to stand strong, eventually it too was abandoned and the Sinhalese capital shifted to the west of the island.

Polonnaruwa is situated 140km north-east of Kandy and 104km south-east of Anuradhapura. Although nearly 1000 years old, it is much younger than Anuradhapura and generally in much better repair. Furthermore, its monuments are arranged in a reasonably compact garden setting and their development is easier to follow. All in all, if you're something less than a professional archaeologist you'll probably find Polonnaruwa the easier of the two ancient capitals to appreciate. Going by bicycle is the best way to explore it and you can rent one at several places in the town.

Orientation

Polonnaruwa has both an old town and a spread-out new town to its south. The main areas of ruins start on the northern edge of the old town and spread north. Accommodation is mostly in and around the old town. The main bus and train stations are in neither the old town nor the new town but in Kaduruwela, a few kilometres east of the old town on the Batticaloa road. However, buses from anywhere except the east go through the old town on their way in, so you can get off there anyway.

The ruins at Polonnaruwa can be conveniently divided into five groups: a small group near the Rest House on the banks of the tank; the royal palace group to the east of the Rest House; a very compact group a short distance north of the royal palace group, usually known as the quadrangle; a number of structures spread over a wide area farther north – the northern group; and a small group far to the south towards the new town – the southern group. There are also a few scattered ruins outside these groups.

Information

There's an information counter (☎ 24850) at the museum, near the Rest House. It's open from 7.30 am to 6 pm daily. You can get maps and brochures here and buy tickets to the site; the entry charge for non-Sri Lankans is US$15. Officially the site closes at 6 pm, but in practice you can stay till dark. Tickets are not checked at the

POLONNARUWA

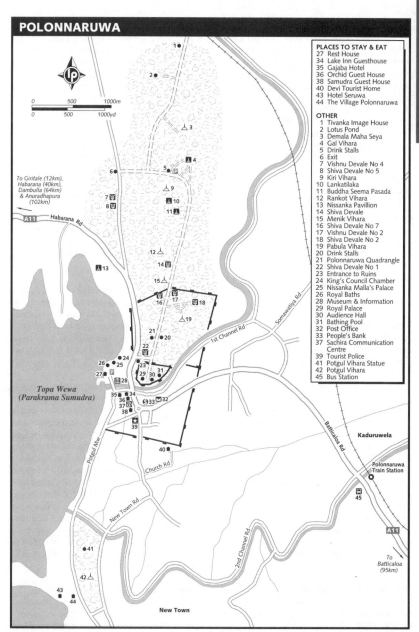

0   500   1000m
0   500   1000yd

To Giritale (12km),
Habarana (40km),
Dambulla (64km)
& Anuradhapura
(102km)

A11   Habarana Rd

Topa Wewa
(Parakrama Sumudra)

Somawathiya Rd

1st Channel Rd

Potgul Mw

Church Rd

New Town Rd

2nd Channel Rd

Batticaloa Rd

Kaduruwela

Polonnaruwa
Train Station

45

A11

To
Batticaloa
(95km)

New Town

PLACES TO STAY & EAT
27 Rest House
34 Lake Inn Guesthouse
35 Gajaba Hotel
36 Orchid Guest House
38 Samudra Guest House
40 Devi Tourist Home
43 Hotel Seruwa
44 The Village Polonnaruwa

OTHER
1   Tivanka Image House
2   Lotus Pond
3   Demala Maha Seya
4   Gal Vihara
5   Drink Stalls
6   Exit
7   Vishnu Devale No 4
8   Shiva Devale No 5
9   Kiri Vihara
10 Lankatilaka
11 Buddha Seema Pasada
12 Rankot Vihara
13 Nissanka Pavillion
14 Shiva Devale
15 Menik Vihara
16 Shiva Devale No 7
17 Vishnu Devale No 2
18 Shiva Devale No 2
19 Pabula Vihara
20 Drink Stalls
21 Polonnaruwa Quadrangle
22 Shiva Devale No 1
23 Entrance to Ruins
24 King's Council Chamber
25 Nissanka Malla's Palace
26 Royal Baths
28 Museum & Information
29 Royal Palace
30 Audience Hall
31 Bathing Pool
32 Post Office
33 People's Bank
37 Sachira Communication
    Centre
39 Tourist Police
41 Potgul Vihara Statue
42 Potgul Vihara
45 Bus Station

Rest House group or at the southern group, but the other three groups are within a single big enclosure and you have to enter at the official entrance on Habarana Rd, just north of the Royal Palace. You are supposed to proceed through the site one way; backtracking will invariably mean more ticket checking. Although the ticket technically only allows you one entrance, if you ask a ticket collector he/she will sign and date your ticket so you can enter again. This way you could visit the site in the morning, take a break over midday to avoid the heat, and head back to the site in the late afternoon.

Solo women should exercise a little caution when wandering around some of the more remote ruins.

The post office and People's Bank are in the centre of the old town along Habarana Rd. You can use IDD and Internet facilities at Sachira Communication Centre at 70/B Habarana Rd. It's open from 8 am to 9.30 pm daily.

Rest House Group

A delightful place for a post-sightseeing drink is the Rest House, situated on a small promontory jutting out into the Topa Wewa. Concentrated a few steps to the north of the resthouse are the ruins of the royal palace of Nissanka Malla, which aren't in anywhere near the same state of preservation as the Parakramabahu or royal palace group.

The royal baths are nearest the Rest House. Farthest north is the King's Council Chamber, where the king's throne, in the shape of a stone lion, once stood. It is now in the Colombo Museum. Inscribed into each column in the chamber is the name of the minister whose seat was once beside it. The mound nearby becomes an island when the waters of the tank are high; on it are the ruins of a small summer house used by the king.

Royal Palace Group

This group of buildings dates from the reign of Parakramabahu I. There are three main things to see.

Royal Palace Parakramabahu's palace was a magnificent structure measuring 31m by 13m, and is said to have had seven storeys. The 3m-thick walls have holes to receive the floor beams for two higher floors, but if there were another four levels, these must have been made of wood. The roof in this main hall, which had 50 rooms in all, was supported by 30 columns.

Audience Hall The pavilion used as an audience hall by Parakramabahu is notable for the frieze of elephants around its base. Every elephant is in a different position. There are fine lions at the top of the steps.

Bathing Pool In the south-east corner of the palace grounds the Kumara Pokuna, or Prince's Bathing Pool, still has two of its crocodile-mouth spouts remaining.

Quadrangle

Only a short stroll north of the Royal Palace ruins, the area known as the Quadrangle is literally that – a compact group of fascinating ruins in a raised-up area bounded by a wall. It's the most concentrated collection of buildings you'll find in the Sri Lankan ancient cities.

Vatadage In the south-east of the quadrangle, the *vatadage*, or circular relic house, is typical of its kind. Its outermost terrace is 18m in diameter and the second terrace has four entrances flanked by particularly fine guardstones. The moonstone at the northern entrance is reckoned to be the finest in Polonnaruwa, although not of the same standard as some of the best at Anuradhapura. The four entrances lead to the central dagoba with its four seated Buddhas. The stone screen is thought to be a later addition to the vatadage, probably by Nissanka Malla. The new museum has a wonderful model, made to scale, of this building as it probably looked in its heyday.

Thuparama At the southern end of the quadrangle, the Thuparama is a gedige, an architectural style which reached its perfection at Polonnaruwa. This is the smallest

POLONNARUWA QUADRANGLE

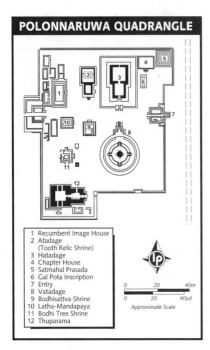

1 Recumbent Image House
2 Atadage
   (Tooth Relic Shrine)
3 Hatadage
4 Chapter House
5 Satmahal Prasada
6 Gal Pota Inscription
7 Entry
8 Vatadage
9 Bodhisattva Shrine
10 Latha-Mandapaya
11 Bodhi Tree Shrine
12 Thuparama

0   20   40m
0   20   40yd
Approximate Scale

gedige in Polonnaruwa but also one of the best, and the only one with its roof intact. The building shows strong Hindu influence and is thought to date from the reign of Parakramabahu I. There are several Buddha images in the inner chamber.

Gal Pota The 'Stone Book', immediately east of the Hatadage (see below) is a colossal stone representation of an ola book. It measures nearly 9m long by 1.5m wide, and from 40cm to 66cm thick. The inscription on it, the longest such stone inscription (of which there are many!) in Sri Lanka, indicates that it was a Nissanka Malla production. Much of it extols his virtues as a king but it also includes the footnote that the slab, weighing 25 tonnes, was dragged from Mihintale, nearly 100km away!

Hatadage Also erected by Nissanka Malla, this tooth-relic chamber is said to have been built in 60 days.

Latha-Mandapaya The busy Nissanka Malla was also responsible for this unique structure, which consists of a latticed stone fence – a curious imitation of a wooden fence with posts and railings – that surrounds a very small dagoba with stone pillars around it. The pillars are shaped like lotus stalks, topped by unopened buds. It is said that Nissanka Malla sat within this enclosure to listen to chanted Buddhist texts.

Satmahal Prasada This curious building, about which very little is known, has apparent Cambodian influence in its design. The construction consists of six diminishing storeys (there used to be seven) like a stepped pyramid.

Atadage This tooth-relic temple is the only surviving structure in Polonnaruwa dating from the reign of Vijayabahu I. Like the Hatadage, it once had an wooden upper storey.

Close to the Quadrangle

Continuing along the road leading north from the quadrangle, a gravel road branches off to the right, just before you reach the city wall. Most of the following structures are on this road.

Shiva Devale No 1 Immediately south of the quadrangle, this 13th-century Hindu temple indicates the Indian influence that returned after Polonnaruwa's Sinhalese florescence. It is notable for the superb quality of its stonework, which fits together with unusual precision. The domed brick roof has collapsed, but when this building was being excavated a number of excellent bronzes, now in the Polonnaruwa museum, were discovered.

Shiva Devale No 2 Similar in style to Shiva Devale No 1, this is the oldest structure in Polonnaruwa and dates from the brief Chola period when the Indian invaders established the city. Unlike so many buildings in the ancient cities, it was built entirely of stone, so the structure today is seen much as it was when built.

Pabula Vihara This vihara, also known as the Parakramabahu Vihara, is a typical dagoba from the period of Parakramabahu (r. 1153–86). It is the third-largest dagoba in Polonnaruwa.

Northern Group

You will need a bicycle or other transport to comfortably explore these very spread-out ruins, which are all north of the city wall. They include the Gal Vihara, probably the most famous group of Buddha images in Sri Lanka, and the Alahana Pirivena monastic group, which is the subject of a Cultural Triangle restoration project. The Alahana Pirivena group consists of the Rankot Vihara, Lankatilaka, Kiri Vihara, Buddha Seema Pasada and other structures around them. The name of the group means 'crematory college', since it stood in the royal cremation grounds established by Parakramabahu.

Rankot Vihara After the three great dagobas at Anuradhapura this is the next biggest in Sri Lanka. There is an inscription nearby that states that Nissanka Malla watched the workmen as they constructed the dagoba. The building is in clear imitation of the Anuradhapura style, and stands 55m high. Surgical instruments found in a nearby ruined 12th-century hospital are said to be similar to those used today.

Buddha Seema Pasada This is the highest building in the Alahana Pirivena group, and it was the monastery abbot's convocation hall. This building also features a fine *mandapaya* (raised platform with decorative pillars).

Lankatilaka Built by Parakramabahu, and later restored by Vijayabahu IV, this huge gedige has 17m-high walls, although the roof has collapsed. The cathedral-like aisle leads to a huge standing Buddha, which is now headless. The outer walls of the gedige, decorated with bas-reliefs, show typical Polonnaruwa structures in their original state.

KELLI HAMBLET

Moonstones are a striking feature of many temples in Sri Lanka's ancient cities region. The animals, plants and other motifs depicted in the elaborately carved semicircular rings all have symbolic meaning.

Kiri Vihara The building of this dagoba is credited to Subhadra, Parakramabahu's queen. Originally known as the Rupavati Cetiya, the present name means 'milk-white' because, when the overgrown jungle was cleared away after 700 years of neglect, the original lime plaster was found to be still in perfect condition.

Gal Vihara Near the Kiri Vihara you come to a group of Buddha images that probably mark the high point of Sinhalese rock carving. They are part of Parakramabahu's northern monastery. The Gal Vihara consists of four separate images, all cut from one long slab of granite. At one time each was enshrined within a separate enclosure. You can clearly see the sockets cut into the rock behind the standing image, into which wooden beams would have been inserted.

The standing Buddha is 7m tall and is said to be the finest of the series. The unusual position of the arms and sorrowful facial expression led to the theory that it was an image of the Buddha's disciple Ananda, grieving for his master's departure for nirvana, since the reclining image is next to it. The fact that it had its own separate enclosure, and the later discovery of other images with the same arm position, has discredited this theory and it is now accepted that all the images are of the Buddha.

The great reclining image of the Buddha entering nirvana is 14m long and the beautiful grain of the stone of the image's face is to many people the most impressive part of the Gal Vihara group. Notice also the subtle depression in the pillow under the head and the sun-wheel symbol on the pillow end. The other two images are both of the seated Buddha. The one in the small rock cavity is smaller and of inferior quality.

Demala Maha Seya Not far north of the Gal Vihara is the (unsigned) huge Demala Maha Seya, which looks like a flat-topped hill but is in fact an unfinished attempt by Parakramabahu I to build the world's biggest dagoba. It was largely overgrown but has now come in for some Cultural Triangle restoration work.

Lotus Pond A track to the left from the northern stretch of road leads to the unusual Lotus Bath, nearly 8m in diameter. You can descend into the empty pool by stepping down five concentric rings of eight petals each.

Tivanka Image House The northern road ends at this image house which, with the lotus pond, is one of the few surviving structures of the Jetavanarama monastery. Its name means 'thrice bent', and refers to the fact that the Buddha image within is in a three-curved position normally reserved for female statues, as opposed to the more upright male form. The building is notable for the carvings of energetic dwarfs cavorting around the outside and for the fine frescoes within. Some of these date from a later attempt by Parakramabahu III to restore Polonnaruwa, but others are much older.

Southern Group

The small southern group is close to the compound of top-end hotels. By bicycle it's a pleasant ride along the *bund* (dyke) of the Topa Wewa.

Potgul Vihara Also known as the library dagoba, this unusual structure is a thick-walled, hollow, stupa-like building that may have been used to store books. It's effectively a circular gedige, and four smaller solid dagobas arranged around this central dome form the popular Sinhalese quincunx arrangement of five objects in the shape of a rectangle – one at each corner and one in the middle.

Statue The most interesting other structure in the southern group is the statue at the northern end. Standing nearly 4m high, it's an unusually lifelike human representation, in contrast to the normally idealised or stylised Buddha figures. Exactly whom it represents is a subject of some controversy. Some say that the object he is holding is a book and thus the statue is of Agastaya, the Indian religious teacher. The more popular theory is that it is a yoke representing the 'yoke of kingship' and that the bearded, stately figure is Parakramabahu I. The irreverent joke is that what the king is really holding is a piece of papaya. There is a similar statuette in the museum at Panduwasnuwara (see that section later in this chapter).

Museum The museum near the Rest House is first class. It's designed so you walk from one end to the other, passing through a series of rooms, each dedicated to a particular theme: the citadel; the outer city (the monastery area and the periphery); and Hindu monuments. The latter room contains a wonderful selection of bronzes. Of particular interest are the scale models of buildings, including the vatadage, which show how these places may have looked in their heyday, complete with roofs. To enter you'll need a current round ticket or a one-day ticket to the site (you can buy one-day tickets at this museum). The museum is open from 7.30 am to 6 pm daily. It's worth visiting before you head out to the site. The information desk can provide regional and local information.

Places to Stay & Eat

Just off the main road in the old town the *Lake Inn Guesthouse* (☎ 22321) has basic, clean, but dim rooms for Rs 150/300 a single or double. The friendly owners also have a restaurant next door with cheap and delicious food (rice and curry costs Rs 55), which you'll enjoy as long as you don't peek in the kitchen.

Samudra Guest House (☎ 22817, fax 25126) has some clean and some grotty rooms costing Rs 220 for singles, and Rs 275 to Rs 380 for doubles. The hosts are friendly and there's a pretty garden out the back.

For the desperate, the *Orchid Guest House* (☎ 25253) nearby has six bland but clean-enough rooms for Rs 275 for singles and Rs 330 to 380 for doubles.

The *Devi Tourist Home* (☎ 23181) at Lake View Watte, is about 1km south of the old town centre and down Church Rd (there's a 'Devi Tourist House' sign on the main road). The friendly owner is one of Sri Lanka's small Malay population. He has four clean rooms for Rs 440 to 660. Breakfast is

Rs 105 and dinner Rs 175 to 250. Bicycles are available for rental for Rs 100 per day, and a laundry service is available.

In the old town at Kuruppu, beside the tank, is the friendly and good *Gajaba Hotel* (☎ 22394, fax 24592). There's a lovely leafy garden and 23 clean rooms (including two rooms with air-con and hot water for Rs 1225). Singles cost from Rs 612 (with shared bathroom) to 750, and doubles are Rs 735 to 850. There's also a restaurant with tasty food – rice and meat curry costs Rs 300. You can also hire bicycles here for Rs 150 per day.

On a promontory by the tank and just a short distance from the heart of the ancient city is the *Rest House* (☎ 22299), with superb views over the waters. There's a fine terrace overlooking the lake where you can sip tea or a cool drink. The rooms, with hot water, are large and well enough kept, and cost US$33 for singles or doubles – add US$8.50 for air-con. Book ahead. There is a bar and a restaurant with tasty food (dinners cost around US$7 to US$9).

Finally, there are two government-built, air-con tourist hotels in a lakeside compound just over 2km south of the old town. *The Village Polonnaruwa* (☎ 22405, fax 25100) has average rooms around a central courtyard and clean, OK-quality rooms in ugly 1970s brick bungalows. The rooms cost Rs 1600 (no hot water) and the bungalows cost Rs 2000 with air-con and hot water. Nonguests may use the tiny pool if they purchase a drink or a meal.

The *Hotel Seruwa* (☎ 22411, fax 22412), run by the Ceylon Hotels Corporation, has plain, clean rooms with balconies or terraces overlooking the lake. All rooms have hot water. A single or double costs Rs 2000, or Rs 2675 with air-con. Nonguests may use the pool for Rs 75.

Getting There & Away

Bus Polonnaruwa's main bus station is actually in Kaduruwela, a few kilometres east of the old town on the Batticaloa road. Buses to and from the west pass through the old town centre, but if you're leaving Polonnaruwa and want to make sure of a seat, it's best to start off at Kaduruwela (see Getting Around below for transport to Kaduruwela).

CTB buses start at 5 am and run about every half hour to Kandy (Rs 39). The first air-con bus to Kandy leaves at 6 am and the last at 4.30 pm (Rs 80). The route is via Dambulla and Kandy, and the trip takes four hours. There are other buses just to Dambulla (Rs 8). CTB buses for Anuradhapura leave at 5, 7, 8 and 8.45 am and then approximately every 45 minutes (Rs 30, three hours) until 2.45 pm. There are no air-con buses. Alternatively for Anuradhapura, you can go to Habarana and pick up another bus there, but a lot of people do this and seats are rare if you board a through-bus at Habarana.

There are CTB buses to Colombo (Rs 55, six hours) from around 1 am and going every 45 minutes until 7.30 pm. The private intercity air-con buses (Rs 120) leave from near the train station at 5 am and run on the half-hour until 7 pm.

Train Polonnaruwa is on the Colombo to Batticaloa railway line, and is about 30km south-east of Gal Oya, where the line splits from the Colombo to Trincomalee line. The train station is at Kaduruwela near the bus station. Trains from Polonnaruwa to Colombo (six to nine hours) depart at 7.25 and 10.50 am, and at 7.30 pm. Tickets cost Rs 73.50 in a 3rd-class sleeper (Rs 53.50 for a seat) and Rs 172 in a 2nd-class sleeper (Rs 147 for a 2nd-class seat only). To get to Trincomalee, catch the 10.50 am train and then change at Gal Oya (which you should reach at about 11.55 am). To get to Kandy catch a Colombo train and then change at Polgahawela.

Getting Around
There are frequent buses (Rs 3) between the old town and Kaduruwela, where the bus and train stations are located. A three-wheeler from the bus station to the old town will cost you Rs 100.

Bicycles are the ideal transport for getting around Polonnaruwa's not-too-widely scattered monuments, which, as an added

bonus are surrounded by shady woodland. Bicycles with gears can be hired for about Rs 200 a day from a couple of places in the town's main street. Before you rent though, check the brakes and the tyres, ensure the lock works, and, if you have a bag, check there is a carrier in working order. Some guesthouses also hire bicycles (usually gearless) for Rs 100 to 150 a day.

A car and driver can be hired for about three hours for around Rs 500, which is long enough to have a quick look around the ruins.

DIMBULAGALA
Off the Polonnaruwa-to-Batticaloa road, about 8km south of Mannampitiya, a rock called Dimbulagala or **Gunners Quoin** stands out of the surrounding scrub. There are hundreds of caves cut out of the rock in a Buddhist hermitage that has been occupied almost continuously since the 3rd century BC. Check the security situation before venturing here.

GIRITALE
☎ 027
If you're travelling by car, Giritale, 12km north-west of Polonnaruwa on the Habarana road, is the type of place you shouldn't plan to come to on your honeymoon, but it's an OK base for visiting Polonnaruwa and possibly other places in the region including the Minneriya National Park (see that section later in this chapter).

Places to Stay & Eat
There are two cheapies on the busy Polonnaruwa road. The *Woodside Tour Inn (☎ 46 307)* has a pretty garden setting. Its eight dark but clean enough singles and doubles cost Rs 330/660. The *Hotel Hemalee (☎ 46 257)* has an inflated view of itself if it thinks its clean, bare rooms are worth Rs 550/770 – try bargaining.

Flashier options overlook the Giritale tank. The *Giritale Hotel (☎ 46311, fax 46086)* has 34 plain air-con rooms and eight luxury singles/doubles from US$39/43. There is a swimming pool and restaurant with great views.

The ugly 1970s monster *The Royal Lotus Hotel (☎/fax 46316)* has air-con rooms for US$45/50. Once again there's a pool and restaurant, but here each bedroom has great views.

A few steps up in the posh stakes, *The Deer Park Hotel (☎/fax 46470)* has luxury cottages and four 'presidential suites'. Rooms cost from US$67/80. The grounds are lovely and there's a pool, but none of the rooms have views. There is also a herbal healthcare centre (a body massage costs Rs 1000).

MEDIRIGIRIYA

Near Medirigiriya, about 30km north of Polonnaruwa, is the **Mandalagiri Vihara**, a vatadage virtually identical in design and measurement to the one at Polonnaruwa. Whereas the Polonnaruwa vatadage is crowded among many other structures, the Mandalagiri Vihara stands by itself on top of a low hill. Note, however, that some who have gone to the effort to get out here have found it disappointing, so don't come here expecting too much.

An earlier structure may have been built around the 2nd century AD, but the one that stands here today was constructed in the 8th century. A granite flight of steps leads up the hill to the vatadage, which has concentric circles of 16, 20 and 32 pillars around the central dagoba. Four large, seated Buddhas face the four cardinal directions. This vatadage is noted for its fine ornamented stone screens. There was once a hospital next to the vatadage – look for the medicine bath shaped like the bottom half of a coffin. People added herbs to the bath water if they were sick.

This site is on the round ticket, so someone will materialise to check your ticket. If you don't have a round ticket you'll have to buy a ticket (US$8) from the museum in Polonnaruwa *before* you come. Tickets are *not* sold at the site. Check the security situation before venturing here.

Mandalagiri Vihara is best visited as a day trip. There are no places to stay or eat here, nor are there any worth mentioning in nearby Medirigiriya.

Getting There & Away

Without your own transport, getting to Medirigiriya is time consuming. It is about 24km north-east of Minneriya, which is on the Polonnaruwa-Habarana road, north-west of Giritale.

To reach Medirigiriya by bus from Polonnaruwa, Habarana or Dambulla involves at least one change at Giritale or Minneriya, from where you can catch a bus or maybe a three-wheeler or taxi to Medirigiriya. The vatadage is then another 3km from the Medirigiriya bus stop.

MINNERIYA NATIONAL PARK

Minneriya is a recent addition to Sri Lanka's national park list, so it doesn't get 4WD-loads of visitors like some other parks. Spread over 8890 hectares, the park is dominated by the Minneriya Tank, but there's plenty of scrub and light forest to provide shelter to its toque macaques, sambar deer and leopard – to name a few. The dry season, from June to September, is the best time to visit. By then, water in the tank has dried up exposing grasses and shoots to grazing animals; elephants, in numbers up to 150, come to feed and bathe; and flocks of birds, such as little cormorants and painted storks, fish in the shallow waters.

The entrance to the park is along the Habarana-Polonnaruwa road, but you have to buy tickets from the Wildlife Office at Ambagaswewa (US$15 for adults). You can arrange safari tours through any of the hotels in Habarana (see the following section).

HABARANA
☎ 066

This small village on a crossroad is centrally placed between all the main ancient-city sites and has a hotel complex principally aimed at package tourists, although some better-heeled independent visitors also use it. It's also a good base for visits to the Minneriya National Park. Habarana also has the nearest train station to Dambulla and Sigiriya. Elephant rides around town can be arranged for a pricey US$20 per person per hour.

Common Langur *Presbytis entellus*

Also known as the Hanuman or grey langur, this slender, long-tailed and long-limbed monkey is a joy to watch as it bounds through the tree tops with remarkable agility. Its black face sports a fringe of pale hair, and the Sri Lankan race has a pointed tuft of hair on top of the head. Troops of this tawny grey monkey are usually around 15 to 20 strong. There is a loose hierarchy with only subtle displays of dominance from the males. All langurs are herbivorous – they mostly forage in the trees but will descend to the ground to collect fallen fruit. Most activity occurs in the morning, the rest of the day being used for resting and preening.

Size: Body length to 70cm, tail 80cm, weight 12kg. Females are smaller. **Distribution:** Widespread and abundant. **Status:** Not endangered.

Purple-Faced Langur *Presbytis senex*

The purple-faced langur is distinguished from the common langur by its black-brown body and limbs. White whiskers surround its dark face, and its throat is white. This species of langur is endemic to Sri Lanka. Several subspecies have been proposed, including the shaggy bear monkeys of the montane forests. Open forest, dense jungle and temples are all prime habitat. These langurs are not exclusively arboreal, walking on all fours along the forest floor when searching for fallen fruit. Wary of humans, family troops, comprising 10 to 15 monkeys, are always on the lookout for leopards or territorial invaders from neighbouring troops.

Size: Body length to 70cm, tail 80cm, weight 13kg. Females are smaller. **Distribution:** Abundant but fragmented populations from the low plains to montane forests. **Status:** Unknown.

Toque Macaque *Macaca sinica*

Noisy troops of these monkeys occupy most parts of the island. The lips and pointed ears of the tawny toque macaque are black and the eyelids have a bluish tinge. The top of the head bears the distinctive thatch of hair parted down the middle. It spends much of its time in trees, and it feeds on fruit, seeds, leaves, insects and birds' eggs. Keen to deny others in the group, individuals will take more than they can eat in a single sitting by stuffing their cheek pouches full! A troop usually consists of 20 or 30 macaques led by a dominant male. During his reign he enjoys most of the mating activity but will be constantly challenged by other males.

Size: Body length to 60m, tail 70cm, weight 8kg. Females are considerably smaller. **Distribution:** Widespread and abundant. **Status:** Not endangered.

Slender Loris *Loris tardigradus*

The striking slender loris is a small, slow-moving, brown-grey primate. The large close-set eyes, telling of its nocturnal nature, are ringed with black. According to superstition, they have the power to induce love! The slender loris has a pointed snout and rakish limbs. Its grasping hands and feet allow the firmest of grips to be held for hours. Deliberate movement along branches, one hand or foot at a time, permits a stealthy approach to catch prey. Insects, amphibians, reptiles, birds and small mammals are snatched in a lightning quick lunge. Fruits and leaves supplement the diet. It is usually solitary, but is occasionally found in pairs.

Size: Body length 20cm to 30cm, weight 250g to 350g. **Distribution:** Dense rainforest to open woodland. **Status:** Unknown.

Golden Jackal *Canis aureus*

The cunning jackal is a well-known fringe dweller. The golden jackal's tawny coat is flecked with black, while the top of the head and the legs are golden. The pointed snout ends in a black nose, the eyes are bright and yellow, the ears pointed and alert and the tail tipped with black. Shy and shrewd, the jackal is mostly nocturnal; eerie howling at dusk signals the night's activity to come. Notorious as a scavenger, the jackal is also an opportunistic hunter of small mammals, birds, reptiles and insects. Often solitary, a breeding pair may cooperate in a hunt, and occasionally a large pack will congregate and run down larger prey such as a deer.

Size: Body length to 100cm, shoulder height 45cm, weight 11kg. **Distribution:** Widespread. **Status:** Not endangered.

Sloth Bear *Melursus ursinus*

Sloth bears are typically black with a white v-shaped blaze across the chest. Powerful forearms end in great curved claws used for climbing and ripping apart termite mounds. The long white muzzle has a protruding lower lip that can form into a funnel, and nostrils that close. These adaptations allow the bear to suck termites and ants from their nests. Insects make up most of the diet but they are also opportunist omnivores, raiding crops and bee hives, scavenging carrion and eating fruit. The animal was first classified as a sloth from skins sent to the British Museum. The mistake was corrected in 1810 when a live specimen reached Europe.

Size: Body length to 1.7m, shoulder height 90cm, weight 150kg. **Distribution:** Found in the forests and grasslands of the low country, the sloth bear is restricted to protected reserves. **Status:** Threatened.

JASON EDWARDS

Leopard *Panthera pardus*

The widespread distribution of the leopard attests to the adaptability of this predator. Contrasting coat markings allow the leopard to stalk its prey unnoticed. The usual colouring is a tawny yellow dappled with black spots and black rosettes, each rosette surrounding a centre of tawny brown. The leopard is an agile climber and will drag its prey high up a tree to avoid scavengers. Its diet can be quite diverse, from insects and amphibians to large deer, although some leopards become partial to certain meats. This solitary creature roams within a defined territory, and most activity, particularly hunting, occurs at dawn or dusk.

Size: Body length to 2.3m including tail, shoulder height to 80cm, weight 50kg. Females are smaller. **Distribution:** Populations are now fragmented and restricted to protected reserves. **Status:** The leopard is highly endangered in Sri Lanka due to habitat destruction and hunting.

WAYNE LAWLER/AUSCAPE

Common Palm Civet *Paradoxurus hermaphroditus*

Civets are cat-like hunters related to weasels. Common palm civets are long-bodied with short limbs and a very long tail. The coat is a speckled grey with indistinct longitudinal stripes or spots of lighter colour. The head is dark, with white markings over the eyes, and the limbs are covered in dark fur. Strong, retractile claws aid climbing and running. By day, palm civets retreat to tree hollows or drains, roofs and out-buildings. They forage for fruit and raid crops but will occasionally devour insects, small mammals and birds. The palm civet is also known as the toddy cat because of its penchant for the fermenting sap of the coconut palm.

Size: Body length to 1.1m, including a 50cm tail, weight 4kg. **Distribution:** Widespread. **Status:** Not endangered.

DAVID TIPLING

Common Mongoose *Herpestes edwardsii*

Lightning speed, bristling hair and ample boldness are the mongoose's protection when attacking a venomous snake. Long bodied and short legged, mongooses look like ferrets, with a pointed snout, short ears and tiny bright eyes. Each hair exhibits alternate bands of black and white, resulting in a speckled grey body colour. The teeth are adapted for tearing meat. Mongooses prey on snakes, frogs, birds and small mammals and also eat birds' eggs and fruit. Their front claws are adapted for digging and they will pursue their prey through burrows if necessary. They actively hunt both day and night, usually alone but sometimes in pairs.

Size: Body length 90cm, including a 40cm tail, weight 1.5kg. **Distribution:** Widespread. Mongooses prefer open forest, scrub and areas near cultivation, where snakes and rats are abundant. **Status:** Not endangered.

Indian Pangolin *Manis crassicaudata*

An armour plating of large, overlapping scales distinguishes the Indian pangolin. The grey scales, made from modified hair, cover the top of the head and the top and sides of the body. Shy and nocturnal, the pangolin ventures out at night to raid termite mounds and ant nests. Powerful front claws rip the nest apart, and the long sticky tongue removes eggs, larvae and insects. The long tail counterbalances the upper body when the pangolin is running and digging and is also used as a fifth limb when climbing in pursuit of tree ants. When threatened, the pangolin curls itself into a ball, its tail tightly enveloping its vulnerable belly.

JEAN-PAUL FERRERO/AUSCAPE

Size: Body length to 75cm, tail 45cm. **Distribution:** Widespread but not abundant. **Status:** Unknown. The pangolin is hunted for its meat, which supposedly has medicinal qualities.

Asian Elephant *Elephas maximus*

This giant of the jungle holds a special place in Buddhist and Hindu beliefs, and it is a veritable workhorse of the Sri Lankan economy. The Asian elephant is smaller than the African elephant, it also has a rounder back, smaller ears, one 'lip' rather than two on the tip of its trunk and four rather than three nails on its hind feet. In Sri Lanka, most females and many males are tuskless. Asian elephants congregate in family groups of up to 10 led by an adult female. Males, banished from the family group upon maturity, may form bachelor herds. Elephants retire in the heat of the day to digest the 200kg of vegetable matter consumed nightly.

DENNIS JONES

Size: Shoulder height of males to 3.2m, females to 2.8m. **Distribution:** The Asian elephant avoids open ground, preferring protected forests. **Status:** The Asian elephant is threatened by habitat loss, habitat fragmentation and poaching.

Wild Boar *Sus scrofa*

This pig-like wild boar is closely related to the slightly hairier wild boar of Europe. A strip of long black bristles, which rises when the animal is excited, runs down its spine. The elongated tusks of the upper and lower jaw, more pronounced in the male, are formidable weapons used mostly for self-preservation. Apart from solitary mature males, wild boars are gregarious, with sounders comprising between 15 and 20 individuals. Opportunistic omnivores, boars eat fruit, roots, tubers, small animals and carrion. They are common in open forests, scrubland and near cultivation, where they can be pests. They are active in the morning and evening.

DAVID TIPLING

Size: Body length to 1.2m, shoulder height 90cm, weight 230kg. Females are considerably smaller. **Distribution:** Never far from water, wild boars are widespread and abundant. **Status:** Not endangered.

DENNIS JONES

Sambar Deer *Cervus unicolor*

The sambar is a big, brown, shaggy-coated deer with a mane. Even the young are rather drab, without the spots seen on other deer. Although much more active by night than day, sambar can be observed at dawn and dusk, usually near water. A matriarch hind will lead a small family group of 10 to 20 deer. The mature male, or stag, leads a solitary life apart from the brief rutting season (November to December). Prior to the rut he develops a pair of three-tined antlers that are used in ritualistic combat for females and are shed and regrown annually. The sambar's diet consists mainly of grass, supplemented with leaves, fruits and berries.

Size: Shoulder height to 1.5m, weight 300kg. Females are smaller. **Distribution:** Widespread but fragmented. Sambar prefer thick forest and are partial to wallowing in water. **Status:** Not endangered.

DAVID TIPLING

Chital Deer *Axis axis*

This spotted deer has a reddish brown back and sides dappled with white spots arranged in rows. Chital graze in herds of 10 to 30, which may include two or three mature stags. Chital frequent open forest and places where forest meets grassland or cultivated land. They eat grass, leaves, forest fruits, shoots and flowers. Feeding occurs mostly around dawn and dusk but can extend well into the day. Often they can be seen feeding with langurs; the chital feed on fruit dropped by the monkeys, and both gain security from the extra eyes, ears and noses ready to sense danger. Stags sport a pair of three-tined antlers prior to rutting.

Size: Body length to 1.7m, shoulder height 90cm, weight 90kg. Females are considerably smaller **Distribution:** Widespread. The chital is always found near water but rarely on steep hillsides. **Status:** Not endangered.

DAVID TIPLING

Five-Striped Palm Squirrel *Funanbulus pennantii*

As its name suggests, this squirrel bears five pale stripes which run the length of its grey-brown body. The long, bushy tail is speckled grey. This squirrel is more commonly seen in cities, towns, gardens and parks and by roadsides than in native forest. Apart from scavenging scraps from tables or domesticated animals, these squirrels eat fruit, nuts, flowers, shoots, insects and birds' eggs. They are usually seen in groups of four to 10. Their scurrying and bounding is accompanied by shrill, high-pitched chatter, and much flicking of the bushy tail. Females mate promiscuously before building an untidy nest high in a tree or roof.

Size: Body length to 30cm, including a 15cm tail. **Distribution:** Widespread and abundant. **Status:** Not endangered.

Indian Flying Fox *Pteropus giganteus*
This fruit-eating bat has an impressive 1.2m wingspan. The body fur is reddish brown, while the head is a shade darker with a black fox-like muzzle. Daytime isn't just a time of rest for the bats – mating, squabbling and birthing result in a surprising amount of noise and activity. Camps (groups of roosting bats) can number up to several hundred bats. Very large trees are the favoured location, and camps can last for several years, an impressive amount of guano accumulating beneath. Soon after sunset the flying foxes decamp, flying tens of kilometres to known feeding grounds; they have an excellent recall of routes as well as superb night vision.

LAWRENCE WORCESTER

Size: Body length to 30cm, wingspan 1.2m, weight 1.5kg. **Distribution:** Found throughout the country. **Status:** Not endangered.

Mugger Crocodile *Crocodylus palustris*
Muggers prefer freshwater habitats. They can be seen on the banks of rivers, lakes and marshes and have adapted well to dams and irrigation canals. They avoid fast-flowing waters and prefer water less than 6m deep. If a mugger's pond dries up, it will march great distances overland to reach water. Muggers feed on fish, amphibians, birds and mammals such as young deer. They can hold prey underwater because a valve in the throat prevents inhalation of water. Muggers are social creatures, especially during mating season. Posturing, bubble blowing and tail thrashing accompany courtship and the establishment of dominance and territory.

DAVID TIPLING

Size: Body length to 4m. **Distribution:** Mugger crocodiles are found in rivers, lakes and freshwater ponds and are more common inside national parks. **Status:** This species is threatened and is still a target for poaching despite the success of farm rearing.

Water Monitor *Varanus salvator*
This lizard is distinguished by its sheer size and its colourful markings – black with pale yellow dappling on its back and a pale yellow belly. The head is long and flattened. It is an expert swimmer, using its tail for propulsion and steering, its limbs tucked to its sides. It is commonly observed scavenging and is extremely partial to carrion. It is also an effective predator of fish, amphibians, snakes, birds and small mammals and is particularly fond of crocodile and bird eggs. It swallows its prey whole, mostly unchewed. Water monitors are quite gregarious at certain times. Males perform ritualistic combat to ascertain dominance prior to mating.

RAY TIPPER

Size: Body length to 2m, including tail. **Distribution:** Always found near water, the water monitor is common in mangroves and has adapted well to the fringes of human settlement. **Status:** Not endangered.

JOE MCDONALD/AUSCAPE

Indian Cobra *Naja naja polyocellata*

The Indian or common cobra is the famous hooded snake associated with the subcontinent's snake charmers. It is usually brown or yellow-brown with white markings on the back of the hood, and rings irregularly and indistinctly banding the body. This highly venomous snake avoids confrontation and will usually retreat. A strike is made with an upward movement, the snout curling back so the fangs protrude. The cobra then hangs on and chews its victim, injecting more and more venom secreted from glands behind the eyes. Cobras are mostly nocturnal and feed on amphibians, reptiles and mammals, particularly mice and rats.

Size: Body length to 1.5m. **Distribution:** Widespread. The cobra is fond of water and cultivated areas. **Status:** Not endangered.

ANT PHOTO LIBRARY

Olive Ridley Turtle *Lepidochelys olivacea*

This ocean-going reptile is found throughout the tropical and subtropical regions of the Indian, Pacific and southern Atlantic oceans. The skin and thin shell are a soft olive green. This turtle feeds on invertebrates such as molluscs, jellyfish and crabs, supplementing its diet with seaweed when prey is scarce. Males are distinguished by their long tail, which extends beyond the carapace, and, apart from a brief scramble from nest to sea upon hatching, are completely aquatic. Females make an annual pilgrimage to the nesting beaches. Hauling themselves across the sand and above the tide line, they will scoop out hollows and each lay 100 or so eggs.

Size: Body length to 75cm, weight 45kg. **Distribution:** Olive Ridley turtles spend most of their time within about 10km from shore. **Status:** This turtle is vulnerable to fishing nets. It nests en masse on only a few beaches worldwide and is highly susceptible to natural disasters and poaching by humans.

THE ANCIENT CITIES

Places to Stay & Eat

The **Rest House** (☎ 70003) has four pleasant, clean rooms in a garden setting at Rs 735/920 a single/double. It's right on the crossroads where the buses congregate. The food is OK, but overpriced; breakfast costs Rs 400, and lunch and dinner cost Rs 780.

The Village (☎/fax 70046) has air-con and non-air-con rooms in cottages, and two suites. The non air-con rooms in the cottages cost US$36/56. It also has a swimming pool. Readers have recommended it as a good spot for families.

The Lodge (☎/fax 70011, **e** lodge@ keells.com), next door, has spotless, air-con lodges set in lush gardens from US$92/116. There's a swimming pool, attentive service and good views to the tank.

Getting There & Away

Buses leave from the crossroads outside the Rest House. There are many departures in all directions, but if you are embarking on a long-haul trip, it's best to start as early as possible.

The train station is several kilometres from town along the Trincomalee road. Many trains pause here on their way to/from Colombo. There are trains departing for Trincomalee at 11.37 am (Rs 13/49 in 3rd/ 2nd class); for Polonnaruwa at 5.13 am (Rs 10.50/28.50); and for Colombo (coming from Polonnaruwa) at 10.15 am, and 12.37 and 9 pm (Rs 43.50/120) or at 8 pm (coming from Trinco), which also has 1st-class seats (Rs 208).

RITIGALA

Deep inside the Ritigala Strict Nature Reserve off the Anuradhapura-Habarana road are the partially restored ruins of an extensive monastic and cave complex. The ruins lie on a hill, which at 766m isn't exactly high, but it is nevertheless a striking feature in the flat, dry landscape surrounding it. The true meaning of Ritigala remains unclear – gala means rock in Sinhala, but riti is open to conjecture, although the most popular theory is that it comes from the Pali arittha, meaning 'safety'. Thus Ritigala, it can be argued, is a safe rock, a place of refuge – and

so it seems to have been for kings since as long ago as the 4th century BC. In 1971 it was a hide-out for young insurgents of the People's Liberation Army (JVP), who were eventually defeated by government forces.

History

Ritigala also has a place in mythology. It's claimed to be the spot from which Hanuman leapt to India to tell Rama that he had discovered where Sita was being held by the king of Lanka. Mythology also offers an explanation for the abundance of healing herbs and plants found on Ritigala. It's said that Hanuman, on his way back to Lanka with healing Himalayan herbs for Rama's wounded brother, dropped some over Ritigala, where they flourished. However, the truth is more prosaic: Ritigala has a climate that's wetter and cooler than its surrounds, hence vegetation that wouldn't survive in the plains below thrives here.

Monks found Ritigala's caves (and probably the cooler climate) ideal for a non-worldly existence, and more than 70 such caves have been discovered. Royals proved generous patrons, especially King Sena I, who in the 9th century made an endowment of a monastery to the *pamsukulika* (which means, literally, 'rag robes') monks.

Ritigala was abandoned following the Chola invasions in the 10th and 11th centuries, after which it lay deserted and largely forgotten until it was rediscovered by British surveyors in the 19th century. It was explored and mapped by HCP Bell, the indefatigable archaeological commissioner, in 1893. Today it has been partly restored by the Archaeology Department.

The Site

Ritigala has none of the usual icons: no bodhi tree, relic house or Buddha images. The only embellishments are on the urinals at the forest monastery, which is a bit of a puzzle, although it's been conjectured that by urinating on the fine stone carving the monks were demonstrating their contempt for worldly things.

The Ritigala site covers 24 hectares. Near the Archaeology Department bungalow are the remains of a *banda pokuna* (tank), which apparently fills with water during the rainy season. From here it's a scramble along a forest path via a donations hall to a ruined palace and the **monastery hospital**, where you can still see the grinding stones and huge stone baths. It's interesting to note that, even today, Ritigala is well known for its healing plants and locals still gather and use them. A restored flagstone path leads upwards; a short detour takes you to what is often described as a stone fort – or, to be more accurate, a lookout.

The next group of ruins of note are the double-platform structures so characteristic of forest monasteries. It's here you can see the **urinal stones**, although they almost certainly weren't always in this exact spot. The two raised stone platforms are supported by stone retaining walls. The platform orientated to the east is rectangular, while the western one is smaller and square; unlike its counterpart, it may have had a roof of some sort. How exactly these platforms were used is anybody's guess, but scholars think they were used for meditation, teaching and ceremony. Someone from the Archaeology Department bungalow will accompany you (but will expect a tip, say Rs 300) and he/she may be reluctant to take you beyond this point – although the ruins extend right up to the top – because of wild animals and dense vegetation.

You'll need at least 1½ hours to see the site properly. If you don't have a Cultural Triangle round ticket, entry will cost the rupee equivalent of US$5. The staff at the Archaeology Department bungalow also act as ticket sellers/checkers.

There is nowhere to stay or eat here.

Getting There & Away

Ritigala is 14km from Habarana and 42km from Anuradhapura. If you're coming from Habarana, the turn-off is near the 14km post. It's a further 9km to the Archaeology Department bungalow. The road is impassable in the wet season (October to January), and at other times you need your own transport. As this is a very isolated area, you are advised to go in a group of three or more

people. A van from Habarana costs about Rs 1000 return with waiting time.

AUKANA

The magnificent 12m-high standing Buddha of Aukana is believed to have been sculpted during the reign of Dhatusena in the 5th century AD. Kala Wewa, one of the many gigantic tanks he constructed, is only a couple of kilometres from the statue, and the road to Aukana from Kekirawa runs along the tank bund for several kilometres. Aukana means 'sun-eating', and dawn, when the first rays light up the huge statue's finely carved features, is the best time to see it.

Note that although the statue is still narrowly joined at the back to the rock face it is cut from, the lotus plinth on which it stands is a separate piece.

The Aukana Buddha is well known and is frequently visited despite its isolation. Few people realise, that there is another image, also 12m high, although incomplete and of inferior craftwork, at Sasseruwa, 11km west, on the site of an ancient cave monastery in the jungle. A legend relates that the two Buddhas were carved at the same time in a competition between master and student. The master's more detailed Aukana Buddha was finished first and the Sasseruwa image was abandoned by the disappointed student.

There is a Rs 100 entry fee that includes a camera charge.

Getting There & Away

A direct bus to Aukana leaves Dambulla at mid-morning. Alternatively you can get any bus to Kekirawa and take an Aukana bus (there are a few daily) from there. Aukana is also fairly close to the railway line from Colombo to Trincomalee and Polonnaruwa. There is an Aukana railway halt only a short walk from the statue, but it's unlikely that express trains will stop there. Kalawewa station is only about 4km away and trains do stop there. A van from Kekirawa will set you back about Rs 900 for a Kekirawa-Aukana-Kalawewa (or back to Kekirawa) circuit; a three-wheeler costs about Rs 500. From Habarana, a van will cost about Rs 1800 return.

ANURADHAPURA

☎ 025

For over a thousand years, Sinhalese kings, and occasional south Indian interlopers, ruled from the great city of Anuradhapura. It is the most extensive and important of the Sri Lankan ancient cities, but its size and the length of its history, and equally the length of time since its downfall, make it more difficult to comprehend than younger, shorter-lived Polonnaruwa.

History

Anuradhapura first became a capital in 380 BC under Pandukabhaya, but it was under Devanampiya Tissa (r. 247–207 BC), during whose reign Buddhism reached Sri Lanka, that it first rose to great importance. Soon Anuradhapura became a great and glittering city, only to fall before a south Indian invasion – a fate that was to befall it repeatedly for over 1000 years. But before long the Sinhalese hero, Dutugemunu, led an army from a refuge in the far south to recapture Anuradhapura. The 'Dutu' part of his name, incidentally, is from 'Duttha' meaning 'undutiful', for his father, fearing for his son's safety, forbade him to attempt to recapture Anuradhapura. His son disobeyed him, sending his father a woman's ornament to indicate what he thought of his father's courage.

Dutugemunu (r. 161–137 BC), set in motion a vast building program that included some of the most impressive monuments in Anuradhapura today. Other important kings who followed him included Valagambahu, who lost his throne in another Indian invasion but later regained it, and Mahasena (r. AD 276–303), the builder of the colossal Jetavanarama Dagoba who is thought of as the last 'great' king of Anuradhapura. He also held the record for tank construction, building 16 of them in all, plus a major canal. Anuradhapura was to survive for more than another 500 years before finally being replaced by Polonnaruwa, but it was again and again harassed by invasions from South India – invasions made easier by the cleared lands and great roads that were a product of Anuradhapura's importance.

Orientation

The ancient city lies to the west and north of the modern town of Anuradhapura. The main road from Kandy, Dambulla and Polonnaruwa enters the town on the northeastern side then travels south to the centre, which is a spread-out affair with two bus stations – the old bus station (intercity express buses leave from nearby this station), and the new bus station, 2km farther south. Buses heading for the new bus station usually call at the old one on the way through, and will also let you off anywhere else along their route.

The ancient city is spread out and has few concentrations of related structures as is the case in Polonnaruwa. Nevertheless, there is one important starting point for exploring it, and that is the sacred bodhi tree, or Sri Maha Bodhi, and the cluster of buildings around it. As at Polonnaruwa, a bicycle is the ideal vehicle for exploring Anuradhapura. This is particularly so at the time of writing, as the numerous roadblocks put in place after the bombing of the Temple of the Tooth in Kandy in early 1998 make travelling around by car frustrating. However, you can't take a bicycle everywhere; near the bodhi tree shrine you will have to park your bike and walk. There are plenty of cold drink stalls scattered around the site – as well as plenty of people willing to act as a guide.

Remember to remove your shoes and hat before approaching a dagoba or the sacred bodhi tree.

Information

A US$15 entry ticket (or a round ticket for the Cultural Triangle) is needed by foreigners visiting the northern areas of the ancient city. Both types of ticket can be bought at the ticket office (open from 7 am to 7.30 pm daily) near the archaeological museum on the west side of the city. You will have to fork out an extra Rs 30 for the nearby Folk Museum, and Rs 50 for the Isurumuniya Vihara. Generally, entry to the bodhi tree area costs Rs 75, but if things aren't busy perhaps no-one will approach you for the money.

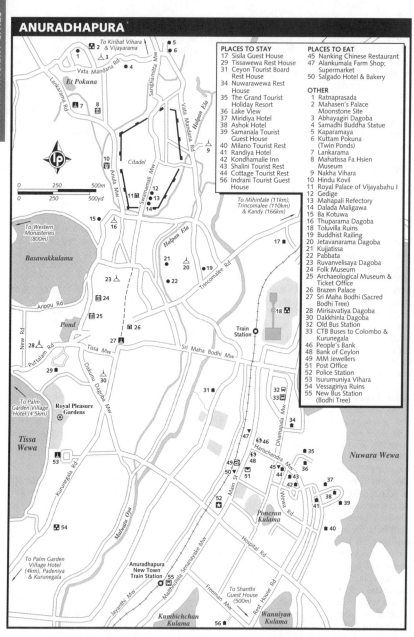

ANURADHAPURA

PLACES TO STAY
17 Sisila Guest House
29 Tissawewa Rest House
31 Ceyon Tourist Board
   Rest House
34 Nuwarawewa Rest
   House
35 The Grand Tourist
   Holiday Resort
36 Lake View
37 Miridiya Hotel
38 Ashok Hotel
39 Samanala Tourist
   Guest House
40 Milano Tourist Rest
41 Randiya Hotel
42 Kondhamalie Inn
43 Shalini Tourist Rest
44 Cottage Tourist Rest
56 Indrani Tourist Guest
   House

PLACES TO EAT
45 Nanking Chinese Restaurant
47 Alankumala Farm Shop;
   Supermarket
50 Salgado Hotel & Bakery

OTHER
1 Ratnaprasada
2 Mahasen's Palace
  Moonstone Site
3 Abhayagiri Dagoba
4 Samadhi Buddha Statue
5 Kaparamaya
6 Kuttam Pokuna
  (Twin Ponds)
7 Lankarama
8 Mahatissa Fa Hsien
  Museum
9 Nakha Vihara
10 Hindu Kovil
11 Royal Palace of Vijayabahu I
12 Gedige
13 Mahapali Refectory
14 Dalada Maligawa
15 Ba Kotuwa
16 Thuparama Dagoba
18 Toluvila Ruins
19 Buddhist Railing
20 Jetavanarama Dagoba
21 Kujjatissa
22 Pabbata
23 Ruvanvelisaya Dagoba
24 Folk Museum
25 Archaeological Museum &
   Ticket Office
26 Brazen Palace
27 Sri Maha Bodhi (Sacred
   Bodhi Tree)
28 Mirisavatiya Dagoba
30 Dakkhinla Dagoba
32 Old Bus Station
33 CTB Buses to Colombo &
   Kurunegala
46 People's Bank
48 Bank of Ceylon
49 MM Jewellers
51 Post Office
52 Police Station
53 Isurumuniya Vihara
54 Vessagiriya Ruins
55 New Bus Station
   (Bodhi Tree)

To Kiribat Vihara
& Vijayarama

Vata Mandana Rd

Et Pokuna

Lankarama Rd

Sanghamitta Mw

Vata Mandana Rd

Halpan Ela

Citadel

Anula Rd

Swarnamali Mw

0 250 500m
0 250 500yd

To Western
Monasteries
(800m)

Basawakkulama

Halpan Ela

Trincomalee Rd

Aripu Rd

Pond

New Rd

Puttalam Rd

Dakunu Dagoba Mw

To Palm
Garden Village
Hotel (4.5km)

Royal Pleasure
Gardens

Tissa
Wewa

Kurunegala Rd

Mahawa Oya

To Palm Garden
Village Hotel
(4km), Padeniya
& Kurunegala

Jayanthi Mw

Anuradhapura
New Town
Train Station

Kumbichchan
Kulama

Maithripala Senanayake Mw

Sri Maha Bodhi Mw

Tissa Mw

To Mihintale (11km),
Trincomalee (110km)
& Kandy (166km)

Train
Station

Dhampala Mw

Harischandra Mw

Main St

L Nuwa Rd

Poncran
Kulama

Hospital Rd

Freeman Rd

To Shanthi
Guest House
(500m)

Rest House Rd

Wanniyan
Kulama

Nuwara Wewa

The main post office is along Main St. MM Jewellers, opposite the post office, has Internet facilities. It's open from 8 am to 6 pm Monday to Saturday, and to 12.30 pm on Sunday. The People's Bank nearby can change travellers cheques, but you can't get cash advances on credit cards. It's open from 9 am to 4 pm.

The Sacred Bodhi Tree

The sacred bodhi tree (Sri Maha Bodhi) is central to Anuradhapura in both a spiritual and physical sense. The huge tree has grown from a sapling brought from Bodh-gaya in India by the Princess Sangamitta, sister of Mahinda who introduced the Buddha's teachings to Sri Lanka, so it has a connection to the very basis of the Sinhalese religion. This sacred tree serves as a reminder of the force that inspired the creation of all the great buildings at Anuradhapura and is within walking distance of many of the most interesting monuments. The whole area around the Sri Maha Bodhi, the Brazen Palace and Ruvanvelisaya Dagoba was once probably part of the Maha Vihara (Great Temple).

The sacred bodhi tree is the oldest historically authenticated tree in the world, for it has been tended by an uninterrupted succession of guardians for over 2000 years, even during the periods of Indian occupation. First-time visitors may be puzzled to find not one but several bodhi trees here; the oldest and holiest stands on the topmost platform. The steps leading up to the tree's platform are very old, but the golden railing around it is quite modern. Railings and other structures around the trees are festooned with prayer flags. Thousands of devotees come to make offerings at weekends and particularly on *poya* (full moon) days. April is a particularly busy month as pilgrims converge on the site for *snana puja* (offerings or prayers). You must remove your shoes and your hat before entering this site.

Brazen Palace

So called because it once had a bronze roof, the ruins of the Brazen Palace stand close to the bodhi tree. The remains of 1600 columns are all that is left of this huge palace, said to have had nine storeys and accommodation for 1000 monks and attendants.

It was originally built by Dutugemunu over 2000 years ago, but down through the ages was rebuilt many times, each time a little less grandiosely. The current stand of pillars (now fenced off) is all that remains from the last rebuild – that of Parakramabahu, around the 12th century AD.

Ruvanvelisaya Dagoba

Behind the folk museum, this fine white dagoba is guarded by a wall with a frieze of hundreds of elephants standing shoulder to shoulder. Apart from a few beside the western entrance, most are modern replacements.

This daboga is said to be Dutugemunu's finest construction, but he didn't live to see its completion. However, as he lay on his deathbed, a false bamboo-and-cloth finish to the dagoba was organised by his brother, so that Dutugemunu's final sight could be of his 'completed' masterpiece. Today, after incurring much damage from invading Indian forces, it rises 55m, considerably less than its original height. Nor is its form the same as the earlier 'bubble' shape. A limestone statue south of the great dagoba is popularly thought to be of Dutugemunu.

The land around the dagoba is rather like a pleasant green park, dotted with patches of ruins, the remains of ponds and pools, and collections of columns and pillars, all picturesquely leaning in different directions. Slightly south-east of the daboga, you can see one of Anuradhapura's many monks' refectories. Keeping such a number of monks fed and happy was a full-time job for the lay followers.

Thuparama Dagoba

In a beautiful woodland setting north of the Ruvanvelisaya Dagoba, the Thuparama Dagoba is the oldest dagoba in Anuradhapura, if not Sri Lanka. It was constructed by Devanampiya Tissa and is said to contain the right collar-bone of the Buddha. Originally in the classical 'heap of paddy rice' shape, it was restored in 1840 in a more conventional bell shape.

It stands only 19m high and at some point in its life was converted into a vatadage or circular relic house. The circles of pillars of diminishing height around the dagoba would have supported the conical roof.

Northern Ruins

There is quite a long stretch of road, which starts as Anula Mawatha, running north from the Thuparama Dagoba to the next clump of ruins. Coming back you can take an alternative route through the Royal Palace site and then visit the Jetavanarama Dagoba.

Abhayagiri Dagoba This huge dagoba (confused by some books and maps with the Jetavanarama) was the centrepiece of a monastery of 5000 monks, created in the 1st century BC. The name means 'fearless Giri' and refers to a Jain monk whose hermitage once stood at this spot. When Valagambahu fled the city before an Indian invasion, he was taunted by the monk and so, when he regained the throne 14 years later, Giri was promptly executed and this great dagoba was built over his hermitage.

After a later restoration by Parakramabahu, the dagoba may have stood over 100m high, but today it is 75m high. It has some interesting bas-reliefs, including one of an elephant pulling up a tree near the western stairway. A large slab with a Buddha footprint can be seen on the northern side of the dagoba, and the eastern and western steps have unusual moonstones made of concentric stone slabs. At the time of writing the dagoba was under further restoration.

Mahasen's Palace This ruined palace north-west of the Abhayagiri is notable for having the finest carved moonstone in Sri Lanka. Photographers will be disappointed that the railing around it makes it almost impossible to achieve an unshadowed picture. This is a peaceful wooded area full of butterflies, and makes a good place to stop and cool off during a tour of the ruins.

Ratnaprasada Follow the loop road a little farther and you will find the finest guardstones in Anuradhapura. Dating from the 8th century AD, they depict a cobra-king, and demonstrate the final refinement of guardstone design. You can see examples of much earlier guardstone design at the Mirisavatiya Dagoba.

Towards the end of Anuradhapura's supremacy, the Ratnaprasada (Gem Palace) was the scene of a major conflict between its Buddhist monks and the king of the day. Court officials at odds with the king took sanctuary in the Ratnaprasada, but the king sent his supporters in to capture and execute them. The monks, disgusted at this invasion of a sacred place, departed en masse. The general populace, equally disgusted, besieged the Ratnaprasada, captured and executed the king's supporters and forced the king to apologise to the departed monks in order to bring the monks back to the city and restore peace.

To the south of the Ratnaprasada is the Lankarama, a 1st century BC vatadage.

Samadhi Buddha Statue After your investigations of guardstones and moonstones, you can continue east from the Abhayagiri to this 4th-century-AD seated statue, regarded as one of the finest Buddha statues in Sri Lanka. This is a site to which visiting dignitaries and heads of state are inevitably brought to admire.

Kuttam Pokuna (Twin Ponds) The swimming pool-like Twin Ponds, the finest ponds in Anuradhapura, are a little east of Sanghamitta Mawatha. They were probably used by monks from the monastery attached to the Abhayagiri Dagoba. Although they are referred to as twins, the southern pond, 28m in length, is smaller than the 40m-long northern pond. Water entered the larger pond through the mouth of a *makara* (dragon-demon) and then flowed to the smaller through an underground pipe. Note the five-headed cobra figure close to the makara and the water filter system at the north-western end of the ponds.

Royal Palace If you return south along Sanghamitta Mawatha, you'll pass, after about 1.5km, through the Royal Palace site.

Built by Vijayabahu I in the 12th century AD, after Anuradhapura's fall as the Sinhalese capital, the palace is indicative of the attempts made to retain at least a foothold in the old capital.

Close to it are a deep and ancient well and the Mahapali refectory, notable for its immense trough (nearly 3m long and 2m wide), which the lay followers filled with rice for the monks. In the Royal Palace area you can also find the Dalada Maligawa, a tooth-relic temple that may have been the first Temple of the Tooth. The sacred Buddha's tooth originally came to Sri Lanka in AD 313.

Jetavanarama Dagoba

The Jetavanarama Dagoba's huge dome rises from a clearing back towards the Sri Maha Bodhi. Built in the 3rd century AD by Mahasena, it may have originally stood over 100m high, but today is about 70m, a similar height to the Abhayagiri, with which it is sometimes confused. It has been under reconstruction for a number of years.

The Jetavanarama Dagoba is made solidly of bricks, and an early British guidebook calculated there were enough of them to make a 3m-high wall stretching all the way from London to Edinburgh. Behind it stand the ruins of the monastery it formed part of, which housed 3000 monks. One building has door jambs over 8m high still standing, with another 3m underground. At one time, massive doors opened to reveal a large Buddha image.

Buddhist Railing

A little south of this dagoba, and on the other side of the road, there is a stone railing built in imitation of a log wall. It encloses a site 42m by 34m, but the building within has long disappeared.

Mirisavatiya Dagoba

Mirisavatiya Dagoba is one of three very interesting sites that can be visited in a stroll or ride along the banks of the Tissa Wewa. This huge dagoba, the first built by Dutugemunu after he captured the city, is almost across the road from the Tissawewa Rest House. The story goes that Dutugemunu

went to bathe in the tank, leaving his ornate sceptre implanted in the bank. When he emerged he found his sceptre, which contained a relic of the Buddha, impossible to pull out. Taking this as an auspicious sign he had the dagoba built.

To its north-east was yet another monks' refectory, complete with the usual huge stone troughs into which the faithful poured boiled rice.

Royal Pleasure Gardens

If you start down the Tissa Wewa bund (bank) from the Mirisavatiya, you soon come to the extensive royal pleasure gardens. Known as the Park of the Goldfish, the gardens cover 14 hectares and contain two ponds skilfully designed to fit around the huge boulders in the park. The ponds have fine reliefs of elephants on their sides. It was here that Prince Saliya, the son of Dutugemunu, was said to have met a commoner, Asokamala, whom he married, thereby forsaking his right to the throne. Atop the rocks there was once a platform intended for looking out over the tank.

Isurumuniya Vihara

This rock temple, dating from the reign of Devanampiya Tissa (3rd century BC), has some very fine carvings. One or two of these (including one of elephants playfully splashing water) remain in their original place on the rock face beside a square pool fed from the Tissa Wewa, but most of them have been moved into a small museum within the temple. Best known of the sculptures is the 'lovers', which dates from around the 5th century AD and is of the Gupta school (the artistic style of the Indian Gupta dynasty of the 4th and 5th centuries). It was probably brought here from elsewhere, since it was carved into a separate slab. Popular legend holds that it shows Prince Saliya and Asokamala.

One bas-relief shows a palace scene said to be of Dutugemunu, with Saliya and Asokamala flanking him, and a third figure, possibly a servant, behind them. There is also a fine sculpture showing a man and the head of a horse. The image house south of the pond has a reclining Buddha cut from the rock. The view over the tank from the top of the temple is superb at sunset. You can't miss the resident colony of bats. You'll be asked for a 'donation' of Rs 50.

South of the Isurumuniya are extensive remains of the Vessagiriya cave monastery complex, which dates from much the same time.

Museums

Anuradhapura's **archaeological museum**, open from 8.30 am to 5.30 pm except Tuesday and public holidays, also houses a ticket office for the ancient city. It's worth visiting the museum's gorgeous old building let alone seeing the exhibits inside. There's a restored relic chamber, as found during the excavation of the Kantaka Cetiya Dagoba at nearby Mihintale, and a large-scale model of Anuradhapura's Thuparama Vatadage, as it would have been with its wooden roof.

Everyone rushes to see the carved squatting plates from Anuradhapura's Western Monasteries, whose monks had forsaken the luxurious monasteries of their more worldly brothers. To show their contempt for the effete, luxury-loving monks these monks carved beautiful stone squat-style toilets, with their brother monks' monasteries represented on the bottom! Their urinals illustrated the god of wealth, showering handfuls of coins down the hole.

A short distance north of the archaeological museum there's a **folk museum** with dusty exhibits of country life in Sri Lanka's North Central Province. Tickets cost Rs 25; it's open 8.30 am to 5 pm, Saturday to Wednesday (closed public holidays).

The modern, Chinese-built **Abhayagiri (Fa Hsien) Museum** (open 8.30 am to 5.30 pm daily; entry is free) just to the south of the Abhayagiri Dagoba, which is arguably the most interesting of all, also has its very own collection of squatting plates. (And on the subject of toilets, there is a clean toilet block for visitors here.) In addition, you can see items of jewellery, pottery and figurines. There is a bookshop selling Cultural Triangle publications.

The Tanks

Anuradhapura has three great tanks. **Nuwara Wewa** on the east side of the city, covering about 1200 hectares, is the largest. It was built around 20 BC and is well away from most of the old city. The 160-hectare **Tissa Wewa** is the southern tank in the old city. The northern tank and the oldest, probably dating from around the 4th century BC, is the 120-hectare **Basawakkulama** (the Tamil word for tank is *kulam*). Off to the north-west of the Basawakkulama are the ruins of the **Western Monasteries**, where the monks dressed in scraps of clothing taken from corpses and, it's claimed, lived only on rice (see Museums, earlier in this section, for more details).

Places to Stay

Nothing, apart from one of the two rest-houses, is very convenient for the ancient city. Nor are many places very near the bus stations.

Places to Stay – Budget

Sisila Guest House (☎ 35139, 260/34 Malwatta Rd, Jaffna Junction) is a bit run down but it has oodles of old-fashioned appeal and a rambling garden. There are six slightly grimy but reasonable rooms for Rs 200/350 a single/double. There is a 10% discount for students with an international ID card.

Shanthi Guest House (☎ 35876, 891 Mailagas Junction) is in the south of town, 1.5km east of the new bus station and the Anuradhapura New Town train station. It is one of the longest running budget-traveller haunts in Anuradhapura, and some rooms look their age, but it's friendly and well set up with bicycles (Rs 150) and motorbikes (Rs 600) for hire, a laundry service, various excursions on offer and inexpensive food. If you phone you can get picked up from the train or bus station for free. Rooms with shared bathroom cost Rs 200/300; singles or doubles with bathroom cost Rs 400.

The *Indrani Tourist Guest House* (☎ 22478, 745 Freeman Mawatha) is actually down a side road south of Freeman Mawatha. It's a family home set-up with rooms for Rs 330/550. It's pretty basic, and nothing special.

The friendly *Lake View* (☎ 21593) has eight rooms, some with hot water; the ones in the front of the building are best. Singles cost from Rs 300 to 450 and doubles from Rs 350 to 550.

The *Milano Tourist Rest* (☎ 22364, 596/40 JR Jaya Mawatha) has eight clean, modern and relatively spacious rooms for Rs 220/330· with shared bathroom or Rs 400/550 with private bathroom. The service is almost too attentive, but the food is tasty and there's a bar. You can hire bicycles for Rs 100 per day.

Along and near Harischandra Mawatha are several more guesthouses, which may be noisy during the daytime. The *Cottage Tourist Rest* (☎ 35363), just past the roundabout, has rooms with shared bathroom for Rs 350/450 and rooms with private bathroom for Rs 450/550. It's reasonably clean, but it's nothing special.

The Grand Tourist Holiday Resort (☎ 35173, 4B2, Stage 1, Lake Rd) is at the end of a lane that leads off Harischandra Mawatha, almost opposite the Cottage Tourist Rest. Grandly titled, it is in reality a pleasant bungalow with an unobstructed view of the lake from an attractive veranda. There are four rooms for Rs 550 for singles, Rs 660 to 770 for doubles; book ahead. Meals are available (vegetarian rice and curry for Rs 250, and breakfast Rs 165). It's a quiet spot.

The *Kondhamalie Inn* (☎ 22029, 42/388 Harischandra Mawatha) has 20 assorted rooms. The rooms in the modern wing cost Rs 550/825 – add Rs 200 for air-con. The rooms in the older house look worn by comparison, and cost Rs 440/550. Bicycles can be hired for Rs 150 a day, and inexpensive food is available.

The *Samanala Tourist Guest House* (☎ 24321, Wasala Daththa Mawatha) has clean rooms for Rs 550/770 surrounding a courtyard, and a pretty garden fronting on to the tank. The friendly family makes good food and also hires bicycles and motorbikes.

The *Shalini Tourist Rest* (☎/fax 22425) has a gingerbread-house-like annexe with a restaurant upstairs. Singles or doubles cost from Rs 500 to 935 (with hot water). There's also a single room for Rs 440. You can rent a bicycle for Rs 150 a day, or take a tour of Anuradhapura's ancient city for Rs 550 (Mihintale and Anuradhapura combined, Rs 900). The friendly owners will pick you up (or drop you off) for free at the bus or train station if you make arrangements in advance.

The *Ceylon Tourist Board Rest House* (☎ 22188, Jayanthi Mawatha) is primarily for pilgrims, but you might get in. A spotless single or double with bathroom costs Rs 743 (Rs 495 with a shared bathroom). Mixed dorm beds cost Rs 200 (women may not feel too comfortable). All rates include one dinner per person.

The *Ashok Hotel* (☎/fax 22753) is an ugly block with hospital-ward-like rooms and corridors. Still the rooms (Rs 880/990) are large and reasonably clean and some have a balcony with views of the tank.

The *Randiya Hotel* (☎ 22868, fax 22017) has 10 rooms for Rs 825/1070 (Rs 260 extra if you want air-con). It's a modern, pleasant place and the rooms are clean.

Places to Stay – Mid-Range

The *Miridiya Hotel* (☎/fax 22519, ℮ info@galway.lk) has rooms with air-con for US$26/28 a single/double (B&B). You may share the pool with wildlife and sometimes the staff can be aloof, but there's a pretty garden running down to the tank. (Non-guests may use the pool for Rs 100.) This place is popular with groups.

Anuradhapura's other resthouse, the *Nuwarawewa Rest House* (☎ 22565, fax 23 265, ℮ quiktur@lankacom.net, New Town), backs on to the Nuwara Wewa. The Nuwarawewa too is pleasant in its own ugly 1960s way. The rooms have air-con and cost US$33 for a single or double whether or not they face the tank. It has a good, clean swimming pool in the garden. The set menu is expensive (US$7.50 for dinner) but you can get around this by choosing to eat a la carte.

The *Tissawewa Rest House* (☎ 22299, fax 23265, ℮ quiktur@lankacom.net, Old

Town) is one of those old places with class that the Sri Lankans can do so well, and has the considerable advantage of being right in there with the ruins. But since it is in the 'sacred area' it can't provide alcohol, although you can bring your own with you. A big veranda looks out on gardens with lots of monkeys, which have no qualms about stealing your afternoon tea. The quaint rooms cost US$32/34 with fan only and US$34/36 with air-con. They are mostly enormous, but there are a couple that are not, so check before you sign in. You can hire bicycles here (Rs 150 per day). As with all resthouses, the set menu is relatively pricey, but the a la carte menu is reasonably priced (Rs 147 for the vegie fried rice and Rs 180 for 'devilled' meals). Guests can use the swimming pool at the Nuwarawewa Rest House. The resthouse is popular with groups, so it would be wise to book ahead.

Palm Garden Village Hotel (☎ 23961/2, fax 21596, **e** *pgvh@pan.lk, Puttalam Rd, Pandulagama)* is Anuradhapura's top hotel. Accommodation is in chalets and rooms set in 38 hectares of beautiful gardens complete with tennis courts – and resident deer. The centrepiece is a stunning swimming pool. Singles and doubles cost US$83; suites cost US$108. Meals are priced accordingly; US$7.35 for breakfast and US$10 for dinner. Foreigners with resident visas pay US$38 for a single or double and US$50 for a suite.

Places to Eat

There's little in the way of eating places apart from the places to stay.

Nanking Chinese Restaurant, a renovated older-style house near the cluster of guesthouses along Harischandra Mawatha, has the usual fare: vegetable fried rice (Rs 65), sweet-and-sour chicken (Rs 190) and fried prawn and veggies (Rs 200). It's open from 11 am to 9.30 pm.

Salgado Hotel & Bakery on Main St is an old-fashioned place serving Sri Lankan breakfasts (Rs 55), short eats (around Rs 15) and biscuits.

Also on Main St, *Alankumala Farm Shop* (279 Main St) is a busy spot serving Chinese lunch and dinner packets for Rs 90,

rice and curry from Rs 50 and short eats. It's open from 8.30 am to 10.30 pm, closed Sunday. There's a *supermarket* next door.

Getting There & Away

Bus Anuradhapura has an 'old' and 'new' bus station. The new bus station is where most CTB buses leave from. There are departures to Trinco from 7.50 am (Rs 30, 3½ hours); to Kandy via Dambulla at 6 and 7.45 am, and then every hour until about 3.45 pm (Rs 45, three hours); and to Polonnaruwa every hour from 5.30 am (Rs 32, three hours). Private express buses leave from near the old bus station. Departures to Kandy via Dambulla are every half hour between 5 am and 6.30 pm (Rs 75, even if you get off at Dambulla rather than Kandy, three hours); Kurunegala buses leave every half hour from about 6 am (Rs 65, two hours); and those to Colombo leave every half hour between 5 am and 8 pm (Rs 120, five hours). CTB buses to Colombo (Rs 58) and Kurunegala (Rs 40) also leave from near the old bus station.

Train Trains to Colombo Fort depart at 5 and 9 am, and 2.35 and 11.15 pm. First class is only available on the latter two. You can reserve a sleeper seat up to seven days in advance. Prices are Rs 42/60 for a seat/sleeper in 3rd class, Rs 116/144 in 2nd class and Rs 275 (only sleepers available) in 1st class. The trip takes about 4½ hours. For Matara (8½ hours) and Galle (seven hours) catch the *Rajarata Rajini* at 5 am. Prices to Galle are Rs 65 in 3rd class and Rs 178 in 2nd class. You can also travel between Anuradhapura and Kandy by train (taking any train), changing at Polgahawela.

Getting Around

Like Polonnaruwa, the city is too spread out to investigate on foot. A three-hour taxi trip costs about Rs 500 and a three-wheeler about a third less, but a bicycle (Rs 150 a day) is the nicest way to explore the ruins leisurely. You can hire them at resthouses and several guesthouses.

Numerous buses run between the old and new bus stations, via Main St.

MIHINTALE
☎ 025

Eleven kilometres east of Anuradhapura on the road to Trincomalee, Mihintale is of enormous spiritual significance to the Sinhalese because it is where Buddhism originated in Sri Lanka. In 247 BC King Devanampiya Tissa of Anuradhapura met Mahinda, son of the great Indian Buddhist emperor Ashoka, while deer hunting around the hill at Mihintale, and was converted to Buddhism.

Each year a great festival, the Poson Poya, is held at Mihintale on the Poson full-moon night (usually in June). Exploring Mihintale does involve quite a climb, so you would be wise to visit it early in the morning or late in the afternoon to avoid the midday heat.

The Hospital
A ruined 'hospital' and the remains of a quincunx of buildings, laid out like the five dots on a dice, flank the roadway before you reach the base of the steps. The hospital consisted of a number of cells. A *bet oruva* (large stone trough) sits among the ruins. There are examples of these troughs in the museum. The interior is carved in the shape of a human form, and into this the patient would climb to be immersed in healing oils. Clay urns for storing herbs and grinding stones found at the site can be seen in the museum. Inscriptions have revealed that the hospital had its specialists – there is reference to a *mandova*, a bone and muscle specialist, and to a *puhunda vedek*, a leech doctor.

The Stairway
In a series of flights, 1840 ancient granite slab steps lead majestically up the hillside. The first flight is the widest and shallowest. Higher up the steps are narrower and steeper. If you have a problem with stairs, the Old Road from the west avoids most of them.

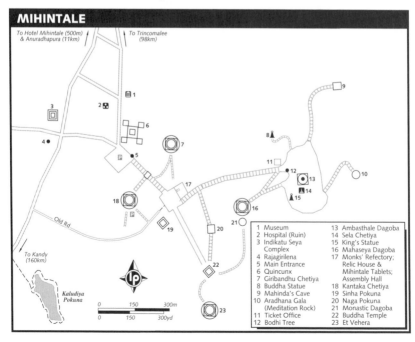

MIHINTALE

To Hotel Mihintale (500m) & Anuradhapura (11km)

To Trincomalee (98km)

Old Rd

To Kandy (160km)

Kaludiya Pokuna

0   150   300m
0   150   300yd

1	Museum	13	Ambasthale Dagoba
2	Hospital (Ruin)	14	Sela Chetiya
3	Indikatu Seya	15	King's Statue
	Complex	16	Mahaseya Dagoba
4	Rajagirilena	17	Monks' Refectory;
5	Main Entrance		Relic House &
6	Quincunx		Mihintale Tablets;
7	Giribandhu Chetiya		Assembly Hall
8	Buddha Statue	18	Kantaka Chetiya
9	Mahinda's Cave	19	Sinha Pokuna
10	Aradhana Gala	20	Naga Pokuna
	(Meditation Rock)	21	Monastic Dagoba
11	Ticket Office	22	Buddha Temple
12	Bodhi Tree	23	Et Vehera

Kantaka Chetiya

At the first landing a smaller flight of steps leads to this partly ruined dagoba off to the right. It's 12m high (originally it was higher than 30m) and 130m around its base. A Brahmi inscription found nearby records donations for the stupa. While exactly who built it is open to conjecture, Devanampiya Tissa (r. 247–207 BC) had 68 cave monasteries built, and the dagoba would have been constructed near these. King Laji Tissa (r. 59–50 BC) enlarged it. So the dagoba was built sometime in between, and is certainly one of the oldest at Mihintale. It is noteworthy for its friezes (see the boxed text 'Sculptural Symbolism'). Four stone flower altars stand at each of the cardinal points, and surrounding these are well-preserved sculptures of dwarfs, geese and other figures. Excavation on the dagoba began in 1934 at which time there was virtually no sign of it to the untrained eye. You can see a reconstruction of its interior design in the museum in Anuradhapura.

South of the Kantaka Chetiya, where a big boulder is cleft by a cave, if you look up you'll see what is thought to be the oldest inscription in Sri Lanka, predating Pali. Through the cave, ledges on the cliff face acted as meditation retreats for the numerous monks once resident here.

The Relic House & Monks' Refectory

At the top of the next flight of steps, on the second landing, is the monks' refectory with huge stone troughs, which the lay followers kept filled with rice for monks. Nearby, at a place identified as the monastery's relic house, are two inscribed stone slabs erected during the reign of King Mahinda IV (AD 975–991).

The inscriptions lay down the rules relating to the relic house and the conduct of those responsible for it. One inscription clearly states that nothing belonging to the relic house shall be lent or sold. Another confirms the amount of land to be given in exchange for a reliable supply of oil and wicks for lamps and flowers for offerings. Also known as the Mihintale tablets, these

---

Sculptural Symbolism

The four *vahalkadas* or solid panels of sculpture at the Kantaka Chetiya are among the oldest and best preserved in the country and the only ones to be found at Mihintale.

Vahalkadas face each of the four cardinal directions and comprise a series of bands, each containing some sort of ornamentation. The upper part usually contained niches in which were placed sculptures of divine beings. At either end of each vahalkada is a pillar topped with the figure of an animal, eg, an elephant or a lion. How or why these sculptural creations came into being is subject to speculation, but one theory is that they evolved from simple flower altars. Others suggest they were an adaptation from Hindu temple design.

The cardinal points in traditional sculptural work are represented by specific animals: an elephant on the east, a horse on the west, a lion on the north, and a bull on the south. In addition to these beasts, sculptures also feature dwarfs, which are sometimes depicted with animal heads, geese (said to have the power to choose between good and evil), elephants (often shown as though supporting the full weight of the superstructure), and *naga* (serpents), said to possess magical powers). Floral designs, apart from the lotus, are said to be primarily ornamental.

---

inscribed stones define the duties of the monastery's many servants; these include which servants gather firewood and cook; which servants cook but only on firewood gathered by others, and so on. There are also rules for monks: They should rise at dawn, clean their teeth, put on their robes, meditate and then go to have their breakfast (boiled rice) at the refectory, but only after reciting certain portions of the scriptures. Looking back from the relic house you get an excellent view of Anuradhapura.

The Assembly Hall

On the same level as the Relic House, this hall, also known as the convocation hall, is where monks met to discuss matters of common interest. The most senior monk would have presided over the discussions and the raised dais in the middle of the hall was apparently where this person sat. Sixty-four stone pillars once supported the roof. Conservation of this site began in 1948. The main path to the Ambasthale Dagoba leads from here.

Sinha Pokuna

Just below the monks' refectory on the second landing, and near the entrance if you are coming via the old road, is this small pool surmounted by a 2m-high rampant lion, reckoned to be one of the best pieces of animal carving in the country. Anyone placing one hand on each paw would be right in line for the stream of water from the lion's mouth. There are some fine friezes around this pool.

Ambasthale Dagoba

The final narrow, steep stairway leads to the place where Mahinda and the king met. The Ambasthale Dagoba is built over the spot where Mahinda stood. Nearby stands a statue of the king where he stood. On the opposite side of the dagoba from the statue is a cloister and behind that a large, white sitting Buddha. The stone pillars that surround the temple once supported a roof. There's a Rs 100 entry fee for this area. You must remove your shoes and hat, and umbrellas aren't allowed. The shoe-minder will expect a small consideration.

The name Ambasthale means 'mango tree' and refers to a riddle that Mahinda used to test the king's intelligence (see the boxed text 'Mahinda's Riddle').

Nearby is the Sela Chetiya, which has a stone rendering of the Buddha's footprint. It's surrounded by a railing festooned with prayer flags left by pilgrims who have also scattered coins here.

Mahaseya Dagoba

A path to the south-west of the Ambasthale Dagoba leads up to a higher dagoba (arguably the largest at Mihintale), thought to have been built to house relics of Mahinda. From here you can see excellent views. You may be asked for a donation.

Mahinda's Cave

There is a path leading north-east from the Ambasthale Dagoba down to a cave where there is a large flat stone. This is said to be where Mahinda lived and the stone is claimed to be where he rested.

Aradhana Gala (Meditation Rock)

To the east of the Ambasthale Dagoba is a steep path over sun-heated rock leading up to a point where there are great views. A railing goes up most of the way.

Naga Pokuna

Halfway back down the steep flight of steps from the Ambasthale Dagoba, a path leads to the left, around the side of the hill topped by the Mahaseya Dagoba. Here you'll find the Naga Pokuna, or 'snake pool', so called because of the five-headed cobra carved in low relief on the rock face of the pool. Its tail is said to reach down to the bottom of the pool. If you continue on from here you can eventually loop back to the second landing.

Et Vehera

At an even higher elevation (309m) than the Mahaseya Dagoba are the remains of a

---

Mahinda's Riddle

Before Mahinda could go ahead and initiate King Tissa into the new religious philosophy, he needed to gauge the king's intelligence. He decided to test the king with a riddle. Pointing to a tree he asked him the name of the tree. 'This tree is called a mango', replied the king. 'Is there yet another mango beside this?' asked Mahinda. 'There are many mango trees', responded the king. 'And are there yet other trees besides this mango and the other mangoes?' asked Mahinda. 'There are many trees, but those are trees which are not mangoes', said the king. 'And are there, besides the other mangoes and those trees which are not mangoes, yet other trees?' asked Mahinda. 'There is this mango tree', said the king, who as a result passed the test.

▲ ▲ ▲ ▲ ▲ ▲ ▲ ▲

stupa called Et Vehera (literally, the stupa of the elephant). The origin of the stupa's name is open to conjecture, but it may have been named after the monastery nearby. The Mihintale tablets mention Et Vehera and its image house. There are good views from here, especially of Kaludiya Pokuna.

Museum
There is a small museum on the road leading to the stairs, virtually opposite the ruins of the hospital. It's open from 8 am to noon and 1 to 5 pm daily except Tuesday and public holidays. Entry is free. There are several rooms, each one dedicated to particular finds, including bronze figurines, fragments of frescoes and remnants of stone tubs from the hospital. The collection includes a replica of the interior of an 8th-century dagoba and a 9th-century gold-plated ola-leaf manuscript. Pottery fragments from China and Persia are also on display.

Indikatu Seya Complex
Back on the road leading to the Old Rd, and strictly speaking outside of the site proper, are the remains of a monastery enclosed in the ruins of a stone wall. Inside are two dagobas, the largest of these being known as Indikatu Seya (literally, Dagoba of the Needle). There is evidence to suggest that this monastery was active in fostering Mahayana Buddhism. The main dagoba's structure differs from others in Mihintale, one point of difference being that it is built on a square platform.

Nearby is a hill that's been dubbed Rajagirilena (Royal Cave Hill) after the caves found here with Brahmi inscriptions in them. One of the caves bears the name of Devanampiya Tissa. A flight of steps leads up to the caves.

Kaludiya Pokuna
Farther south along the same road is the Kaludiya Pokuna (Dark-Water Pool). This artificial pool was carefully constructed to look realistic, and features a rock-carved bathhouse and the ruins of a small monastery. It's a peaceful place.

Places to Stay & Eat
The *Hotel Mihintale* (☎ 66599), run by the Ceylon Hotels Corporation, is on the main road near the turn-off to the site. There are 10 air-con singles or doubles for US$31. The rooms are mostly large and clean and the setting is pleasant. Moderately priced meals are available. This is a good place to pause for a cool drink after visiting the site.

Getting There & Away
It's a fairly short bus ride (Rs 10) from Anuradhapura's new bus station out to Mihintale. A taxi there and back, with two hours to climb the stairs, costs about Rs 500; a three-wheeler is about Rs 400. It will take about half an hour to cycle here .

YAPAHUWA
This rock fortress rising 100m from a plain is similar in concept to the much-better-known Sigiriya. Yapahuwa (pronounced yaa-pow-a), also known as Fire Rock, was built in the early-13th century as a fortress against the invading south Indian armies. Between 1272 and 1284 it was the capital of King Bhuvanekabahu I. It is believed that invading Indians carried away the sacred tooth-relic (now in Kandy) from Yapahuwa at that time, only for it to be recovered in 1288 by Parakramabahu I.

Yapahuwa's steep ornamental staircase, which led up to the ledge holding the tooth temple, is its finest feature. (The other is the lack of tourists, unlike Sigiriya, its busy twin.) One of the lions near the top of the staircase has been replicated on the Rs 10 note. The porches on the stairway had very fine pierced-stone windows, one of which is now in the museum in Colombo; the other is in the museum onsite. Reliefs of dancers, musicians and animals are evidence of south Indian influence. The view from the top of the staircase is wonderful. Climbing right up to the top of the rock is not really feasible as it's very overgrown.

There is a museum, of sorts, to the right of the entrance to the site. On display are stone sculptures, fragments of pottery and the pierced-stone window, but all signs are in Sinhala. Behind the museum is something more fascinating – a cave temple that contains some 13th-century frescoes. Also in the temple are wooden Buddha images and, interestingly, one image made of bronze. The temple is usually locked but a monk will open it for you if you ask, although you are expected to make a donation. Photography is not allowed in the temple or in the museum.

Entry to the site is Rs 150. A guide will attach himself to you in anticipation of a tip.

Getting There & Away

Yapahuwa is 4km from Maho railway junction, where the Trincomalee line splits from the Colombo-Anuradhapura line, and about 5km from the Anuradhapura-Kurunegala road. It's possible to take a three-wheeler from the Anuradhapura-Kurunegala road to the site, although occasional buses do travel from here to Maho and back. A three-wheeler from Maho to the site costs Rs 150 one way. A three-wheeler from the main road and back would cost about Rs 600 with waiting time. Trains stopping at Maho are infrequent and the timetable on this stretch is subject to change. If you want to stop off here, it's best to check the current times and fares.

PADENIYA

About 85km south of Anuradhapura, and 25km north-west of Kurunegala, where the Puttalam and Anuradhapura roads branch off, is the Padeniya Raja Maha Vihara, which is worth popping into if you're passing by. It's a pretty, medieval temple with 28 carved pillars and a stunning elaborate door (said to be the largest in Sri Lanka) to the main shrine. There is also a clay image house and a library, as well as a preaching hall with an unusual carved wooden pulpit. A donation is appreciated.

PANDUWASNUWARA

About 17km south-west of Padeniya, on the road between Wariyapola and Chilaw, are the 12th-century remains of the temporary capital of Parakramabahu I. It's nothing on the scale of Anuradhapura or Polonnaruwa, but it's worth stopping in if you're heading past. The sprawling site, covering some 20 hectares, hasn't been fully excavated. The turn-off to the site is at Panduwasnuwara village, where there is a small museum (open from 8 am to 1 pm and 1.30 to 5 pm daily except Tuesday). Entry is free. The curator is helpful and friendly (which is just as well, seeing as most of the signs are in Sinhala).

Approaching the site, the first thing you'll see is the moat and the massive citadel wall. After that the road swings to the right and past the remains of the palace, where there are signs in English and Sinhala. Nearby, and indeed throughout the site, are the remains of image houses and dagobas as well as evidence of living quarters for monks. Follow the road past the school and veer left; you will shortly come to a restored tooth temple with a bodhi tree and, beyond that, the remains of a round palace (that was apparently once multi-storeyed) enclosed in a circular moat.

There are many stories about who lived in this palace and why it was built. Legend has it that it kept the king's daughter away from men who would desire her, as it had been prophesised that if she bore a son, he would eventually claim the throne. Another story is that it was built to house the king's wives and, intriguingly, that there was once a secret tunnel that led from the king's palace and under the moat to the queen's palace. However attractive these stories are, they are merely that, and it remains the fact that no-one really knows why this place was built.

Buses run between Kurunegala (via Wariyapola) and Chilaw on a regular basis, and it would be possible to be dropped off at Panduwasnuwara village and to walk the remaining 1km. However, it's far more practical to come with your own transport.

ARANKELE

This 6th-century forest hermitage, 23km east of Panduwasnuwara, is claimed to have housed the great sage Maliyadeva and his followers. The ruins of the hermitage include moats, stone walls, an ancient hospital that has retained its stone herbal baths and grinding stones, and an ancient sewerage system. The usual entry to the site is via the *sakman maluwa* (stone-paved medita-tion walk), which is shaded by trees. A her-mit community of monks still lives to the west of the complex and devotees bring of-ferings of food, drink and other necessities daily. It's quite hard to get to by public transport – you won't miss much if you can't afford the time.

RIDI VIHARA

Ridi Vihara, literally the 'Silver Temple', is so named because it was here that silver ore was discovered in the 2nd century BC. Al-though not on the usual beaten track, it's well worth a visit to see its wonderful fres-coes and the unusual Dutch (Delft) tiles in the main cave.

Legend has it that King Dutugemunu, who reigned in the 2nd century BC, lacked the funds to finish an important dagoba in Anuradhapura. The discovery of silver ore at the place now known as Ridigama al-lowed him to complete the work and as a token of his gratitude he decided to estab-lish a temple in the cave where the ore was allegedly discovered, and to put in this cave a gold-plated statue of the Buddha. The golden statue is still in the main cave, called the **Pahala Vihara** (Lower Temple), secure inside a special case. Also within the Pahala Vihara is a 9m recumbent Buddha that rests on a platform decorated with a series of blue-and-white tiles, which were a gift from the Dutch consul. The tiles depict scenes from the Bible, including Adam and Eve being banished from the Garden of Eden, and the transfiguration of Christ. Here you can see what remains of a beautiful piece of ivory carving over the lintel. Unfortunately, this and other pieces of art have been sub-ject to vandalism over the years.

The nearby **Uda Vihara** (Upper Temple) was built by King Kirthi Sri Rajasinghe. The entrance has a Kandyan-period moon-stone. It's interesting to try to pick out some examples of the clever visual tricks used by the fresco artists. In one case, what appears to be an elephant at a distance reveals itself on closer inspection to be a formation of nine maidens. Hindu deities and images of the Buddha are represented in the caves.

The huge boulder that looms over the whole temple complex is attractive to the local wild bee population; you can see their nests bulging below the overhang. It's said that those who enter the temple with impure hearts will get stung, so watch out.

Just beyond the temple courtyard is what used to be a hermit's retreat. It now only houses a small shrine, but there's a skilfully carved pillared porch.

Although there are no signs banning flash photography you should, of course, refrain from using a flash inside the caves in order to preserve the frescoes. You'll be asked to make a Rs 100 'donation'. Remember, this is not an entertainment for tourists but a working temple, and you should dress and behave appropriately. Cover your shoulders and legs, remove your shoes and hat and conduct yourself as you would be expected to in a place of worship.

Outside the temple complex you can see an abandoned dagoba at the top of a smooth rocky outcrop. On the way up, to your right, is an ancient inscription in the stone, said to have been etched on King Dutugemunu's behalf. An easy 10-minute walk starts to the right of this dagoba (as you are walking up to it). Head past a modern pavilion to an abandoned bungalow; nearby, on the top of the cliff, is a slab from which you get the most magnificent views.

Getting There & Away

Ridi Vihara is south of the Kurunegala-Dambulla road. If you are coming by car from Kurunegala, the turn-off to Ridigama village is on your right just past Ibbaga-muwa village. The temple is about 2km from Ridigama via Temple Junction. Buses run between Kurunegala and Ridigama vil-lage (Rs 10, approximately every 45 min-utes). From the village you can take a three-wheeler to the temple (approximately Rs 300 return, including waiting time).

KURUNEGALA
☎ 037

Kurunegala is an important crossroads town on the routes between Colombo and Anura-dhapura, and Kandy and Puttalam. The

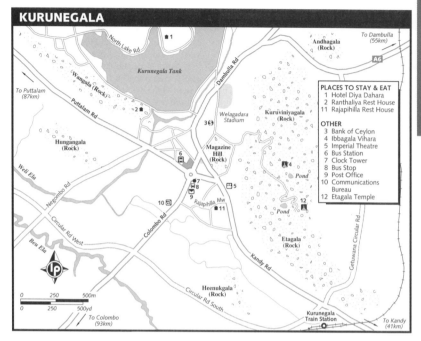

KURUNEGALA

PLACES TO STAY & EAT
1 Hotel Diya Dahara
2 Ranthaliya Rest House
11 Rajapihilla Rest House

OTHER
3 Bank of Ceylon
4 Ibbagala Vihara
5 Imperial Theatre
6 Bus Station
7 Clock Tower
8 Bus Stop
9 Post Office
10 Communications
    Bureau
12 Etagala Temple

town itself is not particularly interesting, but the region around Kurunegala is rich in archaeological sites and temples.

The large, smooth rocky outcrops that loom over the low-rise buildings are a striking feature of this city. Named for the animals they appear to resemble (tortoise rock, lion rock etc), the outcrops are not surprisingly endowed with mythological status. It's said that they were formed when animals that were endangering the free supply of water to the city were turned into stone.

There's a road going up **Etagala**, a large black boulder on the eastern side of the city. The views are extensive from here. On the way up you pass a small shrine, **Ibbagala Vihara**, and at the head of the road there is a **temple** named after the rock itself.

The post office is on Colombo Rd. Check your emails at the communications bureau at 56 Colombo Rd. You can change travellers cheques at the Bank of Ceylon (open 8.30 am to 4 pm daily, to 1 pm on Saturday), 450m north of the post office.

Places to Stay & Eat

Rajapihilla Rest House (☎ 22299, fax 074-691782), in an old colonial bungalow, is handy to the bus station, but it looks like it hasn't been cleaned since it was in British hands. It goes without saying the rooms are grim – but cheap enough at Rs 440 a single or double. Rice and curry costs Rs 125.

Sitting on the veranda of the *Ranthaliya Rest House (☎ 22298, fax 074-690032)* overlooking the tank is a pleasant way to end the day. The rooms are basic and many have a small veranda with OK views over the lake, but at Rs 615/860 for singles/doubles, they're a bit overpriced.

Hotel Diya Dahara (☎/fax 23452, 7 North Lake Rd) is a clean, modern well-run place. The rooms with hot water and balcony (Rs 990/1980) are expensive for what they are, but there's a pretty garden, and a good restaurant beside the lake. Lunch buffets (Rs 315), for which you need to book ahead, are served daily.

Getting There & Away
The bus station is a large, busy place. The private bus station is at the northern end of the enormous yard, near the large buildings that house administration. When you arrive you may get dropped at the bus stop near the clock tower.

Intercity express buses to Anuradhapura leave every half hour between 6 am and 5.30 pm (Rs 60, four hours). CTB buses to Chilaw leave every half hour between 6 am and 7 pm (Rs 21.50, 2½ hours). There are regular CTB and express buses to Colombo (Rs 55, express) and Kandy (Rs 35, express). There are also buses to Negombo (Rs 40, 3½ hours, first bus 5.30 am and last bus 6.30 pm,).

DAMBADENIYA
This small town was, for a short time in the mid-13th century, the site of the capital of Parakramabahu II (r. 1236–70). There is little to see in terms of palace remains, except for six ponds. About 400m east of the centre of town is a **temple** (Vijayasundarama) with wall paintings said to date from when Dambadeniya served as a capital (but there are swathes of recent 'restorative' paint work). It is also where the tooth relic was exhibited. More archaeological excavation work in this area has been scheduled.

If you have your own transport you may enjoy a detour to a little-visited site called **Panavitiya**, where a small resting place (called *ambalama*, which means 'rest hall') was built in the 18th century. Ambalama rest halls belonged to an era when people travelled long distances on foot. The structure is very simple. A stone platform (4m x 3m) supports a wooden pillar frame, with raised planks running around the sides, so people could (and still can, actually) sit facing into the centre.

The twenty-six carved wooden pillars support a modern tiled roof. The original also had a roof, judging by the tile fragments that were discovered buried in the ground. Unfortunately white ants have invaded some of the pillars. The carvings depict lotus flowers, wrestlers, two women greeting one another, snakes in combat, dancers, deer, and men chatting.

To get to Panavitiya, look carefully for the Quinco Highland Sales Outlet sign (there's a white milk bottle with the sign) 4km north of Dambadeniya. The turn-off is opposite this sign. Panavitiya is 3km down this road, near a temple.

The East

There's little open to tourism in the east, largely because of the civil war, but what isn't off-limits gives you a taste of what this area has to offer: long clean beaches, great surf, colourful towns and shrubby parks teeming with wildlife. It was always much less developed for tourism than the west and south coasts and conveniently, it's at its best climatically from about May to September, when the monsoon is making things unpleasant on the 'tourist' coasts.

However, the signs of ethnic violence appear at the beginning of your journey east. The bus will probably be a rattling has-been, that crawls along at a snail's pace. Then there are the police/army checkpoints – up to nine to Trincomalee, around six to Arugam Bay – where the passengers file off and on. If you're heading to Trincomalee you can't help but notice the roads deteriorating, the bullet-ridden house shells, kilometres of barbed wire and soldier after soldier. Arugam Bay is easier to get to and less confronting, but you'll still go through spots where the vegetation is cleared on both sides of the roads to deter would-be attackers.

The security situation could develop either way. New troubles might close Trincomalee again or, who knows, peace might even break out along the whole coast. If you're interested in travelling east, make sure you've done some research. Scan the local newspapers, speak to travellers, and find out the latest situation from your embassy. If you're the type of person who likes to go where there may be risks, consider registering with your embassy in Colombo first.

TRINCOMALEE
☎ 026 • pop 52,000

Trincomalee (or Trinco as it's called) really didn't stand a chance of peace when Sri Lanka's ethnic jigsaw started to fall apart. For one thing, it's highly strategic, as it has one of the world's finest harbours. For another, before the troubles began the population of the town and surrounding district

Highlights

- Snorkelling around Pigeon Island just off the beautiful Nilaveli beach
- Catching waves and rays and watching fishermen haul in their catch at Arugam Bay
- Spotting wild elephants from the road that cuts through Lahugala National Park on its way from Monaragala to Pottuvil

was almost equally divided between Sinhalese, Tamils and Muslims. The town is currently controlled by government troops, and the trickle of tourists who do make the journey are usually passing through town en route to the beach at Nilaveli. There's a busy market area, but the town is dusty and depressing. There's little tourism infrastructure. At the time of writing both the main road from Anuradhapura and the Habarana road were open, although the many checkpoints make bus travel slow.

History

Trincomalee has the most convoluted colonial history of any place in Sri Lanka. The Dutch (or rather the Danes, because Danish ships were used in the Dutch-sponsored visit!) first turned up here in 1617, but their visit was a brief one. At that time the Portuguese were the dominant European power in Sri Lanka, but even so they did not arrive in Trincomalee until 1624, when they built a small fort. The Dutch took it from them in 1639, but promptly handed it over to the king of Kandy, with whom they had a treaty. In 1655, the treaty conveniently forgotten, the Dutch took it back, but in 1672 they abandoned it to the French who handed it back to them. Finally it was the turn of the British, who took Trincomalee from the Dutch in 1782, but lost it to the French who gave it back to the Dutch just one year later. Confused?

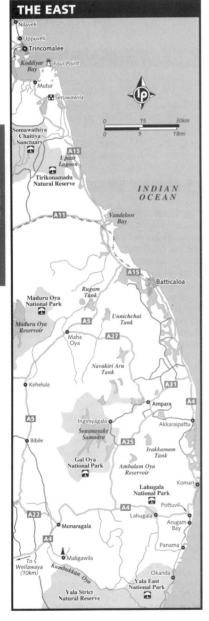

THE EAST

Nilaveli
Uppuveli
Trincomalee
Koddiyar Bay   Foul Point
Mutur
Seruwawila
Somawathiya Chaitiya Sanctuary
A15
Upaar Lagoon
Tirikonamadu Natural Reserve
A11
Vandeloos Bay
A15
Batticaloa
Rugam Tank
Maduru Oya National Park
Unnichchai Tank
A5
Maduru Oya Reservoir
Maha Oya
A27
Navakiri Aru Tank
A31
Kehelula
Ampara
A4
A5
Inginiyagala
Akkaraipattu
Senanayake Samudra
A25
Bibile
Irakkamam Tank
Gal Oya National Park
Ambalam Oya Reservoir
Lahugala National Park
Komari
A4
Pottuvil
A22
Lahugala
Arugam Bay
Monaragala
A4
Panama
Maligawila
To Wellawaya (10km)
Kumbukkan Oya
Okanda
Yala East National Park
Yala Strict Natural Reserve

INDIAN OCEAN

0   15   30km
0   9   18mi

Much of this back-and-forth trading was of course a result of wars and political events in Europe. In 1795 the British were back again and the Dutch, months away from the latest news in Europe, were totally uncertain whether to welcome them as allies in their struggles with the French or to fend them off as enemies of themselves and their friends, the French. After a bombardment lasting four days the British kicked the Dutch out and Trincomalee was once again a British possession. When Singapore fell to the Japanese in WWII, Trincomalee became strategically important to the British, thereby opening itself up to become a military target. It was bombed in 1942 by the Japanese, but it remained in British hands until 1957.

Fort Frederick

Originally built by the Portuguese, Fort Frederick, on the spit of land pointing east into the sea, is used by the military, but usually visitors are allowed to walk through the fort in order to visit the Koneswaram Kovil, a temple at the end of the spit. You are not allowed to bring a camera and few foreigners come here these days. The views of the harbour from the road leading up to the temple are spectacular. Close to the fort's gate is a **stone slab** inscribed with the double-fish emblem of the south Indian Pandyan empire, and a prediction of the 'coming of the Franks'. You've got to search to find it, as it is built into the fort's entrance arch on the right-hand side.

If you follow the road through the fort, about 100m from the gate a large building with a veranda stands on your right. This is **Wellesley Lodge** (although nobody in Trinco seems to know it!), where the Duke of Wellington (the 'Iron Duke' of Waterloo fame) recovered from an illness in 1799 after taking on Tipu Sultan in India. The boat he would have been on, if he hadn't been ill, went down with all hands in the Gulf of Aden – his poor health was fortunate for him but not so for Napoleon.

Swami Rock

At the end of the road through the fort is Swami Rock, also known as 'lover's leap'.

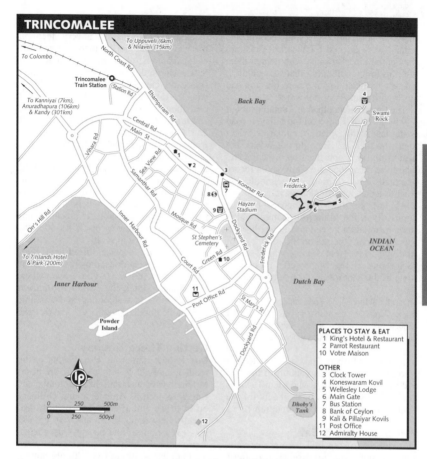

TRINCOMALEE

PLACES TO STAY & EAT
1 King's Hotel & Restaurant
2 Parrot Restaurant
10 Votre Maison

OTHER
3 Clock Tower
4 Koneswaram Kovil
5 Wellesley Lodge
6 Main Gate
7 Bus Station
8 Bank of Ceylon
9 Kali & Pillaiyar Kovils
11 Post Office
12 Admiralty House

A Hindu temple, the **Koneswaram Kovil**, occupies the end of the spit; you must leave your shoes at the foot of the steps leading to the temple itself. The temple is, however, popular with pilgrims. When the Portuguese arrived here in 1624 there was an important Hindu temple perched atop the rock, so with typical religious zeal they levered it over the edge. Scuba divers have found traces of the old temple under the waters over 100m below, and recovered the temple *lingam* (phallic symbol of Shiva), which is now mounted in the new temple precincts.

Other Attractions

Somewhere in **St Stephen's Cemetery** on Dockyard Rd is the grave of PB Molesworth, who was the first manager of Sri Lanka's railway system. In his sparetime, he also dabbled in astronomy. While living in Trinco he discovered the famous Red Spot on Jupiter.

Trinco's **Dutch Bay** can suffer from a very dangerous undertow, so take great care if you decide to swim there. The best beaches in the Trinco area are north of the city, particularly at Nilaveli (see North of Trincomalee later in this chapter).

At **Kanniyai**, 8km north-west of Trinco, there are some hot wells that according to legend were created by Vishnu to distract the demon king Rawana, who named them after his mother, thinking that she had died. There's no place to soak here but you can slosh with buckets of hot water.

The **Commonwealth War Cemetery** about 4.5km north of Trinco on the Nilaveli road is the last resting place for many servicemen who died at Trinco during WWII. It's beautifully kept and the friendly caretaker who lives next door can show you a record of exactly who's buried where, should you wish to locate a particular grave.

About 12km south of Trinco, Sri Lanka's largest river, the **Mahaweli Ganga**, which starts near Adam's Peak and flows through Kandy, reaches the sea on the south side of Koddiyar Bay. Near Mutur, which stands beside one of the Mahaweli's mouths, a stone at the foot of an old tree announces:

This is the White Man's Tree, under which Robert Knox, Captain of the ship *Ann* was captured AD 1660. Knox was held captive by the Kandyan king for 19 years. This stone was placed here in 1893.

In fact it was Robert Knox's father (Robert Knox Senior) who was captain of the *Ann* and Robert Knox Junior who spent 19 years in Kandy. (See Books in the Facts for the Visitor chapter for more information.)

Places to Stay & Eat

Most places to stay in Trinco are cesspits and not much fun for women travellers. Head north for better options (see North of Trincomalee later in this chapter).

Votre Maison *(☎ 20288, 45 Green Rd)* has stayed open through Trinco's most difficult times and it looks it. It's basic and grimy. Single/double rooms (no mosquito nets) with scary shared bathrooms cost Rs 125/250. There's no food available but there are IDD facilities. It's not recommended for women travellers.

7 Islands Hotel & Park *(☎ 22373)* is the best option for women travellers in town. To get there follow Orr's Hill Rd to the end of the promontory, where a sign indicates

the turn-off. The driveway up to the hotel, located on top of the hill, is very steep, but the views once you get there are magnificent. Spacious, clean rooms cost Rs 370/620 a single/double. Meals are available (rice and curry from Rs 100). A three-wheeler from the train or bus station will cost about Rs 60.

King's Hotel & Restaurant *(☎ 22302, 263 Central Rd)* actually has two street frontages, one on Central Rd and the other on Main St. Half the hotel is a bar and eating place, which you enter from Central Rd. The other side is where the rooms for rent are. The place is seedy and is not recommended for female travellers. The rooms themselves are passable if box-like, and have bathrooms for a rip-off Rs 400/800. Some rooms have air-con.

Apart from the places listed here, there are a few basic eateries, mostly to be found near the bus station. If you are anywhere near King's Hotel, the **Parrot Restaurant** *(96 Main St)* is welcoming and passable (vegetable noodles cost Rs 60, and rice and curry Rs 70).

Getting There & Away

Bus Expect numerous checkpoints on all roads in and out of Trinco. There are buses to Trinco from as far afield as Colombo and Kandy as well as Anuradhapura. Ordinary buses to Colombo leave Trinco fairly frequently between 6.45 am and 7.30 pm (Rs 70, seven hours), and air-con buses leave approximately every 45 minutes between 6.30 am and 4.30 pm (Rs 140, 6½ hours). There are no air-con buses to Anuradhapura, but there are regular buses between 8.30 am and 1.30 pm (Rs 50, four hours). Ordinary buses run fairly frequently to Kandy (4½ hours) from 7 am and air-con express buses leave approximately every 45 minutes between 10.30 am and 4.30 pm (Rs 120, four hours).

The trip to and from Dambulla takes three hours (Rs 35). Any of the Colombo or Kandy buses will drop you off there. If the Anuradhapura-Trincomalee road is closed, which it has been in the past, head for Habarana, 80km south-west of Trinco.

From here the road leads to Anuradhapura, Dambulla, Colombo, Kandy and Polonnaruwa. This is a major transport hub.

You can get a bus up to Nilaveli but the service is a bit infrequent – you may be better off taking a taxi or a three-wheeler. The Nilaveli Beach Hotel (see Places to Stay & Eat in the North of Trincomalee section), will arrange a pick-up for you if you call.

Train There are two trains daily between Trinco and Colombo Fort via Habarana leaving at 9.45 am (arriving at Fort at 5.45 pm) and 5 pm (arriving at 4 am). Fares are Rs 61 in 3rd class (sleeper Rs 79) and Rs 168 in 2nd class or Rs 193 in a 2nd-class sleeper. The vegetation for some distance either side of the track on the approach to Trinco has been cleared to remove cover for any would-be attackers.

NORTH OF TRINCOMALEE
☎ 026

Heading north, you'll pass a few more police and army roadblocks as the road cuts through marshes to **Uppuveli** and on to **Nilaveli**. Small houses protected by barbed-wire fencing line the beach and road, but there are few people around. There's not much to see, and less to do up in these parts, but the beach is beautiful – it stretches 6km to Uppuveli, continues to Nilaveli village, 15km north of Trincomalee, and halts at a lagoon mouth about 4km farther north. Beware of the currents near the lagoon mouth, and all along the beach. It's too dangerous to swim at all during December and January. You can hire boats to take you out to **Pigeon Island**, not far north of the Nilaveli Beach Hotel, where there's good skin diving and snorkelling. See the boxed text 'Responsible Diving & Snorkelling' under Hikkaduwa in the West Coast chapter for some advice.

Places to Stay & Eat
Given the paucity of tourism in the area, places to stay here have a neglected, deserted air about them; aid workers are often their sole custom. All places serve meals.

Uppuveli About 4km out of Trinco on the Nilaveli Rd is a signpost for *The French Garden (☎ 21705)* . It's a laid-back, friendly spot right on the beach with bungalows and rooms from Rs 300 to Rs 400. The rooms are basic, but clean enough.

Hotel Club Oceanic (☎ 22307, Sampaltivu Post), about 3km out of Trinco, has a sad, abandoned look, but it's a good spot. Singles/doubles cost Rs 440/770. The rooms are clean and spacious and some have a balcony overlooking the sea. There's a pool and an unkempt garden, but the staff are friendly.

Nilaveli Signed from the main road as you head towards Nilaveli, *Hotel Coral Bay (☎ 32272, fax 32202, 389 Fishermans Lane)* has 10 clean rooms. The three air-con rooms cost Rs 660/1300, fan-only rooms cost Rs 550/1100. All rooms have hot water and all overlook the beach.

The beach-front *Nilaveli Beach Hotel (☎ 32295/6, fax 32297, Ⓔtangerinetours@eureka.lk)* is 18km from Trinco and is really the only place along this stretch of coast that receives a regular stream of guests (many are foreign nongovernmental organisation workers on holiday). It's well maintained and well run with a swimming pool, bar and restaurant.

Single or double rooms on the beach side cost Rs 1361, rooms with views over the tennis court cost Rs 620 – more for air-con (Visa, MasterCard and AmEx cards are accepted). It would be worth checking current prices if you are planning to go there; tourism seems to be picking up along this stretch of coast, which means prices may rise. The food is delicious (rice and curry costs Rs 250). A boat to Pigeon Island costs Rs 675 per boat. Bring your own snorkelling equipment. The hotel is about half a kilometre from the turn-off on Nilaveli Rd.

Getting There & Away
Buses from Trinco have an infrequent timetable; you may want to fork out for a three-wheeler (about Rs 330 to Nilaveli) or a taxi (about Rs 450). If you are going to stay at the Nilaveli Beach Hotel you can arrange for a pick-up from Trinco (Rs 450 one way).

THE EAST

BATTICALOA
☎ 065

The east coast has many lagoons and Batticaloa (Batti to its friends) is virtually surrounded by one of the largest. You must cross bridges and causeways to enter or leave the town. Batticaloa was a chief centre of Tamil Tiger control until the government retook it in 1991. So secure did the Tigers feel here at one time that they even started building their own monuments, one of which has now been turned into a clock tower.

Batti has an interesting little Dutch fort, but is most famous for its 'singing fish'. Between April and September a distinct, deep note (described as the type of noise produced by rubbing a moistened finger around the rim of a wine glass) can be heard from the depths of the lagoon. It is strongest on full-moon nights. Theories about its cause range from shoals of catfish to bottom-lying shellfish.

If for some reason you're contemplating going to Batticaloa, contact your embassy and get advice on the security situation in the area and the safest means of visiting it.

Places to Stay & Eat

There is a lack of tourist accommodation, which isn't surprising given there is no tourism. Reportedly the best place to stay is **Riviera Resort** (☎ 23447, ℮ *rivi1@sltnet.lk*) on New Dutch Bar Rd, Kallady, 1.5km from town. There are three rooms for Rs 400 and a smaller room for Rs 300. Meals are available. Riviera Resort is on the lagoon, about 500m from the ocean east of Lady Manning Bridge. You should book at least a week in advance.

GAL OYA NATIONAL PARK

The Gal Oya park (260 sq km), to the west of Ampara, surrounds the largest tank in Sri Lanka, the Senanayake Samudra. March to July is the best time to see wildlife here. The beloved jumbo is the star attraction – around 150 elephants have been spotted at one time – with the best viewing being between 6.30 to 9.30 am and 4.30 to 6 pm.

The usual way of seeing Gal Oya is to take a small motor boat around the lake (you can hire one from the park ranger), watching the animals and birds on the shore and drifting right in close to herds of elephants.

You can stay in the wildlife bungalow beside the Ekgal Aru tank, east of the park but you'll need to be organised and book it through the Department of Wildlife Conservation (☎ 01-694241, fax 698556), at 18 Gregory's Rd, Cinnamon Gardens, Colombo 7.

To enter Gal Oya, you'll need to go to Inginiyagala (reached via Ampara). If you're coming from the south, you can take the turn-off (to Inginiyagala) near the 27km post before you reach Ampara. Whichever route you take you will need a 4WD. You should check the security situation in the area before contemplating a visit.

MONARAGALA
☎ 055

This small town, also known as Peacock Rock, is a junction point between the hill country, the south and the east coast. Unless the security situation south of Batticaloa improves, anyone heading to/from Arugam Bay must pass through this town (it's not up to much – do pass through it).

Maligawila

At Maligawila, about 15km to the south of Monaragala via Okkampitiya, stand two huge, ancient statues that, combined with Buduruwagala, make this corner of Sri Lanka fertile ground for monument hunters. One of the statues, an 11m-high Buddha, is reckoned to be the world's largest freestanding Buddha figure. The other, 1km away, is a 10m-high Avalokitesvara (a divine being who chooses to reside on the human plane to help ordinary people attain salvation). Thought to date from the 6th or early 7th century AD, and attributed to King Aggabodhi, the statues had lain fallen for centuries before being unearthed in the 1950s, and were raised and restored from 1989 to 1991. The Avalokitesvara had been broken into over a hundred pieces. Both statues are made of crystalline limestone.

Places to Stay & Eat

Places are listed in order from the Wellawaya end of town. They are all on the main road.

Silva's Guest House *(☎ 76296)* is basic but passable. Rooms with bathroom start at Rs 300.

At the ***Victory Inn*** *(☎/fax 76100)*, there are better rooms for Rs 400/700 a single/ double, though these are overpriced.

The pick of the bunch is the ***Wellassa Inn Rest House*** *(☎ 76815)* with a pleasant garden setting. Clean rooms with bathroom cost Rs 400. This is one of the better places for rice and curry (Rs 130). It's about 500m from the bus station, in the direction of Wellawaya.

Apart from these places there are a few basic *eateries* near the bus station, which is at the Pottuvil end of town.

Getting There & Away

A bus to Pottuvil (for Arugam Bay) leaves Monaragala at 11.30 am (Rs 35, 3½ hours), though there is occasionally a bus at 2 pm as well. Ignore the touts with boring tales that the 11.30 am Pottuvil bus isn't coming, or that it's too long a journey, or whatever. Their ploy is to get you into a taxi or three-wheeler (certainly a hellish ride) for around Rs 1000. Colombo-bound intercity buses leave at 6.15 am daily (Rs 200). There is a CTB bus to Badulla at 6.45 am (Rs 16) and a direct bus to Ella at 9 am (Rs 30) but you can always catch a bus to Wellawaya, which leave approximately every 20 minutes between 5.45 am and about 5 pm (Rs 16), and change there – it's a transport hub.

ARUGAM BAY

☎ 063

Arugam Bay is a fishing village 3km south of the small town of Pottuvil at the remote southern end of the east coast. It has probably the best surf in Sri Lanka, which forms near a low promontory a little further south, and because of this it has developed into a hang-out for low-budget travellers. There's a wide, sweeping beach in front of the village itself which is good for swimming; and south of the surf promontory a

long, deserted beach leads down to 'Crocodile Rock', from where wild elephants can quite often be seen.

The best surfing is between April and September and during this 'season' the number of travellers – most of whom are die-hard surfers – visiting the area increases. When the season ends the place empties and some guesthouses and restaurants shut up shop, but this may be just what you're after.

Since the troubles began, Arugam Bay has been on and off the 'safe' list, not only because of incidents in Arugam Bay itself and Pottuvil, but also because vehicles on

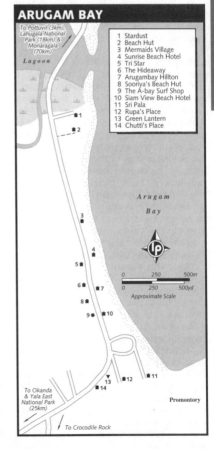

ARUGAM BAY

To Pottuvil (3km),
Lahugala National
Park (18km) &
Monaragala
(70km)

Lagoon

Arugam
Bay

1 Stardust
2 Beach Hut
3 Mermaids Village
4 Sunrise Beach Hotel
5 Tri Star
6 The Hideaway
7 Arugambay Hillton
8 Sooriya's Beach Hut
9 The A-bay Surf Shop
10 Siam View Beach Hotel
11 Sri Pala
12 Rupa's Place
13 Green Lantern
14 Chutti's Place

Approximate Scale
0   250   500m
0   250   500yd

To Okanda
& Yala East
National Park
(25km)

Promontory

To Crocodile Rock

the road leading there through Monaragala have been attacked at times. The army usually turns back travellers when they consider the area dangerous, but that doesn't guarantee it's safe at other times. Get advice on the security situation in the area and the safest means of visiting it before coming here.

Information

There's no bank in Arugam Bay so you'll have to head to Pottuvil. Along Main St there you'll find the Bank of Ceylon, which takes travellers cheques and gives cash advances on Visa cards.

The nearest post office is on Main St in Pottuvil. In Arugam Bay you can use the Internet facilities Siam View Beach Hotel (see Places to Stay & Eat later).

Lahugala National Park

Just inland from Pottuvil, tiny Lahugala National Park (1554 hectares) has a superb variety of bird life and lies on an 'elephant corridor'. The pastures watered by the Maha Wewa and the Kitulana Tank attract elephants at any time of year, but around August, when surrounding areas are dried out, the elephants start to move in, eventually forming the largest concentrations found anywhere in Sri Lanka. A good viewing time is from 4.30 to 6 pm. With the October rains most of them drift back to their regular haunts. You may see elephants from the Monaragala-Pottuvil road.

Lahugala also has an evocative 'lost-in-the-jungle' ruin called the Magul Maha Vihara, with a *vatadage* (circular relic house), a dagoba (Buddhist monument) and numerous guardstones and moonstones. It's about 4km back towards Pottuvil. A kilometre south of the ruins you can see the remains of a circular structure that may have been an elephant stable.

Although Lahugala is officially closed, some travellers still visit and you can organise trips by taxi for jumbo spotting and twitching. A round trip from Arugam Bay (for three hours) should cost Rs 800 per vehicle. Make sure you've asked around about the security situation in this area before embarking on a trip.

Yala East National Park

Yala East National Park (180 sq km) is entered at Okanda, 25km down the coast track south of Arugam Bay via the small town of Panama. It has large numbers of water birds, particularly in the Kumana mangrove swamp, where many nest in June and July, plus elephants and the occasional leopard. Like Lahugala, Yala East is officially closed but some travellers are still heading there. A round trip (for three hours) from Arugam Bay costs Rs 1200 per vehicle. Find out what the security situation in the area is prior to embarking on a trip.

Surfing

During the surfing season itinerant surfboard renters set up shop in the main street (Rs 200 to 250 per board per day). The A-bay Surf Shop rents boards (and bicycles for Rs 100 per day).

Places to Stay & Eat

All the spots to the east of the main road have prime views of the beachfront. There are sometimes power cuts, so come prepared with a torch (flashlight).

Down at the very far end of the beach, where the fishing village is, you'll find three cheapies. *Chutti's Place* has five shoebox-sized rooms (with shared bathroom) but you'll pay shoebox-sized prices: Rs 150 per single or double. *Rupa's Place* (☎ 48258) has seven grotty huts for Rs 200, all with shared bathrooms. At least the family is super friendly. Another friendly family (shame about their dog) runs *Sri Pala* (☎ 48251), with three rooms and three cabanas for Rs 220 to 380 each. The shared bathroom is bearable but there are no fans in the cabanas (there are fans in the rooms).

Sooriya's Beach Hut (☎ 48232) has no-frills treehouses and rooms – all with shared bathroom – for Rs 100 per person. It's blessed with a long, rambling garden, a well-stocked library and mouth-watering food.

The *Beach Hut* (☎ 48202) has three cabanas with shared bathrooms, and three rooms with private bathroom. It's simple 'service with a smile' accommodation – and you can't complain about the prices: Rs 150 per cabana, and Rs 200 for a room.

The *Tri Star* (☎ 48200) has boring, worn singles/doubles for Rs 330/440. It's only for the desperate.

Sunrise Beach Hotel (☎ 48200) has five basic, but slightly small rooms for Rs 400/500. There's a beachside restaurant.

Mermaids Village has an inflated opinion of its three basic rooms if it thinks Rs 600 is reasonable; bargain hard. No meals are served.

Arugambay Hillton (☎ 48189) has a friendly owner and eight rooms squashed around a sandy garden. Rates range from Rs 500 to 800. The cheaper rooms are a bit grubby, but the more expensive rooms have spotless bathrooms and the owner's pride and joy – spring mattresses.

The Hideaway (☎ 48259) has four cabanas and five rooms all priced at Rs 750 per single or double – they're spacious and clean but they have little character. There's a large garden and a restaurant.

The *Siam View Beach Hotel* (☎ 48195, fax 48196, e ArugamBay@aol.com) has an assorted mix of accommodation: several fancy rooms (all with hot water) for Rs 950; two cabanas on 'legs' (Rs 500); two cabanas without 'legs' (Rs 500); rooms for those counting their rupees (Rs 300); and a patch of lawn for tents. There's a billiard table, Internet facilities, booze, a chunky generator (if needed) and nightly videos.

Stardust (☎ 48191, fax 072-286482, e sstarcom@eureka.net) is the first place you reach after leaving Pottuvil. It's a Danish-owned, well-run, stylish place with a pretty garden. There are two types of cabanas: simple grass huts for Rs 1300 and fancy cabanas for Rs 1800. Single rooms cost Rs 800, the 'luxury' rooms (if luxury means no hot water or air-con) cost Rs 3600. The food is pricey, but to-die-for. Try the homemade ice-cream (Rs 130), Danish-style burger (Rs 520) or the muesli (Rs 240).

As for food, *Green Lantern* has cheap eats such as rotty with meat, vegetables and egg for Rs 35. Other cheapies pop up during the season but they were closed at the time of writing. The food at *Sooriya's Beach Hut* gets good reviews, and consider splurging on the delectable delights at *Stardust*.

Getting There & Away

Badulla and Wellawaya are the best starting points for reaching Arugam Bay. You may be able to get a bus direct to Pottuvil. Otherwise, go to Monaragala, where there is a bus to Pottuvil at 11.30 am (Rs 35, 3½ hours). Buses between Pottuvil and Arugam Bay cost Rs 3 and there are three or four daily in each direction. A three-wheeler one way should cost about Rs 100. At times there may be direct buses from Monaragala to Arugam Bay.

Heading off, you can pick up a bus to Monaragala from Arugam Bay's main road. There's one leaving at 7.30 am daily, but the timetable changes so ask at your guesthouse. If you're flushed with cash, a taxi to the Bandaranaike International Airport costs Rs 6500. To Colombo costs Rs 220 by CTB bus, or Rs 350 with an intercity express.

THE EAST

Jaffna & the North

The north of Sri Lanka, with an overwhelmingly Tamil population, has been the hub of the Tamil rebellion (see the History section in Facts about Sri Lanka). It has consequently been off the travel map since the mid-1980s, except for a brief spell at the end of the 1980s when the Indian Peace Keeping Force (IPKF) imposed an uneasy cease-fire and a few travellers were able to visit Jaffna.

At the time of writing, the Jaffna peninsula and the region north of Vavuniya were off-limits and dangerous. Although government forces control Jaffna, they are not in control of the region surrounding it, and even in the controlled areas there are regular outbreaks of violence. For details of the dangers, you need only read any of Sri Lanka's daily newspapers. You'll need clearance from the Ministry of Defence to go to the Jaffna peninsula. The Jaffna peninsula is very cut off from the rest of Sri Lanka. There is no land route or rail line from Colombo, although domestic flights between Colombo and Jaffna have resumed.

Even before the troubles, the north was the least-visited part of the country because of its relative remoteness and dry, flat landscape. If you could travel to this region, there would be basically two areas of interest for the visitor: the Jaffna peninsula at the northern tip, and Mannar Island, which was the arrival and departure point for the ferry to/from India until 1984.

JAFFNA

Before the troubles escalated with the 1983 riots, Jaffna was an industrious place with a fairly distinct culture and a population of 118,000. About 750,000 people lived on the whole Jaffna peninsula. Since 1983, the population has been much reduced by war casualties and by many people fleeing the area (there was a huge exodus just before the government forces captured Jaffna in December 1995, although people eventually started returning in April 1996).

The Portuguese, who arrived in Sri Lanka in the 16th century, took over the Tamil kingdom centred on Jaffna just as they took over other coastal kingdoms. Jaffna was the longest-lasting Portuguese stronghold on the island, and only surrendered to the Dutch after a bitter three-month siege in 1658. The Dutch handed it over to the British in 1795.

Since the early 1980s Jaffna has been fought over by Tamil guerrillas, Sri Lankan government troops and the Indian Peace Keeping Force (IPKF) – a period surely worse than any other in its history. It's now a shadow of its former self.

Jaffna Fort

Jaffna's fort, centrally positioned near the lagoon-front, beside the causeway to Kayts island, was built in 1680 by the Dutch, over an earlier Portuguese fort (the outer works were not built until 1792). It has seen much fighting during the unrest, with government forces often holed up inside it.

Architecturally, this is probably Asia's best example of Dutch fortifications of its period. The star-shaped fort, built on a grass-covered mound, is 22 hectares in area. Surrounded by a moat, it is grander than the Dutch headquarters fort in Jakarta, Indonesia. Within the fort is the King's House, the one-time residence of the Dutch commander and an excellent example of Dutch architecture of the period. There's also the 1706 Dutch church, Groote Kerk. Nearby

Life in Jaffna

The sounds of Jaffna were one of the first things I noticed when I arrived in early 1999. On one level, Jaffna is quiet and there are few cars on the roads. After 17 years of conflict, trucks, buses and 4WDs used by aid agencies are the only vehicles on the roads. The few private cars in use are old, dating back to before the conflict; most have been run on a variety of fuels, including coconut and vegetable oil.

Now the majority of people move around the peninsula by bicycle, and the silence is reinforced by the 8 pm curfew. This same silence is spasmodically broken by the sounds from the nearby temples, music from the ubiquitous ice-cream van, and the occasional burst of gunfire.

There is no denying that life in Jaffna is difficult for people on many levels. Many items available in Colombo are now available in Jaffna – but only at a price. At the rebuilt local market many stalls are empty; the only produce on sale either transports well from the south of Sri Lanka or is grown in Jaffna. Farmers do not produce on a large scale, as there is only a small demand, and land use is limited because of mines. Fish processing factories stand idle, testimony to both the once-lucrative fish export trade and to the effects of many years of conflict. Fishing is now tightly controlled by the government forces, and permitted for just a few hours each day. As the day's catch is brought in it is checked – there is a fear fishermen may carry ammunition and weapons for the separatist Liberation Tigers of Tamil Eelam (LTTE). Against this scenario, doctors working in Jaffna talk of protein deficiencies among the people of the peninsula.

The streetscape of Jaffna tells the story of civil war: Virtually every building seems to have been shelled, many having been damaged beyond repair. Some families who have returned to Jaffna have found their own homes destroyed, and have moved into the houses of friends or relatives yet to return to the peninsula. For those without friends or relatives, there are over 100 temporary camps, supported by both aid agencies and the government, housing over 18,000 displaced people. Makeshift roofing is often the only repair work that has been done, as the cost of building materials in Jaffna is high. And while the provision of electricity is improving, there is still at least one power failure a day.

In Sri Lanka, people use either gas from gas bottles or wood for cooking. To refill a gas bottle is expensive at Rs 430. Wood is problematic because of land clearances during heavy fighting as well as the presence of land mines.

It is very hard to write about life in Jaffna. Living here, I see people going about their daily business: They try to make a living and feed, clothe and house themselves and their families as best they can. They seek an education for their children and worry about the future.

But I am constantly reminded that everyone now living here has been a refugee in Sri Lanka at least once in their lives, and there is no guarantee this won't happen again. Constant uncertainty is a fact in their lives, and all around are reminders that this conflict is far from over.

Maxime Bodin (former volunteer in Jaffna)

on the outer wall, there used to be a small British-period house in which the writer Leonard Woolf, Virginia Woolf's husband, lived for some time. It features in his autobiography *Growing*.

Other Attractions

Most of Jaffna's Hindu *kovils* (temples) date from the British era. Their architecture is generally typical of the south Indian Dravidian style. The most spectacular juggernaut (extravagantly decorated temple 'cars') festival is traditionally held from the **Kandaswamy Kovil** on Point Pedro Rd in the Nallur district of the city during July or August. The original Kandaswamy Kovil, torn down by the Portuguese, has been variously described as dating from the

15th century, the 10th century or even earlier. Its successor is topped by a typically Dravidian *gopuram*, the tall 'entrance tower' alive with technicoloured characters.

There are other important kovils outside the city limits.

AROUND THE PENINSULA

The Jaffna peninsula is almost an island; only the narrow neck of land occupied by Chundikkulam Bird Sanctuary and the causeway known as Elephant Pass (where once elephants waded across the shallow lagoon, but now more famously a battleground) connect it with the rest of Sri Lanka. The terrain is low lying, and much of it is covered by shallow lagoons; there are a number of islands off the western side of the Jaffna peninsula.

The peninsula looks quite unlike other parts of Sri Lanka. The intensive agriculture (the peninsula is famous for its mangoes) is all a result of irrigation, and instead of the southern coconut palms, Jaffna substitutes the rather stark-looking *palmyrah* (tall palm tree).

Popular beaches in peaceful times include **Kalmunai Point** near Jaffna and **Palm Beach** on the north coast. However, this area has never had the sort of touristy beach resorts that are found further south. The best-known beach is tranquil **Casuarina** on Karaitivu island, where the water is very shallow and you have to walk a fair distance out from the shore.

The **Kandaswamy Kovil** at Mavidda-puram, 15km north of Jaffna near Keeri-malai, has a juggernaut festival rivalling that of its namesake in Jaffna.

At **Kantarodai**, about 3km west of Chunnakam, which is north of Jaffna about half way to Kankesanturai, there are nearly 100 curious miniature dagobas (Buddhist monuments) crammed into a tiny area not much over a hectare – the largest is only about 4m in diameter. Discovered in 1916, they are thought to be over 2000 years old.

ISLANDS

Kayts, Karaitivu and Punkudutivu are joined to the mainland by causeways over the shallow waters around the peninsula. Close to the town of Kayts, at the northern tip of Kayts island, stands the island fort of Hammenhiel, which used to be accessible by boat from Kayts. The name means 'heel-of-the-ham' – the Dutch thought that Sri Lanka was shaped like a ham.

Delft

Delft, named after the Dutch town, is 10km off Punkudutivu and 35km from Jaffna. Ferries, when they run, go from Siriputu. The island bears traces of the Portuguese and Dutch eras (such as the Dutch garrison captain's country house with a stone pigeon-cote) and for its bleak, windswept beauty.

The small **Dutch fort** is only a short walk from the ferry dock. Behind that is a beautiful beach with many exquisite shells. On the island are hundreds and hundreds of walls which, like the Dutch fort, are made of huge, beautiful chunks of the brain and fan coral of which the island is composed.

Mannar Island

Mannar is probably the driest, most barren area in Sri Lanka. The landscape features many baobab trees, probably introduced from Africa by Arab traders centuries ago. Mannar, the major town on the island, is at the southern end, joined to the mainland by a 3km causeway. It's not interesting apart from its picturesque Portuguese/Dutch fort. Talaimannar, near the western end, is about 3km from the pier that was the arrival and departure point of the ferry for India that operated until 1984. A little farther west, an abandoned lighthouse at South Point marks the start of Adam's Bridge, the chain of reefs, sandbanks and islets that almost connects Sri Lanka to India. In the Ramayana, this is the series of stepping stones that Hanuman used to follow Rawana, the demon king of Lanka, in his bid to rescue Sita.

Language

SINHALA

Sinhala is somewhat simplified by the use of many *eka* words. Eka is used more or less similarly to the English definite article 'the' and *ekak* is used like 'a' or 'any'. English words for which there is no Sinhala equivalent have often been incorporated into Sinhala with the simple addition of *eka* or *ekak*. So, if you're in search of a telephone it's simply *telifoon ekak* but if it's a specific telephone then you should say *telifoon eka*. Similarly, English definitions of people have been included in Sinhala simply by adding *kenek* – if you hire a car the driver is the *draiwar kenek*.

Two useful little Sinhala words are *da* and *ge*. *Da* turns a statement into a question – thus if *noona* means a lady then *noona-da* means 'This lady?' or 'Is this the lady?'. *Ge* is the Sinhala equivalent of an apostrophe indicating possession; thus 'Tony's book' in Sinhala is *Tony-ge pota*. *Ta* is like the English preposition 'to' – if you want to go 'to the beach' it's *walla-ta*.

As in many other Asian countries, Sri Lankans do not use the multitude of greetings that you find in English ('Hello', 'Good morning', 'How are you', 'Goodbye'). Saying *aayu-bowan* more or less covers them all. Similarly, there isn't really a Sinhala word for 'Thank you'. You could try *stuh-tee* but it's a bit stiff and formal – a simple smile will often suffice. Appreciation of a meal can be expressed by *bohoma rahay*, which is both a compliment and an expression of appreciation. *Hari shook* translates as 'wonderful', 'terrific' or even 'fine'. A side-to-side wiggle of the head often means 'Yes' or 'OK'.

For a more comprehensive guide to Sinhala, get a copy of Lonely Planet's *Sri Lanka phrasebook*.

Forms of Address

In Sinhala there are over 20 ways to say 'you' depending on the person's age, social status, sex, position and even how well you know them. The best solution is to simply avoid saying 'you'. The word for Mr is *mahaththeya* – 'Mr Jayewardene' is *Jayewardene mahaththeya*. The word for 'Mrs' is *noona* and it also comes after the person's name. Any non-Eastern foreigner is defined as white *(sudha)*, so a male foreigner is a *sudha mahaththeya*.

Sinhala is officially written using a cursive script and there are about 50 letters in the alphabet.

Pronunciation

The transliteration system used in this guide to represent the sounds of Sinhala uses the closest English equivalents – they are approximations only. Listening to Sri Lankans is the best way to learn Sinhala pronunciation.

When consonants are doubled they should be pronounced very distinctly, almost as two separate sounds belonging to two separate words. The letters **t** and **d** are pronounced less forcefully than in English, and **g** is pronounced as in 'go', not as in 'rage'. The letter **r** is more like a flap of the tongue against the roof of the mouth – it's not pronounced as an American 'r'.

Vowels

a	as the 'u' in 'cup'; **aa** is pronounced more like the 'a' in 'father'
e	as in 'met'
i	as in 'bit'
o	as in 'hot'
u	as in 'put', not as in 'hut'

Vowel Combinations

ai	as the word 'eye'
au	as the 'ow' in 'how'

Greetings & Civilities

Hello.	*hello*
Goodbye.	*aayu-bowan*
Yes.	*owu*
No.	*naeh*
Please.	*karuna kara*

Thank you.	*stuh-tee*
Excuse me.	*sama venna*
Sorry/Pardon.	*kana gaatui*
Do you speak English?	*oyaa in-ghirisih kata karenawa da?*
How much is it?	*ehekka keeyada?*
What's your name?	*oyaaghe nama mokka'da?*
My name is …	*maaghe nama …*

Getting Around

When does does the next … leave/arrive?	*meelanga … pitat venne/peminenne?*
boat	*bohtuwa*
bus (city)	*bas eka*
bus (intercity)	*bas eka (nagaraantara)*
train	*koh-chiya*
plane	*plane eka*
I want to get off.	*mama metina bahinawa*
I'd like a one-way ticket.	*mata tani gaman tikat ekak ganna ohna*
I'd like a return ticket.	*mata yaam-eem tikat ekak ganna ohna*
1st class	*palamu veni paantiya*
2nd class	*deveni paantiya*
3rd class	*tunveni paantiya*
timetable	*kaala satahana*
bus stop	*bas nevatuma/ bas hohlt eka*
train station	*dumriya pala*
ferry terminal	*totu pala*
Where is (a/the) …?	*… koheda?*
Go straight ahead.	*kelinma issarahata yaanna*
Turn left.	*wamata herenna*
Turn right.	*dakunata herenna*
far	*durai*
near	*lan-ghai*
I'd like to hire …	*mata … ekak bad-data ganna ohna*
a car	*kar*
a bicycle	*baisikel*

Around Town

bank	*benkuwa*
chemist/pharmacy	*faamisiya*
… embassy	*… embasiya*

Signs – Sinhala

Entrance		
	etul veema	ඇතුල්වීම
Exit		
	pita veema	පිටවීම
Information		
	toraturu	තොරතුරු දැන්වුම
Open		
	virutai etta	විවෘතව ඇත.
Closed		
	vasaa etta	වසා ඇත.
Prohibited		
	tahanam	තහනම් වේ.
Police Station		
	polis staaneya	පොලිස් ස්ථානය
Rooms Available		
	kamara etta	කාමර ඇත.
No Vacancies		
	ida netu	කාමර නැත.
Toilets		
	wesikili	වැසිකිළ
Men	*purusha*	පුරුෂ
Women	*sthree*	ස්ත්‍රී

my hotel	*mang inna hotalaya*
market	*maakat eka*
newsagency	*patara ejensiya*
post office	*tepal kantohruwa*
public telephone	*podu dura katanayak*
stationers	*lipi dravya velendoh*
tourist office	*sanchaaraka toraturu karyaalayak*
What time does it open/close?	*ehika kiyatada arinne/vahanne?*

Accommodation

Do you have any rooms available?	*kaamara tiyanawada?*
for one person	*ek-kenek pamanai*
for two people	*den-nek pamanai*
for one night	*ek rayak pamanai*
for two nights	*raya dekak pamanai*
How much is it per night?	*ek ra-yakata kiyada*
How much is it per person?	*ek keneh-kuta kiyada*
Is breakfast included?	*udeh keh-emat ekkada?*

hotel	*hotel eka*
guesthouse	*gesthaus eka*
youth hostel	*yut-hostel eka*
camping ground	*kamping ground eka*

Some Useful Words

big	*loku*
small	*podi, punchi*
bread	*paan*
butter	*batah*
coffee	*koh-pi*
egg	*bit-taraya*
fruit	*palaturu*
ice	*ais*
medicine	*beh-yit*
milk	*kiri*
rice (uncooked)	*haal*
rice (cooked)	*baht*
sugar	*seeni*
tea	*te-eh*
vegetables	*elavalu*
water	*watura*

Time & Days

What time is it?	*velava keeyada?*
day	*davasa*
night	*reh*
week	*sumaaneh*
month	*maaseh*
year	*awurudeh*
today	*ada*
tomorrow	*heta*
yesterday	*ee-ye*
morning	*udai*
afternoon	*havasa*

Monday	*sandu-da*
Tuesday	*angaharuwaa-da*
Wednesday	*badaa-da*
Thursday	*braha-spetin-da*
Friday	*sikuraa-da*
Saturday	*senasuraa-da*
Sunday	*iri-da*

Numbers

0	*binduwa*
1	*eka*
2	*deka*
3	*tuna*
4	*hatara*
5	*paha*

Emergencies – Sinhala

Help!	*aaneh!/aayoh!/ amboh!*
Call a doctor!	*dostara gen-nanna!*
Call the police!	*polisiyata kiyanna!*
Leave me alone!	*mata maghe paduweh inna arinna!*
Go away!	*metanin yanna!*
I'm lost.	*mang ivarai/ mang vinaasai*

6	*haya*
7	*hata*
8	*a-teh*
9	*navaya*
10	*dahaya*
100	*seeya*
200	*deh seeya*
1000	*daaha*
2000	*deh daaha*
100,000	*lakshaya*

one million	*daseh lakshaya*
ten million	*kotiya*

TAMIL

The vocabulary of Sri Lankan Tamil is pretty much the same as that of South India – words have the identical written form in the traditional cursive script – but there are marked differences in pronunciation between speakers from the two regions. The transliteration system used in this guide is intended to represent the sounds of Sri Lankan Tamil using the roman alphabet – as with all such systems it is an approximate guide only. The best way to improve your pronunciation is to listen to the way Sri Lankans themselves speak the language.

Pronunciation
Vowels

a	as the 'u' in 'cup'; **aa** is pronounced as the 'a' in 'father'
e	as in 'met'
i	as in 'bit'
o	as in 'hot', eg, *rotty* (bread)
u	as in 'put', eg, *ulluh* (seven)

Vowel Combinations

| ai | as in 'eye' |
| au | as in 'how' |

Consonants

Most consonants are fairly similar to their English counterparts. A few which may cause confusion are:

dh	one sound, as the 'th' in 'then' (not as in 'thin')
g	as in 'go'
r	a flap of the tongue against the roof of the mouth – not pronounced as an American 'r'
s	as in 'sit'
th	one sound, as in 'thin'

Greetings & Civilities

Hello.	vanakkam
Goodbye.	poytu varukirehn
Yes/No.	aam/il-lay
Please.	tayavu saydhih
Thank you.	nandri
That's fine, you're welcome.	naladu varuheh
Excuse me.	mannikavum
Sorry/Pardon.	mannikavum
Do you speak English?	nin-gal aangilam paysu-virhalaa?
How much is it?	ahdu evvalah-vur?
What's your name?	ungal peyr en-na?
My name is …	en pay-yehr …

Getting Around

What time does the next … leave/arrive?	
eppohlidur arutur … sellum/vahrum?	
boat	padadur
bus (city)	baas (naharam/ul-loor)
bus (intercity)	baas (veliyoor)
train	rayill
I want to get off.	iranga po-orem
I'd like a one-way ticket.	enakku oru vahlay tikket vaynum
I'd like a return ticket.	enakku iru vahlay tikket vaynum
1st class	mudalahaam vahuppur
2nd class	irandaam vahuppur
luggage lockers	vai-dhu pehna saamaan

Signs – Tamil	
Entrance	
vahli ullay	வழி உள்ளே
Exit	
vahli veliyeh	வழி வெளியே
Information	
tahavwel	தகவல்
Open	
turandul-ladur	திறந்துள்ளது
Closed	
adek-kappatulladur	
அடைக்கப்பட்டுள்ளது	
Prohibited	
anumadee-illay	அனுமதி இல்லை
Police Station	
kaav'l nilayem	காவல நிலையம்
Rooms Available	
arekahl undu	அறைகள் உண்டு
Full, No Vacancies	
illay, kaali illay	
நிரம்பியுள்ளது, காலி இல்லை	
Toilets	
kahlippadem	மலசலகூடம்
Men	aan	ஆண்
Women	pen	பெண

timetable	haala attavanay
bus/trolley stop	baas nilayem
train station	rayill nilayem
Where is it?	un-ghe irukkaradhur?
Where is a/the …?	… un-ghe?
Go straight ahead.	neraha sellavum
Turn left.	valadhur pakkam tirumbavum
Turn right.	itadhur pakkam tirumbavum
far	tu-rahm
near	aruhil
I'd like to hire …	enakku … varaykhur vaynum
a car	kaa
a bicycle	sai-kul

Around Town

| bank | vanghee |
| chemist/pharmacy | marunduh kadhai-karehr |

... embassy	... *tudharahem*
my hotel	*en udehr hotehl*
market	*maarket*
newsagency	*niyuz ejensee*
post office	*tavaal nilayem*
public telephone	*podhu tolai-pessee*
stationers	*eludhuporul vanihehr*
tourist office	*toorist nilayem*
What time does it open/close?	*et-thana manikka tirakhum/mudhum?*

Accommodation

Do you have any rooms available?	*arekil kidhekkumaa?*
for one/two people	*oruvah/iruvah ukku*
for one/two nights	*oru/irandu iravukku*
How much is it per night/per person?	*oru iravukku/oru naba-rukku evvalavur?*
Is breakfast included?	*kaaleh setrundeen sehrtoh?*
hotel	*hotehl*
guesthouse	*virun-dhinar vidhudheh*
youth hostel	*ilainar vidhudheh*
camping ground	*tan-gum idahm*

Some Useful Words

big	*periyeh*
small	*siriyeh*
bread	*rotti*
butter	*ven-nay*
coffee	*kahpee*
egg	*muh-tay*
fruit	*paadham*
ice	*ais*
medicine	*marunduh*
milk	*paal*
rice	*areesee*
sugar	*seeree*
tea	*teh-neer*
vegetables	*kaay-karahil*
water	*neer*

Time & Days

What time is it?	*mani eh-tanay?*
day	*pahel*
night	*iravu*

Emergencies – Tamil

Help!	*udavi!*
Call a doctor!	*daktarai kuppa-ravum!*
Call the police!	*polisai kupparavum!*
Leave me alone!	*enna taniyaahu irukkaviduh!*
Go away!	*pohn-goh!/ tolandu po!* (informal)
I'm lost.	*naan valee tavuree-vittehn*

week	*vaarem*
month	*maadhem*
year	*varudem*
today	*indru*
tomorrow	*naalay*
yesterday	*neh-truh*
morning	*kaalai*
afternoon	*matiya-nem*

Monday	*tin-gal*
Tuesday	*sevvaay*
Wednesday	*budahn*
Thursday	*viyaalin*
Friday	*vellee*
Saturday	*san-nee*
Sunday	*naayru*

Numbers

0	*saidhu*
1	*ondru*
2	*iranduh*
3	*muundruh*
4	*naan-guh*
5	*ainduh*
6	*aaruh*
7	*ulluh*
8	*uttu*
9	*onbaduh*
10	*pat-tuh*
100	*nooruh*
1000	*aayirem*
2000	*irundaayirem*
100,000	*lah-chem*

one million	*pattuh lah-chem*
ten million	*kohdee*

SRI LANKAN ENGLISH

Like every other country where English is spoken, Sri Lanka has its own peculiar versions of some words and phrases. Life can be a bit confusing if you don't have a grasp of some of the essentials of Sri Lankan English.

Greetings & Questions

Go and come – farewell greeting, similar to 'see you later', not taken literally

How? – How are you?

Nothing to do – Can't do anything.

What to do? – What can be done about it?; more of a rhetorical question.

What country? – Where are you from?

People

batchmate – university classmate

baby/bubba – used for any child up to about adolescence

to gift – to give a gift

paining – hurting

peon – office helper

uncle/auntie – term of respect for elder

Getting Around

backside – part of the building away from the street

bajaj – three-wheeler

bus halt – bus stop

coloured lights – traffic lights

down south – the areas south of Colombo, especially coastal areas

dropping – being dropped off at a place by a car

get down (from bus/train/three-wheeler) – to alight

hotel – a small cheap restaurant without accommodation

normal bus – not a private bus

outstation – place beyond a person's home area

petrol shed – petrol/gas station

pick-up (noun) – 4WD utility vehicle

seaside/landside – indicates locations, usually in relation to Galle Rd

two-wheeler – motorcycle

up and down – return trip

up country/hill country – Kandy and beyond, tea plantation areas

vehicle – car

Food

bite – snack usually eaten with alcoholic drinks

boutique – a small, hole-in-the-wall shop, usually selling small inexpensive items

cool spot – traditional, small shop that sells cool drinks and snacks

lunch packet/rice packet – portion of rice and curry wrapped in plastic and newspaper and taken to office/school for lunch

short eats – snack food

Money

buck – rupee

purse – wallet

last price – final price when bargaining

PLACE NAMES

Sri Lanka's often fearsome-looking place names become much simpler with a little analysis. *Pura* or *puram* simply means town – as in Ratnapura (town of gems) or Anuradhapura. Similarly *nuwara* means 'city' and *gama* means 'village'. Other common words that are incorporated in place names include *gala* or *giri* (rock or hill), *kanda* (mountain), *ganga* (river), *oya* (large stream), *ela* (stream), *tara* or *tota* (ford or port), *pitiya* (park), *watte* (garden), *deniya* (vegetable garden), *gaha* (tree), *arama* (park or monastery) and *duwa* (island).

Not surprisingly, many towns are named after the great tanks (artificial lakes developed for irrigation purposes in the dry regions) – *wewa* or *kulam*. The same word can appear in Sinhala, Sanskrit, Pali and Tamil! Finally *maha* means 'great'. Put it all together and even a name like Tissamaharama makes sense – it's simply '(King) Tissa's great park'.

Pronunciation

Pronounce each name as a series of clearly defined syllables (stress generally falls on the second last syllable), eg, Anuradhapura (a-nu-ra-da-**pu**-ra), Polonnaruwa (poh-loh-na-**ru**-wa).

Gazetteer

English
    Sinhala   **Tamil**

English / Sinhala	Tamil
Adam's Peak	
ශ්‍රීපාදය	சிவனொலிபாதம்
Aluthgama	
අළුත්ගම	அளுத்கம
Ambalangoda	
අම්බලන්ගොඩ	அம்பலாங்கொடை
Anuradhapura	
අනුරාධපුරය	அனுராதபுரம்
Arugam Bay	
ආරුගම්බේ	அறுகம் முனை
Aukana	
අවුකන	அக்குறணை
Badulla	
බදුල්ල	பதுளை
Bandarawela	
බන්ඩාරවෙල	பண்டாரவளை
Batticaloa	
මඩකලපුව	மட்டக்களப்பு
Belihul Oya	
බෙලිහුල්ඔය	பெலிகுல ஓய
Bentota	
බෙන්තොට	பென்தோட்டை
Beruwela	
බේරුවල	பேருவலை
Chilaw	
හලාවත	சிலாபம்
Colombo	
කොළඹ	கொழும்பு
Dambadeniya	
දඹදෙණිය	தம்பதெனிய
Dambulla	
දඹුල්ල	தம்புல்லை
Dimbulagala	
දිඹුලාගල	திம்புளகல
Ella	
ඇල්ල	எல்ல
Galle	
ගාල්ල	காலி
Giritale	
ගිරිතලේ	கிரித்தல
Habarana	
හබරණ	ஹபரண
Hambantota	
හම්බන්තොට	ஹம்பாந்தோட்டை
Haputale	
හපුතලේ	ஹப்புத்தளை
Hikkaduwa	
හික්කඩුව	ஹிக்கடுவை
Horton Plains	
හෝර්ටන් තැන්න	
	ஹோட்டன் பீளெயின்ஸ்
Induruwa	
ඉඳුරුව	இந்துருவ
Jaffna	
යාපනය	யாழ்ப்பாணம்
Kalpitiya	
කල්පිටිය	கற்பீட்டி
Kalutara	
කළුතර	களுத்தறை
Kandy	
මහනුවර	கண்டி
Kataragama	
කතරගම	கதிர்காமம்
Kitulgala	
කිතුල්ගල	கித்துள்கல
Kurunegala	
කුරුණෑගල	குருநாகல்
Mannar Island	
මන්නාරම් දූපත	மன்னார் தீவு
Matara	
මාතර	மாத்தறை
Medirigiriya	
මැදිරිගිරිය	மதிரிகிரிய
Mihintale	
මිහින්තලය	மிகிந்தலை
Mirissa	
මිරිස්ස	மிரிஸ்ஸ
Monaragala	
මොණරාගල	மொனறாகலை
Mulkirigala	
මුල්ගිරිගල	முல்கிரிகல
Negombo	
මීගමුව	நீர்கொழும்பு
Nilaveli	
නිලාවෙලි	நிலாவெளி
Nuwara Eliya	
නුවර එළිය	நுவரேலியா
Padeniya	
පාදෙනිය	பாடெனிய
Panduwasnuwara	
පඬුවස්නුවර	பண்டுவஸ்நுவர

Polonnaruwa
පොලොන්නරුව   பொலன்னறுவை
Puttalam
පුත්තලම   புத்தளம்
Ratnapura
රත්නපුරය   இரத்தினபுரி
Ritigala
රිටිගල   றித்திகல
Sigiriya
සිගිරිය   சீகிரிய
Sinharaja
සිංහරාජ   சிங்ஹராஜு
Tangalla
තංගල්ල   தங்காலை
Tissamaharama
තිස්සමහාරාමය   திசமஹாரம

Trincomalee
ත්‍රිකුණාමළය   திருகோணமலை
Unawatuna
උණවටුන   உணவட்டுன
Uppuveli
උප්පුවෙල   உப்புவெளி
Weligama
වැලිගම   வெலிகம
Wellawaya
වැල්ලවාය   வெல்லவாய
Wilpattu National Park
විල්පත්තු ජාතික වනෝද්‍යානය
යාල்பத்து தேசிய புகல் அரண்
Yapahuwa
යාපහුව   யாப்பஹுவ

Glossary

aluva – rice flour, treacle and cashew-nut fudge

ambalama – wayside shelter for pilgrims

ambul thiyal – a pickle usually made from tuna; translates literally as 'sour fish curry'

amudes – loincloths worn by gem miners

arrack – distilled *toddy*, often very potent

Aurudu – Sinhalese and Tamil New Year, celebrated on 14 April

Avalokitesvara – the *Bodhisattva* of compassion

Ayurveda – traditional system of medicine using herbs and oils to heal and rejuvenate

baobab – water-storing tree *(Adansonia digitata)*, probably introduced into the dry northern regions of Sri Lanka by Arab traders

bed tea – early morning cuppa served to you in bed

bet oruva – large stone trough

Bhikku – Buddhist monk

biryani – delicate north Indian dish of spiced rice with meat, hard-boiled egg and pickles

bodhi tree – large spreading tree *(Ficus religiosa)*; the tree under which Buddha was sitting when he attained enlightenment

Bodhisattva – divine being who, although capable of attaining *nirvana*, chooses to reside on the human plane to help ordinary people attain salvation

bonda – deep-fried potato and lentil ball in lentil flour batter

Brahmi – early Indian script used from the 5th century BC

bund – built-up bank or dyke surrounding a *tank*

Burgher – Sri Lankan Eurasian, generally descended from Portuguese-Sinhalese or Dutch-Sinhalese intermarriage

cadjan – coconut fronds woven into mats and used as building material

Ceylon – British colonial name for Sri Lanka

chena – shifting cultivation whereby land is cultivated until its fertility diminishes; it is then abandoned until it is restored naturally

chetiya – shrine

Chinese rolls – deep-fried pastry rolls filled with vegetables or meat

Chola – powerful ancient south Indian kingdom that invaded Sri Lanka on several occasions

coir – mat or rope made from coconut fibres

copra – dried coconut kernel used to make cooking oil and also exported for use in the manufacture of confectionery

crore – 10 million of anything, but most often rupees

CTB – Central (formerly Ceylon) Transport Board, the state bus network

Culavamsa – the 'Minor Chronicle', which continues the history commenced in the *Mahavamsa* up to 1758

curd – buffalo-milk yogurt

curd vadai – deep-fried lentil patty with yogurt

cutlets – deep-fried meat or fish balls

dagoba – Buddhist monument composed of a solid hemisphere containing relics of Buddha or a Buddhist saint

devale – a complex designed for worshipping a Hindu or Sri Lankan deity; devales are sometimes found near Buddhist shrines

dhal – thick soup made of split lentils; in Sinhala, *parripu*

dharma – the word used by both Hindus and Buddhists to refer to their respective moral codes of behaviour

dorje – hourglass-shaped Tibetan thunderbolt symbol

Dravidian – south Indian group of peoples and languages; Tamils are included within this grouping

DUNF – Democratic United Nations Front

EPDP – Eelam People's Democratic Party

gala – rock
ganga – river
gaw – old Sinhalese unit of distance
gedige – hollow temple with extremely thick walls and a corbelled roof
gopuram – soaring pyramidal gateway of a Hindu temple; a style of *Dravidian* architecture found principally in South India
guardstones – carved ornamental stones that flank doorways or entrances to temples
gurulu – legendary bird that preys on snakes, used as an image in carved *raksha* masks

hodhi – curry with a thin gravy
hopper – popular Sri Lankan snack or meal; a regular hopper is like a small, bowl-shaped pancake, fried over a high flame, while string hoppers are made of tangled circles of steamed noodles
howdah – seat for carrying people on an elephant's back

iddli – south Indian rice dumpling
illama – a gravel-bearing stratum likely to hold gemstones
IPKF – Indian Peace Keeping Force; the Indian Army contingent that was present in Sri Lanka from 1987 to 1990 with the aim of disarming Tamil rebels and keeping the peace

jaggery – hard, brown sweet made from *kitul*
Jataka Tales – stories of the previous lives of Buddha
juggernaut – huge, extravagantly decorated temple 'car', dragged through the streets during Hindu festivals
JVP – Janatha Vimukthi Peramuna or the People's Liberation Army; a Sinhalese Marxist revolutionary organisation that rose up in 1971 and again in the late 1980s

kalu dodol – coconut milk, *jaggery* and cashew-nut sweet
Karavas – fisherfolk of Indian descent
karma – Hindu-Buddhist principle of re-tributive justice for past deeds
kavun – spiced flour and treacle batter-cake fried in coconut oil

kiri bath – a dessert of rice cooked in milk; it also has ritual significance
kitul – sap from the kitul palm drawn off from the tree; in liquid form it's known as treacle, and when boiled down as *jaggery*
kolam – masked dance-drama
kool – a speciality of Jaffna consisting of a boiled-and-fried vegetable combination dried in the sun
korma – curry-like braised dish
kotthu rotty – *rotty* chopped up and mixed with vegetables, eggs or meat
kovil – Hindu temple; most Sri Lankan kovils are dedicated to the worship of Shiva
kul – spicy chowder dish, popular in Jaffna
kulam – Tamil word for *tank*

lakh – 100,000; a standard unit of measurement in Sri Lanka and India
Laksala – government-run arts and handicrafts shop
lamprai – rice and curry wrapped up and cooked in a banana leaf
lingam – phallic symbol; symbol of Shiva
LTTE – Liberation Tigers of Tamil Eelam, also known as the Tamil Tigers; separatist group fighting for a separate state of Tamil Eelam in the north and east of the country

Maha – the north-east monsoon season
Mahavamsa – the 'Great Chronicle', a written Sinhalese history running from the arrival of Prince Vijaya from India in the 6th century BC, through the meeting of King Devanampiya Tissa with *Mahinda*, and on to the great kings of Anuradhapura
Mahaweli Ganga – Sri Lanka's biggest river, which starts in the hill country near Adam's Peak, flows through Kandy and eventually reaches the sea near Trincomalee
Mahayana – the 'greater vehicle' of Buddhism; a relatively later adaptation of the teaching emphasising the *Bodhisattva* ideal, which teaches the renunciation of *nirvana* in order to help other beings along the way to enlightenment
Mahinda – son of the Indian Buddhist emperor Ashoka, credited with introducing Buddhism to Sri Lanka
mahout – elephant rider or master
Maitreya – future Buddha

p
pe
danc
pirive
monast
pittu –
grated c
slightly ro

makara – mythical beast that is a cross between a lion, a pig and an elephant, commonly carved in the balustrade of temple staircases

makara torana – ornamental archway

mallung – shredded green leafy vegetable mixed with grated coconut and lightly stir-fried, eaten as an accompaniment to rice and curry

mandapaya – a raised platform with decorative pillars

masala – mix (often spices)

masala dosa – curried vegetables inside a lentil and rice-flour pancake

mawatha – avenue or street; abbreviated to 'Mw'

moonstone – semiprecious stone; also a carved stone 'doorstep' at temple entrances

mudra – symbolic hand position of a Buddha image

naga – cobra deity

naga raksha – a *raksha* mask featuring a 'coiffure' of writhing cobras

nirvana – the ultimate aim of Buddhists, final release from the cycle of existence

nuwara – city

ola – palm leaf used in manuscripts and traditional books

oruva – outrigger canoe

oya – stream or small river

PA – People's Alliance; a coalition including the *SLFP* founded in 1994

paddy – unhusked rice

padma – lotus flower

Pali – the language in which the Buddhist scriptures were originally recorded

palmyrah – tall palm tree found in the dry northern region

pappadam –thin, round crisp bread eaten with curries or as a snack

arripu – red-lentil *dhal*

rahera – a procession, usually with ers, drummers and elephants

na – centre of learning attached to ery

steamed mixture of rice flour and oconut, sometimes made with asted wheat flour

plantain – banana; there are many different varieties in Sri Lanka, some of which are eaten as an everyday fruit while others are reserved for special occasions

pokuna – artificial pond

pol – Sinhala word for 'coconut'

poya – full-moon holiday

puja – literally meaning 'respect'; offering or prayers

raksha – type of mask used in parades and festivals

Rakshasas – legendary rulers of Sri Lanka, led by *Rawana*

Ramayana – story of Rama and Sita and their conflict with *Rawana*

rasa-kavili – sweets

Rawana – the 'demon king of Lanka' who abducts Rama's beautiful wife Sita in the Hindu epic the *Ramayana*

red rice – partly hulled rice

relic chamber – chamber in a *dagoba* housing a relic of Buddha or a saint and representing the Buddhist concept of the cosmos

rotty – elasticated, doughy pancake; also a small parcel of vegetable or meat wrapped up in a rotty

Ruhunu – ancient southern centre of Sinhalese power near Tissamaharama; it continued to stand even when Anuradhapura and Polonnaruwa fell to Indian invaders

sambol – chilli side dish, often made with coconut or onion; the general name for any spicy-hot dish

samudra – large *tank* or inland sea

Sangamitta – sister of *Mahinda* who brought the sapling from Bodhgaya in India from which the sacred bodhi tree at Anuradhapura grew

sanni – devil-dancing mask

Sanskrit – ancient Indian language, the oldest known member of the family of Indo-European languages

sari – traditional garment worn by women

school pen – ballpoint pen, often requested (or demanded!) from tourists by Sri Lankan children

short eats – plates of pastries and savouries, such as *bonda*, *Chinese rolls* and *vadai*, served at tea shops

sikhara – a dome- or pyramid-shaped structure rising above the shrine room of a Hindu *kovil*

Sinhala – language of the Sinhalese people

Sinhalese – the majority population of Sri Lanka, principally Sinhala-speaking Buddhists

SLFP – Sri Lanka Freedom Party

stupa – see *dagoba*

sweetmeats – sweets

Tamils – a people of south Indian origins comprising the largest minority population in Sri Lanka

tank – artificial water-storage lake or reservoir; many of the tanks in Sri Lanka are very large and ancient

Tantric Buddhism – Tibetan Buddhism with strong sexual and occult overtones

thali – south Indian meal consisting of rice with vegetable curries and *pappadams*

thambili – also known as the king coconut, an orange-coloured drinking coconut

Theravada – orthodox form of Buddhism practiced in Sri Lanka and South-East Asia, which is characterised by its adherence to the *Pali* canon

tiffin – colonial English expression for lunch

toddy – mildly alcoholic drink tapped from coconut palms

toddy tappers – people who perform acrobatic feats to tap *toddy* from the tops of coconut palms

TULF – Tamil United Liberation Front

UNP – United National Party, the first political party to hold power, in Sri Lanka, after independence

vadai – deep-fried lentil or flour patty

vatadage – circular relic house consisting of a small central *dagoba* flanked by Buddha images and encircled by columns

Vedas – Hindu sacred books; a collection of sacred hymns composed in preclassical Sanskrit during the second millennium BC and divided into four books: Rig-Veda, Yajur-Veda, Sama-Veda and Atharva-Veda

Veddahs – see *Wanniyala-aetto*

vel – trident; Skanda, a god associated with war in Hindu legend, is often depicted carrying a vel

vihara, viharaya – Buddhist complex, including a shrine containing a statue of Buddha, a congregational hall and a monks' house

Wanniyala-aetto – the original people of Sri Lanka prior to the arrival of the Sinhalese

wattalappam – popular dessert of Malay origin, made with *jaggery*, eggs, coconut milk and cardamom

wewa – irrigation tank, artificial lake

Yala – the south-west monsoon season

YMBA – Young Men's Buddhist Association

Thanks

Many thanks to the travellers who used the last edition and wrote to us with helpful hints, useful advice and interesting anecdotes:

Karen Achten, Jonas Aeberhard, James & Sandy Alexander, Solange Alves, Mandy Andrews, Peter J Andros, John Appleby, Hazel Armstrong, Christoph Arndt, Louise Arthur, Jo Ashwell, Peter Astbury, Agnes Aubert, Jane Austin, Alison Ball, Gordon Barclay, Janina Bard, Adam Barry, Vlady Beckerman, Carina Beresford, Ava Billings, Pat Bishop, Ralf Bornhak, T Brown, Susan Buie, RG Burgess, Prior Butler, Simon Byrom, Pat Callaghan, Julia Camm, Mary Capoci, Victoria Careford, Ken Chalmers, Mathieu Christe, C Clarke, Alex Clerk, Ted Corbett, Tui Cordemans, Emma Davey, Don Davidson, Emma Dawson, Jeroen De Jong, Michel De Lange, Gaetane De Volder, Tine Defoor, Carlos Deprez, Nik Devlin, Stefan Dischler, Rodney H Donaldson, Philip Dove, Brenda Drinkwater, Bram Dumolin, Frank Dux, Chris Earp, Stuart Eggleton, Alon Eisenstein, Becca Evans, Marion Faerber, Detlef Feussner, Jason Field, Greg Firkins, Gary Fishman, Jens Foell, Andrew Forsyth, Lawrence Foster, Shiela & Mike Francis, Bernd Friese, Edward Galvin, Balazs Garamvolgyi, Dave Gerrish, Simon Gibbon, Lynda Gibson, Nadia Giguere, I & S Gillespie, Jim Godfrey, Dan Goldthorp, Dr JJ Gordon, Leon Greer, Josine Grosveld, Steven Gumm, Nigel Hadden-Paton, Christopher Hall, Elaine Hamilton, Andrea Harley, M Harley, Sarah Haveland, Robert Hazell, Anita Hecker, Ogg Heinrich, Kalugalla Hena, A Henderson, Sibylle Hergenroether, Damitha Hewavitharana, W Hewison, Valerie Hill, Samanera Hiriko, Laurian Hirling, Gro Hoen, Urula & Sven-Erik Hoflin, S Hollwarth, Howard R Houck, Laura Hughes, Yvan Ivanov, Richard & Ann James, Glenys E Jarvis, Neil Jebb, Prem Jeevan, Simon Jerks, Craig Johnston, Menna Jones, J Judge, Tuva Kahrs, Georgina Kelly, Sandy King, Rudolph Klee, Brenton Klemm, Thorsten Koehler, Diederich Koehn, Sascha Kriese, Max Kuhn, Bouwe Kuik, Luke Lantman, Steve Lawrence, Steve Laws, John Le Bras, Phillip Leather, Christelle Lecu, Terence Ledger, Martin Liebermann, Marion Lievestro, Kelvin Lim, Vanessa Lindley, Sandy Lloyd, Fiona MacKay, Matt MacKay, Rian Maelzer, Jennifer Magarity, Vic Magedera, Delian Manchev, Janssens Marleen, David Martin, Ben Mason, Julie Maynard, Gregory McElwain, Suzanne McKay, Walter Michel, Banlul Miller, Sarah Milne, Andy Minett, Karen Mitchell, Naomi Mockett, Silke Moessner, Cath Mole, John Molyneux, Julie Morrison, David Morse, J Mortimer, Christine Myles, Corrado Nai Fovino, Sophie Niall, Peter O'Hagan, Jonte Olssen, Sachiko Osada, Eric Pantekoek, Sarah Paten, Sasha Pattinson, Robert Patton, Don Pavey, Anna V Pfeil, NC Phillips, Jim Pilston, Oliver Pogatsnik, Horst & Tina Poos, Katrien Poppe, Steve & Barbara Pretice, Mr Priyadarsin, Steve & Athena Pullin, Noortje Rabelink, Bobby Radic, PA Ratcliffe, Roger Rawlinson, Kevin Redslob, Kieran Reid, Steve Richards, David Roberts, Rick Roberts, Low Puay Hwa Roger, Jaimie Sach, Steve Samuelson, Jurgen Sause, Mrs & Mr Scanlon, Manfred Scheu, Michael Schmitt-Rabiger, Anne Schneider, Ekkehard Schwehn, Veronica Sheridan, Walter Silva, Dr G Silvestro, Richard Simpson, David Smallwood, Angela Smith, Damian Smyth, Fenwick Snowden, Roger & Ann South, D Stainthorp, Herman van der Steen, Zoe Stephens, SP Sumathipale, Shinsuke Suzuki, Edwin Theuerzeit, Anne Thomas, Dianne Thomas, Jeremy Thomas, C Turner, Kate Turner, Dana Uhl, Suzan Vaessen, Simon Van Evelinigen, IJ van Geest, Leendert van Nieuwenhuijzen, Jay van Rooy, Marie van Walle-Willems, Paul Vanderwert, Rene Vasington, Els Vroom, Joanna Watala, Fred Wegley, Angelika & Udo Weiss, Ella Wheatcroft, Phil Whitchurch, Marleen Wijnen, Laurence Wild, Leslie Wildesen, Bart Willemsen, Kahren Williams, Mark Woolnough, Richard Zanre, Azwardeen Zarook, Bernd Ziermann

LONELY PLANET

ON THE ROAD

Travel Guides explore cities, regions and countries, and supply information on transport, restaurants and accommodation, covering all budgets. They come with reliable, easy-to-use maps, practical advice, cultural and historical facts and a rundown on attractions both on and off the beaten track. There are over 200 titles in this classic series, covering nearly every country in the world.

 Lonely Planet Upgrades extend the shelf life of existing travel guides by detailing any changes that may affect travel in a region since a book has been published. Upgrades can be downloaded for free from **www.lonelyplanet.com/upgrades**

For travellers with more time than money, **Shoestring** guides offer dependable, first-hand information with hundreds of detailed maps, plus insider tips for stretching money as far as possible. Covering entire continents in most cases, the six-volume shoestring guides are known around the world as 'backpackers bibles'.

For the discerning short-term visitor, **Condensed** guides highlight the best a destination has to offer in a full-colour, pocket-sized format designed for quick access. They include everything from top sights and walking tours to opinionated reviews of where to eat, stay, shop and have fun.

CitySync lets travellers use their Palm™ or Visor™ hand-held computers to guide them through a city with handy tips on transport, history, cultural life, major sights, and shopping and entertainment options. It can also quickly search and sort hundreds of reviews of hotels, restaurants and attractions, and pinpoint their location on scrollable street maps. CitySync can be downloaded from **www.citysync.com**

MAPS & ATLASES

Lonely Planet's **City Maps** feature downtown and metropolitan maps, as well as transit routes and walking tours. The maps come complete with an index of streets, a listing of sights and a plastic coat for extra durability.

Road Atlases are an essential navigation tool for serious travellers. Cross-referenced with the guidebooks, they also feature distance and climate charts and a complete site index.

ESSENTIALS

Read This First books help new travellers to hit the road with confidence. These invaluable predeparture guides give step-by-step advice on preparing for a trip, budgeting, arranging a visa, planning an itinerary and staying safe while still getting off the beaten track.

Healthy Travel pocket guides offer a regional rundown on disease hot spots and practical advice on predeparture health measures, staying well on the road and what to do in emergencies. The guides come with a user-friendly design and helpful diagrams and tables.

Lonely Planet's **Phrasebooks** cover the essential words and phrases travellers need when they're strangers in a strange land. They come in a pocket-sized format with colour tabs for quick reference, extensive vocabulary lists, easy-to-follow pronunciation keys and two-way dictionaries.

Miffed by blurry photos of the Taj Mahal? Tired of the classic 'top of the head cut off' shot? **Travel Photography: A Guide to Taking Better Pictures** will help you turn ordinary holiday snaps into striking images and give you the know-how to capture every scene, from frenetic festivals to peaceful beach sunrises.

Lonely Planet's **Travel Journal** is a lightweight but sturdy travel diary for jotting down all those on-the-road observations and significant travel moments. It comes with a handy time-zone wheel, a world map and useful travel information.

Lonely Planet's eKno is an all-in-one communication service developed especially for travellers. It offers low-cost international calls and free email and voicemail so that you can keep in touch while on the road. Check it out on **www.ekno.lonelyplanet.com**

FOOD & RESTAURANT GUIDES

Lonely Planet's **Out to Eat** guides recommend the brightest and best places to eat and drink in top international cities. These gourmet companions are arranged by neighbourhood, packed with dependable maps, garnished with scene-setting photos and served with quirky features.

For people who live to eat, drink and travel, **World Food** guides explore the culinary culture of each country. Entertaining and adventurous, each guide is packed with detail on staples and specialities, regional cuisine and local markets, as well as sumptuous recipes, comprehensive culinary dictionaries and lavish photos good enough to eat.

OUTDOOR GUIDES

For those who believe the best way to see the world is on foot, Lonely Planet's **Walking Guides** detail everything from family strolls to difficult treks, with 'when to go and how to do it' advice supplemented by reliable maps and essential travel information.

Cycling Guides map a destination's best bike tours, long and short, in day-by-day detail. They contain all the information a cyclist needs, including advice on bike maintenance, places to eat and stay, innovative maps with detailed cues to the rides, and elevation charts.

The **Watching Wildlife** series is perfect for travellers who want authoritative information but don't want to tote a heavy field guide. Packed with advice on where, when and how to view a region's wildlife, each title features photos of over 300 species and contains engaging comments on the local flora and fauna.

With underwater colour photos throughout, **Pisces Books** explore the world's best diving and snorkelling areas. Each book contains listings of diving services and dive resorts, detailed information on depth, visibility and difficulty of dives, and a roundup of the marine life you're likely to see through your mask.

OFF THE ROAD

Journeys, the travel literature series written by renowned travel authors, capture the spirit of a place or illuminate a culture with a journalist's attention to detail and a novelist's flair for words. These are tales to soak up while you're actually on the road or dip into as an at-home armchair indulgence.

The range of lavishly illustrated **Pictorial** books is just the ticket for both travellers and dreamers. Off-beat tales and vivid photographs bring the adventure of travel to your doorstep long before the journey begins and long after it is over.

Lonely Planet **Videos** encourage the same independent, tough-minded approach as the guidebooks. Currently airing throughout the world, this award-winning series features innovative footage and an original soundtrack.

Yes, we know, work is tough, so do a little bit of deskside dreaming with the spiral-bound Lonely Planet **Diary** or a Lonely Planet **Wall Calendar**, filled with great photos from around the world.

TRAVELLERS NETWORK

Lonely Planet Online. Lonely Planet's award-winning Web site has insider information on hundreds of destinations, from Amsterdam to Zimbabwe, complete with interactive maps and relevant links. The site also offers the latest travel news, recent reports from travellers on the road, guidebook upgrades, a travel links site, an online book-buying option and a lively travellers' bulletin board. It can be viewed at **www.lonelyplanet.com** or AOL keyword: lp.

Planet Talk is a quarterly print newsletter, full of gossip, advice, anecdotes and author articles. It provides an antidote to the being-at-home blues and lets you plan and dream for the next trip. Contact the nearest Lonely Planet office for your free copy.

Comet, the free Lonely Planet newsletter, comes via email once a month. It's loaded with travel news, advice, dispatches from authors, travel competitions and letters from readers. To subscribe, click on the Comet subscription link on the front page of the Web site.

Lonely Planet Guides by Region

Lonely Planet is known worldwide for publishing practical, reliable and no-nonsense travel information in our guides and on our Web site. The Lonely Planet list covers just about every accessible part of the world. Currently there are 16 series: Travel guides, Shoestring guides, Condensed guides, Phrasebooks, Read This First, Healthy Travel, Walking guides, Cycling guides, Watching Wildlife guides, Pisces Diving & Snorkeling guides, City Maps, Road Atlases, Out to Eat, World Food, Journeys travel literature and Pictorials.

AFRICA Africa on a shoestring • Botswana • Cairo • Cairo City Map • Cape Town • Cape Town City Map • East Africa • Egypt • Egyptian Arabic phrasebook • Ethiopia, Eritrea & Djibouti • Ethiopian Amharic phrasebook • The Gambia & Senegal • Healthy Travel Africa • Kenya • Malawi • Morocco • Moroccan Arabic phrasebook • Mozambique • Namibia • Read This First: Africa • South Africa, Lesotho & Swaziland • Southern Africa • Southern Africa Road Atlas • Swahili phrasebook • Tanzania, Zanzibar & Pemba • Trekking in East Africa • Tunisia • Watching Wildlife East Africa • Watching Wildlife Southern Africa • West Africa • World Food Morocco • Zambia • Zimbabwe, Botswana & Namibia
Travel Literature: Mali Blues: Traveling to an African Beat • The Rainbird: A Central African Journey • Songs to an African Sunset: A Zimbabwean Story

AUSTRALIA & THE PACIFIC Aboriginal Australia & the Torres Strait Islands •Auckland • Australia • Australian phrasebook • Australia Road Atlas • Cycling Australia • Cycling New Zealand • Fiji • Fijian phrasebook • Healthy Travel Australia, NZ & the Pacific • Islands of Australia's Great Barrier Reef • Melbourne • Melbourne City Map • Micronesia • New Caledonia • New South Wales • New Zealand • Northern Territory • Outback Australia • Out to Eat – Melbourne • Out to Eat – Sydney • Papua New Guinea • Pidgin phrasebook • Queensland • Rarotonga & the Cook Islands • Samoa • Solomon Islands • South Australia • South Pacific • South Pacific phrasebook • Sydney • Sydney City Map • Sydney Condensed • Tahiti & French Polynesia • Tasmania • Tonga • Tramping in New Zealand • Vanuatu • Victoria • Walking in Australia • Watching Wildlife Australia • Western Australia
Travel Literature: Islands in the Clouds: Travels in the Highlands of New Guinea • Kiwi Tracks: A New Zealand Journey • Sean & David's Long Drive

CENTRAL AMERICA & THE CARIBBEAN Bahamas, Turks & Caicos • Baja California • Belize, Guatemala & Yucatán • Bermuda • Central America on a shoestring • Costa Rica • Costa Rica Spanish phrasebook • Cuba • Cycling Cuba • Dominican Republic & Haiti • Eastern Caribbean • Guatemala • Havana • Healthy Travel Central & South America • Jamaica • Mexico • Mexico City • Panama • Puerto Rico • Read This First: Central & South America • Virgin Islands • World Food Caribbean • World Food Mexico • Yucatán
Travel Literature: Green Dreams: Travels in Central America

EUROPE Amsterdam • Amsterdam City Map • Amsterdam Condensed • Andalucía • Athens • Austria • Baltic States phrasebook • Barcelona • Barcelona City Map • Belgium & Luxembourg • Berlin • Berlin City Map • Britain • British phrasebook • Brussels, Bruges & Antwerp • Brussels City Map • Budapest • Budapest City Map • Canary Islands • Catalunya & the Costa Brava • Central Europe • Central Europe phrasebook • Copenhagen • Corfu & the Ionians • Corsica • Crete • Crete Condensed • Croatia • Cycling Britain • Cycling France • Cyprus • Czech & Slovak Republics • Czech phrasebook • Denmark • Dublin • Dublin City Map • Dublin Condensed • Eastern Europe • Eastern Europe phrasebook • Edinburgh • Edinburgh City Map • England • Estonia, Latvia & Lithuania • Europe on a shoestring • Europe phrasebook • Finland • Florence • Florence City Map • France • Frankfurt City Map • Frankfurt Condensed • French phrasebook • Georgia, Armenia & Azerbaijan • Germany • German phrasebook • Greece • Greek Islands • Greek phrasebook • Hungary • Iceland, Greenland & the Faroe Islands • Ireland • Italian phrasebook • Italy • Kraków • Lisbon • The Loire • London • London City Map • London Condensed • Madrid • Madrid City Map • Malta • Mediterranean Europe • Milan, Turin & Genoa • Moscow • Munich • Netherlands • Normandy • Norway • Out to Eat – London • Out to Eat – Paris • Paris • Paris City Map • Paris Condensed • Poland • Polish phrasebook • Portugal • Portuguese phrasebook • Prague • Prague City Map • Provence & the Côte d'Azur • Read This First: Europe • Rhodes & the Dodecanese • Romania & Moldova • Rome • Rome City Map • Rome Condensed • Russia, Ukraine & Belarus • Russian phrasebook • Scandinavian & Baltic Europe • Scandinavian phrasebook • Scotland • Sicily • Slovenia • South-West France • Spain • Spanish phrasebook • Stockholm • St Petersburg • St Petersburg City Map • Sweden • Switzerland • Tuscany • Ukrainian phrasebook • Venice • Vienna • Wales • Walking in Britain • Walking in France • Walking in Ireland • Walking in Italy • Walking in Scotland • Walking in Spain • Walking in Switzerland • Western Europe • World Food France • World Food Greece • World Food Ireland • World Food Italy • World Food Spain **Travel Literature:** After Yugoslavia • Love and War in the Apennines • The Olive Grove: Travels in Greece • On the Shores of the Mediterranean • Round Ireland in Low Gear • A Small Place in Italy

Lonely Planet Mail Order

Lonely Planet products are distributed worldwide. They are also available by mail order from Lonely Planet, so if you have difficulty finding a title please write to us. North and South American residents should write to 150 Linden St, Oakland, CA 94607, USA; European and African residents should write to 10a Spring Place, London NW5 3BH, UK; and residents of other countries to Locked Bag 1, Footscray, Victoria 3011, Australia.

INDIAN SUBCONTINENT & THE INDIAN OCEAN Bangladesh • Bengali phrasebook • Bhutan • Delhi • Goa • Healthy Travel Asia & India • Hindi & Urdu phrasebook • India • India & Bangladesh City Map • Indian Himalaya • Karakoram Highway • Kathmandu City Map • Kerala • Madagascar • Maldives • Mauritius, Réunion & Seychelles • Mumbai (Bombay) • Nepal • Nepali phrasebook • North India • Pakistan • Rajasthan • Read This First: Asia & India • South India • Sri Lanka • Sri Lanka phrasebook • Tibet • Tibetan phrasebook • Trekking in the Indian Himalaya • Trekking in the Karakoram & Hindukush • Trekking in the Nepal Himalaya • World Food India **Travel Literature:** The Age of Kali: Indian Travels and Encounters • Hello Goodnight: A Life of Goa • In Rajasthan • Maverick in Madagascar • A Season in Heaven: True Tales from the Road to Kathmandu • Shopping for Buddhas • A Short Walk in the Hindu Kush • Slowly Down the Ganges

MIDDLE EAST & CENTRAL ASIA Bahrain, Kuwait & Qatar • Central Asia • Central Asia phrasebook • Dubai • Farsi (Persian) phrasebook • Hebrew phrasebook • Iran • Israel & the Palestinian Territories • Istanbul • Istanbul City Map • Istanbul to Cairo • Istanbul to Kathmandu • Jerusalem • Jerusalem City Map • Jordan • Lebanon • Middle East • Oman & the United Arab Emirates • Syria • Turkey • Turkish phrasebook • World Food Turkey • Yemen **Travel Literature:** Black on Black: Iran Revisited • Breaking Ranks: Turbulent Travels in the Promised Land • The Gates of Damascus • Kingdom of the Film Stars: Journey into Jordan

NORTH AMERICA Alaska • Boston • Boston City Map • Boston Condensed • British Columbia • California & Nevada • California Condensed • Canada • Chicago • Chicago City Map • Chicago Condensed • Florida • Georgia & the Carolinas • Great Lakes • Hawaii • Hiking in Alaska • Hiking in the USA • Honolulu & Oahu City Map • Las Vegas • Los Angeles • Los Angeles City Map • Louisiana & the Deep South • Miami • Miami City Map • Montreal • New England • New Orleans • New Orleans City Map • New York City • New York City City Map • New York City Condensed • New York, New Jersey & Pennsylvania • Oahu • Out to Eat – San Francisco • Pacific Northwest • Rocky Mountains • San Diego & Tijuana • San Francisco • San Francisco City Map • Seattle • Seattle City Map • Southwest • Texas • Toronto • USA • USA phrasebook • Vancouver • Vancouver City Map • Virginia & the Capital Region • Washington, DC • Washington, DC City Map • World Food New Orleans **Travel Literature**: Caught Inside: A Surfer's Year on the California Coast • Drive Thru America

NORTH-EAST ASIA Beijing • Beijing City Map • Cantonese phrasebook • China • Hiking in Japan • Hong Kong & Macau • Hong Kong City Map • Hong Kong Condensed • Japan • Japanese phrasebook • Korea • Korean phrasebook • Kyoto • Mandarin phrasebook • Mongolia • Mongolian phrasebook • Seoul • Shanghai • South-West China • Taiwan • Tokyo • Tokyo Condensed • World Food Hong Kong • World Food Japan **Travel Literature:** In Xanadu: A Quest • Lost Japan

SOUTH AMERICA Argentina, Uruguay & Paraguay • Bolivia • Brazil • Brazilian phrasebook • Buenos Aires • Buenos Aires City Map • Chile & Easter Island • Colombia • Ecuador & the Galapagos Islands • Healthy Travel Central & South America • Latin American Spanish phrasebook • Peru • Quechua phrasebook • Read This First: Central & South America • Rio de Janeiro • Rio de Janeiro City Map • Santiago de Chile • South America on a shoestring • Trekking in the Patagonian Andes • Venezuela **Travel Literature**: Full Circle: A South American Journey

SOUTH-EAST ASIA Bali & Lombok • Bangkok • Bangkok City Map • Burmese phrasebook • Cambodia • Cycling Vietnam, Laos & Cambodia • East Timor phrasebook • Hanoi • Healthy Travel Asia & India • Hill Tribes phrasebook • Ho Chi Minh City (Saigon) • Indonesia • Indonesian phrasebook • Indonesia's Eastern Islands • Java • Lao phrasebook • Laos • Malay phrasebook • Malaysia, Singapore & Brunei • Myanmar (Burma) • Philippines • Pilipino (Tagalog) phrasebook • Read This First: Asia & India • Singapore • Singapore City Map • South-East Asia on a shoestring • South-East Asia phrasebook • Thailand • Thailand's Islands & Beaches • Thailand, Vietnam, Laos & Cambodia Road Atlas • Thai phrasebook • Vietnam • Vietnamese phrasebook • World Food Indonesia • World Food Thailand • World Food Vietnam

ALSO AVAILABLE: Antarctica • The Arctic • The Blue Man: Tales of Travel, Love and Coffee • Brief Encounters: Stories of Love, Sex & Travel • Buddhist Stupas in Asia: The Shape of Perfection • Chasing Rickshaws • The Last Grain Race • Lonely Planet ... On the Edge: Adventurous Escapades from Around the World • Lonely Planet Unpacked • Lonely Planet Unpacked Again • Not the Only Planet: Science Fiction Travel Stories • Ports of Call: A Journey by Sea • Sacred India • Travel Photography: A Guide to Taking Better Pictures • Travel with Children • Tuvalu: Portrait of an Island Nation

LONELY PLANET

You already know that Lonely Planet produces more than this one guidebook, but you might not be aware of the other products we have on this region. Here is a selection of titles that you may want to check out as well:

South India
ISBN 1 86450 161 8
US$19.99 • UK£12.99

Goa
ISBN 0 86442 681 X
US$16.99 • UK£10.99

Sri Lanka phrasebook
ISBN 0 86442 597 X
US$7.99 • UK£4.50

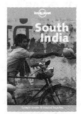

India
ISBN 1 86450 246 0
US$24.99 • UK£14.99

Kerala
ISBN 0 86442 696 8
US$15.95 • UK£9.99

Healthy Travel Asia & India
ISBN 1 86450 051 4
US$5.95 • UK£3.99

Read This First: Asia & India
ISBN 1 86450 049 2
US$14.95 • UK£8.99

The Age of Kali
ISBN 1 86450 172 3
US$14.95 • UK£6.99

Maldives
ISBN 0 86442 700 X
US$15.99 • UK£9.99

Available wherever books are sold

Index

Abbreviations

WG – Wildlife Guide

Text

Boxed Text

Bold indicates maps.

MAP LEGEND

CITY ROUTES

Freeway	Freeway
Highway	Primary Road
Road	Secondary Road
Street	Street
Lane	Lane
	Roadblocks
	Unsealed Road
	One-Way Street
	Pedestrian Street
	Stepped Street
	Tunnel
	Footbridge

REGIONAL ROUTES

	Tollway, Freeway
	Primary Road
	Secondary Road
	Minor Road

BOUNDARIES

	International
	State
	Disputed
	Fortified Wall

HYDROGRAPHY

	River, Creek
	Canal
	Lake
	Dry Lake, Salt Lake
	Spring, Rapids
	Waterfalls

TRANSPORT ROUTES & STATIONS

	Train
	Metro
	Tramway
	Bus Route
	Monorail
	Cable Car, Chairlift
	Ferry
	Path in Park
	Walking Trail
	Walking Tour

AREA FEATURES

	Building
	Park, Garden
	National Park
	Market
	Beach
	Campus
	Cemetery
	Urban

MAP SYMBOLS

CAPITAL National Capital	Bus Terminal, Stop	Mountain or Hill	Snorkelling
CAPITAL State Capital	Cathedral, Church	Mountain Range	Stately Home
City, Large Town City	Cave	Museum, Gallery	Stupa
Town Town	Cinema	Pagoda	Surf Beach
Village Village	Embassy, Consulate	Parking Area	Synagogue
Place to Stay	Golf Course	Pass	Taxi
Camping Ground	Gompa	Petrol/Gas Station	Transport (General)
Place to Eat	Hindu Temple	Police Station	Telephone
Point of Interest	Hospital	Post Office	Temple
Airfield	Internet Cafe	Pub, Bar	Theatre
Airport	Lighthouse	Ruins	Toilet
Bank	Lookout	Shelter	Tomb
Bird Sanctuary	Monument	Shipwreck	Tourist Information
Buddhist Temple	Mosque	Shopping Centre	Zoo

Note: not all symbols displayed above appear in this book

LONELY PLANET OFFICES

Australia
Locked Bag 1, Footscray, Victoria 3011
☎ 03 8379 8000 fax 03 8379 8111
email: talk2us@lonelyplanet.com.au

USA
150 Linden St, Oakland, CA 94607
☎ 510 893 8555 TOLL FREE: 800 275 8555
fax 510 893 8572
email: info@lonelyplanet.com

UK
10a Spring Place, London NW5 3BH
☎ 020 7428 4800 fax 020 7428 4828
email: go@lonelyplanet.co.uk

France
1 rue du Dahomey, 75011 Paris
☎ 01 55 25 33 00 fax 01 55 25 33 01
email: bip@lonelyplanet.fr
www.lonelyplanet.fr

World Wide Web: www.lonelyplanet.com *or* AOL keyword: lp
Lonely Planet Images: lpi@lonelyplanet.com.au